H U
with the
TWENTY-TWO

by

Charles S. Landis

Author of

.22 CALIBER RIFLE SHOOTING
TWENTY-TWO CALIBER VARMINT RIFLES

Martino Publishing
Mansfield Centre, CT
2012

Martino Publishing
P.O. Box 373,
Mansfield Centre, CT 06250 USA

ISBN   978-1-61427-249-6

Cover design by T. Matarazzo

Printed in the United States of America On 100% Acid-Free Paper

HUNTING
with the
TWENTY-TWO

by

Charles S. Landis

Author of

.22 CALIBER RIFLE SHOOTING
TWENTY-TWO CALIBER VARMINT RIFLES

A Samworth Book on Hunting

SMALL ARMS TECHNICAL PUBLISHING COMPANY

GEORGETOWN, SOUTH CAROLINA, U. S. A.

1950

TYPOGRAPHY, PRINTING, AND BINDING IN THE U. S. A. BY
KINGSPORT PRESS, INC., KINGSPORT, TENNESSEE

Contents

Foreword

THE PERFECT RIFLE FOR HUNTING SMALL GAME AND VARMINTS IN settled and semi-settled agricultural and grazing districts should be quiet, safe to shoot there and inexpensive; and, owing to the small size of the vital areas of most of such game, should be superlatively accurate. Its bullet should, whenever possible, either expand and remain in the game, or destroy itself completely upon impact with earth, sod, stones or rock. It should kill well, yet not cause needless mangling or suffering.

The .22 caliber rifle, both in the rim fire and in the flatter-shooting center fire, gives the least report, throws the lightest and smallest projectile, is among the most accurate of all calibers, and is the least expensive to shoot. In the .22 long rifle caliber, it is also the easiest to supply with factory ammunition, which can be purchased at nearly any village hardware store. In center fire, it is cheap to reload, has very light recoil, and causes but little annoyance to farmers and stock raisers. In Eastern farming or estate country, the .22 caliber, both rim and center fire, is the quietest and yet the most effective of all our rifle calibers for either field or woods hunting of small game. In short, from the thoroughly practical standpoint of being usable where any sort of rifled firearm may be shot, it has more advantages and fewer disadvantages than any other caliber.

Further, the use of a .22 caliber rifle in the field or in the forests is much like the use of a 20 gauge shotgun on quail or a fine fly rod to dangle dry flies before trout or small mouth black bass. It is the equipment of the man of appreciation and discernment who wishes to develop and depend upon skill rather than upon force and smashing power.

After all, most of us go hunting for sport. We wish to enjoy ourselves to the full while gunning, consequently we do not wish to be stopped, neither do most of us wish to annoy landowners. Nevertheless, we need a weapon of precision, great mechanical refinement, X-ring accuracy, and yet which is of a type which appeals to those who have substituted skill and ability in hunting and shooting for the 30″ killing pattern of the 12 gauge shotgun.

The real story of what has been done, can be done, and what you can do if properly equipped and instructed and shooting a splendidly accurate, properly sighted, precision-built .22 caliber rifle in field and forest has never been adequately told in a book exclusively devoted to hunting and shooting small game and varmints with .22 caliber rifles. The author went into this as much as space permitted in 1931 in *".22 Caliber Rifle Shooting,"* but that work is now out of print, the issue having become exhausted.

This book, by text and illustration, covers the subject. It is in no part a work of fiction. The shooting related in this book actually occurred. It tells you exactly how to hunt successfully, and to shoot each common variety of North American small game and varmints, where to find them, how to locate and hunt them, and gives numerous examples of rifles and cartridges which produced unusual results.

For the youth or the man with his first .22 caliber rifle, for the small bore target shot who has enjoyed only one-half of an experience with a .22 rifle (the remaining half to be found afield), and for the crank rifleman, reloader, small bore ballistics shark and experimenter, this book is a *must.*

Read this work in the spirit in which it was written, that of sportsmen writing one to another; of old timers in the game of field shooting giving their experiences, their hunting lore, their ammunition developments, their misses and their long range hits. This is the book for any small game and varmint hunter who has a rifle and wants to use it more successfully. If you can read this work without learning anything about hunting with the small caliber rifle, you certainly know game shooting with the .22 rifle.

May it bring you many happy days in the field. You, and you, and you!

C. S. Landis

Wilmington, Del.
    1949

CHAPTER 1

The Squirrels of America

OF ALL SMALL GAME WHICH MAY BE SHOT WITH THE .22 RIFLE, TREE squirrels are the most gamy, interesting, and supply the most sport. Ask any backwoods boy! Ask any rifleman born and brought up in timbered areas or in wooded mountain country! Ask any old squirrel hunter! Though he live a thousand lives, there are few things a man will accept in trade for good squirrel hunting with a small bore rifle, once he has become really expert at that sport.

The youthful experiences which most of us have had who were so fortunate as to be reared in hardwood timber country are something which cannot be duplicated though a man may travel around the globe. The gathering of chestnuts, often amid the scolding of gray or red squirrels; the roasting of chestnuts and popcorn before the evening fire; the peeling of apples and roasting them with sugar on top; and the getting up early and going for gray, black or fox squirrels the following morning, is a part of life for which there is no substitute and when night comes again and the bag of squirrels is brought home, and spread out for examination on the kitchen table before skinning—that completes the perfect day. What more can a man ask? One can possibly develop better rifles, but there is no substitute and no improvement upon good squirrel hunting!

THE GRAY SQUIRREL

The gray squirrel is the most widely distributed and hunted, is the best known, and is the most toothsome for the table, of all the 48 or 50 varieties of squirrels in North America. Of these, eight varieties are gray squirrels—three in the West, five in the East. The Western gray squirrels are less widely known than the Northern and Southern varieties of the Eastern gray squirrel. They are as large or slightly larger but live in much taller trees. Possibly because of the much greater height of the Northwestern and the California timber, these Western gray squirrels develop longer tails with wider feathering, which gives them better balance when climbing and gives more sailing power if one happens to fall. These squirrels may look smaller when viewed so far aloft, but do not let that fool you, as they are as large as the other gray squirrels.

These three Western gray squirrels of the coastal portion of Washington, Oregon and California, include the Columbia gray squirrel found in all three states; the Anthony gray squirrel of the Southern mountains of California; and the pretty black-footed gray squirrel in the Pacific-side districts of California. These are mostly acorn-eating squirrels, but pines, spruce and other coniferous trees supply some food.

Because of the great vertical distance to which squirrels can climb in this area, the hunter requires first class rifle equipment and the telescope sight is a great help both in spotting and shooting the squirrel.

East of the Rockies and the Mississippi, we have five varieties of gray squirrels, the most numerous, and the one most familiar to the public, being the Northern gray squirrel common in the Allegheny and Blue Ridge districts of Pennsylvania, and found in Delaware, Maryland, Eastern New York, in New England, particularly in Western Massachusetts, Vermont and New Hampshire. Do you remember W. Dustin White's Vermont gray squirrel shooting stories and his squirrel photos of 10 to 25 years ago? Up in Southern Ontario we find gray squirrels in considerable numbers and eastward throughout Southern Canada—often scattered as to habitat. The gray squirrel of the North varies in numbers according to its food and environment, including suitable and sufficient den trees. Two things are always necessary to a squirrel population, food and den trees. Also, the importation of occasional stock for breeding purposes from outside districts is helpful to increased numbers of young squirrels.

Among the other factors to consider are whether there is adequate and suitable cover, and whether the local stock has been depleted by overshooting, migration or other causes. At times gray squirrels of the Northern race migrate in large numbers. On such occasions, hundreds or even thousands move across the country without any regard for the wishes of hunters, and for no apparent reason whatever, as they have been known to forsake entirely areas that were abundantly supplied with food. Frequently they are drowned in large numbers when attempting to swim wide, swollen rivers. A notable instance of this occurred in Connecticut a few years ago when a westward migration of squirrels undertook to cross the Connecticut River while it was at flood stage. They apparently migrated elsewhere at that time also, as they have been more plentiful in the covers of Delaware and Pennsylvania ever since that westward migration. This habit of migrating is not peculiar to the Northern race of gray squirrel, but is characteristic of all gray squirrels, except perhaps those of the Pacific coast.

The adult Northern gray squirrel is a foot and a half long and weighs from one and a half to slightly in excess of two pounds, old gravid females being the heaviest. Yearlings will average about a pound each, while squirrels of August, September and October litters run from eight to 10 ounces each when they come down to feed and play. The average weights of Northern gray squirrels, counting both old and young, taken in the early season will probably be from 14 to 18 ounces, but as the season advances, the average will run higher, as the young squirrels will be nearer maturity, while both old and young will have put on fat in preparation for winter.

Squirrels shot in the early fall while the weather is still hot and they have not accumulated much fat are vastly inferior in table qualities to the squirrels with fat covered kidneys that are killed later in the season after hard frosts have fallen. In dressing a squirrel, be sure to remove the musk glands that lie between the shoulders and the ribs, as these are the source of the so-called "wild taste" of the meat. These glands have the appearance of dirty gobs of oily fat, and are thus easily identified. Also, if you are so unfortunate as to kill a pregnant female, or one that has been suckling young, be sure to cut or scrape from the abdomen all of the whitish granular fatty substance found thereon. This is the milk gland, and the flesh of the possessor will be flavored like rotten wood unless every trace of it is removed. After a fall of fattening on corn, acorns, beechnuts and hickory nuts, the meat of a properly dressed squirrel is firm, sweet and tasty.

The Southern gray squirrel is the other common race of the Eastern species, and is found from Virginia southward, being quite abundant in that state and in the Carolinas and Georgia. According to the Biological Survey and other authorities, it is generally called the cat squirrel throughout much of its range.

Mention should also be made of the Northwestern or Merriam gray squirrel of Minnesota, which was named for the well known naturalist Dr. C. Hart Merriam. The habits of this squirrel are similar to those of the gray squirrels of New England and the Middle Atlantic States. It frequents for the most part the deeper and darker woods, and is seldom or never found on poles or trees at the edge of the forest, in striking contrast with the habits of the fox squirrel of Minnesota.

In the far South are two additional varieties or sub-species of gray squirrel; the Everglades gray squirrel of Florida, and the Western far Southern gray which is known as the Louisiana or Bayou gray squirrel, which inhabits the gums and other trees of the bayou country. It is in many respects a swamp squirrel, as is the Everglades variety, simply because so many of the trees in such areas are standing in water or are largely surrounded by water and stand on small mounds or rises of ground in flat, wet country. Many such trees are also found in the coastal districts of South Carolina, which is also the best wild turkey country. The fact is, wild swamp or mountain areas which are good squirrel areas are always, or at least often, also good turkey and in some instances, good black bear country. All feed on beech or oak mast, meaning that they feed on beechnuts and acorns, and in the North, where there are still some few chestnuts, they all feed on chestnuts, particularly the squirrels.

Some claim that gray squirrels are active only in the daytime. Others that they are active only from about break of day to about 9.45 A.M., and from about 3.30 P.M. to dusk. Actually, you may find gray squirrels out feeding at any time especially in the winter season. I have hunted and shot them off stark dead chestnut snags in New Jersey, around 11 to 12 o'clock at night, on bright moonlight nights, 35 years ago. The author has known a few hunters who shot very fair bags of gray squirrels between 7 P.M. and 11 P.M., principally because that was the only time they had to go hunting—after work. Maybe it was not exactly legal, but in some areas we find numerous persons who have not been brought up to obey any sort of game laws.

Corn is perhaps the favorite food of Northern gray squirrels. They seem to prefer it in the milk stage, but continue to feed on it even after the kernels have hardened and the ears are ready to husk. In the North, beechnuts, hickory nuts, black walnuts and chestnuts are their staple foods, supplemented infrequently by butternuts or white walnuts. Poplar seed, mushrooms and haws are also eaten freely. A squirrel feeding on haws should be drawn immediately after being shot, else the flesh will be bitter to the taste. In the spring, squirrels feed largely on buds, principally those of maples and poplars, and to a lesser degree those of oaks and other trees. In addition to corn, the main foods of squirrels in the South are hickory and pecan nuts, acorns, pine seed or mast, cypress seed, mulberries, wild grapes, and berries of both black and tupelo gums and of dogwood. The flesh of these three last mentioned berries is not eaten, but the hard pits are cut open and the kernels extracted. Observers report that in this section black walnuts are practically never eaten by squirrels of any kind, presumably because hickory nuts, acorns and other preferable foods are too abundant. In the South, the hickory nut is decidedly the favorite food of squirrels, with acorns a close second, particularly those of the overcup, the willow, the water and the laurel oaks.

Southern gray squirrels feed on buds in the spring in the same manner as those of other sections.

In years gone by, the chestnut furnished the main denning sites and the main food supply of the Northern gray squirrel. When the chestnut blight destroyed the chestnut timber in the Allegheny and Blue Ridge mountain ranges during 1910 to 1913, it dealt the gray squirrels the greatest single blow they have ever suffered. In the years which followed, the beeches and the hickories became the main food trees of the gray squirrel, but at times they will feed greedily on the acorns of the crimson oak, and then about two weeks later on those of the pin oak. The author has a 70 foot pin oak in front of his bedroom window, and his pet gray squirrels feed greedily on its acorns every late September and early October. However, in the swamp areas of Delaware, the pin oaks are about the last of all the trees to which squirrels resort for food. On the other hand, beginning with the late summer corn constitutes the first and beechnuts the second seasonal source of their food supply.

Far too many people have distorted or erroneous ideas of the sport which is associated with gray squirrel shooting with a .22 rifle, because they see only the hand-fed pets in city parks and have no idea of the wildness, the craftiness, the cunning and the hiding ability of real wild gray squirrels of rocky, mountain country and of very dense, dark, swamp areas, where the squirrels have been hunted for many generations and rarely see any men except in the hunting season or during lumbering operations. As a general rule, the higher the timber and the rockier the ground beneath the nut trees, the wilder the gray squirrels which inhabit that timber. According to the author's rather extensive experience in hunting squirrels, those of the woodlot of limited area, while wild and hard to stalk in many instances, are not as difficult to stalk or locate as are those of mountain or deep swamp country. Further, the average ranges will be longer in the country of the two latter types.

THE BLACK SQUIRREL

The black squirrel is a particularly shiny and handsome cousin of the gray squirrel. It is, in fact, a melanistic gray squirrel. It has so much black pigment in its skin that its pelage or fur is coal black and shiny, almost like the feathers of a crow.

Northern gray squirrels are of two types, viz: the slim, sleek, handsome silver grays, and the fatter, heavier bodied and sturdier reddish grays. These are but color phases, the colors not being controlled, however, by the age or sex of the animals. I have had litters of reddish gray semi-tame squirrels that subsequently became silver gray, and others that were silver gray from birth. On the other hand, I have had reddish gray squirrels that were so born and never afterwards changed color. A reddish gray sire and a silver gray dam produced silver gray offspring, while a silver gray sire and a reddish gray dam produced reddish gray offspring. So draw your own conclusions as to the cause of the color phases.

Black squirrels are usually long and rather slim, and those found in Northern Pennsylvania, and perhaps elsewhere, are generally rather wild. During his later years, Dr. Ellis E. W. Given, who was an accurate and accomplished amateur naturalist, often spoke of the black squirrels he had hunted near Renovo, Pennsylvania, and always affirmed that these blacks were both slimmer and wilder than the gray squirrels of the same region. Around Orillia, Ontario, and other sections of that province, black squirrels are abundant, and photographs taken of them in that area show them to be sleek, fat, often pot-bellied in contour, shiny black, and at least as large as large gray squirrels.

The naturalist John Burroughs claimed that gray squirrels and black squirrels interbreed freely. The author has never seen specimens or their skins, nor photographs, of black squirrels which showed them to be partly gray and partly black. They are gray or they are black, but they are not like octoroons, Eurasians, or anything of that sort.

Both the gray and the black squirrels eat the same kind of nuts and buds, and occupy the same districts at times. It is claimed that both gray and black squirrels may be found in the same litter, but not squirrels that are born with intermingled gray and black hairs, or patches of both.

The principal feathered enemies of both gray and black squirrels are the larger hawks and owls, the chief offenders being the goshawk and the red-tailed hawk and the great horned owl. No hunter need be told that the tremendous size of the legs and feet of a red-tailed hawk is required for the catching of a few small field mice or field rats. Any such claim is absurd on the face of it.

Among the furred predators the chief enemies of squirrels of all species are foxes, both red and gray, wildcats, house cats, weasels, raccoons and dogs. Snakes, especially large colubers and large rattlesnakes, are very destructive on squirrels. Gray squirrels and black squirrels show more fear of house cats and of weasels than they do of any other animals, and it is well that they do. One of their main enemies, however, is the touring automobiles which often run over and crush them on highways traversing good squirrel woods. A gray squirrel is really not so fast, either on the ground or aloft. In some areas, particularly those where the squirrels are used to seeing many people and have become accustomed to automobiles, the author feels sure that from 10 to 25 per cent of their numbers are killed annually by automobiles alone. Three such kills which occurred within a quarter of a mile of the author's house were reported to him within a few months before this was written.

THE FOX SQUIRREL

Standard works on natural history list five species or sub-species of fox squirrels. These are: (1) the Southern or black fox squirrel, ranging the Southeastern states, including Florida; (2) the Northern or white-bellied fox squirrel, ranging from Central Virginia and West Virginia to Pennsylvania, and westward; (3) the yellow-bellied fox squirrel, ranging the Mississippi valley to Wisconsin; (4) the Texas fox squirrel, ranging the gulf coast of Texas, Louisiana and Mississippi; and (5) the Western fox squirrel, ranging the western part of the Mississippi valley adjacent to the Great Plains. Some of these will be hereafter discussed in more detail in Chapter Five dealing with their hunting.

THE RED OR PINE SQUIRREL

The red squirrel is the noisiest of the tree squirrel family. He is always either "singing" his challenge or coming out on the end of a limb to chatter it. He is also the smallest of the various species which are ordinarily shot as "game," and when in motion is the fastest.

The red or pine squirrel is red or chestnut color on the head, back and tail, has a blackish tinge along the sides, and is grayish white and white on the sides and under parts. The older reds, especially the males, are often colored with yellow, orange, or even rather dark tints beneath the under jaw. This is the badge of the Grandpappy or the Great Grandpa, who has probably spent three to six years or more scolding at and "sassing" every intruder that ventured into his neck of the woods and especially those who came near his den or his feeding grounds.

In my younger days I shot hundreds of red squirrels, most of them with the rifle. I have shot many running, usually with a .22 rim fire slide action repeater, sometimes hitting them as often as three or four times before getting a bullet far enough forward to make an instant kill. How they travel—when scared or angry! The pine squirrel is almost twice as fast as a gray, will invariably whip a gray, and can run one down as if the gray were tied, even when both are on big timber.

Red or pine squirrels are of the Northern and of the Southern varieties and the former appear to be a bit larger, and possibly also a bit darker in color. The Northern pine squirrel, or one of his cousins, ranges almost as far North as Hudson's Bay. A friend of mine who has made trips up almost to the Southwest tip of the Bay, reports that these red squirrels were the only squirrels he saw so far North. This was in 1937 and in 1938. Pine squirrels are widely scattered; they are found in Michigan and Minnesota, are especially plentiful in some parts of Pennsylvania and throughout almost the whole of Allegheny and Blue Ridge Mountain ranges. They feed considerably upon pine cones, both fall and winter, and on the seeds of fruits like cherries and apples, but their main food today is the hognut hickory nut which is of practically no use to anyone and yet is quite prevalent in our Northern woods. Red squirrels also pick up an ear of corn at times, but are by no means as destructive to corn as gray squirrels and fox squirrels.

The dens of red or pine squirrels are often in dead snags, chestnut, pine or oak trees, adjacent to the nut trees upon the seed of which they feed. They also build nests at times, I have seen these even in apple trees. Once in a while a family of red squirrels will take up residence in an old attic or barn, but this is comparatively rare as compared to the numbers which normally den in heavy timber. Red squirrels quite often den in old hollow trees along the edge of woods, or in fence corners, and will even den up in rocks if no other refuge is present—but where food is plentiful.

Pine squirrels provide much excellent rifle shooting sport, especially to boys and young men, and at times of the year when gray and fox squirrels are protected riflemen can sharpen their shooting eye on red squirrels, crows, woodchucks, and an occasional hawk. Red squirrels are gamy little animals, and usually come out and "sing" if the hunter keeps quiet for a few minutes. They run out on a limb or sit in a crotch where a large limb joins a tree trunk, and scold and express their defiance—in squirrel language—which often sounds as if it is a bit profane and certainly is vociferous whenever an intruder ventures near. Red squirrels are either much tamer than gray squirrels or else as wild as hawks, depending upon how much they have been hunted, the surroundings and their age. Also, upon the weather; as squirrels are usually wild on windy days!

Red squirrels are fond of black walnuts and consequently often come out to single trees standing alone more than do gray squirrels. When so seen an old red looks pretty large to a 10 to 15 year old boy, who can get a terrific kick out of shooting a mess of them, even though they weigh but six to eight ounces when fully grown. A very few old pine squirrels weigh nine to 10 ounces, but these will be orange or even red under the chin and often also on the belly, and

OUT ON THE END OF A LIMB

High up on the tree, sways a feeding squirrel. He is busy "cutting" nuts which fall with a "tump" on the leaves. As he stops for a moment, the rifleman brings the crosshairs of the scope to rest on ear or shoulder and then— "sphat" goes the rifle!

Compliments Leo Luttringer, Jr.

will be numbered among the patriarchs of their tribe. I have weighed dozens and dozens of them in my youth. I will never forget the first one I shot at; it was fully 60 yards off and well up on an enormous tree. Viewed over the open sights of the boy's .22, it looked like a speck in the distance, but down it came like a plummet and I found, after running up, that the bullet had struck it exactly in the right eye. Even though that was the only squirrel I managed to kill that season, it in no wise dimmed my then youthful enthusiasm. The second one I hit also came down and in running to retrieve it I fell over a log at least 20″ in diameter, lying horizontally, raised somewhat above the ground level and believe it or not I never saw that log until I nearly broke my neck over it. Don't tell me a red squirrel does not look as big as a tom cat and as important as a bear, to a youthful rifleman—I've been there!

The red squirrel is generally thoroughly damned by the naturalist who, more often than not, spends eight to 10 months a year in some college, at which location he often has little or no opportunity to examine closely or watch the natural habits and food gathering of any sort of squirrels.

It may be true that red squirrels kill a few small birds, rob a few birds nests, and eat an ear of corn now and then, but half a century of keen observation of what squirrels do has failed to convince me that red or pine squirrels the whole year through, do 10 per cent of the damage in dollars that is done by our common robin to ox-heart cherries, strawberries and similar fruits and berries in the two months during which berries and cherries ripen. I have seen cherry crop and berry crop one after another, 25 to 100 per cent ruined by robins, blackbirds and catbirds—but mostly by robins; and cherries and strawberries mean real money to fruit and berry farmers. I spent my youth on a fruit farm, which was adjacent to mighty fine squirrel woods and there is no comparison between the destruction caused by robins and the small amount usually done by pine squirrels. Yet our public has been ballyhooed about the virtues of one, and the viciousness of the other. It is so unfortunate the public is continually misinformed about the relative destructiveness of the different species of wild life.

Squirrels are unquestionably the most interesting, most crafty, most amusing and the most gamy of our woodland small game, other than the wild turkey and the ruffed grouse.

Take red and gray squirrels out of the average Eastern woodland and what have you left? Listen reader, I will tell you what you have left; you will have rotting slab piles, blackened stumps, second growth timber, empty beer cans, sandwich wrappers, and hot dog skins. After the squirrels are all gone, most of the rest is simply not worth the taxes.

Any time you think you are a real "hot" rifle shot, try picking off a half dozen pine squirrels from old oak, chestnut or hickory snags and boles that rise 70 to 120 feet into the sky, and when you are standing at least 60 yards from the foot of the trunk, maybe on a hillside, and your shoe soles are slippery. You will find there is a great deal to rifle shooting you just do not pick up at this belly shooting with a 12-pound match rifle.

The whole squirrel family is a developer of riflemen. There are so few things left today which do develop *riflemen* that it is not a bad idea to pay a bit of attention to the conservation of one item that will always develop riflemen—tree squirrels. Do not be too hard on the red or pine squirrel; in many a thousand acres of woodland and farm lots he is the last stand of the squirrel family.

Some claim he has chased all of the robins out of the woods. Let's look at it a little more sensibly. If you have ever lived in the country, or in a country town, you have likely looked out of the back window and watched a robin feeding her young. Possibly you have taken out your watch and counted the number of times Mrs. Robin has arrived at the nest bearing a big fat worm in her bill and then jammed it down the opened mouths of three to five ever-hungry, squalling youngsters. Probably you were surprised at the number of times she arrived and left within 10 minutes.

All right. Under the circumstances and remembering the quantity of food it takes to fill the craws of four or five hungry little robins, would you build your nest in an apple tree right back of the house, with a lawn and a garden on one side—both fine places for fat worms and a grub now and then, and with an ox-heart cherry tree on one side of those and a fine patch of luscious strawberries on the other, from any of which you could reach your nest in five or 10 seconds—or would you build your nest a mile or more away in the woods and have to fly back and forth—two miles for the round trip? It is not red squirrels that make Mrs. Robin build her nest right beside the dinner table—it is plain common sense and a disinclination to work too hard.

Maybe the red squirrel is no angel; maybe he does not belong to The Society of the Cincinnati; maybe his great granddaddy did not come over in the Mayflower; maybe he is a mischievous, chattering, busy little rascal. What if he does race down the fence line now and then and come back with a cheek full of cherry pits? He is at least 90 per cent worthwhile, and for young riflemen is just the thing to keep them out of the corner pool room. He is 100 per cent American and furthermore, is more of a sporting proposition than 90 per cent of the city slickers who condemn him—and call him names!

The red squirrels as to habitat are divided scientifically into three groups. These are the Douglas group in the Pacific states and West of the Rockies, which group is scientifically further subdivided; the Fremont group in the Southern Rockies; and the Hudson group with its Latin names, which includes the Northern and Southern reds, both of which are numerous. There are also a Minnesota variety, an Alaskan red squirrel, a Black Hills piney, and various lesser groups, all different in but slight essential characteristics, or probably not at all so far as the hunter is concerned.

THE ABERT SQUIRREL

The Tuft-eared or Abert squirrel is a large tree squirrel resembling in color and size the Eastern gray squirrel. It has definitely tufted ears like those of the European tree squirrel, which it more closely resembles than any other American species. Along the back runs a brownish red band of color above sides of gray. The under parts are white, with a black line separating it from the gray of the sides. The tail is broad and bushy, white beneath, mixed gray and black above, and black at the tip. The ears are tall, and the tufts, especially in winter, are long and prominent. This is the typical squirrel of the great yellow pine forests of the lower Rocky Mountain region.

It is found in Old Mexico, south of the border, and in the high country of New Mexico, Colorado and Arizona, and generally at elevations between 5,000 and 10,000 feet, for which reason it is not often seen by those living in the lowland farming country of these states. This squirrel lives and feeds in areas even much higher than the range of the marten, the prize furred game of the British Columbia and Alberta trappers, which usually lives at an elevation of between 4,500 and 5,500 feet.

Between twenty and twenty-five million squirrels, mostly gray, red and fox squirrels, are shot or trapped annually by our registered and farmer hunters, totaling eight to ten million gunners. This makes somewhat less than three squirrels per gunner annually, but that beats killing one-fifth of a woodcock, one-fourth of a quail, and one-fiftieth of a wild turkey, which might leave you holding the bag with either the feet or the neck. States in which the squirrel kill is very large in numbers include Pennsylvania, Indiana, Ohio, Minnesota, Missouri and Illinois. River bottom shooting is the rule in the latter, walnut grove shooting prevails in Indiana, and hardwood forest shooting in Pennsylvania, Maryland and Delaware. The per-capita kill in some of the smaller states is higher than in many of the larger, and is likely to be relatively more important where there is no open season on deer, bear or wild turkeys.

A general review or outline of the tree squirrel family, its distribution, and its hunting is given above, but stripped of too much naturalist lingo to enable the hunter to obtain a good practical view of the squirrels he will hunt, and what the requirements may be of the arms and ammunition he should use for them.

As you read on and into the actual hunting of squirrels in the following chapters, the author hopes you will experience a good share of the enjoyment and healthy recreation he has experienced for more than 50 years and in many a squirrel woods.

It will be a sad day for the youth of this country when a trip into what was once a famous squirrel woods reveals nothing but empty distances, and all one hears is the hum of locusts in what has become a silence of death. Man has in too many instances done to the forests what the atomic bomb some day may do to man!

I, for one, would rather listen to the rustling of the leaves, the sound of falling bark, the noise of scrambling feet, and then the "Quack, Quack, Quaahh! ! ! ! of the gray squirrel, or the Czeeeee! Czeeeee! ! Czeeeeee! ! ! ! ! of the angry little red, than to have to sit and gaze out over a valley from which one recognizes nothing but the barking of a farm dog or the lowing of a patiently waiting milch cow.

A forest which is really worth while has *life*. That life is squirrels! Destroy them, and you emasculate nature, which should remain lovely, fruitful, abundant and undefiled!

CHAPTER 2

Hunting Squirrels

MILLIONS OF GUNNERS HAVE HUNTED AND SHOT SQUIRRELS WITH 20, 16 and 12 gauge shotguns. They have located the beech, hickory, oak and walnut trees upon which squirrels feed. They have still hunted squirrels, walked them up on wet days, and have trailed and treed them with squirrel dogs. Everything about such squirrel hunting is sport except the actual shooting, which is often much too easy if the squirrel is close and sitting, and on the other hand will result in too high a percentage of lost cripples if the squirrel is more than 50 yards distant.

Rifle shooting at squirrels is an entirely different proposition. The hunting is just as much fun but of necessity, because of the weapon used, largely still hunting and individual precision marksmanship when you find your squirrel. You will observe, particularly if using a telescopic sight on your .22 rifle, that a feeding squirrel is in almost constant motion. With a .22 rifle you cannot merely fire at waving branches, or let drive at "the center of the ball." If you adopt such tactics you will almost certainly miss the squirrel entirely or shoot at the tail, at which a rifle shot is not fatal.

In squirrel hunting with a rifle it is necessary to pick out a definite vital spot upon the squirrel, take careful aim—with the sights set for that distance, and then hit that spot. Squirrels can be shot with the small bore rifle so successfully, if using proper ammunition, that the percentage of cripples which escape, even on shots up to 80 and 90 yards, will be quite small. Squirrel hunting with a rifle is definitely a *sporting proposition*. Everything about it is sportsmanlike. You must develop a degree of skill, rely upon your own ability as a hunter, very definitely rely upon your own rifle shooting, and when you have made a nice bag for the day, you can display them with a pride that no one ever felt in presenting a half dozen gray or fox squirrels each riddled by a shotgun charge.

Squirrel hunting with a .22 caliber rifle is probably the most thoroughly enjoyable form of small game shooting with the rifle in all outdoors. An "educated" squirrel is definitely smart, and is extremely clever. Furthermore, he is smarter than the average hunter and that makes outwitting him and cleanly bagging him a definite personal accomplishment which no rifleman can well pass up.

In driving for deer, with a rifle, you normally have a tremendous amount of hunting, walking, crashing through second growth and brush, and then a wait on a stand during which you almost freeze to death. You are either exhausted and sweating to the point where you often care little what happens, if only you could stop and catch your breath, or else you are, for two or three hours at a time, a shivering, quaking, human icicle. You find it impossible to dress comfortably for both driving and watching. And to top it all off, you may get one, two, or three shots during the season; probably no shooting at all.

Compare this with squirrel hunting with the rifle. If auto or bus transportation is available close to the average squirrel woods, you have little or no exhausting walking or hunting. The weather is usually pleasant and mild in squirrel season. You enjoy the most beautiful colors in all outdoors and you hunt cautiously, carefully, slowly and comfortably. When you find squirrels feeding, playing, or in the vicinity of dens, it becomes still hunting from a chosen position.

You may expect three or four, to eight or 10 shots on the average day of squirrel shooting, and you can repeat this daily, almost every nice day, throughout a shooting season. In other words, 20 to 50 shots a year at squirrels, when using a rifle, are not unusual for a skilled hunter in a good squirrel neighborhood. What more could one ask? Better still, every squirrel bagged will come as the result of a good accurate aim and a properly placed bullet.

I could give you a long list of instructions for squirrel shooting with a rifle, but such would soon become dull reading. How much more fun it is really to go hunting in your reading, with a squirrel hunter who has had a lifetime of experience in shooting squirrels with the .22. In this book we are going to take you along to the beechnut ridges and the hickory knolls. We will take you on actual shooting trips, with the author using a .22 scope sighted rifle. We will tell you of the good shots and of the missed chances; the easy shots and the hard, running shots which often present themselves. We will talk of the pleasant days in the woods and of the times when conditions were not so favorable to the hunter.

None of the shooting trips or individual shots described in this book are or were imaginary. They occurred just as written down here. The author has hunted squirrels for more than 50 years and has had a lot of experience in this line, because it is his favorite sport with the rifle. He has had more than a generation of time in which to learn the ways of squirrels and how to hunt them. In the beginning of his squirrel hunting days, he was instructed in the sport by the two outstanding squirrel hunters of his locality and by many others who were better than average.

The author has had, in addition, 40 years or more of match shooting experience with rifles and pistols, much of it in company with the best in the nation. In such background you pick up many of the fine points of using an accurate rifle.

If some of the squirrel shooting averages given in this work appear a bit high remember that plenty of practice and experience, both as a hunter and as a rifleman, has preceded this shooting. Many others have had very similar experiences and the averages quoted elsewhere in this book for other forms of small game and varmint shooting with rifles and by other hunters are just as high, or higher.

Read these stories thoughtfully and with the idea that you will not only enjoy them, but that you will find out from this book what to do and what not to do when squirrel hunting with a .22 caliber rifle.

Nearly everyone learns faster and more thoroughly by going along and watching the shooting of a veteran with the small bore rifle. The author has had the pleasure of starting many young men shooting squirrels with a .22 rifle; they all enjoyed it and most of them became very expert at the game. So should you! Read on and by the time you have reached the point in this book where we go to other forms of small game and varmint hunting possibly you will see why the author has begun *"Hunting With the Twenty-Two"* with a number of chapters on squirrel hunting with the rifle.

It is the No. 1 sport which may be enjoyed in timbered country with a small caliber rifle. Regardless of your age, strength, walking ability, or past experience, it is a sport at which you can become proficient if you will but apply yourself as directed.

Boys like squirrel shooting better than almost any other sport. A careful boy with a .22 rifle almost *never* gets into trouble. Reason, he has keen eyesight, is a quick thinker, has the courage to rely upon his own ability and skill, and he is not then in the company of older vicious companions who would lead him into trouble. The best time of anyone's life is when he is a growing boy. Buy him a good .22 and let him go hunting by himself and learn squirrel shooting. It never lands the boy in jail.

Squirrel shooting will appeal particularly to professional and technical men whose conception of shooting includes at all times the idea of precision shooting. Squirrel shooting provides that for every day spent in the woods. Squirrel shooting with a rifle should appeal to almost everyone who wants something different, something more personal, something more pleasant and less nerve wracking or physically exhausting than many other forms of sport.

We hand you now a pair of carefully made and nicely fitted shoe pacs, which are quiet in the woods, a hunting coat, your license, a copy of the game laws, and a .22 rifle equipped with an accurate telescope sight. We want you to go along hunting in the pages of this book, and as a final send off here is a box of cartridges and a fare-you-well. May the sun come up bright through the fog and as you gaze out across the valley, up on the mountain, with the author, may you hear the quack, quack! Quaah! of the gray squirrel, the noblest Roman of them all, and the variety of small game which will add many pleasant days to the experience of a man's lifetime.

Now then, I hope you enjoy the hunting, and especially, that you will most thoroughly enjoy the *shooting*. No better sport is to be found in woodland valley or on the mountain!

TWO MEMORABLE DAYS WITH THE HI-SPEEDS

Eleven days of rain, six and one-half inches of rainfall, and three days of terrific gales had lashed the territory in which I usually shot gray squirrels. The tropical hurricane had roared the length of the nation, had smashed much of New England, had taken a toll of more than 600 lives and had destroyed millions of dollars worth of property.

The frisky gray squirrels had taken to their dens and literally "pulled the holes in after them!" Even the woods runs became roaring creeks. Cornfields were washed and ankle deep with mud. Leaves had been beaten down from the trees, old snags used as dens had rocked and creaked in the gale. Nature had pulled the covers over its head!

Finally, the sun shone forth! It always does. No matter how bleak the previous day, nor how widespread the damage during the hurricane, a morning follows in which the air is calm and the sun comes out bright, warm and cheerful. By mid-day the undergrowth was beginning to dry, so I shouldered my .22 match rifle—the 52 Winchester-Hoffman, and started for the woods. It looked like a good afternoon and evening for gray squirrels. They would need to come out and feed. Most of them would likely be hunting the dryer spots and leaping over bunches of wet grass and weeds, but they would be working into the edges of the cornfields, if I knew anything about the ways of squirrels. They knew where it would dry first, and where there would be plenty for them to eat.

At 1:30 P.M. I was in the edge of the squirrel woods. It was surprisingly dry, considering the rainfall that had occurred; good drainage and a wind over night, had been the reason.

Within 15 minutes a gray squirrel raced across the leaves and immediately up and away into the thick leafy branches of a group of poplars; up the rear side of the tree of course. There had been no frost as yet to bring down the poplar leaves, nor even to turn them in color. I would hardly have gotten a shot, even with a shotgun. He had hidden for a moment, then made a dash for a "better-'ole."

Soon, one appeared on the ground from nowhere, made a few hops toward some high second-growth brush, and just as he was about to disappear I pressed the trigger. Nothing happened! In some manner I had let the striker down. This was the beginning of one of those days, when quite a few things occurred which had been unforeseen, or else just happened.

I hunted out into and down the cornfield, took a stand behind a shock at the lower end and before very long a large gray hopped up on the lower rail of the only fence bars around and frisked in the sun. Then he jumped down onto the ground, then up on the post at one end, then back onto the rail again. By that time I had moved up into offhand shooting distance.

The crosshairs settled on his neck and the rifle cracked! It pinned him fast to the post at the end of the bars. He finally dropped off and kicked a bit. By the time I got there the squirrel was dead. The range was about 30 yards. The bullet, a Remington Hi-Speed hollow point long rifle had blown out the whole throat and had broken the spine at the base of the neck, driving up from the underside. Finely pulverized flesh, which looked like brains, was spattered against the post at the end of the fence rail. Bullet expansion had been excellent as there was not more than an inch of flesh to expand upon, on a side shot. This was a fine big gray with some browning fur on its back and under parts and was very fat around the kidneys. Cornfed squirrels always wax fat and are good eating.

After hunting around for a time, I shot a yearling gray off a limb of a poplar tree, the squirrel being not over 12 feet from the ground, and little more than 10 yards from the edge of the corn. It was a wild and crafty squirrel and took a good deal of careful stalking. This one was "bunched up" and headed partly away from me when shot, the bullet entering the ribs on the left side, blew out the throat, and came out through the left eye. A most peculiar course as it went in the left side and came out of the left side, yet went through the center of the neck. At the moment of bullet strike, this gray was vigorously chastising a flea back of his ear, using a hind foot to scratch it.

As this seemed to hunt out the field, I trudged down the run and made the rounds of the lower field, or rather, the woods adjacent thereto. I saw one gray, on the ground, in the woods along the run, but only for a flick or two of his tail and he was gone in the undergrowth.

Then I hunted out a couple of old den trees down the run and saw nothing, after which I took a course up on the far side of the run along an old woods path. There was good big timber along there, and it should have been a logical spot for winter dens.

Suddenly, while walking along a dim woods path, I was attacked by black hornets from some source unseen. Likely the storm had damaged or knocked down a nest, and they were taking it out on the first passer-by. I was wearing a pair of the large Soft-Lite Lens sport glasses containing the lightest, pinkish shade of Bausch & Lomb lenses, ground with my prescription. These glasses are fitted with detachable fine wire safety gauze made up by hand for me by the American Optical Co. The side clips at the temples keep out most of the wire grass, twigs, sharp branches, briars and all other things that may blow into or jam their way into the eyes and damage the sight. They are especially valuable in hunting in brush where a man at any moment is likely to be punched in an eye by some sharp twig or thorn that he did not see in time.

A big black hornet banged against the middle of the right lens, directly over the pupil of my right eye—my shooting eye. When he discovered this did not work, he climbed up on the frame and stung me on the right eyebrow and then on the forehead. Another landed with a "plop" and stung the same eyebrow and added a second sting for good measure on the forehead. That made four hornet stings above one eye, but my shooting glasses had saved my eyes and probably the eyesight—this being the second time, in my experience, that heavy shooting glasses have saved that right eye from serious or painful injury.

Being stung by hornets is very painful, and also quite nauseating. Mud poultices soon helped with the swelling on the forehead, but for the rest of the day all I could see out of the right eye was a dull blue. Squirrel hunting under such conditions had to be conducted under handicaps. I was not sure that I could avoid falls over sharp corn stubs as I walked up the field. Before long I had a good offhand shot at a gray squirrel sitting about 10 feet up on a limb of a poplar and only 25 yards off, and apparently completely missed him. I could not see the crosshairs and could only dimly see the outline of the squirrel.

Soon a squirrel jumped from one poplar to another and down over the limbs but I could not get an aim on it through the glass.

Finally, near sundown, I came upon three large squirrels, feeding together on the corn on the ground, and while I could see a tail wave every now and then in the scope, I could not see well enough to get a shot. Finally I noticed one jump down off a corn stalk, where he was feeding by himself, a fine large male, quite angry and disturbed at being interrupted at his meal, and he stood up on his hind legs like a chuck to look me over. He took a bullet through the neck, the lead blowing out the throat and smashing the spine and one front foot—the one on the far side. That made three squirrels and I called it a day, although I had seen 10 or 11, all told but only had the four shots.

A weak dioxogen solution, 1 per cent mercuric oxide and various other home remedies had cooled off the right eye by the following day, but I was still pretty groggy. It looked like a grand afternoon for squirrels, so I was on the grounds by 1 o'clock.

Within 15 minutes a good sized squirrel showed up in a crotch about 30 feet up a beech den tree and some 30 yards off. It was an offhand shot and at the moment I was starting to slide down a bank to cross a watercourse. One could scarcely be off balance worse and of course I missed. Normally, it was a very easy shot. But I had to shoot then or never, as the squirrel had seen me and was ready to run. After the shot he ran about three feet, misjudged the direction of the whizzing bullet and came right back to the crotch from which he had run. The second shot caught him directly through the ribs, from the left side, went on through and smashed the spine before it emerged on the right side, also through the ribs. This was an instant kill but the shot itself was more difficult than the previous one, as the animal presented a much smaller area to the marksman. This was especially so in a vertical direction, which is the more important one, particularly when the sight line is one and one-half inches above the bore.

As they say around Allentown, "That makes no nevermind," *if* you have bagged the gray squirrel.

It was still before 1:30 P.M., a good start for possibly a long afternoon's shooting.

Within half an hour I got another shot, at a very large, female gray which came sneaking up through the corn rows and sat up like a woodchuck and watched me. Scope sighted rifle, safety goggles, hornet-stung forehead and all, I suppose I looked like something that had wandered out of a sniper's post and was probably a fearsome looking object to the squirrel. All I needed to complete the assembly, was a gas mask. This gray took a bullet directly between the forelegs, as the crosshairs rested on the tip of its nose, as it stood up straight as a picket pin, in the corn row. It gave a perfect shot.

The bullet had then come up to about one inch below the line of sight. The squirrel was all yellow and dark shaded around the lower jaw and was fat as butter around the kidneys, when dressed. I always carry a pocketknife which is used to dress the squirrels as soon as shot, or a Bean light trout knife, which is sharper and almost as convenient to carry, in its sheath. It also makes a fine skinning knife. A squirrel's hide is very elastic and quite tough. It takes a good knife to cut it, and on a shot which traverses most of the length of the body—a shot you want to avoid when possible by the way, even a high speed .22 long rifle bullet will normally stop under the elastic hide at the far end.

I have always made it a habit to examine carefully and more or less to dissect the inedible portions of a squirrel, so as to note exactly the course, penetration and apparent expansion of the bullet, as this in many ways is valuable to a hunter in determining where to aim and how to place the bullet so that it will surely make a killing wound, not cause excessive suffering, and yet not spoil too much meat. By being careful and holding his shots well, an experienced rifleman can often go through a season with 90 per cent of his shots which hit, falling within a one and one half inch area, on squirrels. This includes all sorts of shots at all ranges and includes sitting, standing with arm rest, and offhand shooting. Shooting from the kneeling position is seldom advisable for most hunters, and prone is simply impossible for most squirrel shooting due to the angle of fire, up into the air, and also to undergrowth in the woods and grass in the fields of corn.

Two squirrels in the hunting coat by 2 P.M. seemed like a good omen. It is like getting two strikes over on the batter. From then on he who serves them up can take his time and choose his course of action. If there is a squirrel or two around that has outwitted you time and again, this is a good time to waste a half hour trying to knock down his ears. If you have a section of the woods that has not been thoroughly explored and hunted, this would be a good time to give it a whirl.

But in this instance I had the one most desirable district to cover. The idea was to hunt it thoroughly before the corn was all cut off, or before someone else got there, or before it was posted. Saturdays are often poor times to hunt squirrels. Too many hunters are out, and they often break down bars, fence rails, cut barbed wire or otherwise do things which provoke a farmer. I prefer to hunt more or less alone and to keep as quiet as I can, while hunting.

Within a short time, after the previous mention, a gray squirrel raced down a poplar and perched precariously on the top of a small, dead stub, about two feet above the ground level, and partly hidden in grass. I took an offhand shot, all that was offered, at some 25 yards, and missed. It was a downhill shot and I think I shot over or under. The squirrel made a jump into the poplar thicket and was out of sight for good. I never saw that one again. It was only a yearling, but yearling squirrels seemed much wilder, especially in the cornfields that year, than the old squirrels which normally are much wiser and craftier.

The next shot was unexciting. It occurred along the edge of the bushes, and was at a medium sized animal, which was shot through the ribs. The range was only 15 yards. I do not recall when I ever shot so many gray squirrels at such short ranges as during the year of the big storm. I would rather have them farther off, as then the bullet will be up level with the line of sight, or maybe just a trifle higher. The rifle had been sighted in for 50 yards, with the bullets grouped in the upper half of the 10-ring of the 100-yard target, which gave a sighting about five-eighths inch above the line of sight at 50 yards.

Before long another hunter, whom I had met before, showed up. He had a single barrel shotgun. It seems that he had pieced the two halves of two different guns together and was therefore using a hybrid weapon which had the one virtue of being light and handy. Otherwise, it was not very prepossessing.

We discussed various things, off where it would do no harm, and then walked down the field together. Squirrels would work out into the cornfield, among the shocks, and shielded by the grass, and a hunter would not see them generally until one ran sneaking down a corn row or put on a burst of speed for the nearest line of trees.

Down near the end of the cornpatch *three* squirrels suddenly made a break for shelter, although I only saw two of them at the moment. These had both been feeding on one ear of corn. My companion fired at and killed a very large male squirrel back of me, but his shot made the one I was aiming at put on a sudden burst of speed, and in addition it got down below my line of sight as the ground level was lower where it was going. So I swung onto the other squirrel, which was a bit smaller, and fired just as he made a frantic leap to the butt of the nearest hickory. The bullet pinned him fast to the tree trunk, about a foot from the ground from which position his plume whirled around in a circle, which always means a hard hit on a gray squirrel. So I walked up and picked this one up from where it had in the meantime fallen to the ground and found it shot squarely through the ribs, from side to side.

"You shot that squirrel while it was running hard, and with a rifle, didn't you?" asked the rather astonished gunner.

"Yes," was the reply, "I get one that way occasionally. But it is difficult to shoot squirrels running on the ground, especially if they are partly hidden by the grass," I added as an afterthought.

"Just the same, it is the first time I ever saw that done!" said he. "I miss a good many myself with the shotgun. I am going home now, before I make a fool of myself in front of you, but before I go I *would* like to see you shoot *another!*"

He looked rather longingly at the "bump" in my rear coat pocket where four squirrels and a lunch made the coat stick out quite prominently.

It may have been just natural enthusiasm of a sportsman watching rifle shooting that was a bit more successful, just then, than he had been accustomed to—largely because of better equipment. But there was also a peculiar glitter to his eye as he said this, and I could at once see a vision of the boy who stood on the burning deck and who did not feel much like jumping in; the water, it appears, was both deep and wet.

In this instance I was wondering what would happen on that next shot especially if the squirrel ran hard, and in addition I still was not seeing things any too clearly and that is no help, especially on moving game. It is a wise man who knows when to quit. I figured it was probably a good time for me to take a walk down along the run, and do a little shooting down there, alone. But just then a foolish squirrel came out and ran up and down on the fence rails at the only bars around, and these bars of course had to be directly on my way to the lower woods. Consequently, I could not get out of attempting another shot, as my companion very graciously stepped back and made it his special duty to signal me as to every movement of the squirrel while I attempted a stalk within offhand range, from cornshock to cornshock.

I do not mind saying that I felt a bit relieved when the squirrel dodged behind the bars and raced into the woods. Meantime, the shotgun shooter moved down toward the other end of the corn rows, saw a squirrel on the ground, and apparently missed it, as he waved his hand in a disgusted movement as he left, and did not stoop down to pick up anything as he passed that spot.

About that time I reached the bars and stood up back of the post. Within five minutes a gray came across the leaves, apparently looking for mushrooms, upon which they often feed considerably, and when he saw me started rapidly for a small tree in which there was a squirrel nest. I held ahead and as his head came into view in the scope and the nose approached the cross-hair intersection, blazed away and turned him upside down with a complete flip-flop. The bullet "thwacked" against his left side, entering low down in the ribs, cut the heart in half, as I discovered upon dressing the animal a few moments later, and the H.P. came out the ribs on the right side, on its way cutting up both front legs considerably, and breaking the spine between the shoulders. The range was around 30 yards or less, as he was coming my way pretty fast, and a gray squirrel gets over the ground.

This made five squirrels in six chances; The last two, both clean kills, were shot running and the last one was hit through the heart. But the other shooter had by that time left the cornfield feeling, I assume, that his day's work was done.

These were good sized squirrels, fat, and in fine condition. The looks of the cornshocks, indicated why; ear after ear was either completely stripped of kernels or at least 50 per cent shelled and eaten. The worst of it was that the corn which was not eaten was largely destroyed, or at least unfit for sale as most of the grains had been chewed down part way to the cob. A tyro squirrel shooter can always discover *where* squirrels are feeding on corn on the stalk or in the shock, by walking along any cornfield near a woods, or a line of trees, or even a grown up fence row or a stone pile, and noticing whether ears of corn, partly eaten, are strewed here and there on the ground, hauled up into the lower branches of trees or left balancing upon a fence post or rail, or whether ears have been pulled partly out of the husk and chewed and largely shelled off. Some of this damage may have been done by ringnecked pheasants if the corn is simply partly eaten out of the ears and the ears are on the ground only, and on the stalks, but in that case grains will be eaten cleanly and not chewed off at the outer portion or large end of each grain. But if they are chewed materially and not cleanly shelled, it is squirrels, either gray, fox or red, which are doing the damage. They usually feed on the corn the hardest after 5 P.M. or on moonlight nights.

Perhaps we can show you here, a photo of what a cornshock looks like after the squirrels have been working upon it, for a time.

Up to the time mentioned above, I had shot 18 gray squirrels, in 20 shots, during the open season of that year and of these, 15 had been fired at with a .22 rifle, and 13 of those had been killed and bagged. Two required two shots each, one being struck by two bullets, the other having been missed on the first shot and bagged with the second. Eleven of the thirteen squirrels had been killed cleanly with one shot each, and not a single squirrel had been shot back of its middle, except the one mentioned. None had been gut shot or struck through the hams, either of which is always unfortunate, and no squirrels had been shot and killed which had previously been wounded.

Most of the shooting was strictly offhand, without a rest of any kind, and a sling strap had not been on the rifle, therefore had not been used. For most offhand shooting in green timber, with nearly all the leaves still on the trees, early in the season in those localities in which the squirrel season comes in earlier than it should, and with much undergrowth in the cornfields, a sling merely adds useless weight to the outfit, it gets caught on snags and in brush and worse still it sways beneath the rifle and causes the muzzle to describe a larger than normal arc, at the exact moment you may want to fire hurriedly. In late season squirrel shooting, in high and large timber, with the leaves all or nearly all off the trees, the underbrush down by heavy frosts, and nothing much between you and a squirrel and most of them by that time wild, hungry and hard to approach, a sling begins to show its advantages, especially in the case of shots from the sitting position and when a sort of impromptu arm rest is possible. In that case most shots will be at ranges of 35 to 100 yards, and occasional chances may be taken by a thoroughly competent rifleman at still greater distances, if necessary.

But, careful stalking and better placing of your stand with relation to the hickory trees, nests, den trees and down logs, and also the nearby rail fences used as squirrel highways, will generally put you well within .22 rifle range of the average gray squirrel which shows up.

It has been my experience that squirrels living in mountain country where there are large boulders and irregular rock piles, old chestnut snags for den trees, and not much second growth on the forest floor, will be harder to stalk, more difficult to kill, and will take closer watching after they strike the leaves, than will squirrels in more settled and more thickly populated and more open farming communities.

In the farming districts, the squirrels are more accustomed to the daily presence of people, autoists, farmers, farm animals as well, and to noises and sudden approaches. A squirrel soon gets tired of racing wildly for the nearest tree when there is no real need for running. The corn or the beechnuts are inviting and he no more likes to be chased from a full dinner table than would you.

But even so, I would much rather hunt and shoot squirrels in virgin timber that is both old and high than in short scrub with occasional trees or in cornfields and around their edges. The conditions are much better adapted to successful rifle shooting. The best rifle for shooting a squirrel running across a tree top, up or down a tree trunk, or down a cornrow, is a light repeater with jack sights. And by far the best one for taking the long range shots, is the telescope sighted match rifle, single shot or repeater.

But, as suggested before, "squirrels are where you find them!" It

TIME FOR A PHOTO, BEFORE GOING HOME

An Ohio hunter, who, with his scope sighted .22 repeater, has bagged four grey and fox squirrels. Even the dog seems to feel that all is well, and is not at all averse to taking his full share of credit for the success of the day's hunt.

Photo, Courtesy, Ohio Div. of Conservation and Natural Resources

behooves a man or a boy bent on shooting squirrels, be they gray, fox, or pine squirrels, or any other variety, not to quarrel with conditions as he finds them but to accept the situation as it is and to plan his campaign of shooting so as to give him the maximum number of suitable shots, under light, weather, outside influence and other conditions, so that he may possibly handle most of them successfully.

In this respect, you must look where you are shooting and to the background. You must discover the highways used by the squirrels in getting to and coming from, the feeding grounds—be these rail fences, worm fences, lines of trees—crossing from tree to tree, or on the ground to the field, from the nearest nest or den tree. But the main thing is to discover their feeding grounds and what time of day they are most certain to be out in force.

Remember, you are planning on shooting individual squirrels. Unfortunately in the wilder districts, an intruder is likely to be immediately barked at, by the old dam. The squirrel that is feeding industriously and then speeding for home, in a bee line, is also likely to be the old dam. The big, tough, short-tempered chap, who does not like to be disturbed at table, is generally father. He may also be a grandfather or worse. The squirrels which are racing up and down tree trunks with wild abandon and chasing each other over and around logs, without much attention to what else goes on (except in mating season) will usually be this year's young squirrels which may not as yet have acquired much sense.

In the order of their ripening, you will likely find gray squirrels feeding upon the following: Field corn in the milk, ripened field corn on the stalk, and then a bit later in the shock—in which case squirrels will usually be denned temporarily in trees within 10 to 100 yards of the corn fields. But they may come down from a quarter of a mile up the mountain, or even from clear at the top of the mountain, if nuts and mushrooms are non-existent or scarce.

They also feed very extensively upon beechnuts, especially early in the season, and when so feeding make excellent marks for a .22 rifle. Beechnut trees are easy to hunt out and the ground beneath them is usually fairly even and level and easy to cover with the eye. A bit later they are feeding upon chestnuts, if there are any chestnuts; upon small, sweet acorns, shellbarks and on hognut hickory nuts—all hickory nuts are bitter when they are not fully ripened and squirrels will not feed upon them extensively if they have other feed like corn or beechnuts until they do ripen. Squirrels, in this particular, have more sense than small boys who like to eat green apples. Hunt your shellbark and hickory nut trees in late October and early November, rather than in mid-September, if the local shooting season permits hunting gray squirrels in several of these months. Squirrels also feed considerably upon persimmons, upon mushrooms found usually in damp portions of the woods after rains, even upon small berries or cherry seeds and fruits on occasion. A squirrel will eat a wide variety of foods if it needs to, but its main menu today consists of corn, beechnuts and hickory nuts; also acorns, often from pin oaks.

In a year of "no nuts" meaning few if any chestnuts, beechnuts and hickory nuts, squirrels will invariably attack the corn early and late and will keep this up in fields along the foot of mountain ranges, ridges or wood lots, day after day until the corn is removed or destroyed.

Meanwhile, the chap who hunts the mountain tops and the hill-sides, keeping largely to the den trees and the hickories and chestnut stubs, will come home often with a puzzled look on his face and an empty coat, even when his friends are shooting plenty of squirrels.

Many of the squirrels may have migrated for the time being, down along the creek bottoms and the occasional trees that line the streams in the farmer's fields. Or they may be seen racing along rail fences or crossing the automobile highways, from one fence line to another, or one grove of trees to another.

In past years chestnuts were the greatest gray squirrel food in the Alleghenies, the Blue Ridge, and the wood lots of the Middle Atlantic and adjacent states. Every mountain side, every wooded field, and every creek bottom had its stand of chestnut trees. They were the feeding, the playing and the living quarters of the squirrels of the community. When the chestnut blight hit the East, gray squirrels suffered an almost irreparable loss, not only in food, but because it gradually wiped out their den trees. This made a housing shortage in Squirrel Land.

Beechnuts, butternuts and hickories, and also white oaks, chestnut oaks, red and black oaks, would grow around and among them, or adjacent to them, but the old lightning and fire-blasted chestnut snags were the ancestral homes and the food reservoirs and Frigidaires of the gray squirrels. They were also the locations of many "bee tree" honey caches, and at times the homes of raccoon and opossum.

Blown down chestnut trees, chestnut logs, two to four feet or more in diameter in most instances, were the highways of the gray squirrels from here to over there. They also made fine seats to sit upon (when dry) by the squirrel hunter, or good places to lie down back of and take a snooze while passing the time which was dull and monotonous, between 10.30 A.M., usually the end of the morning shooting, and 2.30 or 3.00 P.M., the beginning of the afternoon fun.

Many a time I have so slept for hours, the sun glimmering in gold and silver, down through the gloriously-colored leaves of the trees colored by old Jack Frost in every known shade of red, brown, yellow and lemon. Lying there in the warm sun, covered with dry leaves, and with my head on my arm, warm and dry in the Duxbak outfit, I could sleep in peace without an alarm clock or the call to meals.

But any good thing can be overdone! I once woke up suddenly two or three hours after darkness set in, a mile up on a mountain side, somewhere on the "flat" which was higher on the down side than on the side next the real mountain, and a third of a mile wide. I thought I must be dead. It was as dark as the inside of a cow. I soon discovered that I was not in Heaven because I had neither wings nor a nightgown. I luckily was not in Hell, because by that time I was really much too cold to have been there. I certainly was not in my own bed so—where was I? All at once it came to me that I must be up on the mountain, so, how to get down? There were no woods roads, and about one-third of the area was in choppings; two of these were below me. If you ever have tried to get down off a mountain side, in pitch darkness and without matches or a flash-light, and have to find your way without moon or many visible stars you will realize the difficulties of the problem. I made it in about half an hour, by lining up an occasional lamp in a farmhouse in the distant valley, down below, and by holding my hands in front of my eyes to try to protect them from branches, briars, and from bumping too sharply against trees.

But an even more annoying experience once happened to a squirrel hunting friend of mine, and on the same mountain. He had also fallen asleep. When he awoke he somehow sensed that all was not well immediately back of him. It was just at dusk and an owl was hooting most mournfully in the distance. When he turned his head he looked directly into the glaring eyes of a large wildcat which was then sitting on a rock ledge within a couple of feet of his face, and it then immediately spit at him!

Story is that he threw away his gun, ran wildly down the mountain, and did not get the shotgun back until the following day when a heavily armed "posse" of shooting friends went along and helped to rescue it.

One does not hear so many tales of wildcats scaring squirrel hunters these days, but foxes often trot silently past the shooter in the half light of dawn or dusk, and then bark sharply as they reach the more open valley and begin their hunt for mice, rabbits, quail nests or maybe a tasty ruffed grouse, if still in the wooded country. Or maybe a fine plump Plymouth Rock from the flock of Farmer Brown, who lives along the foot of the mountain.

But the squirrel hunter sits up far above the abode of Farmer Brown and he can look off far into the distance, some times, if the timber is not too thick, and in his mind's eye, possibly, he can look back years and years before the coming of the age of the motor car, the radio, the submarine and the bombing plane, when painted Senecas, Iroquois, Delawares and other braves flitted silently along the mountain paths on moccasined feet, and along the tortuous shallows in the creek bottoms and he will see the .22 match rifle, his pet squirrel arm, turned mysteriously into a flintlock Pennsylvania rifle, his headdress will assume the proportions of a coonskin cap, his Duxbaks will be transformed into buckskin, and on his feet will be the beaded moccasins such as worn in the years gone by.

The timber crown will rise suddenly to virgin timber height, there will be no sawdust piles in the hollows below the mountain springs; deer, squirrels, and turkeys will again roam the forest in the numbers they actually were in, many, many hundreds of moons before, and there he will sit and dream and see these things with himself all as an integral part of it. And it will all be a wonderful dream, and to some it can seem so very, very real, especially to youthful hunters whose imaginations may still be fired by the visions that march down the forest aisles.

But for you and me, my friend, evening comes, it gets cool on the mountain after the sun goes down, and also in the ordinary wood lot of more open farming areas, and while the poplars, the oaks, the buttonwoods, the beechnuts and the hickories flame in the setting sun we must regretfully, ever so regretfully, turn our faces to the West, and the path that leads us home.

Gone are the days of the American frontier! Gone are the dreams of youth! But never gone are the visions of the squirrel hunter as long as he is able to shoulder his rifle! It may be only a modern .22, but it is still a rifle, the weapon of the expert shot the world over, and the means by which the squirrel hunter in North America periodically renews his youth.

So long as we live, may each of us be able to carry the rifle up the Indian path that crosses the squirrel woods, out on the mountain!

CHAPTER 3

Science in Squirrel Shooting with Rifles

WEBSTER'S DEFINITION OF SCIENCE MAY BE CONDENSED INTO THESE few words: "Science is systematized knowledge of acknowledged truths and laws as demonstrated by experiment and observation."

Science in squirrel shooting is therefore the application of systematized knowledge of natural laws and ballistic facts as demonstrated by experiment and observation to belong to small bore rifles and ammunition, plus the practical working knowledge of squirrels and their daily habits under different conditions of food and weather, that is acquired by hunting.

In a nutshell, it is simply using your brain in the woods, first: to locate the squirrels; and second; to shoot at those squirrels, individually, so that you may bag them with the first shot.

Possibly the first thing the reader will ask himself, if he has had but little training in ballistics, or lacks experience in rifle shooting at game in the woods, is, "What can I do to make myself a successful squirrel hunter with a rifle?"

Obviously, he is reading this book, possibly he has read ".22-Caliber Rifle Shooting" by the same author, published in 1931 or "Twenty-two Caliber Varmint Rifles, published in 1947 and should in this or other ways, have obtained at least some knowledge of the ballistics of the .22, and of how to hunt and shoot squirrels with a rifle. In case he is a newcomer to the game, and to refresh the memory of the more experienced, we will attempt to give a bit of practical application of science to squirrel shooting.

We will assume that the hunter has a .22 caliber light sporting rifle, either single shot or repeater, or that he has a .22 match rifle probably converted into a sporter. In the first case his rifle is likely equipped with open or peep sights, in the latter it will have peep and bead metallic sights and a rifle telescope adapted to hunting, but in a mount adjustable by very small and exact divisions.

He has probably also purchased a couple of boxes of .22 long rifle high velocity ammunition containing hollow point bullets and has discovered, ere this, they are loaded with lubricated bullets, of alloyed lead, each having a small hole in the nose. The bullet is rather flattened on the front end, and if he will take a pocketknife and cut one of these bullets down the middle, he will find that the bullet is pierced down its center by this hole, for about one-third to one-half of its length; when fired this has the result of causing the bullet to mushroom or spread out to a materially larger diameter, even when penetrating nothing but the tough hide and the flesh of the squirrel. A direct hit on the larger bones will cause considerable shattering of the bony structure. A gray squirrel is normally from one inch to two and one-half inches in thickness, in the foreparts, which is the area at which aim is usually taken. An experienced shot does not fire at a squirrel turned lengthwise toward him if possible to avoid this. He does not wish to mangle the meat of the lower back or the hams, the more desirable and edible portions of the squirrel.

Ballistic engineers have very carefully designed and alloyed this bullet so that it will expand promptly and efficiently in small animals or the larger birds. It will make a hole in the hide, where it enters, varying from the diameter of the bullet to that of a dime, and where it emerges from the size of a dime to that of a quarter. How much it expands will depend upon the range, which determines the remaining velocity of the bullet, and upon the toughness of the bones which it meets in passing through the squirrel.

Before this the hunter has probably learned this bullet weighs 37-grains (the solid nose bullet weighs 40-grains), and that it has a muzzle velocity of approximately 1,350 f.s. when it leaves the rifle. This does not mean it will travel 1,350 feet in the first second after it leaves the rifle, it means that it is traveling *at the rate of* 1,350 f.s. as it passes out of the muzzle.

Air resistance is encountered immediately, even when passing up the barrel, and this cuts down velocity almost immediately after emerging from the muzzle. At 100 yards from the muzzle of the rifle the velocity is *then* 1,075 f.s. which is almost exactly the *muzzle velocity* of the older and standard velocity .22 long rifle cartridge—one which is preferable in some cases, due to its much lighter report.

This little 37-grain, high speed lead bullet, which is today the best buy for the money in .22 rim fire ammunition, of types suitable for small game hunting, develops an energy of 161 foot pounds at the muzzle (Winchester figures), and still retains 95 foot pounds at 100 yards. You will seldom kill a squirrel at that distance, so it stands to reason and is a fact of ballistics, that the little bullet will be traveling somewhere between 1,075 f.s. and 1,350 f.s.—most likely about 1,175 to 1,200 f.s. when it strikes the squirrel. It then has an energy of around 125 foot pounds which will be partly dissipated in the body of an animal weighing one to two and one-fourth pounds.

Some of this energy will be dissipated in the form of heat; more of it will be used up in cutting a hole in the tough hide—try your knife on it and see how tough it is and how easily it stretches, even in a young fox or gray squirrel. Then additional energy will be transformed into other forms in tearing through the tough muscles and the bony structure. Whether the bullet or its main fragments emerge from the squirrel will depend upon the range and the angle at which the bullet strikes and the bones encountered.

But before all these scientific changes occur you must first hit the squirrel! This may be easy and it may be very difficult. Science enters again, plus much sport! To hit squirrels, which are small and very active and usually pretty wild and difficult to approach, especially in dry weather and in mountainous country, the very first thing to do is very accurately and properly to sight in the rifle.

That means, *with the ammunition you will use*, the rifle must group its bullets in an area, the center of impact of which will be so located as compared to the position of aim on the squirrel, that you can hit and kill the squirrel at the maximum spread of distances, both close and far, without changing the holding materially, or the sighting at all. This sounds a bit complicated and indefinite but actually it is simple.

Careful ballistic experiments have shown that the .22 long rifle rim fire, H.P., high-speed type of cartridge may be sighted for 75 yards and when so sighted the bullet will not be more than one inch above or below the line of sight, at any distance between 10 yards and 83 yards, if the rifle be scope sighted, and very little more than this if sighted with peep and bead sights which do not set up quite as far above the bore.

If you happen still to have some of the low-velocity .22 long rifle hollow points, the rifle may be sighted for 60 yards, and the bullet will not strike more than one inch above or below the line of sight between 10 yards and 70 yards from the muzzle.

But experience and theory do not exactly agree on the desirability of sighting a .22 rim fire squirrel rifle for such long range. For one thing, especially early in the season, when many leaves are still on the trees and most of the squirrels are feeding along cornfields, or are on the ground running around among second growth, or are going up and down tree trunks, when seen they may not average more than 25 to 35 yards from the rifle, and possibly a shorter range sighting would be preferable. Many find it so.

If the 75-yards sighting be used, and most of the shots are between 20 and 40 yards from the gunner, the average bullet will strike somewhere between one-fourth inch and one inch above the line of aim. In other words, practically every shot will be striking high.

Experience—not ballistic, but field experience—has proved that it is desirable to have the bullet strike a bit high, in squirrel shooting, because this results in a very high percentage of shots striking and cutting the spinal cord, which of course, causes paralysis, and usually nearly instant death, and as squirrels are rodents and tenacious of life, this is a desirable factor in favor of high grouping. On the other hand, if one shoots at the head of the squirrel, and the bullet goes high, he is likely to shoot over the animal and have a miss, as he would likely aim for the butt of the ear. If the squirrel is crouching and is flattened on a limb, or is partly hiding behind a branch or the trunk of the tree, one is likely to shoot high as there is little allowable vertical deviation, so it is not always desirable to have a too-high sighting. It is well to remember at all times, that if a squirrel is well hidden, and peeping across a limb, all one sees is plenty of tail, which is likely to draw the shot if you do not have a telescope sight.

If the sighting is excessively low, the rather high trajectory of the .22 long rifle cartridge, which is about three inches over 100 yards for the .22 long rifle H.P. high-speed loads, will cause excessively low shots beyond 40 yards.

So we will gather up a bunch of rifle targets and seek the nearest 50 yards rifle range and see what we can do about sighting in that rifle for effective squirrel shooting. It may be better to take 100-yard targets for use at 50 yards than the standard 50-yard targets, because a bead front sight covers quite a bit of area, and may completely cover the 50 yards bull, and in addition more of the 100-yard targets are printed one on a sheet than 50-yard targets. It is less confusing to be able to aim at but the one bull on the paper.

You will not be using the target shooter's 6 o'clock hold beneath the bullseye but will aim directly on the bull, so that the top of the bead is in the middle of the bull, as the hunter must aim *at* what he is trying to shoot, not somewhere thereabouts. To use the 6 o'clock hold and sight in for that, and then go hunting, will invariably result in most of the bullets going two to three and one-half inches above the point of aim, which of course will give misses on gray squirrels flattened on limbs or running or hopping on the ground while feeding.

Target frames are readily obtainable on most target ranges and of course are in the club house or in the target shed, and the targets are attached to the frames by thumb tacks or large clips. If no frames are available, two widths of a wide board, nailed onto cross pieces, will answer nicely—they can be hung onto a wire or to a frame, or stood up against a backstop. If no regular 50 yard range is available, step off 52 to 55 paces and go to it!

Most target shooters would sight in the rifle prone and then add a bit of extra elevation for offhand. But more than likely you are not accustomed to prone shooting, the rifle may not be fitted with swivels or a sling, and you may not be at home in shooting prone.

The automobile that takes us out to the range makes an elegant semi-offhand, semi-sitting, rifle rest. Just turn the car at right angles to the range and rest the arms and the back of the left hand on a blanket thrown over the hood of the car, and you have a perfectly practical arm rest from which very steady and successful shooting may be done. The engine should be shut off, to prevent vibration and excessive heat. A bench rest, or a table with a chair to its left side, and a small box or a folded blanket or small cushion on the front of the rest or table, will also make an excellent and secure shooting rest.

A scientific fact of much interest to the squirrel shooter, is that a rifle, even a .22 rim fire, regardless of whether it is a heavy match arm or a light repeater, will shoot high from any table or auto or bench rest, if the barrel rests on anything solid and unyielding. The nearer the muzzle it is rested, (and also the thinner the barrel of the rifle) the higher the rifle will tend to group, the more the barrel will vibrate, especially toward the muzzle, and the higher the center of impact will be *above* the normal center of impact when the rifle is shot offhand, or with a body rest or arm rest against the side of a tree.

Experienced riflemen always rest the back of the left hand on a cushion or a folded blanket, rather than to rest the rifle barrel itself, when sighting-in a rifle for hunting, especially if it must be used on small game which presents as small an area in a vertical direction, as does the average squirrel. They are very careful to let off each shot when the sights are properly aligned, one with the other and both with respect to the bullseye. They are careful to maintain the tension on the sling, if one be used, as uniform as possible. They are observant to see that they do not push down or pull back hard for one shot and hold very lightly for the next.

The rifleman will fire five or 10 shots in a group, after firing a couple of warming shots into the ground, and will then examine his group to see how its center of impact corresponds with, or superposes over, the bullseye. He will fire repeated groups and change the sighting, lowering the sighting if the rifle shoots too high, raising it if too low, moving the rear sight to the right—or the front one to the left, if the arm groups to the left, and vice versa, until the group does center pretty close to the middle of the bullseye. He might decide to set it a bit high purposely.

Riflemen have learned that .22 rifles, as well as other calibers, shoot higher: 1. With an increase of temperature; 2. When the light is stronger; 3. At a high altitude than at a low altitude. The amount of moisture in the air, and that absorbed by the powder, will affect vertical grouping and will also affect the accuracy of shooting. Further a very heavy barreled and rigidly stocked rifle is likely to show smaller deviations from changes of temperature, or of moisture, especially if its stock is of dense grained walnut, than is a light barreled rifle or one poorly stocked.

The old timer, and the ballistic expert, will try to sight in the rifle when the sky is partly overcast and not so much sun is on the sights or the target, because it always seems more overcast and quite dark, comparatively, in the woods, especially if the timber be high and thick with leaves. It is likely to be especially dark in woods down along runs and in second growth. Obviously, you want the rifle sighted for the light condition and the temperature where you will do your squirrel shooting. This is likely to be an average temperature throughout the day, of about 50° F. in the Middle Atlantic States, during the normal squirrel shooting hours, with 15° to 20° lower on very frosty mornings, and 20° to 25° higher on very warm, Indian summer afternoons.

A frosty morning, means a low shooting rifle. The chill of evening coming on results in a low shooting rifle. The hunter who moves from a dense dark woods out into the edge of a cornfield, in the bright sun, to shoot squirrels feeding along the edge of the cornshocks or the boundary fence, will normally find his rifle grouping higher than in the darker woods. This change of grouping will usually be from one-half inch to one inch at 50 yards, with a one and one-half inch change in vertical in extreme cases. Be certain you will get this change, with the changes indicated in light and weather. They will be less with a telescope sight than with iron sights, *if* the scope mounts are of rigid and heavy construction. Notice, I said the *mounts*, not the scope!

The experienced squirrel shot will keep these things in mind if he is wise, and most of them are, and he will aim lower on the body or at the lower edge of it if the day gets very warm and the rifle had been sighted for a cool day, or a dark, cool day. And on a foggy morning or a very cold, windy morning (which latter is normally a miserable day for squirrel shooting) he will be very careful to aim about the top line of the back or just above it. On the other hand, with a very even shooting rifle, consistent that is in daily variations, he will not *overdo* this matter of holding high or low.

The Drug Store Cowboy may not bother with such refinements, but then the Drug Store Cowboys are not, as a rule, expert rifle shots of the type who shoot but once at a squirrel and expect to hit it about the same place as the usual aiming point, at least four times in every five shots.

The man who has had the advantages of an engineering or other technical, scientific or chemical education and training, will see the need of most of these as soon as they are pointed out to him, and the experienced ballistic engineer or match shooter will attend to such things as second nature.

Having by this time, sighted your rifle to group to center at 35 yards, if most of your shots will be within 40 yards, or to group one-half inch to one inch high at 50 or 60 yards if you expect long shots as well as close range opportunities, you are about ready to go squirrel shooting. If you have difficulty to remember how much high or low the rifle is shooting, at any range, and with a given sighting, it is a good plan to carry a homemade, small scale trajectory graph, with each 10 yards listed so much high or low, in the patch pocket of your coat or shirt.

Obviously, it is almost useless to hunt squirrels where there are no squirrels or so few of them, and these so wild from overshooting, that one can seldom be seen. The real problem is to find a woods in which there are many squirrels, and in which hunting is permitted, or in which you can obtain such concession.

One method of finding such a location is to interview country town or farm boys, the hired men on farms, the rural mail carrier, or salesmen who often drive through the area in question. I know that during the last few years it has become nationally popular to slander our young people, and to paint them as being wild, lazy, criminally inclined and habitually untruthful. Maybe some are worse than the paragons of virtue I associated with in my youth, and some of whom became sainted hypocrites in later years, but you can not prove it by me. When I want to find quail or gray squirrels, I always ask the farm boys, because I have found them to be usually truthful in such matters.

It is presumed that we have now located a suitable place to hunt squirrels. There are pine squirrels, gray squirrels, black squirrels—a form of the gray—and fox squirrels. It is well to recall, that the feeding habits of several of these species will be found to vary quite a bit—red or pine squirrels will hang around pine trees, apple trees and walnut trees but grays are not so likely to do so—and the dens of all may depend quite often, largely upon the local timber.

Better set the alarm clock for one and one-half hours earlier than you want to be in the woods, after a normal, short drive. It is best to wear old hunting clothing because that is not conspicuous, and to be shod in shoe pacs, sneakers, moccasins, or at least *rubber heeled* Army shoes. The idea is to keep the feet dry in the morning, and to be able to move around in the woods a bit, now and then, without sounding like a moving van or a bull on a rampage.

You will need your hunting license, your license certificate, a box or two of cartridges (you might prefer to use both high-speed and low-speed cartridges during the day), a small lunch, a good skinning and dressing knife, and it is a good idea to put a heavy double bag (one bag inside the other) in the rear game pocket of the hunting coat, in which to carry bleeding game—like dressed squirrels. A small camera can also go along, in its case. You do not require a lot of heavy shotgun shells, or even a shell vest, unless you wish to wear one to keep warm, and to protect the stomach and abdomen in case of a fall on a snag or on rocks. It is excellent for that purpose.

Remember that all squirrels must come from a nest or a den tree. Be near one or more of these half an hour before daylight. It takes the average gray squirrel 20 to 30 minutes to come out and run around after the usual hunting party has crashed through the woods. I am not in favor of smoking, talking, shooting at anything whatever except hawks or other predators, or fooling with a flashlight, while hunting squirrels. The idea is to keep quiet and to make every shot a kill. This conclusion requires but little scientific knowledge; it is just plain, common sense.

It is obvious that a squirrel may be seen first, when it is between you and the sky, or when it is between the shooter and the rising sun. The gunner should be posted accordingly. It should be obvious that the squirrel will soon move from his den tree toward the cornfield, or the nut tree, or the cache in the ground, or to the nearest water, and once he starts will lose little time on the way. On very cold mornings he may come out and preen a bit in the warm sun, before feeding or before running out onto the tips of the limbs to cut off nuts, which then will be buried when he has decided he has put enough of them down. The sound of falling nuts, especially if it is not windy or very frosty, is a pretty sure sign that a nut-cutting squirrel is hard at work. Look for shaking limbs. Several squirrels may feed on one tree at the same time. These are likely to be the old ones and the young brood. "Cuttings" on stumps, down logs, on rail fences or posts, will help to locate where the squirrels sit and feed.

Remember, we now have two things to do: locate the first squirrel, then bring down that squirrel. Another gray may appear, to present a better opportunity, in the interim. It sounds simple and easy, once you have found the squirrel, but the frisky little fellow may have other ideas. Once dead, he will be dead a long time and he is not inviting disaster. Never forget that the most obvious characteristic of all squirrels, is *curiosity;* which transcends that of almost all other game animals.

He seems to ask himself: "What is he doing there? Is he dangerous to me or my brood? Let's call him unprintable names, then slip around the tree trunk and hide! What business has he here? I think I will comment unkindly about his ancestors, maybe then he will leave!" And so, "Quack! Quack! Quaah! Quaah! Quaah! Quaah!"

An owl may hoot off in the distance, in the eerie gloom of the woods. The water drips from the trees. Leaves come sailing down in a ghostly manner. The whole forest seems mysterious and weird and maybe your hat starts to rise at every little noise. There it goes again, "Quack! Quack! Quack! Quaah! Quaah!" Sounds a bit closer this time, not so high in the trees, the bark is angrier and more vigorous. The squirrel is gaining courage. Then farther up the hill, comes a fainter, "Quaah! Quaah! Quaah!" This means, "It's true, he is that kind of a so-so! Bark at him!"

The tyro imagines that he hears a wildcat, or a raccoon, or a fox, or a mountain lion, but brother, it is only an angry gray squirrel, possibly 30 or 40 yards off, barking, and another, possibly 100 yards off, adding his angry "two cents."

The barking gets louder and more urgent—if you should happen to see him his tail would be whipping sharply with each bark, and he would be stirring around uneasily on the limb. But you do not see him, and soon there is the sound of falling bark, then the squirrel runs unexpectedly down the tree and off into the bushes. You missed that chance for the moment by not being ready and by not having a woodsman's eyes. The chances are too, that you were examining trees too far away from you.

Just then there is a low sound on the rail fence, the squirrel's highway, 20 yards back of you. You glance around and there is a gray, plume in the air and whipping sharply back and forth because he is annoyed at the intrusion. You move very slowly, very carefully around, keep an eye on the feet at the same time, to avoid breaking twigs, the rifle comes up a bit at a time and, when it comes level with the squirrel, he gives a jump or two and perches on a post.

The rifle gives a sharp "splat," the bullet lands with a solid "plop" and down goes Mr. Gray Squirrel on the far side of the fence. There is a bit of scurry and all is still. If you are certain of the shot there is no reason to move; if not, go over at once and retrieve the game— and look for him sneaking up the rear of the nearest tree trunk, as you move along. Squirrels at times, exhibit the most remarkable vitality, particularly if the bullet failed to expand, or if not hit in an immediately fatal spot. And sound of movement in the leaves, not all in exactly the same spot, is also a bad sign. It means you have no time to lose. But, you have been lucky this time.

You pick up the squirrel *by the hind foot*—keep your hands away from his jaws if there is the least bit of life, and start dressing him. That is, if no *fleas* are in evidence, ready to leave the carcass. If so, snap the animal away from you and walk away from there and give them time to leave. Not many squirrels have fleas, but some do, and here is where you act as host, if you are going to accumulate visitors. They may jump on your leggins and climb up the legs.

Slit the squirrel from crotch to throat, remove all of the organs, entrails and bladder first, then kidneys, stomach, lungs, heart, the small kernels in the arm pits, and shake out the blood. Note the hole of entrance and the hole of exit. If you have made a clean shot, you have reason to congratulate yourself. If the animal is shot in the hams, or to the rear, in the back, as well as in the chest or head, pin no roses upon yourself but try to keep your aim where it belongs next time, and never shoot at a squirrel facing directly toward or away from you, if on all four feet, if at all avoidable. Now you can resume your original post, let the squirrel dry and drain a moment, keep off any blow flies which may be attracted, and then put him in that double bag in the rear coat pocket.

Your shooting may now be resumed. First, you have the problem of locating another squirrel. You may recall that a gray came down a tree about 30 yards off, another answered 100 yards up the hill, so there are at least two more, feeding, hiding or just sitting up in curiosity, rather close to you.

If the leaves are very wet, you might wish to change your position a trifle to command more of the ground where the squirrel ran across and down the large trees he might have again climbed. You may want to get midway between the upper and the lower squirrel. If so, take it easy, and do no moving around for the present that may be avoided.

In about 20 minutes you hear a slight noise, about 25 yards to the left, on the leaves. Yes, there is a young squirrel hopping lightly across the ground. Bring your rifle up slowly, hold ahead of the squirrel and when his nose comes into the field of the glass or you see it across the sights, let him have it as he walks into the bullet.

Unless you remember to hold a foot to a foot and a half ahead, at least, he will get across and past the field of the scope, or out of your metallic sight line, before you can shoot. In which case you will then have to change your position a bit and try to pick him up again.

But if lucky, and you *remembered* that bit of ballistic advice, that the bullet is *below* the line of sight for the first 10 to 25 yards, as a result of which you held on the upper line of the head of that squirrel and then naturally the bullet landed somewhere between neck and tummy.

A squirrel so shot usually pitches over, kicks a bit, then lies quiet. Might as well go pick him up *unless another squirrel is in sight and within rifle range.* If there is, try to get a shot at the other before you leave your present position.

By this time the sun is probably shining across the top of the hill, things are livening up in the woods, and the day is at hand in earnest. You can see much better than you could three quarters of an hour before.

Before long you spot a squirrel washing his face, or eating a nut in the first large crotch of a big hickory, some 60 yards down the woods. He is simply out there for a sun bath, and if you are careful and no one else comes along, he is not likely to leave soon.

This will be a very simple and practically a certain shot, for an experienced squirrel hunter who has a first class, scope sighted rifle, and there is opportunity for an arm rest of some sort. But the tyro is likely to become over anxious, shoot too scon, and spoil such an opportunity.

It is presumed he has a rifle with the sight line one and one-half inches above the bore. His bullet will strike, if let off perfectly, from one-half inch to one inch above the aiming point on the squirrel. The rifle will probably be shooting a one and one-half inch group, at 60 yards, with hollow point, high-speed ammunition, which means the bullet in the chamber might strike any place between one-fourth inch low to one and three-fourths inches high, but not more than three-fourths inch on either *side* of the point of aim, or rather, the exact point of center of impact when the rifle fires.

An arm rest, on the *side* of a tree, is likely to give an excellent vertical but considerable side motion. A rest on a log, across a fence, or sitting with a tree rest on the side, is likely to give more vertical than horizontal. If anything *slips*, just as the shot is fired, the shot will nearly always go low and to the right, for a right-shoulder shooter. It is a good idea to bear that point in mind. Keep your feet well braced and take a full breath, then let out about one-third of it, just before getting off the shot. It makes for the best average delivery.

If the rifle is sighted lower, or even to strike center at 60 yards, then the big handicap is the possibility of shooting low on the squirrel. Right here it is well to mention that you can forget all hope of "barking" a gray squirrel with a .22 rim fire rifle. I never have done so in 50 years of squirrel shooting. I never accomplished it but once, when I happened to cut off the left front foot of a red squirrel with a .25–20 rifle and it came down and died from shock, hence you are not going to kill that squirrel by hitting the crotch or limb he is sitting upon. You want to hit that squirrel in the area of the shoulder if on a side shot, and in the throat or chest, between the shoulders, if he sits up and looks toward you.

Choosing the shot from the ballistic standpoint would indicate that you ought to guard against excessive sidewise movement of the rifle and get off the shot when the squirrel is sitting up straight and presenting the greatest area in a vertical direction. Remember you do not *know* the squirrel is 60 yards off. He might be 50 yards or 70 yards, or 75 yards. He is also pretty well up on the tree, and the bullet will travel the course of the hypotenuse of a right angle triangle, plus the arch of its trajectory. Plenty of science to think of in this shot!

Maybe you get red in the face, have a touch of buck fever—you have plenty of time to get it—and have to attempt that shot three or four times, then wait a bit and start all over again, before you get the shot fired; but a moment later, when the far-off answering "plop" of the bullet on the squirrel brings its signal and the animal falls whirling head down to land with a resounding "tump" on the wet leaves, you may feel like standing up straight and letting out a resounding "whooie!"

Daniel Boone or the famous Deerslayer, never felt better!

You would not trade that moment for a million dollars. Compare the difficulty of the shot with that of slaughtering a moose, standing like a horse or a cow, 200 yards across a barren! There is no comparison! That is why some of us prefer squirrel shooting with a rifle to anything else invented for sport with the rifled tube.

Not a moment to lose, you *must* chase over and pick up that squirrel.

You arrive—and there is no squirrel!

The thing to do now, is to hang your hat up above some spot which you have set down in your mind, as the exact spot that squirrel should be. Good idea here, to look up carefully to where the squirrel was sitting, note the slope of the hill, whether the tree leans uphill or downhill, whether it leans back toward where you were standing or in the opposite direction, and then you look down and there are *two or three bright red drops of blood on the leaves!*

Ah, looks as if you have scored a 10 on that one! Glance down the hill some 15 to 30 feet, and, sure enough, there is his plume sticking up above the leaves. You have bagged him after all!

It is odd how they roll some times, but gravity acts on a dead squirrel the same as on a living body, and the squirrel bounced, most likely when it struck the leaves, then rolled.

So, you go down and pick him up by the brush, and let him hang limp in your fingers, and see the hole in the ribs on one side and the larger hole where the bullet smashed its way out of the shoulder on the far side. *Some shot*, and do not let anyone tell your grandmother differently!

By that time, in your own mind, you are at least as expert as

WHERE TO AIM TO KILL A GRAY SQUIRREL

Two ⅞″ white target pasters were placed on this life size photo of a young gray squirrel, to indicate the exact spot at which aim should be taken: 1. For a brain shot at base of the ear, or a fatal, high neck shot: 2. For a shot in the heart or lung area. A group was then fired at each from 50 yards, by C. S. Landis, Jr., using the author's Model 61 Winchester fitted with Weaver 330 hunting scope, and Remington Hi-Speed, .22 long rifle, H.P. ammunition. Ten of the 11 shots struck the ⅞″ pasters and all would have been almost instantly fatal.

anyone you know, and three or four times as good as you thought you were when you entered the woods.

So you walk up the hill a few yards and sit down hoping to see something of that squirrel that barked some time before. You sit there for 30 or 40 minutes and nothing at all comes in view. There are no sounds in the woods, except the distant cawing of crows. You get fidgety and have about decided to move. Three or four times you *almost* leave, when suddenly a gray's head appears from around a tree trunk not over 20 feet away. His head is pointed *down* as he hangs there, uncertain as to what to do. What an easy shot!

Ever so slowly up comes your rifle, the squirrel draws back and then looks out another time, possibly two feet farther down the tree, and this time you hurriedly let drive. Not a darned thing happens! That squirrel disappears as if the ground had swallowed him up. Actually, the little animal has merely flashed around the trunk, raced up to the dense cover of the leaves at the top, and is securely hidden. You probably will not see that one for the remainder of the morning.

Well, Napoleon met his Waterloo—so have you!

Anyone could sell you for thirty cents! Is your face red? Are your knees wobbling, and would you like to sink right down into the ground? The whole trouble, brother squirrel shooter, is that you forgot the ballistics and science that goes with rifle shooting. Your bullet had not as yet risen to the line of sight, and you shot just under that gray squirrel's nose. Had he been coming up the tree, instead of going down, things would have been different, as then the bullet would have struck about where the neck joins the shoulders. What you should have done, was to have aimed one inch higher than the spot you wished to hit.

Be sure you *always* remember this. Always aim high, clear over the squirrel's ears, on any shot within 15 yards, and certainly within 10 yards. This does not mean to aim six inches high, but just over the level of the ears or back if the rifle *is sighted for long range shooting*. If it is sighted for about 35 yards, has iron sights and no telescope, you will not undershoot more than one-fourth inch to one-half inch and you should score on that squirrel.

We might as well move on! Nothing, as a rule, is to be gained by sticking around after that sort of miss. The sun is now coming out pretty warm and squirrels are likely to be feeding mostly on the ground. We will slip up to that clump of beech trees, around the brow of the hill. The forest is open there, the boys said that there were many beechnut cuttings on the stumps all over that area, and the shooting should be good, early as it is in the season. Also, it will be possible to obtain a view of considerable of the woods floor, from the elevated area, and other squirrels may come out on den trees farther down the hill but will be within fair range of the beech trees on the brow.

As you go, everyone will wish you luck. Watch the leaves and sticks underfoot, and may heaven help you to remember what you have been told, when the next gray squirrel comes feeding over the hill.

Never forget that "cuttings," fresh, frequent and ample "cuttings" on stump tops, down logs, fence rails, and scattered here and there under the trees, near the trunks or the first large limb, will be the gauge of the abundance of feeding squirrels in that area. It is always a good idea to know whether you are shooting in a part of the woods in which the squirrels are feeding, in which they are merely denning, in which they are both denning up and feeding, or whether they are merely passing through from den trees to feeding grounds.

It seems that there is just one thing you have forgotten. Before walking up over the hill, better retrace your steps to the old hickory, take your hat down off that sapling and put it back on your head.

When hunting gray squirrels, the most important thing (speaking figuratively), is to *keep your hat on!*

CHAPTER 4

Shotgun vs. .22 Rifle on Squirrels

SHALL YOU CHOOSE A .22 CALIBER RIFLE, OR YOUR 12 GAUGE SHOT-
gun for squirrels; more particularly will you use the shotgun or the
rifle when the cover on the trees is very dense, and still green; when
there is much second growth and underbrush; or when the squirrels
are feeding almost altogether upon the ground?

Here is a discussion of both sides of this problem, with the author
giving both favorable and unfavorable factors, concerning each of
the two styles of squirrel hunting.

This will be a comparison of the actual *results* with the 12 gauge,
full-choke shotgun, as compared to the scope-sighted .22 rifle used
with high-velocity, hollow point ammunition. If you are undecided
on this question, be sure to read the following chapter carefully.

On the question of pure sportsmanship, between shotgun and
rifle, there is no debate. On the matter of satisfaction to the shooter,
there is little argument; but in the matter of practical results, in the
matter of adequately filling the game bag, one must at times, if but
a single firearm is taken, decide whether it will be for a squirrel
hunt *only*, or whether dove, quail, rabbit, ruffed grouse or ringnecked pheasant shooting may also be a part of the day's program,
possibly at other hours of the day.

In the latter case a shotgun is indicated, in fact just about required. For squirrel shooting alone a rifle is normally adequate—for
a good rifle shot. This I shall attempt to demonstrate as we go along.

Today, squirrel hunting may provide a wide variation in natural
conditions and therefore in shooting. Due to a wet season, lack of
early frosts, or of both, leaves may be very dense upon the trees and
they may still be green, particularly upon the bushier beechnut
trees. Squirrels will then be very difficult to see long enough for a
shot when not moving around. This is definitely not favorable for
rifle shooting. The little animals may nearly all be feeding upon the
ground, especially just before a storm, or if a very heavy frost has
brought down a heavy fall of nuts—beechnuts, hickory nuts, or
small, sweet acorns, and the squirrels are busy burying these for the

43

winter. This also provides difficult shooting because the squirrels are running about on the leaves, and undergrowth may largely hide their movements from the rifleman.

On the other hand, after the leaves have mostly fallen squirrels may frequently be seen upon den trees in early morning or late afternoon, often at quite long ranges, and they may also be spotted upon logs or while feeding upon the ground, when too far off for a shotgun but yet well within the range of a good .22 rifle. Then too, very high timber provides great difficulties for the shotgun user but excellent opportunities for the rifleman. There is always the problem of hunting and of obtaining shots well within .22 rifle range, but at very irregular distances, often up to 60 to 100 yards.

The start of a recent squirrel season presented me with a number of difficult problems. My son and I discussed them, pro and con, at length, the evening before the opening day, which in this instance, was September 15th.

The woods we were to hunt had suddenly become a squirrel heaven because it was flanked on one side by two heavy stands of corn. Gray squirrels had flocked into this timber and had come out and fed on the uncut corn until possibly $50.00 worth of damage had been done in one field and $25.00 worth in the other. The farmer and his son, were both pretty angry. They wanted to get rid of some of those squirrels. As we had hunted this district for years for doves, and later in the year for quail, rabbits and ringnecks, we were only too glad to vary the program and to take advantage of a golden opportunity. We felt sure that many other hunters would be on the grounds to do likewise. The presence of many hunters is not favorable to successful rifle still hunting.

Finally, the young man closed the argument. "Listen, Dad," said he. "You will have all fall to use your rifle, and when shooting conditions will be much more favorable to getting results. But tomorrow the woods will be full of hunters, all banging away. The squirrels will soon become wild and will hide. The underbrush is thick and high in that tract of woods and if they happen to feed much upon the ground you won't see them long enough for successful rifle shooting. You say it will rain all night and much of tomorrow morning. Everything will be dripping wet and your rifle scope will fog and maybe become useless. Let's take the shotguns this time and maybe we can get some doves after the squirrel shooting stops late in the morning."

So, we decided to use shotguns for the opening day's shooting.

Finally, the alarm went off. I got into my clothes, including the Bean Maine hunting shoes with rubber bottoms and leather tops, which are both light and quiet on such a morning and also dry and

warm. Soon the door opened, the young man came in for his breakfast but it was still raining outside.

Then we drove to the grounds. It was dark as we walked down
over the hill, through the corn stubs, an excellent place for a hard
fall when one does not see his way. The underbrush in the woods
was mighty wet that morning!

I took up my post in a small grove of poplar trees in one edge of
the woods some 30 yards from the edge of the upper corn, now cut,
and in which grove I had seen two or three grays chasing around a
day or so before. I sent the younger hunter up the line some 200
yards, along the edge of the only corn still standing and where I
felt his younger eyes would soon locate some game.

You are never quite alone in brushy timber, wet with rain, at
daylight and with a mist falling. There is the matter of mosquitoes.
In this locality they grow so big and vicious that when a New Jersey
mosquito comes across they pounce upon him and beat up the poor
little fellow. Then, there is the matter of those big black ants; these
my dear reader, may at times, present the problem of ants in one's
pants. Every now and then maybe a spider drops down the back of
one's neck. This all goes with September squirrel shooting. Why
worry? Just slap! But slap quietly.

I took my stand down hill, sheltered on three sides by poplar tree
trunks and so that I could look up toward the sky line and see squirrels trading up and down the tree trunks. I could reach nearly
everything within sight, with the Ithaca 12 gauge, Model 37, full
choke, ventilated rib, trap gun, I was using. I had a Winchester
Repeater shell loaded with my favorite dove load of 3–1⅛–7½ ch.
in the chamber, and two Dominion Imperial Long Range Duck
Loads, 3¾–1¼–6 ch. in the magazine, for longer range shots.
(Federal law permits but three shells at a loading and a plugged
magazine for dove shooting, also for ducks.)

Within half an hour or less a medium size, this year's silver gray
squirrel came down my side of a poplar, flattened against the tree
trunk, saw me as the gun came up slowly, and lost most of his front
portion from the first shot at 15 yards. Just one of those shots you
have to take as you find them and hold off a bit to prevent excessive
mangling of back and hams.

After dressing this one, I rather sensed that something was back of
me. I looked up and there was a larger gray sitting on a limb,
tightly against the tree trunk and some 30 yards off. I had heard him
working in the tree and on the ground, but had been unable to see
him previously. He took a load of 6s in the ribs, but I had to step
on his head when I picked him up. A good sized squirrel and hit in
the spine!

Attracted by the shooting, a young man came along who lived just above the woods, and shot twice at a gray, out of my range and also out of my sight. It fell into a small run and was fished out—a very wet gray squirrel. Load sounded very light for a squirrel charge. Gun was evidently a Winchester pump, from the sound of the slide.

Before long a very large squirrel was observed feeding some 40 or 50 yards off, on a walnut tree. He came down to the shot with the Imperial and landed with a pronounced "tump" in high weeds. I went over, crawled through a barbed wire fence, was snagged top and bottom as usual, finally wiggled loose, and after a five minute search there he was, stone dead. A very large gray squirrel, with plenty of reddish fur on him, and the whole of the underparts a deep yellow, indicating age.

These big fellows are usually cross and ill-tempered, and scrappy. One generally pre-empts a large tree or end of a woods, for his exclusive feeding, and other and smaller squirrels stay out of reach of his teeth.

This was three squirrels with three shells, from one spot, in a small grove far enough removed from either cornfield's center to indicate that it might not be such a good location. However, squirrels are where you find them!

Two young chaps, by that time, were opening up every now and then down along the timber that flanked the run. I heard my son fire two single shots out along the corn-flanked woods and then a double, just far enough spaced to indicate he was aiming carefully.

For nearly an hour past I had heard stampings and thumpings back of me in a small pasture field and end of the cornfield. It sounded much like deer, but the area had supposedly been without deer since the days of the Indians. Two cows habitually grazed that field, and one, a large spotted animal, was there now.

Before long a soft pattering and swishing of the undergrowth back of me caused me to turn around and I saw a handsome buck deer walking cautiously toward me, on a small cow path along the run. This path ran within 40 feet of my stand. The buck tossed his head, straightened up and simply walked past on the path, without even noticing me at all and apparently quite unconcerned and altogether unafraid. When he came to the barbed wire, he bounded over, without effort, and not at all hurriedly.

I spent all of my time, while he was in sight, trying to accurately count all of his points. At first I thought he was a 12 pointer, then 10, and finally decided he had five prongs on the left antler, and possibly six on the right antler, which was the larger. He was not very fat nor especially large, for such a rack, just a good sized buck in his summer coat.

Within five minutes, four of us were talking it over. Two had seen four deer, one had seen three does, and I had seen only the buck. My son had three squirrels and had been unable to retrieve a fourth which had fallen in the middle of a large briar patch. One hunter had nothing and the other had one and had lost one which fell onto the top of a stone pile. The four of us, together, had shot at possibly 15 gray squirrels, with those doing the most moving around and shooting having the least luck.

Nothing more transpired during the next half hour, except repeated shooting down towards the woods run, so I slipped down there intending to hunt down the hollow past the fence paralleling the upper corn. This corn was farther from the woods, being some 50 yards out, and was likely fed upon more in late afternoon and on moonlight nights than in the morning.

Before long I saw a gray feeding in the top of a hickory. The leaves and twigs were very dense, and 15 minutes passed before I shot. He grabbed onto the twigs and hung there apparently all in, but a second shot brought him to the ground, as another hunter was approaching from down the hollow. To leave it drop of its own accord merely invited a shot and a claim of ownership from another hunter. Soon the other man came up and showed two squirrels as the result of the two shots he had fired, he complained it was all that he had seen. He was smoking a pipe which was belching a cloud of smoke like a fire engine of the old days. I never could see the logic of smoking while hunting in the woods and then expecting to see much. Game has a much keener sense of smell than most persons.

Gaining the level of the cornfield, some 15 minutes later, a pigeon or a dove flushed from beneath a large and very bushy poplar tree. I ran out to see which and nearly ran over a good sized squirrel that was out feeding on the nearest cornshock. I was between the tree and the squirrel, and of course it tried to run past me. A hurried shot, aimed ahead to strike only the head, was entirely too successful when the animal put on a sudden burst of speed, so one minute he "was" and the next he "was not."

Before long we called it a day, as an hour or so of steady hunting in the cornfields failed to raise any doves. Result of day's shooting for both of us: four bagged and one shot-up for me, and three bagged and one shot and unrecovered for the son. I found later that one of the other young men bagged three, after a good deal of shooting. Insofar as I could determine the fourth, and also two other hunters, bagged nothing. The one down the run had a pair. Just average first of the season shooting with shotguns. A high percentage of kills by some, and not too much sport by anyone.

My first three shots could have been handled easier and cleaner with a .22 rifle, the fourth might have been, but it was rather unlikely, and the fifth would have almost certainly been lost.

For the kind of day, the squirrels were coming out quickly, and were not as wild as might have been expected. As a rule, squirrels which are feeding on corn, and accustomed to people, are rather tame.

As a comparison take the second day's shooting—the afternoon of the following 24 hours. On this occasion I carried the scope sighted .22 rifle.

I reached the grounds a little later than I had hoped to and met the farmer's son, who wanted to talk about the deer.

I walked down along the edge of the standing corn where my son had hunted the previous morning. Soon a gray squirrel jumped down off a cornstalk where he had been feeding on an ear some six feet from the ground. He was highly indignant at such intrusion and his language was terrible. He rushed into the cover of some underbrush and vines, some five or six feet distant and accidentally collided head-on with a sapling beneath the brush that set him back on his tail, and his chatterings and growlings and whimperings and rushings around indicated that a gray squirrel's nose hurts just about as much as a human nose struck briskly under similar circumstances.

I think I will get that gray to carry a flashlight in the future— then he may see better where he is going. Anyhow, he seemed to think it was all *my* fault. Soon he popped out on a limb, about three feet from the ground, and in an opening in the undergrowth, just 30 feet or so in front of me. Such a shot with a scope sighted .22 rifle, calls for a great deal of care. In the first place, you must move ever so slowly or the animal will run back of the tree trunk and get away before you can fire; if you aim quickly, so as to attract his attention, or to startle him. You must also aim some one and one-fourth inches above the spot to be struck, as the scope is one and one-half inches above the line of the bore, and the bullet has not as yet had chance to rise much toward your point blank sighting. And with a five power scope, such as I was using, such distance is magnified five times. It all looks pretty complicated and an aim that will kill the squirrel will appear to indicate a certain miss by shooting over.

At almost the exact instant the rifle was to fire, the squirrel made one quick move and was out of sight, *down* the trunk and into the briars. I doubt that he was scared, he probably decided to go down and try to sneak out into the corn. I heard him moving around now and then in the undergrowth but could not get a shot. I would likely have killed this gray squirrel with a shotgun. A movement backward more than three rows of corn would have made accurate aim out of the question. Just a poor setup of a shot, which occurred unexpectedly. It is a situation the rifleman meets now and then along the edges of cornfields—a squirrel *too close* to be handled successfully.

After a time I shouldered the 52 Winchester-Hoffman sporter (with Hart speed action, of which too much good can hardly be said; I have used mine without a trace of difficulty for some 18 years) and the 5A scope sight, with *coarse* crosshairs, which is my favorite reticule for squirrel shooting. I moved down toward the poplar grove.

Just as I looked across a fence, about 100 yards down a lane, a pure silver gray, but in part an albino—the whole animal was about the color of lime dust, but of peculiar appearance—walked briskly across a flat stone pile. It was not hopping, as a squirrel usually moves, but was walking briskly across an open space of some 40 to 50 yards. I held the crosshairs in front of his nose, but he walked through the field of the glass before I could fire. I then held farther ahead of him and as his head came into view fired and the bullet struck him about three-fourths inch back of and below the butt of the ear, making a perfect spine shot. The animal was a male, in good flesh and apparently about a year old. It could have been of the first spring litter of the current year. I have never before shot or seen a squirrel of that color, and it was not dusted or dyed by anything. It was an offhand shot at 30 yards.

The Remington .22 long rifle Hi-Speed hollow point bullet went right on through and mangled the front leg on the far side. He was traveling at possibly a 60° angle to the line of fire.

Normally, this is not a very easy shot with a rifle. The squirrel moved pretty fast, he was rising somewhat due to the slope of the ground, and the stones were uneven. That made a triple movement to allow for; no chance for a rest, and certainly none for a prone shot. I have not killed two per cent of my squirrels in prone shooting. In fact, prone shooting ability might just as well be forgotten in woods shooting on squirrels.

While dressing this animal, I had a presentiment that a squirrel was working in a hickory tree to the right of a woods path, some 25 yards to the right of where I had shot this one. Looking up, I saw one flattened in a crotch, on the other wide of a barbed wire fence bisecting the woods, and so obvious of my presence that a stalk would have been foolish. The shot was some 45 or 50 yards.

Every squirrel hunter who is a rifleman, knows how to best handle such a shot. Raise the rifle very slowly and quietly. Edge to the nearest tree. Stand still a moment, get the rifle up on the *right* side of the tree, if a right handed shooter, be partly concealed from the squirrel by the tree trunk, and get a part rest, part offhand, semivertical shot off successfully. It is the most common shot in shooting squirrels with a rifle from high timber or on den trees. You want to know exactly where your rifle groups on such a shot and it will not be the same as on a shot near the ground, at the same horizontal distance. Be careful you do not undershoot or overshoot because the squirrel is nearly always giving you an angling shot, much wider in vital area than vertical.

The bullet hit this one high in the right shoulder, as I wanted to be sure I did not undershoot this one, since he was half hidden by the limb. He dropped like a plummet. The same shot is very deadly on woodchucks. He too lost the off front leg. The spine was blown in two. The tree acting as a semi-rest was only a sapling and had quite some motion when I leaned against, or even rested against it, and such a situation presents a problem in which you have to gauge the sway of the tree, the motion of the crosshairs, whether the squirrel will move his position before you can let off the shot, and try to make all three work out successfully. Obviously, you press the trigger just a moment *before* the crosshair intersection bisects the spot you want to strike.

After a few years of gray squirrel shooting with a rifle, one does these things as instinctively as he puts on his shoes. But the tyro needs to be told how to handle the problem.

Within two days I had made five kills on gray squirrels with five shells and cartridges, all within 100 yards of the same spot, and had seen a very fine buck deer, presenting a perfect chance had there been an open season, all in the same area. This is what some call "a game pocket." Normally, I would not have judged it worth 30 minutes' hunting. Being adjacent to the corn, was most of what had made it a game pocket.

I went over and spent half an hour where I had shot the three squirrels the previous morning, and as I rather expected saw nothing.

Next I hunted down the lower run, and saw a gray feeding along on some low undergrowth three or four feet above the ground. He saw me too. When I slowly raised the rifle he started to run for the nearest trunk, some six or eight feet away and as the rifle cracked his body suddenly dropped about two inches as a small twig snapped under his weight. I thought I had completely missed him by over-shooting, but soon saw him hanging tail down, gasping, on a twig four feet farther along. He jumped off that, then climbed a large poplar 50 yards off and began to bark at me. "Quack! Quack! Quack! Quaahhh! Quaah! Quack! Quaah! Quaah! Quaah!" He kept it up for 15 minutes. I could not see him; foliage was too thick. Finally I moved closer and he crawled up over a limb and hung on. I took a hurried, long range, offhand shot, and had the satisfaction of hearing the solid "plop!" of the bullet, and then the "tump!" of the animal's body thudding upon the ground, which at that point was nearly bare of leaves although thickly covered with brush. He fell as if he had been shot in a well-filled tummy, and so it proved to be.

The first bullet had gone through sidewise, in the kidney region and due to the very little resistance offered to the passage of the bullet, as the ball passed just under the spine, it had not expanded at all. The wound had closed and had bled but little. When they strike in this spot, few bullets will be found to have expanded, and seldom will the squirrel be bagged unless shot again. The second bullet had gashed the skin a bit across the knee of the right hind leg, made a center shot on the middle of the body, gone through and blown out the ribs on the far side and smashed the shoulder and leg. For a place about one inch long, the stomach content had been almost blown *through* the ribs on the far side. A perfect mushroom and an instant kill; but a pretty difficult offhand shot!

After dressing this squirrel, I walked down to the run to wash the blood off my hands. Then I noticed a medium sized squirrel dash across on a log over the run, about 30 yards downstream, jump off the log and hide back of and beneath same at the exact instant that a sharp-shinned hawk, of small size, shot past its tail. The hawk curved sharply when it saw me, kept on past my head, some five yards off, and flew up the woods along the run. After giving both a chance to settle down, I walked slowly up through the woods but could find no trace of the hawk.

Then I came back and watched the log for a time. Nothing came along, so I moved a bit closer, got into a higher position on the bank, where I could see over more of the forest floor area, and stood there and waited. Suddenly a very large gray squirrel appeared out of a knot hole in the log, took a hurried look up the run toward where the hawk had disappeared, and then dashed across toward my end of the fallen tree trunk. The rifle was aimed ahead of his nose and the hollow point bullet struck exactly amidships, went on through and smashed the off front leg as it emerged. The squirrel turned a back flip-flop off the log, wriggled forward about twice its length and gave up the ghost.

This made four kills with five bullets. By this time it was getting dusk. The sun was still up a trifle above the horizon, but it was getting dark in the damp woods. So I started for home.

In walking up past the edge of the cornfield, where the first squirrel had been seen, I made a stand. After a wait of 15 minutes, during which faint scurrying was heard in the underbrush, I suddenly noticed a gray squirrel perched on a limb, but backed up against the tree trunk, on a very large maple some 75 or 80 yards off and about 25 yards into the woods. This was across a trash-filled shallow ravine and a stalk appeared impossible.

A squirrel at 80 yards makes quite an offhand shot. The only possible "arm rests" were single cornstalks. These were tall, brittle and rather spindling. If you touch one, it immediately starts to sway back and forth, and even if the arc is only a couple of inches, by the time it is magnified by the rifle telescope and transmitted out to the chord of an arc with an 80-yard radius, your crosshairs appear to be wobbling and swaying back and forth over all outdoors.

It is some trick to "steady" such a cornstalk long enough to get a steady aim and let off the shot. You sort of take him on the fly, so to speak, as the crosshairs intersection is about to pass the squirrel— you obviously must start pressing the trigger an interval before the crosshairs rest for a moment on the spot to be hit—or maybe a bit above it.

In the meantime, the squirrel is taking all this in, and has possibly changed its position a couple of times.

But in this instance the gray squirrel was so hypnotized by my efforts to steady that cornstalk for an 80-yard shot that he simply sat there and looked goggle-eyed, and when the rifle cracked even a Republican had good luck!

Later investigation proved that the bullet landed just an inch below and behind the butt of the ear, and he came down as if the heavens had fallen upon him. So I beat down the brush, found a path across, and paced it out 78 long paces to the foot of the maple; and he was up about 50 feet.

Even though I was one short of the legal bag limit for the day, that ended a perfect three hour's squirrel shooting—five shots, all kills, and only one required a second bullet.

On quite a few different occasions I have shot and killed five and six straight on gray squirrels, using the same .22 Model 52 Winchester-Hoffman with Hart Speed action. Once or twice I have killed 10 straight with it. And at this writing, have an unfinished long run of 14 straight. (It ended at 15.) On one occasion, I shot and killed 13 straight gray squirrels, using a single shot Stevens target rifle with a Pope barrel. There is no reason why any other experienced rifleman should not be able to do the same, provided —and mark well the provideds—his rifle is very carefully sighted in for some one definite range and the shooter knows what that is; that he remembers the trajectory of the cartridge he is using over 75 to 90 yards; and that he uses common sense in choosing the time to shoot, and the exact spot on the animal at which to aim. Almost any experienced rifle shot can tell within an inch or less of exactly where he has hit a gray squirrel, long before it hits the ground, by the way he got off the shot, by the actions of the animal after being shot, and the sound of the bullet when it landed. He needs a bit of luck too, that the squirrel does not decide to run or materially change its position at the exact instant the rifle cracks. One gains knowledge with increased experience and I have been shooting squirrels with the .22 rifle for most of my lifetime.

The rifleman, to be consistently successful on squirrels, needs to be both a rifleman and something of a woodsman. And of course he needs to be a hunter. He must be able to sense where squirrels will be at any given time and how to get close to them and fire without the squirrel holing up. He also needs to develop a fair knowledge of the feeding, playing, nut-burying and loafing habits of squirrels. All these have a bearing on what a squirrel is likely to do, at any given instant.

Patience and silence in the woods are the prime requisites of a squirrel shooter. Patience is something most persons must acquire. If the average squirrel will not come out until 20 or 30 minutes after you have taken a stand in a woods, and most of them will not once they have been shot at, wait at least 15 minutes longer than you think you should before moving off from a good looking location to one which may be as good, and may not be. This idea of staying "put" 10 or 15 minutes longer than seemed called for has bagged for me many a gray squirrel. It is really astonishing how many squirrels will come into view within five or 10 minutes after your patience becomes exhausted. Their patience either becomes fagged just about the same time, or their curiosity overcomes better judgment after that interval.

Anyone can have a bad day in the field, with either shotgun or rifle. You may have a run of hard luck for two or three days or even a week. But in the long run, staying qualities and perseverance, for anyone who is in fair health and not congenitally a nitwit, should bring you a good day with either rifle or shotgun. I believe I have shown here that one is just as likely to have good luck, and to do accurate shooting, with a .22 rifle as with the 12 gauge.

Over the season things will average up. If you grasp the fundamentals of squirrel shooting with the rifle, find what they are feeding on and then hunt there, whether it be on beechnuts, hickory nuts, small acorns, chestnuts, shellbarks, corn on the stalk, or whatever else it may be. They invariably spend a great deal of time seeking food or burying it for winter use.

They do not often loaf on the bread line. They do their playing, loafing, washing up, and resting on, in, or around the den trees or nests in tree crotches, and on logs on the ground. Never forget that squirrels have main highways, side highways, and individual paths to reach any spot, just as do people. These highways are along any fence which is of wood; up and down any leaning tree, especially if it is a dead tree; and on top of any long log, or any series of logs lying, more or less, end to end. They always cross streams, if possible, on fallen logs or on overhanging branches, as they do not like to get wet and are particular about keeping their tails dry. Incidentally, they swim well if it becomes necessary. But if they fall into deep water after being shot, they immediately sink except in the late fall or winter season after they have become excessively fat.

They feed in early morning, usually best on foggy mornings, and up to 9.30 or 10.30 A.M. Then they retire and come out again to feed from 2.30 or 3 P.M., occasionally from 3.30 P.M., until nearly dark. Very few have I found just at nightfall, but I have seen them out playing and feeding on moonlight nights. Occasionally, on dark days, or windy, stormy, rainy days, they may be found out at all hours of the day, but they will not come out early on a dry, windy and cold morning. Generally you might as well hunt birds or rabbits during the time from 10.00 A.M. to 2 P.M.

Hunters in the South, however, state that in the winter season when squirrels are feeding on the ground, midday on a clear sunny day is the very best time to find them, particularly in the oak flats. If at that season they are feeding in trees, such as gums, the best time for hunting them in that section is just before nightfall.

I prefer evening shooting to morning shooting because I generally get better shots then, find more squirrels which offer a shot, and the leaves and underbrush are usually dry and not uncomfortable to tramp through. Many prefer the morning, but the shooting is likely to be for two hours instead of three.

One thing you will often notice when still hunting with the rifle is that you may hunt for an hour under supposedly perfect conditions, and not a squirrel is seen, and not a shot is fired nearby or in the distance. Then within ten or fifteen minutes, squirrels appear to come out everywhere and it sounds like a battle. They may stop coming out just that suddenly, and then, within another half hour, may appear again. The cessation of rain, following by the sun coming out warm and comfortable, the lifting of fog, the stepping up or the slowing up of any breeze there may be, all play a part. So do noises in the woods, the passing of teams or automobiles, or the farmer driving out to his fields.

Every hunter, regardless of his skill and experience, will have unfortunate days afield. Things simply do not break right. You arrive just a day too late—although that usually happens with ducks. Others may have shot the game you understood was feeding in that locality. (It may have been shot just the week before the beginning of legal gunning season.) A wind springs up at the wrong moment and increases in velocity as the day wears on. The woods may turn out to be so dry that you can not move three feet without being heard by every squirrel within 200 yards. Maybe it rains so hard everything has holed up. A Norther comes along and squirrels remain indoors until the sun comes out warm and comfortable. And so it goes; just one piece of bad luck after another.

Unless you are seeking meat, or the conditions are not propitious for rifle shooting, you will not need a shotgun. Remember there is a great deal of difference between the skill of the average 14-year-old boy and his $10.00 .22 single shot sporting rifle, and that of the match rifleman who is also a woodsman, a squirrel and woodchuck hunter, and has a real outfit and knows how to use it.

The one is in the Grammar School age of squirrel hunting development. The other is the Professor in the School of Technology and Engineering. It is a long road, from one grade to the other, of skill in the woods, and part of it is a stony road, but if there is rifle shooting in the "Happy Hunting Grounds," I'll take the .22 at gray squirrels, for much of mine!

CHAPTER 5

Hunting Fox Squirrels

As stated in chapter one five distinct species or subspecies of fox squirrels inhabit the United States. While generally similar in size and appearance, these are wholly different in their coloration and habits. A much larger squirrel is native to Indo-China. Museums in this country contain specimens of this foreign squirrel that, including tail, measure more than three and a half feet in length. This squirrel frequents tropical forests and is dark brown in color. Nothing like it is to be found in North America.

THE NORTHERN FOX SQUIRREL

A Southern sportsman Henry E. Davis, of Florence, South Carolina, who has had much experience with fox squirrels, writes:

"The Northern fox squirrel is found from central Virginia northward and westward, and is an animal of hardwood forests. In the mountain valleys of Virginia, he is often encountered on the edge of a forest of oaks, and is frequently met with in a hickory or other nut-bearing tree standing alone in a clearing at a considerable distance from any timber. In short, he more than any other squirrel will seek his favorite food far away from the protection of any woods. In Highland County, Virginia, where I have done much woodchuck hunting, they are very common, and the local landowners assert that they drive the gray squirrels out.

"The Northern fox squirrel is generally of a grizzled or yellowish gray color, with a considerable amount of red on parts of his body, and with white underparts. In other words, his coloration is rather similar to that of the common gray fox."

THE YELLOW-BELLIED FOX SQUIRREL

In the upper Mississippi valley region, the Northern fox squirrel is replaced by the yellow-bellied fox squirrel, which is the characteristic species of that region. The two species are similar in color with the exception of the underparts.

THE FOX SQUIRREL

This photo, which was taken in Georgia, gives an idea of the size and appearance of the Fox Squirrel, of which good photos appear to be almost unobtainable. This animal can stand a fair amount of shooting—such calibers as .22 long rifle, High Speed, H.P., .22 W.R.F. Hi-Speed H.P., and .22 Hornet with reduced loads, being most suitable.

Photo courtesy Biological Survey

The best shooting of Northern and yellow-bellied fox squirrels is to be had in western Virginia, West Virginia, Ohio, Indiana, Illinois, a small section of Minnesota, and another spot in the Ozark mountains of Missouri. The hunting of these two species will be considered first.

"The largest squirrels I have ever seen, big husky reddish squirrels at least 30 per cent larger than the finest shown in recent photographs sent you, were two fox squirrels shot quite some years ago on my uncle's farm, 30 miles north of Indianapolis, Indiana," wrote Harrell V. Noble, prominent pistol, revolver and rifle match shooter, in a recent letter to the author. "These fox squirrels were killed around Christmas holidays. My cousin bagged one, I the other. After eating their fill of nuts all fall, they came in and fed from a corn crib near the barn. They were *fat* and they should have been for they had fed on corn to the bursting point for more than a month of real cold weather. Under such circumstances squirrels put on fat and the meat also becomes firm and sweet. As I recall, these squirrels ate or destroyed at least one-quarter of the corn placed in that crib, in the early fall before the remainder of the corn was consumed by stock."

Comment, almost verbatim, from Charles W. Hymer, well known trade representative, who has for years been a very enthusiastic squirrel hunter follows: "On our home farms near Greencastle and Crawfordsville, Indiana, and in adjacent and nearby areas, there were many fox squirrels. Some of the larger and better farms contained up to 1,200 acres, most of them were posted and were largely covered or dotted with sugar maples and shellbark hickory and black walnut trees. These would be found standing singly or in clusters in the rich farming country thereabouts, and at times as many as 50 or more shellbark hickories would be fed upon at one place by gray and by fox squirrels, even within the limits of one field. The fox squirrels greatly outnumbered the gray squirrels in that area, possibly six or eight to one.

"In Indiana, wooded sections contained many large den trees. Many of these were hard sugar maples and in time these became hollow, and of course then provided fine homes for the squirrels.

"The fox squirrels were more inclined to come out and feed upon single shellbark hickory trees, or upon the black walnut trees, than gray squirrels and three of us used to hunt them in Indiana with .22 caliber rifles. Fox squirrels were so plentiful in those days that we did not purposely shoot the old squirrels but picked out the young ones, which since they were smaller and had much more tender meat, were preferred for eating. In those days, when the timber was large and abundant, a bag of 20 squirrels for a small party was not infre-

quent. Today, of course, some of the large sugar maple, walnut and
hickory timber has been cut, but there is still enough for squirrel
dens and for cover. Even today, the squirrel shooting throughout
most of that central-state district is just fine. The season now is from
about August 10 to October 8, and so by the time I get out there the
boys have thinned them out. However, when I have opportunity,
I like to get down among the black walnut trees and the shellbark
hickories and maples and have a whirl at the fox squirrels. That is
really sport!"

For some reason we hear less of the fox squirrel shooting in Missouri, Illinois, and Virginia, than we do in Indiana and Ohio; possibly because two of these states have more of a Southern type of
climate, and the other is more famed, at most seasons, as a quail
and duck shooting state. In any case, the Northern and yellow-
bellied fox squirrels are animals of the open woodland and the individual large nut tree. They may even be found at times on telegraph poles. They do not keep to the dense woods, as does the gray
squirrel except when the latter is feeding along cornfields. According
to H. C. Russell, sales manager of Federal Cartridge Co., who is a
firearms enthusiast and collector, in Minnesota it is quite common to
see fox squirrels along the edge of woods and even far out on individual trees at a considerable distance from woods.

The author has seen a good many fox squirrels on comparatively
small individual trees, and in small stands of young timber, in open
wood lots in northern and in central Ohio. Fox squirrels seem to
prefer their own company to that of gray squirrels. Harrell V. Noble
quoted above, and now living a few miles out from Dayton, Ohio,
writes: "I understand that almost all squirrels up to about one and
one-half miles west of my property are fox squirrels. Thereafter only
gray squirrels are to be found for the next two or three miles. From
then on, it may be either."

On his uncle's place in Indiana, there are many little pine or
red squirrels and also the large fox squirrels. There are numerous
walnut trees on that farm and some good stands of large trees
which make fine woodland. The red squirrels chase the fox squirrels.
One of the fox squirrels in a photo he sent the author, he reports
had three close and deep scars from such castration attempts, which
proved unsuccessful. These scars he credited to red squirrels.

Further information on timbered country usually inhabited by
fox squirrels in numbers is suggested by the following Noble comment to the author: "On my uncle's farm there are three or four
acres of black walnut trees which all bear heavily. This wood lot
adjoins a 30-acre dense woods which contain many oak, beech and
hickory trees. The second woods is then about 450 yards from an-

other 20-acre wood lot which is fairly open. There are one or more cornfields near his woods, and it is estimated that he loses an acre or two of corn to the squirrels, in a fall." The fox squirrels seemed so thick in the fall of 1944, when Noble was there, that the number killed in two or three days made no difference in the shooting the following day. One man can usually see three to seven fox squirrels at some time during the daylight hours, often hanging from a tree, at a 45 degree angle. Noble remarked, "I have only seen fox squirrels so far on my place of 10 acres. I recently picked up about a peck of corn that these squirrels had pulled down. I saw lots of squirrel tracks in the snow last winter but I own no hollow trees to my knowledge, so they must live in open nests."

The author can recall seeing only one article in all of the sporting magazines within the last 40 to 45 years, which was entirely about the hunting and shooting of fox squirrels. Yet there have been many articles about hunting gray squirrels, some about black squirrels and of course mention of pine or red squirrels.

Considering the prevalence of fox squirrels in so many states, and their wide range throughout Central, the Western portion of the Eastern States and so many of the Southern States, it is unusual that more information and more photographs of fox squirrel shooting are not available. They are so large, and slow and deliberate in their movements as compared to gray or black squirrels and especially as compared to the little red or pine squirrels, and they are of sufficient size as to make them a matter of interest as food, even though as such they do not rate equally with gray or black squirrels.

The yearling Northern and yellow-bellied fox squirrel usually weighs from one and one-half to two pounds, large old ones from two and one-half to three pounds, and many probably going to three and one-half or even more. The author has shot gray squirrels weighing two to two and one-half pounds in both Pennsylvania and Delaware, and others nearly as large in New Jersey.

He has seen but one fox squirrel, when hunting, surveying, motoring, or riding on trains, in Pennsylvania, and that one had lost a front foot and lived always in a single tree, along the waterfront at Harrisburg, in a residential park area. It was kept and fed by a man living there. A trolley once ran over and severed the foot. The author has shot at least one squirrel in Delaware which appeared to be a large fox squirrel, the same being shot fairly well down the state, and once saw one on a stump, about 15 or 20 miles below Wilmington, which was unquestionably a fox squirrel—a few having previously been imported into Delaware, but this squirrel jumped down off the stump and disappeared. It did not appear to be greatly alarmed. A neighbor advised the author that he had seen and shot a few fox squirrels near Milford, Delaware. There were a few down that way.

There are of course thousands of gray squirrels shot which, from their large size and reddish-brown fur, appear to be crossed with fox squirrels, but in most instances it is probably nothing but a different color phase of the gray. However, these gray-brown grays are nearly always broader and heavier around the rump and shoulders than the average silver gray squirrel.

A .22 caliber rifle for fox squirrels should be a trifle more powerful than the one used for grays. The .22 long rifle hollow point, high-speed cartridge is about the weakest that is suggested, others being the .22 W.R.F., and especially if obtainable in H.P. style, and reduced loads in the .22 Hornet, K-Hornet, .218 Bee, .22/3000 and R-2 calibers, same being three and one-half to five grains of No. 80, or its equivalent. Three and a half to four and a half grains of Unique would be good. Shoot for the head or ribs; avoid the *hams*.

A rifleman who has lived for many years in the Carolinas and of course has hunted there extensively, recently wrote the author in regard to southern squirrel hunting as follows:

"The Southern gray squirrel is not nearly as large as the Northern gray and a majority of those bagged around here are about the size of young Northern squirrels. Some are quite small.

"The Southern fox squirrel is considerably larger than the Northern species. Some Southern fox squirrels are quite large and solid-bodied animals; a full grown one will weigh close to three pounds and may run heavier than this in some instances. I have a postal scale which registers to two and one-fourth pounds and a fully grown fox squirrel quite obviously weighs much more than this will register, when laid on the scales.

"Fox squirrels are like darkies in that they come all shades and colors; ranging from solid black to bright red, some being as red as a red fox. One is apt to find a certain shade predominating; here along the lower Pee Dee River in South Carolina the prevailing color is gray although some are silvery and look almost white. In Onslow County North Carolina, about 150 miles to the North, the prevailing shade was a very dark gray ranging to almost a solid black; in fact I shot specimens which were coal black with the exception of their white nose and ear tips. Those Onslow County squirrels had considerable red streaked or mixed in with the black and some had a decided red cast.

"The brightest specimens I ever saw came from Hyde County, North Carolina, and these were a bright, rich red just like the Northern red fox. They were splendid looking animals. I understand that red is the prevailing color in Oklahoma, for their fox squirrels.

"It would be interesting to start a collection of the various phases of the fox squirrel and compare these hides. I commenced to make such a comparative collection, on three different occasions, but someone always came along and asked for the hides then on the board.

"This Southern fox squirrel is quite different in his habits from the Southern gray squirrel. He stays in different timber and type of ground, mostly in the pine sections along or in the swamps. He does most of his foraging on the ground and when you scare one he will run off along the ground for a considerable distance, probably passing several good trees and will seldom jump or climb into the first tree handy as will the gray. Despite his much larger size, the fox squirrel can hide on the opposite side of a limb much better than can a gray. When you have a fox squirrel treed you do not see the tail hairs sticking up or his sides showing, or his tail hanging an inch or two below a limb. He will carefully flatten out and have all of himself well behind cover.

"Squirrels must have been a terrible pest to the early settlers in this area, and also up North. I have often heard my grandfather tell about the heavy migrations of gray squirrels in the North and how they damaged the cornfields when the milk was in the grain. When I came to the Low Country of South Carolina, I promptly experienced first-hand evidence of just how much damage a large number of squirrels can do. Or even a few, given time and opportunity. We planted three acres of corn in a small field, surrounded by woods, and as soon as the corn reached the 'milk' stage, the squirrels came in and destroyed most of the crop. They were helped some by raccoons. The squirrels worked on the corn during the daytime and the coons by night. They only eat fresh, unopened ears and tear back the husk to get at the end of the ear, eating the grains at the tip of the ear or cob and leaving the balance open to crows, insects and other pests. The farmer on a small farm in the South, whose fields are surrounded or bordered by woods or swamps will lose a large portion of his corn crop to squirrels every year and is obliged to turn out and shoot as many as he can of the squirrels.

"Until about the year 1920, squirrels were a serious factor on any of the farms located along the Pee Dee River or in this heavily wooded section of the country. I often have a neighbor tell me about how he 'got ketched up with his shooting' by having a regular job of keeping the squirrels out of their cornfields when he was a young man. 'Job' it was, as he had to be there in the field at daybreak and stay until dark, doing nothing but run back and forth and shooting squirrels. Then, at night, he would have to stay up two or three hours and load shells for the next day's engagement. You could not call it squirrel hunting; they simply came in on him in countless dozens.

"He killed squirrels by the hundreds and after a week of it the ground along the edge of the field was covered with dead and decaying squirrels—remember the average temperature was high, almost like that of Northern summer, and some places you could not put your feet down without stepping on one. Even so, all the outer rows of corn would be eaten up for some distance into the field. Had they not protected the crop in this manner they would have lost it entirely, and it was a large planting of about 20 acres, which is two to four times the size of most Middle Atlantic and New England cornfields, on average size farms, many of them being cut up into two to five acre fields.

"This shooting and protection of corn against squirrels had to be kept up daily, seven days in the week, for almost a month, after which the corn had hardened—what was left of it, and the squirrels then left it alone for a time. But in the winter, that is well into the winter, they would start eating the hardened grains whenever they could get at them.

"Squirrels are rather plentiful all over the less settled sections of the South. In Onslow County a neighbor living across the river had a swamp run between two large cornfields and during the roasting ear stage this patch of timber filled up with gray squirrels which fed on the corn. This farmer did no shooting himself, nor did he permit his neighbors to hunt on the place. He 'hired the shootin' privilege' to some persons from up state, and a car full of sports came down there to shoot these grays. In one full day's shooting, it is known they killed and picked up over 300 gray squirrels from this swamp, using an entire case of shotgun shells to kill them. They had the back of their car piled full of squirrels."

The Southern Fox Squirrel

Speaking of the Southern fox squirrel, Henry E. Davis, already quoted, has this to say:

"The Southern fox squirrel is the wildest and craftiest of the entire race of squirrels. He is essentially a denizen of the deep pine forests, and unless such timber has all been destroyed, is never found any distance therefrom. In the days of the great virgin long leaf forests, his favorite haunts were the pine lands surrounding small cypress ponds, which furnished suitable den trees, drinking water, and a portion of his food, as the seeds of the cypress are cut out of the balls and greedily devoured by both gray and fox squirrels. Another favorite den tree of this big squirrel was an immense dead long leaf pine, which for several years after it died had a very thick layer of spongy sapwood between the bark and the solid heartwood of the tree, and after this layer began to separate and spring away from the heartwood, the squirrels made their dens in the crevices thus formed. Frequently, large dead pines were found with rotten cores and into these, well above the ground, woodpeckers of various species drilled large holes for nesting sites. Nearly always these nesting cavities were appropriated by fox squirrels as dens. This squirrel also builds nests after the manner of the gray squirrel, but larger, and uses for this purpose leaves, twigs and Spanish moss. Both nests and dens are usually lined with shredded cypress bark, which somewhat resembles jute but is softer, silkier and warmer. The presence of fox squirrels in an area is frequently betrayed by the evidence that the cypress bark has been freshly stripped from the small pond cypresses found therein.

"This fox squirrel does not, as a rule, feed on corn in the fields and stays away from human habitations. His main foods are pine mast, acorns, hickory nuts, various wild fruits, gum berries and cypress seed. In the early spring, like other squirrels, he subsists largely on buds, being particularly fond of those of the red maple. He is rather solitary in his habits, and is usually found alone. Occasionally two or three young specimens may be found in an oak, hickory or other feeding tree, but rarely are two adults ever so found. He feeds on the ground more than any other squirrel, and no hunter without using a dog can attain any success in hunting him. Other squirrels feed early in the morning or late in the afternoon, but this fox squirrel has no definite feeding time. In fact, some hunters claim that 2 P.M. on a clear fall day is about the best time to locate one.

"Since the pine timber has been cut on the ridges in the great river swamp of the Pee Dee valley in South Carolina, a few fox squirrels are killed every year in this area by hunters of gray squirrels who occasionally encounter them in the cypress or oak flats of the swamp. This, however, is not typical fox squirrel range. The noted hunter Fleetwood Lanneau, now a civil engineer of Flat Rock, North Carolina, who spent eleven years as the keeper of a large game preserve in Great Pee Dee River swamp in Darlington County, South Carolina, states that he never saw a fox squirrel outside of the pineland sections of that vast swamp during all the time he was there, but that they were abundant in such sections. One of the finest ranges in existence for these Southern fox squirrels today is the Sand Hills State Forest, containing some 92,000 acres of pinelands, mostly long leaf, in Darlington and Chesterfield Counties, in South Carolina. This wooded region has the pines, the oaks, (mostly turkey, black jack, and blue jack) the gums, the pond cypresses, and the small streams and ponds that make up the ideal habitat for this wild, pineland dweller, and he thrives there in abundance.

"Three distinct color phases of this fox squirrel are found in the central Pee Dee valley, viz: (1) silver or brownish gray back, white abdomen and under parts, and black head, with white ears, nose and feet; (2) coal, glistening black, with white ears, nose and feet; and (3) grizzled red or tawny on a black ground color. Squirrels of type three are very rare, while those of type one are the most common. Both sexes are represented in all the types, but among the coal black specimens, females seem to predominate.

"This squirrel is a past master in the art of hiding, and can put a gray squirrel to shame in this respect. Let one climb a big thick pine, even if it has no Spanish moss on it, and you will hardly ever locate him, either with your naked eye or with a telescope. He will keep all of himself, including his tail, behind the limb or trunk away from you, and he will remain that way regardless of how you turn or move your position. One of his favorite tricks is to climb to the very crown of the pine, and then get up on top of it, thus putting a mat or wall of straw between you and himself which you can not possibly see through. The best, if not the only, way to kill him when he hides in such a tree is to conceal yourself and wait until he moves out, which it may take several hours for him to do.

"Another peculiar habit of this squirrel is that sometimes if you happen to fire into the section of the tree where he is hiding, he will suddenly leap to the ground, even if the tree is 100 feet high, and run off. In fact, running on the ground is one of his common stunts, and I have known one to run a road ahead of a fast trotting horse for a half mile before taking a tree.

"This fox squirrel is one of the hardest species of small game to kill with a shotgun. In the first place, up a tall thick tree, if you happen to locate him, he presents a very small target, and unless you have a good full choke gun, the chances for hitting him with an adequate number of shot to insure a kill are rather remote; and in the second place, he is exceptionally tenacious of life, and the number of shot necessary to kill is unusually large.

"For a hundred years, or probably more, a favorite sport in South Carolina has been to hunt this handsome and cunning squirrel with a trained dog and a good rifle. Several could be secured in an afternoon by this method, and these expert old marksmen with their gilt-edge percussion rifles with double set triggers always took head shots if available.

"A very singular characteristic of this fox squirrel is that if one is mortally wounded he will frequently sink his front claws into the wood of the limb where he is, and will die in such position. It is generally impossible to dislodge with a shotgun one that has thus clutched a limb. I have known of one that swung thus for seven days in the top of a big long leaf pine until a buzzard succeeded in pulling him off.

"A young Southern fox squirrel is very good eating, but an old one is very tough and the meat is dry and insipid unless the animal is very fat. The bones of this squirrel are a vivid red color, both in the raw and in the cooked state.

"Many regard this squirrel as the handsomest game animal of America, and I am inclined to concur in their opinion. It makes an interesting and hardy pet, but must always be kept in a cage and can never be handled. In the mating season the old males are apt to be very pugnacious and brook no trespasses. I had a friend who kept four magnificent specimens in a cubical wire cage with 10 foot sides. One day he entered the cage, as he had been accustomed to do daily for a long period of time, to change the water supply. One of the females happened to be in heat, and the old male sprang on his owner's head and inflicted some rather severe wounds before he could be subdued. After the rut was over, he again became quiet and even-tempered.

"The call of this squirrel is a coarse 'Hakka, hakka, hakka,' repeated several times, but it is very seldom heard, as he is rather inclined to be taciturn. A fox squirrel never 'cusses' and scolds as a gray squirrel does. If a hawk or an owl comes too close, he is likely to utter a coarse chatter of one or two syllables, and he will do the same thing if a bullet or load of shot discharged into a tree strikes so near as to make him disclose his hiding place. Otherwise, he keeps absolutely mum. One stunt he is very apt to pull, however, is to run down the trunk of the tree on the opposite side from the hunter and then run off on the ground. He is a rather poor jumper from one tree to another, and unless the trees are closely interlaced, he can not ride their tops after the manner of a gray squirrel; hence he usually prefers to use the ground as his highway of escape.

"Owing to the toughness and dry quality of the meat, some hunters of the gray squirrel refuse to shoot a fox squirrel when they chance to meet him on a hunt.

"Southern fox squirrels are said, as a general rule, to be considerably larger than those of the other species of fox squirrels, and this is no doubt true. I have known of one specimen of the Southern species that weighed in excess of four pounds.

"The chief predators on this squirrel are the fox, the bobcat, the red-tailed hawk, and the barred and great horned owls. The worst of these is the red-tailed hawk, and I once saw one of these with a full grown black fox squirrel in his talons that he managed to bear away to a distance beyond the range of a Hornet rifle. In some states this hawk is protected by statute as being beneficial, the benefits being that he eats a few rats. So do rattlesnakes. Actions like this are what cause the public to have no respect for the opinions of so-called scientific experts. How a predator that will strip a wood of every squirrel can be classed as beneficial, no sane man can understand! In hunting squirrels, both of the gray and of the fox species, red-tailed hawks usually work in pairs. Unless taken unawares and at a disadvantage, as when on the ground, a squirrel can frequently escape capture by a single hawk, but he has no chance against a pair. When he dodges around the tree or a limb to avoid his first assailant, he runs right into the clutches of the second."

In all my hunting, I have never attempted to "bark" a squirrel, but I have seen it done. On one occasion, my younger brother, Rev. W. Emmet Davis, D.D., now of Newport News, Virginia, and I were hunting in the swamp of Great Pee Dee River in Florence County, S. C. Each of us carried a Springfield sporter of .30–06 caliber, with a good supply of both full power and short range loads. Incidentally, I may say that the Whelen short range load in this caliber, consisting of the 150 grain service bullet ahead of 18 grains of #80 powder, is one of the best cartridges I have ever used on squirrels. It has a muzzle velocity of 1508 feet, is very accurate, kills instantly without undue multilation, and with it I have bagged quite a number of them. On this particular hunt, we ran a big gray squirrel up a very large oak, and it flattened against a big limb well up in the tree. Emmet is the best shot I have ever seen in action with a rifle, and as he raised his rifle, he remarked: "Watch me bark this one." With the report of the rifle, the squirrel was thrown several feet into the air and came down dead, without a scratch on it. The cartridge employed was the old regular service 150 grain load. Recently I visited Emmet in Virginia and reminded him of this incident, which he remembered well. He then told me that he had performed the feat several times with the same cartridge and load.

The old timers of my acquaintance, who used for their squirrel shooting heavy percussion rifles of about 40 caliber carrying a round ball, never, so far as I can find out, practiced "barking" squirrels, but prided themselves on their ability to make successful head shots with such weapons. One of the old hunters whom I knew well and who was a splendid shot, used to boast of his ability with such a rifle to burst an egg floating in the current of the nearby river or to split a bullet on an upright knife blade. Another old fellow who lived next door to me for many years could, with his percussion rifle, take off a turkey's head at 50 yards or kill a hovering bumble bee at ten paces. Neither of these cold chaps, however, ever made any mention of barking squirrels, and I feel sure such feats were unknown in the section in which I was reared.

In hunting squirrels with a rifle, the very finest sport to be had is by employing a dog. As a matter of fact, this is the only way to hunt fox squirrels successfully. Where the timber is densely grown, as in the great river swamps, a dog is of no help, as the squirrel easily shifts from tree to tree and hence can not be located when the dog barks "treed." Further, in such territory there are too many hollow trees that afford refuge for the quarry. But in the pinelands and on cut-over swamp ground, it is quite another story.

Throughout the Carolina Low Country are large areas of pine lands interspersed with ponds and streams. Usually, such areas harbor many gray and fox squirrels, but the best still hunter, regardless of his hunting ability, can not make a respectable day's bag in such a squirrel range. However, after the leaves fall, a good squirrel dog in such territory will give even a tyro the opportunity to make a good showing. If the timber is large, the shooting may be rather difficult, as the squirrel will generally go as high as he can and will manage to keep pretty well concealed. An eye and an ear may be all you can see if the pine is a big one some 125 feet high, and to hit such a target will require good holding. All the shots will not be so hard, but they will be plenty sporty.

While I have never owned a squirrel dog, I have hunted with one occasionally for more than fifty years. In my boyhood days, the old plantation negro foreman had a very good one that I used on many successful hunts, but only in the pine lands. For the past several years, I have used a dog on squirrels several times each season, and always with good results; and I hope to have the same pleasure this season.

A few years ago I was talking to a friend from upper South Carolina, and he was amazed to learn that squirrels could be successfully hunted in the Low Country without a dog, as he had never heard of such a thing in his section of the state.

No particular breed is necessary to make a good squirrel dog, provided he will bark when he trees the squirrel. My brother on our plantation has a fox terrier that has been trained for the purpose, and I expect to use him some this season. However, I would generally prefer a dog with some hound blood in him, as he will be a better trailer—and sometimes a long trail may be necessary. I once saw a coon hound trail and run a squirrel nearly a quarter of a mile from a cornfield before treeing it. We killed the squirrel. Hunting over the high cut-over land of a great river swamp a few seasons ago, two of us by the use of a full blood coon hound squirrel dog bagged some eight or ten squirrels one cold winter afternoon, and if they had been out and feeding, the kill could easily have been doubled.

On the property of one of the clubs to which I belong is an area of at least 2,000 acres that is ideal for the use of a dog for squirrels, but such use is forbidden by the club rules. No sound reason can be given for such a rule, but it was put over by some cranks in former years and has never been revoked. I also am a member of the club that leases the adjoining property, which has been logged in recent years. Following the timber operations, I have enjoyed several fine hunts for squirrels with a dog on the latter property, and it is the only practical way to hunt the property now.

When speaking or writing of hunting squirrels, we should not forget Tennessee, Alabama, Mississippi and Louisiana as states in which they abound. Particular attention should be given to Louisiana, as more hunters have written of squirrel hunting in that state than probably in any other of the Gulf states.

During the War of 1812 with England, we had an example of the accurate shooting of riflemen trained on squirrels, when "squirrel hunters from Tennessee" inflicted the most frightful losses on British regulars and won the battle of New Orleans with the most lopsided casualties ever known in an important infantry engagement.

The greatest drawback to the shooting of gray and fox squirrels in some sections of the deep South for food as well as for sport is the prevalence of grubs under the skin, on the back of the neck, shoulders, or even on the head under the skin on the top of the head.

One rifleman above quoted writes on that subject as follows: "I never saw this affliction of squirrels until I came down into South Carolina. In fact, until then I did not know that these grubs would infest the squirrel. In Onslow County, North Carolina, I never encountered the infestation, nor did I ever hear of it spoken of there. All the afflicted squirrels I have encountered or examined had these grubs in or around the neck area and the larvae seemed to be every bit as large as the similar grubs in rabbits in the North. These infestations are very prevalent among both cat and fox squirrels (the gray squirrel in the South is commonly called the cat squirrel), and we also have a few flying squirrels although I do not know whether these are infested with grubs, but likely they are.

"These infestations cured me of all taste for squirrel here in the deep South, but as a matter of fact I had about stopped eating them anyhow, as this is country a bit too hot for the meat to taste real sweet and be firm."

Much the same condition and situation as to squirrel meat exists in August and September in Delaware, in which period it is soft and insipid, and may even spoil before the hunter gets home with his game, even if dressed as soon as shot. In fact, the author has had a number of squirrels spoil in the hunting coat pocket, within a period of four to six hours, in very warm weather within 10 days or so after the opening of the squirrel season in Delaware, September 15. Consequently, this rifleman's comment could be applied with almost equal force to more Northern squirrels, in places where a squirrel season which could have been made to open late except for political reasons, spoils a sport which would be tops if enjoyed six weeks later.

Quoting again: "Throughout the South, rabbit meat is likewise most unappetizing on account of lack of cold and frost, at least until well into the middle of real cold winters. Very few white folks will eat rabbit here in coastal South Carolina and invariably they are lean and flabby fleshed and generally full of fleas, as well as grubs. But squirrel is universally eaten and liked hereabouts, but not by this rifleman. I have seen squirrels which had the head swollen to twice normal size from grubs beneath the skin and then they are a most grotesque looking animal. The hawks must manage to snatch most of such infected animals as then they are most sluggish in their movements and I have even encountered squirrels which were blinded of one eye, temporarily, through the swollen area. Very frequently you will find and shoot squirrels here that have got rid of the grub or grubs, and then the infested area is covered with large scabs and patches of bare hide. I am not sure that these grubs infest every squirrel found locally, but the infestation is sufficiently general to interfere greatly with the sport of squirrel shooting in this vicinity, particularly by those who are not accustomed to picking up shot game that is found to be so unattractive."

In this connection, the following statement from Henry E. Davis is of interest: "During my hunting career spanning a period of more than fifty-five years, I have killed, I would estimate, more than 2,000 cat or gray squirrels and a number of fox squirrels. Most of my squirrel hunting has been confined to eastern South Carolina, where such game has always been abundant. Many of the squirrels I have killed were shot for hunting club stews, as frequently the club held meets when it was required that we live off the land, on which occasions fish or squirrel was the principal meat on the menu. In my early days, I used a shotgun, but for the past twenty-odd years I have hunted such game with a rifle exclusively.

"In all my experience, I have never seen but one squirrel that was infested with a grub or 'wolf,' and that was over fifty years ago in Williamsburg County, South Carolina. In fact, this infestation seems to be limited to a belt some twenty or thirty miles in width extending along the seacoast of that state. I have never heard of it in the interior counties lying along the Santee, the Black, the Lynches, and the two Pee Dee Rivers. At the club houses of the preserves along the upper Great Pee Dee River, I have seen during the past thirty-five years hundreds of squirrels that had been killed by members and guests, and not a single instance of grub or wolf infestation was reported. The case would be quite different, however, I am reliably informed, in Horry, Georgetown, Charleston and other coastal counties if the squirrels were shot before hard frosts and the advent of the winter season.

"I quite agree with Mr. Landis that no finer sport can be found anywhere than is afforded by rifle hunting for tree squirrels. If you want to enjoy it in its finest form, get a good squirrel dog and try your luck with Southern fox squirrels in big pine timber. They will make you hold a rifle as you have never held one before in order to secure a respectable bag for the number of shots you fire."

CHAPTER 6

Hunting Black Squirrels

MANY WHO CALL THEMSELVES NATURALISTS ASSERT RATHER DIS-
paragingly that the black squirrel is "merely a melanistic strain of
the gray squirrel." Whether this is true or not, the fact remains that
the black squirrel is a common and abundant resident of certain of
the less thickly populated areas of the Northern Middle Atlantic
States and Southern Canada. It is crafty, hardy, difficult to approach or stalk, and withal not at all easy to bring to bag.

It was formerly very plentiful in Crawford and Erie Counties,
Pennsylvania. The author has frequently heard his father, who was
very familiar with that section, mention the great numbers of these
squirrels he saw in those counties about eighty years ago. At that
time this was probably the most sparsely settled portion of that state,
and being a region composed of miles of rugged mountains covered
with heavy timber, it afforded a range that appealed especially to
these squirrels, which seem to take particular delight in the dark
fastnesses of the deep woods.

Today a short season of very good black squirrel shooting is found
in Southern Ontario. Some of it is still to be obtained in Northern
and Northwestern Pennsylvania, but apparently very little in the
state of New York.

The following account of black squirrel hunting with the .22 rifle
is by John L. Cull, a staff editor of *Rod & Gun in Canada*, whose
summer home is in the heart of the black squirrel country at Orillia,
Ontario, which is quite some distance north of Toronto, where he
lives in winter. These crow-black squirrels frisk and play around the
Cull home and along the lake at Orillia, and hunting them in that
area is just as common as hunting gray squirrels is with you. Mr.
Cull is a gray and black squirrel hunter of long experience, and has
been an enthusiastic .22 rifleman all his life. His description of this
most unusual and interesting form of squirrel hunting will show you
the black squirrel in his native habitat and how he is hunted today
in Southern Ontario. Now the story by Mr. Cull:

A Day with the Nut-Crackers of Ontario

By John L. Cull.

During a recent fall the Ontario authorities proclaimed a short open season on black and gray squirrels, the first for several years. To people who watch the big black squirrels as they frisk around our homes, climb trees and scamper across lawns, the idea of shooting such friendly animals seems like slaughter. But drive out into the country a few miles from town, locate a few of these same squirrels near their dens in the tops of tall trees, and if they have been shot at occasionally—just enough to make them scary—the hunter will find a very different proposition. If he will restrict himself to head shots he will find that it takes all his skill and marksmanship to locate the quarry and bring it down.

A friendly rivalry had long existed between Fred, my shooting partner, and I as to the respective merits of our scope-sighted rifles; a .22 long rifle on his side backed up by youth and a keen eye; and the .22 Hornet with a few more years experience behind the trigger which I could supply. We had attended shooting matches for turkeys and geese in the country each fall and occasionally had to shoot off a tie to see which had won the bird, while scores on the target might only vary a point or two with the advantage either way. This of course when using iron sights. So it seemed fitting to test ourselves during the open season for squirrels, head shots alone to count.

October 21 dawned damp and cool, after an overnight rain which meant that the squirrels would be out looking for breakfast and that we could move quietly on the wet leaves underfoot. We piled into Fred's car about 7 a.m., with rifles, field glasses and lunch. I had been out a day or so before to look the country over, and had located a bush which harbored a number of blacks, all of a satisfactory wildness. Although only a few miles from town, the concession road ran some distance without any crossroad, and we did not know what lay on the other side of the bush. We parked the car on the grass at the side of the road and sat quiet for a few minutes to allow the excitement of our arrival to die down. It was not long before we saw a black run up a butternut tree some 100 yards away, and by the aid of the glasses we watched his progress up the trunk and his arrival at a round opening, into which he vanished. Here was a chance to see which would score first blood. We separated and moved slowly over towards the tree, making no noise on the wet leaves under our feet. Soon out came a head, affording an easy shot at some 35 yards, but we had found by previous experience that no matter how dead he might be killed, there was no chance of his falling outside, but instead would slide down out of sight. Suddenly

ONTARIO BLACK SQUIRRELS

Four fine big black squirrels—a bag of which any rifleman would be proud. Note the size and weight of these melanistic cousins of the gray squirrel.

Photo: Courtesy, J. L. Cull

he whisked out and around the trunk, stopping to peer over a branch. I had a good view of his head, but Fred on account of his position to one side, called that he could only see a shoulder, usually a deadly mark, but under the terms of our contest, not to count. Here I had a chance to demonstrate why I preferred the Hornet to the lower velocity .22 long rifle. I was using a special handload, developing greater speed than the factory load, and more destructive on such a small object as a squirrel's head. In practice I had found that the explosive effect of the hollow point bullet would take the whole head off, killing instantly and without damaging any of the meat. As Fred called "take him" I settled back against a tree and placed the post of the scope on his ear. I must have held a trifle high, as at the sharp report the squirrel leaped into the air, to fall with a satisfying thud to the ground. When I advanced to pick him up, I was surprised to find no mark of the bullet, until closer examination revealed a slight scrape in the fur across the top of his head. I laid him down on a fallen log and called to my friend to come over, which he did, and I turned to exhibit my kill, only to see him vanish out of sight into a hollow log, having recovered from the stunning shock of the "crease." I mentally erased the score which I had chalked up to my credit, and we moved on a bit.

Soon we saw another black making his way towards us along the ground jumping over logs, running up a tree trunk, only to leap again to the forest floor and proceed in our direction. He appeared to be carrying something nearly as big as himself, and when he got closer we saw that it was a whole ear of corn which he had filched from a neighboring barn. There was no building in sight, so he must have carried it at least half a mile to where we saw him. He would stop and lay the corn on the ground, sit up and take a look around as though he suspected our presence, and then take up his prize and go on. Each time he stopped, up would come our rifles, but never would he pause for the extra moment needed to give us a shot. Finally he reached the fence close to the car, ran across the road, and up into a huge lightning-blasted trunk into which he disappeared, to show up again in a few minutes minus his load. In the meantime another black appeared with another ear of corn, following the same trail along the forest aisles, except that we noticed that he stayed in the tree branches longer. Finally he arrived at the last big tree between him and the fence, and running down the trunk, hung head-down some 20 feet in the air, with the corn gripped in his jaws. I saw Fred's rifle whip up, a sharp report, and the ear of corn flew into a dozen pieces, while the squirrel maintained his position head-downward for several seconds. The shock of the bullet tearing the cob from his jaws must have stunned him, but when he did recover, he made tracks for another part of that forest. Yes, there was a chance passed up to make the first score, but both of us had a taste of the unusual, and either would have preferred to see what a squirrel would do when his meal was shot out of his mouth, rather than tally the first hit of the contest. So far, we were even, one try each and no score. Ten minutes later another squirrel arrived via the tree route with another ear of corn, surely not the one we had shot at. He did not seem at all frightened by the reports, only took care to keep moving all the time. As he disappeared on the far side of an oak, we wondered whether these squirrels had been shot and kept on the run during the earlier part of the season. Soon I saw a black fluffy tail waving in the wind, and made him out crouched in the fork of his tree some distance away. A head shot messed his skull up quite a bit, but we slipped him into the game bag as one to my credit. Suddenly a black appeared on the fence not 10 feet behind us, stopping and running, but at no time did he give us a stationary shot. Here I saw Fred make one of those hits which caused me to envy his skill. I saw his rifle go up and the muzzle follow the leaping squirrel along the fence rail. At the report he jumped into the air, shot through the shoulders. Nice work.

For a while there seemed to be a letup in the game. Nothing larger than a red squirrel, which seemed pretty small after the larger blacks. We noticed that the red squirrels chased the blacks out of the trees, and often shot the little red fellows just to stop their persecution. However this red one was lying flat on a branch a few feet above the ground and about 60 feet away. I was minded to try out a trick of the old-timers, but knew it was performed with the heavy lead bullets then in use, and doubted whether the light high-speed bullet I was using would be effective. Carefully I held about an inch below his shoulder and touched off the sensitive trigger. The bullet entered the branch, forcing a piece up with sufficient force to drive it against the animal's heart, bringing him stunned to the ground without a mark, and a rap on the head put an end to his activities. Nothing spectacular about it, just a matter of hitting the branch where I wanted to. Red squirrels did not count this day, though I was glad to see just what the Hornet bullet *would do* under these circumstances. I had tried it often enough with the ordinary long rifle cartridge, but all it did was to jar the game off the branch.

Thinking we had better move to a fresh spot, we strolled along among the trees, and I kept my eye on my companion for fear he would pull off another stunt without my noticing it. Suddenly I saw him stop, peer into a tree top, then raise his rifle and whistle to draw my attention. I sidled carefully over, and saw what he was watching, another red squirrel with a nut in his mouth, as he chipped away with his keen incisors and the nut scraps flew. "Watch me take that nut from him," and sure enough at the report the nut scattered in all directions. Like the black robbed of his ear of corn a little while before, this one made never a sound for several seconds, but when he recovered from the shock to his jaws, he let loose a flood of squirrel invective which resounded throughout the tree tops.

The next one we saw was on a small branch of a pine tree directly overhead. Only his nose showed through the glasses, although his tail waved gaily in the breeze, but he kept the branch between him and danger. We watched for about 15 minutes, but he seemed in no hurry, so I fired a shot into the branch underneath him. This brought him up erect, and gave my partner a chance to score another, a head shot this time, to even up the record. However my turn came soon afterwards. I saw a big gray squirrel, the only one we had seen so far, sitting on a boulder near a tree stump, and a good long distance off. Here was a chance to get in some fine work, so I lay down on the damp leaves, got the sling adjusted and tightened, rested the muzzle on a convenient log, and cut loose. After several years' use of the Hornet I have got accustomed to either missing or killing cleanly. This time I used a solid point bullet and held for the shoulder. The squirrel leaped some two feet into the air at the report of the rifle, and threshed around in a circle at the foot of the tree. On examination I found that my bullet had passed through his neck, tearing out the whole backbone, but despite the shock he was able to move by muscular contraction. We paced the distance from shooter to squirrel, and found it to be about 80 yards, the longest shot that either of us had that day.

By now we were beginning to think of lunch, so as the sun had appeared from behind the clouds, we went back to the car and made ourselves comfortable at the side of the road, while we waited for the water to boil in our pails.

While we sat in the sun, enjoying a few minutes' rest, we saw a gray squirrel run along the fence and stop not 15 feet from us. I stretched out a hand for my rifle, but withdrew it at my partner's comment of "too easy." He stayed within 50 feet of us for several minutes, finally frisking off across the road into the lightning-blasted stump which had received the ears of corn earlier in the day. We noticed that he was not a pure gray, but tended to shade into brownish black in the hindquarters, sure sign of a melanistic strain.

A few more shots of no great interest netted us a couple more blacks and as the light began to fade, we made our way home, each well pleased with his choice of rifle and ammunition, and each confident that he had an edge of the other when it came to marksmanship.

CHAPTER 7

The Last Day of the Squirrel Season

PROBABLY YOU ARE ONE OF MILLIONS WHO NEVER MISS THE FIRST DAY
of the hunting season. It is often exciting and game is sometimes
then plentiful. The main drawback is that on that day the woods
are usually overrun by hunters and a still hunt by yourself is sometimes impossible, due to the yelling, shooting, and tramping around
of the multitude.

How about going shooting on the last day of the season? Game is
less plentiful, much more wary and harder to find. But most of the
time you will run across comparatively few other gunners and there
may still be sufficient game to provide excellent sport if you can
but locate it.

Here is the true story of the last day of a recent hunting season.
Squirrels were not overrunning the woods, but there were enough
of them to provide real sport. And it was *sport!*

Read this chapter and see whether you don't wish that *you* had
been along!

Few of us are likely to sleep well the night before the annual opening of the gray, black or fox squirrel season. Some wake up half a
dozen times, and then toss around in bed before the old alarm clock
finally goes off with a whirr! They are so anxious to get out into the
autumn colored woods that they live over in their dreams the wildest
hopes and anticipations of the squirrel hunter.

In much the same manner the *last* day of squirrel season has the
same appeal to the veteran disciple of the grooved bore, but with
this difference! Toward the end of the shooting season those squirrels that still remain in the oaks, the beechnuts and the hickories,
or are industriously running around on the leaves and are busy burying nuts in the ground, are still alive because they were smarter,
trickier, craftier, and more wide-awake at all hours than the hunters. On the last day of the squirrel season, a foretaste of winter has
come. The leaves are on the ground, and if any are still aloft they
are only in small bunches and here and there on a tree that sheds
its leaves later than normal. Young and foolish squirrels of a month

or so before have long since gone into hunting coats, and have furnished the piece-de-resistance to many a squirrel potpie, succulent roast, or squirrel fry that has proved to be a toothsome change from the foods of domestic sources.

Any young squirrels that now remain are practically grown and wiser than their parents—for verily is not the younger generation always smarter, in their own mind, than the wisest, of the squirrels that are so old that they are yellowed under the chin? Young squirrels too are not as pugnacious as old squirrels, and are not so inclined to rush out onto a limb and "bark" angrily at every intruder who may venture incautiously near their abode.

On the last day of the season, the hunter who has luck on squirrels—when the bushy tails are few, wild as hawks, and crafty beyond all measure—will bag them by knowing most of what is to be learned about locating, hunting and shooting squirrels, and by knowing definitely the zero of his rifle.

He will hunt the old den trees, usually old chestnut snags or weathered oaks or hickories, maples that have become rotted at the core, and gum trees that are old and knotted. He will watch always for squirrels feeding on the ground, where they have buried beechnuts, small sweet acorns and hickory nuts or shellbarks in small "caches" for their winter food. He will watch too along any backwoods or mountain field, where some unhusked corn still remains in the shock for winter husking, and especially will he hunt such places if the nut crop for the fall has been largely a failure.

On the last day of a recent squirrel season the writer went gray squirrel hunting. He chose the early afternoon for the start of the hunt because the days had become chillier and that day the late fall sun had come out warm and bright to warm the sunny nooks in the woods, the small section of rail fence that flanked the poplars, and the hickories and the oaks which adjoined the cornfield in which he had shot successfully at the beginning of the hunting season. In such times gray squirrels come out to run around, play, and feed, right after lunch time and will feed all afternoon, and in fact, are "out" more then than in later evening when the winds get cool and the shadows settle into the shady nooks by 4 or 4.30 P.M.

No longer is it good squirrel hunting policy to go shooting after 3.30 P.M. because by then the sun is getting rather low in the West, the squirrels have played and fed, and possibly have returned to their leafy nests high in the crotches of trees, or nests lodged in the limbs near the tops of the half-naked oaks, hickories and maples.

At 1.30 P.M. I slipped quietly into the woods, after asking permission of the farmer. He was sorting apples in his barn; red, ripe shiny and juicy-looking "Smokehouse," "Baldwins" and other fruits of the nearby orchard, and he seemed glad to let me hunt, because verily those squirrels had taken a heavy toll of his corn shocks.

I walked down through the cornfield to the edge of the woods, and soon a small gray flashed among the brush, lingered a moment —but not long enough to permit an aim, and was gone in a dense tangle of briars.

At least there was one gray squirrel left in the woods. But—as is often the case he refused to come out again. I believe this was the same small gray that I had seen on three different occasions and at which I had never been able successfully to get a shot. He always saw me first, and always managed to get off without the firing of the rifle. Once I had stalked him from the depth of the woods and he had come down out of the field, after jumping off a corn shock, had disappeared and then had suddenly reappeared some 15 feet on the other side of a large hickory behind which I was standing quietly. I could only see the rear part of his silky coat and his bushy plume, for the tree, but on he came out of sight, jumped onto the tree trunk, ran up opposite my face and suddenly stuck his head around within four feet of my nose as I was slowly leveling my rifle. One flash and he was gone! Had that squirrel been 25 to 50 yards off, he would have been an easy shot.

As this one could not be located by sitting out of sight, on first one and then on the other side of the briar thicket in which there were probably stumps, I walked up along the field, heard a squirrel run into the woods from the edge of the field, but could not see him long enough for a shot, as he dodged for a flash through the under-brush. The wind was blowing pretty hard by that time, and I stood by a cornshock, hoping he would come out.

I had a .22 long rifle low-speed hollow point in the rifle chamber, as I wanted again to compare results.

In about 10 minutes I saw a moderate-sized squirrel, squatted more or less back of a limb, almost entirely out of sight and with his gray tail blowing in the breeze as he arched it over his back. You can not kill squirrels by shooting at the tail. The tail is about two-thirds of the total "ball" made by a squatting or hiding squirrel and is always the most prominent part, and usually the one sticking up the highest above a limb. But the rifle telescope showed clearly which was the body and which was "brush."

It was a long shot, fully 50 yards to the tree and the tree was pretty high. A limb was between me and the squirrel, and there were some reddish leaves upon it. The squirrel, from his perch aloft, had all of the advantage and saw me clearly and a closer stalk was out of the question. So I risked an offhand shot, got the bullet off too low in an endeavor to avoid shooting at the tail, and to just scrape the top of the limb so it would cut well into the body. I heard the faint "tump" of the bullet on the animal, but saw at once from its actions, and could tell anyhow from the sound, that it was not a center shot. The squirrel rushed down the tree trunk, through second growth, passed twice through the field of the scope, then stopped once and I had to raise the scope to get onto him—as I wanted to catch him the instant he appeared in the field, falling and running down the tree, and finally he reached the ground, without a second shot, and scrambled off to safety among some down logs.

Well, that was that! Things were not going so well! Two grays seen and nothing to show for it!

So I walked slowly up to the end of the field to a shallow hollow from which I had shot possibly eight or 10 squirrels, the same season, all within an area of 100 yards. A very large gray ran up from a briar patch, dodged back of a tree trunk, flashed into view twice, through the brush, and then came into sight very craftily and thought he was hidden sitting on a limb next the trunk. I raised the rifle slowly, aimed on the chest and the high-speed "sphat!"

The bullet landed with a solid "thwack" on his tough hide, he whirled around the limb, hung a moment, and dropped to the ground with a soft "tump." Five minutes later I was pretty well briar-scratched but holding up an unusually large gray squirrel, a big old rascal, which dressing showed was shot directly through the heart. The spine also was broken. Yet he still showed a trace of movement as I lifted him by a back leg. Never pick up a squirrel by the head or the tip of a front paw. And never reach into a hole in a tree, into which one has gone. They may bite viciously at a finger, even if it is with their last breath. An old buck and especially an old female squirrel is scrappy to the last!

I stood quietly by that tree and 10 minutes later saw a gray hiding in the top of a tall poplar 40 yards off, down farther in the woods. The tree was swaying in the breeze, and the squirrel was pretty well hidden around the head and upper part of the shoulders but his plume and rear parts were showing—but of course I did not want to fire a bullet at those. I waited a minute or two, and he raised up for a more comfortable "hold." I had an arm rest by that time and took full advantage of it. One soon learns to lean the body against a tree and to get a rest for the left side of the arm or wrist, to steady the muzzle. And to prevent body sway on a vertical shot.

When the rifle cracked the squirrel turned end over end, hung on a moment, then dropped head down to the leaves. Nothing stirred, so I felt he was safe enough. Anyhow, a squirrel which drops head down from a rifle shot seldom escapes.

I walked over and there he was, lying on his belly, spread out, and dead. Dressing the little fellow showed that the bullet had cut off the large artery that leads out from the top of the heart.

The heart was completely deflated, or empty of blood, and the bullet had gone across through the chest, after entering just beneath the right elbow, had smashed the spine between the shoulders, and had come out about three-fourths inch back of the left ear, yet had not broken the neck, as it was traveling upward and forward at a sharp angle and had cut the spine at the center of the shoulders. I now had a nice pair of squirrels, fat as butter, "corn fed," hale, hearty and ripe for the frying pan. Verily a good start on the last day of the shooting season. It was just 2.30 P.M. and 2.45 P.M. when I picked up those two gray squirrels.

I stood a while at the intersection of two small woods runs, but nothing came along and no squirrels barked in the woods. Then I walked down through the woods, and came out on the lower side of the tree from which the Winchester had brought down the sunning squirrel, that had gotten off into the bushes. After a 15 minute wait at the edge of the corn I saw a very large gray jump up onto a cornshock and take a look at me, some 30 yards *out in the field*. He had hidden there as I came up through the trees. It was a peach of a shot, but a large house was almost directly in line and some 200 yards off across a hill top. Such a shot obviously should never be risked.

I walked slowly and carefully through the corn, keeping behind the shocks as much as possible, until I got up above the shock on which the squirrel had been seen and into which he had popped, when I came slowly out of the woods. That squirrel never left the cornshock until I got up within about eight feet of it, when it dashed wildly and in a zigzag course down the cornrow, onto the nearest small tree and on the second jump on that the bullet struck him directly in the middle. He hung on there for a moment, on the far side of the trunk, then dropped slowly from the tree and "tumped" on the leaves. I picked him up gleefully as he was by far the largest squirrel I had shot during the season. The high-speed hollow point had cut the last rib on the left side, went directly through his "corn fed" tummy—which was stuffed with partly digested corn, and emerged from the far side, making a hole of exit about the size of a quarter. This squirrel would *not* have been bagged by a solid nose, .22 rim fire bullet, as it would not have expanded, and a squirrel so shot can often struggle along for a hundred yards and hide. Yet this was an absolutely "center shot" on the flashing ball of gray as it wheeled around the tree trunk. Possibly a 30-yard shot, and yet it had started only three yards from my nose. Growth in cornfields often prevents shooting at a squirrel dashing along on the ground, between the rows of corn stubs.

About that time a man hunting with a shotgun showed up at the upper end of the field where I had shot the two grays an hour before. The only thing the matter with him was that he was just an hour too late. He was using early fall hunting tactics on the last day of the season, partly because he could not get away from town any earlier, and contrary to his hopes, things had not worked. You have to be in or along the squirrel woods at the right time, or you do not find many squirrels out playing around or feeding.

He said he had been waiting down in the woods for about an hour, but had seen nothing stirring around except a small, migrating bird, so he had come out to the edge of the corn to see whether a squirrel might work out that way to feed and had heard my rifle crack.

He was a bit skeptical when I answered a question about what luck had come my way, by holding up three fingers. This in squirrel shooters' language, means one squirrel for each finger held up. It is better than yelling or talking loudly around where people are hunting. So, I pulled three squirrels out of the paper bags I had them in to keep them from bloodying up the hunting coat, inside, and showed him where a single bullet had killed each squirrel, and that all three had been struck within an inch of the same spot.

"Well, I'll be darned," said he. "I've heard of such shooting, but I never actually believed it. I thought it was mostly talk. But now I have seen it. You know, I wish I could shoot squirrels like that. I would not care if I only got one squirrel. I would feel proud!"

We separated to hunt a few minutes until dusk, then started toward the car and home. Suddenly, "Kak! Kaak! Kaak! Kaak! Kaak—K! K! K! challenged a big ringnecked pheasant rooster, in the field above the woods. He challenged a couple of times. It sounded good too as in another two weeks that challenge might be changed to a frightened "rattle" as the ringnecked pheasant season would then come in. In about five minutes he came, racing and then flying, and cackling and crowing loudly, the whole way down the hill. Someone was apparently walking along the path through the field, near the top of the hill, and it both disturbed and annoyed Mr. Ringneck.

The last glimpse of a gray squirrel was of one racing across the leaves, over the top of a stump, then up a tree to safety. Seed for another year! You cannot expect squirrels next year, unless a "seed crop" of breeding game is left to furnish the supply.

So, with the final dying down of the gold of a setting sun, fading rapidly to dusk in the West, we set out for home. Home from the chase! Home, with hunting-coat bulging with enough gray squirrels to satisfy a reasonable man. And each one shot, as it should have been, with a single bullet.

What more could any rifleman want for the season? Twenty-one gray squirrels bagged in 24 shot at, and the last 16 out of 19 chances with the .22 Winchester.

In like manner, down into the past goes the end of every gunning season. For 50 of them has the author trod the paths in the golden-brown squirrel woods. Hunting on the mountain; hunting on the flats; hunting on the ridges; hunting in the valleys. But in every instance, hunting squirrels, the chosen game of the expert rifleman to whom one shot, should mean one squirrel. May it always mean that to you, if you too, love the "spat" of the .22 rifle!

CHAPTER 8

Shooting the Daily Bag Limit versus Making a Long Run of Clean Kills

IN SMALL GAME HUNTING FAR TOO MANY HUNTERS MAKE STRENUOUS efforts to kill the daily bag limit of game as often as possible. With much pride they freely proclaim "I got the limit!"

These efforts to kill the limit are responsible, possibly more than any other one thing, for the exceedingly low bag limits now placed on nearly every species of small game in practically every Northern or Western state in the United States today.

Killing the limit frequently is the surest way ever designed by man to shoot out a good squirrel woods. In addition, much of the game so killed is not eaten but is given away or wasted for the reason that the average small family today is unable, or does not wish to cook and eat one, two or three daily bag limits of squirrels or rabbits, if brought home at the end of one shooting trip, and particularly if shot in warm weather. How much more sport it is diligently to try to kill two, three or five squirrels with the expenditure of only that many .22 rifle cartridges and forget all about killing the daily bag limit, regardless of whether it may be large or small?

After all, rifle shooting on squirrels is, or at least can be made, strictly a sporting proposition. When the author was only ten or eleven years old, he was given by his grandfather, Adam Singer, a single barreled gun and thirty-five handloaded shotgun shells. He had previously received suitable and expert instruction in the use of a rifle and of a shotgun from this grandfather, who was the best rifle shot on game and the best wing shot in the field in an area of about 120 square miles. With these shells, and considerable good advice on the matter of the advisability and necessity of making a kill with every shot at the rats which infested the barn at the end of our lot, was the proviso that *if* I showed sufficient proficiency in the use of a gun to be able to return daily the remains of sufficiently freshly-shot rats to show better than a 50 per cent kill and miss ratio, I could then go hunting in the field by myself, but until I could show 50 per cent of kills, I was still under adult instruction afield. It was pointed out with distressing clarity that trapped rats, alibis, and rats which were hit and ducked back in, would be scored as misses.

No youngster with a consuming desire to go hunting alone ever was placed in a hotter spot. When the supply of rats gave out, I returned three loaded shells, and was credited with 29 dead rats, two cripples which ducked back in, and one miss. By that time I had learned that a rat shot in the nose would kick back into the hole even if he had lost the whole front of his head, and that it was better to wait until they stuck the whole head out and fire for the base of the ear. A rat shot just back of the ear would kick forward and a young fellow fast on his feet and who started for the rat at the crack of the gun, could grab him before he sometimes slipped down out of sight under the barn floor.

The idea of making a kill with every shot, if possible, paid dividends. The first time out alone, the author killed, bagged and brought home, a big rabbit (shot running), a ruffed grouse and a dove, and he was not 10 per cent as proud as his grandfather, who was then well past 80, but who was quite determined to leave at least one shooter among his descendants.

It was probably a good thing all around that the author had a fairly successful day. It was probably even more fortunate that he had to undergo such a strenuous training period because ever since he has endeavored to kill the highest possible percentage of the game shot at, rather than make the largest possible bag.

Making long runs of straight kills on gray squirrels, using a .22 caliber scope sighted rifle and hollow point ammunition, is not too easy a proposition. It is much easier to make a high average of *kills*. For instance, even for a man who will kill 80 to 95 per cent of the squirrels shot at, during a season, or a number of seasons counted consecutively (and not too many will actually do this), there is always the chance that a squirrel may suddenly change its position. It may move its head, jump down off a stump, jump along over the leaves while feeding on the ground, or something may scare it, in which case it will run up to the first large limb, or more likely hide behind a tree trunk. If this occurs while letting off the shot it may be too late to stop the pull and a miss is certain to result. There will be misses due to change of elevation of the normal group, to the first shot out of a cold, oily barrel, or to having roughly whacked the telescope. A telescope sight *base* screw may come loose, which will always cause unexplainable shots until discovered and corrected. A squirrel may be missed at very short range while feeding on the ground, due to undershooting because the rifleman will forget for the moment that the rifle will group one inch to one and one-half inches *below* the normal line of sight, at very short range, because the line of the bore is that far below the intersection of the crosshairs. The sight magnifies the apparent size of the squirrel by the magnifying power of the rifle telescope, and it appears entirely improbable to a tyro in the woods that he must aim so far above a squirrel so close that through the scope it looks almost the size of a tomcat. Nevertheless, one *must* aim well over the back on a very close range shot or one *will* certainly undershoot.

There are unexpected occurrences which cause misses at most inopportune times right in the middle of a long run, for instance: a squirrel sees the hunter and starts to run, and a small dead limb breaks under its weight and it drops a few inches before catching on to the next lower limb. Or, a hawk suddenly darts at the squirrel which immediately whips back of a tree trunk, or, another squirrel, unseen by both the hunter and the other squirrel gets playful, makes a dart at it, and the squirrel makes a wild jump out into space. I have seen at least three squirrels badly stunned that way, one just this last year, which jumped and landed on hard ground, almost at the author's feet, when another squirrel rushed it. All these things and many more, have occurred to squirrels which the author has been hunting.

The writer once was sitting against the butt of a chestnut tree resting, expecting to see a ruffed grouse come out and sun itself and drum on a log along a stone pile, in the woods, which place was a favorite drumming ground for local grouse (in Pennsylvania). He would then have walked up, flushed the bird and fired at it with his shotgun, which was then on his lap.

What *did* occur was that while he was practically dozing three gray squirrels suddenly ran squalling and fighting down the back of the small chestnut tree, circled the tree and two of them, one after the other, landed on his left shoulder and jumped off to the ground. The third put on the brakes and showered him with bark as it scrambled wildly up the trunk as he jumped to his feet and started shooting. He missed the first squirrel and killed the other two. The only time the author was more startled in the woods was when a ruffed grouse whizzing along out of space like a bomb or a shell, and with a terrific rustling and flapping of "brakes" tried to alight upon his head, from the rear, while he was sitting on a rail pile in the woods, eating his noonday lunch, which was spread out upon his lap, upon its newspaper wrapping. Of course the author ducked, then jumped to his feet, spilling the lunch and missing the grouse as it dodged back of a tree. The author was at the time under the impression he was being struck by a large hawk or an eagle, it occurred so suddenly and unexpectedly. Odd things happen at times in the woods, even when hunting small game.

Killing more than five gray or black squirrels, without missing a shot, when using a rifle, is unusual. I say this after having had a lifetime of gray squirrel hunting, in most of which I have killed a satisfactory bag of squirrels, always with a rifle except when merely picking up a gray or two when primarily hunting ruffed grouse, quail or pheasants. At times I have had very liberal bags of squirrels over the year, but never have made a practice of shooting large daily bags of squirrels.

In the late summer and early fall of 1941 the author attended the National Matches at Camp Perry, Ohio, and while there served as an instructor in the small arms firing school staffed by the F.B.I. Captain Baughman, of the F.B.I. was in charge, and the late, Major (then Captain) C. A. Lloyd, for many years coach or team captain of the most celebrated U. S. Marine Corps Rifle Teams, was Chief Range Officer.

Our local squirrel season then opened on September 15 (which was six weeks to two months too early) and after a few days afield, I sent a collection of bullet fragments and mushroomed .22 long rifle high-speed H.P. bullets to Merton Robinson, Ballistic Engineer of Winchester for examination so that he could observe at first hand, exactly how much mushrooming of .22 hollow point high-speed bullets does occur when shot out of a .22 long rifle Winchester rifle and when they strike and enter a squirrel at different angles and places.

Quoted from a letter to him, of September 25, 1941, is the following:

"I fired five shots at squirrels, last week, from my Winchester-Hoffman match rifle sporter with Hart speed action and 5A scope. These five were killed cleanly, four being cut across the heart, or through the aorta artery at the top of the heart, and one was in addition shot directly through the center of the forehead. That sounds like a good shot, but actually it was a 50-yards offhand hit, firing at a gray squirrel of which I then saw little but the tail, and being able to see nothing else after a time, I fired at the portion of the animal which appeared to be the left flank, hoping to hit the heart area. The bullet did so, and in some manner the projectile then deflected so that the portion enclosed drove up through the neck, and the head, and came out directly under the skin after having penetrated through the exact center of the forehead, being both a heart shot and a brain shot, something very rarely accomplished with a single bullet from a .22 rifle. It took me fully 20 minutes to find that squirrel in the deep leaves, as the range was greater than estimated, the woods being full of second growth.

"The squirrel from which the entire bullet was recovered, completely mushroomed, was struck directly on the point of the right elbow, as the animal was doubled into a knot, giving a flea biting on its rump 'the works.' The bullet went diagonally back through the body and blew all of the entrails out of a rather large hole in its side, in the opposite flank. The entrails were not much torn, and when pushed accidentally, back into the body most likely the bullet embedded in them, was returned to the body cavity, as it was found, when dressing the animal, directly between the kidneys.

"No experienced squirrel hunter, using a .22 rifle, will purposely shoot through a gray, black or fox squirrel, so that the bullet will penetrate the ham or hams, from the rear, nor will he shoot it through the throat, from in front, when the animal is on all fours, as in either case the hollow point bullet will destroy most of one or both hams. In very few cases, will a high velocity .22 long rifle hollow point bullet completely penetrate even a young squirrel endwise, as it will be found in the hams, after striking bones, or it will be found in the shoulders, neck or head, when penetrating from the rear. But such type and velocity of .22 bullet will almost always cleanly penetrate the animal on a side shot of any sort, and will go clear through the tough and flexible skin on the far side. A shot which strikes on an elbow or a kneecap, and then drives on into the body, will seldom penetrate clear through on a side shot, and never on an endwise shot, and a bullet through the bones of the neck, or the skull, plus some body volume, may leave fragments just under the skin on the far side.

"A .22 long rifle round nose, solid nose bullet, of any sort, at any standard velocity, is not a good killer on gray squirrels, and the hunter may have to fire two, three, four or five shots, even if fairly well placed, before killing the animal, or bagging it, unless some of these happen to strike the brain, the vertebrae in the neck, break the back ahead of the kidneys, break both shoulders, or cut through the upper half of the heart.

"An experienced rifle shot, but one who is no better rifle shot than myself, will go through a normal season with·75 to 85 per cent of the bullet holes in the squirrels he bags, grouped within the same one and one-half inch to two-inch area even when some are shot running, or otherwise in motion, as when feeding on outer limbs, or on the ground, or moving up or down a tree trunk. In such instances, aim is taken just ahead of the point of the nose. Such shooting will be partly offhand, other shots taken with an arm rest and shooting at everything which offers a good, reasonable and safe chance, up to 50 or 60 yards, and at good motionless chances often at much greater distances. The longest kill I can recall making was about 145 yards, paced. The average kill on gray squirrels is about 35 yards to the base of the tree, and the squirrel is usually 30 to 90 feet up. Those shot while feeding on the ground, and some days most of them will be so feeding, or those which have jumped up onto stumps to look around or eat a nut, are usually considerably closer and therefore are much more difficult to hit, because the angular distance through which they normally move, while feeding on the ground, can easily be two or three times the width of the field of the telescope sight, during the period while one is taking aim and letting off the shot. That often makes it necessary to take aim two or three times before getting off the shot at a moving gray squirrel."

This long run, started in 1941, continued through 1942, 1943 and into the season of 1944. At the end of the 1943 season, 14 squirrels had been killed successively, without a lost squirrel and with the firing of but 15 cartridges. The 12th squirrel had to be shot twice. It was a yearling gray sitting on a limb about 25 feet above the ground. It was a very cold, raw morning and very dark in the woods; so dark, that the squirrel looked black. There was much high brush between the rifleman and the tree and the range looked longer than it was. The author was shooting at a dark object, in poor light, against a very dark background. Temperature was below normal by possibly 25 degrees. Everything called for a resultant low shot. I held therefore with the crosshairs on the level with the top of the shoulder and creased the squirrel half the bullet width, across both shoulders. It dropped back of the tree, partly stunned, then in about 15 minutes appeared within 10 feet of where it had been sitting, and careful aim at the usual spot, made a clean kill in the heart area.

Of the fourteen squirrels bagged, over the years 1941-'43, inclusive, during which very little time for hunting was available due to constant work on smokeless powder and high explosives plant engineering and writing on explosives, four were killed at 80 to 85 paces. Three of these were shot from approximately the same spot, on the same tree, or an adjoining one, and the same distance away. One was shot directly at the butt of the ear, and the bullet came out under the opposite eye. The other two were heart shots. In the last of these instances, nothing but the head was seen, and the squirrel would not raise up out of a crotch, any further, after a 20 minute wait. As a matter of fact, I was not quite sure it was the head of a squirrel until I saw the eyelid move. One can see such things clearly through a good rifle scope.

The other long shot was at a very large male gray squirrel which was seen at quite a distance and then carefully stalked from a range

A Perfect End to a perfect day with .22 rifles and squirrels.

of about 150 yards until reaching a tree some 80 to 90 yards off, after which he moved around some in the tree tops and was finally killed when he stopped to bite into a hickory nut. That was the largest squirrel of the fourteen—a very old one yellowed under the chin.

Three of the squirrels in this long run were killed while in motion. This is not always as difficult as it sounds. One was shot running on a down log, toward me, and coming fairly fast. It was an angling shot, I held an inch or two ahead of the nose and he ran right into the bullet. The difficulty was in finding this one, as he fell stone dead into some briars and brush about as high as my head and thick as hair on a dog.

Another was running along on the lower rail of an old rail fence, a mean shot always, and this one, shot through both lungs, threshed around a bit, and got under some down stuff where I finally found him, lying helpless.

A person may accept all sorts of running shots. Probably the most difficult to handle, on the average, is a squirrel hopping along while feeding on the ground, in fairly dense, dark timber, with under-growth four inches to two feet high. You see him only here and there, and about the time you are ready to shoot he has either hopped out of the field of the scope or has gone behind a sprout. I saw two or three on the ground, feeding, close up and in high sprouts, at which I never did get a shot, simply because they were too close and at the slightest movement of the gunner would dodge out of sight, often not to re-appear. Another mean shot is a squirrel which comes racing along an old rail fence, too close to the gunner, while you are watching a longer piece of the same fence farther off. I lost one such last year without a shot simply because I only saw him for about two seconds, He saw me then and was off into the sprouts before I could turn around to the left to fire. I may have killed this one a day later, at least the next one killed was shot off the same fence about 50 yards farther along, the following day out.

Probably when Satan really sticks up his old horned head and whispers in your ear, "You better not fire at this one, you will break your long run," is when you are out in an open field, or in a cornfield, without a blade of cover, feeling as naked as September Morn, and you have looked toward the nearest woods, and in the middle of all that cover, fairly high up on a maple your eye picks out a thumping big gray squirrel squatting on the third big limb from the bottom, backed tight against the trunk, facing directly at you and intently watching you.

There, Mister Squirrel Shooter, is your big temptation. Are you going to take it, or are you going to sneak off and let him sit? You know, just as surely as the Creator made little green apples, that you cannot sneak up on that squirrel as much as five yards, no matter how slowly you move your feet, before he slips around that maple trunk and then goes up and rests comfortably in the top where you cannot see him, but where he can still see you.

I had a shot like that two or three years ago, where, on account of moving slowly so as not to startle the squirrel into movement, it must have taken me four to six minutes to get the shot off. But I felt confident I had killed that squirrel before I saw him start whirling over and over on his way to the earth. It was a good 80 yards or so, and I had to wade through elderberry bushes, briars, trash and finally through a small swampy morass, before I started climbing again to the base of the tree. I felt like yelling when I picked up that squirrel drilled just exactly *right;* and the chances were probably 20 to one I would either miss or hit him just anywhere at all.

Shooting a long run in the Swiss Match is much easier than making a long run on squirrels. I won the Small Bore Swiss at Sea Girt one fall in a high wind, and took second the previous year, and long runs were not common either day, but when you are out in the woods and are in the last portion of a long run on game with the rifle, you tighten up, sometimes a good deal worse than you might on the rifle range shooting prone, simply because you have days or even maybe two or three years to think about it, and you are every now and then asking yourself, "How long will this run keep up?" "Will I miss the next one—or will it be the third or fourth from now?"

Maybe about that time you hear a very slight rustle on the ground, and you look into the brush about 15 yards below you, and there is a gray tail just going over a little hump, and then you cannot see hide nor hair of him any more. There are a few mushrooms there in that damp spot, and squirrels like mushrooms for a change. Now what to do? You can be certain you can not walk up on him from the rear, because the speed with which that tail crossed the rump is fairly definite proof he saw you first as he fed across that level space down below you. You think a moment and decide that maybe if you circled up and around him and came in from directly in front, he'd be looking *back* and he would likely feed or walk right up toward you. I have shot quite a few in just that way. But it will take 20 or 30 minutes of careful stalking, and he will probably be feeding on a young hickory in the hollow by the time you get around ahead of him, so look all over that area for a squirrel on the move. Meantime, you look around for a good long, last look over all the trees above you and there, about 35 yards off, is one sitting cautiously on a limb backed up against the trunk where there had not been even a squirrel's whisker five minutes before.

You say to yourself, "Saved again!" Such a shot is so easy for a good careful *rifleman* that if you miss the spot you aim at, by three-fourths inch you ought to be booted.

You slowly raise the rifle, rest your left arm carefully against the tree trunk (but do not rest the rifle barrel), place those crosshairs on his left forearm about a third of the way above the joint, and you drill him through the upper part of the heart or through the aorta artery coming out of the top of the heart, just as surely as those little apples spoken of above get ripe eventually. One more squirrel is added to the long run as you hear that definite "tump" on the leaves.

During the twenty-nine years I served as gun editor of seven sporting magazines and trade journals, thousands of correspondents wrote me concerning practically every subject under the sun connected with rifles and shooting, but only a few of these reported long runs on squirrels. One man reported having killed thirty-three woodchucks without a miss with a .25 caliber Remington semi-automatic rifle. The chances of anyone equaling such a run would be very small.

John G. W. Dillin, author of *The Kentucky Rifle* and who in his day was one of the very best offhand match rifle shots in the United States—a most excellent training and help in shooting squirrels with the rifle—reported something like, as I recall now, thirteen or fourteen straight kills on fox squirrels in Kansas and Nebraska when a boy. Mixed in with these, I believe, was one hawk. He said the fox squirrels then were tame and were found along watercourses, and they are sufficiently larger than a gray or a black squirrel to present a fifty to one hundred per cent larger vital area. On the other hand, they are harder to kill instantly, being larger and tougher, and when you find a wild one, he is likely to be very hard to outwit. As I recall, these were shot with a .25 Stevens rim fire. It has been several years since John passed on the comment; at any rate, it was the best small game shooting he had done with a small caliber rifle, and it was done back in the days when men wore sideburns and hunters were comparatively few and far between in that country.

As a general rule, a man of skill and experience will find himself killing four out of five, or five out of six, every now and then, but I have found it difficult to get beyond seven straight. It is more difficult to do this when the shooting is strung over several weeks or seasons and there are wide changes in temperature and humidity, or you have to change ammunition. World War II made a lot of substitutions in the kit of the rifle shooter. You used what you could get, were glad to get it, and saved ammunition. In such instance, the idea of shooting for a long run fits right in with your other plans and problems. In any case, hunt *carefully* and with every shot or change of hunting area planned carefully in advance. For some odd reason, shots between 45 and 60 yards appear rare at least in my present hunting district. They are either a bit closer or materially farther. You get the big kick out of the distant kills, but most of them will be made from den trees with which you are quite familiar and from which you probably can find a place of concealment or a good place to stand quietly, next to a tree trunk, so that you are not too close, or materially too far, or so that a herd of cattle or a farm house or traveled road is not directly in the near distance. And if you will make a rough drawing or careful notes of the exact trajectory of the .22 long rifle standard velocity and high velocity ammunition and sight your rifle, as directed in the first edition of *.22-Caliber Rifle Shooting*, or in this book, and will carry that in your gun coat patch pocket at all times, you can readily refer to it in the woods, and know at a glance, just where to aim to *kill* a squirrel at any distance at which you are likely to shoot at him.

Always remember this: the large vital area presented in the body of the squirrel when standing up, or running up or coming down a tree trunk, or when hanging on the side of a tree, is vertical, or up and down; and when he is feeding along on the ground, moving along on a rail fence, crouched on a limb of a tree, or flattened on anything which is horizontal, his long vital area is horizontal and then his vertical area is not over three-fourths inch to one and one-half inches in most instances, within which an instantly vital or paralyzing shot may be made. It is risky to take an 80 to 120 yard shot on a gray showing but half an inch of his back over a limb, because even a slight misjudgment of range will cause a sure miss, but if that squirrel sits up, you can likely bring him down with a hit anywhere within three and one-half to five inches vertically, and stone dead, within a one and one-half to two and one-half inches vertical space between the eyes and the kidneys somewhere so as to cut the spine. If very close to you, beware of the high vertical and the small horizontal—he is likely to run to one side.

Finally, when are you justified in passing up a shot, when making a long run, without feeling that you have actually for all practical purposes missed one? The author would personally feel that he was obligated to fire at any squirrel when seen under conditions which would include every possible shot he would normally chance in the field, when not in the middle of a long run. I think that will answer it about as well as it can be answered.

It is always difficult to make a long run on gray squirrels feeding on the ground in cornfields or when up on cornshocks out in such fields. Nevertheless, this is one of the best places extant for killing a good mess of squirrels. Surroundings, undergrowth and background are almost certain to make such shooting with a rifle difficult, due to the little animals moving around rapidly in weeds while on the ground and because of the open background when firing at them on cornstalks or cornshocks. However, a hunter sitting in cover with an available arm rest can make sure shots on squirrels out in the cornfield, on those in trees lining the woods' edge of such field, and on those that come down a fence row and stop on the top of posts for making observations before quitting the fence for the field.

Shooting squirrels off den trees is always more deliberate and generally easier, even at 70 to 90 yards, than when shooting at them within 40 feet feeding on the ground.

The most difficult shots are *directly* overhead, at squirrels hiding on the upper side of large limbs, and on trees more than 80 feet tall. I will take off my hat to anyone killing eight straight all under or rather *over* those conditions. If you must take such chances, breathe fully two or three times, expel about 75 per cent of the oxygen in your lungs, then start your aim and put it through as rapidly as possible before you get completely out of breath. If you feel about strangled, regardless of everything take your rifle down and start all over again. You are almost *certain* to flinch badly if completely out of breath just as you let off the shot. If your lungs are too full of oxygen the strain is terrific and you will not be able to hold on a barn, let alone the vital area of a squirrel.

This matter of shooting for consecutive kills works out just as well on gray squirrels, red or pine squirrels, black squirrels, fox squirrels, Western tree or ground squirrels, gophers of the plains country, woodchucks, marmots, or jack rabbits. It is not likely to be so satisfactory when firing at coyotes, hawks, or varmints of any sort. In such instances, one does not wish to be under unnecessary strain or keyed up more than normal, and he will shoot at any range at which a disabling hit appears even remotely probable, or even possible, and he may have to do rapid fire shooting at a running object at great distances. But, care in taking that first shot *always* pays dividends. Volume of fire means almost nothing to the *expert* rifleman in a squirrel woods, unless he is using a light repeater and is shooting at running squirrels by preference. Accuracy of placement of the first shot fired is the prime essential.

The ability to make kills at long range, on squirrels, sometimes leads to the most astonishing, unexpected and amusing results. At one time, near the end of a particularly long sustained and severe dry spell, a young man passed a very warm and lazy day hunting gray squirrels on Peters Mountain in Central Pennsylvania, at a spot about a mile and a half west of what was known far and wide as "The Cold Spring." He was hunting old and very large chestnut snags used as den trees on the flat of the mountain, and as usual was carefully still hunting, alone.

For three weeks, practically no one had killed any gray squirrels on that mountain, using a shotgun. The only exception of which this young man was aware was a man who habitually used a Daly 10 gauge weighing 10½ to 11 pounds, and loaded with four and one-half to five drams of powder and very coarse shot in large quantity. This gave a load of maximum range. Moving around in the exceedingly dry leaves and then killing squirrels was entirely out of the question at the moment, as the leaves were practically all off the trees and on the ground, and a man could be heard walking for nearly a quarter of a mile even if slipping along very stealthily.

By sitting quietly for hours at a time, within 50 to 60 or more yards of the most promising den trees, chosen as such by examining the visible holes in the tree trunks for rubbed places, and fresh claw or tooth marks, showing recent occupancy, the young man killed three squirrels, all shot in the heart or in the heart area, and all three bullet holes could have been covered with a quarter placed on the same area on each squirrel. The squirrels were in his coat pocket when he went to the Cold Spring to eat lunch.

While there a young friend came along, who was known as one of the best hunters and best wing shots in the valleys around, but who was quite cast down because he had not been able to get sufficiently close to even one gray squirrel for the previous 10 days, to have killed it. When asked what luck he had had, the rifleman pulled out his three squirrels, laid them down, called attention to the bullet holes as proof that they had been shot with the scope sighted .22 rifle he was carrying, and then the other hunter after a moment said, "I have heard for some time that you have been killing squirrels right along on the flat here, where it has been too dry for us shotgun hunters to get up close enough to get a shot, but I did not believe most of it, except of course for possibly an accidental hit now and then, but now I have seen what I never expected to see—a man who can shoot squirrels through the heart *consistently*, and at an almost unbelievable range, because I do not believe you can sneak up on them any closer than I can, on these dry leaves. And *I* have not gotten any for more than a week!"

Shortly after reaching home that evening, by which time he had four squirrels, the young hunter with the .22 was called upon by three or four of the veteran hunters of the community, all of whom demanded to see the squirrels shot with the rifle. Upon being shown the skinned squirrels, none of which contained evidence of shot pellets, but all of which had been shot through the chest with a .22 rifle bullet, the men left.

Upon going over town the next day the young man was startled to learn that he had shot a mess of squirrels, by shooting them through the heart at a distance of over a quarter of a mile, because *it was not possible* for the best hunter in the area to get any closer to that many squirrels in one day, under the then existing conditions. Verily, the adding together of two and two sometimes leads to the most astonishing result.

These squirrels had been killed that day with a Pope-Stevens Schuetzen at ranges of 60 to 110 yards, by sitting them out at den trees and carefully touching off the set trigger at exactly the right moment. No one had told an untruth; a group of veteran shotgun hunters had simply formed a group deduction from all of the available evidence, and had figured that a young rifleman could not do anything that they could not do. All the rifleman had said was, he had shot them at ranges beyond ordinary shotgun killing distance, had shot them off old chestnut den trees down the mountain, on the flat and that, while he did not always shoot a squirrel in the heart he usually tried to, and that he was using a very accurate .22 rifle, with set triggers and a reliable telescope sight. The veracity and ability of the hunter who had met him was so highly regarded locally, that a rather amusing tale of the general type of the James Fenimore Cooper's *Deerslayer* rifle shooting resulted.

It has been the author's experience over many years that gray squirrels living on very remote and rocky, mountainous areas, having high timber and old snags as den trees, and which see comparatively few people except in hunting season, are invariably very much wilder and much more difficult to approach, especially very late in the season, when the trees are bare of leaves, and during very dry weather, than are squirrels that live out in open woods lots and wooded country, which is flat, or swampy, and in which farms are much more thickly studded, and in which people are moving around daily close to the squirrels due to farming or lumbering activities and are usually paying little or no attention to the squirrels.

Anyone who can make a run, of even five or six gray, black, or red squirrels under such circumstances can pat himself on the back, regardless of the ranges, or who sees what, and he can feel that he has obtained just about the most satisfying rifle shooting that can fall to the lot of the man who hunts squirrels in the woods with a .22 rifle.

You will never forget the experience. Even though your years may creep up to 70, 80, 90, or 100, and even though you may have traveled to many parts of the world, and have experienced many delightful enjoyments, you will not feel that you have reached the zenith of achievement until you have killed squirrels at ranges that others thought impossible or have had such a long run of straight kills that you did not think it possible. Then, and only then, will you appreciate how much real sport can come to the man or the woman, who takes an accurate rifle into the woods and does his very best; try it! That, to the author's idea, is real rifle shooting.

The long run of 14 straight on gray squirrels, which was carried into the first day of the 1944 shooting season, was soon to come to an end. The season opens much too early, September 15, and in '44 that happened to be one day after the severe tropical hurricane which came up the coast from the Carolinas. It smashed and flooded houses, piers and ships and blew down forests. Fortunately, most of it swept out to sea 30 miles below the author's property but we caught the rain and enough wind.

The first two squirrels located after this storm passed were feeding in the leaf-covered tops of beechnuts and hickories. No shots were obtained. Every now and then a limb would shake, cuttings would trickle down, or a gray tail would be glimpsed for a moment. But you cannot shoot squirrels with a rifle unless you can first see the exact spot on the squirrel you want to hit.

Having no luck in the lower woods, I next tried the upper stand of timber. After listening to cuttings pattering down for an hour, I suddenly saw a squirrel sitting on a limb, crouched ready to run. His right hip and the tail curled over his back were all that showed plainly. It was a 45-yard high, offhand shot, directly into the morning sun. Nevertheless the author tried to miss the point of the knee and drive a bullet into the far shoulder or the lungs by a shot cutting diagonally upward and forward through the body. The most unfortunate place to hit a squirrel with a rifle bullet is in the middle of the upper joint of a hind leg. This is the "ham" and is where you find most of the toothsome flesh.

I got this shot off well, he slumped to the crack of the .22 rifle, hung on for about 10 seconds, and then dropped to the leaves. The bullet had struck the extreme edge of the ankle joint, slashed up the inside of a hind leg, cut a slash an inch long across the abdominal wall, entered the left chest at the right spot, cut off the aorta artery just above the heart, and had gone on through the left shoulder and out the point of the shoulder about an inch and a quarter below the butt of the ear. It required a heel squeeze neatly on its head, but actually died from internal hemorrhage. The bullet had plowed so far along the underside of the squirrel that it looked when dressed out as if it had been hit in half a dozen places. It was a pure silver gray, weighed about one and one-fourth pounds, and was in splendid shape, but had been completely castrated at some early date.

This shot made 15 squirrels straight, killed with 16 cartridges, all shots being hits. The weather was by then dark, wet, windy, and not very comfortable. It was damp in the woods. Fortunately there were no mosquitoes, a happy circumstance but seldom to be counted upon in Delaware. The natives have a good time claiming that they had the first signer of the Declaration of Independence. What they overlook mentioning is that they also had the mosquitoes which bit the first signer! Their descendants are still with us, and how they have thrived!

My luck now suddenly changed. During the remainder of the afternoon I saw a few more squirrels, but only one presented a chance for a successful shot. When on a proper hold the bullet struck below the nose of this one, which was facing downward on a tree, I became convinced that the rifle had changed its center of impact and was shooting lower than and to the right of normal. A test made on a small yellow leaf put up on a stump as a target at 20 yards showed my deduction to be correct. Two shots were fired, and both bullets cut into the same hole an inch and a quarter low and a quarter of an inch to the right. The rifle was shooting abnormally low. This may have been due both to the swelling of the fore end, which caused it to press tighter to the metal, following the storm, and to the darkness of the woods. Excessive moisture in the air should have caused the rifle to group a bit higher. Before my next hunt, I devoted some time to practice which presented targets at approximately the same height, angle, and in the same sort of background, as squirrels, hawks and crows. Such practice trains one's muscles, especially in the neck and shoulders, and it trains the rifleman to breathe properly when firing up into the air.

What a help that is, was seen the next trip out when the author finally saw a large gray squirrel feeding in the top of a 75 foot beechnut which was situated somewhat farther up a hill, than his stand near another beechnut which he happened to be watching. This squirrel suddenly showed up while watching another gray feeding on the near side of the same tree. The foliage was so dense that seeing either of them was mostly luck. Firing strictly offhand, and very high into the air, I centered that one with the first shot, at fully 75 yards, and probably 90 feet above my head. That is a *shot*, any time and any place! Try it in your spare moments. The bullet entered just back of one foreleg, high up and came out the far side right against the back of the front leg, cutting off the spine cleanly, and severing the artery above the heart. It was a nice clean kill; the squirrel never kicked after stricking the leaves.

Next one was shot off the same tree, while standing farther down in the ravine and the target probably 85 yards from the rifle. I first saw what looked like the end of a corncob, beneath the tail which was waving and guessed it was his head as he peered at me through the leaves. However, it happened to be one hind leg, and I shot the squirrel through the ankle, the bullet grazing up across the underside of the body. The squirrel kicked up a fuss, and after a moment, I saw more of the squirrel and fired again, the bullet cutting across the breast and tearing off the whole right shoulder and pulping the front leg attached to that shoulder. The squirrel dropped to the ground, moved up the hill slowly toward a groundhog hole and stopped. It was then too dark in the shadows on the ground, to see the animal through the scope or with the naked eye; both were tried. I walked up, it moved up over the hill, was run down and shot hiding a foot above the ground, in a hollow chestnut snag. The bullet entered the front of the chest and came out of the throat. Figure out how that could happen! These two long shots were made while hunting with a captain and a trooper of the state police.

The remainder of the '44 shooting season brought the year's total up to nine squirrels, one miss and two lost cripples. One of the latter and the misses were on shots at running game. Included in the bag were a hawk, a chuck and five crows, followed by two misses on crows. This totaled 23 squirrels, two lost cripples and a miss, in consecutive shooting, and the following season I started off with four straight kills, making 27 squirrels in 30 consecutive chances. That is a 90 per cent average, including shots at moving game. Some of it was moving fast!

This 1944 shooting included two very satisfactory shots. One, which may be mentioned elsewhere, was a clean offhand shot at 64 paces, at a pure silver gray hanging head downward barking at the author. The bullet struck the throat, about an inch under the base of the ear. The last shot of the year was at a gray crossing a root of a black oak, on the ground practically, at a distance paced carefully of just 85 paces. The squirrel was probably eight or 10 feet lower than the rifleman. The animal had his back humped up and that offered the best shot. It would soon have been out of sight below a higher bit of ground.

The bullet struck in the middle of the back, with a resounding "sphatt!" The squirrel dropped on its side, switched its tail sharply up and down, four times, like a vitally hit woodchuck, and then rolled over the edge into the bed of a small stream. I will remember that shot, a long time! It brought to a close the squirrel shooting with the .22 rifle for the year 1944.

Within 200 yards radius I had killed two rabbits, five crows, one red and four gray squirrels, and from the 1943 season my last remembrance had been the raucous cackling of a cock pheasant, flying down off an open hill to the cover of the squirrel woods.

I hope that it will be possible in the years to come, to slip into the old hunting clothes, grasp the favorite scope sighted rifle, and lose one's self for a day down by the rippling little run, where the ground pine grows in clumps. On the hill stand the hickories which grew there when more rugged men trod those slopes. Down from the open hill, comes a rivulet in a ravine into which deer sometimes glide softly and with cautious step. On the top of the 90-foot sycamore, now dead in most of its branches, crows will sway in the wind and caw and shout hoarse abuse at intruders. Sixty yards off is a favorite tree behind which one can stand and pop them off with beautiful precision.

In the black oaks, in the hickories, the beeches, roam the gray squirrels full of life and action and color. It is one of the few spots locally into which one can stroll and almost immediately turn back the calendar, one to five centuries—turn it back to the days when only the Indians roamed the woods. It has been variously estimated that a high of 3,000,000 and a low of 300,000 Indians were all that lived in this whole country which is now the United States. Most of the Indians stayed along the Eastern watercourses and on the plains in the West where the bison roamed. In such districts there was most of the game they could use, and it was easier to go from place to place to find it.

Today, in such a hardwood grove, by the use of a bit of imagination and by putting present cares out of mind, one can forget most of the headaches which civilization has brought us. You have your favorite .22 rifle and its accurate and deadly ammunition. You can spend days in such a spot or grove without regret, living life as only the hunter, nature photographer, or naturalist can live it today. You look into the forest toward the setting sun, and you are sorry only because it is evening and others expect you to come home. As you trudge your way toward the car, on the way back to town, there is one thought always uppermost—on the first day on which you can return with your rifle, *you will be back*. The Indian was right; there *is* a happy hunting ground. Only the foolish man must die to find it!

The 1945 squirrel season started with abnormally warm weather. With the rush of work in the final preparation of the last of the copy for *Twenty-two Caliber Varmint Rifles*, and the hot weather and everything, the author did not go squirrel hunting until the 28th day after the season opened.

Normally this is not a particularly auspicious season's curtain raiser. In many areas, all the game you find a month after the opening of the season you could easily place in your vest pocket, or even the watch pocket, in some sections.

However, after it started to clear off a bit, we arrived in the pet "game pocket" woods, about 8 A.M. and walked down along the old run. Feed seemed to be almost non-existent. There were scarcely any cuttings on stump tops and down logs. No crops had been planted or harvested in the fields adjoining the woods. Rank weeds were everywhere.

Eventually I came upon a man of about my own age, who was apparently waiting out a gray squirrel, and finally he saw it and shot it, a very small one of the fall litter of '45. He was using an automatic shotgun and said that made three for himself and his son. He added that another larger squirrel had gone up a beechnut tree next to the one where he had bagged his squirrel.

I overlooked saying that I had seen a gray tail hanging for a moment below a large limb pretty high up on a poplar, two large trees to the south of the beechnut in question. He was hiding and apparently his foot slipped, but only for a moment.

Finally the other hunter left, saying he had to take his son to a football game and they had better get going as it was a long drive.

I waited out the gray I had located, and finally up popped his head over the top of the limb, but only a small part of the head. He just hung there and would not show more, so, after 10 minutes or so, I put a bullet—a Remington Hi-Speed .22 long rifle hollow point into his throat and lifted him right out of the tree. The Winchester 52 Hoffman sporter had made an X. The whole lower jaw was torn off, and a small hole was in the top of the neck where the bullet came out. The throat was torn out, so that the whole lower section of the head, from nose to about one and one-half inches toward the chest, was gone. It could not have been that I shot the squirrel in the back of the neck and it came out the throat, because it would have been physically impossible to shoot it from my position in the back or in the top of the neck, unless I had adjusted my skyhooks and had ascended vertically and then shot earthward. But, with my usual nonchalance, I had left my skyhooks at home! The tree was 15 yards distant, and the squirrel 60 feet up.

After a short wait, without seeing anything more, I walked back up through the woods, waiting out a hickory tree that in other years had always produced game and in half an hour suddenly saw an abnormally large gray feeding on the ground and coming diagonally toward me. The squirrel was about 15 feet from the foot of the hickory, it was a cold, frosty morning, undergrowth was reasonably bare of leaves by then, and the squirrel presented a nice open shot on the ground.

This squirrel was giving a 45° angle shot, and moving forward its own length every second or two, but fortunately at an even rate of speed. The range was about 30 to 35 yards. The bullet struck exactly on the point of the right shoulder, at which point it was aimed, traversed diagonally through the chest cavity, blew the heart to pieces, leaving only a small fragment, tore up both lungs and the liver and emerged from the body rather far back in the ribs on the left side.

This was an abnormally large male, fully developed, a pure silver gray, and a very fine fat, handsome squirrel. He was all reddish and yellow beneath the chin. The first one shot was about a pound in weight, a castrated male of the first litter of this year. The other was grandpa, and he looked like a scrapper.

That made two, with two cartridges. Not bad, to start the season, no sighting shots, and the rifle had not been fired for some months. Both shots were Xs; temperature was about 40° F.; the first was killed at 8.45 A.M. and the second at 11.15 A.M.—the latter at a time of day which theory says *all* squirrels are safe in bed, with the covers pulled up over their heads, and taking a noonday siesta. The wind was gradually increasing.

After this shot I walked up the woods a way, saw a sharp-shin hawk closeby in the woods hunting gray squirrels, but even though I hunted this one for some time I could not get a shot at it. So, I went down the woods again.

After a bit I saw a large gray squirrel down a sort of lane, between the trees on the ground feeding along rapidly toward the foot of a hickory tree which, if it climbed 10 to 20 feet, would place the squirrel at a particularly bad angle for a shot, due to buildings in the distance. The shot on the ground was strictly an offhand shot, I was not near a tree at the moment, the squirrel saw me and I had to shoot thus or let the squirrel get into an area in which a shot could be dangerous—if it ricocheted.

I took the shot offhand, as the 30 yard shot had just been, and called my shot one to one and one-half inches at 12 o'clock and guessed the range at 75 good yards. The bullet struck the squirrel in the left front leg, it threshed around for a short interval over an area of about 30 feet, and then disappeared up a hickory behind which it had found refuge. I found the squirrel had shed no blood on the leaves, even where it had rolled around. I stood quietly in one place, and finally spotted it about 65 yards off, and about 60 feet up in a poplar tree, hidden behind a clump of leaves on some limbs, sitting curled up in a ball, quite motionless, and with its tail arched over its back. It saw me and was simply hiding, perfectly motionless. I would not have seen it then had not the light been directly back of it. It was 75 to 100 yards from where it was shot.

I managed to get an arm rest, located the tail carefully and then aimed for the exact middle of the body, as I could not tell which end the head was located. There was not sufficient visibility in the tree tops to tell this even with the telescope sight. The squirrel came down like a falling apple and was found to be perfectly centered, in one side out the other, and with the elbow shattered by the first shot. It was fractured but not badly torn. This shot was paced out on the ground from where I fired the first time to the point of the stick which the squirrel was passing when I fired at it first, and the first shot was 83 paces—paced twice, on level open ground. So, that one took two bullets, at 83 and 65 yards, and it was also an abnormally large male, reddish under the chin. Rather, a sort of deep, reddish brown with some tinges of yellow. The coat on the back was a pure silver gray.

I then walked farther to the west; checked again with the watch, and found I had the two shots at squirrel No. 3, at 11.45 A.M. and 12.30 P.M.

Eventually I saw a very small gray squirrel make a wild leap from one bare beechnut onto the end of a leafless dead limb of another beechnut. He then raced around rather wildly on that bare tree, was apparently just playing and enjoying himself, without a companion. Finally, when he was going rather rapidly up a long, bare limb, onto the top of the tree and soon to spring into an adjoining tree covered with leaves, I led him and fired. I held a bit too high, he walked into the bullet which struck too far forward in the head, and after whirling he fell and lay quiet. As I walked up and was reaching down to pick him up by the tail he suddenly flashed around a small partly dead tree, about four inches in diameter, which had a hollow core, and was up out of sight on the far side. I finally located him coming out for air, about 15 or 18 feet up, and killed him at 15 yards, with a shot through the ribs, high up, which tore off the spine. This bullet shed fragments in the squirrel, although only 15 yards off, and the squirrel weighed only eight or 10 ounces, being a young gray of the last litter.

This one was shot at 1.45 P.M. This now made four straight, with six cartridges, all hits. This squirrel had been shot in a peculiar manner by the first bullet. It had a hole through the front of the head, which made an open wound, about .32 caliber in diameter, just ahead of the brain, and all that held the nose on was a bit of flesh at the tip. The bullet had just gouged out a segment consisting of about 80 per cent of a circle, the other 20 per cent being just open space, and was as large in diameter where the bullet struck as where it came out. Almost anyone would have said that squirrel had been shot in the head too far forward, with a .30 or a .32 caliber, flat nose, solid bullet, and it had just cut a groove right through the bone and flesh, without expanding. It looked as if it had been gouged out that way, by a steel tool, or a flat nose bullet. It was one of the most peculiar looking wounds I have ever seen made by a .22 long rifle, Hi-Speed, hollow point bullet. The squirrel had been stunned, had trouble to breathe apparently, but did not appear to be suffering. It did not as yet quite know what had happened to it.

By that time it was getting very windy, large trees were rocking and bending in the gale so, while I could likely have shot our legal limit of six on a poor day for hunting, 28 days after the opening of the squirrel season, I left, as I had all I could use, and arrived home and in the house by 3 P.M. I had had a 28-yard shot, a 30-yard shot, an 83-yard shot, a pair of 65-yard shots and a 15-yard shot, all hits, and had killed all the live squirrels I had seen that day. Yes, the .22 rifle is a deadly weapon if you have a good one, have it well sighted, know its trajectory, necessary lead on moving grays, and can shoot in the woods.

Squirrels were very scarce the remainder of the 1945 season and this was true in 1946, 1947, 1948 and 1949.

CHAPTER 9

The Woodchuck

As a sporting proposition, the eastern woodchuck or ground-hog, gray or black, provides the best long range shooting with a small caliber rifle to be found anywhere in the United States or Canada. He possesses acute vision, good hearing and a very keen sense of smell, and becomes very wild and difficult to bag when constantly hunted. In such instances, every chuck bagged is indeed well earned.

Fortunately for his future, he is more common over his range than most of the small game protected by law, except possibly rabbits. He is also the permanent home builder for the cottontail rabbit.

The woodchuck is more tenacious of life than any other small game animal. He is the best training for riflemen ever afforded, particularly for those who are not essentially woods hunters and who like to shoot at long range and, in so doing, very carefully place their shots.

In writing of the woodchuck, we will first discuss his life, habits, characteristics and peculiarities, and follow this with suggestions as to the best methods of hunting him.

This chapter is written to please and help both the tyro and the expert. A complete description and critical discussion of most of the .22 center fire wildcat woodchuck cartridges is to be found in *Twenty-two Caliber Varmint Rifles* by this author.

Now for the woodchuck, his life and hunting.

This is intended to be a rather intimate glimpse of the life and habits of the woodchuck, *Marmota Monax*, from his birth in a den in a hillside to his maturity, his fall feeding, hibernation, spring emergence, his mating, his hunting by foxes and men, and finally the end of his normal life cycle.

Much of this data was compiled especially for this volume by the late Dr. Ellis E. W. Given, of Frankford Arsenal Rifle Club, and the other portions are from the author's own observations. This information is intended to assist in locating and still hunting the woodchuck with a long range, flat-shooting .22 caliber rifle.

SIR MONAX

Taking a last look around before turning in and calling it a day. Instantly fatal shots on a chuck, posed like this, are: at butt of ear; half way
between eye and ear; 1″ to 2″ below butt of ear (to break neck); or 2″ below
and 4″ to left of butt of ear, for bullet to drive through both shoulders. In
any one of the four cases, you get your woodchuck with an instantly paralyzing shot, and he will not get back into his den.

When motoring in the country, or when hunting, you may gaze across a field and see one or more short, stocky, small-sized animals, of a grizzly-gray or reddish-brown color feeding in the clover. Each will have a very short, apparently useless and rather bushy tail, and, when resting in the sun on an earth mound at the mouth of a chuck den, will look much like a fat brown rabbit or a red fox curled up ready to sleep. The chuck is both low slung in the middle and fat. He is also heavily built from the waist back. He has the characteristic of drawing himself erect, pulling up his front legs, and letting his forefeet dangle before his chest, thus giving the appearance of being quite rigid. His cone-shaped head will be held at a right angle to his body, as he faces you, and he will watch you intently each minute unless busily engaged in feeding.

If you move, he will likely drop suddenly to all fours and, moving with a suddenness unusual for an animal built so stockily, will then go underground with an unexpectedness that is often startling in its suddenness and completeness—he is there one moment, the next he is gone! At times he may appear rather sluggish and stupid and sit there apparently paying no attention to anyone. But he is probably just sizing you up, and unless you are a better rifle shot than he seems to imagine, you may let him dive in, or lose him by poor shooting; he is rarely a fool!

Marmota Monax is a frequent resident of the fields, fence rows, lands adjacent to truck patches, sometimes the rocky narrows, and the rather heavily wooded plots in the farming and waste lands of the Eastern United States down at least to Western North Carolina, and up into Southern Canada, mostly Southern Ontario, in which section he is often very plentiful. Northeastern New York State, in the general vicinity of Troy; Vermont, Western Massachusetts, Central and Southwestern New York; parts of Northern and Central Pennsylvania, New Castle County Delaware; Western Maryland, and on down the Appalachian mountains country, are his favorite habitats. Out in the Rockies and in British Columbia a slightly different species is known as the Whistling Marmot, and is just as gamy.

The woodchuck of the East is known to farmers and town hunters as the groundhog, and sometimes is referred to as hedgehog, whistlepig, and whatnot. This animal, formerly a woods resident when the Eastern half of the country was far more wooded with heavy timber than today, has since that time followed the passing of the timbered areas out into the open farming sections where he feeds in clover fields, dens up along the sides of washes, in back pastures, along fence rows grown up with blackberry vines, locust sprouts, and poison ivy, and in general sets up housekeeping very close to his favorite good food supply.

The woodchuck was well known to the American Indians, particularly the Eastern tribes of the New England and Middle Atlantic and Central Western areas. The early settlers, noting his somewhat squat shape and general resemblance to the small pig that in their native lands was at times known as the "chuck," called him "woodschuck," or, the woodspig.

During the last 25 years, this rodent of the farm lands, for he is a rodent, has greatly increased in numbers despite fairly brisk hunting and also in spite of government directed efforts for his control.

Well fed and apparently satisfied with life as it is where he sits, he has become one of the greatest of pests to many farmers, truck growers and horse breeders, and to many who live in the country from choice and who like to keep their farms or estates looking nice, free of holes, dens and dirt piles. On the other hand, many like a few chucks around to give life to the locality and to provide rifle shooting sport. The number allowed to exist may depend upon the location of most of the summer dens—there are both summer and winter dens built by chucks. The summer dens are built in or very near their food supply; while the winter dens, with an eye to protection from Northwest winds, are usually in the lee of a bank or hill, with the opening always facing East or Southeast.

The chuck in his free, natural habitat, is subject to no especially devastating diseases, plagues or epidemics. He is peace-loving as a rule but will fight viciously if attacked and woe be it to the dog, untrained in chuck fighting, that attempts to dig him out. A mature and powerful chuck may weigh 12 to 14 pounds; and even heavier weights have been reported in various sporting magazines. The average chuck will probably not weigh over six or eight pounds. Dr. Given, who weighed many as a scientific matter and recovered skulls and skeletons, was emphatic on lack of larger and heavier animals. Some naturalists claim few exceed 10 or 10½ pounds in weight. The author has shot a few very large and heavy chucks, the largest probably being the one referred to elsewhere as the duPont chuck. Another very large one was the Hollingsworth chuck. He has often wished that both could have been weighed just after shooting. The chuck's teeth are much like those of a squirrel, but much larger and more firmly anchored and are really vicious fighting weapons, especially when used on the ear, nose or throat of a dog.

The blood vessels of the chuck are placed deep, his hide is so tough it will turn a sharp knife blade, and his body contains a scant supply of blood in proportion to his mass. With his three-inch teeth, two inches of which are imbedded in the jaw, and with powerful jaw muscles, he is a fighting fool when aroused. He can slash like a skilled swordsman, as anyone knows who has seen fights between dogs and chucks. His feet are strongly muscled, and are used almost daily for hard work in stones and earth. He has five toes on each rear foot and four on each of the front feet. The toes are tipped with non-retractile, horny nails. The adult woodchuck is fairly safe among all other animals of about his own size and weight except the fox.

The ancestral home of the marmot was said to have been South America, but today he actually lives throughout most of the world, except Australia and New Zealand. He varies some in physical form and appearance due to geographical environment.

The entrances to and from his burrow are usually one which is rather prominent due to a mound of earth thrown up in front of it, as a result of underground excavation, and the other hidden well generally, 20 or 30 feet distant, in a depression, under a dewberry thicket, along a fence row, on the far side of a brush pile, or wherever he can pop forth, often unseen, to seek safer quarters elsewhere if the need arises. The chuck is not the sort of fool who digs a hole, and then drags the hole in after him. He digs a series of passages and a den, with at least two and sometimes many more entrances and exits.

There is no question but that he is an occasional danger to farmers, their families, livestock, the hired man, incautious hunters passing by, and to anyone or any animal which might unexpectedly fall into one of these unseen exits and break a leg, sprain a groin, or otherwise become lamed or incapacitated. The author once had a very close shave from a serious shooting accident in which one hunter went down to his crotch in a vertical chuck den along a small run— the bank of which was grown up with short briars, at the exact moment he expected to flush a quail, and being thrown around to an angle of about 180°, he recovered and was pulled out by his companion, although it was found that the muzzle of his gun barrels was then just about six inches away, and pointed directly at the ankles of his companion. Fortunately the safety was strong and was "on"; the sears were not worn, and the gun did not fire, either from pulling both triggers or from the shock of the hard fall. Before stepping and falling down into the vertical den passage, he was faced in exactly the opposite direction walking along on top of a small bank. It was one of those falls that no one expects and no one can foretell or usually avoid. Just the season before this was written, the author's shooting companion wrenched his groin very severely by a somewhat similar fall, while trying to find a down cock pheasant which the author had shot, and which had shed feathers all over the place. This man had to retire from hunting for several days. It is useless to say that such accidents will not happen, or that when they do they are the fault of the hunter, that they would have been avoided had he been watching his footing. Many a chuck hole or den mouth comes up under a briar patch out in a pasture field, or may appear overnight in a locality in which chucks are seldom encountered. Horses are valuable and at times almost unobtainable, and a farm horse which steps into a hole and breaks a leg is usually at the end of his trail; men, too, are today at a premium!

On the other hand, localities which do not contain chuck dens, if in settled areas such as are found throughout most of the East, are often almost entirely devoid of rabbits three days after the gunning season opens. The rabbits have no place to go for complete safety. In any area somewhat hilly, briary and stony, in which chuck holes are reasonably plentiful, it is just about as difficult to shoot out all of the cottontails and pheasant cocks, as to keep cows away from green corn, or kids from green apples. They pop into the chuck dens at the first alarm, and stay there until the coast is again clear. For this reason, primarily, the State of Pennsylvania designated the chuck a game animal and put a season and a bag limit upon his resolute self.

Unfortunately, the woodchuck has been proved definitely to be a carrier of the infected tick which transmits the highly dangerous disease known as Rocky Mountain Spotted Fever. The late Dr. Given and the author of this book jointly wrote the articles on the subject of tick infection that appeared in *The American Rifleman* and in *The Pennsylvania Game News*.

If the groundhog comes out at any time during the day on February 2nd and sees his shadow, it is claimed that he will go right back in again and sleep until the coming of Spring, as this omen guarantees another six weeks of bitter cold, freezing weather. But if it be cloudy or raining on that day, so that at no time can the groundhog see his shadow, this is regarded as a sure harbinger of an early Spring. People begin to joke among themselves, and home gardeners get out their garden tools and their seed. Women flock to the milliners to order spring hats. Local business has a boom in the Lebanon and Lehigh Valleys, and only the coal men are tempted to commit suicide.

To many this is all just an amusing joke, but in Central and Eastern Pennsylvania it is surprising how many, even today, take Groundhog Day very seriously, even though they may joke about it!

The Slumbering Groundhog Lodge, of Quarryville, Pennsylvania, is one of the most famous organizations that makes an annual pilgrimage to a previously agreed on inhabited chuck den, so that there, in full regalia and in solemn conclave, they may arrive at the official weather forecast for the remainder of that winter, and also possibly have a bit of fun. No matter if all the Weather Bureau stations report heavy snows and severe blizzards and it happens to be merely a dark day and the chuck does not show up, every one in the community is cheered by the thought that "Spring is at hand!" But if the sun comes out bright and warm in the early morning, so that even a torpid, hibernating woodchuck would be waked from his long winter's sleep to have a look, all is gloom and black despair. The woodchuck can see his shadow and the worst may be expected. Anxious mothers pull heavy ear muffs down over their youngsters' ears and get out additional red flannels with which to encase their screaming kids. The man of the house grabs the phone and orders an additional truckload of coal. The Slumbering Ground-hog Lodge has a very select membership. They admit but one new member annually except to replace those lost by death. In 1938 they admitted as a non-resident member the then Vice-President of the United States.

Another thriving groundhog club is located near Allentown, Pennsylvania, and the Gobbler's Knob Groundhog Club, near Punxsutawney, Pennsylvania is widely known. Certain it is that the actions of woodchucks on February 2nd have more effect upon the humor, beliefs, superstitions and fears of the general public than any other type of wild life. In Pennsylvania, the groundhog is regarded today as game. It has a closed season and an open season, and is therefore ranked in importance along with the wild turkey, grouse, pheasant, black bear and deer. Our chuck is coming up in the world of sports. He is rifle game like squirrels!

Some years woodchucks stay out very late before retiring for the winter. On October 27, 1945, the author, while driving home from a squirrel hunt with Edgar F. Burkins, almost ran over a very large, very active, fat and grizzly gray woodchuck which raced across the side of the road and hurriedly popped into a hole directly in the west or exposed side of the roadbed. The temperature at the time was about 45 to 50 degrees Fahrenheit in the shade, and it was quite windy and felt cold. Standing in the woods, dressed in Duxbak clothing, the author had been uncomfortable that afternoon. But there was that woodchuck sitting right out in the road, and he dived in with all possible speed when we rounded a little turn in the high-way and nearly ran him down.

As suggested previously, chucks build their dens in accordance with the natural cover and the field crops of that year; also in ac-cordance with the protection a hill will afford for winter dens. Where chucks are numerous, they often den up in groups or families, quite frequently in the choicest portions of some farmer's hay field.

As a general rule, a woodchuck will dig his den in a well-drained area, in somewhat sandy soil, but not too sandy, or in red shale if shale is found locally, but not in solid rock and not in slate. According to John L. Cull, as noted elsewhere, they are never found in Ontario in fields in which there is milkweed. No reason is assigned, but it is probably due to clay soil. Chucks will rarely, if ever, build a den in pure clay, because, first, it is difficult to dig a den in such soil, and second, and what is much more important, clay is non-porous and a den dug in it would be flooded by water that happened to run into it.

The chuck is a first class engineer. He can dig like a small steam shovel or a boring machine, and when he once gets underground in loamy earth, it is often useless to try to dig him out. He can dig and close up the passageway after himself, and dig and then sit in a side passageway in safety, much more quickly than a man can progress with a pick and shovel. When digging, the chuck throws the dirt back between his legs, and often if one comes up very quietly on a chuck working in the mouth of his den, as the author often has done when wearing rubber soled sneakers, he may see dirt come flying out of the mouth of the den in a small cascade. On one occasion— a Sunday morning in May—the author and a friend motored out to a nearby chuck village on a small hillside. Just over the brow was a shallow hollow up which one could walk and in which we had our 200-yard small bore rifle range. On the eastern side of this little ridge, a big fat chuck was sitting, apparently sound asleep, right on the mound of fresh dirt, before his den. The sun was hot. Everything in the sunny areas was boiling and simmering with the heat and the earth seemed a lazy place. I said to my friend, "Stay here and let him watch you, and I will walk up the hollow back of him, slip over the hilltop as quickly and as quietly as I can, and will see how close I can sneak up on him, before he wakes up and dives in." Woodchucks have a very keen sense of scent, and they can undoubtedly sense or feel the vibrations caused by a person walking on the surface of the ground.

I took my time, and when about 50 feet from the chuck, crept slowly forward on tiptoe, and very deliberately put down and then slowly raised each foot from the ground so as to minimize any chance of vibration. I actually got up back of that woodchuck and tapped him on the shoulder with a Winchester 5A rifle telescope which I was carrying in my hand and using as a monocular.

The chuck jumped about two feet into the air, whirled around, hissed like a cat and prepared to fight. Then I noticed more particularly that he was completely covered with an eczema type of hard rash on the forepart of the body and the rest of him, mostly, was covered with a swarm of ticks. He then moved away very slowly and dragged himself down into the den. That chuck was obviously sick, but he was not too sick to fight! Years before, at different times, I had shot and killed a very few large red or pine squirrels which were all broken out with what looked like a bad case of chicken pox—not eczema, but chicken pox. They appeared to be sick and very miserable, and I threw all of them away, or buried them.

A woodchuck may dig his den in dense dark woods, close to a stream of running water, but not because he needs or wants the water—for drinking, washing food or washing himself, or wetting his feet. A woodchuck objects to wetting his feet about as much as a house cat. The slight amount of liquid demanded by his body, is obtained, at least in most part, from the early morning dew on the grasses, especially clover, his favorite food. But he also obtains water from fruits, muskmelon, or whatever he happens to feed upon. The indifference to bullet shock, and pain, characteristic of the chuck is almost certainly due to the comparatively very small amount of blood in the animal, the lack of fluid content of the body to a degree observable in more tender skinned and softer fleshed animals, and a warriorlike toughness which seems to permeate his whole being. A chuck can "take it" like a water buffalo because nature fitted him with a physical design through which the transmission of sudden shock to the brain is very difficult, and because his body tissues are of a type which do not tear readily, and because also, his nervous reactions appear slow and dulled.

I have shot chucks on a small strip of flat meadow land on the farm owned and lived upon in Delaware, years ago, by the publisher of this book, in which a 170-grain national match bullet sawed in four to six places, about two-thirds way down to the bearing portion, failed to expand. The ranges averaged about 50 yards. A bullet going straight through from side to side, through the lungs, would leave a chuck sitting there unconcernedly nibbling at clover for a few seconds until his lungs began to fill up with blood; he would then appear startled, run uncertainly for five to 20 yards, and fall over and die. It appeared that the chuck would feel the pain of the bullet so little he would not stop eating until breathing became difficult. When a bullet expanded, the chuck would be badly torn, and the shot was almost immediately fatal. On one occasion a fat old chuck was shot on top of a hill, along a small ravine, at a range of about 150 or more yards, and the chuck started to move forward just as the rifle cracked. They do this occasionally—move forward for no apparent cause, and in this case the bullet struck in the middle of its immense grass filled stomach. It just turned that chuck inside out, tore a hole about six or eight inches wide through its middle, converted the stomach into a hot, steaming mass of groundup grass and clover leaves, which gave off a most loathsome stench. That animal scarcely moved; hydraulic pressure and nerve shock took effect!

Forty years ago, a few chucks used to den under immense rocks along the Narrows Hill, two miles below the author's boyhood home. Today, they are more abundant; new and tamer chucks moved in, and no longer are they found only in the Narrows and in rocky projections on Peters Mountain, as was the case 30 to 45 years ago.

In some parts of Northern Delaware, chucks feed out in alfalfa or bean or peafields, a good deal at times, and when so feeding will usually be found to have fresh dens in nearby grownup fence rows, which may have a heavy growth of poison ivy or blackberries and wild cherry.

Normally, except in some low, flat, creek bottom meadow lands, as around Greene, New York not so far from the New York State Game Farm, chucks will den up in summer under old chestnut snags, or stumps, out in pasture and grass fields, a very favorite location by the way. They will always pick out dewberry or ground blackberry patches, on the sunny side of rolling hills, or on the East side of such hills; never as a rule, on the North side.

Quite frequently, they will be denned up along the banks which slope down to runs and creeks, and a spare den opening will be 10 to 50 feet out in a grassy meadow from which it will come up vertically so that they can climb out to feed without ever coming into their front den or out of it. These are lovely "booby traps" to step down into and wrench an ankle.

By coming very slowly and carefully over a hill top or hummock crest, one can often shoot down onto one to four or five chucks feeding on such a grassy bottom, but they have a tendency to watch above them and also are invariably careful to dodge if they see a shadow.

There may be dens along any old fence line with chestnut posts, with either chestnut rails, or with barbed wire, especially if such fence runs across a small hill about 50 to 200 yards from the edge of a woods. Some will be denned in the woods, others along the fence, a few out in the open spaces on the hill itself. Others will den under apple tree roots in old orchards; a very favorite place is old abandoned stone or wood springhouses, barns or buildings, including farm houses; and along the walls of canals, particularly the walls or banks on the side next to a river or creek adjoining the canal. They like to den in or under old stone walls used as fence lines, especially in Connecticut and New York state. A den located under an old chestnut snag or stump, or among the roots of a very large old oak, apple or maple, is almost impossible to dig out and the way to get him is to watch from a range of about 100 to 125 yards and shoot him with a bullet aimed at the butt of the ear, or into the sticking place from in front, about two inches below the top of his skull from the rear, or high up through both shoulders.

The woodchuck is immune to poison ivy, poison oak, briars and apparently even to barbed wire. He has a hide like leather, tough feet and is largely insensible to ordinary pain. Also, he wears wide runways through which he travels like a rabbit or a muskrat, and when he rushes through a briar patch it is along these runways, while you would have to crash your way through the real thing. The shorties of this world, and the "aldermen," sometimes have the last laugh. Woodchucks, raccoons and hogs all are good fighters not only because they have a fighting spirit and good teeth, but also because all of them, at proper seasons, are well insulated with a layer of fat right under the skin; most animals cannot bite through it.

With the natural craftiness of the woodchuck and his almost impenetrable dens, one may wonder how the fox can obtain a meal of a succulent young chuck. To do this, foxes hunt in pairs. The fox and his mate together slowly stalk the chuck. They glimpse or possibly first smell a chuck sunning on his mound or upon a stone fence or a log pile or rail pile, from which of course he will soon spot them. One fox wanders around in a small area, seemingly catching mice or interested in some local object. He does this until he catches the interest of the chuck. Next his mate walks slowly toward the chuck which permits a rather limited approach, then ducks underground. From here on, he cannot see the plan of attack. The fox which walked or crept up takes a position above and behind the mound at the mouth of the den.

The woodchuck, inquisitive by nature, and also at times rather garrulous, becomes impatient to see what is occurring, does not expect to be shot at, so sticks out his nose; after carefully scenting the air, out pops the head and if nothing happens then, out comes the chuck! Seeing only the far distant fox hunting away from him, the woodchuck moves away from the den mouth to feed upon the succulent clover; as he senses it, the coast is clear!

But is the coast clear? The fox waiting above the den mouth, makes a swift but silent stalk, then a rush and he is between the chuck and his den openings. The distant fox now comes up on the run and the unequal battle is on. Unless the chuck is very fortunate or an old and seasoned battler he will be snapped up. Some summers ago a local friend saw a fox trot unconcernedly toward him, down along a fence row, with a partly grown chuck swung carelessly across his shoulder. He was holding it by the nape of the neck. Only when the fox saw the hunter, did it vary its pace and run off.

In warm weather, when chuck den mouths are filled with old cobwebs, with piles of old dirt which nearly fill the opening, when there are no blow flies or other insects buzzing around the opening, you can assume that "Mabel doesn't live here any more!" If fresh ground is thrown out so that even the color of it has not had opportunity to lighten, if there are fresh chuck tracks on this dirt, and especially if you saw a sudden slight movement as you slipped up quietly to the vicinity of the den mouth, assume at once that the family is at home and will soon come out to look you over. The chuck madam may be "sweeping out the front hall," or old Mister Monax himself may be about to emerge.

Sit down 50 to 75 yards off, if using a .22 rim fire, or 100 to 125 yards distant if shooting a .22 wildcat, and wait patiently until the head and neck appears. Aim then for the butt of the ear, or center of forehead and the chuck will lie right down and take a long nap, not bothered by foxes.

Some chucks at times show an effrontery and a recklessness in placing a den right in, or near the middle of a truck patch, or right up in the farmer's yard where his dog can get at them, which appears to be plainly suicidal. It seldom is! Some years ago, the farmer might have run a hose down from the exhaust of his car, and gassed Mr. Monax. But more recently gasoline has been too scarce. Chucks apparently come out at night and clean up half a truck patch of strawberries twice the size of the end of your thumb, lettuce, peas and whatever the farmer's wife has set down as just about ready to pick for dinner the following morning. Night feeding is mostly on mild, moonlight nights.

Consequently, if a farmer will not let you come on his farm, or within yelling distance of it in November, he will almost certainly welcome you with open arms in the summer when chucks have cut up his hay field and his truck patch. Only, do not use a rifle of such loud report that it scares the women in the farmhouse, or in the summer kitchen. The .22 wildcats, even those of the lower brackets of wildcats, are plenty large enough, and if it is a farm in which 125 yards shots are seldom exceeded the .22 long rifle high speed hollow point is plenty loud enough. Just remember however, to aim and hold on certain small areas on the woodchuck.

A woodchuck may dig a burrow complete, in the space of one day or a week. He may later on add a gallery or two. For entrance, most chucks adopt a tunnel approximating about 30° below the surface of the ground, passing inward for about four to six feet, seldom more than four to five feet. Cripples, or those killed too far in the den, may lie four to six feet down, at the bottom. In length the den is seldom more than 40 feet, including branches, which

may be to right and left. Both the main tunnel and the branches
extend at varying levels, along which the chuck will dig vertical
outlets. Seldom will the first one be less than eight to 12 feet from
the main mouth of the den. A chuck which has a den in which there
is a vertical outlet somewhat higher than the main entrance and
about 12 feet back of it is pretty difficult to catch by fox or dog, but
he is often then an easy shot by a rifle bullet, as he may go in the
lower entrance and then soon thereafter stick his head out the upper
one for a look-around, and if nothing happens he may pop out and
come waddling down to the front entrance and sit on the mound.

No experienced chuck shooter purposely "brackets" a chuck with
bullets. He tries to center the chuck's head with the first shot fired.
It is not a good idea to rush over and pick him up, if through the
scope he appears quite dead, especially if his head is lower than his
rump. One can often pick off several chucks by discreetly remaining
out of sight, and waiting for the second emergence of the inquisitive
chucks remaining.

The entrances and exits from a chuck's burrow are always located
so that at no time can a stream of water entering any one of them
completely flood the entire underground system. Some part of this
is always above high water mark for that immediate locality. There
in that high spot he sits and contemplates, most likely with contempt,
the work of those industriously "trying to drown him out." You can
sometimes pour barrels of water in and out of the entrances of a
chuck den without greatly annoying the inhabitants. But all of it
is hard work for the chappies outside.

The farmer may still have to depend upon his faithful "two holer"
at the back of the garden, but Brother Monax always equips his
home with a nicely enclosed "one holer" composed of plenty of
finely powdered earth at the end of the principal burrow. It is his
indoor comfort station.

This is recovered with earth as often as needed. When the time
comes to clean out the "cesspool" the whole mass, finely powdered
dirt, excrement, small stones and all, is thrown out of the mouth of
the den, at the main entrance of his burrow, never at the back
safety door. Merriam reported a whole bushel of such objectionable
substance ready for removal at one time.

The woodchuck is a member of that great body who live at home
and board out. No food is ordinarily eaten in the burrow, by him
or by his family. He does not store food underground or in hollow
logs or trees, as do chipmunks, squirrels, and other rodents. At the
time for litter production the male may carry in a few shoots of
succulent greens from outside, for the female, but not otherwise.

The entrance to the average chuck den is slightly elliptical, about eight inches wide and nine or 10 inches high, or a bit less, and is easily recognized by shooters. After the middle of March mating has its fruition. After a gestation period of 28 days, the female brings forth within the burrow her young, about the last week of April, maybe during the first few weeks in May.

The usual litter is four or five, it may be three to nine. Progeny are devoid of hair, except five small hairs over each eye, and weigh less than one ounce. They cannot stand or walk when very small. They are born with eyes and ears closed. Papa woodchuck is immediately asked out in no uncertain terms and out he then stays. More than likely he now spends his time at some "men's club," for he lives a monogamous life both at home and abroad. His return is likely to be in about five weeks, at which time the young venture forth for their first eating of fresh greens. While in the burrow the young are breast fed, but upon going above ground are at once able and willing to eat the foods of the parents.

Dr. Given's medical description of the anatomy which feeds the young follows: "Four small but well developed feeding stations on each side of the ventral surface of the female chest and abdomen, from the level of the front legs to the groins, is the array from which the young of a moderate-sized litter receive an adequate supply of milk." It is each for himself, and the weakling usually suffers most in the food line. Seldom does a dam carry through a maximum litter. Six survivors would be a high average. Four husky young are more usual. The author once shot five, one after the other, as they stuck their heads out of a den mouth. All were of the same size and litter.

They make rapid progress in growth and physical changes and leave the burrow during the first few days of June, or a bit later, according to date of whelping. Sight and hearing are normal and developed when they go above ground. In possession of their various functions when appearing in the surface world, they are ready to play and eat all the growing plants and vegetables or grasses upon which their parents feed.

The dam looks after them during the summer, then drives them from the parental burrow about the end of the hot weather. In some instances a few may be permitted to remain over the hibernation of the first winter. She insists that they go out and dig for themselves, leaving the home burrow for herself and her mate.

By persistent feeding the chucks store up a great amount of fat on all parts of the body by the time cold weather starts to make its appearance. Particularly do the chucks like the luscious second growth grass of late August; if a shower comes up they may stay out and eat right through it, for "Winter Comes!"

The chuck feeds sumptuously from even before sunup until about 10 A.M. after which he may take himself to the top of a stone fence, a rail pile, an old chestnut stump, or whatever is most convenient, and there stretch himself for a snooze in the warm sunlight. If a chuck senses an enemy he may stop motionless while preparing for his sun bath, and remain so until he thinks things have again become safe. Then he stretches out, cradles his head on or between his front feet, and is off to the land of nod. Here he may remain for two or three hours or more. Bright, warm sunshine, right after a brisk summer rain, will bring out the chucks almost any time. The normal coming out time for evening feeding is from 3:30 P.M. to 5:00 P.M., the feeding times of the woodchuck and the squirrel being nearly identical, although chucks are more likely to be out sunning themselves in the middle of the day than are squirrels, which go into nests or dens in old trees to sleep.

The best way to look for chucks, when they are coming out to feed of a morning or evening, is to locate yourself in good light cover, about two thirds your cartridge's accurate and killing range away from the chuck, and a half hour or so before you think the chucks will begin to appear. Try to choose a position from which several or a dozen holes may be watched at one time. Use binoculars or the rifle scope to locate each animal as its nose first appears in the mouth of the den. Shoot only when the chuck mounts the mound at the mouth of the den, or after he comes completely out of the den if other shooters, traffic, cattle, poultry, farmers or wild game do not impose other restrictions. Sometimes you have to take your shots as you can get them. In other instances, you can definitely choose the exact time to fire, and the exact spot on the chuck at which to aim. If facing you, aim at the sticking place; if sidewise, at the butt of the ear or at the neck about two inches below the ear; if farther off, high on the shoulder; if facing away from you, aim at the base of the neck, or the fold of fur when he is a bit hunched up and it shows where neck and body join. *Never* aim at a chuck farther back than the lungs. It is better to let him go, unless you can blow up a distended tummy with a 4,000 f.s. load, using a hollow point bullet.

In late summer and early fall it seems that a woodchuck is out eating almost all of the time. Such voracious natural feedings lead to the progressive growth of his hibernating glands and he becomes less active as summer changes to fall. Chucks are often shot on warm days in November, so late does he come out to loaf in the sun, and to feed, voraciously, for the winter hibernation. At the end of the day the stomach is distended with finely chewed greens. He never bolts his food, it is always finely masticated. This trait permits considerable time in choosing shots on feeding woodchucks *unless* other persons, or yourself, or passing traffic, scares him in.

Not the "Yoo-Hooing" that General Lear frowned upon!; not the angry "chirr" of the red squirrel; nor the "Quack, Quack, Quaah," of the gray, but, suddenly startled by fright associated with annoyance or anger, chucks frequently give a sharp whistle, which is a warning to all other chucks to be on the watch.

At times, when sitting quietly watching for chucks, a rifleman may become conscious of a heavy, pungent, slightly unpleasant odor. You look across on yonder hill, and there, or close by, may sit one, or both of the old chucks. They are "sitting out on the front porch, talking over the happenings of the day" as it were; not really making sounds which are loud, but low throaty sounds which give slight vibrations. Odor is their voluntary signal to other chucks that they are out, all is well, come join the party. If the scent deepens it probably comes from others which appear, and it can be voluntarily emitted by the chuck.

Hibernation of the average woodchuck starts about the third week in September, although the date varies with regions, being affected by both altitude and latitude, but not *all* chucks disappear permanently by that date. I have shot them on warm days right through our squirrel hunting season. When the hibernating period comes along, the chucks body is fattened to last him through the winter. His activities become lessened day by day, his mental forces become obtunded, and when he goes below, he may hibernate in his own burrow or dig a new one for that purpose. About the time of the fall equinox Mr. Chuck curls himself into a hairy ball about four feet below ground, lower if the frost line is lower. He stays there until Spring calls him forth.

The author hates to see the chuck gassed, dug out or poisoned. He deserves a better time of it here and a better fate. He is the best training target for snipers for war the Creator ever produced. For this end alone his future should be kept bright. The rifleman with the flat shooting, low report, light recoil rifle, an arm equipped with telescope sight and every refinement of design and ammunition, will never consent to the extermination of the woodchuck. Today he is one of the very few *free* Americans. Let him sit on his mound and be monarch of his little back pasture. Let him roll in a ball and snooze the winter through, insensible to the cares of the world, while his more highly educated (or are they) neighbors shiver through a long, cold winter too stupid or too foolish to so arrange their political and economic affairs that they will have an adequate supply of food and fuel to last the winter. Too improvident to provide adequate, comfortable and sanitary housing. Examine conditions in any city!

Marmota Monax gives life, action and interest to many a run down and abandoned farm; a bit of land on which the chuck waxes fat, but upon which man would starve due to his own lack of forethought. The woodchuck is a living example of a supposedly stupid animal which can live, increase his kind, his range, and have a future amid surroundings in which man, with all his technical achievements and his development of the atomic bomb, has failed to make a living. The man proves himself the master of the woodchuck through ballistics, but he has failed to prove that he is the woodchuck's equal in maintaining an existence.

The author salutes a sporting game animal which has improved its prospects, while during the same interval of the last 30 years man has devoted most of his efforts to conquest and to the infliction of his own political ideas upon others, when his own house is neither politically nor economically in order. It is true that during this period science has made many of its most notable advances, often spurred by necessity. But on the other hand seldom have those advances been devoted to humane and sensible ends.

In addition, man has most foolishly wasted or destroyed a high percentage of his most valuable resources; his timber, coal, iron, copper and oil. He has rendered his watercourses unfit for fish life and has made many of his forests into waste lands. By making unwise laws and by giving too much authority to politicians he has lost most of his own liberties which his predecessors had been centuries in developing. He has destroyed many of the treasures gathered through 6,000 years of known history, plus millions of years of development as proved by indentations in coal mines. To what effect has man used his ability? Some good, possibly. But millions have met death and who of these has gained anything?

In contrast, consider the woodchuck! He constructs his own castle, finds and harvests his own living, eats, loves, mates, and rests, as he wills. He pays no taxes, fills out no forms in triplicate, has had to consult no ration boards, can obtain materials to enlarge his home without having to seek a permit, fights no inter-colony wars, can live in peace in numbers with his neighbors. He can adapt himself to a rather wide variety of natural conditions. All this of course proves his inferiority, that he is exceptionally stupid, that he ought to be exterminated, even that he ought to be gassed!

It is true that sometimes he eats some of the farmer's produce and his crop. But, does the farmer, and do the farmer's customers, waste as little of the share which remains?

He is only a woodchuck down in the pasture. His meat has little value to many who shoot him. His hide is worth little but for rough leather, and his fur does not adorn the neck of the frivolous. But his engineering is as sound as that of an honor graduate of M.I.T. His construction is as durable and as well laid out as that of our tunnel and mining engineers, he has fewer caveins than do they; his sanitary engineering causes fewer epidemics than ours; his chemistry is practical, he chews his food slowly and normally, eats only the best, thus is seldom sick; he is strictly monogamous, thus seldom has to see a lawyer, and in general appears happy and contented.

In the evening, he sits out on his front porch, and radios his neighbors, using a simple but effective system of transmission which costs nothing and does not wear out. His neighbors all understand the meanings his "radio" transmits, but man would need an interpreter in most instances, to converse with his neighbors. But then, man is so much brighter!

It is true the woodchuck lacks electricity for light, heat or cooking, he lacks porcelain-lined plumbing and Beautyrest mattresses. But, place a group of men, regardless of the University from which each graduated, in the same environment, but without soap, hot water and towels, living under stumps and along ditches, make them eat and dig with their hands, live in earth tunnels, and within three weeks it would be necessary to *delouse* the bunch! Read history.

In summer the woodchuck comes out and harvests the clover, just enough to take care of his needs. One hundred, 200, 300, yes 400 yards off, there he sits on the yellow earth mound in front of his den, and at times he appears just a bit disdainful of man. Possibly he has real reason to be. His world is not bankrupt. He has no inflation. If he has mass unemployment, it is only between meal times. So he sits there quietly, having no particular worries and of course he offers a perfect shot.

If, after 30, 40, or 50 years of practice, you have acquired a degree of skill with the rifle which enables you to stand him on his head and make him frenziedly wave his tail, you can likely class yourself in skill with those who have finished high in the Wimbledon, the Marine Corps, or the Leech, in the Small Bore National Championship, or the Swiss. Having placed in a number of these, the author knows about how steady you have to hold that front sight or crosshairs to make the shot. It takes good even holding. It requires calculation. It takes time and patience, and real ability with a small caliber rifle. It suggests the finest in optics with which these rifles can be sighted. It takes, at times, the knowledge acquired during a lifetime, and a study of the habits and stoutness of the grizzled but unconcerned monarch of the back pasture. It takes the best that you can give to your chosen sport! That is what it takes for successful woodchuck shooting! Never underestimate the acumen of *Marmota Monax*. He will be sitting there, waiting, when you hunt him!

WOODCHUCK AT HIS DEN

Eastern Woodchuck (Marmota Monax) emerging cautiously from his den. Minus the chuck, this view could pass anywhere for the mouth of a sniper's den on the Western Front. The equipment for both is the same. A small caliber, high velocity, scope sighted rifle, and a real rifle shot behind it. There is no more deadly combination in the field of ordnance. This woodchuck would be fair game at any range from 50 to 350 yards. Hold the crosshairs high on the shoulder, then touch it off smoothly and without flinching, and you should bag your game with certainty.

CHAPTER 10

The .22 Long Rifle on Woodchucks

THE SHOT AT A WOODCHUCK THAT STANDS OUT IN MY MEMORY probably more than any other was made one day in company with a Chiropractor friend. We were driving along a back road in his car, when across on an opposite hillside I saw a very large woodchuck sitting in the mouth of his den. This was probably the first ground-hog this friend had ever had an opportunity to see, and it had to be pointed out several times before he could see, and identify it positively, as the den was located in the shadow of some small trees, possibly 10 or 12 feet high, scattered along the brow of the hill.

The sun was shining through the tree limbs onto the chuck, and as he turned toward us, his throat showed up very distinctly, and I very ineptly made the remark, "Watch me kill that chuck right where he stands!" I no more had said this, than I wished I had remained silent, because the range was at least 150–175 yards in an airline, there was no practical means of getting closer, and my rifle was a .22 Long Rifle 52 Winchester-Hoffman with 5A scope. I had a .22 long rifle Hi-Speed cartridge in the chamber. At one-half the distance it would have been largely a sure thing, but across on that hillside trajectory would have to cut quite a figure.

My companion almost immediately suggested that I had no possible chance to make a kill with a .22 Long Rifle at that distance, so why chase him in?

I could not well back down! I therefore rested my arms across the back of the car seat and the window sill, took careful aim on the light area just under the chin (with the sights set for the estimated range), and let off the shot. He had raised up nicely for me, at a low whistle.

At the welcome, "plop!" of the hollow point, upon striking where it was directed, the chuck suddenly "humped" himself, turned slowly around in a very small circle, slumped onto his nose and died. This is the typical result from a shot in the "sticking place," except that as a rule they simply slump forward on the nose and do not have strength to make the turn, before they go down.

Almost anyone who is observant and who has had many years of experience in shooting small game and varmints with a rifle of low recoil will be able to tell, in most instances, within an inch or two of exactly where the bullet landed, without going up to look. While varmints, especially chucks, which are hard to kill instantly, often show marked differences in reaction to shots in the same spot, due to their differences in vitality and ability to withstand shock, nevertheless the effects upon the bone structure, nervous system, and the resultant muscular reactions are quite similar when shots hit a certain area which controls or moves various organs of the body.

When I retrieved this woodchuck shot in the throat, the bullet hole was found to be just an inch to one side of the vertical line of the center of the body, and perfect for elevation. It had cut the jugular vein, and ranged backwards and upwards so that it broke or paralyzed the spine at just about the juncture of the shoulders. The chuck was located a little higher than we were and most of his body was in the mouth of the den, both tending to make a bullet plough through the body backward and upward into the vitals.

I carried the woodchuck back to the car, and after my friend had examined it carefully, he remarked, "That was the most remarkable shot I have ever seen made with a .22 rifle." However it was obvious that it was the last hit he expected to see that day.

When I bagged a second chuck with a bullet one inch below the base of the ear at approximately 90 yards, on the second shot, he changed his mind and his estimate of the .22 long rifle as a hunting cartridge picked up considerably.

For years that friend used to ask me whether I had made any more long shots on woodchucks and whether I still remembered the day we bagged one at such a long distance. I heard about that throat-shot from a good many people, and from widely different sources, during the following 10 days. The range picked up to a half a mile, and in fact if anyone mentioned it as being less than 300 yards, I began to be disappointed. My reputation was suffering. Apparently news travels with the wind!

Many will say, "that was just a lucky shot!" As a matter of fact, it was not in this instance. The rifle happened to have been carefully sighted for 150 yards. A shot into the sticking place, from in front, is more certain to anchor a chuck on the exact spot occupied before he was shot, than even a frontal brain shot—which is likely to permit a chuck to kick around quite a bit, especially if a bit low, so that the bullet just nicks the lower edge of the brain.

A common yearling barnyard hog, weighing 150 to 300 pounds, when butchered, will now and then get up and run around in a circle and squeal, when shot by a .22 bullet through the frontal bone so that the bullet cuts one half its diameter, into the brain itself, just above the nose. A shot rather high in the brain, will bring it down at once. A shot into the brain is a little like a shot into the heart. A .22 bullet can cut quite a nick out of the lower one-third of the heart of a gray squirrel, especially if the heart is practically empty of blood when struck, without killing the animal instantly, but strike the upper two-thirds of the heart, where large blood vessels come out, and down goes your gray, helpless and nearly immovable.

Having always had considerable of a yen for surgery I always immediately examine, and largely dissect, whatever I happen to shoot. It is quite a help in determining the point of aim for successful small bore rifle shooting in the hunting fields. It is not sufficient to guess whether you hit the heart, the brain, the spine, or the lungs; you want to *know*.

This shot mentioned reminds me of another day in Cumberland Valley, Pennsylvania, some miles Southwest of the Susquehanna, opposite Harrisburg. A large woodchuck den was located on a small, sparsely timbered hill, possibly 10 feet above the level of a grassy bottomland along a creek, and about 50 yards back from the edge of the water. I took a partly screened shooting position, back of a stump, which provided an arm rest, a short distance from the mouth of a den which was freshly "used." I sat there quietly in the comfortable position provided by the stump and the ground behind it, and shot and killed five woodchucks, one after the other, each with a single bullet planted midway between eye and ear into the brain. These were four young chucks, about 50 per cent grown, and one very large old chuck. It was the most chucks I had ever killed in one day, up to that time, *from one den.* Then another large chuck came along on a visit, or maybe the "old man" had simply been out at his club. He popped into the hole before I could get a shot, then stuck his head out to look around, after which a bullet aimed for the same spot, as in the other shots, and apparently pulled just as carefully, landed with a resounding "plop!"—for a mature woodchuck has a pretty tough skull.

The chuck simply sank slowly out of sight, rolled to the bottom of the den, and lay there and coughed and sighed. This did not sound so well and I could not get him out! This seems like a rather dismal ending to what should have been a perfect woodchuck shooting day. It was! Yet any rifle which will kill instantly, with one shot each, five-sixths of its chances, is a good rifle and deadly on that game, at that distance, regardless of the caliber and the distance shot over. Rifle shooting is a good deal like boxing. It is not how often you hit them, or how hard you hit them, but where you hit them and the timing—assuming of course the blow delivered perfectly is coming hard enough to drop him. A woodchuck that is hit with a bullet, when it does not know it is going to be shot at, is a good deal more likely to be knocked off its feet and go down than one that is looking at you, intently watching what is going on and all set to run!

Several years ago, the late Gerald Averill, who served as a Warden for the Department of Inland Fisheries and Game of the State of Maine, made a prolonged test on woodchucks, with Western Super-X hollow point ammunition in a sporting rifle chambered for the .22 long rifle cartridge. He used a Model 57 Winchester, box magazine, light repeater, a boy's size but very accurate little "52," and wrote the author as follows:

"The .22 is a poor man's rifle, all right, and I think that up to 100 yards, the Super-X .22 long rifle in the hollow point style will kill varmints just as cleanly as anything. I ran one of the first tests on woodchucks with it, in a Winchester 57 with Lyman 438 scope, and I will defy anyone to get cleaner kills. As I remember it, I killed 52 out of 57 woodchucks, stone dead, at ranges of 50 to 125 yards each, and I would not ask for a better killing combination at such distances!

"These first cartridges were dry bullet loads, and the only fault I had to find with them was that they left some lead in the bore. I overcame that by wiping them off with a bit of chamois saturated with Mobilubricant. Soon after this the manufacturers put out Super-X lubricated ammunition, and then this greasing was unnecessary. At the time the factory was concerned whether my method would increase the back-thrust to a dangerous extent, but I never had any trouble except once, when I did blow out the magazine (a box magazine which might at the moment have been held loosely). This of course was a mere trifle!

"I hardly know whether the .22 long rifle is under or over-estimated. We have a lot of deer killed here in Maine every year with these .22s, and there is no question that a cool shot will kill a lot of game with one.

"One reason for the great popularity of the .22 long rifle is the large amount of ammunition that can be carried in proportion to its expense and its bulk."

The largest two woodchucks I have ever seen or shot were both females, and each was killed with a .22 long rifle hollow point high-speed cartridge. The first, which was the larger, I call for the want of a better name the "duPont woodchuck" because it was shot in a field adjoining property belonging to a man of that name. This enormous woodchuck, which stands out in my memory as surpassing in size all others in my hunting experience, was one I had never

seen before I shot it. In the locality in which it was found was a line
of trees about 200 yards back from a country road, and along such
line was a row of woodchuck dens, but I had never been able to
get a shot at any of their builders. Near to and flanking these trees
was an apple orchard, which the owner living nearby claimed was
raided from time to time by these chucks. One warm day in the
early fall, I hunted along this line of trees, and during my course
killed five red squirrels out of six shots and one woodchuck. Upon
reaching the upper end of the tree line, which was on a hill, I
stopped to scan the adjoining meadow which lay considerably lower
than my position. A sight there greeted my eyes that I shall never
forget. Right out near a stump in the middle of the meadow, which
was covered with short grass of vivid green, was an animal furiously
digging and in so doing, sending a perfect cascade of dirt backwards
between its legs. It was round and fat, and to all appearances would
have easily passed for a black bear cub. It bore no resemblance to
a woodchuck, but shortly it raised its head and then its identity was
revealed. As I had the advantage of elevation, I took careful aim
and placed a long rifle hollow point bullet in the spine near the
junction of the shoulders, and down it went almost like the dropping
of a lead weight.

When I first saw this chuck, I was impressed by its unusual size,
but I did not really realize how large it was until I actually picked
it up. It was lying almost covered with dirt near the mouth of an old
den where it had been digging up some succulent roots when shot,
and it was so heavy that I pulled it out with great difficulty. It had
enormous hind feet, and in color was almost coal black on the back.
I first decided to carry it to the car so that I might take it to town
and weigh it, but after reaching the fence line on the road some 200
yards away, I reversed my decision and refused to carry it the additional 300 yards over the hill to the car. It was just too heavy and
malodorous to be transported by hand any farther. If that woodchuck weighed only 12 to 14 pounds, it certainly felt like 35 or 40
pounds when I started to carry it, and more like 125 pounds when
I threw it down.

The second super-sized woodchuck was one with which I had
long acquaintance and numerous experiences before finally bringing
it to bag. Since the home of this animal was on the property of
Hollingsworth, I have always referred to it as the "Hollingsworth
woodchuck." On this property was located one of my favorite areas
for hunting squirrels. On the point of a pasture hillside, a good .22
rifle shot from the nearest corner of the upper of the two squirrel
woods on this property, this wise and tremendous old woodchuck
dug a cluster of holes with several accompanying lookout mounds,

and there for some six or eight years successfully defied all my attempts to kill it with a rifle. The squirrels in this upper woods were all wild, wary and difficult to stalk, and the few woodchucks resident nearby were even more so. If you crossed the open space between the lower and upper woods to reach the corner of the upper woods nearest the chuck dens, which was the only cover close enough to afford shooting from a wooded area, the chucks, if out eating clover even 300 or 400 yards away, would duck in immediately, and moreover they would stay in. As a rule the only way to kill a chuck on that hill was to wait patiently in the upper squirrel woods for a few hours and then silently crawl over to the fence line near its edge and try to locate one in range feeding in the clover field. Generally, if out, they were either well beyond the range of a .22 long rifle or in line with cattle or farm buildings, all insuperable obstacles to a shot.

After hunting squirrels for some time, about noon on a hot September day, I crawled under a barbed wire fence on the edge of the upper squirrel woods with the intention of going over to a run beside the lower woods to get a drink of water. As usual I got tangled in the fence, and in getting loose made considerable noise. When about 25 feet out in the opening, I suddenly became aware that the "Hollingsworth woodchuck," erect as a levelman's rod, was sitting on the hillside and looking directly at me. It was at least 150 yards away, and was located much farther from the woods than usual. As there were dens up and down a very shallow wash along the slope of this hill, it might be able to dodge into cover almost anywhere in that part of the field. I slowly brought the rifle up and trained the cross-hairs of the 5A scope on the chuck's head. Through the glass it looked enormous, even larger than the huge "duPont woodchuck" previously described. My first impulse was to take a head shot from my position, but on reflection I decided against it. Hitting a chuck's head at 150 yards is less difficult than hitting the inner circle of the small bore target at that range in the Small Bore Palma or the Dryden, provided you know your range exactly. Even in the field, the range habits of a lifetime can not be overlooked or forgotten. Light, mirage, distance, wind drift, all must be borne in mind; forget the breeze for a moment, and you will surely miss. The latter is what influenced my decision against taking the 150 yard shot. Just a few days before we had been visited by a great tropical hurricane, and the light winds of the aftermath seemed to be blowing in all directions at the same time. So I crawled back to and through the fence, then stalked 50 yards through the woods to the corner of the fence, where I sat down with my right shoulder and part of my back resting securely against the trunk of a large oak, and prepared to make the shot.

Owing to the fact that the chuck was from 20 to 30 feet above my level, it was impossible to shoot prone. So I assumed the position that was almost as steady, namely, the sitting position with shoulder rest. Doping the whirlpool winds as best I could, I held the scope crosshair intersection about four inches above the ears of the chuck, which meant five inches above the top of the skull, and about a third the width of the skull into what appeared to be the strongest breeze. As the chuck turned its head, I let off the shot almost as fast as if I had been shooting a 20 gauge shotgun due to the fact that the Hart speed action in my Winchester-Hoffman Model 52 works with such precision and speed. The stricken chuck made a whirling motion until it had completed about one-third of a revolution of its body, and then collapsed head down.

I paced the distance out to the chuck lying dead on the hillside and found it to be 102 paces. On reaching it, I noticed both its color and size. It was very dark brown, but definitely not black, and in weight was but little inferior to that of the "duPont woodchuck." I had no scales with me so had no way to determine its weight. Of course I might have taken it with me, but this would have required that I carry it in my hands more than a mile to a car bus line, and this I never do. Suffice it to say that it was one of those giants of the woodchuck family that are rarely found.

Thus ended the career of the wily old dame that was the mother, grandmother and great-grandmother of the wise and wary wood-chucks of Hollingworth hill. An examination and autopsy showed that the 37-grain hollow point lead bullet entered the left side of the skull about a half inch below and an inch back of the left eye, and traversed the brain and right side of the skull without passing through the skin on the right side of the head. The whole upper skull was wrecked, and the bullet itself was broken into fragments, the largest one of which included the base and weighed 17-grains. Many more grisly details of the autopsy could be given, but these are sufficient to show the destructive power of the .22 long rifle hollow point high-speed load at 100 yards.

About two years after killing the "duPont woodchuck," I shot an exceptionally large male chuck that had completely lost his "tail feathers." There was only the barest trace of a healed-over stub. Apparently the "other man" in the case got a tail hold and refused to let go. The chuck might also have backed into the den one day when the old dame was having one of her conniptions, and she beat him to the draw! He was also badly scarred about the body from fighting. When seen, he was feeding on the top of a hill covered with clover about a foot high. He saw us and started for the subway, but before taking the downhole express he stopped for one last look and that was when the bullet "plopped" on his shoulder! That was also as much woodchuck as I care to carry for more than 100 yards. But it was really only a fair chuck compared to that old "duPont woodchuck." Simply one that had fed for years and years on rich hillside clover, and had made his full growth, scrapping his way up from the lightweights, to the middleweights, then to the heavyweights and finally going down for the count to a .22 long rifle hollow point bullet.

I recall, also, another enormous fat old grandpop woodchuck that fed for weeks on a wide and long meadow back of Conodoguinnet Creek in Pennsylvania. This one took three weeks of stalking before I got a satisfactory shot and I bagged him with a .22 long rifle in the ribs, well across on the other side of the meadow. It was a hair-raising shot, but it was that or nothing that evening. He showed all the symptoms of being about to turn in for the day.

The woodchuck which caused me the scare of my life, was shot from a car along a narrow road about a third of a mile from where the duPont chuck met its end. This chuck had thrown up quite a mound of earth along a fence row, and this in turn was grown up with dewberry bushes and weeds. The chuck happened to be out one day as we drove past, and was killed with a shot at less than 40 yards. I climbed the bank and just as I was about to pick it up by one hind foot, and it really was an enormous chuck, I stooped over with my face probably not over a foot from the ground and at that moment a very large cottontail rabbit jumped out from under my nose and raced up the hill and I practically sat down on my coat tails. Talk about one's hair rising, mine not only rose straight up, it simply lifted the hat! I thought the chuck had come to life and had jumped into my face to bite. Examination showed that the rabbit had actually built a form and had sat there for days and days within not over three or four feet from the mouth of an unusually large chuck den and apparently had been getting along in perfect peace with a pretty scrappy looking male woodchuck; since there was ample feed for both.

I have, on probably half a dozen occasions, while hunting, kicked up a rabbit that ran through a flock of quail on the ground and flushed them, or vice versa, the quail flushed and the noise of their wings caused the rabbit to jump—in which cases I have always shot at the quail—but never before nor since have I jumped a woodchuck and a rabbit at the same spot, although I once knocked down and stunned a rabbit coming out of a woodchuck den mouth, shooting at it in mistake for a young chuck, using iron sights, and firing from one hill to another.

By this time, you may begin to think that the author feels that the .22 long rifle is the one and only woodchuck rifle. Not at all! He does not, but it will kill chucks as dead as any other rifle, under some circumstances, which means the bullet must be placed properly, and the range should not be too excessive.

The .22 long rifle high-speed, hollow point bullet is deadly, almost instantly, if it strikes in the sticking place, in the butt of the ear, in the center of the frontal bone, in the skull from the front; if the animal is shot in the side of the neck, so that the bullet cuts either the jugular vein or severs the spinal cord; if the bullet bores straight through both shoulders, or hits a little high and not more than about two to three inches back of the shoulder, so that it will drive straight on through and forward toward the neck and head; and if the bullet pierces the spine, especially from above and behind. A shot in the heart area may kill instantly and it may not, for the chuck may drag in first, but in any case a well placed shot will kill a high percentage of woodchucks. It is not a rifle, however, for the chap who simply shoots "at the middle of the pile" and trusts to luck to make a kill. Instead of sticking that fuzzy little tail as stiff as a ramrod into the air and then cashing in that chuck is likely to scramble frantically to the nearest hole and flop in and that's that, or will be, two or three days later after considerable suffering.

As mentioned elsewhere, I have been present when my son shot and killed eight straight woodchucks, with a Model 39 Marlin .22 long rifle, using Hi-Speed hollow point ammunition, and doing most of his shooting off the top of a light automobile. The average shot was 100 yards, and most of the hits were high in or just back of the shoulder.

Edgar F. Burkins, who over the years has probably killed as many chucks as anyone in the state of Delaware, tells me that his highest remembered long run of consecutive kills with the .22 long rifle, was 18, which were shot with a Model 52 carrying a Fecker 6X scope in target mounts. But he prefers the .22 Hornet to any other rifle he has used for woodchucks, having had long runs of consecutive kills of 13 and then 18 or 20, with different Hornet rifles. His run of 18 straight chucks with the .22 long rifle was made with solid bullet ammunition. He invariably shoots for the head.

Many experienced woodchuck hunters at times bitterly condemn the use of the .22 long rifle or .22 W.R.F. calibers on woodchucks, regardless of the range or the type of country shot in. They claim it is not sportsmanlike and you lose too many cripples.

It can be said that for long range, open shooting, on bare hillsides or among rocks, on stone fences, and in meadows in which shots may be and often are taken at 200 to 400 yards or even more, by those who will take a shot at almost *any* distance, the .22 long rifle is *not* a good selection, but more persons *have* .22 rim fire rifles for chuck shooting than any other caliber.

One thing to consider in this regard is that thousands and thousands of woodchucks can only be shot at very close range, except in very exceptional instances. The reason is that in many localities large numbers of chucks live along fence rows, grown up quite high with all sorts of trash, such as sumac, blackberries, poison ivy, locust sprouts, and honeysuckle vines. The fields are too wide and too bare to shoot these chucks from the far side of the field, and they do not often feed far out from the fence. The only way to get shots at these chucks is to slip as silently as possible up the fence row, and take a quick shot at any that come out or which are surprised in the mouth of their dens. If some of the trees are large enough, and not too thorny, you can climb one and from there shoot up and down the row.

In many fields, where the grass or weeds are high, dozens of chuck holes may be found in small clumps of head-high briars,— blackberry briars, sumac and greenbriars—and the only way you can often shoot chucks in such a place is to walk up quietly and stand motionless 50 feet or so from a bunch of dens, hold a light .22 pump action or bolt out in the direction of the most frequently "used" den mouths, and when an ear comes up, put a .22 bullet into the butt of that ear. Or, you may be able to climb a tree and shoot into a briar patch from there, or fire across and down, from one hilltop, into a wash and briar thicket at a somewhat lower level. Long range shooting is as impossible here as it is on a city street. Any ordinary shot can place his bullet on a quarter to a silver dollar at that distance—20 to 75 feet—and you do not have to have a Magnum-magnum to make a kill.

Such woodchuck shooting conditions are the regular thing up the Susquehanna Valley, and in any sort of soil which is rich and loamy or slightly sandy, and on which vegetation grows very high and very dense in rainy weather. The same is true in districts in which there are many abandoned farms, grown up with wild carrot, sumac, briars and trash and which are very rarely mown in midsummer as is the case with more highly cultivated farms. For long range shooting you must first be able to see the woodchuck. You may well be within range of two dozen and not see one, unless possibly one suddenly stands up like a ramrod in the high grass, and then most likely drops down again and feeds along before you can get a bead on him.

I do not recall that I ever shot more than two or three woodchucks up the Susquehanna Valley, before I was 25 years of age, although by that time I had killed hundreds of squirrels, rabbits, quail, ruffed grouse and ducks there. The only woodchucks in that region were along the River Narrows hill, which was all rocks and possibly 600 feet above the railroad tracks down below and a few of them on Peters Mountain; and the only ones that were bagged were run in by dogs and dug out by long and laborious work. Any shot obtained was almost certain to be at less than 20 yards and with a rock background. What incentive was there to hunt woodchucks under such circumstances? Since then chucks have moved into that area in some numbers, are now found in briar patches and in washes and on hillsides just as they are at other places, and are providing burrows for rabbits which is their principal game conservation virtue in any locality.

Where there are no woodchucks in the fields and in the woods and choppings and briar patches, the rabbits, and also the ringnecks, have few places to dive into for safety when pursued by a dog. A rabbit that has to stay on the surface is simply a gone gosling when a really fast dog comes upon it out in the open. Woodchucks therefore should have some protection as game, not so much because they are gamy themselves, but for the reason that they provide so much protection for rabbits. They do more to preserve a breeding stock of cottontails than all the importation of Western rabbits since time began. There are no substitutes for chucks and chuck dens for harassed cottontail rabbits, except old board and slab piles, fence post and log piles. We do not have enough saw mills today to provide a sufficient number of these. I always regret to see farmers stage a "gassing" and den-destroying campaign against the few woodchucks on their farms. Obviously at times something of this kind can hardly be avoided, but as a rule a few woodchucks on a farm do very little actual damage. The same men, who will criticise bitterly because their State Game Commission fails to provide enough rabbits for hunting, will destroy the woodchuck dens which are the only real safe refuge those rabbits can find when chased by dogs.

CHAPTER 11

The .22 Hornet on Woodchucks

THE .22 HORNET IS THE MOST PRACTICAL ANSWER TO THE DEMAND
for an inexpensive factory-loaded center fire varmint cartridge that
is really effective as a killer and which has match ammunition accuracy. It is practically the only small caliber center fire on the
market in which the ordinary "store ammunition" will shoot three-
fourths inch to one and one-half inch groups at 100 yards with sufficient frequency to make this the normal expectation. It is also
practically the only one that has a trajectory sufficiently flat to insure
certain kills on all good chances up to 150 yards. The .218 Bee can
not do this, as it lacks match accuracy.

Small caliber center fire factory-loaded cartridges of 10 to 30
years ago had certain undesirable characteristics, all of which mili-
tated against good success when used by the varmint hunter. Excessive erosion, immediate and almost certain corrosion, and an unnecessary number of loud ricochets were obvious drawbacks. You
had to handload to get best results, and also if you wanted to preserve
the barrel. Most of the bulk smokeless powders in use then were
loaded ahead of black powder primers and a small priming charge
of black powder. This combination absorbed moisture in excessive
amounts and this gave large daily variations in point of impact if
the weather happened to change. This added considerably to the
woes and the worries of the expert rifleman who was a varmint
hunter, especially if he were a woodchuck hunter. In years gone by,
the handloaded .25–21 was the best small caliber center fire cartridge for small game and varmint shooting. The .22–15–60 cartridge was almost an exact duplicate of it in .22 caliber. But the
.22–15–60 often was neither as accurate nor as reliable as the .25–21
and was more difficult to load uniformly, especially if a man desired
to shoot less than the full charge, which was about a .22–12–45
combination. The .22–13–45 W.C.F. cartridge was a neat little
trick but not very accurate, otherwise it would have been a fine
squirrel cartridge and a good one for crows, hawks and woodchucks
at moderate ranges. Being more accurate, the .25–20 outsold it.

Then along came the .22 Hornet, which was primarily the .22–13–45 with well made metal-cased bullets. There are a few slight differences in contour, but the principal difference is in primers, powders, and the really remarkable little metal-cased soft point and hollow point bullets which are usually available for it.

Up to 175 yards it is a first class woodchuck cartridge. Sight the rifle to shoot one inch to an inch and a quarter above the line of sight at 100 yards when using a telescope sight, and forget about holding high or low inside of 150 yards, except that at ranges less than 20 yards you must hold high as the bullet has not as yet risen to the line of sight. If you overlook this, you will shoot considerably below that at which you are aiming.

The main advantage of the modern Hornet factory load for chuck shooting is that it kills splendidly on any hit ahead of the middle of the lungs. If you hit a woodchuck back of the middle, it makes but little difference what you are shooting, unless it is something like the soft point load in the .220 Swift, as he will go into his den anyhow. Other advantages of the Hornet are: totally negligible recoil, which permits a perfect let-off of the shot; rifle very easy to clean; arm shoots right where it looks—provided the rifle is well stocked with properly seasoned, dense walnut, has rigid scope mounts, and a good barrel to begin with. If any of these are offside, and they frequently are, any other .22 or .25 caliber center fire rifle may be expected to show more inaccuracy than the Hornet, because the heavier recoil will help produce greater variations from normal, as the vibrations will be wider and sharper.

The Hornet cartridge gives a sharp and quick report, but the report is *lower* than that of any other .22 center fire, metal-cased bullet charge, either commercially or privately made, because the others all use more powder. Therefore, it is logical to expect less complaint and objection because of the report, and fewer people will put a stop to your shooting because of it. This means you can do a reasonable amount of shooting with a .22 Hornet, where many other .22 varmint cartridges would make this impossible. I am stressing this situation strongly, because in settled districts it handicaps more riflemen than any other cause.

The average farm contains horses, cattle, turkeys, barnyard chickens and women, and all of these are at times quite upset by continued or even occasional loud reports of rifles. Persuasive and ingratiating tactics on the part of the shooter, and the use of the softest sounding but effective woodchuck cartridge, are often the only practical remedies, and at times even these will fail.

Another advantage of the .22 Hornet is that the cartridge is light, short, and comparatively inexpensive. Fifty may be carried easily, in a small box in the pocket or they can be carried loose. Either factory loaded, or handloaded, they cost less, than any other .22 center fire, modern load, using metal-cased, expanding bullets.

Most of the faster and larger .22 center fire cartridges use one and one-half to four times as much powder as the Hornet, and most of them use bullets in their full charges which cost two or three times as much as the .22 Hornet bullets. A shooter can therefore decide for himself whether because of personal, financial, or neighborhood shooting conditions, he should choose the .22 Hornet, or some one of the larger and more expensive and more powerful cartridges. The most important requisite of a woodchuck cartridge is that, for both physical and financial reasons, it is "shootable" whenever needed on your chuck grounds. This is 10 times as important as whether every now and then, possibly once a year, you may kill a woodchuck beyond 350 yards. This means 1,050 actual feet—it does not mean an estimated 350 yards, which might be about 190 yards if the shooter is a bit excited or new to his district.

Having used the .22 Hornet for most of my woodchuck shooting, except those woodchucks hunted and shot while gunning for squirrels, ever since the Model 54 Winchester came on the market, I have had a fair amount of chuck shooting experience with it.

The first chuck I recall shooting with the Hornet was running hard for his den in a little hollow in a grass field on top of a hill. I held the crosshairs just under his chin and the bullet hit a bit back in the ribs, as he was really throwing the dust. He slid along on his nose, humped his back once, his little bushy tail waved stiffly a couple of times, and he was through. The bullet hole was about the size of a quarter, and when I squeezed the chuck a bit it went "whoosh!"—inside! On other chucks, if the bullet struck in that area between the eye and the diaphragm—the membrane that holds the lungs up from the abdominal organs—the chuck wilted right down. Sometimes there was not so much "whoosh!" inside; at others quite a bit of destruction occurred among the vital organs —but the bullet holes were almost invariably between the size of a dime and a quarter.

It will do no harm to repeat, that the Hornet rifle is so accurate, with first class factory ammunition especially the soft point loads, that before long you become annoyed when you fail to hit the exact spot at which you aimed on the woodchuck. It is one rifle cartridge with which a man can take aim at the butt of the ear, at the point of the shoulder, in the sticking place, or just half way between eye and ear—and hit that exact spot a surprising number of times. As this copy is being written the author had just returned from a varmint shooting trip with a friend who had recently been laid up by an accident and wanted a change of scene. He called me up, was driven over, and we went out. I had one shot at a crow with the Hornet which, due to continued bad weather, had not been fired for nearly two months. The range was 90 to 100 yards. The bullet struck fairly through the butts of the wings and the bird wilted without moving a single feather. It is just like reaching out and making a dot on the mark with a draftsman's pencil. You must have shot a rifle like that for months and have the holding ability to place your shot where you want it to land before you will believe this is uniformly so, but it is so and under normal conditions the game will go down as if struck by lightning—if you use ordinary knowledge of anatomy in placing your shots. Remember, readers, there are a large number of shooters who can train themselves to place that first shot with almost machine rest accuracy. The eyes are fresh, the nerves are not yet frayed and as a rule, you are rested and your mental and physical reactions are 100 per cent.

I remember once going out with a shooting friend of considerable ballistic knowledge and shooting experience. He wanted to see what a scope-sighted Hornet would do on woodchucks. I shot five chucks with five shots, from his auto, and at least four of these shots were really spectacular. His estimates of the ranges were 125 to 190 yards with only one less than 150 yards. Those chucks simply wilted down, from stone walls, den-mouth observation posts and lookout points. The way their stubby tails stood up and "buzzed" the "all in" signal, the "taps" for that woodchuck, I believe gave my friend a little more of an insight into the extreme deadliness of the super-accurate, .22 center fire, woodchuck rifle, than most persons are privileged to experience, or witness, unless they have such a rifle and have become thoroughly accustomed to shooting it successfully.

The Hornet cartridge also has definite limitations for woodchuck shooting. It is not sufficiently flat shooting for consistent kills at 200 yards and beyond. By that I mean, so that five or six successive kills may be made between 175 and 250 yards, every few weeks, when weather and light conditions are favorable and you do not have measured or paced grounds to shoot over. In other words, where one drives out and hunts wherever he finds game. A cartridge giving still higher velocity is more desirable for the longer shooting. If sharper pointed bullets are used in the Hornet, better windbucking qualities are noted, the trajectory is flatter, and more hits from the same number of shots should occur. But these sharper pointed bullets, while they shoot flatter and drift less in the wind, seldom shoot as accurately in calm weather as the present style of Hornet bullets, and they do not expand as well, as a rule, at Hornet velocities, hence do not kill as well on a given shot.

Consequently, amateur ballisticians can be wrong in this constant demand for a flatter shooting and less wind drift Hornet load. What I would like to see is a .22 Hornet spitzer load, in addition to those on the market, which has not to exceed 1,800 to 2,000 f.s. m.v., all the accuracy of that remarkable Winchester soft point 2,350 f.s. charge, first put out, and a bullet which is so adjusted as to jacket strength, core alloy, and lead protrusion at the point, that it would give just about the same amount of tearing effect and slashing sort of wound as the .25 Stevens rim fire, factory charge, but with the flatter trajectory and less wind drift and more even shooting, of the Hornet rifle. What an extremely fine squirrel rifle that would make. It would kill a lot of woodchucks too inside of 125 yards. This, I feel, is a load that, with the present factory charges, would make the .22 Hornet almost unbeatable as a settled community, poor man's varmint rifle. It would double the usefulness of the Hornet because with the lighter and less-expanding load, cottontail rabbits, squirrels, muskrats, gophers, crows, and such could be shot with less noise, less expense, less racket, less laceration of flesh or pelt, and less danger on a line shot on tree or post; or on the skyline or wherever a bullet might continue on and on.

With two such loads, the present factory maximum and this just suggested, the farm boy and the small town rifleman would be very well supplied. If, some day, he wanted to go farther from home and do woodchuck shooting out in the great "in back of beyond," where the ranges are long and the travel is sparse, then he could tote one of the larger and more powerful .22 center fire rifles, to be suggested in the following paragraphs and chapter divisions; also, to greater length in *Twenty-two Caliber Varmint Rifles*. 'Till then, we will be looking at them, over the crosshairs of the .22 Hornet!

THE K-HORNET, .22/3000 LOVELL, R-2, .22 MAXIMUM-LOVELL, .22 LINDAHL CHUCKER AND SIMILAR SMALL WILDCAT CARTRIDGES ON WOODCHUCKS

These numerous .22 caliber, small size wildcat cartridges made from .22 Hornet, .25–20 single shot Stevens, .219 Zipper and .25 Remington automatic cartridges are all extremely accurate, light, easily carried and cheap to shoot in the field. None of them makes an excessively loud report, although all crack louder than the .22 Hornet factory charge.

The .22 Hornet is a 10-grain cartridge; the K-Hornet a 12-grain case; the .218 Bee (the nearest commercial cartridge) is a 14 to 15-grain cartridge; the .22/3000 type of cartridges are 16 to 18-grain cases; the Maximum-Lovell type will handle one to two grains more

A REAL *Black* WOODCHUCK

This coal black woodchuck, photographed so as to show laceration caused by the bullet, was killed in Wayne Co. Pennsylvania, by J. G. Schnerring, and photographed by Dr. Ellis E. W. Given, now deceased. The rifle used was a .22–4000 Sedgley-Schnerring fitted with Fecker telescope sight. The crow was shot that day at 300 yds.

On September 12, 1945, the author examined the skin of this chuck, which was a small, and young black chuck, in the Academy of Natural Sciences at Philadelphia. At the time it was being kept in a drawer with two other skins of abnormally large woodchucks of ordinary reddish-brown color also contributed by Mr. Schnerring.

The hair of this chuck, even after being preserved for years, was as black and shiny as that of a black skunk, or the feathers of a crow, as can be observed in this photograph. The black chuck was hit only in the head. The skin off the body was not damaged.

powder; the short .22 Lindahl chuckers are 24 to 24½-grain cases; the Pfeifer short cases are also in the medium or low charge class. The whole bunch develop from 2,800 to 3,500 f.s. m.v. The smaller ones do not go up as high as the larger, of course, but often they are found the more efficient cartridges for the charge burned, a point often overlooked by the shooter.

Users are enthusiastic about these cartridges as woodchuck loads. They shoot flatter than the Hornet, especially over 150 to 300 yards; they kill better due to the higher velocity, but every one of them (not including the .218 Bee) is strictly a rifle crank and handloading proposition. Until some factory comes out with ammunition in a variety of these sizes, you cannot walk into a sporting goods store and come out with a box or two of ammunition, all ready to go hunting.

All of these cartridges made from the .25–20 S.S. case are difficult to supply with cases; the reason being that no considerable number of .25–20 single shot rifles have been made by Stevens or anyone else for the last 15 years, and such manufacture is not likely to be resumed. The .25–20s which have been made are repeating rifles for the .25–20 repeater cartridge, which is a shorter, fatter, bottle neck case.

Most of the smaller .22 wildcat cartridges are suitable for Eastern chuck shooting, except where 300 to 400 yard shots are taken *frequently*, and sometimes are necessary or the chuck will dive in. With such cartridges above mentioned, very sharp or pencil pointed bullets are sometimes used. They have a tendency to flatten trajectory and in one make seem to give good accuracy. But the actual killing power of such bullets is often exaggerated—as compared to that obtained with a more rounded ogive bullet at similar striking velocity. A chuck's hide is tough, but the nearside penetration is normally not difficult; it is the hide on the farside which bulges out and gives and is difficult to cut or penetrate. By that time the bullet has completed its killing or wounding. Body contents are usually pulped and shattered due to hydraulic action on the fluids and semi-fluids of the body, usually mostly at velocities beyond 2,900 f.s.

.22 VARMINTER JUNIOR, .219 DONALDSON-WASP, .22 LINDAHL SUPER-CHUCKER, .219 ZIPPER IMPROVED AND SIMILAR-SIZED CARTRIDGES

These cartridges, and others of somewhat similar size, shoulder slope and body design, normally develop from 3,200 to slightly over 4,000 f.s. m.v., depending upon the load used, bullet weight, whether maximum charge or about 80 per cent charge for that case, and similar conditions. The 55-grain bullets will give 3,000 to about 3,650 or slightly higher muzzle velocity, in cartridges of this size. This size case gives higher ballistic efficiency, in many instances, with 55-grain, or with 50-grain Sisk and similar bullets than with 41-grain, 45- and 47-grain bullets as the heavier bullets cause the powder to burn better.

Cartridges of this size case, and slightly larger, usually burn 29 to 37 grains of powder, most times 30 to 35 grains is used, but this is quite a stepup from the 15 to 18 grains of the .22/3000 type of cartridge or the 10 to 13 grains of the various versions of the steppedup Hornet or the K-Hornet.

These charges all crack considerably higher and sharper than the Hornet, K-Hornet and .22/3000 class of varmint cartridges and are in a report range that in many areas is certain to result in complaint from landowners. This is, or at least can be, as important as the range, flatness of trajectory or accuracy of the charge, and may be even more so. I bring this point up time and again, because it cannot be overemphasized in thickly or even moderately settled districts. Remember, there are always persons annoyed or easily frightened in any community. Some are rabid on the subject, particularly if they think anyone is shooting on *their* land. It may be just waste land which maintains nothing but a few colonies or families of woodchucks, dewberries and poison ivy, but *they* live on it and maybe you had better not use too noisy a rifle.

The ease with which .219 Zipper, .30–40 Krag, .303 British, .25 Remington Rimless, can be obtained today, as compared to .25–20 S.S. cases to neck down, and the fact that .25–35, .22 Savage H.P., can be used for necking down in place of the Zipper, or that .30–30 and .32 Special can be used with more necking down operations if needed, or that .32 Remington Rimless and .35 Remington Rimless could be used in place of the .25 Remington Rimless, if necessary but with more work, helps to make cartridges of these head sizes and case strength popular as compared to older, thinner brass of a generation or so back.

THE .22 STANDARD VARMINTER, .22 SENIOR VARMINTER, .22–303 VARMINT-R, .224 AND .228 ACKLEY MAGNUMS AND SOMEWHAT SIMILAR-SIZED CARTRIDGES

These, and the super .22 H.P.s, the .220 Swift with sharper shoulder like the .220 Arrow, the 7mm job made into a .22 like the .22/4000 Sedgley-Schnerring, all make very long range woodchuck, coyote, and wolf cartridges, but actually they are antelope and deer cartridges if used with heavy bullets and in rifles with sufficient twist to spin them.

They are *effective*, but give a very loud and carrying report and a sharp and ear-piercing muzzle blast, when fully charged. This is expecially noticeable on very calm and on very damp days, when shooting around elaborate farms and estates and may easily cause the rifleman to lose his shooting opportunities in such areas, due to the noise and its effect upon farmers and their families.

THE .22–348, THE .22–60 PMVF, AND SIMILAR CARTRIDGES

These very large cases, holding up to 60 to 65 grains of powder, give the flattest trajectory, but the sharpest and most annoying report, and a very short barrel life, due to the heat of the large charge and its erosive effects. They are of a type which is ballistically less efficient, in proportion to the powder consumed, than any of the well-designed small or medium cartridges.

Ray Weeks kept records which proved that a good R-2 Diller-Johnson barrel was superbly accurate up to 6,600 to 6,700 rounds. The Swift class usually lose accuracy rapidly after 750 to 1,500 rounds, and larger cases, particularly those with a not too fortunate shoulder slope design, wear out very much faster than the Swift. Instances have been noted in which .22 varmint type rifles with very long, large-capacity cases and a shoulder slope which directed the powder gases flaming against the rifle barrel walls at the throat and just ahead of the case, lost accuracy badly after 200 to 250 rounds.

All of the medium and larger cases, and some of the smaller ones, with certain very easily expanded bullets, give an explosive effect upon the lungs and tummy of a woodchuck, and the very fast loads give this even at 300 to 350 yards. They are thus inclined to help distribute the chuck as well as to liquidate him. But they are not good cartridges to choose for firing promiscuously at crows on dead tree tops, or at anything in which the bullet is likely to travel two to three and one-half miles or even more across country—in which there may be heavily traveled highways, farm buildings which are inhabited, or fields containing valuable live stock. Almost all of these cartridges are much safer to shoot at woodchucks feeding in back fields, at crows—which you see while hunting chucks and which birds may be feeding in corn fields, stubble, and then in winter on snow and ice covered farms—than cartridges like the .22 long rifle, the .38–40 and .44–40, .38 Special revolver cartridge, the .45–70 and the like, all of which give bad ricochets at times. The bullet of the .22 varmint rifle of very high velocity, if of soft point or readily and *easily* expandable hollow point type, will be shattered to pieces on contact with earth by any cartridge from the .22 Hornet on up, and the faster it is driven the more certain it is not to ricochet. But a full metal-cased bullet will nearly always ricochet and will give very deep penetration, anything from a foot to six feet of pine, depending upon type and load and hardness of core, and should not be used recklessly in farming areas or on estates.

Out on long, bare hillsides, where there is not much of anything but some woodchucks and a few crows, one can shoot almost anything without too much regard to ricochets, but such areas are becoming less common every year.

It pays to look *carefully* as to the background, and especially as to where a bullet would ricochet, and realize that most ricochets go to the right in rifles having a right hand twist, and that includes nearly all of them. Look two or three times before you shoot, even if a chuck or a crow moves off while you are looking and you are likely to have opportunity to shoot in that area many more years than if you shot first and looked afterward. One has to be wrong but once and you do not want to be around when the noise of a speeding or ricocheting bullet arouses the local vote.

When ice is on the ground and the fields it is often dangerous to shoot across a plowed field, because of the small angle with the surface of the field and anything hard has a tendency to bounce and ricochet off ice or frozen snow. Shooting on freshly plowed ground is much safer.

CHAPTER 12

The Best Woodchuck Districts

SERVICE AS A GUN EDITOR FOR SEVERAL MAGAZINES COVERING A
period of nearly 33 years gave me through correspondence with
many riflemen an opportunity to learn of hunting conditions and
experiences in many sections of the country that has proved invaluable over the years. In this way I came to know the shooting conditions in various localities as well as the hunting methods prevailing
therein. Basing my opinion on the information thus obtained, I
would state that the Southern portion of the Province of Ontario,
being that section of the Province lying north of Lake Ontario and
Lake Erie and opposite Western New York and Eastern Ohio, offers
better woodchuck shooting today than any other area of similar size
in North America. Melanism is quite prevalent among the woodchucks of that region. In other words, many of the chucks found
there have a large amount of black pigment in the skin or hair,
causing them to be called "black woodchucks" or "woodschucks,"
their woodland homes being often the cause of this condition. While
these black chucks seem to be more eagerly sought after than those
of lighter pelage, there is really no difference in them except in color.

There are good chuck districts near Troy, New York and extending over into Western Massachusetts and Vermont; East and North-
east of Erie, Pennsylvania; and between Binghamton and Sherburne,
New York, extending through that creek bottom country above and
below Greene, New York. The Mohawk Valley between Albany and
Utica, except in spots, has shown few evidences of woodchucks, or
chuck dens, in the several trips I have made through it, although
there may be more chucks back from the river country. There are
several small but excellent chuck districts in the Catskill Mountains
area of New York and the hilly country West thereof.

Western Massachusetts, Vermont and New Hampshire, as well as
parts of Maine and much of Connecticut, supply good woodchuck
hunting. Northern and to some extent Central, and South Central
Pennsylvania are now better chuck areas than they were 15 or 20
years ago, but dense vegetation in some of these latter districts,

makes hunting chucks much less satisfactory to a rifleman than more open and less heavily grown-up areas. New Castle County, Delaware, parts of Maryland, Western Virginia, Western North Carolina, West Virginia, and areas in New Jersey, Ohio, Indiana, and Westward across the upper Mississippi, afford woodchuck shooting in varying degrees of plentifulness. The whistling marmot in British Columbia and our Rocky Mountain areas, provide Western riflemen with chuck shooting.

The general habits of woodchucks are much the same, but the terrain, the vegetation or lack of it, and the type and density of population make a great difference in the best methods and the proper rifles to use for such shooting.

It is always a good idea to permit the young chucks to be born and to grow up and get fat, before you start the systematic woodchuck shooting for the season. Your chuck shooting will last longer and you will leave your shooting district with fewer regrets.

Woodchucks are as temperamental and as erratic in their feeding habits as the black bass. One trip you find them out, apparently, in almost unlimited numbers; the next time through the district you may only see two or three, or possibly none at all.

Chuck shooting is usually good as the dew starts to dry on the grass in the morning. They feed before the heat of the day, and they feed again after 3:00 to 4:30 P.M., depending largely upon whether it is a very warm day or a cool day. Squirrels and woodchucks have some traits in common. They come out on the warm sunny hillsides and in the warmer portions of cool days, and in the shade and the cooler portions of the very warm, sultry days.

Immediately before a good rain or right after a short, sharp shower, which wets the grass and cools the atmosphere, the chucks will almost invariably be out feeding greedily. If you do not go out any other time, go chuck shooting *then*.

The woodchuck is more sluggish and deliberate and by no means as playful as the gray squirrel. Instead of scampering around and chasing wildly here and there, simply in fun, as squirrels often do on frosty mornings, he lumbers out and feeds busily in the clover, sticking up his head or rising on his hind feet with his front paws draped across his chest for a keen look for possible enemies.

When his locker room is well packed, he takes a station on the nearest stone fence, stump, mound of earth or comfortable post, stretches out and maybe takes a nap in the sun. But that does not say that he is not more or less on the alert, and that you can come along talking to a companion or crashing over sticks and fences and find him dozing there. He can see, hear and smell, and can probably also feel vibrations through the ground.

The best time to hunt woodchucks is when they are feeding or resting. At other times they are usually down in their dens.

Generally, chucks do not like windy weather. On most hunts you will find few out at such times. However, there are exceptions particularly when East winds presage the coming of a storm.

The inclination of chucks to come out and feed when it is calm, cool and quiet, is of great advantage to the rifleman using a moderate or low velocity .22 bullet, because at such times the bullet drift is least, variations from normal in sighting are least, and the chances of making a killing shot with the first bullet are at the maximum. This has saved the reputation of many a woodchuck hunter. If chucks came out only when the wild geese fly and when the mallards are driven before the gale, from the open water back into the sheltered ponds, we would not hear nearly so much as we do about 300 to 450 yard shots on woodchucks.

John L. Cull, of Orillia, Ontario, and of Toronto, is a woodchuck hunter of skill and experience. He is also a camera enthusiast who is keen on outdoor photography of game, and he has considerable knowledge as an amateur naturalist. He is quite familiar with the hunting of both the brown and the black woodchucks of Ontario, particularly in Southern Ontario a hundred miles or so North of Buffalo. Tourist business is bound to increase from the United States into Ontario and Quebec, after the many reconversion problems are solved. Consequently, more people from the States will be going into Ontario to hunt, fish, or shoot varmints, and many of these who have had trouble in their own localities due to scarcity of woodchucks or posted shooting grounds, will go to Ontario to hunt chucks just as they might go there for small mouth bass, grouse or deer.

The black woodchucks and the black squirrels of Ontario will sound very intriguing to many sportsmen in the Northern half of the United States. In late years squirrel seasons in Ontario have been very short and infrequent but their woodchuck shooting lasts from late spring frosts to first fall frosts.

The hunting conditions on woodchucks are much the same in Ontario as in the area from Erie, Pennsylvania, and Buffalo, New York, East to Rochester, Syracuse, Utica, and down to Binghamton, New York, except that Southern Ontario has the very best chuck shooting and today contains the best black woodchuck district in all North America.

The following account by Mr. Cull, who has been associated with the same Canadian sporting magazine as the author and for nearly as many years, will give you a better insight into woodchuck shooting North of the International Boundary, than would otherwise be possible. It is a section which you may find it very much worth your while to visit and hunt. Mr. Cull presents here a very accurate description of the area generally lying between Detroit on the Southwest and that which is North of Cleveland, Buffalo, Toronto, and Rochester, and of the game to be found there and how to shoot it.

This district, away from the large cities is, much of it, quite rural and sparsely settled and is farmed only in the better farming areas. Away from the cities and towns, and while on the back country roads, hunters will be found much fewer than in the United States. Remember that Canada is much the same size as Continental United States, but has today only a million or so more inhabitants than Pennsylvania. The war has also cut down her young manpower, and that means her hunting population. Canada had it worse, proportionally, in both World Wars than had we, in the matter of casualties.

Sportsmen visiting Ontario to hunt woodchucks will often find ruffed grouse dusting in the roads, or roosting in trees, paying not too much attention to chuck hunters in the summertime. Crow shooting in Ontario is altogether a Spring and Summer and early fall sport. They mostly go South in October. See Ray Weeks' account elsewhere in this book.

Altogether, Ontario is a delightful place in which to hunt chucks, crows and other varmints. It will give you a place to look around in, and your early fall grouse or deer shooting. There are, as you will see described in *Twenty-two Caliber Varmint Rifles* and in this work, special Canadian .22 woodchuck and varmint cartridges especially suitable for Ontario and for Western Canada varmint hunting. Among those which were largely developed in Canada were the K-Hornet and the .22–303 Varmint-R.

THE ONTARIO WOODCHUCK
By John L. Cull.

For the benefit especially of readers living South of the International Boundary I would like to give a short description of the environs of the Ontario woodchuck, or groundhog as he is often called up here.

I am only acquainted with that part of the Province of Ontario lying North of Lake Ontario, East as far as Port Hope, West as far as London, and North as far as Haileybury. Roughly this district lies North of Rochester over to Erie, and just across the Great Lakes.

I have not been over all this territory thoroughly, but have covered a lot of it, and have seen chucks in most of the country within the boundaries I have mentioned. They have been seen right beside the main highway leading North from Toronto, and not 20 miles North of that city. I saw two in a field just north of Haileybury, up in the mining country; I saw seven in one field a short distance North of Port Hope; and a few a hundred miles West of Toronto.

However, living as I do in Orillia, just South of the famed Muskoka summer resort district, I am better acquainted with the country within easy motoring distance, say 25 miles in all directions from my home.

The area referred to above is roughly 200 miles square, studded with numerous lakes and streams. Much of the Southern part is under cultivation, with some first-class roads and many concession roads not so good, but quite passable at all times of the year between snows. Some of the gently rolling hills seem to be sandy on top, while the valleys between are well covered with grass and clover. There are many level fields with patches of bush, and as one approaches the Muskoka boundaries one enters the rocky formation peculiar to that location. This country is rather rugged, ledges of rock, swamps and second-growth timber, and small level patches of tillable soil on which the farmer grows what he can, and pastures his small flocks of sheep and cattle.

Groundhog shooting is a favorite pastime of many Canadian sportsmen. Partridges, ducks, deer and rabbits are growing scarcer each year, and it is important that when we get a chance to hunt them, we should be able to make as many clean kills as possible. The man who can consistently knock over a woodchuck, or groundhog as we call them up here, at distances of from 50 to 200 yards with a high-powered rifle, is going to find that he is in pretty good shape to connect with a deer or other species of game when the hunting season comes around.

For the benefit of those who are not familiar with the Ontario groundhog a few words of description may not be out of place. When they first appear in the spring, they are, of course, last year's chucks—usually dark brownish in color, with some gray about the face, rather thin when they first appear, but they soon acquire enough fat to nicely round out their contours. Once accumulated, this fat seems to be an integral part of their anatomy as I have shot chucks all summer and they have all seemed well padded with fat. A shot at one chuck went a trifle high, just nicking the backbone at the shoulder and ripping the skin for several inches, and upon examination there was laid bare a layer of whitish fat at least half an inch thick and extending right around the body. The young ones appear about the first of June, perhaps earlier in more southerly districts. When first seen they are a light brown or orange color, darker on the back, and quite unafraid of man. On his approach they may run for the shelter of their holes but will pop up and sit unconcernedly in the entrance, and allow him to come quite close. They grow fast, being three-quarters grown by August, and gradually changing to a rich reddish brown. It is when they are first grown up that many of them appear to be so black. The patriarchs of the species get grizzled and have a touch of hoar around the face.

As the chuck grows, his contours change. Not only does he attain a truly aldermanic girth, but his proportions alter. When young, his body is rounded much like a rabbit, cat, or small dog. With increasing age and weight he seems to widen sideways. A Goliath of the species may stand 15 inches when erect, with a width of body of nearly nine inches, and yet when you walk across the field to inspect the carcass lying on its back, he is not more than four inches thick. He is always low-slung, with legs about four inches long, and except when frightened, when he breaks into a sort of lumbering but very effective gallop, his body seems to drag along the ground. Examine the location of one of his dens and you will usually find three holes, each some 15 feet apart, and with well-marked trails running from one hole to the others. The grass and clover may be several inches high, but the mark of the body being dragged from home to hole will show a clearance of not more than an inch or so. A chuck in five or six inches of grass would be well hidden, only his curiosity will not allow him to remain concealed, but he must either stand up every few minutes and look around, or seek some slight rise in the ground which will give him a vantage point to see from, and also show him up to the best advantage to the shooter.

The possession of a motor car is almost a necessity owing to the distance from town to the fields in which the chucks are found, and the convenience of being able to travel backwards and forwards along the side roads, picking off the chucks in the fields and returning to get the ones missed the first time. A good pair of field glasses are of great assistance as they enable one to make sure whether the object in the grass is really a chuck or simply a tuft of sod, stump or small stone. An evening meal is also needed as it seems impossible to leave the territory until it is too dark to shoot. A low power telescope on the rifle will add many minutes of shooting at the end of a dark day, as well as helping to make hits at the longer ranges. The glasses are also useful for spotting hits or misses at long range, by noting how the chuck falls, or where the bullet sends up a spurt of sand on missing. Most of the shots will be fired from the front of the car, or from the fences along the roads.

In Ontario we have some extremes of temperature. In winter in some parts temperatures of 10, 15 or even 20 degrees below zero are not unusual. The ice on Lake Couchiching may freeze from 36 to 40 inches thick, depending on whether there is much or little snow to form a blanket. Snow from 18 to 24 inches deep is usual, although drifts may run much higher. I remember jumping into one and disappearing from sight until I floundered out. However, by the middle of March there are bare patches showing on the south sunny slopes of the hills, and a few black chucks are reported as appearing even as early as this, but there is nothing but last year's dead grass to eat and they soon go back. By the time the snow has disappeared, say around the first of April, they are out to bask in the sun, and nibble at any green shoots hardy enough to sprout. As the sun's strength increases, and the acquisition of a meal becomes easier, the chuck stays out longer each day, although it is not until the warm weather sets in that he is out in earnest. He comes out to feed at daybreak, then goes back for a sleep around noon, to re-appear in numbers towards sunset.

Temperatures in summer may run as high as 90 degrees but such warm days are uncommon, except perhaps for a few days in July. However, the warmer the day the more likelihood there is of good chuck shooting.

If a man feels that he just must have some woodchuck shooting, almost any kind of a day will do, except, of course, during a heavy rain. To be sure, the hot dry days of late summer, with the sun on its downward course towards the horizon, and without a breath of wind, are the days one should pick if there be a choice. Those are the days when the chucks come out in great numbers to bask in the sun on top of stone pile, boulder or stump. Even if such an afternoon is followed by a light shower, there will be a few hardy individuals that will stay out until quite a bit of rain has fallen. But if the weather turns cooler and a strong wind gets up, you might as well head for home. Chucks do not like a wind and will not come out when it is blowing.

It is pretty generally accepted that in Ontario, the chuck holes up for the winter about *the middle of September*. Be sure to do your hunting before that date. Of course there are lots of fine warm days later on when a few will be out, and I have even picked off a hardy one in November, but by the first of October they are usually too scarce to justify the long drive necessary to get them.

One place you need *never* look for chucks, is in a *clay field*. Mr. Chuck is no fool, and knows very well that clay is nonporous, and that the first good rain would drown him if he dug his den in clay. Another bete noir of the family is milkweed. If you see this latter growing in a field, drive on to another location.

I have found chuck holes and dens in a great variety of places. Walking along the railway tracks near home I have seen a freshly dug hole only a foot or so beneath the rails. They are to be found along the banks of streams and irrigation ditches, draining fields of grass or clover. Along the country roads their holes may be seen in the sides of ditches, opposite fence posts, under or beside large stones and tree stumps. Abandoned log houses and barns also seem to be favorite places for them to dig their dens. Driving through the country, particularly to the East of Lake Couchiching one sees a number of *deserted* farms with log houses and barns. Nearly every one is a likely location for a groundhog family. I have even crept quietly to a broken window and seen them moving about the earth floor inside the barn. Stone piles are another favored location. Farmers gather up the stones from their fields and pile them in heaps. A gray-brown chuck is very hard to see among these stones, but unless they are frightened their curiosity will not permit them to stay hidden, but they must first peep out and then emerge to sit in full view for the hunter to see.

Part of the area last mentioned lies in the limestone belt, and there are level fields, devoid of much vegetation except scrub, which are flat rock. Crossing this in every direction are numerous cracks, perhaps six inches wide and maybe three feet deep. The sides of these cracks are irregular, and seem to be favorite places for the chuck family to locate in. Looking down into a crack, there is usually a certain amount of surface soil which has been washed down, and the rock in cracking seems to have made lots of pockets and overhangs. It is in these that some chucks live. There is practically nothing for them to eat except the coarsest scrub and grass, so I imagine that they travel to the nearest farm and stock up, making their way home by degrees. Perhaps some which I have shot a few hundred yards away had been out too late and met disaster on the way home. In some places the rocks are piled many feet high, and as a chuck is a good climber one may see him on top of a rock as high as a small house.

The den of the chuck may be a hole under a stump, under a barn, in a stone pile, or may be located in the middle of a field. It has certain characteristics, especially if the ground be soft enough for digging. There are usually three entrances, maybe 15 feet apart, one with a big pile of sand and stones, on which he sits erect to look the situation over; and a couple of more modest ones, coming out behind a tuft of grass or beside a big stone, and never do these supplementary entrances and exits have any sand or earth to draw attention to their location. The holes seem to go *straight down* for a foot or so, and then off at an angle to a common center. I have never dug out this center, but have been told that they make quite a nice nest of leaves and grasses, and it is in here that they pass the cold weather and where the family is raised. This Ontario wood-chuck family may run from three to five, more often the former number. They are seldom seen until they are as big as rats, and some days one may see the old one sitting at the door of her burrow flanked by a pair of the next generation.

By August most of the crops are cut and garnered, and that is the best time for shooting. The days are long and the sun hot, and it is often quiet and practically windless. Mr. Chuck and his family may be out at any time from noon on towards dark, particularly in districts away from traveled roads. I have in mind one side road leading from a well used country road, between two pasture fields, past an abandoned house and tumble-down barn, crossing a tiny rill of the clearest and coldest water imaginable, and finally losing itself in a swamp. There is one occupied farm near its end, but there is so little traffic along this road that the grass has reclaimed it from civilization, and except for an occasional rut, we could hardly tell it from the pasturelands on each side. As we turn off into this grass-grown track, we see perhaps five or six chucks in the field to the South—there are never any in the field to the North, probably because it may be clay.

We notice a big one just inside the fence, but as the car approaches in second gear, he raises up from his feeding, apparently recognizes our motor and ducks for his hole under the boundary fence. Having no traffic to worry about, we park right on the road and sit patiently, one with the field glasses studying the heaps of stone here and there in the field, the tops of stumps, and tufts of grass. In the meantime out comes the Savage .22 Hornet, a full magazine is slipped into its place, and I await a report from my observer. The first shot may be at the head of a chuck seen slowly raising from the crevices of the stone fence. He need only show the top of his head and one eye to get a sight of us, so what he reveals is not a very big target. However, I hold the crosshairs of the scope just where I want the bullet to strike, press the trigger, and hear, "That took the whole top off his head." In the interval of waiting for this chuck to appear, perhaps two or three have recovered from their nervousness and are standing up to get a good view of the visitors. As the rifle cracks, down they go, but finding nothing has happened, they are soon up again, and one after another they fall, to lie in full view in the short grass. If they are too scared to return within a reasonable time, we either have our supper, often having to lay aside a sandwich to have hands free to shoot, or else we drive on a field or two, picking off any ones we see on either side of the road, to return to the original spot and collect the ones we passed up the first time.

We often wonder how much the chucks migrate in this part of the country. For instance we may drive backwards and forwards past a certain field, seeing seven or eight chucks and gathering in the whole of them. We are quite sure there are no more chucks in that field, and yet a week or so later, when we creep slowly along that same wilderness-reclaimed road, there may be half-a-dozen chucks in the same field, near the same holes and furnishing the same amount of sport. I have known this to be repeated in certain fields several times during the season. Do they move about the country early in the morning, entering certain clover-fields, and finding chuck holes in abundance, pre-empt the field until it is their turn to swell the dividends of the ammunition companies? When one can shoot as many as 14, 15 or 16 woodchucks in an afternoon (my Red Letter day chalked up 21 with 22 shots with the Hornet) one does not bother to collect and dispose of the carcasses. After being struck by a high-speed bullet they are seldom attractive things to be handled. I just leave them where they fall, and it is not often that any are to be seen a few days later. My own belief is that there are many more foxes, wildcats, weasels and similar predators living in these woods than even the farmers suspect. If the chuck lies well out in an open field, one will often see a crow making a meal off him, particularly after he has been exposed to the sun a few days to ripen and soften. A hollow point Hornet bullet will blow a hole through the middle of that crow two inches across, and leave but a shell of the head, tail and wings to mark the spot.

Another favorite spot is a field lying a few miles East of Lake Couchiching, off the main traveled road. The best time to arrive is about two hours before sunset. The road runs along the East side of the field, and with the setting sun some 10 degrees above the horizon the chucks stand out in silhouette against the blazing background. It is mighty hard on the eyes to line up a chuck with the sun just behind him. If some shooter has been along a short time before me, I can tell it by the way the chucks make for their holes on my approach. If, however, no one has been along for some time, they usually sit erect, offering perfect targets against the glowing background at distances estimated from 40 to 250 yards. Since the drop of the Hornet bullet at the latter range is something like 11 inches, I do not make many hits at these long distances, just often enough to keep the interest up, and these far away ones do not seem to connect the sound of the distant rifle with anything to be afraid of, as they seldom run before giving the shooter half-a-dozen chances. At the longer ranges the .25/3000 Savage will anchor the chuck with a hold of about five inches high. At the shorter ranges with the crosshairs held for a shoulder hit, there is little excuse for missing one out of 10. In midsummer perspiration may drip into one's eyes, and trickle down the back, and the glare of the setting sun may cause some squinting, but the more unpleasant the conditions are from the shooter's standpoint, the more likely he is to be able to chalk up a good tally. If the day is cold, with no sun, there will be the odd chuck out, but the sultry days, with the sun sinking in a blaze of glory, are the ones when the most kills will be made.

One day I walked across a pasturefield, close-cropped and with a number of chuck holes, and sat down on a convenient rock to watch for a shot. Suddenly close behind me I heard what sounded like a sheep or lamb galloping along the turf. Quite startled, I looked around only to see a chuck coming towards me at full speed. He had not noticed the still figure on the rock until I moved, when he ducked into a chuck hole and immediately stuck his head out to get acquainted; subsequent events interested him no more.

One afternoon I accepted a previously given invitation to a farm which I knew to be well studded with holes and well stocked with chucks. Imagine my consternation to find that they had not waited for me to show up, but had backed a truck up to many of the holes, run a hose from the exhaust into the dens, and gassed the occupants. Fine way to treat a trusting colony of woodchucks, whose only ambitions were to eat clover and furnish shooting for me. Another day as we drove past a sloping field, we caught sight of a young one who had ventured too far from home, and very well he knew it. Up the slope he ran, towards his den, stopping every 10 feet to look back over his shoulder exactly like a child running away from its mother. Because of its youth, we held our fire, and if he was the big one that we bagged there the next spring, he had not increased in wisdom as fast as he had in stature. As we drew up on a grassy side road for supper, we saw a full grown chuck on the top rail of a fence. Rather an unusual place for one to rest; however it did not stay long but leaped to the ground. Here we saw her join five little ones in the grass. Pressure was brought to bear on me not to break up a family like this, but when we came back there a few weeks later, there were no signs of them, so perhaps some other shooter found that the Red Gods had been good to him by handing him six chucks in one place.

Only once have I seen any signs of emotion among full grown chucks, except fear. Shoot one or two, and any others close by will scoot for their holes. But on one occasion I picked off one of two chucks in a pasturefield. They were only some 10 feet apart, and as soon as the first one rolled over, the second ran to it and touched it with its nose. After a minute, during which I held my fire, it started slowly off across the field. A sharp whistle made it pause, and a hollow point Hornet bullet made the pause permanent.

In this locality the chucks certainly seem to be able to recognize me when I drive along. Even before the car comes to a stop they begin to run for their holes, and in some districts there is not one in sight by the time the engine is shut off. In a field there is a large stump perhaps 175 yards from the road. On warm afternoons there was always a big black groundhog stretched out on top, clearly to be seen through the glasses, but not offering a very big target at that range, as they seem to be able to flatten out considerably. Whang! A high-speed bullet would go into the stump beside him, and he would roll off down the reverse side and disappear. Back in a few minutes we could see him ooze up the rough bark and settle down. After a few shots like this he got onto us, and before the car had slowed down his head would come up and by the time the engine had stopped he was gone with a flick of his black tail. It got to be a regular thing to try and get off a shot at him before he disappeared. I do not believe I ever did hit him, but something must have discouraged him, as next spring an examination of the holes around the stump showed spider webs spun across each of them. Perhaps he moved, and was one of five chucks I saw in a nearby field, so close together that all five showed up in the binoculars at one time.

We have mentioned abandoned farms, but have said nothing about the farm which is being worked. Perhaps it is not necessary for me to stay anything, as the farmer will have said it all, and without repeating himself, when he comes out some morning and finds a patch of clover as big as a room eaten down to the roots, or finds the tops of his garden truck, like cabbage, lettuce, peas, beans, eaten off as clean as a cow crops pasture. If this is not sufficient to excite him, walk alongside as he reaps a field of hay, oats or buckwheat. When the knives of his reaper strike stones as large as a turnip, brought to the surface of an innocent-looking field by the chuck as he digs a home, or his horse steps into a den mouth or rear exit and breaks a leg, then you can guess that farming and chucks mix no better than oil and water. The pasturefield is not such a serious problem as neither horse nor cow is too likely to step down into a hole as they graze.

While the majority of my shots at groundhogs have been rather routine affairs, and little out of the ordinary, some few stand out as rather spectacular. Hogs are to be found by the time we have gone three or four miles from home, and knowing the districts in which they may be found, we drive along with eyes on the alert. The following might be an account of a typical groundhog day, easy shots,

OLD WOODCHUCK DEN UNDER CHESTNUT STUMP

This is a perfect example of a well used den under a large chestnut stump. To the author's certain knowledge, chucks have used this den for more than twenty years. They are seen on the mound in the left center and on top of the stump. Author shot his first chuck of 1939 from this location—an old battle-scarred male, almost devoid of hair except for a long orange-red mane, some 3″ long, encircling the shoulders, exactly like the mane of a lion. Two additional chucks were shot from same spot within the following month. This stump is on bare hillside, 125 yards from nearest cover.

Photo by author

hard shots, just as they come.

Having found that they are fairly plentiful in certain fields, we plan our trip so as to go past these good fields. Arriving at the first lot, lying along the railway track, we notice a young one not far inside the fence along the right-of-way. He may be feeding as he goes, which means that he is in several inches of grass or clover, and when his head is down to eat he is really showing a very small area to be hit. An older chuck might be nervous enough to keep watch every few minutes by standing erect, and by that action giving me something definite to shoot at. However, this young one does not know enough to be frightened, so I must either take a shot at what I can see through the grass, or wait until he moves along to where the grass is shorter. Usually I prefer the latter, as it means that he can be seen, and I need not walk over to see if he is dead, or has just slipped down a convenient hole, as he will be lying in full view. I do see this one lying on his back, so we chalk up a hit and move on. The next one is sitting in a burrow dug in the edge of a drainage ditch some six feet above the water. If he gives a quick jerk and rolls down into the water, I can feel sure that his troubles are over.

Next we see a black one sitting erect in a pasturefield perhaps 85 yards away. At the crack of the rifle he subsides, but pops up almost at once. A miss, I think, and try another shot. This time he disappears for good so we walk over to where he was and find two chucks stretched out on the grass. I had killed the first one and its companion had jumped up to see what was going on, and had shared its fate.

Some distance ahead we see a chuck on the road, and at our approach he moves into the ditch and we think he has entered his den. As the car stops we look down and see him not 10 feet away. If he had some salt we could drop it on his tail, but instead we throw a stone near and off he goes at a lumbering gallop. Through some brush, under the fence, and heads for a pile of sand beside a big stone some 50 yards away. Ducks into his den, then turns round and sticks his head out, then emerges and stands erect. I take a steady rest as this is to be a head shot, and a chuck's head is not very large. Of course with the Hornet cartridge, the hollow point bullet striking anywhere near a vital spot like heart or brain means instant death, so I am not surprised to see him subside on the sand, tail jerking a few times and then slowly coming to rest. A minute later another chuck bobs up from a hole on the other side of the stone, and I draw a bead on his head. Another shot, and still I have not connected. Now he has gone down out of sight, so we stop for a few minutes to plan our next move, when out he comes, a young and unwary chuck, to crouch right on top of the stone, a perfect broadside shot. I aim for the bullet to strike the stone half an inch or so below his body, and touch off the trigger. A .250/3000 bullet would make a much more spectacular showing, but the little Hornet bullet glances off the stone and enters the chuck's body in a dozen small pieces. The larger bullet would have raised him three feet in the air, but the Hornet bullet only elevates him six or eight inches. However he is a very dead chuck when he comes down.

Over a slight rise in the road, down into a hollow, and we are approaching the next farm. Our attention is attracted to a small dog of the cur variety, which is dancing about and barking his head off. Of course we stop the car to see what is exciting him so. I have seen some black chucks in my day, but this one was black in color and black with rage. In some manner, while going through the fence, he had managed to get snagged on the barbed wire. The barb had caught in the skin at the back of his neck, and he hung there, hind feet just touching the ground at intervals, jerking and twisting in his efforts to get free. In his rage he had managed to bite his own lips and they were a mass of bloody foam, through which his long yellow incisors showed as he gnashed his teeth. The dog was wise enough not to come within biting distance, but contented himself with a lot of noise. With the aid of a stick I managed to free the little beast, when he made a rush for his hole, over-running it in his hurry, and ploughing a furrow in the sand before he could stop. A few hundred yards further along the road we noticed a pile of fresh sand at the side of the ditch and stopped the car some 10 feet away. Out of another entrance hidden in the grass, and nearer still to us, I saw a small head appear, followed by the rest of a chuck little bigger than a black squirrel. Looked as if he might not be more than six weeks old, and apparently had never had a fright in his sheltered life. If we moved or spoke, he shot out of sight, to re-appear immediately, sit up on his haunches, and stare at us. Had the sun not been behind him, he would have made a nice picture, and until we moved on, some 10 minutes later, he remained in full view and consumed with curiosity as to who we were and what we wanted.

Our farmer friend was trimming out some bushes near the gate, and we asked how the chuck crop was on his land. He said "There's a pair in my woodpile right now, over there—up against the house. They'll be coming inside for a meal, first thing we know." I soon spied his head between two pieces of cordwood, but at the shot, he slipped down out of reach, and I had to help pull the woodpile down to reach him. Not that I wanted him particularly, but the farmer thought he would prefer the body under ground instead of enriching the landscape.

Well, along the road we go for a mile or so, coming to a halt in the shade of a small tree. After a few minutes I sniff—my companion sniffs—we both sniff. I say "Did you bring Limberger cheese with you?" While we are arguing I notice three brownish masses laid out on the top rail of the fence, surrounded by a cloud of flies. Somebody has bagged three chucks and left the evidence where we could see it. Let us move along a piece.

We come to a fence composed of uprooted stumps. The roots have been chopped off, but even so, some of the topmost pieces must be eight feet from the ground. Stretched out in the sun, as high up as possible, lies one of the biggest chucks I have ever seen. Perhaps he was a visitor from the back lots, as he showed very little uneasiness even when we got opposite him, except that we noticed a tensing of his muscles. I had heard that a paunch shot may be as fatal as a lung shot, because the paunch, being full of fluids, transmits the explosive effect of a hollow point bullet to every part of the body. Here was a chance to try it out, so I held in the middle of the abdomen and cut loose. There was a hollow "plop" much like the sound of a kick on a pumpkin, and the chuck rose up into the air, turned right over and subsided in the long grass alongside the fence. Yes, it worked in this case all right. Nothing could have wilted a chuck quicker than did this hit.

The next chuck we see is in a pasturefield perhaps 40 yards away. He lifts his head as we stop, then turns his back and goes on feeding. I have a few solid point copper-cased cartridges with me, and this looks to be a good opportunity to try out their penetration. He is slightly below me, so I hold the post of the scope just above the tail and press the trigger. The chuck collapses as though struck by lightning, with a flip or two of his black tail, and I walk over to see the effect of this bullet. I note where it had entered, striking the backbone, as it happened, and ranging forward, came out near the center of the chest. No wonder he wilted, when the bullet had struck the backbone and probably had penetrated the heart also, judging from the point of exit. And this latter was no larger than the entrance, showing, of course, no mushrooming effect. The 35-grain sharp pointed bullet, driven to at least 2,800 feet per second, had drilled a clean hole through everything in its way. On one or two shots at crows with this same load, I have found it gives clean quick kills, so probably the shock due to extreme speed is sufficient without any mushrooming.

Away to our right we see three chucks, the nearest at least 200 yards away, and the farthest some 50 yards beyond this. I do not often shoot at such long ranges, as it means a long walk across the field to make sure the chuck is dead, and because it is hard to estimate the drop of so small a bullet at these extreme ranges.

However, if the grass is quite short and the chuck easily seen, I do throw a few shots at them. One thing in my favor is that being so far from the road, they are not shot at often, and so not easily frightened. I have to estimate how far to hold over when shooting at say twice the range for which my rifle is sighted, say 100 yards. Here is where I appreciate the value of special equipment on both rifle and scope. I can change the front-sight insert from flat-topped post to a floating bead on a cross-wire, or to a special flat-topped post hanging from the top instead of standing up from below, as described in one of my articles in *Rod and Gun*. With this latter I hold the bottom of the inverted post on the spot I wish to hit at ranges around 100 yards and for longer distances I raise the muzzle until I can see the object clearly and maybe eight inches below the post when reversed from its conventional position. Or if I happen to be using the "X" reticule in the scope, it is easy to raise the muzzle until the chuck shows up directly below the center of the "X" and the necessary distance beneath it. With both these latter sights I can watch for the bullet striking sand, or dirt, as nothing is hidden by any part of the sight, as is so often the case when using other types. And a few hits at these ranges bolster up confidence in both outfit and skill.

Yes, the .22 Hornet is a good all around factory cartridge. Use full loads for chucks and crows, reduced loads for partridge, squirrels and rabbits. A telescope in 3-power with two reticules, one being a crosshair set as an "X," and the other a flat-topped post, help a lot in showing up the chuck when he may be nearly 200 yards away; but at times I find myself leaving the scope at home, and reverting to iron sights—a Watson No. 2 front with flat-topped post or floating gold bead, and a Lyman No. 42 with two different sized apertures, used according to the amount of light left when I shoot.

Up to date I have shot nearly 1,000 chucks, probably 200 with the .250/3000 Savage and the balance with the .22 Hornet cartridge. This is counting only the shots which I felt were clean kills. One summer my total reached 167; another year it was 137; with two other summers totalling over 100 each. However the last two seasons my bag only ran from 20 to 41 so it looks as if I must locate other hunting grounds and give my home district a rest.

I am cherishing a secret ambition to emulate the Iroquois Indian and creep up on a groundhog den, worming my way along the grass, and picking off a few with some .22 Super-X cartridges in my Sportsman revolver. Of course they would need to be close as I am an indifferent shot with a revolver. But it would form a contrast to long range shooting with a rifle equipped with target sights or telescope.

And something that I like to keep always before me is the thought "Let me either kill clean, or miss clean."

It must be all of 40 years since I shot my first woodchuck. He fell to an old single barreled 28 gauge gun using handloaded brass shells and No. 6 shot. I believe he was about 15 feet away. Shortly after that I bought a Marble Game Getter, one of the 1908 models, and its .22 barrel accounted for several chucks. Although the Game Getter's barrels were only 15″ long, and the hollow point .22 cartridges available then were far inferior in energy to present ones of high velocity type, I managed to knock over a number at distances from 20 feet up to probably 60 yards. I did not realize then how lucky I was to make kills with such an outfit, but kill them I did, as well as a number of partridges, squirrels, the odd crow, and many rabbits. The latter I followed on snowshoes until I would come up with them, then shoot.

A Stevens Favorite in .22 rim fire caliber, also laid out a number of woodchucks. It had to be carried on a bicycle, as most of the chuck fields were beyond walking distance from home. After the First World War, but before the Second, I used a couple of Savage rifles in .250/3000 caliber, but as soon as the .22 Hornet cartridge came upon the market, nothing larger would do. Now, after a number of years, when I can look back in my mind's eye to the day when this cartridge dropped 21 chucks with 22 shots, and a summer when a dozen days might average from 14 to 16 chucks per day, I still feel that it is an extremely satisfactory woodchuck rifle.

CHAPTER 13

Crow and Hawk Shooting with .22 Center Fire Rifles

THE AUTHOR IS CONVINCED THAT THE SHOOTING OF CROWS AND destructive hawks with .22 caliber varmint and woodchuck rifles is of more practical value in the conservation and protection of our rapidly disappearing supply of game than any other activity in which the sportsman can engage. It is also a very sporting proposition. Definitely, a rifleman earns every hawk and crow that he kills.

Most game wardens try to do a practical job, and I believe most of them try to do an honest job, within the limits of course of what they have learned they can or can not do by reason of politics or otherwise. There is such a thing as tempering a policy with common sense, and also at times with compassion and a sense of justice. Unfortunately, there are not enough officers of any sort who pay sufficient attention to the latter two features.

As a rule, the average game warden devotes most of his time to other matters than the killing of crows, magpies, owls and destructive hawks. Very few law enforcement officers or game wardens are real riflemen in the sense that you and I regard the term rifleman. A rifleman is a man who is really skilled in the use of the rifle in the field. That presupposes that he has a really accurate and efficient rifle for game protection, and that it is so sighted that a high degree of skill can be put into practical use. Very few game wardens own such an outfit, or ever did own one, and have still less likelihood of soon being supplied with such an outfit by the State or Department by which they are employed. And if they were so equipped, not one in 20 without considerable training and instruction could use such an outfit with any degree of success.

This puts the whole matter of varmint destruction right back on the doorstep of the individual sportsman who is a really skilled and successful varmint hunter and has a proper outfit and, most important of all, knows how to use it and has frequent opportunity to manifest his skill. One of the purposes of this book is to sell you on the idea that such shooting is really worthwhile, how it can best be done, what it can successfully be done with, and the equipment needed to produce results.

There is no question that in most parts of the United States crow, hawk and varmint shooting is a year-round sport. It knows no closed season. It keeps you in constant shooting trim. Knowledge that you are primarily shooting varmints, particularly crows, sharp-shin and other chicken hawks, sets well with most farmers and landowners, particularly those who raise corn, poultry, or anything upon which such varmints live.

The sections herein devoted to crow, hawk and varmint shooting with .22 caliber rifles present a clear picture of the subject, and exact specifications of the rifles, cartridges, bullets, sights, shooting rest and other equipment which will produce deadly and consistent results in the field are all outlined.

Readers should be told and retold the facts in regard to this situation. Our game is being needlessly destroyed 365 days in the year by varmints which constantly persecute and pursue it. It does not make sense to spend millions of dollars of the sportsmen's license money in operating splendidly equipped state game farms, run in most instances by experienced, capable and enthusiastic game keepers, and then turn loose the game produced at an age and at a time of year when it is most helpless to defend itself against winged and ground predators without any systematic and state-wide program for protecting it from these predators after it has been released.

In recent years we have been publicized and ballyhooed by various game producing and protective associations, some of which have made the most extravagant claims of game increase. Yet the shooting conditions the following gunning season, as compared to the past, the three years previous, and the five years previous gunning season, is frequently not only not any better but is often definitely worse.

Also, anyone knows that adjacent to a large game farm such small game as pheasants and mallard ducks ought to be much more common than 50 or 100 miles distant from where either are raised. On numerous occasions friends of the author have hunted the immediate vicinity of large and presumably well handled state game farms, using well trained bird dogs and in some instances have either found very few birds or have raised nothing at all. There is something wrong with such a situation. In a large number of instances it is because varmints of all sorts, hawks, crows, house cats, field-roaming dogs, mink, weasels, and whatnot congregate around the vicinity of game farms and grab and eat practically everything which gets out. The officials try to protect what is inside the wire but what gets out now and then must fend for itself; all too frequently it does not last long.

The same situation exists in regard to coyotes and foxes preying on wild fowl raised in pot holes and small lakes and dams erected by sportsmen's money, and rarely is anything systematically done to kill them off; large owls, hawks, and weasels add their toll. Snapping turtles, mud turtles, water snakes and what have you, live off the game so raised. The sportsman must kill off this varied collection of varmint life or face a future in which there is much talk of abundant game, but very little public shooting of such game, which exists largely on paper and in the minds of people who like to talk effusively without too much attention to all of the facts. The varmint control problem is a most serious one with which the shooter himself must deal.

Mr. Reader you will have to protect some of the game in your own shooting area, or you are not going to have too much game there to shoot. Your scope sighted, small bore rifle is the weapon which will do much of this work for you, with greater success in *your neighborhood* than will any similar expenditure of money, effort or time.

It is necessary to kill crows by the *dozen*—by the *hundreds* annually, to show progress. Shooting two or three a year, is only a drop in the bucket.

The riflemen who have written this part of the book are all particularly skilled at crow and hawk shooting with rifles. Read this section carefully, study each part of it systematically and apply it to your own individual and local problems. Crow shooting, as it is described here, *gets results*.

SUCCESSFUL CROW SHOOTING WITH .22-CALIBER HIGH SPEED RIFLES

By A. R. Weeks.

In every sport the accomplishment of the unusual is that which provides the greatest thrill. This axiom applies to varmint shooting with special force. As the rifleman's skill and equipment improves, his pleasure springs from longer shots at harder targets. An experienced shooter armed with a high velocity scope sighted rifle would no more think of potting an unsuspecting woodchuck at 25 yards, than he would of blasting Junior's cocker. He would, in such instance, walk off a couple of hundred yards or so and then try for the chuck at a range where, if a kill were made, he would feel the satisfaction of having made a good shot.

Fortunately for the modern small bore rifleman, one of the most difficult and exasperating targets—something like four times as hard to hit at any range as a groundhog—is found almost everywhere in gratifying numbers. This target's abundance is in no way due to the fact that it is a particular friend or benefactor of mankind. Neither is it cherished because of any vocal or ornamental qualities. Indeed it is a thief, a bully and a sneak cloaked in a certain brazen insolence. It is hated and feared by all small birds, cussed and despised by man; yet it persists and even increases throughout the land. The very qualities responsible for this survival elect this target, which is none other than the common crow, to the very front rank as game worthy of the rifleman's skill.

Inquiry will reveal that the majority of the casual shotgun and .22 rim fire hunters one encounters while afield have *never* shot a crow, a tribute in itself to this gentleman's ability to look after himself. Since I have been successful in shooting with the rifle a total of over 4,300 crows in the past eight years, using the R-2 type of rifles, Mr. Landis suggested that I contribute something about what I have learned about crow hunting. I do not claim to be a super-crow hunter or that I can do any better than anyone else with comparable equipment and experience. It so happens that because of the nature of my work I have opportunity to shoot some crows several days each week during the year and this adds to my total bag.

Three articles of equipment are essential for successful crow shooting: First; a really accurate rifle having a flat trajectory and with a good telescopic sight attached. Second; a first class crow call. Third; a means of getting around the country. A fourth desirable instrument is a chuck rest. Mine consists of a golf club shaft having a hard steel point on the end and an adjustable rubber topped V-block which can be anchored by a set screw at any height desired. It can be carried by a leather thong on the wrist and being very light is no trouble at all. Thrust into the ground it forms a solid support for the forearm, is invaluable on long shots and much quicker to use than the sling.

To deal with the rifle: since a flat trajectory is imperative, the cartridge must have a high velocity, but flat trajectory is useless unless coupled with extreme accuracy. Few people, until they have actually picked a crow and surveyed his knobby form have any idea of what a scrawny bird he is. Hidden under the coarse black feathers is a body about two and three-fourths inches deep and five inches long. Therefore, despite all other virtues a rifle will consistently kill crows only as far as it will regularly, under hunting conditions, place its bullets into an area of this size or less. Indeed, to allow any margin at all for other inevitable errors encountered in actual game shooting, the vital accuracy requirement is no more than two and one-half inches. Furthermore, the arm must possess the ability to put these shots into the given area *every day*. This entails the maintaining of a constant zero. Accordingly, the 200-yard crow rifle must be quite a firearm. To shoot *many* crows such a 200-yard rifle is required.

To illustrate the paramount importance of superb accuracy consider the following facts. I have worn out several R-2 Lovell barrels. One of these, a 28″ No. 3 Octagon relined by Charles Diller, fitted and chambered by Charles C. Johnson, of Thackery, Ohio, was a perfect jewel. On calm evenings it would consistently group 10 shots into one and three-fourths inches or less, with nine of the shots in about one and one-fourth inches, at a range of 200 yards. I often wondered what it would do in the hands of a bench rest marksman of the caliber of the late C. W. Rowland. It certainly was one of the most accurate barrels on this continent. It was so good, in fact, and I took so much delight in shooting small groups with it that at least one half of its life span was expended in this way when it should have been devoted to field work exclusively. This marvelous accuracy, incidentally, held for 6,600 rounds. The outfit was pure poison on crows up to 225 to 230 yards and killed a good many at 250 yards and beyond.

My game book shows that day after day under all kinds of weather conditions, it registered about 80 per cent hits. When it missed, I knew whose fault it was. Compare this with another of my R-2 barrels. This other barrel, not a relined job, could not be depended upon to keep its shots within a two inch circle at 100 yards, or a four and one-half inch circle at 200 yards. Furthermore, it was exceedingly sensitive to any component change in the loads. While it was chambered by Mr. Johnson in the same way and for the same efficient cartridge as the Diller relined barrel, it blossomed forth as only a 125-yard crow rifle.

As during the time that I used it, I continued to shoot at crows over the same long ranges as before, my percentage of hits dropped below 50 per cent. This of course was most disappointing. Not only that, it soured my disposition and probably jeopardized my chances of a comfortable and happy life in the hereafter. This extended experience conclusively proves that even if a rifle has a velocity of 4,000 f.s. or more, it would still be only a 150-yard crow rifle if at that range it took a two and one-half- or three-inch circle to contain its shots. We now have available rifles whose trajectories are sufficiently flat to make them crow killers at 300 yards but they will not qualify as such until higher standards of accuracy than are now realized are obtained. They will, however, register on woodchucks at extremely long ranges because of the much larger target that a woodchuck presents.

Given an arm of the select type described, it should be equipped with a high grade scope of at least six power. Such telescope sights are expensive but the purchaser has the satisfaction of knowing that they seldom wear out. A high power scope with bright lenses will not only facilitate a much finer aim but will enable the user to discern many crows in the shady interiors of trees where with a small low-power glass they could not be distinguished. As for reticules, the Lee Center Dot is greatly superior to plain crosshairs.

There are a number of good crow calls on the market. All of them will work. At present I am securing fine results with the J. R. Jahn crow call. (This is made for J. R. Jahn, Spirit Lake, Iowa, a very expert trapshooter and one of the most successful crow hunters, with a shotgun, in the United States.) It is practically impossible to learn the use of a crow call by reading the accompanying directions or an article in a book or a magazine. The quickest and easiest way is to allow an expert to actually show you in the course of a few shooting trips. Failing that, the beginner can learn by listening to and trying to imitate the birds themselves and the various calls they use under different conditions. If the rifleman shoots one of a pair, the survivor will promptly put on a fine demonstration of fancy crow talk. This distress call is very effective for shotgun work but in my opinion it keeps the crows milling around too much for successful rifle shooting. However, they may be shot, if close enough, by a shotgun.

When hunting the woodlots as later described, I have the best luck with what I term the "casual" call. It is the talk the crow uses when he drops into a woods and wonders if any friends or acquaintances are around. A series of caws of this inflection and sequence usually brings an answer and if the newcomer does not show up the local inhabitants come out to see where he is. Since they have not been alarmed or excited they usually have no hesitancy in settling down in some convenient tree top for a look around and a few caws. Right there is the rifleman's chance! To me one of the sportsman's most beautiful sights is a jet black crow outlined against the sky with an infinitely blacker Lee Dot forming a medallion on his breast.

The simplest way to shoot crows, but not so simple in war time, such as we have rather recently been through, is to cruise around the rural areas in a car and watch for them in the fields, trees and on fence posts. A point here is worth noting. If the car is stopped *before* reaching a spot opposite a bird he probably will hold his ground. Stop the car directly opposite him or after driving past and almost invariably he takes wing and waits not on the order of his going. If a shot at a crow is available but not seen in time to stop the car as suggested, it is better to drive up the road, noting his location, then turn around and come back with all preparations made.

One of the most productive methods of building up a good day's bag is to work the woodlots. In this system the best available hiding place is selected from which the tallest tree near the woods' edge is visible. To increase the probability of getting more than one shot, it is preferable to locate the stand 150 yards or more away from the tree in which the crows are expected to alight. It is also important to have a steady shooting position from which to aim. I usually lie down under a bush and stick my chuck rest in the ground. If any response to the call is secured, the crows will circle around overhead once or twice and seeing nothing will fly back to the woods to scan the situation. The place selected from which to do the looking is almost invariably this tallest tree. No time should be lost in putting the Lee Dot on one of the black rascals and letting him have it. *Immediately* the shot is fired begin frantically blowing the call. If this is properly done the now alarmed and excited crows, instead of heading for parts unknown, will often circle wildly about and alight again to afford another shot. If the first shot were a hit and any of the surviving brethren saw the deceased fall the chances of more shots are exceedingly good. Whatever his faults, the crow is loyal to his kind. The companion's outraged cries frequently attract all the crows for miles around and on one occasion I killed seven in this fashion before the survivors cleared out. Usually, however, two or three from one stand is about the limit of shooting. It is now opportune for the rifleman to pull up stakes and find another good location. Of course, at many woods he will get no response to his calling. In an area containing a number of likely woodlots it pays to stop for a while and to listen to find in which place the crows are holding forth at the moment. Their cawing and scolding will tell you!

A third method seems to be crow shooting deluxe. In the spring and early summer the birds are widely scattered; each woodlot generally harboring a few crows. But after the young are old enough to keep pace with the parents the various families will drift, in late afternoon, toward a central roosting place, there to be joined by other families to form flocks of 50 to several hundred. These rookeries are usually in sizable woods composed of relatively low but thick trees. In my home district each roost seems to serve an area about 10 miles in all directions. They can be easily located by following bands of crows in the evening. The same one is used year after year. The birds do not go immediately into the roost itself but congregate nearby in favorite clumps of tall trees for the daily pow-wow. Observation will disclose that the same trees are used each day for the council meetings. They will fool around these places for a number of hours, not going into the rookery until dusk. If the hunter takes the trouble to locate these favored trees he can go out before the evening flight begins, find or build an inconspicuous blind 150 yards to 200 yards away, stick his chuck rest in the ground and prepare himself for some really nifty crow shooting. As the families and small flocks drift in from time to time he will get shots at almost every one. I count on getting from six to 12 crows on each visit to the local roost five and one-half miles from home. On September 19, 1943, I had 19 shots, bagging 16 crows. However, it is important not to worry the crows too often in this way and I have found that once every week or so is plenty, otherwise they will organize a new roost some other place. The local roost used to be in a bush only two miles from town, but by over-shooting I forced its abandonment. It is also bad practice to shoot at crows in the actual rookery. Better and more prolonged sport is had at the assembly points. It is also necessary to make certain that the crows never see you prowling around the place. It has been my experience that crows are not unduly alarmed at a rifle report unless they see it is coupled with a human being. Of course they fly at the report but if their sharp eyes can detect no sign of man in the vicinity, they will return. It is also advisable, after the crows are settled for the night, to gather up the deceased or they will thereafter avoid that spot.

The persistent crow hunter will see many examples of this bird's sagacity. As often as not the rookeries are to be found in city parks, golf links or game preserves. Only this past summer on two occasions when I put up families consisting of papa, mamma and three juveniles before I had time for a shot, the offspring being young and innocent, did not follow the parents toward the distant woods, but stopped in nearby trees in spite of vociferous orders from headquarters. On each of these particular occasions just as my Center-Dot was settling down on a victim, through the scope I saw mamma or papa fly headlong down on a victim—the most conspicuous youngster and literally knock him from his perch. What a scolding he got as he was herded off to safety!

I am also certain that individual crows, like many other birds, return to the same locality after migration. About two miles from town, down a road which I often travel, is a large woodlot. From the center of this bush projects a very tall dead elm. It cannot however, because of the general height of the surrounding trees, be seen from a point closer than about 225 yards. Every evening during spring and early summer for some years the dead elm top contained the figure of a crow. He seemed to park there enjoying the sunset as a man sits on the front porch relaxing with the evening paper. I missed this one three times, twice with the Hornet and once with the Lovell and nearly had the sight on him a couple of times more. From then on I will swear he knew my car. He would always fly down into the woods when I was still about 400 yards distant. It got to be a sort of game. I have even taken friends out to show them that he would sit there without budging when cars ahead passed by, but let mine cross the deadline and down into the woods he went. I finally shot him, not without a pang of regret. I killed him by coming up from behind the woods on foot. But now I really miss him as no other crow has adopted the big elm in his place.

There is no crow shooting in my district during the winter. They migrate about November first to the corn growing counties of Kent and Essex near Windsor and Detroit, 150 miles West of my home. Evidently they also fly Southeast across Illinois, Indiana, Ohio and Pennsylvania from Ontario, and may spend the winter feeding in cornfields in Dauphin and Cumberland Counties in South-Central Pennsylvania where the author has shot dozens of crows on the snow in winter.

The crows not killed during the winter invariably return to their home district in Ontario between February 22–25. March and April are good months as the crows are scattered everywhere in pairs and in fours. Also, during this mating time one of a pair killed usually brings a shot at the other and I have frequently killed a whole quartette. During May and early June crows are hard to find. While the nesting is on they are sly and furtive and stick to the woods where they busy themselves raising their own brood and eating the eggs and young of smaller birds. May is a pleasant month and I hunt as much as possible then with the fervor engendered by beautiful days and a long dormant trigger finger, but my records show small bags during these months, especially during May. The cream of the shooting is during July when the young ones, bursting with youthful appetites, are everywhere in the fields with their parents. The average family I find is five, of which three are young crows. As summer wanes the families unite into small flocks, still later into larger and larger flocks until the general roost harbors thousands of birds coming from many miles from all directions. Then comes the sad day when over night the crows have left for the winter feeding grounds.

In the foregoing I have tried to describe some of the successful methods of hunting crows. There is, however, one thing more. We will say that the reader has one of those rare and priceless weapons, a rifle that will *consistently* group into one minute of angle. It will hold its sighting from day to day. It is not sensitive to changes in shooting positions or to minor variations in loads. Its trajectory is so flat that over 200 yards the bullet never rises over one and one-fourth inches above the line of aim nor drops more than one and one-half inches below. It is equipped with the finest telescope sight. The shooter is a good holder and is adept at finding steady shooting positions. There it is—*everything*. According to the gun catalogs and nice diagrams and figures on paper, every crow shot at up to 200 yards is a "dead pigeon." Alas, such is not the case. There is the joker. The joker is a lateral deviation which is very hard to figure and which may be anything from an inch to a couple of feet. It is caused by the breezes that are present in some measure almost every day. In fact, in this area along the north shore of Lake Erie a perfectly calm day is a great rarity. The usual winds seem to run from 10 to 25 M.P.H. The uninitiated will be amazed at the bullet drift encountered under these conditions. Also, it must be remembered that a gentle wind which would not bother much in woodchuck shooting would, if not allowed for, cause a high percentage of misses on a target as small as a crow. I have expended hundreds of shots on life-sized tarpaper crow silhouettes checking the amount of drift encountered from winds of varying strengths and directions. It has as well been my frequent practice to carry one of these dummy crows mounted on a small board equipped with spikes to set upright in the ground. If a miss results from, I think, misjudgment of wind drift, this target is placed on the spot recently vacated by the crow and the shot repeated with the same hold-off. In this way the errors can be discerned and practice like this works wonders. I have often accumulated a nice bag of crows on days when a considerable gale of wind was blowing. Of course the percentage of hits is lower but there is a great thrill in the kills made. Some of these birds were spotted clinging with might and main to fence posts across fields and some were knocked over by shots on which the hold-off was close to two feet. The baseball pitcher with his curve or the golfer with a chronic slice instinctively learns to make a correcting allowance. Just so can the rifleman with constant practice form a sort of mental picture of the curve his bullet will take, due to drift in a strong cross wind. Believe me, windy-day shooting is real fun.

I have written this material with the idea of telling how to shoot a large number of crows. The methods described in this chapter have been devised by Charles Parkinson, of London, Ontario, Canada, and me. Charley is a great hunter and a very fine shot and he and I shoot together a good deal. He would kill as many crows as I do, except that he only goes hunting on Saturdays, which most fortunately, is not the limit of my opportunities. Sometimes he is able to go along on holidays and on the long summer evenings. Parkinson is also an expert wing shot on partridges and pheasants.

At present he is shooting a very accurate Winchester single shot .219 Zipper. He has shot most of the .22 wildcats. We find cartridges like the .220 Swift, .22 Varminter and such to be too noisy for these parts as they tend to arouse the antagonism of farmers. However, for some long range shooting they are necessary.

It is often a question which caliber is to be preferred. I believe that a .22 R-2 Lovell, if of absolutely gilt-edged accuracy will, day in and day out, kill just about as many crows as the larger caliber .22 center fire rifles. But it must be *gilt-edged*. Otherwise, the larger rifles have a real edge.

I have seen very long hits made by Dr. J. G. Kirk, Parkinson and others but the miss ratio becomes higher at extreme ranges, and is seemingly somewhat higher at medium ranges than with an extremely accurate R-2. Both Dr. Kirk and Charley Parkinson think that for some reason, probably increased jump of the rifle, the higher pitched report and greater muzzle blast, it is more difficult to land on a target as small in area as a crow when using the larger cartridge .22s. This despite the fact that from bench rest some of these rifles are exceedingly accurate.

It should be mentioned here, probably, that for crow shooting the rifle should be decidedly muzzle heavy. On one occasion, deciding to stop lugging around so much metal I had a barrel made with a beautiful taper to a comparatively small muzzle diameter. To pick such rifle up and point it around, it sure felt like a honey! But I never could get that rifle to settle down and stay there like the old No. 3, 28″ octagon barrel. It always had to be *held*, something often extremely difficult to do in poor shooting conditions. A crow 175 to 200 yards away is such a very small mark that the bullet must be gotten away absolutely correct or you do not kill the crow. It really requires X-ring shooting.

The greatest number of crows I have ever killed in one day was 29. This I have done on two occasions. Charley Parkinson killed 31 upon one occasion this last year. My best single day's run was 18 consecutive hits at all ranges up to a little over 200 yards. Fired 20 shots that day, and killed 19 crows. On June 12, 1941, I killed nine crows with eight shots, had no misses and made one double, exceeding my previous record of eight crows with seven shots on April 18, 1940. Second best single run for one day, shooting without a miss, was on March 20, 1942 when I bagged 13 without a miss. The longest shots were paced that day, and were from 140 to 230 yards. The best mixed bag was in company with Charley Meredith. We hunted the beautiful hilly area of Southwestern Ontario near Orangeville. That day I fired 38 shots, feathered three crows, killed 16 crows and bagged 15 woodchucks. Some of these shots were at very long ranges, around 250 yards. These "best" days, you will note, were when I had the Johnson-Diller barrel.

THE CROW

THE MOST COMMON TARGET OF THE VARMINT HUNTER

Crafty, with a knack of keeping just out of shotgun range, or of flying a moment before the hunter can aim and shoot, the crow is a favorite target of the rifleman who uses a high velocity .22. Few birds are as destructive to the eggs and young, of insectivorous birds and game birds, including wild fowl, as the common crow. It is with real satisfaction therefore that the shooter places the crosshairs on the butts of the wings of this black rascal, and presses the trigger!

Photo Courtesy, Bureau of Biological Survey

The longest kill I ever made on a woodchuck was at 354 yards. I had three shots at him. The farthest crow was 275 yards. The best work I ever did with the rifle, shooting in an absolute gale—about a 35–40 mile wind according to the Beaufort Wind Table was on July 11, 1942. This was in the Kawartha Lakes district of North Central Ontario. I killed 16 crows and eight chucks out of 28 shots and was holding off a foot or more on the majority of these shots. My best month was July 1941 when I ran up a bag of 169 crows and 96 chucks. I spent two weeks of my vacation then in visiting and hunting with many of the rifle shooting enthusiasts in Southwest Ontario. My best day on chucks was May 6, 1939, when, hunting with Charley Parkinson and "Bus" McLeod, West of London, Ontario, I rang up 33 chucks; Charley got 29 with his Lovell, and McLeod a smaller number with his .257 Roberts which had not as yet been "tuned up."

My scope is an 8X Fecker with 1⅛" objective, in Fecker one-fourth inch mounts and with the crosshairs fitted with Lee ⅝" Floating Dot. Rifle is a Hi-Wall single shot Winchester with single set trigger, which incidentally functions perfectly. The rifle originally was a .38–90 express. It has a Mann-Niedner type firing pin, shortened hammer fall, hammer is also lightened and main spring tension correspondingly increased. The action work was all done by Charles C. Johnson. Maurice Atkinson, of Streetsville, Ontario, stocked it with beautiful crotch walnut from my home district.

With the "bumblebee" barrel this was the finest shooting rifle I had owned up to that time, and in fact, until a .22–303 Varmint-R in 1945, was much the best crow rifle I had seen in action. A rifle which will rather uniformly shoot less than two inch groups at 200 yards, is what is actually required to kill consistently crows at long ranges. In this, I had a rifle and outfit which would fulfill the conditions. I would suggest a somewhat similar rifle to those who would like to accomplish results in field and forest. In the land of the Maple Leaf we have good shooting and we hope to keep it so by practical varmint control. Where there are too many hawks and crows, small game and wildfowl do not have a chance. In the Western duck breeding areas coyotes are also a menace and a slightly more powerful rifle like the .22–303 Varmint-R is the type for shooting coyotes.

Probably our most effective varmint control is with .22-caliber high velocity scope sighted rifles. These should best be in the hands of men who have developed as riflemen until they are very successful field shots. Varmint shooting with rifles is a sport of its own. It needs X-ring equipment and a rifleman who will develop the skill and experience so that he can use that rifle effectively. You will find many things in crow shooting with the .22 that will test your skill and require the best that is in you, but in the sport obtained it is worth the price, and it is worth the effort!

MR. WEEKS' CROW AND WOODCHUCK TOTALS

A. R. (Ray) Weeks of Tillsonburg, Ontario, a contributor to *Rod & Gun in Canada*, and other shooting magazines, has supplied the following records of kills on crows and woodchucks, as taken from his record books on field shooting.

 1941: 604 crows with the rifle; 168 with a shotgun, in wing shooting; 292 woodchucks with rifle.

 1942: 745 crows, all with the rifle; 185 woodchucks.

 1943: 452 crows, all with rifle; 84 woodchucks.

 1944: 557 crows, all with rifle; 111 woodchucks.

 1945: 580 crows; all with rifle; 98 woodchucks.

 All the above with the R-2 rifles.

SUMMARY

This totals 3,106 crows and 770 woodchucks with the rifle within a period of five years.

Weeks reports that his best R-2 Johnson-Diller barrel, which was a relined job on a Winchester Hi-side drop lever action, became inaccurate suddenly, and as mentioned previously, between 6,600 and 6,700 rounds. It fired two 10-shot groups at 200 yards that measured one and three-fourths inches and one and thirteen-sixteenth inches and the barrel then failed after another 100 rounds.

His second Johnson-Diller barrel was the finest he ever owned up to that time, but the first was also a splendid barrel and quite accurate, but a third barrel, as commented upon, bored by a different maker did not give the same degree of consistent accuracy. This was of war time steel and that maker had complained to the author of difficulty in boring such material. Afterwards he obtained much better steel.

The author would like to call particular attention to the rifle barrel rest, light, easily and conveniently carried, which Weeks describes in his story. Very similar rests were used by the late Dr. Franklin W. Mann, and the late Dr. Henry A. Baker, for woodchuck shooting. They have been used to some extent in Scotland for shooting stags. Also, now and then in Ontario, and in New England. I have not heard of them having been used in other places; there could of course, have been instances.

Such portable shooting rests for hunting have been made with a top V rest, or with a U rest on top, in other instances with a bar sliding up and down on a central pin or rod. The rifle barrel rest can be fastened at any desired height to give the proper level of rifle barrel for field shooting. This height will depend upon the build of the rifleman, upon whether he shoots prone or sitting, or possibly kneeling (but usually prone), and upon the distance to the mark and its height above the ground level, as these two distances are the base and the altitude of the triangle the hypotenuse of which is the distance across which the rifleman aims and the path of the bullet is that, plus the trajectory curve.

Rests of this type will be found more beneficial to those of moderate holding ability, and of nervous and excitable temperament, than to the old seasoned match shooting expert. But they are helpful also to him and especially when the ground is muddy or wet and he wishes to assume some other shooting position than flat-down prone.

LATE 1944 AND 1945 CROW SHOOTING
By Ray Weeks.

Regarding additional crow shooting with the R-2, that is after October 15, 1945, I only shot one more that year as the birds migrated while I was up North on a duck hunting expedition. We intended, during November, to make a trip to their wintering grounds in Kent and Essex counties but the early and unusually heavy snow washed out the plan.

I did knock off a few hawks for lack of something better to do, so wound up 1944 with a total bag of 557 crows, 111 woodchucks, 22 hawks and one European hare. The snow was so heavy, and persistent last winter, that the jack hunting cancelled out too.

In 1945 the first crows appeared right on schedule on February, 24 and I had two shots, killing both birds, one at 150 yards, and the other (some poor, unsophisticated brute) at a murderous 35 yards. On March 7 I had a crack at the first chuck, which I overshot on a long try. Saturday, March 10 was a dull day with only light winds and the rifle, still a R-2, performed very well indeed, accounting for 13 crows and one chuck at ranges running from 150 to 235 yards. Another particularly good day was on April 14 when I killed 17 crows and three chucks, the shots running up to 225 yards with five misses. Up to May 5, at which time I began using the .22–303, the R-2 brought down 116 crows, 25 chucks, five jacks and one large predator hawk.

Hunting with the .22–303 this year has been a most interesting, pleasurable but at the same time somewhat disappointing experience. This caliber, to all intents and purposes the Gebby Varminter, is astonishingly accurate and efficient. But, I have come to the conclusion that, if I had to hunt crows for a living in Southwestern Ontario, I would choose no rifle other than the R-2.

In the first place, I have always felt that around 225 yards is what might be called the maximum sure-hitting range on crows, no matter how excellent the rifle or the marksman. This theory was based on the fact that a crow actually presents a two and one-half inch scoring circle. In hunting crows we do not do our shooting from a bench rest so we have to acknowledge some errors in holding. Also there are winds of infinite strengths and directions to dope with plus daily variations in sighting, which all count in this case, no matter how minute. However, every rifleman feels that some little touch of magic is incorporated in his new and wonderfully efficient weapon so I thought that this baby would defy the commonsense reasoning outlined above. Truth to tell, it has done better than could be reasonably expected and is mighty tough on 250-yard crows. This is a fortunate circumstance as a great many shots are had at that very range.

This country hereabouts is quite symmetrically laid out in 40-rod fields. Sentinel crows have a pronounced tendency to park on top of a post across these 220-yard fields. The distance from the road plus an angle across the field usually adds up to about 250 yards. The .22–303 is much more deadly on these shots than the R-2 and even more so if there is much of a wind blowing. Accordingly it is not on this score that I would turn down Varminter-class cartridges as crow outfits.

The entire drawback lies in the loud and wicked report. Witness the following instances: One of my favorite pastimes was to go out to the local crow roost in the evening, park under a certain bush about 175 yards from the daily "pow-wow" trees, ensconce my rifle snugly on the chuck rest and happily indulge in some fancy "armchair" crow shooting. I used to figure on from six to as many as 16 birds in one evening at this pleasant little game. Not so with the .22–303. One shot out of this baby and all the crows clear out to some other woods. Not only that but they will shout vociferous warnings to any latecomers that might be blithely heading to the old stand. I tried moving my blind back to a full 250 yards but still no dice. This reaction occurred so often, and so invariably, that the cause could not be doubted.

Again, when mama and papa still have their three offspring firmly under their wing a scoring shot on one member of the family, from a respectable distance away, is practically certain to bring other cracks at the mourning survivors. I have, in fact, not infrequently killed four out of the five, with the R-2. Such never happens with the big cartridge. The sharp report and the splitting rip of the bullet through the air plus the hellish plop of the missile against the stricken bird instantly banishes all thoughts of kith and kin. The rest disappear in a blur of frantically beating wings.

Some people think that a crow cannot fly fast. I would like to have had these skeptics watch the jet-propelled performance put on by four of these sooty rascals on July 2, 1945. It was a public holiday, "Dominion Day" and I was, in company with my springer "Kim," hunting in the sandy country a couple of miles North of Lake Erie. Kim always goes on these crow hunts but just for the ride, as it were, as he will not go within three feet of a dead one. Anyway, I saw a quintette of the birds parked in a treetop in an old orchard. I sneaked down the bush-grown fence row to within about 200 yards of the proposed victims. Lying on the ground I stuck the chuck rest into the earth and shoved the rifle muzzle out through the golden rod in malicious anticipation of a genuine massacre. A perfect setup, or so it would have been with the R-2. Through the scope I looked the birds over to see which one appeared to be the leader and therefore the one to knock off first. The selected victim had his back to me. The Lee Dot settled amidships and I touched the set trigger. At the crack that crow literally flew into bits and tatters—fragments showering down on the other four. In 10 seconds said four were but specks in the sky. Their home woods was about one-fourth mile distant but they never even paused as they passed over it.

When I went over to inspect the deceased I found morsels of him a good 25 feet beyond the tree. The execution was wrought by a 50-grain 8S bullet marching along at some 3,800 f.s. ahead of 36.5 grains No. 4064. I have noticed, by the way, that a crow struck in the back will usually fly apart in this way. However, I am confident that if the R-2 had been doing the shooting that the remaining birds would not have been terrified to any great extent but would have been more concerned about the unnatural demise of one of their number. Particularly so in cases like this where no human or car are to be seen. Crows are not unduly alarmed by the report of a rifle of moderate intensity, unless they see a man in the immediate vicinity. The first time that I noticed this was when I began shooting the Lovell. One day I was coming down a steep hill, leading into the river valley when I saw a chuck on the hillside about 150 yards to my right. I fired at and killed the chuck, continued on for but a few yards, looked up the river to the left and there were two crows blissfully pecking away at something on the ground and totally unmindful of the R-2's report, the echoes of which had scarcely died. I was so astonished that I could not get unlimbered before the birds saw me and took off. Substantially the same thing has occurred many times since.

I was able to attend an affair which was held near Charlie Meredith's bailiwick at Streetsville. Among the rifles in action were several .280s, .257 Roberts, 7mm, .220 Swift and various wildcats, including my own. Meredith had a splendid bench rest and a fine range rigged up, with butts at 200 and 475 yards. There was not sufficient space available for the full 500 yards. It was a beautiful day for shooting except for a mean 10 to 15 m.p.h. cross wind from 10:00 o'clock. A visitor had two very nice .280s with him and had ambitions to shoot one of those fabled Ross postcard-sized groups at 500 yards. Unfortunately, due to the general scarcity of ammunition most of us had to be content with five-shot groups. I know that I heaved a sigh every time that I wasted one of my good 8S bullets on these paper targets. It is undoubtedly true that a five-shot group does not prove the real accuracy of any 10-shot groups. I knew that my rifle would do well at 200 yards but was pretty skeptical about its performance at 475 yards; five and one-fourth inches. Meredith's .280, built by himself with a pipestem barrel was next with a six inch. The barrel was full floated and visibly whipped up and down at least an inch at every shot. Nevertheless, it put them in the groove. My .22–303 was in a class by itself at 200 yards, producing a group one-fourth inch high and seven-eighths inch wide. I shall print a duplicate of this group in this letter. I am sorry that I have never had 20 or 30 WM bullets to spare for 10 shot groups while this barrel is still in its prime. The other contestant was trying to compete with iron sights and could not get in there with some of the other rifles. The Winchester Model 70s in 7mm and Swift also shot very well.

On September 3,—Labor Day—I set out at 6:30 A.M. determined to break my all time record of 29 crows in one day. Kim and I covered about 150 miles through the very best crow country but crept in at dark with only a measly 19. The .22–303 was working well that day and made a lot of exceedingly satisfactory shots, with very few misses. The record was not broken, for two reasons. In the first place I am coming to the sad conclusion that crows are not as thick around here as they used to be. There are more shooters, both shotgun and rifle, after them and I have myself taken over 4,300, along with their unborn progeny, out of circulation during the past few years. In the second place, as I outlined above, I do not get the multiple shots at a flock with the big cartridge that I did with the R-2. This unhappy circumstance was painfully noticeable that day when I was hunting with the definite idea of reaching a certain quota.

Despite all of this argument which I have been making against the bigger cartridges, I readily admit that there is decided thrill in their range and power. *Furthermore*, I do not have to shoot crows for a living. To my mind, the only real disadvantage connected with their use is the fact that the crack is so sharp and sounds so wicked to the farmer behind the hill that anti-gun agitation will progressively increase as more and more of these ultra modern arms go into action. I know that I have already had several farmers complain to me about this rifle, something which had *never* happened with the R-2.

One of the most delectable of all scenes in vermin shooting, to me at least, is the sight of my Lee Dot settling down on a sharpshin hawk. While these vicious little killers are not uncommon in Southwestern Ontario it is seldom indeed that shots at them are obtained. They are not given to sitting around on conspicuous stubs but stay out of view in thick woods. Each summer for some years a pair of them has made their home in a woodlot bordering #3 highway about eight miles west of Tillsonburg. I have seen these particular hawks dozens of times but have yet to get a crack at them. On one occasion I was driving by this bush when something flashed past the car. It was one of those precious sharpshins, hot in pursuit of a small bird, and gaining with every wingbeat. In sheer desperation the tiny bird flew headlong into a brush pile on the woods' edge. The hawk braked his flight with cupped wings, curved over the pile and landed on the ground on the far side. I leaped out of the car with rifle and cartridges in hurrying hands but the hawk was gone in an instant.

On another morning I again saw one of these same hawks pursuing a bird. This time the intended victim took refuge in a nearby stump fence. The little bird ran for dear life, weaving in and out of the twisted roots. Believe it or not, the sharpshin chased savagely after it on foot. Yours truly made the third member in this strange steeplechase, dashing along rifle in hand, vainly trying for a shot at the slate-blue demon. I did not get it, for suddenly the hawk gave up the hunt and darted back to the bush with characteristic speed.

But once in a while we can send one of these slayers to the place where he belongs. On August 6, 1945 I caught one red-handed. I had taken the day off in celebration of the homecoming from overseas of a former hunting pal. We had hunted all morning with very fair success. A certain road runs along a ridge on either side of which and about 400 yards back lie mile-long, heavily timbered swamps. Plenty of crows were in those swamps and frequently scattered bands worked across from one to the other. Two ancient, tall and gnarled old elms near the road formed a sort of halfway resting place. I had shot a crow out of one of these trees as we came up so we decided to hide our car in some bushes back down the road a piece, eat our lunch in the shelter of some hazelnut bushes within range of the trees and watch for any crossing crows during the process. We also had hopes of the dead one acting as a decoy. About 125 yards to our right was a small swale with a few alders and one lone tree; said tree not being high enough for a crow tree.

We were munching our lunches and reminiscing when we saw a sharpshin coming along in pigeon-like flight, interrupted by typical short glides with drooped wings. It darted into the swale, then up into the low tree with something in its claws. "Blast that little devil," exclaimed George. It was his turn to shoot but as there was no time for argument I dropped to the ground and aligned the rifle. Through the scope I could see the wings of a small bird quivering between the sharpshin's claws. I sometimes have the most disgusting habit of missing shots at around 100 to 125 yards but I thought as I set the trigger, "I'm *not* going to miss this dirty little so-and-so."

At the crack he disintegrated into a cloud of feathers. We went over to see what kind of bird the hawk had cought but the swale proved to have about a foot of black wet muck in it so we gave up the attempt. I felt so good about the whole thing that my batting average on crows jumped about 10 per cent for the rest of the day.

My crow score for the year to date is 580, chucks 98. The crows have now left the district for the winter. This coming Friday and Saturday my friend Charley Parkinson and I plan to follow them West to Kent County and get in one more good shoot. I hope, if all goes well, to increase my year's bag by 30 or 40.

SCREEN SHOOTING

Do not know whether or not I told you about my system of "screen shooting." I have an excellent bench rest and 200 yard range on my own property. On this range the rifle in its rest on the bench, the 100 yard butt and the 200 yard butt are all on the same horizontal plane. I also have it rigged up so that I can put a target in where there is a small hole in the exact center on the 100 yard frame. Through this hole I can see a seven-eighths inch black paster in the exact center of a properly positioned target on the 200 yard butt. The aiming point consists of a black circle with one and one-fourth inches white center, on the 100 yard target. In the center of this circle, of course, is the hole through which I can see the 200 yard paster. This scheme gives the most graphic pictures of the trajectories and wind drifts of various rifles and loads.

I had Pettifer, the photographer, take some pictures of the layout. Bullets passing through the thin 100 yard target paper do not seem to be deflected in any way but will register in exactly their proper locations on the 200 yard target. If there is no wind the 200 yard group is invariably exactly twice as large as the 100 yard group.

Pictures were taken of two such groups. These targets were shot during a fairly strong, variable, and puffy wind coming from 12:00 to 2:00 o'clock and you will note the effect which this wind had on the different shots. This load is, by the way, the flattest yet tried in this .22–303 cartridge. It consists of a 50-grain 8S bullet with 36.5 grains No. 4064. With the scope about one and one-half inches above the bore, this load when one inch high at 100 yards, is still five-eighths inch high at 200 yards. This has checked out on four tests made on widely separated occasions.

Below I will print a duplicate of the 200 yard group shot in the match at Streetsville. Load, 50-grain 8S and 35.0 grains No. 4320.

If there is space I shall also diagram the trajectories of a number of different loads in my rifle as taken through the screens. Most of these loads have been checked at least three times. The beautiful part of this system is that the results will check time after time.

Shown below are some rather interesting groups secured when shooting various loads through the screens in trajectory tests. The 100 yard groups are quite small when it is considered that each shot represented an entirely different kind of powder, charge or bullet weight. At 200 yards the characteristics of the various loads began to show up in decisive manner.

There's the story, my friends. The remaining evenings this week I shall have to devote to the loading of a plentiful supply of ammunition for the weekend trip. We are sure looking forward to giving our sable-feathered friends a good pasting.

P.S. I found yesterday that with 50-grain bullet, 35.0 grains No. 3031 gives precisely the same 200 yard trajectory as 36.5 grains No. 4064.

200 yard group
35 grs. #4320–50gr. 8S bullet 10–15 m.p.h. wind from 10 o'clock
Fired August 15, 1945

Shown below are some rather interesting groups secured when shooting various loads through the screens in trajectory tests. The 100 yard groups are quite small when it is considered that each shot represented an entirely different kind of powder, charge or bullet weight. At 200 yards the characteristics of the various loads began to show up in decisive manner.

.22/303 CARTRIDGE
100 yd. impact—all loads—1" high

200 yd. impacts

Target Centers

| 54 gr. Sisk 38.0 grs #4350 | 50 gr 8-S 35.0 grs #4320 | 50 gr 8-S 36.0 grs #4320 | 55 gr Sisk Ex. 35.0 grs #4064 | 50 gr 8-S 33.8 grs #3031 | 50 gr 8-S 36.5 grs #4064 |

Group #1.—FIRED NOV. 6/45

Shots #1 & #2.—50 gr. 8-S, .223″, plain copper jacket
36.5 grs. #4064
Shots #3 & #4.—Same bullets.
36.0 grs. #4320.
Shots #5 & #6.—Same bullets.
35.0 grs. #3031.
Moderate wind from 5:00 o'clock.

Group #2.—FIRED OCT. 20/45.

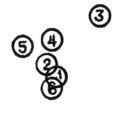

Shot #1.—50 gr. 8-S, .224″, Cadmium-plated. 35.0 grs. #4320.
#2.—   "   "   "   . 33.8 grs. #3031.
#3.—   "   "   "   . 36.5 grs. #4064.
#4.—   "   "   "   . 36.0 grs. #4320.
#5.—55 gr. Sisk Express, .224″   . 35.0 grs. #4064.
#6.—54 gr. Sisk "Wartime," .224″   . 38.0 grs. #4350.
Fairly strong, gusty wind from 4:00 o'clock.

CHAPTER 14

The .22 Caliber Rifles on Crows and Hawks
By Henry E. Davis.

DESPITE ARTIFICIAL PROPAGATION, SHORTER HUNTING SEASONS AND lower bag limits, game is definitely on the decrease in most, if not all, sections of this country today. The genuine wild turkey, grandest of all game birds, is steadily approaching extinction, even in coastal South Carolina, its most favored home. Some of the areas where it formerly abounded know it no more, and even where it still exists, the numbers are scarcely a tenth of those of 25 years ago. To a lesser degree, the same holds true with the bobwhite partridge.

Excessive hunting is but partially responsible for this situation, as it exists where there has been practically no hunting and fullest protection. Adverse weather, flood and flame have contributed, but one of the main causes for this condition is varmints. Foxes, wildcats, hawks, crows, owls, snakes and their kind must eat not merely in open seasons but the year round, and when they take possession of fields and covers, the game vanishes via their maws. This is as inexorable as the laws of the Medes and Persians, yet some crack-brained sentimentalists refuse to see it and still invoke the hoary hoax called the balance of nature. Take it from one who has been dealing with game for more than a half century and who has been managing a great game preserve for years: you can have game or you can have varmints, but you cannot have both in numbers on the same property at the same time.

Space will not permit a discussion of every species of varmints, so what is herein said will relate principally to hawks and crows.

I learned the ways of hawks, crows, owls and company back in boyhood days on a great plantation, and a lifetime of observation has only served to confirm conclusions then reached from actual experience. It is the fashion in some circles to put a halo around the head of the redtailed hawk and to picture him as the beneficent friend who shields the farmer from destruction by the "little tyrants of the field" that such farmer otherwise could not withstand. Well, I own a large farm and my earnest prayer is that I be delivered from the guardianship of all so-called "farmer's friends" whether they be tax-eating politicians and their fawning satellites or game-destroying redtailed hawks!

When I was younger, I killed my share of bobwhites, so let me give you a tip. When you go afield after this fine bird and happen to see an old redtail perched in the top of a tall dead pine standing in suitable cover, take your dog there and you will find your covey. Of course the redtail did not intend to harm them, but was merely protecting them from the rats! No, he was not harming bobwhites, when I have seen him chasing them, and when I have known him to eat every bird out of a covey!

Based on actual experience, I consider the redtailed hawk and the great horned owl among the worst feathered enemies of game we have in this section (South Carolina). The two accipiters, the sharpshin and the Cooper's hawk (we do not have the goshawk this far south), are more destructive of the smaller game birds and young poultry, but they are not as abundant as the redtail and do not so frequently molest squirrels, rabbits, grown wild turkeys and grown domestic fowl. The redtail, despite his apologists, destroys all of these, and not sporadically but consistently.

Recently, one of my friends had a very unique experience. He stopped his car in a strip of woods and just as he did so two hawks, a blue darter (sharpshin) and a redtail, dived into a covey of partridges near at hand. Each hawk missed his aim and the two settled in separate trees not 40 yards away. Seizing his shotgun, my friend killed both hawks, and thereby mightily served the cause of game conservation.

A few years ago, several of us had a flock of 40 domestic young turkey hens of an average weight of eight pounds each. Two redtailed hawks killed eight of these turkeys in just as many days, and both hawks were killed in the act. A pair of redtails killed 19 half-grown turkeys on my farm in one season and escaped unscathed.

On a hunt sometime back I concealed myself in a canebrake and began to yelp like a turkey. A redtailed hawk sailed up and perched about 40 yards away. A charge of No. 6s from the Lewis Magnum ended his turkey hunting forever. Recently, I had a similar experience, but this hawk escaped before I could bring the Hornet rifle into action. With a shotgun I could easily have ended his hunting.

In fact, I could go on and fill this chapter with accounts of the evil doings of this feathered marauder, but shall recount only one more. On one occasion I was hunting turkeys in the swamp of the Great Pee Dee River after the recession of a light freshet. Coming to a depression in a ridge that had been left filled with water by the receding flood, I was struck by the mass of white feathers on the water and stopped to investigate. Lying at the base of a large maple in about eight inches of water was a full grown young wild turkey gobbler with a redtailed hawk lying beside him. What had happened was obvious. During the freshet the turkey had taken refuge in the maple and the hawk had seized him there, and both had fallen into the water and drowned. The raccoons had eaten both the turkey and the hawk, and I had been attracted to the scene by the feathers of the hawk floating on the water. This doubtless is at least a partial explanation of the finding from time to time on our property of the partly eaten carcasses of wild turkey hens the other depredator leaving such evidence being the great horned owl. At any rate, it was the culminating crime of this arch devil, and then and there, like Hannibal of old, I vowed eternal enmity to all his race. Right well has this vow been performed as during a recent three year period a bullet from one of my .22 caliber rifles has ended the bloody careers of just 89 of these sacrosanct killers, and I intend to keep up the good work as long as my eyesight enables me to aim a rifle with accuracy. I know the redtail is positively and distinctly destructive and my advice is to kill him whenever opportunity offers.

To catalogue the sins of the crow, whether of the common or the fish species, is an impossible task. His character is as black as his coat, and like the Norway rat he is all pest. Give 25 crows for two days the free run of a five acre field of watermelons in the ripening stage, and they will make of it an utter ruin. This black pariah, wise and wary, pulls sprouting grain, shucks ears of corn in the milk, steals peanuts from field and shock, and robs pecan orchards. He raids poultry yards and destroys both eggs and young fowl, and from game, song and insectivorous birds he collects heavy toll. As a destroyer of eggs, no creature on earth can surpass a fish crow. Just try to raise guinea fowl or turkeys on a farm infested with them, or even with common crows, and see what will happen. The difference between the two is that the fish crow is vastly bolder and does not hesitate to come right up to human habitations and carry on his robberies there. Then too he will follow a guinea hen or a turkey hen to the nest and rob it just as soon as she has laid the egg and left. The depredations committed by crows on waterfowl in the breeding grounds of Canada are now well known, and in my opinion crows, more than any other factor, are likewise responsible for the increasing shortage of upland feathered game. In fact, a crow does not stop with creatures that wear feathers, but any living thing he can overcome is his legitimate prey. A friend tells me that recently he was attracted by the unusual squeals of a rabbit in a nearby thicket, and went to investigate. Reaching the scene, he found a common crow busily gobbling up a litter of young rabbits, which the frantic mother was helpless to prevent.

Yet, despite all his deviltries, apologists come forward and try to defend the crow with the same old slush as to his being the farmer's friend because he eats a few worms and bugs when he cannot conveniently get anything else. As one farm born and farm reared, and still a farm owner, I prefer the commercial arsenates for worms and bugs, and Jim Crow can not atone for his many sins by excuses like this. When I think of the families of mocking birds, thrashers and others he so ruthlessly destroyed, which, had they lived, would have eaten more worms and bugs in a week than he would eat in a year, his specious pleas fall on deaf ears. He is essentially a sneak thief, a ruthless robber and a merciless murderer, and deserves a bullet wherever found. This is the way I regard him, and the way I intend to continue to regard him despite any sob-sister stuff to the contrary. This "Save the Crow for Posterity" movement is in perfect keeping with all the other vagaries that characterize this insane age. Saddling posterity with every known form of liability is the fashion of the day, and this movement is but another manifestation of such disposition.

Beginning with January 1, 1936, I kept for three years exact records of the game and vermin taken by me with the rifle. These records show in detail not only the game and vermin killed, but the date, the place, the range, and the rifle and load used. Wherever practical, I paced the long shots so as to be sure of the range and not leave it to an estimate. During this period of three years, I killed with a rifle 193 hawks and 528 crows. Of these, 121 crows and 33 hawks were killed with a Winchester Model 52 sporter, using the .22 long rifle high velocity cartridge, both solid and hollow point; 112 crows and 47 hawks with the .22 Hornet; and 295 crows and 113 hawks with the .22–3000 Lovell. From this, it appears that the .22–3000 Lovell alone has taken considerably more than both the other calibers combined; kills at the various ranges have been as follows:

Under 100 yards: .22 rim fire—121 crows, 33 hawks; Hornet, 31 crows, 15 hawks; Lovell, 75 crows, 19 hawks;

100–124 yards: Hornet, 26 crows, four hawks; Lovell, 65 crows, 24 hawks;

125–149 yards: Hornet, 29 crows, 17 hawks; Lovell, 84 crows, 36 hawks:

150–169 yards: Hornet, 15 crows, four hawks; Lovell, 30 crows, 14 hawks;

170–199 yards: Hornet, one crow, one hawk; Lovell, 10 crows, three hawks;

200–224 yards: Hornet, seven crows, four hawks; Lovell, 19 crows, nine hawks;

225 yards: Hornet, two crows, one hawk; Lovell, nine crows, four hawks;

240 yards, Hornet, one crow; Lovell, one crow, one hawk;

245 yards, Lovell, one hawk;

250 yards, Lovell, two crows, two hawks;

275 yards, Hornet, one hawk.

As indicated, the longest killing shot made during this period was at a hawk at 275 yards with a Hornet. The rifle used was a Winchester Model 54 Hornet sighted with Lyman 5A scope, and charged with a load consisting of 11.3 grains Hercules N. 2400 powder, the 40-grain Sisk full-jacketed bullet and Winchester 116 primer. Prior to 1936, with the same Hornet rifle and load I made several kills on hawks and crows at ranges well in excess of 225 yards. However, at ranges beyond 150 yards I found the Hornet to be not as reliable as the Lovell, and especially if there was any wind. For this reason, I used the Lovell more frequently as my vermin rifle.

My best year on varmints was 1938, during which 1 killed 100 hawks and 237 crows. Of these the Model 52 sporter accounted for 92 crows and 28 hawks; the Hornet for 23 crows and 15 hawks; and the Lovell for 122 crows and 57 hawks. That was a good year—I had many opportunities for shooting.

Much of my crow shooting is done on the invitations of farmer friends who, exasperated by their depredations, come in and ask for relief from these pests; and, if possible, I am only too glad to comply with such requests. In such instances I try to reach the scene just after sunrise, which is the best time to call crows, locate a tall open tree in good cover—a dead pine is ideal—and armed with a Model 52 sporter conceal myself about 40 yards from its base. I call with my voice, and as soon as I get adjusted in a good blind, I stage a crow and owl fight; and if there are any crows within a half mile, and they have not been frequently fooled before, I soon have a black mass milling over my head and covering my selected tree. I have had at the same time as many as three different flocks of common crows decoy from different directions, besides a fourth flock of fish crows, with each crow yelling at the top of his voice. Truly bedlam has broken loose when the air is filled with a throng of perhaps a hundred squalling, whirling black forms! Frequently they work themselves into such a frenzy that they will not alight, and at other times they swarm down into the underbrush and some alight almost on top of you. I manage to kill a few of the latter, but I never get any of the former, as I have not been able to develop sufficient skill with a telescope-sighted rifle to kill fast flying crows on the wing. But when they do not become quite so crazy, or do not manifest such extreme caution and freely alight on your chosen station tree,

GOSHAWK SHOT ON HIS KILL

A male Goshawk shot by Bertram Chichester, at a range of 80 yards, and off the body of a ringnecked pheasant it had just struck down and killed. See pheasant and scattered feathers in snow. This Goshawk was killed by a Winchester 52 and a Dominion Whiz Bang .22 l.r. H.P. Bullet.

Photo by Chichester

some real sport is to be had with the Model 52 sporter.

I can recall several separate occasions when I killed with this rifle six crows in succession from a single dead pine. In fact, I did this twice from two separate trees in one morning. On that particular occasion I killed 14 crows before breakfast, 12 with the Model 52 sporter and two at long range with a 2-R Lovell.

Some months ago I called two flocks of crows to a dead pine standing in the edge of a heavily timbered swamp. They perched freely, and I got eight shots with the Model 52 sporter. Six crows dropped to the base of the tree, and the two others flew away, apparently wounded. I did not count them, however, as I did not actually see them go down. All told, I got 10 that day.

Only a few weeks ago, at the instance of a friend who wanted some dead crows to hang up in his field where they were doing much damage in pulling up his corn, I staged a hunt shortly after daylight. Noticing a big dead pine standing some 30 yards back in the very heavy cover of a large creek swamp, I selected it as the scene of operations. After I got set and began to call, two flocks of common crows, one flock of fish crows, and some half dozen hawks came in succession and rested on that lightning-blasted tree. Eight shots were fired from the Model 52 sporter, using high-speed hollow point cartridges, and when the shooting was over, four hawks and four crows lay dead on the ground.

In addition to the .22 caliber rim fire rifle, I always carry on these crow and hawk hunts a Hornet, a K-Hornet, or a Lovell. The long range rifle is used mostly from the car window, and on all shots, whether far or near, that must be taken from such position. A rifle also accompanies me on all of my long car trips, and frequently I take two; and many crows and hawks end their days as a consequence. Once on a round trip of some 230 miles through the Carolina Low Country, I took 10 crows and three hawks with the old .22–3000 Lovell, and four crows with the Model 52 sporter, which I consider a fair day's work.

The Winchester Model 52 sporter, No. 24,267, with speed lock and proof steel barrel, above mentioned, was remodeled by Niedner from a target rifle into a sporter, and then restocked by me with one of the most beautiful pieces of stump black walnut I have ever seen. The barrel is 24″ long and of similar contour to that of the Springfield M-2, with diameters of .637″ at the muzzle and of .850″ at a point three inches from the receiver. The stock is 13¾″ long, with a drop of 1-7/16″ at the comb and 2-9/16″ at the heel, and has a Whelen cheek-piece and a Niedner steel butt-plate. The forearm is of baseball bat shape (such as the author of this book recommends), and is 18⅛″ in length. The bridge was filled in and matted, and one scope base placed on it and the other on the barrel. With the 48 sight and without sling, it weighs 7¾ pounds. It is one of the most accurate arms I have ever shot, holds its zero well, and shows no preference for any particular ammunition. It is by far the best squirrel rifle I ever carried into the woods. I have used almost exclusively the Winchester Super-Speed Staynless greased long rifle hollow point cartridge, because it is easier on the barrel and has fine killing power; but the rifle is just as effective with Super-X. Out of 37 consecutive shots fired with it one summer using Winchester Super-Speed, I got 29 crows and four hawks, a total of 33 kills, and the misses were my fault and not the rifle's.

Besides this special Model 52 sporter, I have two other rifles of this model, a sporter with slow lock and a standard target weight. All three are fitted now with Weaver 440 scopes with Lee Dots, and no better outfit can be found for the .22 long rifle cartridge than any one of the three.

To date I have owned and shot quite a number of rifles for the Hornet and Lovell cartridges. My first good Hornet was a very fine one made from the Springfield .22 caliber target rifle, chambered by Capt. G. A. Woody and restocked by Bob Owen. I next acquired a Model 54, and subsequently a Model 70, in this caliber. Although the Model 54 was extremely accurate, I did not like the trigger pull, so finally sold it. In my hands this rifle brought to bag some 15 wild turkeys. With this rifle I once killed a fish crow in the top of a tree at 257 paces and a common crow on the ground at 277 paces. This latter is the longest shot I ever made with a Hornet rifle. The load used for both of these long shots consisted of 11.5 grains of No. 2400 powder behind the Sisk 6 caliber head 40-grain soft point bullet. This load was recommended to me by my friend the late J. Bushnell Smith, and is really a very heavy one. I would suggest that the powder charge be reduced to 11.25 grains, as I have got good results from such a charge without excessive pressures. After selling the Model 54, I got another Model 70 chambered for the Hornet.

Both of these Model 70 Hornets have been restocked by me, one with a fine piece of French walnut and the other with a piece of bird's-eye maple. The two stocks are exactly alike. They are 13¾" long, of Monte Carlo pattern, with Howe concave cheek-piece and Niedner steel butt-plate. The forearm is 18½" long and of the same shape as that of the standard Model 70 factory stock. The drops from line of bore are: comb, three-eighths inch; at a point seven inches back of comb, three-fourths inch; heel, 1⅜". I gave meticulous attention to the bedding of both barrels and actions, and as a consequence I get the very best performance of which each rifle is capable. Both of these rifles are exceptionally accurate, hold their zero well, and handle all loads with the same scope setting. The scope bases are placed one on the receiver bridge and the other on the barrel a half inch in front of the receiver ring, which is the only installation that is satisfactory with 16″ or shorter telescopes. One October day, with the 40-grain high-speed load in one of these rifles I killed three crows in three consecutive shots at 160 yards. I sight in these rifles to strike one inch high at 100 yards with the factory high-speed 46-grain hollow point load, and so adjusted, they are fairly reliable up to 200 yards with the fastest 40-grain loads.

My best .22–3000 Lovell rifle was built by Lovell in the summer of 1937, and was fitted by me with a stock and forearm of good grade Circassian walnut. The stock had a high comb and Howe concave cheek-piece, and in dimensions and drops followed closely the stocks of the two Hornets described above. This rifle was built on a heavy high-side-wall Winchester single shot nickel steel action, with plain trigger, flat mainspring and lightened hammer, which stopped at half-cock when the action was closed. This last is a very desirable feature. The barrel was 28″ long, had a diameter of 1.10″ at the receiver and for three-eights inch therefrom, where it dropped to a diameter of one inch and then a straight taper to a diameter of .842″ at the muzzle. It had six grooves and six lands, 16″ twist, a groove diameter of .224″, and was tightly chambered for Lovell's standard .22–3000 cartridge. My standard load was first 16.5 grains of HiVel No. 3 powder behind the 45-grain soft point Winchester Hornet bullet, and when it was no longer available I changed to 15.0 grains of No. 4227 powder with the same bullet, each charge fired by the Remington No. 6½ non-mercuric, non-corrosive primer. With both loads, the scope was set so as to have the bullets strike one inch high at 100 yards, and when so sighted in the rifle was good for all ranges up to 225 yards. I found the load with No. 4227 powder even better than that with HiVel No. 3. A more reliable and accurate rifle, in my opinion, can not be built. It weighed 11½ pounds with scope and sling, hence was too heavy for a hunting arm, but for rest shooting at vermin, it was all that could be desired. To show its efficiency, I may say that out of 14 consecutive shots at crows and hawks at ranges running from 100 to 225 yards, I have made 12 clean kills, and the two misses were at the shorter ranges.

But all good things, it seems, must come to an end, and so it was with this super-accurate Winchester. A chance visitor, who came to see my collection of firearms, snapped the hammer and in so doing broke the firing pin. When I sent the arm to Hervey Lovell for repairs, he reported that the bore was slightly rough just beyond the chamber. So I sold it, and ever since have never ceased to regret my action. This was the best rifle I ever owned, and I should have had it rechambered for the R-2 cartridge.

The most accurate .22–3000 Lovell rifle I have ever seen is the Bell rifle, which I own and which is referred to in *Twenty-two Caliber Varmint Rifles* by Landis. This rifle on a Sharps-Borchardt action, has been fitted with a very fine Circassian walnut stock, and I do not use it for the reason that I intend to present it some day to a museum. It is so tightly chambered that it will accept only thin Remington cases.

Another Sharps-Borchardt rifle I own was a very fine crow and hawk rifle in the .22–3000 Lovell caliber. I killed seven crows with it one morning out of seven shots from a car window. None of this was spectacular shooting, but some of it was rather fast and sporty. With this rifle I made the longest shot I ever made with any Lovell rifle. This was on a redtailed hawk which I knocked from the top of a tall dead pine standing 278 paces distant. With the same rifle I once killed a ground hog in Virginia at 277 paces. I subsequently had Jerry Gebby reline this rifle to a groove diameter of .224″ and chamber it for the R-2 cartridge. In this form it is superbly accurate. The R-2 has slightly higher velocity and greater range than the .22–3000 Lovell, but no more accuracy. In fact, the Bell rifle will definitely outshoot any R-2 I have found.

My brother, the Rev. W. E. Davis, D.D., of Newport News, Virginia, has a .22–3000 Lovell with 28″ Savage barrel on a Hi-side Winchester action that is a marvel for long range accuracy. With it I saw him on one Thanksgiving day kill a hawk at a range of more than 200 yards, and a few days before he killed with it a crow on the ground at a range of more than 250 yards. In each case, his load was 16.5 grains of HiVel No. 3 powder behind the Winchester 45-grain soft point Hornet bullet. Recently I loaded for him a batch of cartridges with Remington No. 6½ primers, 15.0 grains of No. 4227 powder, and Remington 45-grain soft point Hornet bullets. He writes that he is getting just as good results with these loads. On this rifle he uses a Lyman 5A scope with Fecker rear mount.

A few years ago I had Hervey Lovell build for me a Maximum Lovell rifle on a fine coil spring model nickel steel high-side Winchester single shot action, with Scheutzen double set triggers. It is exceptionally accurate but very heavy, and I have killed with it a number of crows and hawks at ranges of from 100 to 250 yards. However, I have not found that the Maximum Lovell cartridge has very much advantage over the standard R-2. Both are tops on varmints up to 275 yards. In the R-2 I recommend the use of Remington No. 6½ non-corrosive, non-mercuric primers, as they are slightly larger than the Winchester No. 116 primers and therefore the cases can be used longer as the pockets do not enlarge sufficiently to drop No. 6½ primers. Behind 41-grain bullets, use 16.0 grains of No. 4227 powder, 45-grain bullets, 15.4 grains of No. 4227 powder, and 50-grain bullets, 16.0 to 16.5 grains of No. 4198 powder. The Maximum Lovell will handle from one to two more grains of powder than will the R-2. The barrels for both calibers should be 16″ twist, and with .224″ groove diameter.

For the past few years I have not had the time to do as much shooting as I formerly did, and most of my long range shots on hawks and crows have been taken with a Model 70 relined by Diller to a groove diameter of .224″ with 16″ twist, and chambered by J. E. Gebby for the K-Hornet cartridge. The full power load of 13.2 grains of No. 4227 powder behind the Remington 45-grain soft point bullet is one of the best long range cartridges I have ever fired. I once killed at one shot at a range of 175 yards two crows that were feeding side by side on the ground in an open field. My longest shot with this load was at a redtailed hawk, which I knocked out of a tree 295 paces away. I have killed several hawks with it at ranges from 185 to 225 yards, but the shot that gave me most satisfaction was one taken at a crow that was busy hammering on a nut in the top of a pecan tree. At a distance of 225 yards, that wicked little Remington 45-grain soft point bullet caught him amidships and almost exploded him.

This is my favorite hunting rifle, and I carry it exclusively during the open season for game. With it I have killed two deer, a dozen or more wild turkeys, scores of squirrels and numbers of owls, crows and hawks. At present J. E. Gebby is building for me a R-2 Lovell rifle in hunting weight on a short Mauser action, and this may in time become my all-around hunting rifle. However, it will be something out of the ordinary if it can exceed in general usefulness my relined Model 70 K-Hornet job by Gebby.

At present I am trying out a K-Hornet which I had Gebby convert by rechambering a Model 70 Hornet with standard factory barrel. So far I have used it very little, but am afraid the groove diameter of the barrel is too tight to give the fine performance of my relined job on the same action. The few tests I have made indicate that it is not as accurate as that rifle.

My rifles have full pistol grip stocks, finely checkered on both grip and forearm, and are all equipped with telescope sights and with slings using Whelen quick detachable swivels. On the Hornets, I am using at present Lyman 5A scopes with Fecker rear mounts, which were bought before Fecker adopted his more recent policy of not selling mounts separately, while the two Model 70 K-Hornets carry a special Fecker 6X scope and a Lyman 5A scope, respectively. The new R-2 on the short Mauser action will have a Weaver K-6 scope, with mounts of my own design and make. The other Lovells all carry either Lyman 5A or Fecker 6X scopes. All scopes have either crosshair or Lee Dot reticules. These scopes are never removed from the rifles except in cases of necessity, and as a consequence very little trouble is experienced with changes in point of impact.

Varmint shooting affords fine sport and requires good equipment. For the flat, settled country in which I reside, I believe that the outfits I have described above are just about as near the ideal as can be found, and if I had to confine myself to just one rifle for this class of shooting, I can think of nothing better than my relined Model 70 K-Hornet.

CHAPTER 15

Cartridge Selection for Crows and Hawks

WHAT TO USE, AND WHAT NOT TO USE, FOR CROW AND HAWK SHOOT-
ing; wind drift and stalking technique; the ability of crows to see,
hear or wind the hunter; feeding habits of crows; where to locate
hawks; and how to make use of all this information in crow and
hawk hunting are the subjects considered in this chapter. All of
these matters, and many others that vitally contribute to success
in the field will be discussed therein.

Not all of rifle shooting is aiming and shooting the rifle, but all
of the foregoing matters must be taken into consideration. Rifle
shooting at crows and hawks requires plenty of "know how," and
the purpose of this chapter is to supply some of it.

The selection of the best .22 caliber cartridge for crow and hawk.
shooting requires careful consideration. The matters to be determined are: first, whether the shooter will have to buy a rifle for
the shooting he intends to do; second, if he already has a battery
of rifles, which is the best to use for such shooting; and third, what
is the best cartridge to employ when a rifle of loud report is unwel-
come in the community where it is proposed to hunt, or where on
account of frozen ground or other conditions a cartridge of low
velocity would be dangerous to use on account of ricochets—and
ricochets can be serious around stock or buildings.

In settled country, with much open farm land here and there, the
range of the average shot presented will be between 60 and 175
yards. Many will be offered at greater distances, but the advisability
of taking them will be open to serious doubt, and the doubt should
always be resolved against taking the shot. The shooter who is an
experienced handloader will be in position to use any of the very accurate .22 Lovell cartridges made by swaging down .25–20 single shot
cases and using .22 caliber metal-cased expanding bullets. As the
majority do not handload, however, they will of necessity be confined to rifles for which commercial ammunition is universally available in normal times.

The successful handloader will likely choose a rifle chambered for the K-Hornet, .22–3000 Lovell, R-2 Lovell, .22 Lindahl Chucker, .219 Improved Zipper, .22–303 Varmint-R, .22 Varminter, or the .219 Wasp. Most of these perform well with a rather wide variety of bullets and powders. When loaded with a moderate charge of powder, none of this lot will be too expensive for most riflemen, and the superb accuracy of each will be a source of joy to the shooter.

However, when fully charged, some of these are more powerful than is absolutely necessary for most crow and hawk shooting. The bullets for the higher velocity loads and the large powder charges required run into money. A few of these rifles crack more sharply and more loudly when fully charged than most hunters find desirable in the more settled and builtup districts, or around dairy farms, although this is not so important elsewhere.

The larger cartridges, like the .220 Swift, .22/4000 Sedgley-Schnerring, .22 Express, .22 Varminter, Sr., .22 Marciante Blue Streak, .220 Arrow, and the like, are really deer, antelope, woodchuck and coyote rifle cartridges. They are most effective when fully charged, as are many other smaller cartridges; reduced loads of course, may be used. Midrange charges may be loaded. They are effective at considerably greater ranges, when fully charged, than the more medium size .22 varmint rifle cartridges, have less wind ·drift to their bullets and give flatter trajectories. On the other hand an excess of power for 80 per cent of the shots needed to be taken is not often the best policy but simply an unnecessary waste of energy, money, effort and *barrel life*—also, shooting *opportunities!*

A man should really stop and think what his *average* shot will be in both game and range. And he should also seriously consider *where* his average chance for a shot will be found. After he has found it he should always consider whether it will be advisable for him to risk that shot, with the rifle and ammunition *then* in hand.

It should be obvious to everyone that the most effective rifle for shooting varmints, or otherwise, is that with which the greatest number of kills may be made within a given time.

Today, especially in the Middle Atlantic and New England States, and through Ohio, Indiana, Illinois and lower Michigan, the country is settled so thickly, especially along the main highway routes, that this question of suitable cartridge selection is highly important. It is well known that crows are often much more plentiful in the richer farming areas than in the wilder districts, and there they are often more easily approached. The rich valley farms, large stock farms, institutions, and the like, provide automatically a large amount of crow feed. Crows are quick witted and soon discover which place sets the best table. There they gather, often in enormous numbers. At such place, probably from the protection of out-buildings, a hay stack, or a car parked in a lane, one can obtain most excellent shooting at crows feeding in a bottom with a safe hill background, or along a run, or on a manure-spread corn stubble. But how many farmers, regardless of how much they hate crows, are going to allow you to shoot there for long, or day after day, if you use a rifle that cracks so sharply that it scares the women in the farmhouse, makes the cows jump, frightens the chickens and turkeys, and makes the dog bark? Not many will permit it! The women complain, the farmer suddenly remembers conveniently that the Grange speaker said the cows would not let down milk properly, or the chickens would refuse to lay as many eggs, if they were disturbed frequently.

And so, before long, Mr. Longbottom comes out and tells you regretfully that "much as I would like to see you kill those crows, your rifle makes too much of a row around the barn, and the women are complaining; I am sorry, but you better find some other place to shoot."

So that is that! You motor on down the road; meanwhile the crows flap their wings and caw, derisively.

Possibly two of the State Cops motor leisurely by in their tax-payers' limousine and they too conclude you are making too much noise and you better be given the bum's rush before some one of influence complains to their boss. So, again you move on! Life is no longer what it seemed when you first unpacked that .22/5000 Rifleshooter's Special.

On paper, it was wonderful; along the highway, it kicked up too much fuss and attracted the wrong kind of attention, and *you*, of course, will be the goat!

Bought and paid for, but too many places you just can not use it! I have four high velocity .22 caliber rifles in my gun closets; and they stay there a good part of the time for exactly the above reasons.

This sifts the matter down to the condition that *sensible* recommendation for a crow rifle for use where there are unbelievers, in numbers and of import and influence, is to choose a rifle of not over the R-2, .22/3000, .218 Bee, or .22 Hornet calibers and sizes. You can reload any of these successfully, with very accurate charges, and cheaply. The .22 Hornet is unquestionably the *best* selection for the man who does not reload and a fine selection for the chap who does. The two big items in favor of the Hornet are that it is practically perfect in killing power for both hawks and crows; on soft ground a ricochet very seldom occurs and rarely on frozen ground. On *ice*, almost any bullet *might* ricochet, especially if shooting along level with the surface or nearly so, over an ice-covered pond or bottom. Crows have a habit of feeding on rich bottom land which may be covered with snow and ice. Watch that natural condition when using *any* rifle. Be especially careful with *any low velocity* lead bullet rifle, including all of the .22 rim fires. Another place to be very careful is on a plowed field which has frozen hard on the surface due to having been flooded by a freshet, after which a cold snap set in.

The .22 long rifle, either standard velocity, or super speed types, or the .22 W.R.F. caliber, are good calibers on crows and hawks, within reasonable ranges. They are almost as deadly as any other up to 75 yards, kill well and with fair consistency at 100 and 125 yards *if* a man knows their trajectory over these distances, and are cheap and quiet to shoot. One gets to know the ranges in a field, and can then soon drop a bullet about where it will do the crow the least good. They attract little attention, barring heard ricochets, and many feel that a young fellow out with a .22 rifle is more or less harmless and they might as well let him have a good time, he *might* kill a crow or two. But never forget that the .22 long or .22 long rifle bullet will travel close to a mile, and will shoot through the weatherboarding on a house at 500 yards.

The .22 long rifle cartridge will do pretty good work on crows if you do not expect to make too high a percentage of kills, or take in shots at too great a range. I have fired thousands of shots at crows, with .22 rim fires and .25 caliber low velocity rifles in the Susquehanna River Valley, the valleys that run East from it, and in Cumberland Valley in Pennsylvania. Not many riflemen will kill over three crows a day, if hunting *on foot*, on the snow, and using a .22 rim fire in such country. In fact, the average will seldom be over one a day even for a first class shot. There is always plenty of wind to bother in that area and the crows are usually wild. About as good a place as any is at crows feeding on a railroad track or down in a creek bottom. The difficulty is in getting close enough to the crows for a certain shot before the sentinel crow gives the alarm.

Any old crow hunter knows that it is more difficult to approach a large flock of crows than only one crow to six crows. Then too, you will be willing to shoot prone *only* if the snow be fairly dry, in other words, if the temperature is below about 28° Fahrenheit and if the ground under the snow be frozen hard. Ice water is a bit cold on the tummy and a wet shirt bottom gets very clammy and uncomfortable after a time. When snow is melting, or has melted, there is always mud, slush, water, or wet grass and soggy leaves to prevent prone shooting and you will have to depend upon other shooting positions, which usually means crawling over to the nearest fence line and aiming over a rail, or else edging up to the nearest tree and resting the arm or wrist against that. The vital area of a crow is quite small, he is usually walking around when feeding, and you must hold a bit ahead of the walking crow and let him walk up close to the crosshairs intersection and then let drive! It takes a moment for that .22 long rifle bullet to get out to a crow at 100 to 125 yards. If it hits him is he surprised!

The best crow shooting will usually be obtained by hunting from an automobile on back roads. A few crows will be seen on fence posts and top rails, but it is safer to shoot at those on the ground unless a steep hill in directly back of the crow on the fence. Some few may be shot off corn shocks, but most of the crows in corn stubble fields will be on the stubs cawing and teetering around or walking among the corn rows. A half dozen may be feeding on some shelled corn.

Whether you will shoot from an automobile, or will have to strike out across the fields and take to the shelter of some woods will depend upon whether there are state laws against shooting from a highway and carrying a loaded rifle in a car, and whether such are generally enforced, if they exist. Remember, there is a law against anyone planting potatoes without a government permit, but practically everyone breaks that law. That law and the Eighteenth Amendment were just as much laws as this one about not shooting from this and that—but the enforcement is not always the same.

It can be said here that there is very little danger in shooting from a road from a car provided you do not shoot across the road or do not park on a curve.

Many hunters lose most of their shots by driving too fast along the countryside and passing game or varmints before they see the objects clearly. A good way to get safe and certain shots is to slow up the car in a cut or behind brush, then let one rifleman step out the far side of the car while the car is driven on. The dismounted rifleman can then carefully climb the bank and kill the crow from the protection of the fence.

The .22 Hornet is an excellent rifle for such shooting as the trajectory is sufficiently flat for most shots of this type, the report is not too loud, and you neither scare the other crows very much nor attract unfavorable attention. It is better than any of the low velocity .25 caliber or .32 caliber rifles for crow shooting.

Hawks are very rarely shot on the ground. I do not recall when I ever killed but one or two on the ground. They will then usually be down on a kill, or trying to make one. I have, quite a number of times, seen a large field hawk rise slowly for 30 to 50 feet with a struggling young rabbit in its talons and try to fly away with it, then often have to drop it; and a rabbit so struck dies later from punctured liver or intestines.

Hawks will usually have to be shot off dead tree tops, dead limbs, telegraph poles and very occasionally off stumps, usually the latter in zero weather, or when it is very foggy or hazy, when there is nearly zero visibility and the hawk has to come down to see its game. Some are wild and difficult to approach, others are not. Some will fly right out of the county, usually sailing and flapping their way along, others will give you two or three chances. I believe this often depends upon whether the hawk has been intently watching game or whether it has been merely passing the time. Very often hawks fly just at the moment you are about to shoot. For this reason the man who is fast in getting his rifle to his shoulder, taking aim and firing, will kill more hawks, but will not always kill as high a *percentage* for the shots expended as the rifleman who is more deliberate in his movements.

Never forget that hawks will generally return, time and time again, to a favorite lookout tree. If shot off it, within one to four days another hawk may take its place. There are small areas and certain trees off which my son and I have repeatedly shot hawks. In such case, or when calling hawks to a given stand with a hawk caller, it is important to know the distance to each of their prospective perches from the firing station. This will prevent an error of 50 to 100 yards in estimating a long shot, especially on foggy or hazy days.

The theory that has been advanced that it is necessary to sight in a .22 varmint rifle every day is, fortunately, largely a mistaken theory. Much of this complaint of change of zeros has come from a few who used .22 Hornet-chambered Springfields. The real reason for this complaint is probably the rather general use of very open-pored and cheap-looking walnut in Springfield stocks made since 1914. I have observed and have had more wide changes of zero with Springfields than with any other rifles. I believe that most of this can accurately be blamed on the use of other than first class, dense grain, imported walnut in the stocks. We kill crows, hawks, woodchucks, right along with commercial Hornets and rarely have to change the sighting. In addition, men of widely differing physical build have used one of my Hornets, and have shot equally well and deadly with the *same* sighting. Lack of recoil and good stocking is the answer.

I do not use a varmint rifle for a club, a cane or a crowbar, I do not let it bounce around on an auto floor or seat and I use telescope sight mounts that are famous for holding their zero. It is true that I have had a little more than the average amount of actual shooting under differing weather conditions on the range and in the field, and try to profit as a result of it. That helps to get satisfactory results if one remembers the necessary details. However, I do not here nor elsewhere believe in blaming a cartridge for the things which more properly should be blamed on the stocking or the scope mounts. It is neither fair nor logical.

The things which make a man lose so many shots are the things which, with a little more thought, he will notice that he should not do. For instance, like always trying to sneak up too close for a *certain* kill; firing at a crow walking *rapidly* across a field; or shooting at one which presents the smallest mark in a *vertical* direction, when he ought always to try to shoot at one standing quietly eating, or one that was standing up so that it presented the largest mark in a vertical direction to help out with errors in range estimation.

Another common error made by crow and hawk shooters is to stand foolishly right out in the open, *looking* at a hawk in a tree, 100 yards off, when the rifleman should be getting quietly back out of sight or immediately taking the shot. Too rapid a movement in raising the rifle costs more shots to more persons than almost any other thing; quick movements spell danger to a hawk or a crow.

Talking, whistling, smoking or ambling around carelessly out in the open while shooting crows often scares them off, when a little more care would provide reasonable shooting. Running to get a shot at a bird which is sitting quietly, showing no signs of flying, is another foolish maneuver. Trying to shoot from the prone position at a bird high up in a tree, or failing to take advantage of each possible arm rest or wrist-support position against a tree, a fence rail or a post, are other foolish procedures. If nothing else is handy, the shooter should expel a third of the air in his lungs, hold his breath for a moment, and aim and shoot over the shoulder of his companion; as it is much steadier than taking a long shot offhand.

Going hunting for crows when snow is on the ground and wearing a Duxbak or other canvas gunning coat is just about the worst move a crow shooter can make, in midwinter. Canvas trousers do not seem to make so much difference, for remember the crow is usually aloft—at least the sentinel crow is, and has an airplane pilot's view of you. *White* is the best color for clothing when shooting over snow. Ordinary old business clothes, or blue denim jumpers like many farmers wear while working can be bought large enough and worn over heavier clothing. Garage employees' suits, other than brown ones, are good selections. In other words, you should appear to be a person simply going about his daily chores rather than advertise yourself to the crow as a hunter out for business.

If more than one bird is sitting in a tree and you think you may also get a shot at one of the others, do not shoot the top crow, which will come fluttering and crashing down through the limbs, but shoot at one of those farther down in the foliage or on a lower limb.

On warm days in Fall and Winter, crows like to feed in manure-covered fields, among corn shocks, and along railroad tracks on to the ballast of which corn has been dropped from stock cars. They also feed early in the morning—often being bolder then and settle down back of farm buildings—than later in the day when more people are abroad and when there is more travel on the motor roads. It is usually cold and may be windy at such times, but is more usually simply cold and still. Your rifle will shoot low, almost invariably, under such circumstances, both because the temperature is 20° to 30° less and because in winter the light is poor in early morning. Except on warm days, always use maximum elevation or fairly high holding, for early crow shooting in Winter.

Wind Drift of .22s

As a general rule, the .22 long rifle bullet, regardless of whether it be standard velocity or superspeed type, will be found to have three to five times as much wind drift at 200 yards as at 100 yards, where the crow shooter is much more likely to sight in his rifle. I am not talking now of theoretical drift, but actual drift, which has had to be allowed for at various small bore rifle tournaments, at which I have done most of my .22 rifle match shooting. At Sea Girt I have been so fortunate as to tie for first place, or to win outright, six important matches, which were 200 yard events, or in which the 200-yard stage decided the contest. I could hardly have been guessing them wrong there all of the time. In the Small Bore Dryden or Palma Individual I once scored a 223 with 38 Vs, when the World's Record for that match at the time was a straight with 35 Vs for 45 shots, 15 each at 150, 175 and 200 yards. The V ring was four inches in diameter. The wing butts area of a Cooper's hawk, a redtail, a red shoulder, or a raven, is just about the size of the C-5 V ring. The same area on a crow is smaller, more like that of the two inch 10-ring of the 100-yard scope target.

You must figure out the shot pretty near right, or you will not make a clean kill.

The .22 Hornet will probably show two and one-half to three and one-half times the amount of deflection at 200 yards that it will show at 100 yards with the soft point bullet, and three to four times as much at 200 yards, as at 100, with the hollow point bullet which is also rather blunt nose. The latter loses its velocity faster but often is extremely accurate.

Average wind deflection at 100 yards, in the usual side wind, will be one to six inches, with the standard .22 long rifle, and up to twice this with high speeds. If it is blowing harder than this you will likely think carefully about the matter of wind drift and allow considerably, before shooting. I have fired thousands and thousands of shots at pushedup ice cakes on the Susquehanna River, in my younger days, with .22 long rifle cartridges of all types, and in a few instances in zero weather blizzards which roared down out of the North. I have then observed so much wind drift that I will not set it down here, for no one would believe it. On the other hand, there are many days in which the wind drift, even with the .22 long rifle, is almost negligible. These very calm days are the best ones to pick for your crow hunting, especially if using any of the .22 rim fires; with the fast center fire cartridges it does not make so much difference. Never forget that on the same day you will get two to four times the wind drift at a crow sitting on the top of a tall tree, with a strong side wind blowing, that you will find on a shot along the ground at a crow in the lee of woods that is a windbreak. Consequently it is not safe to conclude too definitely that you only have four inches of wind drift at 100 yards, on a shot at a bird 80 feet up on a dead pine, when you only had about three inches at the same distance at a shot on the snow. Cultivate the habit of watching for the spurt of the dirt or snow or ice thrown up by the bullet, and correct immediately for the following shot.

If several shots at a crow or a number of crows aloft fail to bring results, and you do not know where you are shooting, go off by yourself, away from the game, and target your rifle at an envelope or a can set up at approximately the same distance and see what is wrong. The chances are you will be shooting too low, if the weather is cold, and you will be getting more wind drift than you think possible, if using a .22 rim fire. This low shooting will generally be between two and five inches at 100 yards, if there has been a severe drop in temperature.

When anything goes wrong invariably look immediately to see if the telescope sight *base* screws are loose, and if so, tighten same; you should carry a small screw driver in the hunting coat pocket. Accuracy is entirely impossible if the scope base screws loosen, or if the tang screw or screws loosen, and in the latter case the zero of your rifle will at once change, vertically, and probably also a bit horizontally.

Suppose we do a little actual shooting: One of the simplest looking shots I ever saw was at a large red-shouldered hawk sitting on the extreme tip of a tall, very pointed, evergreen tree on the top of a hill, as two of us were driving homeward from a shooting contest. I looked up and there the hawk was, watching some hens in a nearby poultry run. The day was very foggy and hazy, the most difficult sort in which to judge distance; also, the tree was considerably above our level, which made it look closer than it was. I had along a very accurate Model 61 Winchester, fitted with Wollensak scope, and took a wing-butts aim with the mount readings adjusted for the distance, which never even disturbed the bird. The second shot, held well over its head, brought it down. This was a difficult shot to pace, as the field was covered with slippery ice, especially on the hillside, but my companion went over and got it, and paced the distance carefully, and made it 243 paces. I had never seen a hawk sit in that tree before, and have never seen one there since. This was a very unusual kill for a .22 long rifle, but sometimes such is possible.

I once bagged a bird with the .22 Hornet Model 54, at 240 paces across a level field, covered with snow, ice sheet, and water on top from melted snow. There had been a blizzard, then a thaw, and we were out for hawks. This was on a field of green wheat, iced over.

I saw this bird sitting well up on a tall hickory tree, and as it was quite damp and hazy it was difficult to identify from a distance. The walking was so slippery that it took quite some time to get close enough for a long range shot, but finally I got this off by grasping a swaying birch sprout between the fingers of the left hand, steadying the barrel of the rifle against the young tree, and then finally getting it to swing slowly back and forth in a regular arc by pushing forward and steadying it. The way to get off such a shot is to allow for the movement of the rifle muzzle, your left hand, and the time of travel of the bullet to the object shot at, from the time you begin to squeeze off a shot. If you aim directly at the object when starting to squeeze off, the crosshair intersection will be six inches to a foot past the object by the time the rifle fires and the bullet gets out the barrel.

I suppose it took all of two or three minutes to get that shot off perfectly, but get it off right I did and the bullet struck with a resounding "spank," like smacking a taut pants seat with a chestnut shingle, and a single feather floated off the breast and down crashed the bird. A shot like that gives a rifleman a great deal of satisfaction, when consummated, but there are numberless ways in which the tyro or even the veteran can gum it up. Anything from the slipping of a foot, a jerk in the movement of the tree, a yank on the trigger, or even having the rifle fire a bit before or a bit after you expected it to, will cause a complete miss. This bird fell into snow about 10 feet from the far edge of a deep and fast rivulet, flowing past the foot of the tree on which the bird had sat, and I could not recover it but could see it, stone dead, from a distance of a few feet. It never moved a feather after being struck, except for the floating away of the single breast feather which drifted with the wind.

I think the most I was ever startled when shooting at a hawk was one morning very early as I walked up a lane through a dense woods

VARMINT SHOOTING

When ice and snow cover the ground, and blizzards rage across the land, game becomes weakened, and then hawks and crows are most destructive. The author's son with a morning's bag shot with his Savage Hornet. Four kills in five shots!

Photo by the author

of virgin timber to a small field in which there were occasional wood-chucks. I had hoped to get a shot at one of them, before slipping into the squirrel woods for grays. I looked toward the East, into the brightening, rising sun, and there, about two-thirds way up a dead tree some 200 yards off across the field, was a large bird that appeared to be a bright golden-brown. It was perfectly motionless and its head was back of the tree trunk. I looked it over for quite some time, and finally concluded it could not be a domestic turkey (the farmer had a flock of young turkeys), and it was not large enough for an eagle, and seemed to be probably an unusually large hawk come down from the North. I rested the left arm over the fence, took a careful aim and let drive. The bullet connected with a re-sounding slap—easily heard in the calm morning air and down crashed the bird back of the tree trunk.

Going up, expecting to find a hawk well worth the trouble, I looked down on the smallest, thinnest, sorriest looking, most be-draggled young turkey buzzard I have ever gazed upon. It must have had an awful night of it! The rising sun had so changed the color and appearance of that bird I did not think there was a five per cent chance it was other than a hawk.

A few years ago I was considerably concerned at the appearance of three unusually large hawks, arriving apparently from nowhere, in some open country not very far from my home, and on which I had obtained unusually fine bird shooting for five or six years. It was early in the fall, on the best dove district around. It always contained a covey or two of quail, which liked to dust along a hedge row that flanked a truck patch. From one to five nice ringnecked pheasants always made this field their home, and adjoining along a grown-up ravine there were more of them and also quite a few rabbits. The cottontails often came out and fed in the open fields. Except for squirrels, there was first class game habitat there for every sort of local game bird or animal.

It would be just too bad, if those hawks ganged up on those birds and cleaned them out. Along about that time, a new owner decided to turn it into a "Game Preserve" so called, but if he ever did a single thing to make it a game preserve in actuality, except to tack up signs, I never saw the least evidence of it. There is less game on it now than there was then, which is the usual condition. One day, sitting quietly on a tree, was a large hawk, with 40" wing spread, contemplating his prospects for the immediate future. He was sitting in almost the exact middle of the best rabbit area and the best ringnecked pheasant area, and probably knew it. But just outside the preserve, I stalked this fellow to 150 yards, planted a Hornet bullet in the middle of his back, and blew out the whole breast, and we were one-third closer to being back to the original condition.

The following Sunday a red-shouldered hawk was located on a tree, on the other side of the brushy hollow. The local Game Warden, who was a reasonable chap, was called on the phone, and asked what he would have done under the circumstances—it being Sunday. He replied, "You know what those big hawks do to our game. I would use my discretion!" I figured I would use mine too, but the varmint had left. The following morning that hawk had a sudden and serious accident. *A Hornet stung him!* The other hawk apparently, then left, for I never saw it again.

One of the largest redtails I have ever shot, was sitting on a buttonwood tree, eyeing with interest a few fowls in a nearby yard. He was eyeing them so intently, he apparently paid no attention to me, and I managed to get up within 135 paces and hit him in the wing butts and tore out the whole breast. This one had a 50″ wing spread and was as large as a large Plymouth Rock pullet.

A shot that afforded considerable satisfaction to a rifleman (my son) was a kill at 310 paces, with the Hornet H.P. bullet, and which had to be retrieved after dark, with a flashlight, after ice had frozen thicker on some marshy land. The Hornet has to be handled very expertly to make a kill at such range, as the bullet is then describing a pretty high trajectory, as its really useful range for consistent shooting is about 175 yards.

There are shots which have to be taken under unfavorable circumstances which do not always turn out so well. One was at a Cooper's hawk which offered a good chance at only 50 or 60 yards. I had a rest shot from a car, but the car had moved forward a little too far before I saw the hawk partly hidden in a dense tree, and it was uphill from where we were, so I could not get down properly on the rifle stock to shoot at that angle. I needed to move my head about another inch downward but was unable to make it. The bullet tore across his back and blew off a perfect cloud of feathers. The hawk flew uncertainly up over the hill, coming down lower and lower, and finally pitched over the crest. However, we were unable to go and retrieve same and I never did know for certain whether I had bagged that one.

I think the hawk that made me the most angry of any I ever hunted, was a Cooper's hawk which I killed in Pennsylvania, with a shotgun, after he had been chased off the freshly killed carcass of a ruffed grouse, that I had hunted at odd times, in a small pine woods, for weeks. This grouse was so smart he once outwitted me at least eight or 10 times in one day. I never flushed one that had as many tricks of quick dodging up his sleeve, or which appeared to be so large and in such perfect physical and mental shape. It was never possible to catch him off guard for more than a moment. He fed day after day among some ant hills that flanked one edge of this pine woods, and the ants probably supplied the meat ingredient for a balanced ration, that gave him plenty of life and vigor. I always did believe this grouse got a perfectly fiendish delight in making me look foolish. I was just learning a little about wing shooting then, and *he* knew all the answers.

Yet, this Cooper's hawk zoomed down on him in a small open spot near an old dead chestnut tree, and all that was left was a few bloody scraps of flesh, the leg bones, and some feathers. When the shot made the feathers fly off that hawk, I saw him go down with a world of satisfaction. I have made more spectacular shots on hawks than that, but this one had brought a bad end to a ruffed grouse cock that was the smartest grouse ever to inhabit the Forney Woods in my time.

Crows are often rather amusing when shot in places that incapacitate them for flight, but which wounds do not incapacitate them from sassing the rifleman. I have several times, by accident, shot crows across the root of the tail feathers, on top, so that the feathers were blown off the stern sheets of the black rascal and he was spanked soundly on his most easily wounded feelings.

A shot underneath the tail, or across the underside of the body, back of the wing butts, does not seem to have this effect at all, but a round across the base of the large tail feathers on top, so that the bullet cuts about one-half its depth into the flesh, results in a series of tremendous vertical leaps in attempts to fly, but the crow for some reason can not use his wings, but he *can* use his legs and throat muscles, and certainly does, calling everyone thereabouts all the nasty words he can think up. Such hit is usually the result of rather sloppy shooting, but in firing at crows at long distance and when the wind is blowing across the line of fire you will at times hit them in just about every part of their anatomy.

With a .22 Hornet, an ordinary bag of crows is two or three to half a dozen, in a morning or afternoon. To do better than this, things must come pretty well your way, and you must be shooting in a locality in which there is little automobile travel to interfere, and in which there are several flocks of crows, feeding possibly a half mile to two or three miles apart.

In hunting flocks of crows to shoot at, one will find that he will do better in going after a succession of comparatively small flocks, than one very large one, and give them time to settle down and start feeding well before driving up on them or starting the stalk on foot. Remember that crows hold the sentinel crow entirely responsible for anything that happens to one of their number while feeding.

Except with a longer ranged rifle than a Hornet, the majority, yes 80 per cent of your crows, will be shot and killed within 160 yards. The shots beyond 175 yards may be taken, but in the long run it does not pay because generally you simply scare the flock, that at other times can usually be stalked closer and shot into with greater effect.

We often hear, "using a .22/4000 adds 100 yards to the effective range." It does and it does not! With such rifles, 225 yard shots are reasonably common, but comparatively few are killed at 300 yards and over in comparison to the number of misses. I have not found the .220 Swift to be a really effective crow rifle, nothing like as deadly as the Winchester .22 Hornet. That rifle is the nearest thing to certain death, *on the first shot*, within 125 to 150 yards, I have ever handled. At least three other local hunters, using Hornets in preference to any other rifle, say the same thing.

As we close this chapter, let us consider just a few things about the perfect .22 high speed rifle for crows and hawks. The bullet should completely explode and disintegrate in three inches of feathers and flesh and should not go far beyond the object struck. If a miss, it should fall straight down to the ground, a yard beyond the object shot at. Of course no effective bullet is so obliging, but that is what it should do. The rifle with the least recoil will make the greatest number of effective hits, *all* other things being equal.

The difference in drift in a side wind, between the various .22 calibers and sizes, is relative rather than absolute. It depends upon the bullet used and the charge. No one caliber, in single shot or bolt action style, is confined to any one bullet. The idea that a .22 Hornet bullet will drift all over a 10-acre lot and a .22 Lovell will only drift one inch at 200 yards is in error; someone was just mistaken in his actual zero for the load used.

It has been my experience that not over three to five men in the average rifle club membership are reloaders, and probably not over two of them are so expert at reloading that they can prepare ammunition that is actually as accurate as ordinary .22 Hornet factory stuff; which is really one of the very few commercial hunting loads ever put out with match rifle accuracy.

It has been shown time and time again that actual rifle shooting ability, skill as a hunter and as a stalker, and *patience* in waiting for and properly handling the shot, are far more important in shooting such varmints as hawks and crows than the exact caliber of cartridge used, or its ballistics.

From a practical standpoint it is worse to be overgunned, than to be slightly undergunned, because the man who must use a cartridge giving a very sharp and ear-splitting report, in settled localities, where there is considerable auto travel, even on side roads, and where persons live; of a type who think they own the earth and have little or no feeling for the pleasures or activities of others, regardless of how worthwhile and innocent they may be, is simply going to find before long that he has done himself out of several of his very best previous "private" shooting districts, simply because the actual owners of those areas would not stand for the frequent sharp reports of the rifle he was using.

After all, it resolves itself that you have to shoot crows, where you *can* shoot at crows, and the world being what it is today one has to make the best of it! Never forget that it is always more satisfactory to be able to shoot the rifle you may have, even if it is not exactly what you would most prefer to use, than to own and try to use the rifle of your dreams, and not be allowed a place to shoot.

This is especially so in the Middle Atlantic States and the more thickly populated areas of Massachusetts and southward. In more sparsely settled areas, and where people are broader minded, as they are inclined to be farther Westward, one can do more as he pleases, and use a rifle of greater range, power, and report.

In your case, reader, ponder carefully what you think your locality would permit without complaint from landowners—most of whom have given you permission to shoot. Then stay within that limit, unless shooting hawks or crows within a sparsely settled area in which the sky is the limit and 500 yards is not too far, if you think you can hit a two inch wing butt, at even one-half this distance.

In woodchuck shooting you are likely to get back on the rocky hills and in the briar grown ravines and washes, but in shooting crows and hawks, never forget that these are far more inclined to flock into the easier feeding areas in the richer bottom lands, the creek bottoms, the cornfield back of the barn, and the field which farmer Brown is about to plow or harrow. Let your rifle cartridge, in report and performance, fit these feeding grounds and farm surroundings. Nothing else about your shooting, except personal recklessness has such an important bearing upon your continued, long-time success!

CHAPTER 16

Grouse Shooting with a Rifle in British Columbia

BUT FEW PERSONS IN THE UNITED STATES REALIZE THAT BRITISH Columbia, always called "B. C." out there, furnishes most excellent small game shooting as well as great rifle shooting for bear, goats, sheep, deer and other big game.

Bertram Chichester, of Kelowna, B. C., a frequent contributor to Canadian sporting magazines, a big game hunter and a photographer of motion pictures of big game, is very fond of small game shooting with a .22 caliber rifle and much of his best grouse hunting is obtained at altitudes of from 3,000 to 5,000 feet.

He is also an orchardist of considerable experience, and his place is the home of numerous grouse, pheasants and other small game, including cottontail rabbits. He is close enough to real big game country in the high Rockies to run into ptarmigan, which many believe are to be found only in Alaska.

The following account of his experiences written by him will be found interesting.

BLUE GROUSE SHOOTING IN BRITISH COLUMBIA
By Bertram Chichester.

Our blue grouse hunting in British Columbia mountain country, with all the attendant scenery we have here, is a most fascinating and exhilarating sport. The blue grouse is a bird of over three pounds in weight, heavily feathered to stand the winter climate, and is now getting fairly wary. Years ago the blue grouse were more tame but as a country begins to settle, its game, and especially its game birds of the grouse family, adapt themselves to the new and to them, more dangerous environment, and then become much wilder.

Each fall our blue grouse, which are fine, big, plump birds, are found up on the hillsides and along sparsely timbered ridges. You will find them up to 5,000 feet elevation and more, in spite of the fact that they often nest low down, even within a stone's throw of the lake (O'Kanagan), which has an elevation of only 1,135 feet above the sea.

This gives a range of nearly 4,000 feet up and down the slopes on which one may still hunt the "blues." It is not necessary to have a dog to still hunt blue grouse, but a good ranging bird dog is a help and such dogs love the hills unless they are too old to work on grouse.

These great dusky hooters of the mountain slopes of the Rockies are temperamental birds. Sometimes they will sit tight and let one nearly step on them; then suddenly they really explode from cover on powerful, rapidly beating wings, either to ascend into the tree tops close at hand, or fairly to "zoom" down hill, half a mile or more. So you see it is often a good plan for two bird hunters to shoot together, one with a shotgun, the other with a .22 rifle. This brings to mind one glorious afternoon, in a recent autumn, when I took a young friend on his first blue grouse shoot. The country was up about 4,000 feet elevation, commanding a panoramic view up and down a wide stretch of the O'Kanagan. The weather was clear although it was cool in the shade.

Rex, my setter, was along and working well—a bit too keen, perhaps for he flushed a bird which went high into some firs ahead of us. We advanced cautiously, my friend with the rifle ready, circled, peering up for a shot, while I stood guard on the logical side of the tree for a wing shot—so I thought. Nothing happened, although the dog barked, and we, finally, threw up sticks and strained our eyes for a sight of the grouse. But no, nothing budged! Evidently it was hidden and was staying "put!" We went on, and later stumbled onto a whole flock of grouse. They were all around us; some buzzed off, while others went up into the trees. I spied a head and neck amongst the branches only about 40 feet off. Cecil, my companion, could not make out the head quickly, so he handed me the .22 rifle and I took the shot. The little slug caught the grouse just at the base of the neck, nicking also, a part of its crop. The bird fluttered down and the dog of course was there waiting for it. It could not have lived long anyway.

Then I pointed out a bird perhaps 100 feet up a tamarack. The tree was uphill from us, so the range to the grouse was 40 yards or better. Cecil took the rifle, advanced a few paces, and settled down for a shot from an old log. But, as luck would have it, there were twigs in the way and the grouse began to fidget, so Cecil suggested I take the shot. This I did, just as the bird was tipping forward on outstretched wings, for a getaway.

When the bullet struck down came the grouse! Soon afterward, the dog put a bird into a small tree. The rifleman was quick to fire, bringing down his grouse at the first shot, with a bullet through its back, sidewise. The bird was flapping its last, as Rex and the hunter rushed in for his first blue of the trip.

Now, the ruffed grouse and the Franklin grouse (or fool hen, as it is often called), are much the same size, and I have always found both of them easy to kill with a .22 caliber bullet. I used to shoot many ruffed grouse, long ago, with a small Quackenbush .22 rifle. A thoughtful uncle of mine forgot it when leaving us one time. It is on the wall before me now and will still shoot, after some 35 years of knocking about Western Canada; but, about those grouse!

I was saying that they are easy to shoot! Yes, but do not wound them, or you may not get them. They both have a lot of fluffy feathers so they look large and easy to hit; actually, though, they are a rather small bird in the flesh and if only winged or hit too far back they will lead you quite a chase amongst the willows and perhaps finally hide right under your nose!

Blue grouse should be shot in the head, neck, or the butts of the wings for best immediate effect. When so shot squarely, the bullet and even the cartridge, make little difference, provided they are not too powerful. On the other hand, a .22 solid bullet which strikes too far back in the body of the grouse, or merely cuts the crop, or possibly drills only through the thick breast meat, without getting into the vitals, may easily permit the bird to escape.

I was up in the hills, just back of my place, a short time ago, and shot three large blue grouse, using .22 shorts. There was not a wild berry in any of the crops; they were chuck full of jack pine needles already. It appeared that there would be a hard winter for these birds with no real food that early.

Those birds of the mountains, the "fool hens," with the red, bare skin parts about the eyes, are chumps indeed! I had a wonderful week up in a sheep camp, on a high mountain, this last July, and saw lots of them. The young grouse were running around, some only one-half size. Now I do not know how they act when a coyote comes along, but with me it was dead easy to find a covey quietly, get nearer and nearer until I was right amongst them.

At first the old one would "cluck! cluck!" a bit and the little fellows would "peep!" but when they found I would not molest them, then they merely went on looking for food. They were so tame at times as to run over my feet, and one got busy pecking, chicken-like, at the eyelets in my boots. Wild Birds! Yes,—and No!

These fool hens, and the slowmoving, easily gotten porcupines are both given fairly rigid protection, as they are about all that a man who is lost in the hills could club down for something to eat. Neither are a delicacy, but would be welcome in such a pinch.

Ptarmigan, the little grouse of the top-countries, appear pretty easy to kill. At that altitude, sometimes they need to be. But this leads me to a rather humorous episode:

A party of us were away North. One member had just bagged a mountain goat—about timber line (which is at 7,000 feet here). My partner and I were not far off, so we went over to the lucky hunter to offer felicitations and to photograph the trophy. We were about to go our way, when several heavy shots rang out from above. "That's George, he's got something. Come on!" So away we all scrambled! Another shot! Helter-skelter, along rocky ledges, up and ever up! "Boom!" Excitedly, we hastened our already breakneck pace across the rocks, expecting to find our Pal with at least a grizzly, or maybe, a fine goat with a record head; to our utter astonishment all he had to show for all the cannonading was two plump ptarmigan—about the size of barnyard pigeons. And, blyme, he'd blown their heads off with a pair of full charge cartridges in a .350 Rigby Magnum rifle! What a man!

What a man, indeed! To them, the reports of a heavy magnum were nothing but the shocks of falling rocks, rolling and bouncing down the mountain, or a slide of snow, or shale, so they sat there, unconcerned, while he shot their heads off, one by one, they meanwhile depending upon their excellent camouflage coloring to conceal them from any intruder. But this time it did not work.

Unless they run or fly, chances are you won't see ptarmigan, very frequently, for they know how to hide. If they flush, they do so *suddenly*, like quail, and give out the odd, rather harsh chirp, as they rise, then away they go, bee-lining it for another Alpine ridge.

But there was George—standing calmly with his .350 Rigby and his pair of beheaded ptarmigan. Not a *small bore* rifleman, but yet a rifleman to whom caliber meant nothing more than that it was a means to an end, to bag, neatly, expeditiously, and cleanly, game both large and small. This is probably one of the few times on record of a double on ptarmigan with a .350 Magnum rifle!

In the wintertime, particularly, we have many goshawks, coming down from the mountains, to prey on our pheasants, quail, and so on, in the lower valley of the O'Kanagan. Now these speedy streamlined hawks are devils on game birds. So, whenever I hear a commotion among the pheasants about the orchard, I rush for a rifle. One such time, I could not spot the marauder. The behavior of the pheasants told me plainly there was a hawk around. So I hid myself, and after a short while I began giving out a few imitative hen-pheasant calls.

To my delight, out came Mr. or Mrs. Hawk (I think this one was Mrs.), at any rate just then up got a hen pheasant and be sure the hawk lost no time giving chase. The pheasant flew into some fairly thick pine woods, entering low, while its pursuer swerved up and down in behind the trees.

A moment later, two hen pheasants came out in all haste, towards where I was. They were coming fast when out burst the hawk, swift and straight as an arrow, hot on their tails, and easily overtook one helpless hen pheasant. Just as they passed me, the hawk struck, from behind of course, and down they went together, rolling, flapping a moment, until the hawk got control and pinned its victim under it.

I quickly came out of my momentary trance and levelled the rifle (which movement the hawk noticed, for they were but a few yards from me), but in the split-second that hawk was sizing me up. I pulled, and the hawk wilted from the effects of a .22 long rifle hollow point bullet through the butts of its wings. Believe it or not but the hen pheasant slipped out from under its captor, as she felt those cruel, sharp talons relax their hold, and ran, then flew away! She never as much as stopped to say, "Thank you!" That shooting was with my little Remington 12A with peep sights.

Another time, using the Winchester 52, I again wilted a hawk, this time from a dead pheasant at 80 yards. This hawk had killed the pheasant, eaten part, gone away, then I presume returned to its kill, when I luckily drove home a Dominion Cartridge Company's Whiz-Bang long rifle, hollow point. The bullet entered the rump, passed clean through and came out through the crop, leaving a ghastly wound for such a small slug.

For all such shooting, if we wish to be successful and humane, we should always use the long rifle, hollow point loads in reliable, properly sighted rifles. With open sights, target the arm to hit just at the top of a one inch mark at 35 yards, and with peep sights and fairly small front sight, sight in for say 75 yards. Then hold accordingly when you know your bullet drop.

Use a sling too for the long shots and snuggle right down firm as a rock. One good shot from a steady hold with a good outfit is worth any number of snap shots. Do not neglect having a good smooth trigger pull, use a hone and polish carefully. This is important for accurate shooting.

W. R. Maxon, the Game Warden, came in the other day from a cougar hunt, and we talked of the matter of shooting big game with .22 rim fire rifles. He said he had been called in to shoot two bucks that were doing damage to young fruit trees by rubbing and ripping the trees to pieces. Both bucks were about 100 yards off. One he hit from the side and between the eye and ear; the other he dropped from above, with a bullet at the base of the skull between the ears. These deer both dropped as if poleaxed! They were both good-sized animals, 250 pounds or more apiece. This will give an idea of the killing power of the .22 bullet when properly placed.

CHAPTER 17

Hunting Wild Turkeys with the Rifle

IN RECENT HUNTING SEASONS WE HAVE HAD MUCH PUBLICITY ON THE subject of shooting state-raised or semi-domesticated "wild" turkeys that range a number of the back-country districts of our Northern States. In time, those which survive and their descendants become quite difficult to approach and then provide fair mountain hunting.

Today, however, the real wild turkey districts of the United States are in the old South, and there mostly amid the swamps, lowlands and thickets of the "Low Country." An account of hunting genuine wild turkeys with high velocity varmint rifles is set forth in this chapter.

Having hunted wild turkeys in a number of the wilder mountain districts of Pennsylvania, and having surveyed roads through many more such districts in that state, the author is quite familiar with the hard going and many difficulties encountered in such areas in the effort to get in range of turkeys, whether they be of pure wild or only of hybrid stock. Those who have not hunted mountain ridges, flats and choppings, at elevations of from 1,000 to 3,000 feet, with every imaginable slope and rocky cliff face in between these heights, always underestimate the difficulty of traversing such terrain. In many such mountain fastnesses, you can become completely exhausted before traveling half a mile, and you can rest assured that the turkeys will always select the wildest, roughest and most remote areas in which to feed, forage, loaf and roost. Morning or evenings they may come out to the edge of cultivated lands and corn or grain fields to feed, and may be attracted at certain seasons by the gobbling and putting of domestic turkeys, when a wary Tom may come to the edge of backwoods farms to assert himself and to mate.

However, when the first day of hunting season arrives, gone are most of his foolish ways and ventures. Back onto Jacks Mountain, or whatever his hangout may be when pursued, you may expect to find that he has gone, and from that day on until the morning after the close of wild turkey open season he is seldom anyone's easy shooting.

But, somehow, and for many reasons, primeval hunting in the South, where turkeys have run wild for centuries, and where domestic turkeys seldom if ever have opportunity to inbreed with wild Toms, and where State game farm raised turkeys are not liberated, wild turkey hunting seems more like the real thing. We have obtained a most unusual turkey hunting story from the pen of a past-master in such shooting; no better turkey shooting chapter has ever been written.

In reading the chapter, you will be told how it is possible to do real wild turkey shooting with a .22 rifle in this country today. The old Tom turkey is the most aristocratic and keen-eyed, keen-eared, fugitive from the white man's rifle, to be found south of the Potomac.

This account takes you down to the land of rice, turpentine, cottonmouths, rattlesnakes and gators, wildcats and raccoons; of "hants" and "swamp devils," of mysterious noises booming over the stagnant water, the croak of frogs in the shadows and the swing and swoop of hawks as they stalk their prey.

It takes you into the type of country the Northern rifleman seldom if ever visits, and has rarely heard about and which he finds it difficult to visualize in all of its unusual surroundings and characteristics, but in which, even today, there are a few remaining riflemen of the old school of Southern gentlemen to whom state's rights is a very important subject and to whom private shooting estates are as much a matter of course and are as vital as the actual shooting thereon.

In the account by Henry E. Davis, of Florence, South Carolina, you will find wild turkey hunting as it is today in the South Carolina Low Country. You will also be treated to a most remarkable piece of literary composition.

THE .22 HIGH VELOCITY RIFLE ON WILD TURKEYS
By Henry E. Davis.

From the days of its first settlement, the Low Country of South Carolina has been a veritable hunter's paradise. This region is a fertile alluvial plain bordering the sea for the entire length of the State and extending back some 50 miles into the interior. It is traversed by many noble rivers, each flanked by immense, heavily timbered swamps. Innumerable smaller streams with their attendant wooded swamps thread the entire section, while bays, which are low timbered areas without watercourses, abound. Large portions of the uplands have long since been cleared, and are today the sites of splendid farms, while the lowlands along the tidal rivers in former years constituted the greatest rice plantations of the world. Rice culture has passed from the state, the glorious civilization peculiar to it is but a fragrant memory, and the old plantations have now become some of the world's most notable private game preserves.

Most of the worthwhile smaller game indigenous to North America has always found a home in this favored region. So abundant were deer in colonial times that their skins were among the most important articles of commerce. Official customs records disclose that during one period of 23 years Charleston exported nearly 3,500,000 deer hides, or an annual average of more than 150,000. (*The Carolina Low Country*, p. 71.)

I was born and reared on a great cotton plantation located about 40 miles from the ocean and in the very heart of this Carolina Low Country. Moreover, I sprang from a race of sportsmen, learned to ride, to shoot and to hunt in my early youth, and for more than a half century have ardently kept up my hunting and shooting. In my boyhood, doves and partridges (the absurd nickname *quail* had not yet been invented or used locally) thronged field and forest, wild fowl swarmed the waters of river, lake, pond, slough, lagoon and marsh, while whitetail deer, squirrels and wild turkeys teemed in swamp, bay and woodland.

But this narrative has specifically to do with the wild turkey and its hunting, so to that subject let us come. At the outset, permit me to say that the story does not concern mongrels masquerading as wild turkeys, but deals solely with the pure-blooded aristocrats of our vast swamps and forests that my forebears and I have known since the colonists first set foot on Carolina soil.

The so-called wild turkey of most of our states today is nothing but a domestic hybrid gone wild and bears but little relationship to a pure-blood wild turkey. This, however, is not true of the wild turkey of South Carolina. In the coastal section of this state are hundreds of thousands of acres of heavily wooded river swamps, bays and woodlands on which no domestic turkey has ever set foot, simply because no man could ever live there to own one, and in this territory the true wild turkey flourishes today, though not as abundantly, just as he did when the first settlers came.

Viewed from any angle, the wild turkey inspires respect and admiration. Built tall, lithe and slender, after the fashion of a Greek athlete, he is the very embodiment of grace, caution, alertness and action. His little blue head houses a brain marvelous for sagacity and cunning, and his dark beady eyes never deceive him whether the object be still or moving. I have hunted practically every species of our native game, and in my candid opinion, when it comes to outwitting his foes, a hermit wild gobbler is *sui generis*. The hunter has not yet lived who can stalk such a gobbler to within shotgun range, or can call him to within such range, except in the mating season. During my life span of 71 years, I have seen hundreds of wild turkeys, both alive and dead, have killed quantities of them myself and have seen numbers killed by others, and I have yet to see the hermit gobbler that was brought to bag when given an even break by his slayer. An old gobbler stands nearly four feet tall and is slim and racy, with absolutely no indication of the bulging breast that is characteristic of practically every picture of a so-called wild turkey that illustrates our sporting magazines or adorns the literature of breeders of alleged wild turkeys. I have yet to see in actual life the true wild gobbler afflicted with a rotund, swelled-out front. Further, the head of a thoroughbred is small and of a deep blue color with but little show of wattles or dewlap, and the legs and feet are long and of a vivid pink.

With the possible exception of the peacock, nature presents no more gorgeous creature than an old wild gobbler in full plumage. The whole back and breast are overlaid with a metallic bronze that glistens like burnished brass in the sunlight; the rump feathers are barred with black and gold; the tail coverts are a deep reddish brown; the terminals of both tail and rump feathers are chocolate; and no trace of white is found save in the larger feathers of the wings. The females are similarly marked, but duller, and mature specimens have pronounced reddish breasts. In form and figure, they present the same alert, slim, lithe and athletic appearance as do the males. Large red heads, squat, round, heavy bodies, white or yellowish tips to the terminals of feathers, and the absence of pink legs indicate mongrel blood, and never occur in genuine wild turkeys.

To become a successful turkey hunter requires long experience, infinite patience, a good knowledge of woodcraft, keen eyesight, hunting sense, and a thorough understanding of the ways and habits of these wary birds. Turkey hunting is no sport for the amateur, and if he thinks it is, he is certain to be disillusioned. I once had a friend who was an excellent turkey hunter and who was endowed with an unusual fund both of common sense and of native wit. A young chap betook himself to the local hardware store and bought a complete hunting outfit. He then sought out my old friend and stated to him that he was on his way for a turkey hunt and had come by to have the old hunter tell him how to distinguish a wild turkey from a tame one, as he did not want to make the mistake of killing a turkey that had an owner. After listening to his harangue, the old huntsman said: "Young fellow, your problem is easy. Any turkey you get in range of is sure to be a tame one; so, unless you want to pay for some farmer's property, my advice is not to shoot any turkey *you* have an opportunity to kill." To which advice, any good turkey hunter will say "Amen."

There are three distinct classes of turkeys known to all experienced hunters. These are: (1) mixed turkeys; (2) old gobblers; and (3) hermit gobblers. The first group comprises the hens and the young of both sexes of the season. Usually several hens with their practically grown young band together, and I have known of one such flock that contained more than 50 individuals. The average flock, however, contains some 12 or 15 birds. As a combined sporting and table proposition, the young gobbler is probably the most desirable of all turkeys. The sporting method of taking him is for the hunter to locate and scatter a drove of mixed turkeys, and after waiting an hour or so call up a young gobbler from the scattered birds by imitating certain notes of a turkey.

Considering the second class, it is to be borne in mind that as a rule no self-respecting old gobbler ever herds with a band of mixed turkeys, and as the season advances, even the young gobblers forsake such flocks. In more than a half century of hunting, I have seen just two old gobblers with a drove of mixed turkeys, and one of these was after the mating season had begun. On the contrary, gobblers of two years of age and upwards usually band together in flocks that may contain a dozen or more individuals. When scattered, the members of such a flock can be called up by a good hunter, but it requires more skill than in the case of young turkeys. Frequently old gobblers scattered around midday will not attempt to reassemble until sunset, and sometimes not until early the next morning, and consequently will not come to a call except at these times.

The third and last class is the hermit. This wily old rascal is usually of great age and the largest size, and he absolutely scorns the company of all of his kind. No call can induce him to come to a hunter, and instead of yelping or clucking in reply (a gobbler never answers with a gobble outside of the mating season), he silently and swiftly fades away. My theory as to a hermit is that he is the sole survivor of a former band of old gobblers, and after all his comrades are gone, he makes no new associations. I have killed several of these patriarchs and each of them carried a beard of unusual length and was armed with extra long and sharp spurs, both evidences of great age. On the table, each proved to be tough and sinewy, which was additional proof of age. How long a hermit lives, I can not say, but I know several that have been ranging certain sections of swamp for many years, and to date not a single one of them has permitted himself to get into a position to be shot.

My experience with wild turkeys dates back to boyhood days on the old plantation, when I used to bait them along the edges of the fields of cowpeas and shoot them from a blind. Since that time I have hunted them in practically all of the great river swamps of the low country of my native state from the Savannah River to the North Carolina line, and have been fairly successful in such quest. Fortunately for me, for a long period of years I have enjoyed the privilege of membership in a club that controls some 13,000 acres of the finest timbered land in the swamp of Great Pee Dee River in Florence County, South Carolina, and on this great property I have had full opportunity to follow my favorite pastime of hunting this royal game bird.

For years, I used for their hunting two extra good 12 gauge full choke shotguns, one a W. W. Greener and the other a G. E. Lewis Magnum. But as turkeys became scarcer, I decided it would be more sportsmanlike to pursue them with a rifle. Besides, such a weapon would afford more opportunity to bring to bag some birds that hitherto had proved too wise to come within shotgun range of a hunter despite his most perfect yelping. The problem was to find the rifle and cartridge best adapted to the work in hand, and this was more serious than might be thought. A wild turkey is almost as tenacious of life as a woodchuck, and yet, as McIlhenny declares in his book *The Wild Turkey and Its Hunting*, the good breast meat when struck by an improper bullet will "spatter like soft butter" and the game as a consequence will be ruined for the table. Fleet-wood Lanneau, now of Flat Rock, North Carolina, resided for 11 years at a hunting lodge in Darlington County, South Carolina, located in the swamp of Great Pee Dee River, and as he was the best rifle shot that ever lived in this section, he killed, mostly with a rifle, over 300 wild turkeys while he was so located. He tells me, however, that he shot with a Krag rifle, using its original round nose 220-grain bullet, at least 25 old gobblers as they fed in peafields, and, although he hit every one of them, in no instance did he kill a bird instantly, and many of them flew so far into the swamp after being mortally wounded that they were never found.

The problem as to the proper rifle to use is complicated by the fact that all of our best turkey hunting, especially until near the close of the season, is in the deep river swamps adjacent either to the river itself or to the lakes and streams with which the swamps abound, and a turkey must be killed on the spot or else be irre-trievably lost. Speaking from bitter experience, it is rather disheart-ening to wound fatally a splendid gobbler and have him fly away and finally succumb in a spot so inaccessible that it is impossible to reach him.

The .32 Special has proved to be a good killer, and so has the .30-Springfield, both with heavy round nose full-jacketed bullets at good velocities, but occasionally a tough old gobbler, though fatally wounded, will not be brought to bag by either of them. Despite its

A Rustle Back of the Log—and There He Stands!

Poised, alert to every sound, or the slightest movement, there, on the middle of the log, stands the most highly prized feathered game that may be hunted with the high velocity, .22 center fire rifle, the American Wild Turkey.

Photo by J. S. Ligon, N.M. Courtesy, Biological Survey

high trajectory, some experts, among them Mr. Lanneau, recommend the .32–20 with the flat nose bullet as the ideal load for this game, but I know nothing of it from actual experience. I know the .25 Stevens is worthless for such purpose, and I do not consider the low speed .25–20 any better. I found the .25–35 with full-jacketed bullets to be no good on this game, as it lacked killing power. The .25 Remington was not much better with jacketed bullets, and was too destructive with those of expanding type. I own both the .250/3000 and the .25 Roberts but have never used them on turkeys (except the Roberts on one occasion) for the reason that they are too powerful with expanding bullets, and I have never been able to find a jacketed bullet in this caliber I considered suitable for this particular purpose. After trying out a number of different calibers, I finally settled on the .22 Hornet as the ideal turkey cartridge, and six years of actual use on such game served to confirm my judgment to this effect.

Before relating any experiences with the .22 Hornet, however, I wish to make a few observations relative to the high speed .22 caliber long rifle cartridge. My hunting pal, the late Tom Gregg, of Florence County, South Carolina, was a past-master as a turkey hunter, and he swore by the .22-caliber long rifle hollow point but despite his success with this cartridge, I never could share his enthusiasm. On our trips, he killed a number of turkeys with it, but he never used it on an old gobbler and confined his shots on young birds to ranges not in excess of 75 yards. Even at such short ranges, he lost a few mortally wounded birds, and perhaps would have lost others had they not fallen into water and were thus prevented from running off. A fairly placed shot at short range from a .22 caliber long rifle hollow point in the head, neck or butt of the wing of an old gobbler would put him down for keeps, but fatal wounds elsewhere would permit his escape, as this light bullet regardless of its expansion has too little shocking power for game of such enormous vitality.

My own experience with the .22 long rifle hollow point has been limited to two gobblers, but this was sufficient for me to condemn it. The first was with an old gobbler that had been brought down with a shotgun. While going in a trot straight away from me, at a distance of 50 yards, I sent a hollow point .22 caliber bullet clear through him and he continued to trot for fully 10 feet without slacking his gait before succumbing.

The other was with a large young gobbler, unwounded and in full vigor. Coming out of the swamp at nightfall, I flushed this turkey from the roost in a grove of big pines. He stopped in the top of a tall pine and by placing a tree between us, I managed to approach to within a range of 125 yards. He had settled for the night on a large limb, and had his back to me. I aligned the scope of the Model 52 for a center hit in the back and pressed the trigger. He sprang upward, came straight towards me, and dropped into the crown of a pine, where he was completely obscured by the needles. I fired several shots through the pine top without any taking effect, and he finally sailed out and set a course towards the sunset, which fortunately gave me more light to follow him. As he left the tree, I saw he was fatally stricken, and watched his course as he volplaned to earth. I marked him down by a dead pine a quarter of a mile away, and taking this pine as a guide, I walked straight behind him. About 50 yards beyond the pine, I came on him, and as he was attempting to run off, I sent another bullet through him. Though this stopped him, it did not kill him instantly, and I had to finish him after getting my hands on him. Had this turkey been shot on the river, he would have undoubtedly crossed it before coming to earth and thus would have been wholly lost. No, do not give me for use on wild turkeys any rifle chambering the .22 long rifle cartridge! When I shoot a turkey, I want to retrieve him and not see him fly away to become the prey of foxes or raccoons.

Without doubt, the .22 caliber long rifle cartridge is the ballistic marvel of our age. Its accuracy up to 100 yards is second to none, and weight for weight of bullet, primer and powder charge, it is the most powerful cartridge in existence. Yet notwithstanding all this, it is just too light for best results on wild turkeys.

With the .22 caliber Hornet, however, it is another story. To date, I have owned a number of rifles in this caliber, but have settled on the Models 54 and 70 Winchester as the most satisfactory. I make all of my rifle stocks, and they are of telescope height, of Monte Carlo pattern, with full pistol grip and Howe concave cheek-piece. They fit me, but what is more to the point, they are perfectly bedded and fit the rifles on which they are placed. A Model 54 or Model 70 Hornet so equipped holds its zero almost perfectly, and I have shot one an entire season without making a single change in the telescope adjustment. The most satisfactory sights I have found are the Lyman 5A and Fecker and Unertl 4X to 6X telescopes, with three point suspension rear mounts.

The best loads for turkeys are the standard factory cartridges of 2,400 f.s. velocity for the 45-grain soft point bullet and 2,625 f.s. velocity for the 46-grain hollow point bullet. The latter is preferable for old gobblers. The best hand load is 10.3 grains of Hercules No. 2400 powder behind the 45-grain soft point bullet with Winchester 116 or Remington 6½ non-mercuric rust-proof primer. This is practically equivalent in power to the high speed factory hollow point load.

The most powerful Hornet load and one of the most accurate I have tried is 11.5 grains of Hercules No. 2400 powder behind the 40-grain Sisk-Lovell soft point bullet with six caliber head. I use this exclusively for vermin in a Hornet rifle, but its pressure is too great except for strong rifles like the Winchesters, and it is too destructive to use on turkeys at short or medium ranges. At 100 yards it will demolish a crow and will cut a Cooper's hawk practically in half; but it will reach out and get the game at 250 yards.

A few of my experiences with the Hornet on turkeys may prove of interest. On one occasion, I was sitting in a Ford coupe near an old road running through a peninsula located between two great rivers. A drove of turkeys had just flushed from this site, but I remained in the car as a steady cold winter rain was falling. While I sat there, waiting and wishing for the rain to cease, a magnificent young gobbler came marching along a pine-studded pond, stopped, and stood erect just about 100 yards away. The glass was lowered, a Hornet rifle was slowly eased out of the window, the crosshairs were quickly aligned on the center of his back, and a 45-grain soft point bullet was speeded on its way. At the crack of the rifle, the gobbler flattened with both wings outspread and soon ceased to flutter. The bullet struck to the left of the backbone, and came out through the fork of the wishbone, thus passing through the crop. The hole made both at entry and exit was just about the size of a man's little finger, with no destruction of flesh along the line of passage.

The next shot was at a young gobbler, and the result was equally gratifying. I located a flock of about a dozen birds scratching in an open glade beyond a cypress pond. Taking advantage of the screen formed by the cypresses, I crawled up to within 100 yards of the feeding flock and a soft point bullet from the 54 Hornet neatly laid out a young gobbler. This bullet passed directly through the body without any undue mutilation of flesh.

A few days later I roosted this same drove, and next morning yelped up four of them in a bunch. I was using a dense canebrake for a blind, with the fore-end of the rifle resting on a huge grapevine. The turkeys were coming directly to me through an open swamp, and when about 65 yards away, all four of them stopped. I aimed at the crop of the largest and let drive. The 46-grain hollow point bullet from the high-speed factory load killed like a thunderbolt, and I was pleased to find that it had gone straight through, making a small clean hole without any mangling.

During the same season I killed two more turkeys with the same 46-grain hollow point high speed load, and neither of these was unduly mangled. One of these was killed at 75 yards, and the other at 150 yards, and in both instances death was instantaneous.

Tom and I were hunting one morning and he called up a very large young gobbler. At a distance of 110 yards, I gave him a 45-grain soft point Hornet bullet from the 2,400 f.s. load (it having been agreed between Tom and me that he would call and I would shoot), and he crumpled but struggled on for some 40 yards and stopped stone dead. The bullet struck just back of the ribs and made a neat, clean hole about the size of a lead pencil. About a week later, I called up and killed another turkey from this same flock, and at a range of 75 yards the 45-grain soft point bullet did considerable damage, due apparently to its striking a thigh bone at a steep angle.

With the 45-grain load, I have had one failure to kill instantly. A band of five or six old gobblers had been ranging for weeks a certain section of swamp, and one afternoon I set out to roost them. I found plenty of scratching everywhere, and feeling sure they would roost at a certain pond, I sneaked up to it and waited there until sunset. Hearing and seeing nothing, I slung the old Model 54 over my shoulder and started for the clubhouse. In about a quarter of a mile I reached another noted roost, and pausing for a moment I heard the wing beats of several heavy gobblers as they were flying up for the night. I saw four as they alighted, and marked particularly one bearded veteran that had settled in a tall tupelo about 250 yards away. I got a tree between us and managed to approach to within 120 yards. I peered around the tree and there he stood as tall and slim as a Po-Joe in the top of that tree which was well out in a pond densely grown with tall cypresses and tupelos. My tree was not quite to the water's edge, so I knelt down in order to get a steadier position, and thrust the rifle forward. When I did so, I was disappointed to find that the gobbler had squatted down on the limb, so I could no longer select the spot at which to aim. It was dim twilight, and I could just make out his outline through the Lyman 5A. Taking the best aim possible under the conditions, I eased off the trigger; he sprang fully 20 feet straight up in the air and started up that pond like a feathered cyclone. I marked his course and just as he passed a big cypress fully 300 yards away, he gave way and slanted downward. It grew too dark to find him that night, and I returned at daylight next morning. The pond was nearly a half mile long and covered with about 20 inches of water. I searched for nearly an hour this water near the big cypress and the adjacent land, but failed to find him. A week later, I tramped an edge of the same pond for its entire length, and at a point some 150 yards beyond the cypress where I had seen the gobbler start downward, I found his carcass, with the flesh all eaten by raccoons but with two heavily spurred long pink legs untouched. I took these as souvenirs of a great disappointment. Considering his position and the dim light, I can not say that had I used a 46-grain hollow point high speed load I would have killed this tough old specimen instantly, but I believe I would have done so. Had he been standing and had the light been better, I could have placed the bullet, and under such circumstances the 45-grain soft point bullet would have been adequate. However, since this experience, I am using the 46-grain high-speed load on these old fellows; and if I had the opportunity to shoot one at 200 yards, I am inclined to think I would use the 40-grain soft point high-speed load described above.

To date, I have probably killed more turkeys with the 45-grain soft point factory load than I have with the 46-grain high-speed hollow point load, but I have had absolutely no failures with the latter. For this reason, I am now using it nearly altogether on turkeys.

My last hunt of the past season was one of the most thrilling I have ever enjoyed. The preceding afternoon I accidentally came upon a band of four splendid old gobblers in the very heart of the great river swamp. They eluded me without affording opportunity for a successful shot, and I decided to make another trial after them on the next afternoon, which was the closing day of the season. So I reached their range about 2 o'clock in the afternoon and proceeded slowly to comb the vast swamp in an effort to locate them. While slipping along a water-filled slough, I saw them take wing about 400 yards ahead and head towards the river, which was about three-fourths of a mile away. I marked their line of flight, and followed along a parallel line several hundred yards below it. My course brought me out at the lower and open end of a dense and extensive brake of medium-sized canes. This canebrake was of horseshoe shape with one prong resting on the river bank, and between the prongs lay a dry, open pond filled with low weeds and towering cypresses.

I knew these wise old chaps had sought refuge in the canebrake, so I sneaked over to the edge of the cypress pond along the margin of the prong lying next to the river, and as it was quite cold, lay down in the sunshine at the base of a large tree. After basking there for more than an hour, I gave with a wing-bone call, a coarse yelp of two short notes and in about five minutes repeated it. I then put the call away and awaited developments. In some 10 or 15 minutes, an old gobbler croaked in the canebrake across the pond from me and near its upper end. I knew better than to answer this wary veteran, and I also knew that if I hoped to take him I would have to let him hunt me in the vicinity from which he had heard my call. So I made ready to receive him. About 50 yards from me, near the center of the pond, lay a large sweet gum log with a top made up of many huge limbs. I quickly crawled to this tree top, and found it made an ideal blind, as one of the forks completely screened my body while a broken limb just above formed a shelf that afforded a perfect rifle rest. I cautiously eased the Model 54 up to this shelf and with the 5A slowly scanned the edge of the canebrake along the side from which old Tom had called. About 150 yards away, I saw him steal out of the canes into the weeds along the margin of the pond and come slipping my way with the sly craftiness of a fox. About 100 yards away he stopped and came to attention, and I felt thankful that I was so thoroughly screened from the piercing vision of those telescopic eyes. Between us and just 70 yards away lay a three foot log, and he dropped his head and again stole forward with everything obscured by the log except his back. When he reached the log, he jumped up on it and raised himself to his full height so as to take in all his surroundings. As he stood there, proud, alert and erect, with the sunshine playing on his glorious plumage and producing a sheen as of polished gold, he presented as splendid a spectacle as it has ever been my lot to see. But I had not come merely to admire his regal bearing and transcendent beauty, but rather to take him home with me. So the crosshair was quickly brought to rest at the bottom of the crease that ran down the center of his neck and throat, and I squeezed the trigger. The rifle sharply cracked and the 46-grain hollow point bullet knocked him backwards from the log. In a moment he was up and away, with me in hot pursuit. Before I could give him another dose, he collapsed after a 30-yard run, and when I reached him, had ceased to struggle. He was a magnificent specimen weighing nearly 19 pounds, in prime condition, and with a patriarchal beard.

There were more like him in those canes, the sun was still a half hour high, and the chances for taking another at roosting time were almost certain. But I felt that I had taken my share, so I adjusted my buckskin strap to his head and feet, slung him over my back, picked up my rifle, and took up the long trek of more than two miles to my car; and as I tramped through that mighty swamp, it was with the firm conviction that the wild turkey is the greatest game bird of the world and that his hunting is the most thrilling sport ever indulged in by mortal man.

A post-mortem showed that the bullet had entered the lower part of the crop and had passed straight through to the backbone and had then turned downward to emerge at one of the hip joints. Its course was clean and open without any mutilation of tissue. From this, as well as from other experiences, I believe these standard Hornet mushrooming bullets of 45- or 46-grain weight at muzzle velocities of around 2,600 f.s. are the ideal loads for wild turkeys.

My favorite varmint rifle is the .22 caliber Lovell, using the 45-grain soft point Hornet bullet driven by 16.5 grains of HiVel No. 3 powder. This cartridge thus loaded gives to this 45-grain bullet a muzzle velocity in excess of 3,000 feet per second, and judging by its smashing effect on crows, hawks, woodchucks and the like, its energy, even at 200 yards, is much too great for turkeys. Hervey Lovell in 1944 made me up on a Winchester single shot action a special hunting rifle in this caliber, with 16" twist and chambered to take pointed 55-grain bullets, and I hope to give it a thorough tryout on turkeys (if they can be found) this season. It is my purpose to test several 55-grain full-jacketed bullets of different types, but frankly I do not anticipate any better results than those already achieved with the Hornet high-speed loads.

Now, just a few words as to the weights of wild turkeys. In most of the turkey hunting stories we read, the bird is an old gobbler and he never weighs less than 25 pounds, and some writers even boost him to 30 pounds. Such a bird may be wild, but if so, he is nothing but a barnyard fowl that has gone astray. As a matter of fact, 90 per cent of genuine wild turkeys killed are hens and young gobblers, but a rifle ball or load of shot changes the sex, increases the age, and mightily augments the weight of all such in the vivid imagination of most writers of turkey stories. Based on observation covering a period of fully 55 years, and on data from unimpeachable sources going back for more than 100 years, I state without any equivocation that true Eastern wild turkeys weigh about as follows: Old gobblers, from 14 to 19 pounds, with a 90 per cent average of 16 pounds; old hens, from eight to 10 pounds, with an average of nine pounds; young gobblers, from 10 to 13½ pounds, with an average of 11 pounds; and young hens, from seven to eight pounds, with an average of seven pounds. I have seen one pure blooded old gobbler that weighed 21 pounds, and another that weighed 20½ pounds, and I have records of two that weighed 22½ pounds each, but these were rare exceptions; all of these weights are gross.

The late Dr. Isaac W. Graham and his son, Senator Samuel A. Graham, of Williamsburg County, South Carolina, were leading citizens of that section, were large land owners, and were noted turkey hunters. The father's life span covered a period of 92 years, and the son's nearly 70 years. This gave them a combined hunting life of some 90 years, and this was spent along the great Santee swamp and the adjacent bays and pinelands, one of the world's greatest ranges for the wild turkey. They killed scores of old gobblers, and both of them told me more than once that the average weight of such was 16 pounds, and that neither of them had ever seen but one that exceeded 19 pounds in weight. I have similar information from equally reliable sources, but this is sufficient.

When a turkey exceeds 21 pounds in weight, his ancestry is most certainly tainted with domestic blood. In short, 25 pound wild gobblers of pure blood are fictions of the imagination.

During the past season, a gentleman in western Virginia wrote me for advice as to the selection of a wild turkey rifle. In his letter he stated that all during the season he had endeavored without success to kill an old gobbler that he knew weighed 30 pounds; but he felt sure I would call such gobbler a mongrel. Of course I would call him a mongrel, and rightly so. How can a pure wild turkey exist in a land where fields and pastures of the valleys throng with thousands of domestic birds, and the wild birds of hill and mountain constantly mate with gobblers from such flocks? No, a true wild turkey is never found in such a country.

Whenever I read or hear of one of these wild gobblers of superweight, I always think of a conversation I once had with a Low Country negro. In response to my questions as to the breed of his old nondescript coon dog, he replied: "Well, suh—he pa't houn', pa't kuh (cur), and mixed wid bull." With the rarest of exceptions, this is an apt description of the pedigree of any wild gobbler whose weight exceeds 20 pounds.

THE K-HORNET FOR WILD TURKEYS
By Henry E. Davis.

When the foregoing account was written, I had never used the K-Hornet cartridge on wild turkeys. Since that time, however, I have employed nothing else; hence the picture would not be complete without some reference to its performances on such game.

In comparatively recent years, I have killed 30 wild turkeys with a rifle, nearly half of which were shot with the K-Hornet cartridge. Based on my own experiences, I give it as my deliberate opinion that the best all-around rifle today for hunting wild turkeys is a Model 70 Winchester with a special standard weight barrel of 16" twist and .224" groove diameter, chambered for the K-Hornet cartridge and sighted with a 6X scope of standard make. Considering its size, this is without doubt the most powerful center fire cartridge ever developed. For all loads therein, employ either Winchester 116 or Remington 6½ non-corrosive, non-mercuric primers. Both give most excellent results, and I can not say which is to be preferred. The squirrel load is 8.8 grains of No. 4227 powder behind the Sisk 35-grain full-jacketed bullet. The turkey load for ranges up to 125 yards is 10.5 grains of No. 2400 powder or 12.0 grains of No. 4227 powder, behind the Winchester 45-grain soft point Hornet bullet.

For ranges beyond 125 yards and up to 250 yards, use on turkeys the powerful long range load consisting of 13.2 grains of No. 4227 powder behind the Remington 45-grain soft point Hornet bullet. This load is estimated to give a muzzle velocity well in excess of 3,000 f.s. A charge of 12.0 grains of No. 2400 powder behind the same bullet is practically a duplicate load.

Another very powerful and very accurate load is the Sisk 41-grain Super-Lovell soft point bullet driven by either 12.5 grains of No. 2400 or 13.5 grains of No. 4227 powder. I can not say, however, that it is better at long range than the maximum load of 13.2 grains of No. 4227 powder behind the 45-grain Remington bullet. With the latter load I have killed two deer dead in their tracks with one shot for each. One of these was a six point buck at 47 paces, and the other a spike horn at 77 paces. In each deer the spine was broken, the first in the neck and the second in the back. The second was going directly from me in a slow gallop, while the first was standing still.

With this full power load I have killed several large gobblers without causing any undue mutilation, but I do not recommend its use even on them for ranges under 100 yards. One was shot diagonally through the body as he was going away from me at an angle, while another was shot straight through the body at the point of the hip as he was crossing my position at right angles. The range in each instance was about 65 yards, and the bullet drilled a hole about the size of a finger. I broke another gobbler's neck at 115 yards with the same load, and no flesh was destroyed. However, in January, 1948, I used this load on a large turkey standing in the top of a big cypress about 100 yards out in the water of the swamp, and the bullet, which struck just above the rear end of the breastbone and ranged diagonally forward, made a rather large hole. When I fired, it was after sunset and getting dark and I felt sure I was shooting a gobbler, but when retrieved it proved to be a very large old hen. Fortunately, I had an order for such as a museum specimen, and the hole made by the bullet was too low to ruin the bird for such purpose. In this case I was compelled to use the long range load, as I did not have any midrange loads with me when this shot was offered.

One season I killed four turkeys with the mid-range load recommended above, and one with a W-M 8S 45-grain bullet at the same velocity, and in each instance the results were satisfactory in every way. With the last mentioned load, I killed instantly a young gobbler at 90 yards with a neck shot. Thirty minutes later, with the same 8S load, I shot down a young gobbler at 85 yards, the aim being taken on the butt of the wing. This last turkey recovered sufficiently to get away, and it was several weeks before I found a portion of his carcass. The Winchester 45-grain soft point Hornet bullet would have anchored this gobbler on the spot.

While the W-M 8S 45-grain bullet is exceptionally accurate in a regular Hornet rifle, I have found it also to be quite unsatisfactory on turkeys when used in such a rifle.

For ranges up to 150 yards, I can not say that the K-Hornet is superior to the regular Hornet as a turkey rifle. On the contrary, I would put them on a par up to that distance. In the Hornet, for ranges up to 100 yards, use either the Winchester factory load of 2,400 f.s. velocity or a handload consisting of the Winchester 45-grain soft point Hornet bullet driven by 10.8 grains of No. 4227 powder. For longer ranges, use the factory high velocity loads or a handload of 10.3 grains of No. 2400 powder behind a 45-grain soft point bullet. I much prefer soft point bullets to the hollow points. They are more accurate and hold up better at long range.

With a Hornet using a 40-grain soft point bullet driven by 11.5 grains of No. 2400 powder, I once killed a turkey at a range of some 225 yards, but I do not like these light bullets for such game. Yet they are what you must use in a Hornet if you expect to boost its killing range to any degree. This is where it is definitely outclassed by the K-Hornet. The maximum muzzle velocity obtainable in a Hornet with a 40-grain bullet is about 2,900 f.s., while in a K-Hornet a 45-grain bullet can be driven at a muzzle velocity in excess of 3,000 f.s. The 45-grain weight is amply heavy for turkeys, and when fired from the full power load in a K-Hornet rifle would surely put even a big gobbler down for keeps at a range of 250 yards.

From time to time persons have written me for suggestions as to the use of .22–3000 and R-2 Lovell rifles for hunting wild turkeys. To date I have tested 17 of these rifles and have killed hundreds of crows and hawks with them. However, I have never shot a turkey with either of these cartridges, mainly because my rifles of this class have been too heavy to use for general hunting. A wild turkey has exceptional vitality, but the flesh is tender and easily ruined. For this reason do not employ a 50-grain Sisk bullet in a R-2 rifle on such game, as this bullet is too explosive. Also, do not use a full-jacketed .22 caliber bullet at any velocity, as it will penetrate without killing; at least, this has been my experience. A .25 caliber full-jacketed bullet in the .250 Savage or .257 Roberts is generally all right if given sufficient velocity, but I have seen failures with it.

If, however, a R-2 is to be used on such game, employ only heavy-jacketed soft point bullets, such as the W-M 8S 50-grain and the Sisk-Niedner 55-grain. Load one batch to give a velocity of 2,400 to 2,500 f.s. and use them on ranges up to 125 yards, and load the other batch to give a velocity of about 3,000 f.s. and use them for the longer ranges. You might use the W-M bullet for one load, and the 55-grain Sisk-Niedner for the other, and thus avoid confusion. Different velocity loads for different ranges are essential to prevent undue mutilation. This data as to the R-2 has been compiled after comparing notes with one other rifleman who has used it successfully on turkeys, and his views concur with mine.

Scores of turkeys have been killed in this section with .30 or .32 caliber rifles using heavy-jacketed bullets. In such rifles, use a 170- to 220-grain round nose bullet at 2,200 f.s.

ANOTHER VIEW ON TURKEY RIFLES

Another experienced rifleman wrote the author as follows:

"My personal reaction is that I would not care to use any high velocity 'bust up' cartridge on turkeys, because such bullets spoil entirely too much wild turkey meat. Once you are in a real turkey country and get to working on them, you soon begin to rate them above everything else. They are a grand game bird. A wild turkey is even better eating than a tame turkey and their table value is fully up to their game value. A wild turkey should be drawn as soon as shot. The real turkey cranks also bleed them. With a shotgun, any man who considers himself a turkey hunter always shoots them in the head or neck if at all possible.

"I have shot wild turkeys with the .30/1906, 150 grain service load at 2,700 f.s. and this is a fine load for turkeys; it lays them right down. Also, the 220-grain bullet is fine, even in expanding styles as it does not open up *too* much. The .25 Niedner-Krag is a great turkey cartridge if not speeded up too much or if the turkey is not too close to the rifle. In practice, all the wild turkeys I have shot have been close in owing to the nature of the country; the longest shots I have ever had a chance at were around 100–125 yards. I have passed up far more shots than I have taken at turkeys with the rifle, owing to my having blundered or walked into the flock in the grass and had a 'bust up' deer load in the chamber; under those circumstances there was no sense in shooting as I would have blown the turkey to pieces and he would have been useless to anyone, so why shoot?"

Certainly any rifleman who can carefully read this chapter and not get the wild turkey fever has extraordinarily low blood pressure and ought to do something about it. On the other hand, it is possible to get up quite a sweat thinking of the wild turkey hunting and shooting you are going to have, and then have to conclude finally that you are not so situated as to go wild turkey hunting even once a year. Turkeys are where you find them, and when you find them there; otherwise, they just aren't.

CHAPTER 18

Wolf and Coyote Shooting with .22 Caliber Varmint Rifles

WHAT THE WOODCHUCK IS TO THE EASTERN RIFLEMAN, THE COYOTE is to the varmint hunter of the cattle and sheep country of the Far West.

Crafty, acute of hearing, and with a sense of smell often beyond the understanding of many unacquainted with the ways of the coyote, this animal provides a type of long range rifle shooting that is a real sporting proposition. Windage is a much more important factor in hunting him than in most Eastern rifle shooting of any kind. Only those who were born and brought up amid the nightly wails of coyotes serenading on adjoining hills fully understand their ways, and their shooting can be adequately described only by those who have been expert or professional coyote and wolf hunters.

Once, while attending one of the earlier National Matches, I overheard a Wyoming cowboy announce with great bitterness that "No one would stay in Wyoming who had sense and enough money to ride out of it." I asked him what made him react that way, because I had always felt very kindly toward the idea of a trip to Wyoming and had always liked the riflemen who had come from that state and were acquaintances or friends of mine. "The trouble with Wyoming," replied the cowboy, "is that there is nothing there but miles and miles of rocky waste areas, constant biting wind, bitter cold in winter, and the nightly yapping of too many coyotes." He added that the trip he was then on was the first time he ever had journeyed so far from home.

However, plenty of people like Wyoming and its coyotes. For instance, there was Ed Howard and Allyn Tedmon who knew coyote shooting from A to Z. Who could give you the inside story of varmint rifles on coyotes to better advantage that they?

Ed Howard was a rifleman who shot coyotes in Colorado before the earliest days of the first .22 center fire varmint rifles. When Charles Newton and A. O. Niedner first designed .22 wildcat cartridges and rifles to handle them, Ed Howard stripped off coyote hides and collected bounty money for them.

For years, the late Bud Dalrymple was a professional coyote hunter in the Dakotas and Wyoming.

This chapter covers the hunting experiences of both of these hunters on this little wolf, each of whom specialized largely on special .22 wildcat rifles of considerable range, flatness of trajectory and power, long before most Eastern sportsmen were using such rifle calibers extensively on woodchucks, crows and hawks.

Coyote shooting is a sport that bids fair to continue unabated long after most big game hunting in this country becomes a thing of the past for many men. Coyotes thrive in cattle and sheep country. They have spread all over most of the Canadian provinces which are the best breeding grounds of wild ducks and in these areas have caused untold damage in breaking up duck nests and destroying the young and the eggs.

Coyotes have even moved into the valleys along the Alaskan Highway, and have worked their way northward and westward into the Yukon and Alaska. The coyote bids fair to be with us for centuries to come. He is extending his range constantly, and in many districts is definitely increasing in numbers. Wherever he is, he is a no-good outdoor nuisance. Fortunately in most recent years his pelt, with a small bounty, is often worth $15.00 to $20.00, particularly in the Canadian Provinces where ready money is not always too plentiful in other endeavors. This makes coyote shooting both a sporting and, definitely, a financially attractive proposition.

We shall therefore first hear what Ed Howard, speaking through Allyn Tedmon, has to say regarding coyotes and their hunting. But before we read Howard's story, let Allyn Tedmon tell us something about the man himself.

"Ed Howard was one of the last of our real, honest-to-goodness Westerners. He was a slightly built, wiry sort of a man who could and did handle a 14-pound Winchester 52 match rifle offhand like nobody's business. He, like most all of his type, used little or no profanity; if he did get real tore up over something he might bust loose, but even then it would have a humorous sound to it. You seldom heard any of this filthy-mouth profanity, that is so commonly heard around among both men and women in this country today, from our real old time Westerners.

"Ed operated a cattle ranch in the south end of North Park, Colorado; his home was located a mile or so south of the Rand post office and store. While he apparently made a good enough living at punching cows, yet he really lived to shoot a rifle. His saddle horses, the most important items of equipment a knowing cow man can own, were just saddle horses to Ed. But when it came to his rifles, ah man, this was something different again. The cows' and the horses' main place in his scheme of things was to furnish fodder for the rifles.

"If and when Ed had to make a ride to look for, or over a bunch of cattle, or horses; or if he was forced to get out and fix up a fence, the first thing he would do in any such case would be to get together his rifle and ammunition. After this all-important matter was cared for he would saddle his horse, or throw tools, wire and posts into the spring wagon for the fencing job. But of all things needed the rifle came first.

"As a rifleman Ed was not the ordinary kind who is generally satisfied with some sort of a rifle, not Ed. He was years ahead of his time in that the going rifle of that day usually held little interest for him. He had a 'flock of thirty-thirties' then finally got a Winchester '95 Model .30–40. He wore out, and I mean wore out, four or five of the little Marlin Model 1892 and 1897 .22 rim fire rifles; in his opinion the only twenty-two repeater worth owning. He had at least four Marlin .25–20 rifles but as they simply didn't come up to his ideas of the kind of rifle he wanted he went to the Marlin .25–36, and he used and owned several of these delightful little rifles. And please note that his choice was the Marlin and I mention this for the reason that during this very time that he was using and wearing out Marlin rifles there was a dirty smear campaign on trying to put this fine series of rifles out of business.

"Then came his Niedner .22 and later his Newton .22 and .25 cal. high velocity rifles, all single shots, and all developing breech pressures that are unknown today because back in 1910 we did not have the fine series of powders that are now available. Had Charles Newton had our present powders to work with one can only guess what he would have developed. Ed and Charles Newton became close friends and as Ed once told me; 'Newton and I done a lot of fooling and figuring around.' That's the way he usually underestimated the work that two of our greatest pioneer rifle developers carried on; incidentally he and Newton sat as the main ballistic experts for one of Colorado's most noted murder trials.

"As you will get from Ed's own story he did not like single shot rifles for the job he had to do; that job was to kill coyotes. For several years at least this killing was for the U. S. Forest Service. The main reason the single shot was not satisfactory for him was the difficulty of reloading the gun in winter, and if you haven't lived in North Park brother you don't know what winter is or can be. Thus when the Savage .22 HiPower came onto the market back around 1912 Ed immediately sent for one; in those days we sent to the factory direct. His rifle was fitted with a regular weight Savage barrel screwed in solid; not the little 20-inch light weight barrel regular issue for that, then, new rifle. Of course Ed reloaded for this rifle and soon developed some fast, accurate loads for it. In fact the Savage .22 HiPower was perhaps the most popular rifle in all that area, as it was in northern Wyoming where I lived at the time. In fact after 17 years of use of this .22 Savage HiPower model '99 rifle (I won't say that it was the original rifle or barrel, but this rifle and cartridge) Ed wrote me in early 1929 that; 'My latest pet coyote rifle is a lever action action Savage, .22 H. P. with a special heavy barrel, equipped with a Malcolm 5 power scope. I think it is hard to beat for a coyote gun and I have tried most everything.' There you have it, after all those years the .22 Savage HiPower was still his 'latest pet coyote rifle.'

"When the Savage Model '99 rifle came out in 1915 in the .250–3000 caliber Ed immediately sent for one, as I myself also did. But Ed never did care for the .250–3000, he told me that it tore the hides too badly and as for deer he definitely was convinced that the .22 HiPower had deeper penetration than the 87 grain .250–3000 bullet. And no doubt he was correct. Had he used the 100 grain bullet, as was urged by Newton when Savage took over the .250–3000 cartridge, I have little doubt but what he would have liked the .250–3000. And right here I wish to remind you that both the .22 HiPower and the .250–3000 cartridges as originally issued developed close to 50,000 pounds pressure, according to Whelen's book *The American Rifle*. Occasionally that of the .250–3000 went as high as 55,000 pounds. I shot a lot of this early stuff myself in my original Model '99 which is yet as tight as a drum after 35 years of service. When the 'experts' would moan and wail that over 45,000 was dangerous in this particular rifle, Ed would only grin and shrug his shoulders and say; 'Tain't the way I heard it.'

"Along about this time Newton developed and placed on the market the Newton bolt action rifle which came in .22, .256, .30 and .35 calibers. He sent Ed one of the .22 Newton caliber rifles which Ed at the time understood was one of two in .22 caliber made, his and one to the Ford Motor Company for testing armor plate. He found this rifle a well made and accurate arm. As he expressed it; 'It was a mighty nice little gun.' However, as usual after trying out a new rifle he went back to his old love, the Savage .22 HiPower. Now and then he would pack his super-accurate Springfield bull gun, scope sight of course, when after coyotes or wolves, and please note the difference. Coyotes are small animals weighing from around 20 pounds up to as much as 35 for the big dogs. The wolf, or Lobos, as we call the big, savage greys, will weigh 100 pounds and over.

"Remember that Ed Howard lived in a place and at a time when game was plenty, coyotes were seen daily. I doubt if he could have even made a good guess as to the number of these he killed during the time previous to, let's say, 1930. As to the big grey Lobos it is my guess that he probably killed 40 to 50 coyotes for every Lobo he took. As I now look back to those days coyotes were everywhere, goodness they were stealing chickens on the outskirts of Cheyenne and Denver. The wolves, however, never were so numerous. I have little idea how many Ed saw during his life. I for one, never knowingly ever saw a big Lobo even though my life has been spent in the mountains, the badlands and the plains of Wyoming and Colorado. Ed Howard lived in a game country that you fellows now dream of, but that you never will know for the simple reason that there are too many of you. The wolves are about a memory all over the West; coyotes do still exist in small numbers, so small that the average farmer or ranchman, to say nothing of the average town dweller, seldom ever sees one. Whereas in Ed's lifetime the little fellows were out hunting in daylight, now they make their forays in the dark of night. Coyote hunting as such is a thing of the past.

"One could easily write a sizable book on the doings and experiences of a man like Ed Howard. There was his livestock side that we completely forget. He was one of the original users of our truly high velocity rifle cartridges and as he did practically all his own loading, a report on the loads, the bullets and such that he used would fill many pages. And unlike you of today who load and shoot a rifle, Ed not only poked holes in reams of paper, but he was able, and did use his rifles on game. No doubt but what Ed Howard shot more game from ground squirrels up to elk and bear with small bore .22 and .25 caliber rifles than any other one man in the country. At least if there is another his name has never been in print. Fact of the matter, the average fellow who may read these lines can really have very little conception of conditions as they existed where Ed lived 50 and more years ago. For this reason whatever Ed Howard says is what actually happened; he didn't have to guess, he knew.

"Around about 1908 or 1910 Ed started using telescope sights, he preferred those of 5 or 6 power, and of all the rifles he owned the last time I visited him I can remember only one that he used, a little Stevens Favorite specially made for .22 shorts and C. B. caps, that did not have a scope on it. He was always seeking higher velocity and greater accuracy. Velocity without accuracy interested him not at all, thus when the .220 Swift was put on the market by Winchester, Ed promptly bought one of these rifles. About the same time he obtained another of the same model, Winchester 54, in the .270 caliber. If Ed had any choice in rifle actions it was probably

ED HOWARD AND HIS EARLY .22S

Above photograph, taken in 1936, shows the late Ed Howard and Capt. Allyn H. Tedmon, Jr. Ed is holding his .22 Niedner H.P., the first hi-power .22 he ever owned. Tedmon is holding Ed's .22 Newton rifle, a Winchester Single Shot shooting a .30/40 Krag cartridge necked to .22 caliber.

the lever, but this matter of action he simply left to the factory, what he bought was the cartridge. But as he told me not too long before he left us; 'Now that I have the best coyote rifle I ever owned, (the .220 Swift) the coyotes are all gone.' In one letter a year or so before he went over the range, over there beyond the sunset, I recall his mentioning having killed one coyote all that winter. This might have been his last, as he left in December, 1942.

"Ed Howard was one of the men, along with Dr. Mann, Charles Newton, A. O. Niedner, Leopold and the few others to who you are indebted for our present day high velocity, superbly accurate rifle cartridges. The rifles themselves have made little progress as to design or style, better materials of course, but it is quite evident that the design must have been very sound because when these farsighted and fearless men produced the cartridges, the rifles made good on the rifle range and in the hunting field.

"And if and when that time comes that you may be privileged to drive across that great, sage brush-covered, mountain-circled, high altitude plain known as North Park, where the wind never is still, stop and meditate. This was Ed Howard's home. And if you will listen intently you may hear the echo of the shots he fired during a lifetime spent trying to produce a cartridge with a load that would put all the bullets into one ragged hole."

THE TWENTY-TWO CALIBER RIFLE ON COYOTES
By the late C. E. Howard and as told to
Allyn Tedmon.

Through Allyn Tedmon, I have been asked to contribute comment for this book covering my experiences with .22 caliber high velocity rifles on coyotes. I have used both rim and center fire .22 caliber rifles for over 45 years. Having spent my life in North Park, Colorado, an opportunity has been given me to hunt game of all kinds common to the West that could be shot with the rifle, but as Mr. Landis has asked me to give experiences especially with gray wolves and coyotes, I will confine my comments mostly to the brush wolves.

Twenty-two caliber rim fire cartridges are generally considered only large enough for the smallest game and for target shooting; however with them I have shot everything here that wears hair. One time I especially well remember I rode onto a bunch of antelope and as we needed meat at the ranch I decided to take a shot with the Marlin .22 long rifle caliber, 1892 Model I had under my leg. Sliding down off my horse I fired at the nearest one and as the animal did not drop I threw in another .22 long rifle cartridge, the old black powder kind. Just as I pulled the trigger a second antelope stepped between me and the wounded animal. The second antelope dropped when the little bullet hit it and after running a little way the first animal went down for keeps. The distance was 160 good long steps and I found that the first animal had been hit in the heart while the second had been shot in the back and the spine broken. I do not want to be misunderstood as recommending this long rifle cartridge for such game, yet it is bad medicine if it hits the right spot. I literally wore out several of those fine .22 caliber Marlin repeaters.

My first center fire .22 caliber rifle was a .22–15–45 Winchester center fire single shot. This was when I was 17 or 18 years of age and after shooting at jackrabbits, gophers and the like all day, I would sit up about all night casting bullets and loading more cartridges. I shot this rifle an awful lot; it was a real good killer but not so accurate, nevertheless I managed to kill a wagon-load of small stuff with it, also quite a number of coyotes and several deer and antelope.

Following the .22 Winchester center fire rifle I tried out four different Marlin .25–20 rifles. One of these was very accurate and about 1906 I put a 4-power John Sidle telescope on it. Shooting the standard black powder load, this particular rifle would keep its shots in a five or five and one-half inch group on a still day at 200 yards. Not being satisfied with the .25–20 repeater cartridge I bought a Marlin .25–36 rifle and fitted the Sidle scope to it. I had several of these .25–36 Marlin rifles, found them very satisfactory and killed coyotes, deer and elk; but they lacked what I dreamed of as a perfect coyote rifle.

In the spring of 1910, I think it was, I saw an article in one of our sporting magazines telling all about the then brand new .22 Niedner at the target, so I sat right down and ordered one; it was fall of the same year before the rifle arrived. This rifle had a 26″ hard steel barrel on a Winchester single shot action; I shifted my 4-power Sidle scope to it and later also used a 6-power Malcolm on it. The .22 Niedner was a .32–40 case necked down to .22 caliber and the bullet was made by Niedner from a .22 rim fire short case taken from the machines before being headed up. It weighed 60-grains and had a pointed bare lead tip. The load that Niedner recommended was 25.0 grains of Lighting, he claimed 3,300 f.s.m.v. and I guess it had it all right. This rifle shot so different from my previous ones that I had to get used to it to do any good. It added a good 100 yards to my sure coyote range of the .25–36 Marlin and it was somewhat more accurate, shooting into a four inch group at 200 yards on a good day. The .25–36 Marlin was always deadly on coyotes up to 200 yards and if I could get a good hold on one I figured I could kill it. The .22 Niedner would hit them mighty often up to 300 yards.

I killed 60 coyotes the first winter I used this .22 Niedner rifle and I never made a miss in the first 20 shot at, which is the best record I ever made. I missed the 21st coyote shot at—about 300 yards. My record book shows that the first 45 coyotes on the list were hit at ranges of 50 up to 616 yards, the average being 278 yards; 10 taken as they come run 250, 250, 110, 200, 150, 300, 300, 230, 320, 550 yards.

I killed a number of wolves—big Lobo wolves not coyotes—with this rifle. One I hit three times out of three shots, the first shot running at 100 yards, the next running at 300 yards and the third standing at 300 yards. Another time, in the winter of 1910 or 1911, my brother "H. L." and I were following a pair of large wolves up a timbered ridge, we were on horseback and the snow was quite deep. I had the .22 Niedner and he had a .25–36 Marlin. Suddenly I saw one of the wolves, it proved to be the female, backtracking. She stopped behind a thick bunch of wild currant bushes perhaps 100 yards off and as I could outline her through the brush I took a shot. The little bullet somehow got through the brush and hit her in the ham, breaking the bone but not disabling her. We ran out to the edge of the ridge and saw the wounded one and, across a canyon some 400 or 500 yards, a very large male. I sat down in the snow and fired several shots at the male, all running, and one shot hit him through the muscle of a front leg, cutting a large artery. We followed the female about a half mile and killed her and when we came back to where the male had been wounded we found where he had laid on a snow drift, at least 18″ deep, and the blood from his wound had melted the snow clear to the ground. We went only a short distance when we also killed him. My brother would not shoot at this wolf across the canyon as he considered it out of range for his rifle.

This .22 Niedner was a reloading proposition and I had to get all my bullets from Niedner, they being a baseband style that sat in the case only about one-sixteenth inch, the front of the bullet projecting up into the rifling to where the lands touched the band. The rifle was chambered very tightly and the cases did not expand, so there was no resizing to it. The bullet was a good killer and was just about right for coyotes but would tear them up on close shots, especially if a slashing hit. I killed several deer with this rifle but as I recall they were all close-up shots and were taken while coyote hunting; when I went deer hunting I took the repeater, a bigger gun.

I have shot so many coyotes that I can not remember each single one; however, I do remember shooting a big grizzly with this little rifle. The bear was in a trap and was just raving and tearing around trying to get at us. I have always liked to experiment, so when we were 30 or 40 yards off I tried a shot with my new Niedner .22 caliber rifle. I hit him in the right spot and the bullet tore through his heart and lodged under the skin on the other side; it took all the fight out of him and he lasted only about 30 seconds.

Another time I well remember was on a terribly cold morning while I was riding up Illinois creek from the old Baldwin ranch before sunup. Glancing up, I saw four coyotes coming down the creek toward me, right there I slid off my horse and sat down in the snow. It was so blamed cold that I nearly froze and I could hardly wait as those four coyotes jogged closer and closer to me. Finally when they were 150 or 200 yards off I pulled out of my right mitten and leveled down on the lead one and hit it. When I tried to reload I could not get the cartridge into the chamber, the metal of the gun seemed to burn my fingers and I had to give it up and sit there and watch those other three coyotes run off.

Another time a friend and I were riding along when we saw an eagle on the high point of a hill, a good 500 yards off. He said to me: "Ed, I never was good enough shot to hit an eagle." "Oh, that's easy," I said, and dropping off my horse I sat down in the snow and put the crosshairs where they would do the most good and let her off, and blamed if I did not hit the bird. Just a lucky shot of course, but didn't that fellow look hard at me though.

Along about this time Charles Newton—I knew him well—sent me a new rifle he had just made up to take a Krag case necked to .22 caliber. This rifle was built on a Stevens Model 44½ action, the barrel was a regular single shot Stevens barrel bored for the .22–15–60 Stevens cartridge but rifled .001″ deeper than normal. The load he recommended was 32.0 grains of Lightning powder and a 70-grain bullet he made himself; the velocity he estimated at 3,276 feet per second and the rifle was very accurate. I remember that I broke into print in old *Arms and The Man* in the June issue of 1911 or 1912, I do not recall which, where I gave pictures of some groups I had shot at 200 yards. The largest measured four and one-half inches and the smallest three and one-fourth inches, the average for the eight groups shot being three and three-fourths inches. At 400 yards I shot one group of five and one-fourth inches and another of nine inches, while at 500 yards the rifle gave me two groups of nine and three-fourths and 10¼ inches respectively. That rifle was equipped with a Malcolm scope when it came to me; it was a powerful and accurate outfit, far too powerful for coyotes. After shooting it a while I sent it back to Newton; a picture of this very same rifle appeared in the March 1936 issue of *The American Rifleman*, accompanying an article by H. A. Donaldson.

In 1912 I got my first .22 High Power Savage rifle. They sent me the regular issue with the light takedown barrel and I did not like it, so sent it back and had a regular standard 22″ Savage barrel fitted solid. I also ordered the chamber cut a trifle shorter and tighter. This rifle has a 5 power Malcolm scope on it, in Malcolm mounts as Malcolm used to mount his scopes on Savage 1899 model rifles. It will easily make two-inch groups at 100 yards and I have shot quite a number of dollar-size five-shot groups; in fact the rifle did very well after I had the heavy barrel put on it. I used 26.0 grains of duPont No. 18 powder with the regular Savage 70-grain bullet, but the load that I liked best for coyotes was 28.0 grains of No. 18 powder and the 59-grain Reed bullet. This load gave around 3,000 feet velocity and was very accurate, in fact better than the 70-grain bullet. This outfit had a little higher trajectory than the .22 Niedner and was not quite so sure at 300 yards but it was very good up to 200 yards. The Niedner .22 bullet seemed to retain its speed better and the wind did not affect it as much out at 300 yards as it did the Reed bullet, but I could not interchange bullets as the Niedner was a baseband bullet. I used the Niedner for a long while after getting the Savage but finally went over to the Savage, as the single shot Niedner was such a nuisance to load in cold weather. The .22 High Power is a mighty fine little gun; both my boys and I have found it very good and while we used it mainly for coyotes, on deer we found that it has as good if not better penetration than the Savage .250/3000.

You will understand that out where I live we have plenty of wind. One day when the wind was going its best I jumped a coyote and chased it. After a short run it stopped to look back. Right then I jumped down off my horse and, holding off six or eight feet for the wind, fired, but the coyote ran on down the ridge. I followed along and finally my boy Roy shot it with his .22 High Power and we found that my bullet had gone through both hips but it had never opened up at all, due to the fact that 500 yards is a long ways off. When we used to drive a ridge both ways it took fast shooting and you killed them running or you did not kill them. The boys and I always use scope sights.

My coyote record for the .22 High Power Savage for 1913 shows that the first 16 coyotes were killed at the following distances; 200, 303, 355, 112, 165, 305, 185, 170, 300, 75, 200, 108, 62, 400, 125, and 200 yards, all paced or very close estimates; shooting as much as I did in those days I got so I could estimate the distance mighty close. I always kept the .22 High Power sighted for 300 yards and I could give a lot more figures, but these will give you some idea of what we were doing with .22 caliber high velocity rifles more than 35 years ago. I find so many men who do not know that these 3,000 foot velocity rifles are not new by any means, I myself have been using them for 35 years. This .22 Savage High Power was very popular in my country.

Another experience that I had with the .22 High Power was when I shot a trapped grizzly. This was a good sized bear and he was plumb hungry for a man's leg as we rode up. I put the crosshairs on the place where he lives and shot him twice, the first bullet went through to the skin on the opposite side, the second ranged up and broke his back. It was a mighty dead bear when we got up to him.

About 1914 or thereabouts Charles Newton sent me one of the first .22 High Power Newton bolt action rifles ever made. This is a mighty fine little rifle, I like it very much and shot quite a lot of coyotes with it. I had it fitted with a 6 power Malcolm scope. The load I used most was 32.0 grains of duPont No. 18 powder and the Savage 70-grain soft point bullet. This charge gave over 3,000 feet velocity and was very accurate and was a good killer. The first 20 coyotes shot with this rifle were hit at the following distances; 150, 275, 250, 370, 425, 200, 210, 380, 240, 200, 130, 230, 170, 205, 350, 25, 50, 125, 250, and 175 yards.

I got my Winchester .220 Swift in 1936 and I like it very much, and of course it has a Malcolm scope mounted on it. For a coyote gun it is in my opinion the best one on the market. I reload the most of my Swift ammunition using 38.0 grains of duPont No. 4064 powder and the Sisk 55-grain bullet which is way ahead of the regular factory bullet. I also use the Sisk 40-grain bullet on coyotes and perhaps like it better for this purpose than the 55-grain bullet. I use 42.0 grains of No. 4064 powder with the 40-grain bullet and get about 4,500 feet per second velocity. This is a freak load, for did you ever before hear of the powder charge in a load exceeding the bullet in weight? I shot a two-point buck with this load last year through the shoulders at about 100 yards; the buck ran perhaps 25 yards and fell dead. Of course you get a whole lot of bloodshot meat with such a fast bullet and I do not like this any better than anyone else, but for such as coyotes this drawback does not have to be considered.

We also shot several other deer with the 55-grain Sisk bullet at ranges from 75 to 200 yards and we found that this bullet, or the factory 48-grain bullet for that matter, went clear through on side shots back of the shoulder. A 300-pound brown bear shot at 200 yards with the factory 48-grain bullet was hit in the ribs, the bullet went clear through making a hole on coming out about the size of a half dollar. On coyotes close up, these fast .220 Swift bullets rip and tear in bad shape, especially on a slashing shot. I find they are much more destructive than any of the other .22 caliber high power guns I have used, but not as bad in tearing up a coyote as either the Savage .250 or .257 Roberts. Prairie dogs have very tough hides but when hit with a 40-grain bullet with a muzzle velocity of 4,500 feet per second it just evaporates them. They simply explode and there is grease all around; even the grass is blasted out by the roots where they were standing. It is a funny outfit—blows up on a prairie dog but will shoot through deer.

Now I have given you a few of my experiences with .22 caliber rifles on coyotes and the like and when I come to read it all over I am afraid that you will think that I am one of those hunters who never miss, or at least they try to lead a person to think they do not. Just to prove to you that I am just like everybody else I will relate a couple of things that come to mind.

One time when I was shooting the .22 Niedner rifle I sneaked up on a young, unsuspecting coyote that was out in a meadow catching mice. I really felt sorry for the little fellow as it looked like plain murder, yet as I was getting paid for killing them and also could use the money his hide would bring, I proceeded to level down on him at about 75 yards. He did not know that any danger was near and I guess there was not for I missed him the first shot, and then fired two or three running shots and hit him in the same place; by that time I stopped feeling sorry for him.

Another time I was out and had the .22 High Power Savage with me. There was a notorious stock killing Lobo wolf that went by the name of Three Toes that was working that country. The stockmen had put up a bounty of $175 on him and I was out after him and that $175 if it was possible for me to get it. I was out gunning on snow shoes and after I had walked my fool self about to death I ran onto him in a deep wide draw, or what some of you might call a canyon. As he had a long way to go before he would be out of sight I figured that right here is where I collect that $175. I opened up on him running at about 250 yards with the Savage and finished shooting when he went over the hill at about 600 yards. Firing 12 shots at him, all the damage I did was to draw a little blood on one of his crippled toes. I was using Lyman sights on the Savage at that time and have this as an alibi, but a good alibi has never yet helped me to collect even a small bounty.

Big game can be killed with these .22 caliber high velocity guns, but I use a Winchester .270 for deer and elk for the simple reason that big game is too scarce to take any chances nowadays in wounding one and letting it get away. Years ago when I was shooting the old Niedner .22 rifle I saw 100 coyotes where today I will not see 10, or even one. What are left of them lie up in the timber during the day time and come out to hunt only after dark; we hear them around the ranch every night but it is only occasionally that we see them. Just my hard luck I guess, now that I have about the best coyote rifle I ever owned. I have found the .22 caliber guns mighty fine little rifles for general use and especially for coyotes and the like. Anybody liking the .22 caliber should not have any trouble locating the right cartridge.

COYOTES IN WYOMING AND THE DAKOTAS

Professional coyote hunters get around. Some of them also find opportunity for much rifle shooting. Coyote hunting differs somewhat with the country, but it is still high class rifle shooting regardless of the district.

Bud Dalrymple was a Government coyote hunter of long experience in Wyoming and the Dakotas. He was also a reloading crank, and a man who liked to develop new cartridges and charges. Finally he took up gunsmithing professionally.

Shortly before he passed away, he very kindly placed in my hands an account of his coyote experiences, as we had corresponded for years. This interesting account follows.

CENTER FIRE HIGH SPEED .22S FOR COYOTES

By the late Bud Dalymple.

For that fleet little prairie wolf, the coyote, we must have a very flat shooting rifle. For hunting bear, moose, elk and deer, we can use almost any high power rifle and sight, because most of the shooting is under 200 yards and the game is large and comparatively easy to hit. But the coyote is a much more difficult proposition. His vital area is small, we must have a bullet for use on coyotes which will expand promptly and easily on a very small amount of flesh, even at the longer ranges up to 400 yards or more, and for this work the soft point bullet is better than the open point or protected point bullets.

At the shorter ranges, inside of 150 yards for instance, the open point or protected point will usually expand enough to kill coyotes. But hunters should remember that when game is out there 300 to 400 yards or so even the fastest traveling bullet has slowed up a good deal and unless it expands easily it will most likely make only a small hole through the coyote, or even on big game. This we have learned by shooting the different kinds of bullets into elk, bear, deer, wolves, coyotes, bobcats and other game, at different ranges.

It is easy to deduce, therefore, that it is almost impossible for any manufacturer to design a bullet that will expand correctly at *all* ranges so we must use the one that comes the nearest to meeting our demands, and for coyotes that is the pointed, soft-point bullet.

The pointed bullet holds up better at the longer ranges and is less affected by the wind than the blunt soft point bullets, though on the other hand the pointed soft point bullet does not as a rule expand as well on coyotes as the blunt nose soft point bullet. The round nose or blunt point lacks the flat trajectory of the spitzer. Coyotes are not easily approached especially when hunted extensively. Often we have to shoot at them in a strong side wind and a side wind, even though it be not very strong, has quite a little effect upon the bullet at the longer coyote ranges. For instance, to realize the effect of wind, note the following: Some time ago I was shooting blunt point bullets at a small iron plate at 300 yards while a side wind was blowing, and I hit alongside of the plate three times; then I fired three pointed bullets with the same holding, and scored three hits.

My search for a first class coyote rifle has extended over a good many years. I have tried out all of the different high power calibers as they came out and found that when equipped with proper length of barrel and correct sights they would usually do good work. The Winchester .220 Swift appealed to me as a coyote rifle more than any other caliber. But there were several drawbacks to this cartridge when we tried to adopt it to other actions than the one for which it was originally made.

When we use a semi-rimmed case in a Mauser or Springfield action, the top shell in the magazine hooks onto the next shell and drags it along toward the chamber, then of course we have a jam. With a coyote stepping along at 35 miles per hour that is not going to make one say too many nice things.

The abrupt shoulder of the .220 Swift case and its heavy charge develops quite high pressure; in fact, it seems to develop quite a bit of needless pressure. There is no other shell that we gunsmiths can use for making the .220 Swift Winchester shell, so I decided to build a cartridge similar to the .220 Swift, but have a completely rimless case and one with a more gentle slope to the shoulder.

I purchased a chambering tool for the 7mm shell and ground the shoulder to the desired shape, and also dressed the neck down to .22 caliber. This gives a nicely shaped case that works smoothly and easily in a lot of different bolt actions. I have built-over several different rifles for this new cartridge which I named the .22 Express (very similar in size to the .22/4000 Sedgley-Schnerring), and it has given fine results. As there are a lot of Mausers with ruined barrels, this cartridge fills a definite need for a suitable one to be used in these rebuilt rifles. The .22 Express shells can be made from several different caliber rimless shells, namely, 7mm, 8mm, .256 Newton, .270 Winchester, .30–1906 and .30–1903; the last four all have to be cut to the 7mm length.

There are thousands of good fired .30–1906 cases lying around that can be made into .22 Express cartridges, they can be reloaded a great many times, and a hundred or so of these, necked to shape, will last a rifleman a long time. Such necked down .30–1906–7mm–.22s make a powerful and accurate cartridge.

I have been using mostly the Savage make of barrel blanks of special smokeless steel. They came in 30″ lengths, are just finish-rifled, and are one and one-thirty-second inch diameter so that I can turn them down to any taper and length wanted. I recommend 26″ length, and around three-fourths inch diameter at the muzzle, for a good coyote rifle.

I also put this same barrel on a Krag action and chamber it for the .30–40 cartridge necked down to .22 caliber and this too makes a fine coyote rifle. The shells also can be made from the big .405 Winchester cases. This cartridge I call the .22/4000.

Either of these .22 rifles will handle several different weights and styles of bullets. For best results in hunting, one should use the same weight and shape of bullet, especially for long range coyote shooting, as the different weight bullets usually will not shoot to the same height or even to the same windage, and all this is inclined to cause misses. So, for the .22 Express rifle I recommend the 70-grain S.P. pointed or the 55-grain pointed bullet for coyotes; and for deer the 70-grain S.P. as being the best at all ranges.

For the .22/4000, I recommend the 70-grain S.P. pointed bullet, as this long pointed bullet feeds best from the Krag magazine to the chamber. Of course, a shorter bullet can be used, and I have found the Sisk fullcased ones in 40 and 45-grain are fine for rabbits and small game, but for long range work, even on rabbits, I use the 70-grain in full metal-cased design.

With my heavy 28″ barreled Mauser, fitted with Malcolm 10 power scope and double set-triggers (note resemblance to Hervey Lovell's .22/4000 .22-Hi-Power Mauser rifle—Author), I often kill rabbits at 300 and 400 yards. Also, with my light hunting rifle with Hensoldt 4 power scope, with same reticule as Malcolm (fine cross-hairs with dot center), I kill lots of rabbits, owls, and hawks up to 300 yards. The killing power of these .22 Express and .22/4000 rifles will be a surprise to many, especially to those unfamiliar with the shocking effect of fast-driven .22 caliber bullets, so do not be surprised if your coyote shot with a .22 Express at 300 yards has a bigger hole in his carcass than if shot with a .30–1906 bullet at the same range.

This .22 Express with a soft point bullet will shoot through more steel than a .30–1906, 150-grain war bullet and the recoil is hardly noticed at all. I use a 12″ twist for these cartridges and this takes care of any weight bullet up to 70-grain.

These same barrels, with 16″ twist, used on the heavy Winchester single shot actions and chambered for the .22 Hornet, .22 Lovell, or .219 Winchester Zipper, make fine target and varmint rifles. Also, the same barrels with 12″ twist, fitted to above single shot actions and chambered for the .30–40 necked down to .22/4000, make fine rifles.

A good rifle with poor sights is about as useless as an auto without gas, so I would by all means use a scope sight, especially for coyote shooting. If you like it and can hit them on the run, get a 4 power, but if you expect to do mostly standing or still shooting then get at least a 6 power. You can also do good running shooting with a 6 power regardless of what some tell you, as I have shot coyotes, rabbits and wolves, on the run with a 6 power scope; but a 4 power is better for all around game use.

If possible, have the reticule made with fine crosshairs and dot center. This is far better than any post or plain crosshairs, as the dot does not cover up the game at long range, like the post. When you are shooting beyond the point blank range of your cartridge, all you have to do is to hold the dot over the animal, and you still see him clearly below the dot. A post reticule would cover him up, you could not tell where you were holding in relation to the coyote.

The plain crosshairs are all right for target work but when you shoot running game with them they are no good, as you have trouble to find and hold center with them. The post reticule is the same, and you can not use the same amount of post when shooting at running game; I found that out. I tried all kinds of reticules before I had the dot center made for me by the Malcolm Company over 35 years ago, and since then have used no other reticules for all of my scopes. The next best reticule that I know of for game is the No. 5 reticule in the Zeiss.

Now for the mounts: We want the scope mounted low, as low as the action will permit, even though we have to change the shape of the bolt handle. We also do not want several big thumb screws sticking out to hook on clothing, or catch on the car door as we jump out in a hurry, for that coyote is not going to fool around much after he has decided to move on. We do not even need a windage adjustment, that is, we do not want to change it after we are zeroed, and never do we change the elevation adjustment for different ranges. If we do, then we will be overshooting at and missing good shots at the shorter ranges, and may undershoot at the long ranges.

Before I get too much into other things, I want to say a little more about the advantages of that dot reticule and the best size to make it. The Malcolm people and I were a long time in getting this dot reticule small enough and of correct shape, so that it would be as we wanted it. They spent many an hour making dot reticules before my tests of them in the field, and on coyotes and other varmints, showed that we had exactly the right size.

The crosshairs in the Malcolm scopes that are used with these dot centers are not the common coarse steel or metal wire at all, they are silk spider web and very fine, and the average dot we use does not cover more than one and one-half inches at 100 yards, which is one and one-half minutes of angle. It is very hard to get these dots all exact size and shape. Dots I had put on by other scope manufacturers were not too satisfactory, nor were they as good as the Malcolm manufactured dots. Malcolm guaranteed these dots to stay, even on rifles of heavy recoil, and I have found this to be so. I have used their dots successfully on many high power rifles of heavy recoil such as .270 Winchester, .30-1906-220, .256 Newton, 35 W.C.F. and .405 W.C.F. as well as the .30 Newton and several .25 calibers. I have shot over 60,000 rounds of cartridges with them and never had one of these dots to come loose.

I worked for the Government as a predatory animal hunter for more than eight years, during which I carried the rifle in a scabbard on a saddle for all this time, had my horses to take many bad falls when chasing wolves and coyotes, and never a dot came loose. Also, I had no difficulty with loose dots on reticules I mounted for other government hunters, who used them for similar shooting.

A fine load to use in my 7mm case necked to take the Savage 70-grain soft point bullet, and called the .22 Express, is the Western Cartridge Company's 70-grain bullet and 32.0 grains of duPont IMR No. 4064. At 75 yards, muzzle and elbow rest, I have had groups as small as one-half inch by five-eights inch, center to center.

I keep this Express rifle sighted point blank for 200 yards, and this gives a danger zone from the muzzle to 400 yards. Not long ago I noticed a hoot owl sitting in a tree about 350 yards away, so I took my .22 Express with the 10 power Malcolm and held the dot on his head and almost centered him; then at 400 yards I killed a cottontail by holding just over his back. Both of these shots were made using muzzle and elbow rest, to improve steadiness of holding.

I often rest the rifle over the auto hood when shooting at stationary game or marks at long ranges, as I get more kick out of killing a hawk or a rabbit at 300 or 400 yards than I do a bear at 50 yards.

The life of the barrel of one of these rifles is rather hard to estimate. Both my Mauser rifles in .22 Express caliber have been shot a good many thousand times and the bores look the same as they did when they were first put on the rifles. But I take care of them well; they are more polished now. Often a new barrel shoots better after being fired several hundred shots. For instance, my Mauser .22 Express rifle is far more accurate than when it was first made and some time ago I killed 18 jackrabbits with it out of 20 shots at ranges of 50 to 175 yards. I shot these from an auto as I came home from town one afternoon.

A very fine rabbit load for either the .22 Express or the .22/4000 rifles is a charge of 19.0 grains of Hercules No. 2400 and a 45-grain full metal-cased bullet. It is extremely accurate and I shoot many a magpie at 60 to 100 yards. These very high velocity bullets are much safer to use in settled districts and on frozen ground than the larger caliber, lower velocity bullets. Well do I remember when shooting at a jackrabbit with a .38–40 Winchester some 35 years ago, and the bullet hit frozen ground and ricocheted and went sailing through a farmer's barn and just missed a cow that would have been worth a lot of dollars if killed by *that* .38–40 bullet. You know how this is, some scrub cow that is not worth $20.00, but if killed by a railroad engine or a glancing bullet suddenly becomes a full blooded Guernsey or a prize Jersey thoroughbred and is buried with full military honors; the value of said deceased cow just skyrockets!

I killed a lot of wolves out in Wyoming while I was a government hunter. I killed 12 old wolves out of one district in four months' work, which was a great relief to the stock owners. There were amusing incidents too while hunting wolves. We were moving camp one time when it began to rain and the gumbo was rolling up on the wheels and we could hardly keep going, so I pulled into a place that appeared to be occupied and when I knocked on the door a rough looking chap stuck his head out. It kept raining and getting dark, we had sat there a while (after being admitted reluctantly) and finally I asked him if he would let us stay there over night. Finally he said. "No! there is a place some six miles down where you can stop." I always figured the chap noticed the U.S.G. on my car and figured we were hunting *stills*, as Wyoming had plenty of stills at that time.

Another time I was going to camp and noticed a car slowing up on the road. I held out my hand for it to stop as I was expecting a rancher to come and meet me, and imagine how surprised *I* was as one of the two fellows got out of the car and said, "*You have got us!*" He then began to beg me to let him off said they were only trying to make a few *honest* dollars. I laughed and told them I was hunting wolves, not stills.

The best place to look for coyotes, depends a good deal upon the stock and poultry in that part of the country and also upon the sort of country you are hunting. While working as a predatory hunter, a farmer came to my camp and wanted to know if I would come over to his place and see if I could shoot a coyote that was killing his turkeys—it was taking one every morning. So I took my car and hunted all over his place but saw nothing; then just before I got back to my camp, a coyote ran out of a dry washout, so I shot it and found its stomach full of turkey meat and feathers. Some time later I saw the farmer and he said that the coyote "hadn't bothered him lately" and I remarked "I didn't think it would" and showed him the skin.

If you use a horse with which to hunt coyotes, try to pick one that will not quit you when you jump off to shoot. Carry the rifle in a heavy leather scabbard hung on the left side of the saddle. Have the scabbard under the fender strap, and at proper angle so when you pull the horse around his neck will not be gouged by the rifle butt plate. Never carry the rifle on the right side of the horse as then, when you jump off to shoot, you have to jump around in front of the horse to get the rifle out of the scabbard, and chances are he will rear back and delay the taking of the shot.

When you get sight of a coyote and it is too far off for a chance shot, do not ride straight toward it as this will scare it; go along at an angle and keep crowding a little closer, and if it goes over a rise, so that it is out of sight for a moment, hurry and ride for it, and possibly when you come in view again you can shoot it. Sometimes I have fooled a coyote or a wolf, when two of us were riding together, by letting the other rider stop and stay in sight of the animal, and I would slip around a knoll and likely get within range of it that way. It pays to get out after them early in the morning, also late in the afternoon as that is when nearly all aminals are moving around, and if your rifle is equipped with a good scope of about 4 power you can shoot with accuracy when the light is too poor to use peep or open sights at all.

It is well to remember that a wounded wolf or coyote, if able to travel, will usually make for the nearest gulch or brush, and sometimes when there was no snow I have located the animal by noticing an eagle or a magpie hovering around, as these birds will often follow a wounded animal for a long distance. I once got a big white wolf that I had wounded just by seeing a couple of magpies flying along a deep gulch with timber along it. I rode over and there was the old wolf, bleeding freely from a bullet hole but still able to travel.

Since I have been using the .22 Express and the .22/4000 rifles I have had very few animals get away after being hit. I shot one coyote with the 45-grain open point bullet at not over 120 yards as it ran straight away and the bullet went too low, from a low aim, and just cut a deep gash low in the coyote's breast. His heels were up in the air at the moment, but the coyote simply collapsed and never got up; had a slow moving bullet hit him, that coyote would have kept right on.

Another coyote I shot with the 55-grain S.P. bullet at 300 yards was hit too far back for a vital area, but was killed on the spot and had a large hole torn where the bullet came out. He was hit just in front of the hips. Another was killed at 400 yards with a 70-grain S.P. bullet, which went through just in front of the heart, causing a quick kill.

A coyote was killed at 220 yards, as he ran up a side hill by a 70-grain soft point bullet from the Krag .22/4000. The bullet struck low, quartering through the hips, and he was dead as I got over to where he fell. This bullet, on account of hitting bones, went to pieces quite badly, but still some of it went on through.

It is astonishing the amount of metal these little .22 caliber S.P. bullets will go through. The .22 Express will romp a bullet through a steel plate nine-sixteenths inch thick. The Super-Hornet (similar to K-Hornet type) will punch a bigger hole in a coyote than a .30–30, and the .22 Express will drop a coyote quicker than a .30–1906, especially if a non-vital hit is made. I have cut prairie dogs in two, and have blown pieces 25 feet into the air. A cast bullet can be used for rabbits. When using the light loads in these heavy shells the shells do not need resizing for a long time, as the pressure being low does not cause them to expand enough to become tight. The duPont shotgun powders like Oval or MX can be used in proper charges, as the pressures are not high enough to properly burn the higher pressure IMR powders.

When making these .22/4000 and .22 Express cartridge cases from the larger caliber shells I have found it best to use two different dies, first a die that necks them to .25 caliber, then one that further resizes to .22 caliber. When you try to swage the shell down from .30 or .35 caliber to .22 at one operation, the case has a tendency to buckle.

The shell should be wiped free of dust and grit with a cloth with a *very little* oil on it, this before putting in the dies. Remember, *very little* oil. Too much oil will cause the resized case to have wrinkles and holes.

If you are shooting coyotes and wolves just for the sport, or merely to get rid of them, any time is O.K., but if you want to get money for the hides then do not hunt them until the weather is cold enough to freeze, then the sooner you skin the coyote and the cleaner you keep the fur, the more you will realize from the coyote after you shoot it. Use a stretcher that will stretch the skin to full size, clean off all flesh and burrs before putting on stretcher and hang always in shade. Ship skins turned fur side out. Always remove whole of tail bone (with two small sticks, with bone in U notch of each stick) then slit tail clear to end to prevent water forming in hide of tail, causing fur to slip and become worthless. Riflemen will not become rich shooting coyotes for bounty and hide money, but it all helps out and this wolf and coyote hunting and shooting, using a fine, very accurate, and flat shooting .22 high velocity rifle is real sport. May you have your full share of it!

THE .22/3000 CRANDALL FOR COYOTE SHOOTING IN WESTERN CANADA

We have had coyote shooting in Colorado, Wyoming and the Dakotas, so now we will take you to the snow-covered plains country in the wheat belt of Saskatchewan for a different kind of coyote shooting—stalking and shooting from a blind—both by day and by moonlight.

J. R. Appleby, of the land of the Maple Leaf, is a rifle crank who lives upon and owns a wheat ranch near Estevan, Saskatchewan. Out there of a winter's night, it is cold, with the sort of cold that puts the thermometer bulb almost out the *bottom* of the tube. Cold, so that it is still and crackling and eerie as the Northern Lights flicker across the heavens in irregular, brilliant patterns. Cold, so that the readings on the Fahrenheit thermometer are 20° to 50° below zero, and a man must bundle up and provide himself with artificial heat or literally he will freeze fast to what he is sitting upon!

Estevan is in the open plains country and land around there is rather sparsely settled; neighbors are miles away—so far that one is quite safe from unwanted visits of neighbors' dogs and in most instances the in-laws on both sides—and a man can still do a few of the things which he pleases. The farms in this heaven on earth, insofar as other infestations are concerned, are definitely infested with jackrabbits. With so many jackrabbits there are sure to be quite a few coyotes, because the principal food of coyotes is jacks—where they are in abundance, the coyote follows.

One Varmint Less

The late Bud Dalrymple and a coyote he shot at 287 yards using .22 Express Mauser rifle with Hensoldt scope. Fine crosshairs with dot center in 4 power glass. Bullet was 55-grain Sisk S.P. which tore good sized hole as it emerged on far side of neck.

Just to make things homey, Mrs. Appleby keeps chickens. One winter when cash was low and the chickens needed meat ration, two problems were solved by shooting hundreds and hundreds of jackrabbits for a small bounty or hide return, the rabbit meat was fed to the chickens, the chickens laid eggs, which brought in cash, those which did not were served fried, stewed and roasted with stuffing. As 90 per cent of the roosters are unimportant in the scheme of chicken raising, these were eaten first.

Now then, in the matter of ordnance: The coyote and jack problem was very nicely taken care of by an assortment of loads of different strength and an R-2 Crandall .22–3000, which even bagged them from bedroom windows and from sleds, haystack blinds, and when wandering aimlessly on the plains.

For an account of a kind of coyote shooting, read the story that follows. You will wish that you too could have enjoyed this experience. Mr. Appleby is the sort of rifleman, wheat rancher and reloader who can transport you 2,000 miles and set you down with your rifle, your handloads, your hot water bottle or oven-warmed hardwood bedwarmer, and there you are—2,000 miles from home, 20 miles from people you do not want to see, and you have a long, moonlit, still, cold night ahead of you—just you, and the jackrabbits, and now and then a coyote. "Listen to 'em howl!"

SASKATCHEWAN COYOTE SHOOTING WITH THE .22/3000 LOVELL

By J. R. Appleby.

The coyotes in this part of Saskatchewan are just as wild and hard to approach and shoot as those found anywhere. This is particularly true of the shooting in this area during the last few years, especially since about 1940 to 1949, as they have been fired on a good many times, and learn as they acquire experience in evading the scope-sighted high velocity .22/3000 rifle.

I think one must really know how to get within killing range and then to bag the coyotes. A really good high power rifle with heavy barrel to give super-accuracy is necessary if a man is to be successful in getting enough to warrant continued hunting.

For a number of reasons, a repeater is to be preferred to a single shot rifle, because when there are two coyotes running together one has a chance of stopping the second one as he runs from his fallen mate. However, especially these days, we all have to use the rifle which we may happen to have.

The scope sight is a real help, in fact almost a necessity in coyote shooting if one is to be reasonably sure of killing with the first shot coyotes or wolves 200 to 500 yards away. The scope should in all cases be mounted as low as possible, sighted in for about 200 yards and left at that sight setting, holding off for wind and added elevation if necessary. If there is time, one can of course add elevation for the longer ranged shots, but in that instance he should immediately reset his rifle to standard 200-yard elevation as soon as he takes care of the shot, or he may be away off when the next opportunity presents.

The rifle used in the shooting described in this account is a single shot, falling block action, old, heavy-barreled Winchester chambered for the .22/3000 Lovell—the gentle slope cartridge—which I have used successfully for the last 12 or 14 years. This rifle is extremely accurate and has really no noticeable recoil, but mine has been used now a good many winters, the coyotes are now pretty well educated around this area, and with this cartridge the fairly certain range on coyotes is limited to about 225 yards. It is the writer's intention to purchase a longer ranged rifle in the Model 70 Winchester for the longer shots, and use the .22/3000 Lovell for the jackrabbit shooting and the chances under about 250 yards.

But to get down to cases on some recent coyote shooting. One morning in early November, 1942, my wife prepared to go over to her mother's about three miles away so I got out the car and slipped in the .22 coyote rifle and away we went. Sure enough, on the way home a coyote showed up about 500 yards away. After loading the .22/3000 I turned the car across the field and drove about 300 yards. My coyote kept going a few yards, then stopped to look around; this is the common procedure. As my scope was still on my .22 rim fire Cooey rifle, I was very doubtful about hitting this coyote. However, raising the rear sight one notch I held just over the coyote's shoulder and let go and he dropped at 265 yards. He fell on the spot and stayed down. A coyote is tenacious of life and often gets up and runs and hides, if possible, when shot in other than a fatal spot. This was a very fine coyote with a lovely fur. My little 50-grain bullet had hit him just in front of the shoulder going diagonally through his neck, hence his very sudden demise.

My next chance was about two weeks later. Early one morning I was going out, and there was a coyote about 150 yards from the house. By the time I got the rifle and loaded it, he had moved off to a little over 200 yards. I sat on the door step with knees on elbows and back against the door sill. I took careful aim and missed. He had been standing side on, too! No second chance with a single shot rifle, under such circumstances. I had put my scope (Goerz) on in a hurry and had only tested it at 40 yards. Three shots at the end of an oil drum at 250 yards failed to hit the can—after this miss at the coyote. So I really got to work and shot-in the rifle at 100 yards. Then took a shot at the oil drum and hit a white mark I had put on it, as an aiming mark. This mark was only one-half of an ordinary envelope.

The next chance at a coyote was two days before Christmas. I had a man helping me to fill up the barn loft with hay and oat sheaves, and when going in with a load we spied two coyotes crossing my brother's land about half a mile away. We unloaded our load of hay and oats and took the hayrack back to the stack, where I left Bob to load it while I changed the team over to the bobsleigh, called at the house for the rifle and went over to where the coyotes seemed to be heading. About a mile from home I spotted them on a knoll, near a bunch of horses, so, driving as though to pass them about 150 yards off, I kept on with my team at the walk. As I expected, the coyotes moved on clear of the bunch of horses. I rested the rifle in my left hand over the edge of the sleigh box, got one of them in my scope and waited then for them to stop and look around. This they did after a few yards. Of course it was only a couple of seconds work to finish my aim and fire.

Mrs. Coyote did not go down, but lurched, then ran. She only went about 50 yards, however, before going down and was dead before I reached her. Of course Mr. Coyote ran, and although I followed him for a mile, and he stopped a few times, I saw it was no use and let him go.

A few days after New Years (1943), I went out looking for a colt, driving my old faithful hunting team (from which I have shot a good many coyotes and jackrabbits) and sleigh. I did not find the colt this time but had picked up five jackrabbits with the .22 and was passing a slough with some willows around it when out loped a big coyote only 50 yards off. My rifle was lying on a robe on the sleigh floor, so before I could get it the coyote was behind some more willows. Letting my experienced team walk quietly along, I watched for him to come out in the open. But he was too clever. When I drove past the willows he was nowhere to be seen in the open but I spotted him at the other side of the slough where he had doubled back and crossed the open country back of me.

He only stayed there a second, then ran behind some bushes but this time he made a break for the open and when I got the team around the end of the stand of bushes he was about 200 yards away and loping right along. A coyote travels with fair speed at a lope and will put distance between him and you in short order.

Stopping the team, I followed him with the scope, waiting for the animal to stop, before firing, and this he did about 250 yards away.

Firing almost instantly I had the satisfaction of seeing him go down. But he was up again, almost instantly, running for dear life. Putting my team to the gallop I followed him knowing that he was done for, but coyotes have so much vitality that they will put up quite a fight for life, in trying to escape, when given a few moments of opportunity.

I knew he was done for when he went into some bushes, a sure sign that he is hard hit, and then he hid after running only a couple of hundred yards after being fired upon. On my close approach he ran or walked out and I gave him the mercy shot at about 50 yards. These cast alloy bullets and about 4.0 grains of No. 80 powder are very accurate at about 50 yards or so. My first shot had hit him diagonally through the middle. It shows how tough a coyote is as those 50-grain Sisk Hi-Speed S.P bullets are very destructive on coyotes, considering their small size.

Only a few days later, one morning when it was 42° below zero I stepped out of the kitchen door about daylight to do the chores, when our dog Bruce, which had come out with me rushed off barking furiously, and there was a big coyote running away from just about where I missed one earlier in the winter.

This coyote went over a hill about 600 yards away and without waiting to feed or to milk I harnessed the team, hitched them to the sleigh and taking the hot water bottle wrapped in a robe as well as my rifle, away we went.

The snow was too hard for tracking so we missed finding the coyote and after driving around three or four miles decided the hunt had been a failure and headed for home. But I kept my eyes open all the way. About a mile from the house I spotted the coyote still on my own land. Driving so as to head him homeward if anywhere, I had no trouble to get within about 200 yards from where he was then standing in some high weeds. I suppose he must have thought himself invisible in this cover. He never moved when I stopped the horses for the shot and the scope showed him up as plain as you please. A quick aim for the shoulder and "zing!" went the bullet. He did not drop but ran heavily for 40 yards or so, then pitched down on his head a very dead coyote. After warming my hands on the hot water bottle, I drove over and picked up the largest coyote on my list, and a real beauty too. He was hit low down about an inch behind the shoulder.

A week or so later, the skins of these four coyotes were taken to town where they sold for $50.00 after collecting $2.50 each in the way of bounty.

Then, one nice clear moonlight night in February, 1943, I looked out of the window and saw a coyote at the offal of a steer, about

170 yards from the house. As there was a solid white blanket of snow, he showed up as a shadowy figure—they do under such circumstances and lighting. I took a careful aim out of the window but at the crack the coyote ran to beat blazes and as far as I could see him, he was still going. Well, a half an hour later, I looked again, and there to my astonishment was another coyote at the same bait. This time my wife held the curtains back out of the way of the aim and the shot and, putting everything into it, I took careful aim and let off the shot and had the satisfaction of hearing the bullet strike, and he just sort of disappeared in the moonlight. On going over he was still alive but a bullet from my little Cooey .22 finished him quickly. My shot from the window had broken his back. This proved to be my last chance at coyotes that winter but it was the very best coyote of all, bringing $18.00 for the pelt, besides the bounty.

This coyote shooting was lots of fun as well as being profitable. I have often thought that a single shot rifle, or a good repeater, for a cartridge like the .22 Hornet or the .22/3000 Lovell could be used with very deadly effect for sniping in a war such as the last one, on any front, in Europe or in the Far East, and without making much fuss. A man's head, or the helmet covering his head, would be an easy target at 200 yards, and there would be little report, muzzle blast or disturbance to disclose the position of the sniper using this super-accurate rifle of the coyote hunter.

A man can shoot a rifle of this type with a degree of accuracy which is entirely unbelievable to those millions who have not had an opportunity to become a real rifleman in the field. If he is armed with a small calibered light recoil, super-accurate rifle which reaches right out and taps whatever it is used upon, he acquires and displays a degree of accuracy and deadliness that must be experienced or observed in field shooting or war, to be thoroughly understood.

I have actually shot hundreds of jackrabbits with this rifle, mostly with reduced handloads, and many dozens of coyotes, using the high velocity charges, and have shot other game or varmints as opportunity presented. As time goes on one appreciates what can really be done afield with an extremely accurate and flat shooting high velocity .22 rifle. Until he has had that experience, he never fully appreciates first grade accuracy on living objects.

1949 WOLF AND DEER DEPREDATIONS

Quite frequently the author receives clippings, letters, or comments from Canadian friends regarding the wolf and coyote scourge which has spread clear across Canada toward the Gaspe Peninsula on the East.

Lee Straight had a column in *The Vancouver Sun* of March 8, 1949, in which he said: "Coyotes are reported very numerous along the Silver-Skagit logging highway from Hope to the United States International Border. Eric Nordgren, out prowling around since a recent freezeup started, ran across many deer *kills*. At first these were mostly blamed on cougar, but Eric soon found that it was coyotes in most instances. He even arrived in time to send a .22 rifle bullet whistling after one.

"His father, Jonas Nordgren, says bobcats are as numerous as ever in the Hope area and are 'killing too many grouse.' Jonas shot one of the bobcats at his Coquihalla Camp at Othello."

A few years back the author supplied a deer hunter friend with a single box of .30–1906 ammunition for a deer hunt.

He shot a nice buck with a cartridge from this box, but it was the last buck he had been able to kill for four years, due to gray wolf depredations on his shooting grounds. Said he: "I spent the last part of my trip on my island after deer. The night we had gone in, I had paddled around to a marshy bay and had seen two pairs of tracks, buck and doe, that were quite fresh. After coming back from my moose trip, we never saw them again, although we combed the island from one end to the other.

"We did see a very large track which might have been the big buck we have hunted there for the last seven or eight years. My guide says he is the biggest buck he has ever seen. I have seen him twice but never got my sights lined up on him. Last year I stood eight days before the season opened with my rifle strapped to my shoulder, and saw him three times as he went bounding away. However, this year, this one track led down to the water and he apparently had left the island. Ordinarily, before the influx of the gray wolves four years ago, we could count on about 20 deer being on our island, which is 2½ miles long by a mile wide. This year these five tracks, plus a little fawn, were all we saw and none of these was fresh when I settled down to hunt on the island. Of course I came home without a deer for the fourth year, having meanwhile paid non-resident license fees of $164.00

"As I recall I told you in previous correspondence that about four years ago there was a tremendous influx of wolves from the North which decimated the deer herd, killing easily two-thirds of the deer in two years. This year, hunting one favorite spot on a lake surrounded by muskeg swamp, instead of finding scores of fresh deer signs, we found one solitary fresh sign, and four gray wolves following it. Only one deer was shipped out of Kipewa the whole season (1948). Even at a club camp (10 members or more) in the Southeast corner of the lake where they hire a dozen guides and have a lot of swamps surrounded by hardwoods and which is ideal ground for deer driving, *they did not get a single deer*. The answer of course is that the gray wolves have killed off or have driven out the deer.

"One thing that should be mentioned is the Quebec bounty of $15.00 on a gray wolf which is insufficient for one thing, because of the difficulty of trapping these animals, or of seeing them to shoot them, and also because this $15.00 bounty applies only when the wolf is taken on a farm. You can deduce how effective this is, if you take the proportion of farm area in that district to the area of the bush. My estimate of it is that the proportion of farm or farmable area is about one thousandth of one percent. When a trapper does catch a wolf he is faced with the alternative of getting $1.50 for the hide or of perjuring himself in a sworn statement that he took the wolf on a certain farm. The farmer of course is always complaisant as he wants to see the district rid of wolves, so you can imagine the choice he makes!

"Quebec Province has pushed along their open season on moose to October 8 in our zone, whereas moose mate around September 15. The result is that when the season opens the moose will not answer the call and all the sportsman can do is to go into the bush in the hope of running across a moose. Snow does not usually lie well until well into November and tracking is out of the question. Up to the time I left on October 17, only one head had come out and comparatively few hunters were in the bush."

Here he gave a drawing of the track of that big buck deer, which he estimated to weigh 325 pounds and whose track measured 6″ in length back to the dewlaps and 3″ in width. Modern Pennsylvania hunters will rarely if ever see such a deer and not many within 75 pounds of this weight.

This data is given as a specific instance where a small pack of wolves, most times probably four, killed a very high percentage of the deer on private shooting grounds within two years.

George F. H. Konig, big game hunter and high power rifle authority, of New York City, told the writer that on his last and also a very recent trip to the far western mountainous area of Canada, in British Columbia, Alberta and I believe also in some places in Saskatchewan, big game was found to be almost non-existent in much of the high, mountainous, plateau and rocky ridge country where a very few years ago such game was very abundant. Mr. Konig has hunted this area frequently over a period of 30 to 40 years and could readily arrive at an accurate conclusion of the damage done by wolves to all varieties of big game in those areas. Only persistent poisoning, trapping and shooting of the wolves and coyotes with high velocity, super-accurate wildcat rifles of .22 caliber and upward will control this menace. Not until they have been shot and killed off for a period of years, will game come back in numbers.

SHOOTING FOXES WITH VARMINT RIFLES

By Byron E. Cottrell.

Throughout northern Pennsylvania, New York State, and the New England states, some of the finest sport has been hunting foxes with a good foxhound and a heavy shotgun. This really is sport, but I think a rifleman can get even more out of it by using a light-weight modern varmint rifle, such as a six or seven pound Varminter or .220 Swift. I tried this years ago with a lightweight, accurate, little Savage M. 20 in .250–3000 caliber. In any kind of open country I like it better than a shotgun, and I have killed several running foxes with it in timber. I have killed a lot of foxes with a .270 ahead of a hound, but it is larger than necessary. I have also used the .22 Varminter, but this particular rifle was heavier than I liked to carry on this kind of a hunt.

Hunting foxes is a lot different than hunting woodchucks. In fox hunting one does a lot of traveling, generally in mighty cold weather (if in this area), and often in rather deep snow, and one does not want to carry around a 10 pound rifle. Shooting is not at the very long ranges that are common with woodchucks, and to get the most out of it one ought to have a special rifle for the purpose. This is just what I am getting made up right now.

The action will be a Springfield altho there are others that would be as good; a good Mauser in short action might be even better, but for me I will stick to American made actions such as Winchester 70, Remington 30, or Enfield, for all my rifles. I know they have real steel and good workmanship. The barrel will be light, and 20 inches long, chambered for the .220–250 (Varminter). The stock will be small and light, like a stock for a lady's rifle, it will be a little shorter than my standard stocks, so it can be handled fast with heavy clothes on. Sights will be a Lyman 48 rear, and a gold bead on a small lightweight ramp. A lightweight hunting scope could be used, but I prefer the iron sights, not because I like them better than the scope, but I can shoot them well, and the rifle is much easier to carry without a scope. The rifle will be drilled and tapped for target scope blocks, so I can use a scope for some other shooting if I wish. This other shooting likely would be squirrels or turkeys, and I would want a Unertl 3x or 4x Small Game scope.

Such rifle made up as it should be will shoot more accurately than you might think. V. Gipson is going to make up this rifle, and

I have seen a similar arm he made that would shoot 1-inch ten-shot groups at 100 yards with a target scope. Gipson knows how to make these lightweight barrels so they are *straight* and with a minimum of strains in the steel. Such rifle will easily make 2-inch 100-yard groups with the iron sights; and this is all that is needed. I do not recall ever shooting a fox beyond 300 yards, and the most of them are well under 200. At the present time the damage to the skin is not to be considered, as the fur is of little value anyway. But I have shot valuable foxes with a .270 and standard 130-gr. ammunition, and by carefully sewing up the skin *before* stretching the damage was not great.

I have missed foxes with a rifle that I could have killed with a good shotgun, but I have killed many more with a rifle that I could not possibly have gotten with a shotgun.

One time I was waiting at the edge of some woods at the top of a hill. In front of me was a large open field. There was but a few inches of snow. The dog was coming towards me, but a long ways off, and I was not watching as closely as I should have been. Anyway the first thing I knew the fox was running past me at not more than 40 yards. I fired with the .270 and missed. The fox turned and ran back past me even closer, and the next shot stopped him. I had him half skinned before the dog came up. Another time I stopped a large dog fox at around 100 yards running across a field with a single shot from the .250-3000. I have killed them running at 200 yards, but generally at this range they were standing. If they are not being crowded by the dog, and do not know of your presence, a little short whistle will stop them. I have done this many times, and never had it alarm the fox, but you want to be ready to shoot without making any motions, as they will spot any movement quickly and then they will not stop again!

Before getting a special rifle made up, if you have a varmint rifle that does not weigh more than 10 pounds take it out and give it a try. But the light rifle is just what the Doctor ordered.

COMMENTS FROM ELLWOOD EPPS CONCERNING FOXES

"As you know I am a rifleman, at present using mostly a .22 Marciante Blue Streak in a 12-pound rifle made up for a customer of mine, by Charles C. Johnson.

"I have rarely gone out for foxes with a shotgun. On that type of shooting I have followed different tactics from many of the boys. Generally we get behind the fox and track him along and watch where he starts to wander around in a circle, at which point he is looking for more feed or a place to lie down. You proceed from there, very, very cautiously, using a pair of binoculars if you have them along and when seen you try to pick off the fox with a rifle bullet before he leaves in a hurry.

"The type of rifle to use for long range fox shooting, one seldom sees on the market any more, unless built to order in some one of the .22 wildcat calibers or a .25 caliber.

"Most of the more powerful .22 caliber varmint rifles tend to tear and destroy the fox pelt too much, and this is important when the fox fur is of considerable value. At the present writing fox hides are so cheap they are hardly worth skinning after being shot, but there is a bounty on fox and they are very thick in Southern Ontario. I often use my .256 Newton rifle for shooting foxes, loading a full metal jacketed bullet, and have the rifle sighted with a Lyman Alaskan rifle telescope.

"As to the proportion of red fox and gray fox in this area, there are really relatively but few grays. I would estimate there are 300 to 400 red foxes to each gray fox, and up until the last three or four years it was very unusual to see foxes running in the wild, in this section of Ontario, but since that time it has often been quite possible to see three or four foxes in a day's hunting by auto and on foot, and without the help of a fox hound.

"As to the average range at which most of us shoot at foxes, I would say as close as 150 yards. A chap was in my shop the day before I received your last letter on this subject. This man shot two foxes at 232 yards with a .22 Savage H.P rifle. He finds this kills the foxes very well but if the hides were worthwhile he would not bother using this type of rifle. Prior to that, when hides were more valuable, he shot a .25–20 up to 150 yards and at such distances it made a most excellent fox rifle. It killed them very cleanly with any decently, well-placed shot and did not rip the hide. On the other hand, on the poorly placed shots but yet which hit the fox, the fox proved very tenacious of life and was hard to get up to and finish off with succeeding shots. I believe the first fox I ever shot was with a 7mm rifle. The bullet struck in the hind-quarters—which is very liable to happen when the fox is in motion, especially when running and dodging down through bush or in a field. This 7mm bullet tore off one leg completely and tore up the spine and messed up the fox in general, and the fox dragged itself into the bush (woods or scrub) before I could get there and I had quite a chase. It took a shot in the head with a pistol to finish it off.

"I have had relatively little experience, in fact practically no experience trapping foxes, but Mervin Batkin of Clinton, Ontario, has done a good deal of trapping of foxes and can give you accurate and useful information on that subject. Lloyd Stein of Lucknow,

Ontario, can also give some firsthand information on fox hunting.

"As to the very best calibers of rifles for foxes, we are in a fairly settled locality here (at Clinton), the town has about 5,000 population, and there are farms hereabouts, mostly on hills, and it is rather bare on these hills. One should stick to the smaller calibers so that the bullet may have a fair chance to disintegrate upon impact, and combining all the factors makes it rather difficult to select the very best fox rifle.

"The rifle should have a flat trajectory and get the bullet out to the fox quickly, so that running foxes or those at distant and unknown ranges be hit, and yet the bullet should not tear so excessively that the pelt be totally ruined. Yet the fox must be killed.

"I think that if I were going to hunt foxes for the pelt, that a .25–20 with handloaded ammunition, and in a good bolt action rifle would be my choice. In my shop I could make up such a rifle, if required. It would give almost sure kills up to 250 yards, when not too windy on the bare or cut-off hillsides, or even where grass is high, and the bullet would not mess up the foxes too badly. On the other hand, we load in our shop, a good many .30–30 cases using the pointed military type bullet for foxes in less settled areas than around here, as for instance, East and South and North of here, and they tell me when they come in for more ammunition that the large, long, .30-caliber pointed full metal cased bullet kills foxes very well and does not tear up the hide as do the soft point .30–30 hunting bullets intended for deer and other big game.

"For a rifle for fox shooting, a .22 or a .25 caliber rifle should preferably be loaded with a full metal cased bullet, if the bullet is traveling faster than 2,300 f.s. in the .22, and the same applies to the .25 and the .30 calibers. Preference in a fox rifle should be something in .25 caliber, shooting a fairly flat trajectory full metal cased bullet of about 87 grains at a muzzle velocity of around 3,000 f.s. This to permit long range hits and kills, especially when there is some moderate wind blowing. The bullet at this velocity will give good shocking effect without too much tearing of the hide.

"At present one could use almost anything, as the hide is worth so little, there *is* a bounty and the main incentive is to hit and kill the fox so that our rabbits, grouse and pheasants shall not be further thinned out. We also have some jackrabbits."

COMMENTS FROM MAURICE ATKINSON, CUSTOM GUNSMITH OF STREETSVILLE, ONTARIO.

"Until quite recently foxes were very scarce in this area. The planting of ringnecked pheasants and the general trend of the local farmers to go into the chicken-raising business has increased the numbers of foxes to the nuisance point.

"When foxes find game or domestic poultry so as to provide a steady food supply for their young, we have an increase in foxes, and before long, a steady decrease in the game birds and fowl upon which they feed.

"I have shot but three red foxes in the last five years—I have never seen or heard of a gray fox around here. Of these foxes, one was a grown pup shot at close range with a .22 Hornet in 1944. No. 2 was an adult fox shot with the same rifle in 1945. This was shot running ahead of a hound.

"No. 3 was another adult red fox shot with a standard .219 Zipper while sneaking away from hunting companions.

"You will recall the day you and I and Ray Weeks were hunting woodchucks together and I went over and stalked a fox den for quite a while but patient waiting produced no shooting. The young foxes did not come out on the sidehill bank in which they were denned.

"This is rather typical of our fox denning country. Flat open fields usually covered with mixed grains or with hay, and some of the land in open pasture dotted with thistles and other short cover. The foxes den in the breaks in the small banks and in the washes, where there are such. Ontario is not a rocky and stony country until we get much farther North in the Province where many large rocks and rock piles are found.

"Some customers of course use their .22 caliber varmint rifles for foxes, as well as for crows and for woodchucks, which with us are quite commonplace. My gunsmithing business and my other work usually keeps me pretty well tied down or I could give you more data on personal fox shooting, and on work on woodchucks."

CHAPTER 19

Hunting Prairie Chickens with a Rifle

SHOOTING PRAIRIE CHICKENS WITH A RIFLE IS PERHAPS A NEW IDEA
to many of you, but it should not be so, as it is just as logical to
shoot such game with a rifle as it is to shoot crows when the latter
are feeding on the ground. Further, it is just as logical as was the
shooting of wild geese with a rifle when they were feeding on green
wheat in the days when such shooting was legal—and it still should
be legal.

In the prairie chicken country, particularly in Canada, are tens
of thousands of acres of prairie land in which, when you are there,
you are absolutely alone. In other places there is a wheat farmer or
a homesteader every here and there, but in the Canadian prairie
provinces are found plenty of places where you could be farming
50 to 100 miles from a railroad, and five, 10 or 20—perhaps 50 or 80
miles, from your nearest neighbor. What is to prevent your doing
a little rifle shooting in such a country when you feel like it, and
where you do not need to worry about a ricochet if you should happen to have one?

Then too, all prairie country is not perfectly flat. Much of it consists of slight declining dips and gentle swelling little rises. Pot holes,
watercourse ravines and small patches of this and that abound in
addition to the long, rippling fields of wheat.

So, where it is legal—and except where you can not shoot from
a highway generally it is legal—there is little or nothing to prevent
you from stalking, shooting and killing your prairie chickens with
a .22 high velocity rifle. You can spot a chicken in the distance and
at the proper moment shoot it exactly as you would a crow, a woodchuck or a prairie dog, if you happened to be hunting any of these
in their respective localities.

The present chapter shows and tells you how to hunt the prairie
chicken with a .22 caliber rifle and recommends a most excellent
cartridge to use for the purpose.

The Perfect Prairie Chicken Rifle
By E. B. Hutchinson.

Long range prairie chicken and pheasant shooting, using a .22 caliber or small bore rifle, is a challenging and thrilling sport. When the rifleman considers the wind which drifts the tiny bullet much like a sharp-breaking outcurve thrown by a speedball pitcher, when he takes into account the looped trajectory over the greater ranges, and other similar physical and ballistic difficulties to which small bore rifles are heir under distance conditions, then the full import of the word "challenging" strikes home.

Late in the season the birds are wary, hard to approach, but all in all offer excellent long range shooting. Ringnecked pheasants, in their districts, seen feeding out in a field or on the prairie, offer almost identical shooting conditions; if anything, they are somewhat harder to kill instantly.

To meet the challenges which a hunter finds in the fields, manufacturers and custom gunmakers have placed several .22 caliber rifles on the market. The rifles which appear most suitable are those chambered for the .22 long rifle and the .22 K-Hornet cartridges. The first, as you know, is a commercial case and load while the latter is a custom gunmaker's chamber and a handloader's cartridge.

The .22 high-speed long rifle with hollow point bullet is an ideal rim fire cartridge. It is accurate, is inexpensive, and has sufficient killing power for ranges up to 200 yards when used on prairie chickens. The 36- or 37-grain bullet drops quickly beyond the 90- to 100-yard mark and is sensitive to wind. In order to counteract these characteristics one must be a fair judge of distance, of bullet drop, and wind drift. Over and above that there is a definite knack in aiming with the telescopic sight, but, when once this ability to hold the crosshairs at the proper level above the bird is mastered the killing range of this cartridge is surprising.

This preamble and explanation is given to suggest that the rifles used are not the ordinary over-the-counter light weight .22s with open sights. They are target models, chambered for the long rifle cartridge, equipped with 6X or 8X telescope sights, and weighing from eight to nine pounds. As ultra accuracy is desired for long range hunting different brands of ammunition should be used and tested in the rifle you are proposing to shoot, to discover which make and brand will give the most uniform and satisfactory accuracy.

The shooting methods in prairie chicken hunting with .22 rifles will depend upon the relative skill, experience and cleverness of the rifleman. The rifle may be fired in the prone or sitting positions with the gunsling, out in the open prairie country. The sitting position normally gives the best view of the game, but to obtain close groups when firing a rifle in this position a good rest is essential. The rest favored by the writer, after doing a good deal of experimenting along such lines, consists primarily of two steel rods 30″ long. The rods are in three sections so that a sufficient number of sections may be used to provide the proper height of rifle rest for the different shooting positions, and particularly for the one which you are about to use.

When using the chicken shooting rest, the forearm of the rifle is supported by a U-shaped bracket lined with soft rubber. The rubber is backed by a metal band about one inch in width, so supported that the weight of the rifle causes it to grip more snugly. The bracket is supported by the rods which are fastened to it by means of swivel joints which permit it to swing through a vertical plane. The rods are crossed in an X-shape through a sliding collar and terminate in two soft rubber supports. As this rest is often used on the hood of an automobile the value of non-scratch supports may be appreciated. For ground use harder pointed rubber tips are placed on the rods. The complete rest weighs one pound and this slight addition to one's equipment may be easily stored in the kit box when not in use.

While .22 rim fire rifles are satisfactory for prairie chicken shooting one always has a longing for a high-speed, super-accurate small bore rifle, with a flat trajectory and light recoil, and also not too sharp a report. A rifle which may be expected to give a one inch group at 100 yards when fired from an auto window, which has so little recoil that it jumps but little when fired, and the group center of which can be kept constant in location on the target is required for such shooting. One needs for this prairie chicken shooting a small bore which is slightly more powerful but which primarily has a much flatter trajectory over 200 yards, than the .22 rim fires, so that small game and varmint shooting may be done at a good distance without at the same time blowing the game which is of edible variety to pieces. Quite obviously, a .220 Swift or a .22 Varminter rifle, with full charge is entirely too powerful for prairie chicken, or for ringnecked pheasant shooting because the bullet would "explode" the game and ruin the meat.

The .22 K-Hornet introduced in 1940 possesses many of the characteristics needed in a rifle which must reach out and kill chickens parading and strutting around and feeding at quite some distance from the shooter—and to anyone living in the prairie country of Canada, like myself, where prairie chickens are still reasonably plentiful, but often quite wild in season, such a rifle is a treasure of great price. A feature that the reader may not think of at first thought is that the K-Hornet chamber permits the use of factory

Hornet ammunition. The rifle is superbly accurate at 150 and even to 200 yards and more, the bullet kills well but at greater distances than 100 yards does not tear as much as some of the still higher velocity bullets do at extreme ranges. The factory load does two things for the rifleman; when fired in a regular Hornet chamber it provides him with a ready supply of empty cases to reload and fire-form in the K-Hornet chamber, and when loaded to be expanded to full K-Hornet caliber length by firing in the K-Hornet chamber. A factory load has a muzzle velocity in this caliber, some 150 f.s. less than the .22 Hornet produces in the standard .22 Hornet chamber, but it groups well, can be used with proper sighting for the closer-in shots, and when expanded by firing just once, it is then ready for re-loading with the regular 41-grain, 45-grain or other .22 K-Hornet charges.

A consideration of all of these features caused me to have a rifle built for the .22 K-Hornet cartridge. Not only would it be probably the very best prairie chicken rifle on the market, but it would be fine for jack rabbits, prairie dogs, crows, hawks, arctic and barred owls, and it would be quite sufficient on well placed shots on coyotes inside of about 175 to 225 yards. The extreme distance at which it would be found effective would depend upon numerous things; the stillness of the air at time of shooting, the angle at which the shot was presented—the greater dimension should be a full width in a strong side wind the greater dimension had best be placed up and down, if convenient, when shooting on a still day or a late evening which the wind has lulled. One must take his shots as he finds them; but by calm, cool, expert choice of the time, place and position from which to fire, and then to fire at the exact moment if possible when the aim taken will probably insure an instant kill or at least a disabling shot, a very much higher ratio of kills to shots taken will be yours.

After most careful consideration it was decided to forward the writer's Winchester single shot .22 Hornet rifle to G. B. Crandall at Woodstock, Ontario, and have it re-chambered for the K-Hornet cartridge. A supply of K-Hornet ammunition was obtained for testing and for sighting in. The rifle showed real gilt edged accuracy with factory and with handloaded cartridges—all tests produced results far superior to those obtained when using the standard .22 Hornet rifle cartridge in its original chamber. The new load has a higher muzzle velocity and a flatter trajectory, especially beyond 150–175 yards.

Being convinced that the K-Hornet would deliver the goods, arrangements were made to have a fine Winchester Model 70 Hornet rifle re-chambered for the K-Hornet. With considerable shooting

A 400-YARD SHOT

It was a long shot with the .22 Express but the 70-grain bullet caught up with him!

Photo by Bud Dalrymple

in prospect a reloading set was obtained from Mr. Crandall together with a B & M Handbook on how to load your own ammunition. Reloading .22 cartridges proved to be a fertile field for experimenting, and the handloaded ammunition was extremely accurate. The re-chambered jobs were very smooth, in fact, none of the heavy handloads have ever given the slightest extraction trouble.

This Model 70 re-chambered for the K-Hornet cartridge and equipped with an 8x Lyman Targetspot scope is the most accurate and satisfactory small bore rifle I have yet tested for use on small game and varmints. During the first year I had it, over 90 hawks and a large number of crows were shot with it. The killing power of the high-speed, light weight bullets up to 200 yards is truly amazing. The ammunition for chicken shooting is all handloaded, this being necessary to obtain the desired loads for shots at varying ranges.

Having regard to this factor I fired some 5-shot groups, Nos. 1 and 2 being shot at 100 yards, and No. 3 at 200 yards. All groups were exceptionally small. The load used for Group 1 consisted of 9.0 grains of No. 2400 powder behind the 45-grain bullet in K-Hornet cases. The trajectory is low, and it is the perfect load for such shooting. It is used at long range with the full metal-cased bullet. Group 3 represents results obtained with the top-speed load at 3,200 f.s. with 12.8 grains of No. 2400 behind the 41-grain pointed bullet, in K-Hornet cases. This load is deadly up to 200 yards, while even beyond that range the remaining energy is sufficient to make clean kills without destroying the bird, or mangling its splendid meat.

Few realize the excellent eating qualities of the prairie chicken unless they have shot and eaten a good many of them, particularly when spiced with cold, tangy, Canadian fall and winter air, and an appetite such as one obtains while hunting in the brisk breezes that we have here at times in the wheat and corn country of Canada.

The rifle hunting of prairie chickens is almost identically like that of crow shooting with the rifle, except that the birds are somewhat larger, a slate-gray or buff color, which may vary from dark to light when viewed in different lights, with the sun shining on the bird or when it is standing so that it silhouettes, or is squatted or standing in shadow. Chickens feed and roam at will in wheat stubble, in cornfields, along and in patches of cover around pot holes, small lakes, wherever food, their natural cover or water is present. Their habits are in the main rather close to those of ordinary barnyard chickens or guineas which have been allowed to run wild; or like ringnecked pheasants that are feeding or roaming the same or similar country.

Depending upon the time of the year, and upon whether corn is shocked, whether the rows are grown up much with weeds, whether the wheat is cut short and the field is clean, or whether the stubble is four to six inches high, or even higher in clumps, the chicken sticks up its head to look around, but normally its appearance is much like that of a light gray-barred grouse, if you can imagine such. It may be found singly early in the season, or one may spot a covey of young chickens, with one or two old birds, or later on in the season chickens may be found ganged up in flocks of 40, 50 or 60, to even 200 birds, and when so flocked in large numbers they are normally very wild and hard to approach, as they run and fly quickly. Obviously, a flat shooting, very accurate, scope-sighted .22 rifle will pick off numbers of chickens standing around, while feeding or assembled in flocks.

The amount of settlement in the area hunted, types of roads and how heavily they are traveled, cover if any, background, watercourses and general types of feeding grounds all have a bearing on the hunting, also, the local sentiment as to shooting chickens. Remember that in grain bearing time they do destroy a good deal of both corn and wheat, and eat much of it, if they are sufficiently plentiful. This does not make farmers regard them too kindly when wheat and corn are selling at high prices and every bushel is worth real money.

On the other hand, there is the food angle to consider. Homesteaders and wheat ranchers in the far back areas are not convenient to the corner butcher, the poultry dealer, or the chain grocery. Food is a problem with all, particular with beef and pork scarce and in many areas for years strictly rationed. The prairie chicken fills the pot in many an instance and takes its place on the dinner table of the farmer who has had the problem of feeding the world.

There is also, as mentioned, the sporting angle. Prairie chickens are much more gamy than ringnecked pheasants. They can be shot with a shotgun if you can get close enough. Late in the season, when they are collected in large flocks, that is not always so easy. But the chicken standing out there feeling perfectly safe, 100 to 175 yards from the car or the farmer working in his field, is at times literally "duck soup" for a good rifle shot with proper rifle, scope and ammunition, and especially if he has the small portable rest mentioned early in this chapter.

The K-Hornet makes a sharp report, but especially with somewhat reduced loads is not what is known as a "noisy" cartridge. The bullet is not too liable to ricochet, especially if of expanding type. It is no more dangerous to shoot at a prairie chicken than at a crow or a coyote. And when you do get a good shot at a coyote, his hide, bounty and everything often come to $15.00 to $20.00 per coyote bagged. Not bad for an afternoon's sport!

It is not the number of chickens you kill, but the satisfaction felt upon making a perfect long range shot that maintains one's interest in long range bird shooting in the field. The little K-Hornet cracks, down goes the bird in a cloud of feathers, or possibly only one, two or three float in the breeze, but down it goes, struggling but soon to lie still. Others nearby usually take wing with a roar, much like that of rising grouse. There are no hoarse cries as when crow shooting. Chickens are *game;* the very finest of game birds. Old "Meat in the Pot" can readily pay for itself, particularly when one considers the price of domestic chickens, eggs, beef, and the fact that there is always the chance in many localities of bagging enough coyote hides over the winter to pay for the rifle, or the rifle telescope.

With the K-Hornet recoil is absolutely no factor. You can squeeze them as you hold them. And you can call your shots with a nicety and an accuracy that will astonish you; just like dotting a map with a pencil point. You can place the bullet right where you want it to go. If the wind is blowing, and on the wind-swept prairies wind is often a factor, you can learn to hold into the wind a few inches with remarkable accuracy. Also, the shooting of a few shots, or even one to three per day, will soon show you exactly where you are grouping, if you get to missing and cannot understand it.

All one has to do is to lay a prairie chicken down on a white piece of card, bristol board, or even on a white pine board, and outline the body with a pencil, then make the outlines somewhat heavier so they can be seen from the firing line through the telescope sight, put on some small mark like a thumb tack, a postage stamp, or a small Dennison sticker for an aiming point, and you can carry your target with you in the back of the car, on a farm sled, in a wagon, a sleigh, or any form of conveyance. One can always shoot at clods of dirt, small stones if present, or an envelope pinned to a flat background by a couple of thumb tacks.

Sight in your rifle carefully, have it shoot one inch high at 100 yards. Then it will shoot very slightly below the mark at 200 yards. With your K-Hornet you can literally "take your chicken or leave it" as you wish, and as your bag and season suggests.

One thing is certain, much as we all like to shoot crows there is no comparison between the relative desirability of a crow and of a prairie chicken after you have bagged it.

Then too, if shot with the rifle, it gives that chicken a distinction and also you as a rifleshot, that no amount of shotgun shooting could impart to the picture. Also, it greatly improves your ability as a hunter and stalker of small game. When you shoot small game with the rifle you really earn it, and having earned it in the field, you will have the satisfaction of knowing that you kill your birds as a sportsman and as a rifleman only can at long range, with the individual small caliber bullet, and with the skill that years of training and practice with the grooved bore have imparted.

Chicken shooting is at the same distances as crow shooting, woodchuck shooting or even coyote shooting, in some instances. Your little rifle has sufficient power and killing effect to bag them as far as you can hit them, and as you are only shooting at the one variety of game, you can gauge your load and velocity to the work to be accomplished and the distances at which, in your hunting district, such shooting will be done.

All this makes chicken shooting exciting, sporting, and well worth while. And when you have gathered your bag, it is not something which you must then throw away. From stubble field to table, the prairie chicken is one grand game bird. The K-Hornet is the rifle to use on him.

CHAPTER 20

Fun with the .22 Caliber Rim Fire Rifle
By Henry E. Davis.

As stated in Chapter 17, today with but few exceptions game is on the decrease, and predators are on the increase. Some desirable species are on the very verge of extinction, while others are barely holding their own.

The present critical situation respecting wild life is but a repetition of the age old story of the weak succumbing to the strong—the predators have attained the ascendancy, and as a consequence the game is disappearing. At the very foundation of any program for game conservation and restoration lies the problem of reversing the condition—for game to increase, predators must decrease, and must be kept decreased. This chapter will therefore deal in a measure with the role the .22 caliber rim fire rifle in the hands of both youths and adults can play in this program of predator control and eradication. It will also indicate the sport that can be had in executing such a program.

The youth of today can have more sport with his .22 caliber rim fire rifle than his father ever dreamed of. In his father's day such rifles were not common and the ammunition therefor was not satisfactory. But along came Mr. Burns of the Remington Arms Company and changed the whole picture by inventing non-corrosive primers; and the arms companies responded by putting out accurate rifles to handle the new ammunition. So now the American boy with respect to his rifle and its fodder, "is the heir of all the ages in the foremost files of time."

My own experience illustrates the point. I grew up on a large Carolina Low Country plantation, and the rifle of my boyhood was a .40 caliber caplock of modified Kentucky pattern. Up to 100 yards it was quite dependable, but too large in bore for small game. About the time I was grown a .32–20 Model 92 Winchester was added to the family arsenal, but it was of no more practical use than was the caplock. In those days .22 caliber rim fire rifles were rare in our section, and went by the contemptuous name of "parlor rifles."

One day in my early twenties I chanced to enter a village hardware store and immediately fell for a new Savage repeater, chambered for the long rifle cartridge on display therein.

This rifle had a slide action and a box magazine, and had just been put on the market. I bought it and promptly gave it a trial. Even with its crude open sights it proved quite accurate; but if you loaded it, you had to fire it, as the .22 long rifle cartridge as then made was not crimped. Hence when you tried to extract a live load from the chamber the bullet remained in the barrel. Despite this fault, I derived quite a lot of pleasure from it. I recall distinctly the thrill experienced when one cold winter afternoon, following a crawl of some 300 or 400 yards behind a worm rail fence, I tumbled a hawk with it—out of the top of a tall tree at more than 125 paces. This was about as good as I had ever done with the old caplock. My 12 year old brother, however, subsequently badly beat this performance by killing with the same rifle a redtailed hawk at a distance considerably in excess of 200 yards. Many years later he duplicated this feat with a Model 52 sporter that had been remodeled by Niedner.

My two brothers, who were several years my junior, became so enthused over the little Savage that I finally gave it to them, and later bought for myself another just like it.

At this time I was acting as private secretary for a distinguished judge, and when I told him what I had done he threw up his hands in holy horror, exclaiming:

"You have done the worst thing you possibly could have done. In my opinion a small boy should not be entrusted with such a dangerous weapon as a parlor rifle. He is too young, too irresponsible, too careless, and too ignorant to have such a gun. Ten chances to one, he will either shoot himself or someone else; and I am quite sure he will kill all the song birds he can find."

He was so earnest and so sincere that I felt momentarily that I had done wrong in putting this .22 caliber rifle into the hands of that 12 year old boy;—but upon sober reflection, I felt that I knew that boy, and that I had done the right thing for him.

The old judge was one of the dearest friends I ever had and one of the greatest judges I have ever known, as he adorned the benches of both State and Federal appellate courts, but he erred in the dire prophecy he made respecting the gift of that .22 caliber rifle. The boy who was the younger recipient of that gift, now a learned Doctor of Divinity, developed under the guidance of a sportsman father into a capable hunter and an expert shot with both shotgun and rifle, and into an apostle of game conservation whose influence has been felt in every community in which he has lived.

In voicing the attitude mentioned, the old judge was but giving expression to the opinion of the average man and woman respecting a boy and a .22 caliber rifle. The desire to shoot and to hunt is born in nearly every normal American boy, and it should be developed under proper guidance rather than be supressed. My father was a good hunter and a good shot, and I began handling a gun under his instruction when I was 11 years old, and I had killed both deer and wild turkeys before I was 15 years old. Every sound and healthy American boy deserves the same kind of training.

The two Savage rim fires mentioned were bought before the days of non-corrosive ammunition, and as a consequence were awfully hard to keep clean. In addition, the oils and greases of that day were not effectual against rust. Hence, the barrels wore out or rusted out and had to be replaced, but we had a lot of fun using them. I remember well a 65-mile trip I once took in a motorboat down the Waccamaw River, and the numerous alligators I shelled with that old Savage. They were hard to hit from a moving boat and when the little leaden pills did connect they merely glanced from the plate armor of these river pirates without doing any damage. A few hits, however, always made one submerge.

Throughout the warm season of the year the bushes and low trees that fringe and overhang the streams of the Carolina Low Country fairly swarm with snakes. This condition obtains down into the lower tidewater regions and among the ditches and canals of the old abandoned rice fields, where the tides now ebb and flow as they did in the days before man barred them out and made these fertile marshes grow his crops. All of the non-poisonous water snakes will be there, sprinkled with a goodly proportion of the deadly cotton-mouth moccasin. All are legitimate game, as all are deadly enemies of fish and other forms of useful life.

If you want some real action with the .22 long rifle cartridge, get a leak-proof boat and a good paddler, and drift the margins of one of these streams on a clear day in the early spring. A motorboat is too fast, too noisy, and too hard to stop quickly for best results. You want a paddler who can ease a boat along without noise, and who can place and hold it so as to give steady shots. Thus fitted out, you will enjoy more shooting than you ever enjoyed before in such a brief period of time. Snakes alone can keep you busy if the weather is favorable, but to prevent monotony you will have just as many chances at turtle heads, and if you keep a good lookout you will have the opportunity to add many bullfrogs to your day's bag. Turtles are the sworn enemies of fish, and the snapper is likewise a scourge to young ducks. Bullfrogs are likewise not at all averse to dining on duck; and some folks consider their hind legs a delicacy.

A few years ago, the editor of one of the daily papers in this State, who was a noted rifle shot, spent part of his summer vacations in the very sport just mentioned. Such sport surely burns up ammunition, but in so burning it, the cause of conservation of both fish and game will be promoted. Many are the anglers of my acquaintance who when fishing these streams in a boat, always carry a .22 caliber rim fire rifle within easy reach so as to be able to dispose of snakes and their ilk. It is nothing unusual for such a fisherman to kill with his handy rifle a dozen or more snakes on a single short outing. One such individual recently furnished me a score of 19 killed in a few hours, and that too without seriously interferring with his fishing. This same angler once had the pleasure of taking Dale Carnegie, the lecturer, for a day's outing on Little Pee Dee River, as fine a bass and bream stream as flows in any man's land. The superabundance of snakes so impressed Mr. Carnegie that he soon forgot all about fish and went all out for snakes. It is but fair to say, however, that in his zeal he cast aside not only his rod and reel, but also his .22 caliber rifle, and with a .410 gauge shotgun in hand rode that river for hours prepared to deal death to any snake that dared to allow his boat to come within range.

But ability to handle a boat quietly and efficiently is not by any means all you require in your paddler if you want a safe and successful boat hunt for snakes. He should in addition be sober, steady and dependable in any emergency. Under no circumstances should he be a superstitious nitwit who by his antics might turn an expedition of pleasure into one of peril. My friend the judge, had an eccentric paddler of this type who manned his boat on all his fishing trips. This superstitious African could handle a boat with the best of them, but he was mortally afraid of a caterpillar. Snakes held no terror for him and if by chance a big moccasin fell in the boat he nonchalantly dispatched and pitched him overboard with his paddle. If, however, a caterpillar fell in the boat he frantically went overboard and made for shore. No sensible man should risk his life by attempting to shoot snakes with such an individual handling the paddle.

Snakes lying up in bushes or low growing trees present rather large targets and hence are easy to hit. Successful shooting of turtles, however, requires more skill and steadier holding. The black-villain of the tribe, the snapper, shows little more than the tip of his snout above the water line, and hence presents a difficult shot. Other species expose more of the head above the water, and so furnish better targets.

Some years ago, my shooting pal and I decided to devote the Fourth of July holiday to ridding two fish ponds of turtles. We killed well over 100, and in so doing we considered the day had been well spent. We could have used a couple of boys to aid us in this good work, but they were not available. Any boy would enjoy shooting the aquatic predators mentioned, and his fun would have constructive value. Of course, he should be rather mature and not given to taking chances with his own safety before taking up boat hunting for snakes, turtles and frogs. Before reaching this stage he can spend many a pleasant and useful hour shooting them with his .22 caliber rim fire rifle from the stream borders.

In appearance one of the most repulsive of reptiles is the four-banded coluber or chicken snake, and appearance is but an index of its evil ways. This ruthless robber grows to a length of seven feet and is one of the heaviest of North American serpents. It is equally at home in the trees or on the ground, on land, or in the water. It devours the eggs and young of every ground nesting bird, wild or domestic, including turkeys, and those of many that do not so nest. I know of an instance where a pair of six foot specimens were shot as their heads protruded from the hole to a wood duck's nest in a hollow cypress tree located in the middle of a mill pond some three-eighths of a mile wide.

A fisherman happened to see the duck fly from the nest, and on investigation found and killed these two nest robbers. A big one will gobble up a half dozen baby chicks at a meal, and will come back for the remainder of the brood. They are partial to oak trees and take heavy toll from the squirrels that are born in such places.

One of the shots that stands out in my memory was made on one of these treetop prowlers. A flock of blue jays suddenly went wild one summer afternoon in the top of a tall hickory tree, standing in the yard of my old home. Hearing the commotion I picked up the Savage repeater, and went to the back porch to investigate. By watching the excited jays, I discovered the object of their attack to be a big chicken snake stretched along one of the upper limbs. The bullet caught him near the neck, and his tree prowling for squirrels, young birds and eggs was ended. The range was about 50 yards.

The summer after I gave my brothers the Savage repeater, I spent my vacation with them in the old home. In the grove in front of the house and about 75 yards from it stood an enormous red oak. On its south side about 30 feet from the ground, was the stub of a limb some two and a half feet in diameter that had been broken off years before. This stub was hollow, and the lower side projected so as to form a sort of platform. This hollow proved to be a veritable den of chicken snakes. Nearly every day about noon, one would be found sunning on the platform, and the Savage would promptly knock him off—minus a head or with a broken neck. Altogether, we killed between 20 and 40 of these snakes on that one broken limb that summer. No large ones were killed; the average being about three feet in length. This was the largest concentration of them I have ever witnessed, and they really gave us some nice offhand practice.

Every now and again some apologist comes along and tries to defend even such a reprobate as this slithering thief. One afternoon, I was handling, along with another driver, a pack of hounds on a deer hunt. As we came to a canal, a huge chicken snake lay stretched out on the log on which we had to cross. Sensing my movements, the other driver exclaimed, "Don't kill him, he is a good snake," to which I replied, "He will be as soon as I can pull this trigger." Thereupon I shot his head off with a Stevens Favorite .22 caliber rifle I always carried for just such "critters." A few months later the wisdom of my action was demonstrated when two giants of the same species were found gorged with turkey eggs in two nests in the same swamp. Needless to say they suffered the same fate as their relative. Like most people, I have a natural aversion to snakes. I concede that the king snake and a few others are beneficial, but many of the non-poisonous species are decidedly harmful.

In addition to those already mentioned, the list of the harmful should include the black snake, the constrictors, and the coachwhip if you want to protect game and song birds. The corn snake is said to be beneficial but as to this I feel like Donald declared he felt about Sandy's piety, "I have my doubt about it." It always seemed to me that this alleged benefactor charged too much for his services. It is quite true that he will catch many of the mice and rats he chances to meet, but it is equally true that he will eat every egg and baby chick he comes across. If you have no poultry, keep him; but if you do have poultry shoot him, and poison your rats. I shot a big one by lantern light one night in a coop of baby chicks and he had already swallowed several. Regardless of how efficient he may be otherwise, no board of directors would keep a cashier who was known to be embezzling the funds of the bank; and this, it would seem, is a parallel case.

Barring the cottonmouth, the venomous snakes, except in the sections where they congregate for hibernation, afford rather infrequent targets, and as a consequence hunting them with a .22 caliber rifle would be rather dull sport. In those regions where they congregate for hibernation, however, much action could be obtained either in the spring or the fall. But, remember a rattlesnake is a dangerous creature, and whoever hunts it had better keep ever on the alert and be sure he is not in position to be struck by one snake while he is drawing a bead on another one. When it comes to meeting, on his own ground in a Southern swamp, a great six-foot canebrake rattler or an even larger diamondback, I believe, I would prefer Mr. Carnegie's weapon, but I would want it to be of at least 12 gauge and charged with number six shot.

This brings to mind an incident that occurred many years ago. A friend of mine, who was noted for his coolness and physical courage, was hunting fox squirrels with a caplock rifle in the Southern pine woods. Coming to a large prone log, he briskly stepped up on it and was horrified to see lying a short distance in front of it some half dozen huge rattlesnakes. Realizing the utter inefficiency of his weapon against such an aggregation of certain death, he quietly withdrew without firing a shot. With a good .22 caliber rim fire repeater he could doubtless have taken care of the situation, but he could have done it more easily and with less danger to himself with a 12 gauge repeater.

In our hunting club was a member with a young son who became the pet of the club. His father was a fine shot, and little Bill insisted that he be taken on every hunt, even though he was too small to use a gun. It was sufficient if he were to go along and carry the squirrels, or to sit with father on a deer stand; and when father downed a buck Bill's joy knew no bounds. But there came a day when Bill was big enough to learn to shoot, so his father gave him a Remington rim fire bolt action single shot rifle and started his training. He proved a most apt pupil, and ere long with that little Remington could stop in its tracks either a running rabbit or a racing squirrel. Fortunately for Bill, the family lived on a large Southern farm where both game and pests were plentiful, thus affording him abundant opportunities to practice on living targets.

On the morning of his thirteenth Christmas, he armed with the little rifle and accompanied by an older brother and Old Red, a fighting hound, started out on what was to prove a rather unusual adventure. At the rear of the farm was an extensive and rather thick swamp that was under fence as a pasture. After assisting his brother in rounding up a brood sow with a litter of young pigs, he decided to take Old Red and explore that swamp by himself. Accordingly he worked his way through a canebrake, and when he reached a convenient opening he decided to rest and do more reconnoitering before proceeding. So he sat down with his back to a tree and with Old Red at his feet. Immediately in front was another canebrake and from its interior suddenly came an unusual noise. In a few moments two rather large animals came into view on the trunk of a tree just above the cane tops, and rapidly climbed up into the limbs. Being of Scotch descent, Bill quickly sized up the situation and said to himself, "I certainly am in luck today. Yonder go two big coons, and here is my chance to make $10.00 out of their hides."

The range was rather long—about 95 yards—but he knew how to adjust his sights and he knew in addition that he must kill the lower one first so as to keep the upper one from jumping out. So he elevated his rear sight, stretched out behind his tree, and opened fire. Before letting go the lower one absorbed four solid bullets, which was the only kind Bill had available. He then turned to number two and proceeded to pour in the hot lead. After repeated hits this one climbed into a fork from which it could not be dislodged. This required Bill to go to the root of the tree in order to finish the kill. On arriving there and looking up he was amazed to find he had been shooting bobcats instead of raccoons. A brain shot speedily finished number two, and with it safe in the bag, search was made for number one. Nowhere could it be found. Old Red was put on the trail but that was one day he was not spoiling for a fight, and he refused to follow it. A few days later this cat was found dead with four bullet holes in its side. An autopsy on number two disclosed that it had dined on pig the preceding night.

So Bill's ability to shoot a rifle was already paying dividends in the way of conserving the family meat supply. He got quite a thrill out of bagging two cats in one day, but being a thrifty Scot, he was not wholly reconciled to the loss of the $10.00 he felt sure were his when he thought he saw two big coons going up one tree.

Before he had discarded knee trousers Bill had accounted for many deer, not a few of which were shot on solitary hunts taken by him on the old home farm. In a few short years the little pet of the club became its best hunter, woodsman and marksman, and with it all he lost none of his modesty and gentility.

With such a background it is no wonder that he made a fine record as a paratrooper in the great War. The great adventure over, he returned home unscratched, and now holds a responsible position with a great railroad system. But he is still the ardent sportsman, and quite ready to join a hunt either for game or varmints whenever the opportunity offers.

Just now I am having the pleasure of assisting another young fellow to develop into a hunter and rifleman. This is my young friend Jimmie. He manifests the same desire to excel that characterized Bill, and barring no untoward events he will untimately attain to just as high a degree of success. A few years ago, I happened to make a social call one afternoon in the home of Jimmie's parents. He was then a boy some 10 or 12 years of age. Knowing my keen interest in hunting and in rifles, he proudly exhibited a brand new automatic .22 caliber rim fire rifle he had just bought with money he had earned himself. I examined his treasure carefully and then said,

"Jimmie do you really want to learn to shoot a rifle?" and received the reply "I certainly do." I told him if this was his ambition, he would do far better if he sold the automatic and bought a rifle more suited to his needs. This he promptly decided to do. So together we scanned the ads in *The American Rifleman* until we found a good Model 52 at a reasonable price, and this he bought. In a short time the rifle came and we rigged it up as best we could for hunting purposes. This done, I suggested a crow hunt and Jimmie eagerly assented.

We went out to a large farm where crows of both species, fish and common, were rather abundant and there planned our attack. The new rifle was first sighted in at 65 yards with high speed long rifle hollow point ammunition, and we then went down to a dead pine in the edge of the swamp of a large creek bordering the farm. After screening ourselves, I began to call. Soon the air around the top of that dead tree was alive with a whirling mass of squalling crows. One settled on an upper limb only to die at the crack of Jimmie's rifle. Another perched and met the same fate from the same source. This one, however, lodged; and the survivors suddenly became silent and vanished. A second shot brought down the crow that had lodged, and Jimmie retrieved them both. With his eyes beaming, he turned to me and exclaimed, "I like to shoot ducks, but this crow-shooting is the finest, most thrilling sport I have ever had." Right there another full-fledged crow shooter took his place in the ranks of those who are helping the cause of game conservation so greatly by depleting the ranks of this arch despoiler.

That fall and winter we operated as a two-man team in our war on crows, and in so doing followed the technique I had long employed in such hunting. In brief, this was to take both .22 caliber rim fire rifles and one or more .22 caliber center fire rifles on every trip. In all the stories of crow shooting I have ever read never once has mention been made of the sport a .22 rim fire rifle chambered for the long rifle can afford; and yet in this Southern country it is the cheapest to use and withal the most efficient weapon to employ on crows. Just before daylight on a fall or winter morning, Jimmie and I would leave home and drive to a spot near which a flock of crows was accustomed to roost. We would then locate a tall open tree, preferably a dead pine, and make our blinds on opposite sides; it being agreed that he would take the shots on certain limbs while I would take those on the others. This system always worked, unless the crows had been made wary by too much shooting on prior occasions, and we frequently would get five or six at a tree. When the flight stopped we drove to another locality and repeated the performance. In going from one locality to another we frequently got a shot at a crow or a hawk with the Hornet, K-Hornet or R-2 that we had along and these rifles appreciably increased the size of our bags.

Take a typical case. Jimmie's father had bought from T. G. Samworth his plantation known as Exchange on Great Pee Dee River and Mr. Samworth had bought and moved to his present plantation of Dirleton located lower down on the same river. I happened to be at Exchange one Friday night, so Jimmie and I decided to give the crows a round next morning. Just before sunrise we drove out armed with two Model 52s, a Model 70 K-Hornet and a R-2 Sharps-Borchardt. We drifted rather slowly down the dirt roads and with the two center fire rifles took several crows and a few hawks.

When we reached the avenue at Dirleton, we stopped to look over a lettuce field and found the ground black with crows of both species. Jimmie smashed one on the ground with the R-2, and then we took the two rim fires and left the car in search of a good tree to which they could be called. About 200 yards away in a dense grove of large pines we located a tall dead pine. So we made for it, and took our positions. I put on a typical owl fight, which always sets crows crazy, and in a few minutes the air above us literally swarmed with crows. With those two rim fires we took six off that pine before the whirling throng became aware of what was happening; and then the cawing ceased and the living slunk away. We returned to the car and started on our return trip. A part of the road ran through an old field thickly grown to large pines. Just as we came to the old field a crow called, and we stopped the car. No convenient dead pine was in sight, and not thinking that we would have a chance to repeat with the rim fires the performance at the Dirleton avenue we did not get out of the car. Thrusting my head out of the window, I started an owl fight. (I call with my voice, and can easily beat any mechanical crow-call.) Instantly bedlam broke loose, and a black gang took possession of the pines in that old field. Jimmie knocked out three with the R-2, while I accounted for two with the K-Hornet, before the drove bade us farewell. This flock decoyed unusually well, and if we had handled them with the rim fires we no doubt would have made a bigger bag. Our whole outing covered a period of about two hours and we killed 15 or 16 crows. My young protégé was jubilant when he got back home and if I had not fired a gun I would have felt amply rewarded by the fun he had enjoyed that day. This was the largest bag Jimmie and I ever made on a single hunt, but we have staged many others in which we had just as much fun.

Jimmie is now a college student but he is the same loyal friend, enthusiastic hunter, and perfect gentleman. When he came home

for the holidays last Christmas, he promptly sought me out to arrange a crow hunt. I was only too glad to comply and we had a nice
and successful shoot.

When he comes home this summer we plan to take that Model
52 and have a good gunsmith convert it into a sporter. Then I am
going to stock it just like mine. This accomplished he will be even
better equipped to hold up his end of our two-man crow team, and
I feel sure with it he will sound taps for a goodly quota of these black
villains.

I have made almost as good a record when hunting alone with the
combination of a rifle for the .22 long rifle cartridge and a rifle for
a good .22 caliber center fire cartridge as I have made when hunting with a shooting partner. On one hunt just after daylight I killed
12 crows in a brief space with the .22 caliber long rifle cartridge,
and added two more to the bag with the R-2 I carried for the long
shots. I have had as many as 10 shots on a flock of crows at one time
at one dead tree. If you keep concealed and they do not come too
thick and fast, it is nothing unusual to kill a half dozen from one
tree. However if you are so unfortunate as to kill one and it lodges
in the tree, your shooting there is over, as the survivors promptly
leave. On the other hand if one is killed and falls to the ground in
such position as to be seen the others become more frantic, and con-
tinuously alight, thus affording more shots. Writers whose experience with the crow has been in the Northern section of its range give
it great credit for wariness and sagacity. This doubtless is true in
that region, but it definitely is not true in the Carolina Low Country. The crow is a rogue in the latter region, wreaking havoc on
crops of many kinds. The amount of damage a comparatively small
flock can do in a watermelon field, a pecan grove or a collection of
peanut stacks is incalculable. But killing them presents no problem,
if an amateur has not previously frightened them. Just take a good
rifle and a supply of .22 caliber long rifle hollow point cartridges for
it, and go to a nice open tree to which you can call and then proceed to call them. You do not need a particularly good blind, but all
you need is to put the crosshair on him when he alights and press
the trigger while he is yelling at the top of his voice.

With a wild turkey it would be quite a different story. He has 10
times the sense of a crow, and you had better be well concealed and
ready to shoot when he comes; for in his case, as the mountaineer
said, you are dealing with a combination of steel spring and chicken
hawk. He will never stand still and squawk like he is crazy while you
in plain view calmly raise a rifle to blow his head off.

Another pest that in certain places furnishes good sport with the
.22 caliber rim fire rifle is the common rat. I have a friend who has

had an unusual amount of sport with a Model 57 Winchester in late afternoons shooting rats at a certain place along the wharves of a coastal city. In interior towns the best place for such shooting is the garbage dump at the incinerator. Of course, this kind of shooting calls for extreme care as to proper back stops, and should not be indulged in where they are not available. However it is a most worthwhile form of pest control, and should be encouraged where no danger to human life would be involved.

Fifty-five years of active experience with game of many kinds in one of the finest game regions of our great country has given me sufficient background on which to found a decided distrust of hawks and owls. Some of the apologists see red when you prove beyond a reasonable doubt that one of their particular favorites is nothing but a wolf in sheep's clothing and with a bloody record for killing desirable game of many kinds. Some years ago when Ray P. Holland, then editor of *Field and Stream*, reported the wholesale slaughter of both ducks and Hungarian partridges in western Canada, by so-called beneficial hawks, he was ridiculed, and against his actual observations in the field were cited the findings of some armchair stomach-examiner. I have received similar treatment when I reported wild turkeys killed by redtailed hawks.

But what do I care as to the findings of Prof. John Smith when I saw a certain hawk or owl kill a desirable species of game. Recently while hunting wild turkeys in the swamp of Great Pee Dee River I happened to see a large bird fly from the ground and make off into the swamp. Upon going up to investigate, I found the half eaten body of a full grown gray squirrel. I thereupon resolved that I would kill that predator whether I found any turkeys or not. So I backed up against a tree and settled down to wait the killer's return. In about an hour a barred owl sailed up and looked over toward the squirrel on the ground. It gave me infinite satisfaction to center a crosshair on his worthless form and to see him collapse when that Model 70 K-Hornet spoke. It was too late then to get a turkey, but we had one less game destroyer on our hunting property.

With the destruction I have seen wrought by the redtailed hawk on both game and poultry during my long years afield, it is useless for anyone to tell me he is beneficial, because forsooth he catches a few rats. If this is all his apologists can offer, shoot him, and get a fox terrier, which will kill more rats in a week than a hawk will in a year and will not eat up your poultry and game to boot.

In shooting hawks, however, the .22 caliber long rifle cartridge is definitely not in its element. I have killed with it a great many hawks that came to a crowcall, but as a general proposition, hawk shooting must be done at ranges from 100 to 250 yards. This is where

SOUTH DAKOTA VARMINT HUNTING

This coyote was shot at three times. First hit in foot. Then missed. Then 70-grain S.P. bullet from Mauser .22 Express stuck the coyote in neck at 327 paces. Scope was 10 power.

the Hornet, K-Hornet and R-2 rifles shine, particularly the latter two.

The first .22 caliber rim fire rifles I acquired were accurate, but leaned too much to the boy-size type. Finally I decided to have a rifle of this caliber made up to suit me. Accordingly I bought a Model 52 target rifle and sent it to Niedner for remodelling. He cut the barrel off to a length of 22″, turned it down considerably and fitted a ramp front sight and a Lyman 48 rear sight. He also fitted and sweated a blank in the rear sight slot, and matted it. He next installed target scope bases, one on the filled-in receiver bridge; and the other on the breech of the barrel and drilled and tapped the rear upper tang for a screw running through the stock from the rear end of the guard. I then stocked it with a nice walnut blank, giving it a full rounded forend, pistol grip and cheek-piece. It proved exceptionally accurate, and my brother, who now owns it, recently declared that "its equal has never been built."

To date I have had eight of these rifles remodelled for myself and others. Six of the jobs were by Niedner and two by Sedgley, and all have been most satisfactory. On two the standard weight barrel of 28″ length was left untouched, while on two it was merely shortened to 24″. On two it was turned down considerably and shortened to 24″. The other two had respectively the light 22″ barrel already mentioned and a standard barrel cut to 22″. The latter is the poorest rifle in the lot. The better two are a speed lock model with a turned down barrel of 24″ and the one with the light 22″ barrel, which incidentally has the old slow lock.

I have never used a factory made Model 52 sporter, but if they can come up to the target models I have had converted to sporters they are real rifles. At present I have three of these converted sporters, two with 24″ barrels and one with a new 28″ standard barrel recently installed by the factory. Each rifle now carries a Weaver 440 scope with Lee Dot mounted in handmade mounts somewhat similar in design to the Parker-Hale and Hill mounts. The bases are of standard target-type and are placed on the filled-in receiver bridge and the breech of the barrel. Each rifle is fitted with a custom stock of ample and proper dimensions. A rifle equipped as described is just about tops as a hunting arm in this caliber. In fact, I know of nothing that could be done to improve it. Two of these rifles have their scopes adjusted to handle high speed solid ammunition while the third is sighted in for high-speed hollow points.

While I have two rifles sighted in for solid bullets, I have not found such bullets altogether satisfactory in the field. The only reason the rifles are so sighted is because I had a supply of the solid bullets and hollow point ammunition was not available during the war years and I had to husband what I had on hand. The solid bullets kill only fairly well on crows and hawks. They are fine for snakes, turtles and rats, but are no good for squirrels. The very best squirrel cartridge I ever fired was the .22 long rifle high-speed greased hollow point cartridge made by Winchester prior to World War II.

On two successive hunts I fired 16 shots at squirrels with this cartridge and made 15 kills. In considering the .22 caliber rim fire rifle as an arm for sport this discussion has dealt exclusively with the long rifle cartridge. This was done purposely. The .22 short is in no sense a sporting cartridge, even though it be accurate. It just lacks power, and is a wounder rather than a killer. The .22 long is hopelessly inaccurate and has nothing to commend it. How it has managed to survive is a marvel. Further the Winchester .22 Special costs considerably more than does the .22 caliber high-speed long rifle and while more powerful, is without its accuracy.

Quite appropriately the .22 caliber long rifle cartridge has been called "the mighty midget." Considering its size and its ability to perform, it is without doubt the most remarkable cartridge that has ever been developed. For all forms of the smaller pests at short ranges it is the ideal load, and either youth or adult can get more genuine pleasure out of its use on such targets than he can obtain with any cartridge in existence today.

If America is ever to become in fact a nation of riflemen it will be because boys like Bill and Jimmie have been developed in their youth into crack shots by ample practice with these .22 caliber rim fire rifles on the predators that threaten the ruin of all of our useful wild life. A nation of such riflemen means a nation that will survive. He who would disarm the free citizens of America repudiates the very activities that brought this nation into being and have nurtured it through all of its years, and is in fact, if not in name, a traitor to the future of his country.

CHAPTER 21

The Twenty-Two in the North Woods

By Lloyd Melville.

THROUGHOUT A LARGE PART OF NORTHERN CANADA'S WOODED AREAS the .22 rifle is an integral part of the woodsman's equipment. It belongs in his outfit along with his axe, snowshoes and toboggan. If he will occupy a fixed camp in the deep wilderness for any considerable amount of time, whether he is a trapper or not, he should have a .22 to protect his outfit, food and blankets from the rodents that are certain to be a nuisance around camp. Occasionally they come in swarms like the plagues of Ancient Egypt. If he intends to occupy his camp for a period of several months he should take at least 500 cartridges in with him.

One year, up on the Mushhootogamink River, I saved my food supplies and blankets from a swarm of mice that came in such numbers that my two mouse traps were useless. I shot 24 of them in one day. Other times salt-hungry snowshoe rabbits have trooped around my camp and have eaten the guy ropes off my tent; the ropes off my toboggan; the bottom out of a brand new packsack and gnawed at the handle of my favorite axe till they ruined it. Another year the red squirrels started destroying my food supplies and cutting my blankets to get material for nests. I had to shoot more than 100 of them in a few weeks. The porcupine is something to be reckoned with. One got into my camp on the Wanebegon River, ate the leather sling off my 7mm Mauser and had started to eat the stock when I returned to camp. Not every man will have to contend with such numbers but every one should be prepared for them.

The .22 rifle is practically the only gun used for grouse and rabbit shooting in the North. The ammunition is light to carry, it is effective and it does not mess up the meat. In the case of grouse a man who places his bullets in the head or in the big joint of the wing will not lose any cripples. A head or shoulder shot will stop a rabbit in his tracks. While I was on expeditions in the Hudson Bay country no native white man there would think of starting on an extended trip without his .22. It was his insurance against hunger if anything should happen to his food supply. I have seen them take some nice ducks, including eiders, with them. When I was up there only the white men carried .22s. The Indians and Eskimos carried 12 gauge shotguns.

On one of my trips up the east coast of the Bay we collected a number of specimens of birds and mammals for a museum. One of these was a species of loon rare in these parts. It was impossible to get within 200 yards of him. So the man with the .22 sat on the rocks at the edge of the water, adjusted the sights, and broke the loon's neck. Dr. Pentland, the biologist, took the skin for the museum; and we took the body for the pot because we wanted to enjoy an oldtime Cree Indian feast at which the loon was the greatest treat. We parboiled him for an hour and roasted him for half a day in a beanpot buried in hot gravel. We kept repeating these processes till the bird was shrivelled and worn, but we never did eat him because he remained tougher than whalebone.

During the last three decades the .22 rifle has replaced the high powered rifles at the Fall goose and turkey shoots in the Northern farming settlements and villages. All the oldtimers will remember that in the early days the rifles at these shoots have ranged from .30–30s to .45–90s. They shot at three-inch bullseyes, at 100 yards and the bullet nearest the center tack won the turkey. The range and rules are still the same and there has been a steady increase in the number of better quality bolt action, clip-loading repeaters among the patrons of the turkey shoots; this means greater accuracy on the range and in the game fields. Fewer cripples will be lost to suffer and die in the woods.

As hunting arms these new rifles are a lot more accurate than the older models, and extend the range at which small game up to and including foxes may be killed. But, unfortunately, the thousands of wilderness trappers, prospectors and others cannot enjoy the full benefits of these new models, except by taking two rifles to the woods. These opinions are not mine alone. They are supported by the opinions and experiences of a majority of the leading trappers and explorers that I have met during the last 40 years. I have met them on the traplines and waterways across the rough western end of the Laurentians from the Great Lakes to the Northern Clay Belt; and across into Quebec and on down the rivers to James Bay.

The choice of a trapline gun is governed by the type of country and length of trapline. The trapper must modify his personal tastes to suit conditions, so that he will be able to conduct his operations successfully. Under the new Ontario laws most trappers get the exclusive trapping rights on one township—36 square miles of country—per man. With small lakes and ponds dotted all over it and creeks crisscrossing it, it will require a 50-mile trapline to cover it efficiently. Operating from one headquarters camp and a couple of branch camps he must patrol that line regularly, on foot throughout the season. From the first of November till early March he must be out on the line every day, crossing hills and valleys and swamps; traveling through dense woods, thick brush and open places. Because beaver and otter traps must be set under the ice, he must carry an ice chisel with a four-foot handle, and still have one hand free. This means that his rifle, axe, all other necessary equipment and the furs he collects along the line must be carried in his packsack.

Thus his choice of rifles is limited to one of the tubular magazine models. He will carry the magazine full at all times and be ready to seize opportunities when they come. At the most unexpected times a mink will appear, a few yards from him; or a weasel (the ermine of commerce) will run in circles. He must get his takedown rifle out of the pack in seconds, assemble it and fire. Four decades ago the Marble's Game Getters were popular—a short over and under, with a .22 rifle barrel and a .44 barrel for shot. They were splendid bush guns because they were accurate enough for ordinary woods shooting and fitted in packsacks without being taken apart. Smith & Wesson and Colt revolvers with six-inch barrels were popular too, and they were the handiest of all guns because they were carried in leather holsters with flaps to exclude the rain and snow. My first .22 was a cheap revolver with a four-inch barrel. It was not accurate enough for grouse or rabbit shooting, but with it I could kill all live animals caught in traps instantly with one shot. All of the above guns played their part in making life a little easier for the woodsman. But since the U. S. outlawed the Game Getters and Canada outlawed revolvers we can only speak of the Good Old Days.

Many progressive trappers prefer to shoot all live animals found in traps. It is more humane, and the bullet makes a small, clean hole that does not damage the pelt. By contrast, it takes several blows on the head with a stiff club to kill a majority of animals caught in traps—even the smaller ones. When the job is done the scalp is a bloody, gelatinous mess that dries very hard. That part of the pelt is damaged. The fisher is the toughest of all animals and when a club is used never gives up the ghost till his skull has been completely pulverized. Several years ago, when trappers were getting from $100 to $150 for a fisher skin, a friend of mine trapped one on the back 40 of his farm. He "killed" it with a club and placed the "dead" body beside the trail while he reset the trap. When he turned to pick up his prize he saw the animal going down the trail, running for his life! And he never saw it again. One .22 caliber bullet properly placed would have saved more than $100 for that farmer, and would have prevented needless cruelty to the animal.

For shooting small furbearing animals, either in traps or running free along the trail, the standard, smokeless long rifle cartridge with solid bullet will give the most satisfactory results. Animals in traps are always shot at a distance of a few feet. Even when running free small animals such as mink and ermine are rarely shot at more than 20 yards. At these short ranges the standard velocity stuff can be depended upon to kill cleanly without damaging the pelts.

Hollow point bullets are strictly pest killers and should never be used on small furbearers under any circumstances as they will damage the valuable pelts. They will ruin any small game, including grouse and rabbits, if such game is not shot in the head, so save them for the rodents that damage your camp and equipment.

The High Velocity stuff is more than likely to tear too large a hole in small furbearers where it emerges, and cause financial loss to the shooter because the pelt will be graded as damaged. Since one seldom meets, along the trail, any animals for which the High Velocity stuff would offer appreciable advantage over the standard, and since it is not advisable to mix loads for this type of shooting, I do not advise carrying it on the trapline. It does not increase the effective range of the takedown or trapline rifle because the accuracy of such arms is limited to about 50 yards at best. They do not possess the finest long-range accuracy to begin with, and bumping one around in a packsack does not improve its shooting qualities, but to the credit of the average woodsman, let me say here that he keeps his rifle in pretty good shape. When he comes into his camp in wet weather he dries and cleans his gun; when he comes in out of the bitter cold he wipes the gun, lays it carefully and covers it with several thicknesses of woolen blankets to prevent it from collecting moisture as the fire warms the cabin. The High Velocity ammunition comes into its own when a good rifleman who is not after small furbearing animals uses it in a good gun with fine sights. It will reach out farther and it is a better killer. A good shot, with a good rifle can kill foxes consistently at more than 100 yards with it. It is possible to hit them at longer ranges; but the hunter should remember that when you get away out there the bullet has lost a considerable amount of its velocity and killing power, and this, combined with a certain amount of drift off the vital point aimed at, will result in a percentage of the wounded animals escaping.

The .22 Winchester Rim Fire is a great gun for the North. The cartridge is slightly larger than the regular .22s and requires a specially chambered gun to handle it. It is a better killer than any other rim fire .22, due to higher velocity and flat pointed bullet. The latest loads give a muzzle velocity of 1,450 f.s. and mid-range trajectory height of slightly more than 2½″ on a 100-yard range. I owned one of them for several years and used it on a variety of small game. I used it also for shooting hogs before sticking them at butchering time. The biggest hog will drop as if struck by lightning, and he will bleed as well when stuck as if he were stuck in the customary way. To my way of thinking it is a lot more humane to shoot them first.

For instant kills on small and medium game, a reliable rule is to draw an imaginary X on the animal's head; place the bases of the lines on his eyes, the upper tips on his ears, and place the bullet where the lines cross. But do not try this method on a bull moose—he has too much bone between his face and his brainpan. Once I shot a big bull as near the intersection of the X as I could put my finger, and the .303 bullet did not even give him a headache! ! ! I had to wait till he turned broadside, and I shot him behind the shoulder.

The .22 rim fire cartridges were *not* designed for big game shooting, and they should never be used for that purpose except in dire emergencies. Yet, on occasions, they have killed every species of big game in Eastern America, south of the Arctic. It should be clearly understood that these animals were standing in a position that offered a clear shot for the heart or brain, and the hunter scored a bullseye. Shots at big game should *never* be taken under any other conditions, and then only by men who know what they are doing and are capable of placing their bullets where they want them.

One of our best local trappers learned this lesson a couple of years ago. He was walking along the road about three miles from my home, where I am writing this, and a bear came out on the road. The trapper was carrying a singleshot .22 and tried for a heart shot at 100 yards. The enraged bear charged and the man would have been badly mauled or killed if a car had not arrived and allowed him to jump on the running board at the right moment. On the other hand I could tell of a great many cases where cool headed riflemen, shooting under ideal conditions, have killed their game.

A few years ago my friend, Merrill McClelland, was shooting grouse up on the hills. When he had his legal limit of the birds in his game bag, he started home. He had a singleshot rifle and *one*

.22 long rifle cartridge. He saw a big timber wolf standing on a knoll 40 yards away. He took careful aim for a heart shot and scored a bullseye. The wolf died before he got 15 feet. I saw the skin when he came home.

The most thrilling adventure that has come to my attention occurred in the fall of 1947. This section of the country was overrun with bears at that time—there were so many of them that the natural food supply was not nearly enough for their needs and they became a dangerous nuisance. Hardly a week passed that they did not break into a house somewhere. One night when it was as dark as the inside of an infidel, Alex Nadon arrived at one of his branch camps located in a dense forest of big trees. Shortly after Alex had lighted his kerosene lamp a bear started walking around and around the cabin, occasionally scratching at the walls. It was quite clear that the bear was big, hungry, and meant to do something about it. Alex's position was not pleasant, for his big rifle was away in another camp and his supply of kerosene would not last more than one hour. He decided to fight it out while he still had light. So he filled his Winchester .22 repeater full of cartridges. The bear had settled down to sniffing at the wall outside, smelling the groceries that were stored in the camp at one side of the cabin. Alex walked out through the door which is in the center of one end, and went around the corner. It was impossible to see even an outline of the bear but he could tell by the growls that bruin was up on his hind legs. Pointing for where the bear's lungs should be, he emptied the rifle as fast as he could pump it and ran back into the cabin to refill the magazine. By this time the bear was bawling and tearing at everything he could get his paws on. Alex went out and emptied the rifle the second time. Gradually the bear became quiet, and in the morning was dead beside the cabin.

Fox shooting in the North is entirely different to that described by riflemen whose stories appear in the magazines that we read. We get close enough to shoot them with our trapline .22s, mostly by accident, partly by careful stalking. Once, in midwinter I walked onto the ice at the end of a lake that is half a mile wide by a mile long. An inch of fresh snow showed the tracks of a fox that had come down the lake that morning and had gone down the valley that I had come up. Far up the lake I could see a dark speck coming my way fast and soon I could see that it was a fox following the trail of the one that had come along earlier. I took a stand in the trees near the lake where I could watch the ice. The fox came on at top speed and never looked up till the movement of my rifle coming up caught his eye. He skidded to a stop a few feet from me but that was too late—he died where he stopped.

On another trapline a fox fattened for a time by stealing the baits out of my mink traps. Then he committed the crime of eating three quarters of a fine, dark mink that would have brought me $35. I followed his tracks in the snow for a couple of miles, and suddenly, as I rounded a sharp point that jutted out into a lake, I saw him on shore 100 yards away, digging for a mouse. I was able to edge along on the ice till I got within 40 yards of him—and planted a bullet at the base of his ear.

Still another time, when the snow was unusually deep, a thieving fox began raiding the caches of beaver carcasses that I was saving for mink and fisher bait. One sunny morning when I was making my rounds I saw him digging in the snow for one of these caches. Little more than his hind legs could be seen and I was able to get quite close before he got nervous and backed out of the hole he had dug. When his head came in sight I was ready and squeezed the trigger.

The best red fox I ever got was a complete surprise. I had just stepped out of my cabin door when I saw him standing, broadside, little more than 100 feet away. One .22 long rifle bullet high in the shoulders anchored him to the spot.

The newer high intensity .22 caliber center fire rifles have opened up a whole world of fox and wolf shooting for the men of the North. The man who can afford one of these rifles, fitted with a good scope, and who also has a pair of binoculars, can enjoy a lot of shooting and make a profit on it. This statement is made with the reservation that some good, full jacketed bullets become available for them. Soft points are too destructive at short and medium ranges. In Ontario the provincial government collects a royalty on the pelt of every furbearing animal killed, including foxes and it is a punishable offence to allow a pelt to spoil. A fox shot at medium range with a soft point bullet would be more than spoiled; he would be obliterated. Our game wardens would frown on much of that type of shooting and it would be poor business from the standpoint of the woodsman who has been accustomed to getting cash for fox pelts.

Several years ago there were a lot of .22 Savage Hi Power rifles around. I used one for a season and they were satisfactory on fox away out at about the limit of range at which we could hit them. They were excellent on otter at ranges over 100 yards, and did very little damage to the pelts at those ranges. The otter pelt is a lot tougher than fox skins.

Then the Hornet came along and made quite a hit with several of my friends, but practically all of them have dropped the Hornet in favor of the newer .218 Bee. The latter has considerably more range and is a swell gun for the trapper to have in his camp. Both of the above cartridges have a big advantage over higher powered rifles in the comparatively mild report—one can do a lot of shooting on his grounds without scaring away too many animals.

I have done a little shooting with the .220 Swift. It is perhaps the greatest rifle in existence for varmint shooting but it is too closely related to the atomic bomb to be of any value to a trapper.

A considerable amount of fox and wolf shooting is available not far from my home, much of it in open country and my choice of a rifle for it would be a Winchester Model 70, using a .22 Varminter and the 63-grain bullets which are available. With a Weaver K4 scope in a Stith Master mount, a man would get shooting to write about!

Grouse and grouse hunting have not changed in the last 50 years. The birds still feed on the same hills, around the same fields, the same abandoned farms, along the same old roads, and along the banks of the same streams and lakes. They like the leaves of white clover and wintergreen and similar plants. They also like the wild cherries, high bush cranberries and the wild berries that are found in abundance across most of Canada's northern timberlands, particularly in the second growth stuff that has grown after a forest fire.

Large numbers of them live on the farm on which I grew up. They fed right up to the edges of the fields but I never knew them to damage any cultivated crops. Their natural food is abundant at the same time the farmers' crops are. In this country they are almost as tame as barnyard fowl. I live in a typical Northern Ontario village with a population of 1700, in a setting of hills, valleys, lakes and streams. Several coveys of grouse can be found in the bush, right at the edge of the village and one can approach within a few feet of them. Yet they are as wild as flappers in more densely populated areas because they have been overhunted.

All predators kill a few for food but as long as the population of these animals is kept within reasonable limits the toll is not too great. Stray house cats are not a problem in the North for they cannot survive long in the snow and the cold; foxes and brush wolves, when they become too numerous, are hard on them; their worst enemies are the great horned owl and the goshawk.

As soon as snow covers the ground their diet is confined to buds of birch trees and they get no variation in diet till the snow leaves in the Spring. During the milder weather, when the temperature is above zero, they walk on the snow a good deal, and feed at leisure. If there happens to be a high, perpendicular sand or gravel bank in the vicinity, that does not get covered with snow they gather there in large numbers to get the coarse grains of sand that help to masticate the food in their gizzards. Sportsmens' clubs that put out grain for them would do an added favor if they also put out a supply of sand. During the more severe weather the birds feed only twice a day, morning and evening. For protection from storms and severe cold they dive into the loose snow and tunnel in three or four feet, horizontally. A sudden rise in temperature accompanied by rain brings disaster. The frosts that follow quickly on the heels of the thaw make a crust on the snow and the birds cannot get under for protection till another storm brings a new blanket for them.

One Winter a grouse saved himself during a spell of 50-below weather by working his way through the flaps of my tent and crawling into my sleeping bag, which was spread out on my bed, ready for use. The evidence was in the bag when I returned some time later.

Both grouse and snowshoe rabbits are subject to periodic epidemics that kill a large percentage of them. These epidemics strike suddenly and end quickly. Today you see grouse and rabbits everywhere, and in three or four days you see their dead bodies. A corresponding percentage of the valuable furbearers then starve. The shortage of furs brings hardship to all trappers, and a lot of them quit trapping till the numbers of the animals increase again. The Indians of the extreme North on the east side of James and Hudson Bays suffer most following the epidemics because, in addition to the loss of cash or barter income from the sale of furs, they lose a principal source of food. The northern tribes do not eat grouse, ptarmigan and rabbit as a main diet from choice, but from necessity. The vast herds of caribou that used to roam that area in countless thousands have perished—only a few scattered herds remain. I have walked miles upon miles of those plains that are crisscrossed with old caribou trails and covered with disintegrating antlers.

The more southerly trappers are fortunate in having an abundance of big game. They eat a number of grouse and fish, with an occasional rabbit for the first few weeks in the woods but as soon as the weather turns cold enough to preserve meat a moose will be shot and will be the principal source of meat for the balance of the season. These men all use sleeping bags and good woolen blankets. The Northern Indians use rabbit skin blankets exclusively—200 skins in a small blanket; 300 or more in a larger one. Thus the scarcity of rabbits brings another hardship to them.

In pioneer days shotguns were used for both grouse and rabbit shooting and one would meet hunters armed with muzzleloaders and others with breechloaders. Such guns are neither necessary nor desirable for shooting small game that is so tame. Some hunters were careful and aimed at the heads—they were rewarded with fine birds. Others pointed at the bird and picked up a mess of mangled flesh, blood, feathers and fertilizer. It took heroic work to salvage anything that was fit to eat.

I cut my teeth on a sawedoff, single barrel, muzzleloader with a 14-inch barrel. An older brother had bought it for $1 when he was in knee breeches, and gave it to me when he left to make his home in the Rockies. When I was 13 I acquired a can of black powder, a box of percussion caps and a pound of shot. On the opening day of the season I hied to the woods and was back in two hours with four big, fat birds, the happiest boy in the settlement. That gun was a lot better than the breechloaders because only a few grains of shot would register on the target, and the meat was never spoiled. It served faithfully for one season.

Then I bought a Winchester Model 1890, using the .22 W.R.F. ammunition. This is a splendid cartridge, with higher velocity and considerably more killing power than the regular rim fire .22s. I used it for several years and found it excellent for both grouse and rabbits, also for a variety of smaller game. Certain body shots with any rim fire .22 produce a strange phenomenon in grouse. They lose the proper sense of balance and literally stand straight up, flapping their wings violently against their tummies, and climb straight up, often away above the tops of the tallest trees, to collapse at the peak of their climb and hit the ground with a thud.

Snowshoe rabbits are found in much the same habitat as grouse. They are hunted very much by the same methods and the same weapons are used. In Northern Canada, at least, that means a .22 rim fire. Trappers shoot them to bait mink, marten, fisher and lynx traps and hunters from the villages shoot them for sport.

I had exceptional opportunities for testing this .22 W.R.F. on small game as our home was on the bank of a fairly big river, just one mile below a large shallow lake, and a band of rushes and pond weeds a quarter of a mile wide ran along the entire shore line. There were hundreds of muskrat houses, built of rushes and mud, in this big feed bed. There were open seasons in Spring and Fall, and at that time it was legal to shoot rats. From the time I was 15 I used to paddle along the edge of the feed bed in the evenings during open seasons and shoot rats off the floating logs. One shot through the shoulders killed instantly, and nine or 10 rats in an evening was a fair average. That brought more money than good men earned in a 10-hour shift in the sawmill—sawmill wages were then $1.75 per day and the worker paid for room and board out of that.

The same fall I set out a few mink, fisher and lynx traps, following directions in the old *Newhouse Trapper's Guide*, and tended the traps after school and on Saturdays. The venture produced one lynx and nine mink pelts. Because local buyers paid ridiculously low prices for furs, I shipped all of mine to Funston Brothers, of St. Louis, Missouri. The Ontario Government had not realized the value of the fur trade and no restrictions were placed on the export of raw furs for seven or eight years after I began trapping. Funston paid the following prices, with small variations through the seven or eight years that we were permitted to ship them: Fall rats 21 cents; Spring rats $1.00; Mink $7.00; Red Fox $8.00; Fisher $17.00; Lynx $25.00. Such prices left no incentive to go to the lumber camps, the only jobs available then, and work unreasonably long hours, sleep in blankets that were alive with vermin, and draw only $16.00 to $26.00 per month.

During the following four or five years I increased my traplines to eight, 10, 25 and 30 miles, and acquired the knowledge of woodcraft that one must have to prosper or even survive in the wilderness. A woodsman must be an expert with a canoe and on snowshoes, and this includes the selection of the ones best suited to his purpose. The straight bottomed canoes with keel are pleasure craft for use on lakes. They are *not* for use on Northern rivers.

He will soon learn that the small, cheap snowshoes sold in most sporting goods stores are worse than useless in the Northern woods. They are too small, and the gut filling will melt under him if the weather turns warm enough to make the snow soft. A pair of them went to pieces on me at Stony Lake, 40 miles back in the bush and all that saved me was an old pair that a trapper gave me. On another occasion when Dan Hill and I made a trip to Detroit Lake, 30 miles in the big woods, his snowshoes went to pieces. I had to get a piece of moose skin from a trapper and lace his frames before we could move from camp.

When a hunter goes into the woods in winter he should have a pair of the best quality snowshoes laced with babiche, and they should not be smaller than 14" x 48". Some 30 years ago the Tubbs Company, of Norway, Maine made the best. Even if you are coming to Canada for a little winter rabbit shooting get *good* snowshoes—you will need them.

The trapper must be able to identify the tracks of every species of animal, know the direction in which they were traveling and be able to judge closely the time that has elapsed since the tracks were made. In short, he must not day dream as he travels; he must train himself to read the signs of wildlife along the trail as carefully and accurately as the expert accountant reads the figures in his books or as the master mechanic reads his blue prints.

He will learn very quickly that he will have to attend to his traps regularly and keep fresh bait in them, regardless of weather. Fur-bearers that live in good game country will not touch soured bait. No doubt old or feeble critters would welcome any kind of food but every trapper will soon find that there are darn few toothless patriarchs in *his* territory. A few are caught, but not enough of them to help much with the budget so the trapper must have some freshly killed rabbits in his packsack to renew the baits where needed. Low temperatures mean nothing to him for he is accustomed to them; he is well fed and warmly clad, and he can shoot rabbits for bait too. The snowshoe bunnies never have dens. In the lowest temperatures they just crouch with all four feet under them, in the shelter of a log or small tree. Modern guns can be used with safety if proper precautions are taken; and modern ammunition will give perfect satisfaction at 40 below, *if proper precautions* are taken; so will rifle scopes. These will be dealt with later.

A knowledge of our wild animals and their habits is important to the woodsman and sportsmen. Skunks, for instance; they have roamed for centuries wherever their fancies have led them, without opposition. They have few, if any, natural enemies, so at times they become too numerous. For 10 years between the middle 30s and 40s they were a curse to people east and north of Lake Superior. They invaded homes and paraded through villages. A pair got into the basement, of a grocery store in Wawa and remained there all winter—unmolested. One got into my basement but I caught him in a box trap and poured an ounce of chloroform in the box—he went to sleep permanently. In the fall of 1940 five of us were hunting moose on the Montreal River. One night six skunks found our tent and proceeded to eat up our supplies and it took a lot of effort to get rid of them without disaster. Shooting them in the ordinary way is no guarantee that all will be well. I have blown their heads off with high powered rifles, but reflexes emanating from nerve centers along the spine caused them to wriggle and squirt their ink.

Then I remembered the unfailing method of the pioneers; a sharp blow with a good club across the back immediately in front of his hips breaks his spine and cuts off the nerve impulses and prevents disaster. The only trouble with this method is that one must have the skunk in *perfect* position with nothing to interfere with the descent of the club and such luck is not always with the man. Why hunters never took to shooting them just in front of the hips is a mystery. Perhaps the answer is that the cartridge must produce the right amount of shock. I am sure the .22 long rifle, high velocity mushroom would fill the bill, but World War II was on when I started experimenting and these were not to be had. The solid bullet .22 is definitely not in that class; neither is the .25 Stevens

Rim Fire. Even the 169-grain Squibb gas check bullet pushed by 25 grains of Hercules Lightning, in the .30–06 fails in a percentage of shots—but it is not too good a killer anyway, and I have dropped it in favor of the 165-grain Ideal .30–30 gas check bullet.

I loaded up one lot of 80-grain, Hi Speed, mushroom .32–20 bullets with 43 grains of Hi Vel #2 in .303 British cases for a velocity of 3,300 f.s. Assuming a prone position 10 feet from the trail which a family of skunks used I laid the front sight on the proper spot and squeezed the trigger. The skunk went up in smoke and his attar of roses filled the atmosphere of the whole valley—it was positively too much medicine.

So I went back to camp in time to see two medium sized porcupines ambling away. I plastered the first one on the seat of his pants and every ounce of him up to his diaphram was atomized except a strip of belly skin and his hind feet. I caught the second one with a raking shot along his spine which laid him wide open and removed his innards. I used the balance of the lot on rabbits that were causing a lot of trouble around my camp and every one exploded into a cloud of head, legs and garbage. My next experiment was with my .30–06 and the 86-grain full jacketed Mauser pistol bullet pushed by 34 grains of Hercules #2400. This load was a trifle too much so I cut the powder charge to 32 grains and got good results— no odor—on the few skunks that I was able to use it on. An epidemic just about exterminated them in this area in 1946 so there can be no more experimenting along that line till the cycle takes another upswing. The .22 Hornet *should* be a good skunk deodorant; and the .218 Bee might be too. It would be interesting to try them.

Foxes have dens but do not use them much in winter, except during the wildest storms. Fishers also have a home den, usually among broken rocks. They travel in great circles making a complete round in about three weeks. They are an animal of dense thickets and like to follow the edge of swamps. Often old dogs follow the trails of the wolf packs, to feed on the carcasses that the big killers leave. During the good years since World War I, their pelts brought up to $175.00 each and it paid the trapper to have his lines in good order when they made their circle. Snowproof cabins two feet long, a foot wide and 30″ high are built along their routes of travel, and baited with beaver meat, porcupine, fresh rabbit or scraps of deer meat from wolf kills. A good strong trap attached to a stout block of wood is used. They are extremely wary and few are ever shot.

The lynx is the most dignified of all furbearing animals, and spends much of his time traveling—I have never known them to remain more than a few days in one locality. Going the rounds of the great circles that they travel they select routes through fairly open timber, and walk sedately, straight ahead, not turning to the right or left. They seldom run, if it is not essential. They catch small game easily, for they are capable of prodigious leaps. Once when John Keast and I were hunting deer in the hardwoods near the Haughton Prairie, shortly after leaving camp, John heard a grouse fluttering—a lynx had just caught it. John was an excellent hunter and decided to trail and shoot the lynx. He never was far behind it and shortly after noon he heard a second grouse flutter, when the lynx caught it. They meandered over the hills and through the valleys from dawn until dark but he never got a glimpse of it and he left its trail less than a mile from the camp where he started.

I shot three of them with my .22 W.R.F., all brought to bay by my dog. The first one ventured too near our barns and the dog put him up on a high rail fence, where he stood spitting defiance at the dog. It was an easy shot to put a bullet at the base of his ear. The second was in a stand of dense timber and the lynx leaped to the bole of a fallen tree which lodged seven or eight feet above the ground, and a broadside shot, high through both shoulders, knocked him flat. The third one crossed the trail ahead of me by only a few minutes, during a heavy snowstorm. My dog put him up a tall balsam about a quarter of a mile from where our trails crossed. The boughs were laden with snow and it was hard to locate the cat but at last I made out the shape of one hind leg and broke it. He dropped about 10 feet and caught on another branch and a second shot broke the opposite front leg. He dropped to the bottom of the tree and rolled on his back. As the dog closed in the cat grabbed one of his cheeks and held on, and started ripping him with the claws of both uninjured feet and if I had not been so close the dog would have been torn to ribbons.

I shot another lynx as he was crossing a logging road through a cedar swamp. He had a small trap clamped on one foot—it had been poorly fastened where it was set. He was not greatly handicapped, but was going at a normal walk and a 7mm bullet through his spine laid him low.

I missed a chance of a lifetime to get a rare movie shot up on the headwaters of the Aubinadong River the last winter I trapped there. The snow was only a few inches deep and there was good ice on the lakes. A mink was doing a good deal of hunting up on the barren shore of a small lake, where one would not expect to find a mink at that season. I made a hasty job of a small cabin to hold my bait and trap. On the return trip in a few days a magnificent lynx was out on the ice with the mink trap clamped on two toes and he did not appear the least concerned about our approach—my Great Dane, an extra big and powerful dog, was trotting at my heels. When we

LLOYD MELVILLE

The author, Lloyd Melville, posed this picture to show how a Canadian trapper carries his rifle in winter. The birch pole is a must item, for testing the ice on lakes and streams. If ice will stand a sharp blow from this pole, it will carry a man. Stop such testing and you will soon be in the Happy Hunting Ground.

were only a few paces away he trotted past me and stood directly in front of the big cat—just looking at him—when suddenly, without warning, the lynx shot his free front paw out and ripped the dog's face wide open. Equally as fast, the dog lowered his nose and sprang forward. He drove his nose between the cat's fore legs and jerked his head upward and crushed the cat's ribs between his powerful jaws. He sprang 10 feet with the cat in his grip and it required the most vigorous application of my axehandle to save that $25.00 pelt. After I got the big cat in my packsack and started down the trail the dog leaped again and seized the packsack, trying to get the cat out, and it required more axehandle to calm him.

I have read in various magazines that lynx kill deer occasionally, but in all my years in the woods I have never seen any evidence to support the statement, and only once did I see where a lynx had stopped to feed on the remains of a deer that wolves had killed.

Only once did I ever find where a lynx had slept. On top of a long, low ridge a small bear had dug a den under a giant white pine years before. The bottom of the den was covered several inches deep with rotten wood. It was as snug as a den can be, and the lynx used it for an overnight stop, regularly every two weeks throughout the winter. It would have been easy to set a trap in the entrance to the den and catch him—but it would not have been fair. However, I did build several trap sets along his trail; he scorned all the frozen baits and probably lived for years.

All standard makes and models of American rifles will function perfectly in the north in any temperature that man can stand to go out in—that is, if the owner will give the weapon the same care and treatment that the local trappers in any given district give their rifles. Every trace of oil and grease must be removed before starting a hunt in cold weather and the gun must be taken into camp at the end of every day's hunt and protected from the air till it has warmed, to prevent condensation of moisture and frosting. When it has warmed it must be checked carefully and wiped to remove any moisture, such as snowflakes, that may possibly have gotten into it and if a hunter feels that the action of his gun needs lubrication he may polish it with a very light dusting of graphite. *But keep oil and grease out of both barrel and action.* If a hunter follows these simple rules his gun will always function and he will not be carried to the morgue.

For the first few years that the Model 1899 Savage was on the market it was the worst offender ever carried to the woods, not that there was anything wrong with the rifle, but because the manufacturer soused the whole interior with a heavy oil that was almost impossible to get out; as soon as the oil was completely removed, this model worked as well as any other. I know, as I burned a lot of ammunition in the .22 H.P., the .250–3000 and the .303—some of it when the temperature was around 40 below.

My experience with the .30–06 Springfield may help some hunter caught with oil in his rifle in cold weather. In the early Spring of 1924 I decided to get a .30–06 Springfield because there were then no good bolt action sporters on the market and I could not afford a custom made job. It took miles of red tape, and the assistance of some influential friends in the United States to get a high serial numbered rifle with a stargaged barrel from the U. S. Ordnance Department, and more miles of red tape, spelled with capital letters, to get it into Canada—individuals are not allowed to import military arms. But I did finally convince the Canadian military bigwigs that I had no intention of going to war with Siam or the Fiji Islands. The reason for relating this portion of the story is that the delay left me two weeks late in starting up the long trail to my trapping grounds, and the rifle was still submerged in cosmoline when I needed the gun. It would not shoot, even after I had done my best to remove the thickened oil. The firing pin assembly had to be removed from the bolt and both of these pieces had to be suspended in first and second pots of boiling water to clean the oil out. That worked and, after I had made a higher front sight out of an old Canadian penny, I got perfect satisfaction from that rifle.

I have never heard of a .22 or other light rifle being wrecked by firing in low temperatures and I have fired thousands of rounds in the Model 90 W.R.F.; Model 1906 long rifle; and a cheap single-shot. All the trappers use their rifles, big and small in almost any weather, but pay strict attention to the rules of safety—they keep the guns in good shape. In addition to the Savages and Winchesters mentioned I have used the following rifles a lot in temperatures down to 40 below, 7mm German Mauser; two Winchester '95s; a .303 British and a .30–40; .30–06 Springfield and a .30–06 Newton. I know that ordinary steel becomes brittle in low temperatures, and have set 40 below as my limit—below that I pass up chances. I have a good thermometer on my cabin door and I watch it.

I know of only two rifles that blew up in cold weather. The first was an Austrian Army rifle brought back from World War I. A trapper friend of mine sent it to a nationally known firm and had them fit it with a fine new barrel and custom stock and sporting sights. It was superbly accurate and for four or five years he did remarkable shooting at furbearers, particularly otter. With full patch bullets it killed well and did no damage to the pelts. Then one frosty day it let go. This is how he told it to me: "I lined the sights on an otter out on the ice, and squeezed the trigger. There was a blinding flash, and a deafening report and I must have been stunned for I lost consciousness for a few seconds but did not fall—when I came out of it I was still standing, holding the splintered stock. All the metal work was blown off."

The second one was a brand new .348 Winchester. The first fall they were on the market a party of three came up, armed with them. The first day out it rained torrents. When they returned in the evening they stood the three rifles up against a tree. They were beautiful guns, a lot better finished than any commercial grade had been up to that time. To a woodsman that was worse than a mistake; it was sacrilege. I tried to advise them to take them into camp but they left them out in the rain all night.

The skies cleared and there was frost that night. Moisture gathered in a barrel and froze there. In the morning the owner stood up gaily and fired at a rock across the river. If his guardian angel had not been on the job, with all his divine powers, that man's friends would have stood up and sung "Safe in the Arms of Jesus." The action was completely wrecked. The moral is clear: take your gun into camp and see that it is dry, inside and out. If you only have time to do one of two things, clean your gun or say your prayers—clean the gun. One who has not experienced the extremes of temperatures that we get in the north cannot realize what they can do to a gun.

When I write of using guns at 40 below I must make it clear that this is the extreme temperature at which I have risked shooting. It is *not* the average temperature at which shooting is done here. It is mentioned for the sole purpose of showing the factor of safety that is built into our sporting arms and ammunition. It is probable that more than 50% of Northern Winter shooting is done when the mercury stands around zero, or some degrees above. But, shooting in 40 below weather *is* done. When I was trapping on the Mississaugi River two Indians found a big male bear sitting in the snow with his back against a tree, and both paws over his nose. He took his paws down long enough to look at the men, and again covered his nose. He would have perished in a few hours. The Indians shot him and followed his tracks back to the den he had left, to see why he came out when the thermometer registered 40 below. A big female had just given birth to a pair of cubs and had chased dad out of the den.

Modern ammunition works perfectly in low temperatures. The center of impact will not be the same as in warmer weather but for the short ranges at which the woodsman uses his .22 the variation is seldom enough to cause a miss. At medium temperatures, say 15 or 20 below, a good .250 Savage or a good .30–06 will still group its shots close enough to normal to kill a fox at 100 yards, although at longer ranges, it might be different, as I have not tried long shots when the temperature was that much below.

Ammunition gives no trouble. I have never heard of a misfire and out of several thousands of rounds fired in frosty weather I have only one hangfire. I had lined the sights on a fox and squeezed the trigger; there was a click and nothing happened, except that the fox moved behind cover. After the fox disappeared I lowered the gun and was about to eject the cartridge, when it went off with as much force as if nothing were wrong. I was using a mixture of English ammo loaded with cordite and American stuff loaded with nitrocellulose powder but do not know which hung fire.

A lot of homicidal shooting has been done in the northern fur lands since the spectacular rise in prices following the First World War. Little of this shooting ever got more than passing notice in the press, and a good deal of it never made the newspaper columns at all. There were two reasons for this; the locale of the various cases was so isolated—and there were no writers or correspondents in the woods; also the more spectacular shootings by city gangsters took the headlines. This period furnished plenty of thrillers for the press, as well as material for countless movies. The shooting in the woods was just as deadly, just as ruthless, and was done for the same purpose—again. The wilderness trappers were a hard working lot and made good money. As they sold their furs only two or three times a season they got this money in considerable amounts. This tempted the hoodlums and the rats. A complete history of their crimes would stock a small library, so I will mention only a few and I bring this phase of woods life in solely to explain why caution became part of the woodsman's nature, and why he does things in a certain way. I know of no one who was ever nervous or afraid of the hoodlums, nor do I know one who ever grew careless and survived a quarter of a century in the big woods.

The first attempted murder and robbery that I will discuss involved two of my friends, and it was from me that they learned about good trapping grounds on the Fire River that were vacant. I had been guiding tourists up in that area and learned about this opportunity. Skiff Thompson and his partner, a young Nova Scotian made their plans in my hotel room and invited me to go along with them but I wanted to see the farther North and went to Northern Quebec. Going north from the railroad on the Okikadasik River as far as it was possible to canoe it, I carried my outfit across a six mile portage over the Abitibi Hills and went down stream about thirty miles and camped. Thompson and his partner did well on the Fire River and sold $1,800 worth of fur at Christmas.

On the way back to camp a man with no apparent means of liveli-
hood invited them into his cabin for coffee. When the squatter
thought they were off guard he grabbed his .30–30 and with the
one shot he had time to fire he shattered the young man's right
arm and hipbone. Before he could fire a second shot Thompson
landed a hay-maker on his jaw and laid him out. The young man
spent four months in the Chapleau hospital, and went home to
Nova Scotia, a hopeless cripple for life. The thug spent a long term
in Portsmouth penitentiary. These two were the only ones of my
friends who were ever bothered by plug-uglies.

Another case concerns a legitimate trapper who had three cabins
on his grounds back of Dalton, Ontario. A gang of poachers who
had been raiding trapping grounds in the vicinity stole food out of
his cabins repeatedly in the winter of 1946 and because he complained to the authorities, they decided to "educate" him, and
give a lesson to other trappers, so they arranged a rendevous at his
main cabin. He did not act as a successful oldtimer would have
acted, for he did not inform the police in advance. He just told his
wife that he was going to keep a date and if he failed to return in
two hours to call the police, and he neglected to give her information that would help the police to convict the murderers. He did
not take a gun with him. They found the body at his camp and
they found two .30–30 soft points in the sand bank behind him.
The police and the residents knew who did it but lacked the evidence to prove it in court.

The seasoned older woodsmen who have had wits enough to
survive a quarter of a century or more deep in the wilderness have
learned the philosophy of the American general who is reported to
have said: "The general who wins the battle is the one who get
there first." And one of them in a similar situation would have
not only notified the police, but would have had his gun with him
—and he would have had it ready, and even if he lost the final argument against superior numbers, he would have brought down one
or two of the enemy to keep him company in his long sleep in the
sandy plains of Dalton.

All of the cases that I mention can be verified if anyone is interested enough to enquire.

Scores of good trappers and woodsmen have placed second in
these deadly debates but they have won a heck of a lot more argu-
ments than they lost. Take the case of the two shady gents who
started out to get rich quick by robbing the trappers on the upper
reaches of the Goulais River—and did not get back. The following
summer a party of canoe men going up the river saw a signboard
nailed to a post in a muddy bay. The inscription read: "The next

men who come through here to steal furs will get the same thing."
The canoe men saw the toe of a man's boot sticking out of the mud,
and found that the owner was still wearing it. The Provincial Police
buried the two men, but no arrests were ever made.

Then there was the case of Louis and Billy, the most bizarre case
in the whole history of crime in Canada—if shooting trapline robbers
can be called a crime. They made two or three successful raids—
but they went once too often. They made their last public appearance at an encampment of trappers from the Wanebegon and the
Mississaugi, who had gathered at Split Rock Chute to wait for the
Spring breakup. They left a supply of food at the encampment,
saying they had some business back in the bush and would return
in five days, but their business was with the wrong man. He had
learned, and practiced, the motto of the Kansas rifle club: "Thou
shalt be handy with thy gun, that thy days may be long in the land
that the Lord thy God giveth thee." A small army, aided by provincial forestry planes hunted for them for weeks when the snow
had gone in the Spring. The searchers failed to find them because
they underestimated the distance that it was possible for them to
travel. A trapper found their bodies on the open beach at Mystery
Lake, a few miles north of Ranger Lake. Their watches and knives
were returned to the widows, who identified them. Their bones lay
as they fell for a number of years, and the local guides did a thriving
business taking tourists to the scene of the shooting. The skeletons
were photographed, perhaps, more than any other two people of
that decade. They were finally buried by the Reverend Carlton
Brooks Miller, of the First Congregational Church, the late Roy
Henry, and a troop of Boy Scouts from Battle Creek, Michigan.

Most woodsmen while out in the wilderness keep cartridges in
the magazines of their heavy rifles at all times. This is contrary to
accepted practice out in civilization, but it works. The woodsmen
have as low or lower accident rate than other people for everyone
knows that his rifle, and every other rifle, is loaded and they treat
them accordingly. There has never been an accident among the
scores of trappers of my acquaintance who have lived with their
guns for decades. While in the woods I keep three cartridges in the
magazine of my rifle and as soon as I leave the cabin I chamber a
cartridge and snap the safety on. It is always ready for instant use,
and this system pays off when unexpected snap shots are offered.
This system works in the woods because the only people who come
to a trapper's camp are other trappers who know guns, and who
know enough to mind their own business. It would not work out
front because too many people are inquisitive. When the woodsman
is leaving his rifle in camp for a considerable time he puts it in a

flannel-lined canvas case, or slips it between the mattress and blankets to prevent rusting.

The subject of proper food and camping equipment is as important to the sportsmen as his firearms and ammunition and no experienced person should miss an opportunity to give information that will help to correct this craze for going light, and living off the country. The laws of nature are immutable. The body requires a properly balanced diet and the moment that food lacks in a single element, trouble starts. A lot more food is required by sportsmen out on hunting trips than they need at home, and if they have not got it, they soon suffer from lassitude.

The successful woodsman takes an abundance of the proper foods when he is going in for a long period for he has read his history and knows the armies of the Crusaders lost more men from scurvy than were lost in battle. The same was true of all navies and the merchant marines till recent years. The white colonies that settled the northern part of America were decimated by scurvy, a deficiency disease; so were the early prospectors in the Klondike and Alaska. This craze is fostered by many fluent but misguided writers. It is true that they can point to Steffanson, but his case is not a shining example for modern campers. I have read his books and have a high regard for the work he did—he taught the white man to look at the natives and learn from them. His system cannot be adapted to the vacations of you and me. He had native companions who knew where game and fish were to be found at the different seasons. He moved from one Eskimo village to another and lived with them. According to his own count he shot 1,000 Caribou in the six years he was in the Arctic. Turn 100 men like that loose in caribou country and what would happen?

I have had personal and bitter contacts with a few of these "live-off-the-country" boys. Several years ago I was head guide for a boys' camp, with a clientele from the upper crust of American society. A new Camp director was sent up. Our camp specialized on extended trips into the wilderness and was proud of its record—thousands of miles traveled on big rivers, great lakes and the inland sea of James Bay without loss or injury of personnel or equipment. The new Director was determined to change everything—no tents to sleep in and no food except what we could gather along the way. He knew nothing about trips or camping, but because he was a bigwig in one of America's universities he thought he could manage a trip. I had spent years in the country and knew that we would get a few heavy rainstorms, flies to bother at night, and absolutely no edible food, except northern pike. This Director was not dumb for he had gone a long way up the ladder of success—he had a fine brain, but did not use it in connection with camping. We took tents and food.

Man has not become thoroughly domesticated in the comparatively short time since he left the soil and discarded his outmoded tools in favour of modern equipment. Back in his subconscious mind is a yearning for the wilderness and the chase, and that is what makes it possible for glib writers to peddle their junk.

I have a letter on my desk that I have not answered. It is from a successful lecturer, and in it he proposes that he and I take a trip across the Labrador Peninsula, and live off the country. Our only shelter would be a small tent, the equivalent of a large potato sack. The Labrador Peninsula is the most inhospitable part of the Western Hemisphere and no man with any experience of camping in the North would undertake such an expedition with any lesser personage than the Angel Gabriel—and with Him he would demand a written contract to see him through.

I will advise this lecturer to go to his public library and read *The Lure of the Labrador Wild*, by Dillon Wallace. Wallace was on the Labrador expedition when Hubbard starved to death. I will tell him to read Philip Godsell's account of a trip he took from Norway House to Hudson Bay, in company with a native Indian. They had little food with them and a big storm delayed them for a long time on the shore of a large lake. It was so rough that they could not fish and in desperation they boiled and ate some liverwort, one of the things glibby recommended in one of the very latest Campers' Guides. It is mildly poisonous and nearly killed them.

I have one of the very latest of these guide books, and among the things recommended for the live-off-the-country boys are caribou moss, bulrushes, and mice. Caribou eat and digest the moss, muskrats eat and digest the roots of the rushes, but please remember that *you* are neither a caribou nor a muskrat and your digestive organs will not handle such stuff. As for mice, the man with no food in his tent will not catch mice—even a mouse has more intelligence than to hang around a starvation camp. But if you want to eat mice —it is your privilege. The only advice a woodsman can give in this, swallow them headfirst—they can not scratch as much on the way down. No competent woodsman would ever consider eating such unpalatable and indigestible rubbish. The principle of going out without proper food or equipment is entirely wrong and can result only in disappointment and misery.

Gazing backward, I see four strong men, in the prime of life, out at break of day, blazing trails, setting traps, skinning animals, and having nothing for the noonday meal but a grouse each (that had been cooked the night before) and tea; men who had never before seen a shortage of food. In October, 1920, we had each poled a canoe loaded with traps and equipment up the Forty-Mile rapids on the Mississauga River, into what was at that time virgin wilderness. We left the nearest farmhouse 50 miles behind us. Willard Townley and I made our winter camp on the east bank of the Mississauga and Mac Bussineau and Victor Broad made camp on the Aubinadong River, six miles above us. Our camps were finished and trapping season opened the first day of November. We planned to spend one week blazing trails and setting traps to hold our grounds against newcomers, and then making a quick trip down river for the winter supply of groceries. On the evening of the fourth I sat with my .30–40 Winchester across my knees, watching four moose feeding a short distance back of our camp. The weather was unseasonably warm, so I let them go—I would shoot one when it got cooler. Fishing was excellent and grouse were everywhere so we had no difficulty in supplementing our meagre supplies of groceries.

On the morning of the fifth the sky was overcast and a cold wind was howling down from the North. By night the ground was white with snow; ice started to form on the rivers. By the sixth the rivers had frozen to such an extent that it was impossible to use canoes; we could not catch any more fish because we did not have tackle for fishing through the ice; the moose left the river flats for their winter feeding grounds back in the hills. We were not worried at first; we were catching plenty of furs, beaver, marten, fisher and mink, all of which were bringing good prices. Mac had a Marble's Game Getter; I had a Winchester Model '90 pump action .22. We would all eat more grouse, and surely the river would open again in a few days. But the cold weather continued till the twenty-first. Mac came to our camp and stayed with us that night to discuss the food question, which had become serious for all of us. During the night it turned warmer and the following started to rain. Mac went back that day for his supplies.

On the morning of the twenty-third we found that the ice had gone out of all the fast water. So Willard and I selected one fisher, a marten and a few mink skins and headed downstream. We made 25 miles on the river that day, cached our canoe high on the bank, and walked to a lumber camp four miles back in the hills. Clarence Day, the fur buyer was at the camp and we sold the few pelts for $200. We bought all the groceries that our canoe would carry. Early in the morning we hired a man and team to haul the groceries to the river. Then we began the long, hard grind up the rapids. We made half the distance that day and stayed with Art McCreight in his camp that night. The worst of the rapids were still ahead of us and a few short portages had to be made where quieter stretches of river were frozen over. The next day was colder and the river began to freeze again but at dark we reached our camp, dog tired. Now we had 200 pounds of flour, butter, sugar, rice, beans, prunes, raisins and figs—there would be no more worry that winter. Luck continued with us as a few days later I got a fine moose near camp.

Mac walked 35 miles across country, over hills and swamps, and through thick underbrush to a lumber camp on the Garden River. There he bought 125 pounds of groceries and carried them back to his camp, in a record time of four days!

When the successful trapper goes into the wilderness for the winter he takes an ample supply of flour, oatmeal, cornmeal, yeast cakes, salt, sugar, butter, shortening, syrup, rice, beans, dehydrated vegetables, prunes, raisins, figs, evaporated peaches, powdered whole milk, a few sides of bacon and a few smoked hams. He bakes loaf bread in his main camp, and has his food supply distributed around among his other camps so that he can live any required time in any camp. He has a bed with bedding, stove and white enamel cooking and eating utensils in each and every camp, and he keeps them clean. He shoots deer or moose for his winter meat; eats a grouse or possibly a rabbit stew occasionally for a change and catches an occasional fish—fishing through the ice is easy. He does *not* eat muskrats, groundhogs, porcupines, black bear or other questionable stuff.

Here is a sample meal that the normal topnotch woodsman can put on. The Bussineau brothers and Cedric Stone invited my trapping partner and me over to their camp on the East Branch of the Aubinadong River for Christmas, 1943 and here is what was cooked and ready when we arrived; 12 loaves of bread; 12 assorted pies; a roast of moose meat; a small roast beaver; four roast mallard ducks, saved for the occasion, and a big pot of dressing; a few cakes and cookies; and a huge kettle of tapioca pudding. We arrived on Saturday evening and remained till Monday forenoon and were given a King's welcome.

No work on shooting is complete without true information on the timber wolf and the game he preys upon. When I was a small boy there were plenty of moose in the district east of Sault Ste. Marie. I saw the first deer reported in our settlement, when I was nine years old. When I was 18 I heard the howl of the first wolf pack, while I was fishing up on the upper reaches of the Little Thessalon River. The deer had those nine years to multiply and they increased to incredible number. Then the wolf packs came.

I ran a trapline back of the settlements a couple of years later and

had my first real contacts with the big gray killers. The work of
setting out traps completed, I set out one morning to shoot a few
wolves. Tracks were most numerous along a high ridge between my
camp and the settlements, so I hied there and proceeded to stalk
along the peaks. By the time I started along the ridge snow was
falling fast. There was nearly a foot of loose snow when I started
and there was absolutely no noise as I walked along. Suddenly I
came on a big doe that had been freshly killed, just a few minutes
before. The wolves had not uttered a sound—there were five in the
pack. The chase had ended in less than 50 yards—a wolf had taken
two or three snaps at her hindquarters, taking a piece out as big as
a man's fist at each snap. At the second or third snap the doe's
hindquarters went down, and another snap let her innards out.
She was still bleeding when I found her.

The wolves had detected my approach and sneaked away. I
followed them, sure that I would get a shot. Less than half a mile
from the doe, I came on the bleeding carcass of a magnificent buck
that the same wolves had just killed—and the chase again was
short. I followed the wolves till near night, leaving them in a swamp.

In years of careful hunting I never got a shot at a wolf in the
woods for they have an uncanny ability to keep out of sight. I had
hunted more than four decades before I saw a wolf in the woods—
though I had seen plenty in open country—and then I got within
10 paces of them, but did not see them in time. I was hunting moose
and watching the hills 300 or 400 yards ahead. The wolves were
sleeping behind a low boulder, and made a clean getaway so I just
got a glimpse of them. So, after years of hunting, all of us trappers
learned that wolves never chase their prey for miles and howl
after him as most people believe. All of their killing for food is done
in one short, lightning charge.

George Jeffries and I saw one wolf kill a fine buck with four
points on each side, on Ranger Lake. The buck came out of the
woods about 100 yards ahead of us, the footing on the ice was
perfect and he was running as he never had before. When he was
about 100 yards from shore the wolf came out, running like the
wind. When they were 300 yards from shore the wolf took his first
snap out of the buck's hindquarter and in a matter of seconds the
buck's hind legs were dragging on the ice. The wolf proceeded to
eat without killing the buck. Recently I read an article by a Wise
Guy who claimed that being eaten alive does not hurt. How does he
know?

What we have learned by following the game trails is that the
wolf is the most intelligent, capable and ruthless killer in this hemisphere. The theory that they kill the weaklings and cripples is pure,

unadulterated bunk. They do not kill the sick and helpless and do not need to. They kill the best, and do not return to eat what is left of a carcass, at least in good game country; that is why they are so hard to trap. The deer gather in yards when the snow is deep, and that is when the wolf packs go berserk. They break into a yard and with wild, savage howls proceed to maim and kill. We have shot cripples that they left, to put them out of misery. This trait lingers on in the cousins of the wolf—the gentle farm dogs that occasionally gather in packs and slaughter flocks of sheep. This massacre is repeated in yard after yard every winter. One winter Dan Hill took me out to his trapping cabin in the Carpenter Lake country for a few days visit. There was a big deer yard around camp and the last night we were in camp all Hell let loose as the howling wolves raced through the woods slaughtering the deer. On our way out the next morning we saw the tracks of a buck that lit out for the settlements, his only hope, and he ran so hard that he ruptured a blood vessel and fan shaped sprays of blood stained the snow. That buck was not a weakling and he had not been wounded—nothing but the finest could run as he did.

This slaughter never ends. And there would be no deer in Northern Ontario today if the Provincial Government had not been paying $25.00 bounty on wolves. The annual take for several years was around *6,000! ! ! !* Had these 6,000 per year been permitted to continue their slaughter, and raise more thousands of wolves each year to increase the slaughter, there would not be any kind of game left in Ontario. The theory that wolves and game have always gotten along well is bunk—they cannot thrive together and their proximity can produce only cycles of plenty and scarcity.

Hunting, fishing and camping are glorious sports and I have enjoyed the cream of all of them. I spent the best years of my life hunting and fishing with my clients, from the Great Lakes to the sub Arctics; I have dined in the Union League Clubs in Chicago and Dayton; I have camped on the most beautiful lakes and streams, and out on the Great Northern Barren Lands; and in the Edgewater Beach Hotel, the Netherland Plaza, and most of the Statler Hotels, and have been a guest in several mansions of the wealthy. For a quarter of a century I enjoyed one of the largest and finest clienteles in the North Country. Pleasant memories of those better days have helped to soften the shock of financial disaster during the depression, and the long, hard struggle back up.

I am no longer guiding but can still extend a welcome and encouragement to visitors who come to enjoy our sports, and I can assure them an enjoyable and successful trip if they take along the proper food, equipment and rifles—and take care of them.

The woodsmen who has done most of his .22 rim fire shooting with utility guns along the silent, lonely trails of the fur country can tell few tales of exciting, long range shots at game. The pictures etched on the walls of his memory are not of spectacular shooting; they are of situations in which the forces of circumstance made ordinary shooting mighty important. The farther the March of Time has carried him from the actual scene, the brighter the pictures appear.

CHAPTER 22

The Twenty-Two in Southern Swamps

By Fleetwood Lanneau.

FOR 13 YEARS I HUNTED IN THE GREAT PEE DEE RIVER SWAMPS OF South Carolina and for 11 of those years I lived in the heart of the swamp and carried a rifle everywhere I went. Game was very abundant at that time and I killed more game—much of it with .22 caliber rifles—than a man will ever have the opportunity to kill again.

The 3,000 acres that I lived on belonged to a relative and during the hunting season he would often bring hunting parties into the swamp. As they always wanted game to take home and were seldom able to kill enough themselves, I was usually called on to make up the deficiency.

For this reason I killed much more game than I would have killed on my own account, especially wild turkeys, as they are an almost impossible proposition for an inexperienced hunter. In fact, it is very hard for a skillful turkey hunter to put such a man in a position to kill one, as he will nearly always give himself away and spoil his chance.

Besides wild turkeys and deer, which are not game for the .22 caliber rim fire rifles, we had much other small game.

For small game suitable for the .22 caliber rifles we had squirrels in countless numbers, wood ducks in the fall and winter and the migratory ducks in the winter, mallards, black ducks and others, in large numbers. These ducks all frequented the creeks and gum ponds that were all over the territory, where they came to feed on the acorns and sweet gum mast. Also, the swamp abounded in fur-bearing animals, otter, mink, raccoon, opossum, and the like, and some muskrats, where there was open water. We also had pests, such as the redtail and Cooper's hawk, sharp-shins and crows, and, in the summer, many bad snakes, mainly the cottonmouth moccasin.

I shot squirrels the year around, as they were my unfailing meat supply. They had no particular breeding season, as you could find young squirrels at all times. They were not listed as game and by many were looked upon as pests, on account of the tremendous amounts of mast that they consumed. Also they did considerable damage to cornfields, where they could reach them.

Conditions being as they were, I carried a rifle the year round, a .32–20 Winchester and sometimes a .30–40 in the hunting season, and a .22 for snakes and pests mostly, during the closed season.

The rifles I used were Winchesters mainly, also one or more each of Remingtons, Marlins, Stevens, Colts, and others, and chambered for .22 short, .22 long, .22 automatic and .22 W.R.F., or .22 Special, as it is often called. The last was my favorite cartridge. I used it in a Model 1890 slide action Winchester and killed much game with it. The inside lubricated cartridge could be carried loose in the pocket and it was much more effective than the other .22 cartridges with heel bullets.

The Marlin in lever action used the .22 long rifle cartridge, but it was not nearly as effective as the .22 Special, and I could not see that it was any more accurate, therefore, I used it very little. In fact, the .22 long rifle cartridge was hard to get at that time, as the dealers confused it with the .22 long, and I have ordered .22 long rifle cartridges from large sporting goods stores and had them send me .22 longs. When I returned them they said they had sent what I ordered, that they were .22 long and made for rifles, therefore, they must be .22 long rifle cartridges.

South Carolina, or, at least, the section I lived in, was not a rifle country. The shotgun was the almost universal weapon for everything and the .22 rifle was considered just a boy's gun, to amuse him and to be discarded as soon as he could handle a 12-gauge shotgun.

The great popularity of the .22 caliber rifle seems to have come to our section after the First World War, also the great improvement in rifles and ammunition dates from about the same time. The .22 caliber N.R.A. Savage did not come on the market until 1919 and the 52 Model Winchester a little later as did the .22 caliber Springfield and the Stevens Walnut Hill class of rifles.

I bought the N.R.A. Savage as soon as it came on the market and also the 52 Model Winchester. I had splendid success with the Savage as a squirrel rifle, using the .22 long rifle hollow points, and restocked it myself for a sporter. My hunting with it was mostly in the North Carolina mountains, where it was better than the lighter rifles I had used so long in the swamps, as the ranges were longer.

Later on we organized a little rifle club here, with the range on my place, where we had weekly shoots for several years. I bought the 52 Winchester for this shooting. I have this rifle still and most of my shooting with high speed cartridges has been with it. I have also restocked this rifle myself for a sporter and it is my squirrel rifle at the present time and is probably the best one I have ever used. It is very accurate and the higher velocities are a considerable advantage at the longer ranges that we have in the mountains.

From my earliest hunting days I have used Lyman sights, tang sights on such rifles as they were best suited to and receiver sights on rifles on higher power. My Model 52 above has the Lyman No. 48 and a fine bead front and I can shoot close groups with it.

To date, I have never used a telescope to any extent, though I have shot other men's rifles equipped with them. My two hunting companions for years used them constantly but I do not like them on my gun and could never see the need of them. Also, I usually killed more game than the other two together, so I had a very good argument for my iron sights.

My hunting has been done almost entirely in the woods and here the ranges are not very long. If I hunted on the plains, it would be an entirely different matter and I would consider a telescope sight a necessity.

I am very familiar with the use of a telescope, as my profession is that of a civil engineer and surveyor, and I have an engineer's transit in use almost every day in the year. I spent one year in Wyoming with the United States Reclamation Service and often in the field coyotes and antelope were constantly within range of me and I would time and again center the cross hairs of my transit on them and think what a fine shot I could make. The transit telescope is 24 power and gives a very clear view.

I have always sighted my rifles in to strike just above where the top of the front sight rests at 50 yards, then at 35 yards or so I can hold slightly low for the low velocity cartridges; for the .22 short it would be about 30 yards. Horace Kephart, whom I knew well and used to shoot with, liked to sight for 35 yards but I would rather hold slightly low with iron sights than try to hold over and I wanted my rifle to be effective up to 60 yards without changing sights.

With high speed cartridges I think 60 yards is about right and the sighting would be effective to 70 yards.

Seventy yards is about as far as you can place your shots with any accuracy on a squirrel, though you can hit his bulk somewhat farther when he sits up. Seventy yards in the woods is a long shot and you would usually overestimate it and think you were shooting nearer a hundred. It is beyond the distance that squirrels are generally shot and, as a regular thing, would require a telescope and a good rest for the average man.

Trajectory figures have never been of much help to me in hunt-

YOUNG FOX SQUIRREL AT PLAY

Young fox squirrels average about the size of mature grey or black squirrels, while fully grown fox squirrels are materially larger and heavier. They are handled to best advantages by charges varying from the .22 long rifle, high velocity, H.P., to the reduced and medium range loads in the .22 Hornet. Fox squirrels are more likely to be found in open wood lots, on individual trees, and along the edges of large tracts of dense timber, than in large areas of heavy boled hickory, beechnut, chestnut, pin oak, or other trees which are the homes of black or grey squirrels.

Photo, Courtesy, Ohio Div. Conservation and Natural Resources

ing. I used to do quite a lot of practicing at impromptu targets in the woods and fields, estimating the distance to a spot on a tree, then shooting at it and pacing the distance and seeing where my bullet struck. In this way I became quite proficient in judging where to hold.

I practiced this way continually with all my rifles, shooting at small stumps or clods in the fields with the larger rifles up to 200 yards, also at objects over open water, though here I could not verify my estimate of distance. My practice shooting was always done offhand and I shot nearly every day.

Up to this point I have written of rifles and hunting conditions in general. I will now try to write something in detail of the rifles and cartridges I used and the results I got with them.

Before I went into the river swamp to live, I lived as a member of my cousin's family at his plantation home, Laurel Hill, about a mile outside of the swamp, and generally spent Saturdays hunting or fishing in the swamp. Also I often hunted quail and doves in the fields and squirrels on the branches during the week, as I could get time off from my duties on the place. This was mostly with the shotgun.

As a boy I had always been a guncrank and had done much shooting, first with air rifles, then with what we called Flobert rifles, using BB caps.

My first year on the plantation I bought a .22 caliber Remington No. 4 rifle with the rolling block action. This was my first good rifle and I got much pleasure and satisfaction from it. I shot the .22 short cartridges in it almost entirely and it was quite accurate. I used it for squirrels and rabbits about the place and it replaced the shotgun on my Saturday hunts for squirrels in the swamp and went with me on my fishing trips in the summer, slung across my back, and was frequently used to kill the big cottonmouth moccasins as they sunned themselves on logs or lay coiled on the banks or were seen swimming in the creek. I must have killed several hundred with this little gun.

I killed many squirrels and some wood ducks with it in the fall, shooting the wood ducks on the water in the creeks and gum ponds. Later in the season I went back to the shotgun. When the mallards and black ducks came in and the turkey season was open, the .22 short would not do for these latter.

As a squirrel gun this little rifle was only fair. Squirrels were so numerous that I could always get a good string of them but too many were only wounded and got away. I hated this but the shotgun gave the same trouble and I did not know how to avoid it, except by using a larger caliber rifle, which I did when I moved into the swamp to live.

I found with the .22 short that I must shoot squirrels in the head or through the shoulders to be sure of getting them and I got to be more particular in placing my shots and in passing up shots that I considered too uncertain.

After I had been living at Laurel Hill for two years, my cousin bought another place, which was a better cotton farm, and I went into the swamp to look after his interests there, as he kept several hundred head of cattle in the swamp the year round and also did some planting.

As my little .22 Remington rifle would not do for a general purpose rifle in the swamp, I sold it and ordered a .32–20 Model '92 Winchester rifle from William Lyman, equipped with his sights and guaranteed tested and accurate. This rifle gave me great satisfaction and I used it for nearly 10 years for everything in the swamp. With reloaded ammunition it was very accurate and while its trajectory was rather high my ranges were seldom over 100 yards and a very flat shooting rifle was not needed. It was at its best as a turkey rifle and I killed a great many with it. As it was accurate enough for head shots up to 50 yards, most of my squirrels were killed that way. A shot through the body would often cut a squirrel in two. There were few wounded squirrels with this gun. For more than a year it was my only rifle and I shot all my squirrels with it.

After using this rifle as an all around gun for over a year, a friend sent me a .22 singleshot Winchester chambered for the .22 long cartridge. While this is always considered a poor cartridge, I got very good results with it in this rifle. The barrel was 24 inches long and rather heavy and up to 50 yards made very good targets. I used it for years and killed quite a lot of small game with it, also many snakes and other vermin in the summer months.

I equipped it at once with Lyman sights and, shortly after getting it, I took it into the swamp back of my house to try for some small game. I had not gone far on a cane ridge before I heard some wood ducks in a long pond that paralleled the ridge on my right. I made my way very carefully to a large tree near the edge of the water and, looking out across the pond, I could see the water in violent motion, but the cypress knees were so thick that I could not see the ducks. After a few minutes I saw a duck swim across a narrow opening through the knees and I trained my rifle through this, with my left hand resting against the tree. Soon another duck started across and I caught him in the sights and fired. At the shot a lot of ducks flew up in the air but settled back down again. This performance was repeated again and again until the ducks moved out of my line of fire.

I did not know whether I had hit a single duck; but when I

waded out into the pond to see I found several ducks floating on the water. I had killed every duck I had shot at.

A .22 rifle was fine for hunting these ducks on the creeks and ponds, as you could often get a number of shots at them before they would leave.

Not too long after this, I took the same rifle to try for the little ducks again on the same chain of ponds. I had been on the pond for a few minutes without finding any ducks when I heard a lot of snarling made by some animals out in the pond. As I had on hip boots, I waded out into the pond, knowing that the animals must be furbearers of some kind. Keeping some large trees in line, I got to one of them and, on looking around, I saw an otter on a large log, facing away from me, and a great commotion in the water showed that another one was beyond the log. When the second one would try to climb onto the log, the other one would fight him off and this was what all the fuss was about.

I shot the one on the log in the back of the head, killing it instantly, at a range of only 25 or 30 yards. It never moved after the shot and never rolled off of the log. The second one dived a short distance and came up, raising its head high out of the water. It got a bullet in the same place and I went out with two fine otter skins. The log they were on was a regular slide and I went back and set a trap on it and got another one that night.

There were several large logs here, cypress and gum, that had fallen across each other. Some of them were hollow and the otters must have had an under water entrance and had a den in them. This was not more than 400 or 500 yards from my house and the otters must have been raised in this den. They were probably the largest animals that I ever killed with this rifle, as I would never use it on such game as wild turkeys or deer.

I shot this rifle a great deal in offhand target practice and for this I often used .22 short cartridges, as they cost less and were just as accurate at short range. In fact, I used the shorts about as much as the longs, as they gave about as good results, especially on snakes and such vermin.

I found when winter came on and the mallard and black ducks came in that this rifle would not do for them. As with the wood ducks, I could often get a number of shots at a flock on the water, especially if I used smokeless cartridges, but I would seldom kill any—they would fly off, even if they were fairly hit. Only a head shot could be depended on to stop them.

I want to say something here about the use of smokeless powder in .22 rifles before the coming of non-corrosive priming. Colonel Whelen, in his book, *The American Rifle*, says that there is no known way to preserve the bore of a rifle from corrosion when using these cartridges but I think he missed one way. I always carried a pull-through cleaner in a small tin box in my pocket, with a strip of flannel soaked in Three-In-One oil in it and would pull it through the barrel a few minutes after a shot and I have never had a particle of damage done to this or any other .22 caliber rifle from the use of smokeless powder.

A friend and I each bought a .22 Winchester Automatic at one time and we used these rifles for years and shot them many thousands of times and the barrels were as perfect at the end of that time as the day they were purchased and the targets they made just as good. We both used this same method.

Of course, this is of no importance now, but it was a few years back. I used smokeless ammunition a great deal in .22 rifles and found it distinctly an advantage, especially in shooting ducks on the water. They would see the puff of smoke from a .22 Winchester Special black powder cartridge and immediately leave; but they could not locate the origin of the shot with the smokeless cartridge and the sharp, light report seemed to bewilder them. I have often killed several ducks out of a flock this way, without moving out of my tracks or taking my rifle from my shoulder.

It was said that smokeless was not as accurate as black powder in the .22 caliber rifles but I could never tell any difference.

After I had been using this Winchester singleshot rifle for a year or two, I had occasion to send an order to a sporting goods house and I included with it an order for a Model 1890 Winchester slide action rifle for the .22 W.R.F. or .22 Special cartridge. I equipped it with Lyman sights and, after a trial, found that I had a treasure.

In fact, this was about the most useful little gun that I ever owned and it was effective on all game that I ever used it on. I never shot a turkey or a deer with it but I believe it would have given a very good account of itself on turkeys. I made it a rule, however, not to use anything less than a .32–20 on this game. Even the .30–40 army cartridge was not as good with full mantle bullets as the flat nosed .32–20 on turkeys. At least, this has been my experience with this rifle, after shooting some 25 turkeys with it. I may have had just an uncommon run of bad luck but this cartridge just would not stop them for me, and the soft nose would blow them up.

The .22 Special cartridge is not rated in the same class as the .22 long rifle, as regards accuracy but I found it to be very accurate up to 50 or 60 yards, at least, in this rifle and it was a killer. It would kill the large ducks in their tracks, something the common .22s would never do, and it was very deadly on squirrels.

I did some trapping in the winter for fur and I took to carrying this little rifle on my trap lines, in place of my .32–20. I would sometimes get a shot at a coon or a mink and it always made good. One day I saw a 30-pound wild cat (Bay Lynx) crossing a pond on a log and killed him with a single shot. I do not think I ever killed an otter with this rifle, as I seldom saw them unless I was specially looking for them, and then I used my .32–20. I would kill a few otters every winter with this latter rifle.

I would see turkeys practically every day while I carried this little rifle and could have shot dozens of them; but I never shot them unless I was specially hunting them and for this my favorite rifle was always the .32–20. I cannot remember ever shooting a wild turkey with a .22 caliber rifle while I lived in the swamp but I did kill six one season with a .22 Automatic rifle with a much weaker cartridge. I will give an account of this later.

When I left the swamp to take up other work I disposed of all my guns but this little '90 Model Winchester and my Parker shotgun. As these would take down and pack in a trunk or a large suit case, I took them with me. The little rifle went to Florida with me on a railroad job and my rodman was so anxious to own it that I let him have it. I still have my old shotgun.

At one time I got a .22 caliber Marlin rifle in lever action. This was chambered for the .22 long rifle cartridge and I used it for a while for general shooting but I could not see that it was any more accurate than my little Winchester and it was not nearly as good a hunting cartridge as the .22 Special.

An objection I had to the Marlin, on account of its ammunition, was that the bullet would often stick in the rifling when unloading the gun and the shell, in pulling away, would spill the powder charge into the action. This does not happen now with present day ammunition.

A couple of years after I left the Pee Dee, I was in Savannah, Georgia, just after the finish of a construction job. I met there a friend who had been a neighbor of mine on the Pee Dee and who had hunted there with me. His father had owned a large rice plantation on the Savannah River, which was now abandoned, and we arranged to go to the old place for a hunt.

We found the old house still standing; but pretty well dismantled by vandals, so we went on up a large tidal creek and camped on a sandy ridge in the big timber.

We found plenty of game there and got some fine duck shooting in the timbered ponds and, after spending several days, planned to go back. We had used shotguns on this trip.

However, we were both lovers of the rifle and, while getting some supplies for our next trip, we looked over some .22 caliber rifles at a sporting goods store and decided to buy a couple of .22 Winchester automatics and use them in place of the shotguns. We did this and had a fine trip but found that the little guns would not kill ducks with the solid bullets we had, as I should have known from my experiences on the Pee Dee with the common .22 cartridge. I shot at ducks time and again sitting on logs from 25 to 50 yards and did not get one. The little rifles were quite accurate and we killed a lot of squirrels but for ducks they were a complete failure. In fact, they used the poorest cartridge for game shooting that I had ever tried, as the bullets were more pointed and harder than the common .22 bullet.

These rifles used smokeless powder and, according to the authorities, the barrels should have been ruined in a short time but I have told how we prevented this. Also we finally got hollow pointed bullets and they expanded well and the little rifles turned out to be very serviceable weapons. We both kept these rifles for several years and they were in perfect condition when we disposed of them.

This little rifle of mine was so convenient to carry that I kept it in my suit case everywhere I went and I often got opportunities to use it. It was a case of extreme portability being worth more than extreme accuracy.

At one time, after finishing another job, I decided to take some time off and spend it camping on the old Pee Dee. I had only my old shotgun and the .22 automatic at that time but thought I could make them do, as I was not anxious to kill so much game as I was to roam over my old hunting grounds again. I camped by myself for two months or more on a fine oak ridge in the heart of the swamp and found plenty of game. I killed a lot of squirrels for camp meat and to take out at times to old friends and I killed 13 wild turkeys, six of them with the little rifle.

I had never shot a turkey with a .22 caliber rifle and was reluctant to try it then but one afternoon there was a flock of turkeys on the opposite side of a ridge from me and one came to where I could just see the top of his back over the ridge, so I thought I would try for him. If I hit him high in the back, it would paralyze him and if I missed him it would not matter. The little bullet tore out about an inch of his backbone and he did not know what hit him.

This encouraged me to try again and one morning I called up a young turkey that lit in a pine 50 yards or so from me. I could not get just the shot I wanted, but had to take a quartering shot. The bullet knocked this turkey out of the tree and when it hit the ground it made off with a tremendous amount of flapping, but it went only 35 or 40 yards and was dead when it stopped.

Another one was killed late one afternoon. I had stopped on an old embankment with a long pond coming up to it on each side and cane ridges alongside of the ponds. It looked like a good place for something to come along about dark—maybe an otter on its way to the river.

It was just getting dark when a turkey flew up from one of the ridges and lit almost over my head. I hesitated to shoot for a while but finally did. The turkey towered up over the trees for 20 feet or so, spiraled around in one or two small circles and then collapsed and fell within a few feet of me.

Another afternoon I was hunting squirrels and, in going through a belt of thick cane, I saw a young turkey standing in a clear place, watching to see what was going to come out. Some cattle had been ranging the ridges and it probably expected to see a cow. I shot at it and it disappeared. I thought I must have missed it but when I went to see it was lying where it had stood, so instantly killed that it had never moved.

I do not remember just how the others were killed but I thought it was a remarkable record for such a feeble cartridge. I have done much worse with a .30–40 box magazine Winchester, using the full mantle bullets.

I failed on only one turkey that I shot at. I got a good broadside shot at a young gobbler but there was a lot of switch cane between us and the bullet was probably deflected. He did not show any sign of being hit.

However, in spite of its good record on that hunt, I would be the last person in the world to recommend the .22 Automatic rifle as a turkey rifle and I have never tried it since.

The first day I set up my tent on this hunt and got my camp in shape I took my little rifle and strolled off to see if I could get a squirrel for the pot. I had scarcely got out of sight of my tent when I saw six or eight coons feeding under a large white oak. I got a little closer to them and killed one on the ground. They dashed off in every direction at the shot, one of them running right toward me. It started up a tree within 10 feet of me and I killed it without using the sights. When I started forward again one that had gone up a tree saw me and tried to climb higher and I killed him as he was climbing, making the third in about five minutes.

When I left the swamp after this hunt I went to Texas for a year on highway work and the little rifle went along. I did not have very much time for hunting while I was there but I made several little trips to the Sabine River and found the swamp lands very similar to the Great Pee Dee in South Carolina, though not nearly so large. I killed some mallard ducks here and a good many squirrels, a good percentage of them fox squirrels. This was new to me, as we did not have fox squirrels in our swamp in South Carolina, though they were plentiful in the pine lands.

After a year in Texas, I was back on the Savannah River again where I spent a year on construction work, and the little automatic was with me here again and gave me some good sport at odd times.

After this work, I spent a year in Wyoming on reclamation work and I shot rabbits and prairie dogs at spare times along the North Platte River.

I finally bought a place here in Western North Carolina, as it is a fine country to live in, and I was able to have a rifle range of my own and to hunt squirrels at times in the mountains and occasionally make a short camping trip in some turkey country.

After I settled down here in Western North Carolina, I began to use the heavy types of .22 caliber rifles. These included the Savage N.R.A., the Winchester 52 and the N.R.A. Springfield, also lighter sporting models, such as the Winchester 57–69 and 72 models and a Marlin lever action, similar to the one I used to some extent on the Pee Dee. I also used two Winchester automatics, one for the .22 long rifle and one for the .22 short.

The Winchester Model 57 belonged to one of my two hunting companions and one of the automatics to the other but I sometimes kept them for a week or so at a time to test them against my various rifles.

All the heavy models shot very close groups from a good rest and the choice between them was mainly a question of cost. The Winchester 52 was a better made gun than the Savage but it cost more than double. It has a better action and triggerpull and a speedlock; but the Savage would hold its own with any of them on a target. The Springfield would have been best for a military shooter, on account of the long travel of the bolt and the military triggerpull.

I found the Model 57 Winchester an exceptionally fine shooting rifle for its size and weight. None of the heavy rifles could outshoot it and I have made 10 shot groups at 50 yards with it not larger than a dime.

I did a lot of experimenting also with the .30 '06, .30–40, .270 Winchester, .250 Savage and .25–35 rifles, trying out reduced loads.

I also did a good deal of squirrel hunting, most of it with the N.R.A. Savage and my .25–35 Winchester, with reduced loads.

Most of my squirrel hunting here was done in the company of two friends, one a doctor, who used the 57 Model Winchester. All of us used all makes and varieties of .22 caliber cartridges and it was always an open question with us as to which was best.

There was no difference of opinion as to the value of the hollow point bullet but a long series of test shooting from a good rest showed that the regular .22 long rifle cartridge, loaded with Lesmoke powder, gave the best groups and also a lighter report than the Hi-speed and both of these are important, so that my friends preferred the old type in the end.

Squirrels are not shot very often at long range and their vital parts are a small target, so that accuracy counts for a great deal and they may have been right in their decision. They are both gone now and that chapter is closed.

I had always been inclined to favor the Hi-speeds, as I like a cartridge that kills quickly and this was my reason for using my .25–35 with reduced loads very often, instead of the .22.

The third member of our party finally used a Hi-speed cartridge but it was the .22 short in a 74-Model Winchester automatic, equipped with a Weaver scope. He claimed that the .22 long rifle Hi-speed mangled squirrels too badly and that the .22 short Hi-speed hollow point was just right.

I have never shot squirrels with this cartridge and, as I have this rifle of his, I may try it out sometime and see if I can agree with him. I doubt it, myself, though it should be about as good as the .22 Automatic cartridge, and both cartridge and gun would be very nearly ideal for snakes. It is also good for bluejays when they molest the other birds around my home. This is all I have used it for to date.

Another experiment I may try some day is to put a telescope on my Model 52 and see how much it may increase my killing range on squirrels.

Some years ago there was a series of articles in *The American Rifleman* called I believe, "Friendly Little Rifles." It was applied there to rifles of the .32–20 class and I found it very interesting and wish I had kept the copies in which they appeared. I have always remembered this title and think it applies particularly well to the various little rifles of .22 caliber in slide, lever and selfloading actions that are used so much in the game fields. These can well be described as friendly little rifles.

I have used most of them and found them all good, my best friend among them being a little 1890 Model Winchester, for the .22 W.R.F. cartridge. This little rifle was my companion on hundreds of small game hunts and, in the aggregate, we must have covered thousands of miles of swamp trails together. It kept my table supplied with meat the year round, as we had young squirrels at all times and they were not protected at that time. In fact, there were so many of them that they were a nuisance at some seasons. They would go into the cornfields in such numbers as to seriously damage the crops and I have seen considerable fields of corn lying in a narrow strip along swamp woods where it was raided by squirrels by day and by raccoons by night to such an extent as to completely destroy the crop. Also they consumed the bulk of the mast crops, nuts and acorns, at least, that better varieties of game required through the winter.

Squirrels were my unfailing meat supply, varied at times by ducks and sometimes venison, the ducks also being supplied by the little rifle.

Some people do not care for squirrel meat, many of them from prejudice alone. I have this prejudice, myself, against rabbits but I think squirrels are the finest of our wild meats and one that I never get tired of eating.

Squirrels are usually ruined in the way they are handled. They are often shot with a shotgun, where they do not bleed properly and where the paunch and intestines are perforated with shot. Then they are stuffed into the hot pocket of a hunting coat and carried around all day and maybe given to a servant to skin and clean that night or even the next morning. Such squirrel meat is little better than carrion.

My squirrels are always shot with a rifle, generally in the head, or well forward, which bleeds them well, and the internal organs are not damaged back of the heart or lungs. Then I skin and clean them usually not more than five minutes after they are shot.

I always carry a leather or rawhide thong about ten inches long, with a small slit near each end that I can thread the thong through, making a noose in each end. I put one noose over one hind leg, run the thong over a low branch or fork of a bush, fastening the other leg, and have the squirrel hanging head down, with its back to me. Then I cut through the tail, close to the body, and strip the hide down. It will tear around the body and meet just back of the fore legs and you can then pull it over the head and pull the fore legs out, cutting off the paws at the wrists. Then pull it on over the head, cutting out the eyes and using the knife around the lips and nose. Next, reverse the squirrel and, catching the point of skin on the breast, the rest can be stripped off in one motion. Now hang the squirrel up as before, only facing toward you. Cut through the pelvic bones and rip it open and let all the works fall out. I can skin and dress a squirrel in this way in half the time it takes to describe it, without getting any hair on the meat and without soiling my hands, except maybe a little blood on my finger tips. Then I put it in a clean bag and start looking for another one.

They can be cooked in many ways. I like the young, tender ones best when broiled. Old ones, if they are used at all, are good stewed. My old rank ones were usually fed to my dogs.

My house had a large, old fashioned fireplace and it had fire in it throughout the winter. I burned ash, maple and oak mainly and these woods seldom popped. Also, I let large quantities of ashes accumulate and when I went out I banked my fires with these ashes and put up a barrier in front of the fire.

I nearly always had a large Dutch oven over this banked fire filled with squirrels or game of some kind, where it would simmer slowly all day and I could easily prepare a meal when I came in. Although I did all my own cooking during these years, I did not fare badly for food and it cost practically nothing. How different it is today!

Picking ducks was always a disagreeable job, so I avoided it by cooking them in their feathers. I would draw and clean them, then put them down on the hot hearth, put wet leaves over them, then ashes, then live coals and in an hour or so they would be cooked through. When taken out, skin and feathers would come off in one piece, leaving the clean, pink meat, with all its juices retained.

Our winters, after January, were often very cold and if I happened to kill a deer at such times, I would keep a quarter and hang it up in a back room, or outside, and live on venison for a change.

While I am writing along this line, I want to tell about the finest wild meat that I think I ever tasted. It was on a hunt with a taxidermist along and we were after specimens. We killed a big, fat old gobbler and the taxidermist skinned him. Then we used what we could of his body to make a hash or stew, excepting some fine breast meat. This we sliced thin across the grain and broiled over a coal fire on a wire broiler, basting it well with butter and a little seasoning of some kind. It was almost too tender to handle and was perfectly delicious.

I started to write more about .22-caliber rifles and have already wandered off on other subjects.

Going back to my little friend, the .22 W.R.F., I wrote about using smokeless ammunition in this rifle with so much satisfaction during my stay in the swamp. After leaving there, I got hold of some cartridges in Thomasville, Georgia, of a different brand from those I used on the Pee Dee and ran into trouble. After using a few, I had a bad escape of gas from one shot but, thinking it was only one defective cartridge, I continued to shoot them. Soon another one let go and nearly put my eyes out. I went in nearly blinded and later, when I went to clean the gun, found the action locked and had to dismount it. Then I found the carrier broken in two and the action pretty well wrecked inside. I got new parts and replaced them myself but I did not use any more of that make of smokeless ammunition.

Shortly after this I disposed of this gun and have never had another one for this cartridge but it would still be my choice of a cartridge for small game. It is really in a class to its self. If I expected to do any more small game hunting in the swamp, I would certainly get another one.

When I hunted in the river swamp, there were hardly more than half a dozen .22-caliber rifles to choose from, one lever action, three slide actions and a few singleshots—no bolt actions. It was not hard to make an intelligent choice. Today there are about the same number of slide actions, the same lever action, and a perfect swarm of bolt actions, automatics and combination actions, also one or two good singleshot target rifles.

The bolt action rifle is on top, as far as popularity goes, today but I cannot say that I am altogether sold on it. I believe for general hunting in the woods I would still prefer the slide action gun. Unless you go into the expensive target rifle class and expect to shoot at long ranges, there is not enough difference in their shooting qualities to count. It used to be that some of the slide action guns could not be cleaned from the breech but I believe they all have removable breechblocks now and can be so cleaned, if the shooter wants to clean at all. Also, any of the slide action guns will make $1\frac{1}{2}''$ groups at 50 yards and that is good enough where most shooting is done inside of that distance.

I have often been asked why I did not use telescope sights in later years, when they have become so popular and are so easy to get. It seems to me that the reason is obvious to any man who has done much hunting in the woods. I like the clean lines and good balance of a well made rifle too much to clutter it up with such an addition, especially where it is not needed. I can see why a man who has very defective eyesight and still wants to hunt could use a low power glass to great advantage but to a man with good eyes whose hunting is entirely in the woods it seems to me it is a handicap. I have never, to date, had a telescope on one of my rifles. I did, not long ago, come into possession of a little Winchester .22 automatic equipped with a Weaver scope, which, after a few tryouts, I proceeded to take off and replace with the old open sights on the barrel. My eyes are 70 years old and not good for open sights but I like them better than a scope for short range shooting.

My old hunting companion, who had owned this rifle, had several other rifles, all telescope sighted, Lyman, Winchester, Weaver and Belding & Mull glasses. A Springfield sporter was equipped with a Belding & Mull scope in a bridge mount and the glass was perfect. For hunting coyotes on the plains it would have been a treasure but it was totally out of place in the woods hunting that we did.

This sight and mount must have added several pounds to an already fairly heavy rifle and it made it as hard to carry in a canebrake or laurel thicket as an engineer's transit. He hunted with this rifle for five or six years, at least, and if he ever killed anything with it I never heard of it. I think he had to pay so much attention to obstructions in the woods in getting this outfit through them that he had no chance to see game.

This man was my most intimate friend for over 40 years. We hunted together at every opportunity from my days on the Pee Dee until the time of his death. He was one of the best woodsmen I ever saw and nobody loved rifles and hunting more. He had a collection of scope sighted rifles for every purpose but I never knew anyone to kill less game for the amount of hunting that he did. I cannot recall that he ever killed a turkey in all the years that we hunted together. He was a very good squirrel hunter and good on ducks and birds with a shotgun. I believe he would have done better if he had stuck to Lyman type sights.

My first and greatest objection to telescope sights is the spoiling of the lines and "feel" of the rifle. The lighter the rifle, the more pronounced this is. Another is the awkwardness of the sight at very close range. Much small game is shot in the woods at from 20 to 25 yards. At this distance the field of the scope is small and the line of sight is so high above the bore that the bullet does not rise to intersect the line of sight. More squirrels are shot at 25 yards than at 75 and at the longer ranges you can usually get closer if you want to.

As I always say, 75 yards is a long shot in the woods and a squirrel head is not too small a mark at this range for a Lyman sight from a good rest. This is about as far as even a good rifle will group that small. If all shooting was this far, the telescope sight would pay, maybe, but this is beyond the average and, a peep sight being nearly as good, what is the use of cluttering up the rifle with a scope?

Another thing I have noticed is that the scope hunters are never sure that their scopes are right. They have little confidence in them and want to test them at every opportunity. If the rifle gets a jolt or if the telescope gets hung in a vine, they are afraid their sighting has been disturbed and it must be tested. I would rather stay with the old reliable iron sights. I could always hit anything with them that was big enough to see, at least as far as the sights part was concerned and I do not see how a scope can do any better.

There was only one condition that used to make *me* wish for a telescope sight and that was in hunting otters. I would often see them swimming at more than 100 yards and sometimes on logs also and I needed a rifle of flatter trajectory, with a telescope sight for this shooting. My wish used to be for a .25–35 Winchester single-shot with their 5-A scope. When an otter was swimming, the glitter of the water made it uncertain just where his head was. The telescope would have cleared this up.

I always used the Lyman sight with the large aperture and shot with both eyes open. I have sometimes lost game very early in the morning before there was light enough to see the rim of the rear sight near the eye. I could see the front sight clearly but could not tell if I was looking through the rear sight at all. A small hunting disc screwed into the sight, with a fairly large aperture, will take care of this. I made a practice of keeping such a disc in a trap under the butt plate of my hunting rifle, together with a small screw driver and broken shell extractor.

It may be said that I have never given telescope sights a fair test and there is truth in this, but I have used them enough, I believe, to satisfy myself that I do not like them on a rifle. I use a fine telescope nearly every day on an engineer's transit, for that is my business, and I know how accurate it is but I think it is unnecessary and in the way *for woods hunting*.

I think it is beginning to be the case that the reverse of what I said above may be true and that it is the iron sight today that does not get a fair test. Too many people start out with telescope sights and have no way of making comparisons for hunting in the woods.

So many men have had military training for the past generation or more that all shooting is looked upon from that point of view, hence, the bolt action rifles and prone shooting. What earthly good would efficiency in prone shooting do a man hunting in cane as high as his head, or in a cypress swamp? He has to stand on his hind legs most of the time and, if he uses a rest, it is against the side of a tree.

In all my rifle practice with rifles of any kind I always shot strictly offhand. This is where practice is needed by nearly everyone and if a man can shoot well offhand, he need not worry about his rest shooting. It is not once in 100 times that I have ever used the prone position in hunting. Occasionally, in shooting at an old gobbler in a peafield from a position on a ridge, and sometimes at a target on a sandbar in the river or on the opposite bank I have used this position but it is seldom that you can ever see anything at all if you get down as low as prone.

In shooting wild turkeys my favorite position was to sit with my back against a big tree, with my elbows resting on my drawn up knees but here you select your position in advance and the turkey comes to you, usually across fairly open ground. This is in a situation where turkeys are scattered and called up.

In my first notes on .22 caliber rifles, I stated that I had never shot a turkey with a .22 caliber rifle in all my hunting while I lived in the river swamp but that I did kill six one season some years later with a .22 Winchester automatic with hollow point bullets and that I had remarkable success with it, but still would certainly not recommend it as a turkey rifle.

The power of the .22 caliber rim fire cartridge has been greatly increased since that time. The .22 long rifle in Hi-speed and with hollow pointed bullets has become a savage little cartridge and as the .22 W.R.F. cartridge has been stepped up proportionately, if not more so, it should be quite an effective load for turkeys. It has about the accuracy of the old .32–20 cartridge, with higher velocity and, of course, flatter trajectory. I found it years ago, with the old loading, an almost perfect cartridge for everything below turkeys and it should be even better today, and capable of including this great game bird. I wish I could give it a try-out but the time for it has passed, in my case.

I have done little hunting for several years. If I do any next season, I will use my 52 Model Winchester for squirrels. This is about as good a rifle as I could get for our conditions here. It is fairly heavy and I have always found it very accurate, though I do not know just what groups I can get at 75 yards with the Hi-speed cartridges. I will have to try it out from a good rest and find out. I will try it out with several brands and find out which it handles best. I would like to have a Model 61 Winchester in .22 W.R.F. to shoot for comparison. I saw an account of a series of tests with this rifle and cartridge by Charles Askins, Sr., several years ago and, as I remember it, the accuracy was remarkable. I take anything coming from Mr. Askins as absolutely reliable and if I had a record of this shooting I would not need to make a test myself.

Mr. Samworth, for whom I am writing these notes, would like me to write something that might interest boys and beginners in the use of .22 caliber rifles on game and in the practice of hunting in the woods. I can only give this from some of my own experiences as a boy, which are as clear in my memory as if they had happened yesterday.

The first thing to consider is the rifle and rifle shooting as subjects in themselves, for a person cannot have much success as a hunter until he has mastered his weapon. The only shots that count are the shots that hit.

Boys raised on a farm usually have some experience in hunting by the time they are six years old. They follow their father or older brothers about after squirrels and rabbits but most often this hunting is done with single barrel shotguns, which is a good thing for the community, because the average farmer shoots his weapons with no regard as to where the bullets will finally land. The average farm boy usually gets a .22 caliber rifle before he is 10 years old and is more or less of a menace to the neighborhood until he is able to handle the family shotgun and passes the .22 on to a younger brother to take his turn at the same game.

They say that in battle a man's weight is fired away in lead for every man killed and, as the effort to kill here is intentional, it probably would take more to kill anyone in random shooting on the farm and generally the farm boy does not have the money to shoot as much as he would like to.

Only in yesterday's paper was an account of a small boy being killed a few miles from here by his uncle, in whose hands a .22 rifle went off accidentally in their home. These accidents are so common as to scarcely cause comment and they are totally inexcusable.

I have written the above in order to stress the fact that safety should be the first thing taught to a boy or a beginner in the use of any firearms and the first rule should be to never let a weapon in your hands, empty or otherwise, point toward another person. If this one rule is observed, no accident is likely to ever happen to anyone of whose presence you are aware. This rule, however, does not protect distant objects from reckless shooting. The .22 caliber long rifle cartridge, as now loaded, is deadly on a man or farm stock at a range of a mile or more and will shoot through the average frame house. Shooters should always bear this fact in mind.

I think for a small boy or other beginner the singleshot rifle is much better to start with. Most of these are now made in bolt action, which is the same action that he will likely want to continue with, later on, in a repeater. The Winchester people are now advertising a new bolt action for boys in which the safety is automatic and goes on as soon as the bolt handle is raised. This should be an ideal rifle for boys. The repeater is not as safe a rifle for a beginner and the selfloading, or so-called automatic rifle, is the most dangerous of the lot. It is very easy to forget to put the safety on when standing the rifle up or laying it down and a fall or a touch on the trigger would mean an accidental shot, maybe with disastrous consequences.

Having selected and secured the rifle, the next thing is to learn to use it properly. The .22-short cartridge is probably the best for the beginner's use and he should start shooting at rather close range and, if possible, under the direction of a good coach, though I did not have this advantage myself. It is a good idea to use regular targets, which can be had from any sporting goods store and to shoot

TREED!

A good squirrel dog in action. He has put one up a tree which is ideal for a sure shot, as this tree stands apart from other big ones and there is small likelihood of this squirrel traveling along the treetops.

Let's hope there are no den holes in this tree.

a regular number of shots at each target and count up the score on each one and also date it. Keep your targets for future reference and you can note the improvement in your shooting from your practice, and can also compare your ability with that of others. The scores will give it to you at a glance.

As the first object is to learn to use the sights and to gain confidence in yourself, it is best to shoot for some time from a rest. After you have learned your rifle thoroughly and know just what it can do, you can take up offhand shooting.

You will find that your scores will be considerably off from your rest shooting at first and can never quite equal them but this is the practical position for the hunter and, if your object is hunting, I would do my entire practicing offhand and shoot from a rest only at intervals, to test your sights or a new lot or a different brand of ammunition, as you will find them to differ slightly in their centers of impact. That is, that different lots or different brands will center a group of shots in a slightly different place with the same sighting.

After you have learned to do good rest shooting, if you will get a box of cartridges of several different brands and shoot them for groups, you will probably find that your gun will shoot decidedly better groups with one particular brand and it is a good idea then to stick to that brand and adjust your sights especially for it. It is also a good idea to repeat this test at intervals of six months or a year, say at the beginning of the hunting season each year, as the manufacturers change their loadings some times and the preference of the rifle may change. If a man wants to get the best out of his rifle, he has to observe these things and it also adds immensely to his interest in the weapon. In larger rifles, using center fire cartridges, the shooter finds this interest in reloading and in adjusting the loads to his particular rifle. He can spend a lifetime at this fascinating subject, never reaching perfection, which he knows to be unattainable but always improving a little.

The next thing in order is the rifle sights. Almost all the small bore rifles are equipped with first class open sights and on some of them you have the option of open or peep sights. For a boy with normal eyes the open sights are good enough for his first rifle. If his eyes are in any way abnormal, the peep sights would be best. If he hopes to shoot in any competition where the shooting is to be from the prone position, for high scores, then the peep sights would be best in any case.

Prone shooting is good practice and it helps in giving confidence, as any rest shooting would but I think offhand practice is best for the hunter and if a man can develop into a good shot offhand, his rest shooting will take care of itself.

After the beginner gets along this far and wants to go hunting, he will have to find a hunting ground. This is not very hard to do in this section. Most mountain farms extend well up on the mountains and the owners will generally give hunters permission to hunt on their land. Most boys have friends in the schools who live on mountain farms and can easily make arrangements to hunt with them and the country boys can teach them a good deal about finding game and getting about in the woods.

It is always best for a beginner to hunt for a while with an experienced hunter, who can keep him under observation and correct mistakes at times and caution him to be careful, as the young hunter in his excitement is likely to run after escaping game with a cocked gun or be careless in getting over a fence or crossing a ditch or ravine with the same, and the older man can impress him with the folly of this. He can also give him good pointers on finding game and finding good positions for a shot.

These things he will find out for himself in time, if he takes to the sport. Almost all my own hunting was self taught. I commenced hunting in the river swamp at 14 and was living there by myself at 16, but few boys of that age would have my enthusiasm these days, or be willing to undergo the hardships or privations that I did for the sake of hunting.

Before a beginner goes into wild areas in the mountains or into the big swamps by himself he should have some training in woodcraft. If he is a Boy Scout, he has, no doubt, been taught something along this line.

A man can easily lose his sense of direction in the woods and if he finds that he is lost and gets into a panic, it can have very serious consequences. I have more than once shot turkeys in big timber and had them fall 100 yards back in big canebrakes and have lost my sense of direction in hunting for them and had a time getting out.

I remember one incident particularly. One rainy afternoon I was going along a trail through a canebrake, containing several hundred acres. At one place this trail crossed the end of an open flat, perhaps 60 yards across. I looked this flat over before I left the cane and saw nothing but, as I stepped into it with my rifle ready, a big turkey ran from behind a brush pile, preliminary to leaving the ground, and I took a snap shot at him, without using the sights. The bullet hit him and knocked him over but he managed to rise and flew low over the cane for 75 or 100 yards and I heard him crash into the cane when he fell. I leaned my rifle against a tree and went after him and it took a good while to find him, as the cane was 15 feet high and tangled so that you could hardly force a way through them. When I started back I soon realized that I was on a wrong course and I knew that I might have to go half a mile or more in some directions, even if I could hold a straight course, to get out and it was nearly night and cold and pouring rain and I was soaked to the skin. So I climbed a tree high enough to see over the cane and I could see a large pine several hundred yards off—the only pine anywhere in that part of the swamp, and I knew its location. Also I could see a long line of heavy mist, like white clouds, and I knew this hung over the river, so I got my course straight again and, by lining treetops one after the other, I made my way out to the trail before dark and back to the little flat and my rifle. But if I had lost my head altogether, I might never have gotten out.

Very often I would have young men spend a few days with me and they would go into the woods with directions as to trails and creeks and woods roads, and would sometimes wind up on plantations miles away and would be sent back. They would cross woods, roads and trails without ever seeing them.

There is little danger of a man getting lost in the mountains, unless he goes into big laurel thickets. They are as bad as cane-brakes, as progress is so slow and difficult and they may extend for miles. A man can get out of most places in the mountains by simply working down hill. A ravine or hollow will eventually take him to water and the streams to the valley, where he will find settlements where he can get directions as to how to return to his camp or car.

It is well to remember, too, that the laurel is on the slopes with a northern exposure, while the opposite slope is usually open hard-wood timber.

It is astonishing how easily people can get turned around in the woods. When we got our place here in North Carolina we built a house in the edge of a body of woods. My father would go out to pick up a few fallen limbs sometimes and would finally come out on some farm half a mile away and not have any idea where he was. Sometimes he would take a little red cart (painted red so that it could be easily found) and when he would get an armful of dead wood he would head for an oak bush with red leaves and again finally make his way out of the woods far off and then a search would have to be instituted for the little red cart. Other members of the family would have similar experiences.

My own sense of direction has never been very good, not nearly so good as that of my old hunting companion who had the tele-scope sighted rifles and I always deferred to his sense of direction to return to a strange camp. On the other hand, he never seemed to be able to find and kill as much game as I could. We seemed to excel along different lines.

I could write indefinitely on the subject of woodcraft but as this is supposed to be for the edification of boys and beginners, it is safe to assume that they will not try to explore the innermost fast-nesses of the big swamps or the wildest parts of the mountains in the beginning but will skirt the edges and hunt from trails and along creeks and on some of the good open ridges and will gradually find their way deeper and deeper into the woods. A little exploring of this easy going will quickly give a fair knowledge of a considerable territory and the young hunter will have a satisfactory hunting ground.

When boys go into the woods to hunt, I think it is best if they can go in pairs. It is safer and they will get more game than if they go in gangs. If possible, hunt from the trails. They will see as much game and make less noise. Late in the fall squirrels are feeding on the ground most of the time and going quietly along a trail a squirrel will often be seen to steal up a tree in easy range. If one boy stops and the other keeps on, the squirrel will edge around the tree from the moving one, giving the one who has stopped a good shot. If he misses, the squirrel will run back around, exposing himself to the one who turned him first. In this way, they will have the advantage of it, as it cannot use the body of the tree to cover itself from either one. If it is shot at and missed and cannot find concealment in the tree, it will try flight and this is where a lot of good offhand practice may show results as you try to catch him as he pauses to make a leap to another limb.

If the hunter is alone and he sees a squirrel steal up a tree, if he will stop and stand perfectly still, it will be only a minute or two before the squirrel shows its head as he tries to investigate and find out what has become of the object of his suspicion. I have killed hundreds of squirrels this way and the range is seldom over 35 yards and as often 15. Plain open sights are as good as anything for such shooting.

The first method used when hunting in pairs is the method of the red-tailed hawk. A pair of them will strike at a squirrel from both sides of a tree and his only hope is to get back to the ground and get under cover.

In hunting in the early fall the squirrels are feeding in the trees and the best plan is to watch the trees they are working in and get them when they come in to feed. Sometimes you can get more than one tree in range at the same time and this is where you can some-times do long range shooting to advantage. A hunter can often kill 10 squirrels this way from one position, which is the legal limit now, I believe, and is enough for anyone. In the mountains here I find six or eight a very good bag. There is not much feed left for them here and they are scattered over a wide territory. The chestnut blight was a bad thing for game in this section of North Carolina.

While I always try to stress the importance of offhand shooting for the hunter, it is best to take a rest whenever you can get it, especially if the range is over 35 or 40 yards. Prone shooting is hopeless for any but exceptional cases but a big fallen log often furnishes a perfect rest. Most often, however, you will have to use the side of a tree. It is best here to rest your hand against the tree, rather than the rifle itself, especially if it is a rifle with much recoil, as resting the rifle against the tree would cause it to shoot away from the rest. Also, resting across a log may cause it to shoot high.

I expended a considerable amount of ammunition during the summer months in shooting snakes. The river swamps are full of them. There are several varieties of moccasins, of which the worst is the cottonmouth, a deadly snake and a vicious one—the only snake that I have ever known to advance on a man, which it will do sometimes in the water. We had miles of creeks and sloughs, acres of gum ponds and several old rivers besides the Great Pee Dee, itself, for two miles or more and a large cypress swamp, which was headquarters for the cottonmouths. I would often take a .22 caliber rifle and follow the creek banks for miles, shooting every snake I saw. They would be on logs, coiled up on the low banks near the water, or stretched out on limbs over the water, or in bushes, offering fine shots. The cottonmouth has a wide, flat head, a fine target for a .22. Sometimes I would put on hip boots and go into Log Swamp and I would kill many cottonmouths there. This swamp was full of old fallen logs and sometimes you could see several snakes on one log. There were many in the willows along the river and altogether they furnished a lot of good sport and it was never ending, as you would find just as many the next trip. Any .22 caliber rifle was good for this shooting, as the ranges were short, and I often used a Winchester singleshot rifle with the .22 short cartridge.

When I went into Log Swamp I used my Model '90 repeater, for the .22 W.R.F., as I was often in 30 inches or so of mud and water and there was always a chance that a big fellow might come at you and you could not move fast and might want several quick shots. While these things were not *game*, they *were* good hunting and you always felt that you were doing a fine thing by killing as many of them as you possibly could.

Not many boys will be able to do much hunting in the big swamps but many can have fine sport hunting things that I never had a chance at. The woodchuck is one. It must be fine sport hunting them with the rifle and in some sections they are numerous and can be troublesome. As they are shot mostly in open country, prone shooting with a telescope can be used to advantage. If a shooter expects to specialize on woodchucks, he can do the same on prone shooting and he will soon advance to a longer range rifle. I can give a man no points on this shooting, as I have had no experience at it. The nearest to it that I have ever had was shooting prairie dogs in Wyoming.

We have a few woodchucks, or ground hogs, as they are called here but there are not enough to furnish any sport. I see one occasionally along the road, or when I am surveying. Not long ago I saw one at work in the end of a beanfield and about 200 yards from me. I was at my transit and the telescope showed up his eyes and teeth and every morsel that he put in his mouth; but I had no rifle and would not have shot him if I could have. They are rare enough in our country to be a curiosity.

In the lowcountry of the Carolinas crows can furnish great sport and if I could hunt there I would be a crow hunter. On a hunting trip near New Bern, North Carolina, several years ago, we found crows in tremendous numbers and if I had been skillful in hunting them, I would have had more sport than in hunting turkeys. There were two varieties, the common and the fish crow. We had some crows in the river swamp and I shot them when an opportunity presented itself but there were not enough of them to furnish much sport. There are so few in this section that I never bother them but when a man kills one he can feel that he has done some good, for they are great destroyers of the nests and young of small birds. The bluejay is another rascal of the same stripe.

If I was in a position to do much hunting today, I would concentrate on predators almost entirely. It would be just as much sport and would help more valuable game. Every wildcat, mink, weasel, crow, owl and most hawks killed would give valuable game a better chance, and do not leave out snakes and bluejays where small birds are concerned.

In hunting in our Southern woods, there is little to rifle shooting but having your rifle properly zeroed for the most practical range and to do good holding. Long range shots are the exception, and there is seldom any wind.

The reverse of this is true in the little shooting that I did in Wyoming. The ranges on prairie dogs were rather long for the rifle I had, a .22 automatic, and there was nearly always wind. I kept my rifle sighted for a somewhat longer range than common and would hold off slightly for wind. As I could usually see the dust where the bullet struck, it gave me a check on my holding and I could do very good shooting up to 100 or 125 yards. One of my rodmen had a .22 W.R.F. rifle, like the one I used so successfully in the Pee Dee swamp, and I used it sometimes. It was a better killer than my little automatic, but did not have as good sights and I could do no better with it.

There were a great many small rabbits in the clay bluffs, also, and I shot some of these. They were very good eating as the camp cook would fix them. There were also many jackrabbits but not many close to our camp. They would have furnished some fine practice for running shots but I did not kill any. Coyotes and prong horn antelope were seen nearly every day but seldom within .22 caliber rifle range, and the antelopes were protected.

This country had been a part of the great buffalo range and their remains were still in evidence. I would often find their skulls, easily identified by the short, thick horns, more or less disintegrated.

There were more muskrats in the North Platte River than in any other place I ever saw. You could stand on a bridge and see them swimming about nearly any time and once when the river was out of its banks I saw them swimming about in the streets of a small town.

What I have said about 'scope sights would not apply to this Western country. The same about prone shooting. Both would be an advantage here and could be used most places. I could have killed many coyotes here if I had had a 'scope sighted rifle of flat trajectory and the time to use it.

For young hunters starting out there are many good books on small game hunting that he can read to advantage and that he will find full of interest. The same is true of camping and woodcraft. There is information enough on guns and ammunition to fill a library and if he is a real gunbug he will devour it.

Of course, a man can never become a good hunter or woodsman through book learning entirely; but he can get many good ideas and much valuable information this way and he can put it in practice as opportunity offers. Few men ever get the chance to learn these things from experience alone, besides, it takes too much time.

How to use a compass and what to do in case he gets lost might sometime be invaluable to a man. You often hear the statement that moss grows on the north side of trees and that one can find a course by this means and this is true to a certain extent but it is not infallible. It is due to the fact that the north side gets little or no sunshine, therefore it retains more moisture, and this is favorable to the growth of moss. A leaning tree and one shaded by a large tree growing near it might have more moss on the south side, just as a fallen log has most moss on top. So, if a man wants to use this to get a course, he should disregard any but straight trees growing to themselves. Books on woodcraft will note such things that a man might not notice for years.

Also, a man cannot make an intelligent choice of a rifle without much reading. He needs to study catalogs and books by experts on firearms to get an idea of what he needs. Only these men can keep up with the incessant changes and improvements in firearms—the average man does not have the time or the means to do it.

A man needs to know something about velocities, trajectories, and the size of groups that various rifles will make, to be able to compare one with another. For instance, tables may show that the .22 W.R.A. cartridge has a heavier bullet and a little higher velocity and flatter trajectory than the .22 long rifle and that its energy and power are greater; but also that the .22 long rifle will shoot into a 1″ circle at a distance where the .22 W.R.F. would only hold a 1½″ circle, and that the .22 long rifle is also considerably cheaper. These points are all pertinent and should be taken into consideration. In my own case, I would try to have both rifles and use them where they fitted in best. If I was hunting medium sized game, I would use the .22 W.R.F., because I would not want to lose any game and the .22 W.R.F. is much the best killer. If I was hunting vermin or pests or doing a lot of random shooting, I would use the .22 long rifle, as it is cheaper and a little more accurate at long range. However, either could be substituted for the other on occasion.

Also, I would always want a rifle for the .22 short cartridge. It is very accurate at short range, is less dangerous in settled country and is cheap to shoot and I would want a rifle especially bored and chambered for this one cartridge. It is just the thing to shoot for amusement and for small vermin around the farm—rats, snakes, bluejays and what not.

Of late years the leading arms companies have been bringing out a class of rifles in bolt actions between the light sporting rifles and the heavy target rifles. These rifles should fill a longfelt want and would be about the same as the .22 N.R.A. Savage rifle that I once converted to a sporter and found to be such a good squirrel rifle. I have never had the opportunity to use one of these rifles.

I think I have given a fair account of my experiences with .22 rifles on game, without going into too much detail on individual cases, also a fair comparison of the different cartridges that I have used. The .22 W.R.F. would still be my first choice for hunting in heavy timber for game, including our furbearing animals and ducks.

The .22 long rifle hollow point in a target grade rifle is better for squirrel hunting in mountain country where the ranges are somewhat longer. I have always found the regular hollow point greased cartridge good enough, on account of its accuracy and light report but am inclined to think that the Hi-speed would get a bit more game.

For plinking, shooting snakes, frogs and small pests like rats and English sparrows, I would use the .22 short in a pump action repeater. The .22 long I would discard entirely, though I have killed much game with it. Also, I think I made the longest shot with this cartridge that I ever made with any of my rifles, though it was a fluke. I will tell of it and end my account.

One day in late summer, as well as I can remember, I approached one of our old rivers from one end and could see its entire length of probably 600 yards over open water.

When I got near the water, a small blue heron flew up from behind some willows and went off down the lake, finally alighting on a small log at the extreme far end. He was so far that when he closed his wings he was invisible but I kept my eyes on the spot and, as practicing long shots was a habit with me, though almost always at inanimate targets, I raised my rifle and, holding at an angle entirely beyond the range of elevation of the sights, I tried to see how close I could shoot to him. He was evidently watching me for, as the rifle fired, he opened his wings to fly but the bullet caught him as he left the log and struck him down. I was sorry then that I had made the shot, as I had had no wish to harm him. But he did not die entirely in vain, for that incident cured me of ever shooting at living targets just to see if I could hit them. This is something that many people need to learn.

CHAPTER 23

Twenty-Two Ballistics and Statistics

THE .22 BB CAP

The smallest of our .22 rim fire cartridges is a stubby, blunt-nosed affair known as the BB cap. It is not as well known today as it was when the writer was a boy. Back around 1900 it was a most popular cartridge, due mainly to the fact that you got a full hundred of them for 18¢ whereas a box of 50 black powder "shorts" cost 15¢—you got just twice as much shooting for your money. The quality of that shooting was not considered, I fear.

In the early part of the century, the country was flooded with cheap imported .22 rifles, mostly from Belgium and invariably chambered for the .22 short cartridge. Some of the cheaper grades had no breechblock, the base of the cartridge being exposed and the hammer, with built-in firing pin, striking directly upon the cartridge rim, as in many present day .22 revolvers. Such rifles were unsafe with the early smokeless powder cartridges, which came on the market about that same time. But they, and the other "Floberts" were just about right for use with the ungreased "BBs"—as they were generally called.

Up until about the year 1905 these BB caps were loaded entirely with fulminate of mercury, as a propellent. In fact, the powder charge consisted solely of an extra strong primer. As the fulminate of mercury primer of that period was composed in large part of ground glass, you can well imagine what such cartridges did to the rifling and barrels. However, the rifling in the barrel was not considered an absolute necessity by the average boy of those days; in fact he seldom knew it existed.

About 1910, some of the cartridge factories commenced loading BB caps with a pinch of black powder and using fulminate only for priming; others continued using fulminate for the propellent charge. Many in the way of these BBs which came out about this time were quite unreliable.

Today, the BB cap is loaded with a 20-grain lead pellet, driven at a muzzle velocity of 780 f.s. This gives a muzzle energy of 24 foot pounds, and has about 40% of the muzzle energy of the special purpose .22 short cartridge when loaded to its standard velocity of 995 f.s. and these Splatterless bullets.

The .22 BB cap has sufficient velocity and energy to make fairly clean kills on such marks as sparrows, starlings and the like, and on head shots only on rats, but it is by no means a reliable cartridge nor one much used by educated riflemen. It can be skipped over without any loss. About the only thing it could be recommended for today is by the city dwelling rifleman for a cat promenading down the back fence, but, even for a shot at the base of the ear which might have to be taken in poor light, a very slight misplacement of the bullet might result in a great uproar among neighbors if the cat managed to pull its freight all the way home. Where you just could not use anything else, it might be tried, but do not expect to make instant kills every shot. Neither the hitting power, projectile expansion, nor the accuracy of the pellet are of high order. The CB cap, next described, has a lot more on the ball.

Matter of fact, you seldom see boxes of BB caps on the dealer's shelves these days, the .22 short is about as far down the line as they now go. But those squarish boxes of BBs, with the 100 cartridges dumped loosely in, are well remembered by all oldtimers. As a matter of passing interest I might mention that we boys *always* made a careful count of those contents the minute we got out of the store, a chap paying out 18 perfectly good and slow to come by pennies had to watch out that he got his money's worth in those days—you trusted neither the Union Metallic Cartridge Company nor the storekeeper.

THE CB CAP

The conical bullet cap, or .22 CB cap cartridge can trace its ancestry to the days of rugged individualism of the '90s and possibly even a bit farther back. It seems difficult now to determine exactly just when it was baptized, or by whom.

It runs in this writer's mind and memory that this cartridge, unlike the BB caps, was always loaded from the first with black powder as a propellent; in fact, its two claims for superiority over the BBs were that it contained a propellent charge of black powder and fired a lubricated bullet. At any rate, by 1910 it was loaded with powder and by that date Stevens was universally recommending it as a load of little cost with some possibilities for target work at the shorter ranges of 30 to 50 feet, in fact as a cellar or indoor short gallery load, although neither Stevens nor anyone else preferred it to the .22 short for serious gallery work.

Informed riflemen of that time mainly objected to this cartridge on account of its short length and habit of "burning out" the chamber when used in a gun chambered for longer cartridges—which it would promptly do with the greatly abrasive primer mixture of presmokeless days.

This CB cap cartridge was mainly used to kill birds the size of sparrows, and on bullfrogs and the like, although it would kill larger birds the size of robins with a very fair degree of regularity. It was a great bullfrog and snake cartridge when used in the famous $2.50 Stevens "Tip Up" pistol or their Diamond Model pistols, much favored for Sunday shooting close to the larger cities and small towns where such practice was frowned upon.

During the last 10 or 15 years, CB caps have been considerably improved in accuracy and reliability. Today they are loaded with a 29-grain bullet, the same or much the same bullet as that in the standard .22 short cartridge. The bullet is lubricated and develops a muzzle velocity of 720 f.s.; has 605 f.s. at 100 yards; develops 33 foot pounds muzzle energy and still delivers 24 pounds of it at 100 yards. It definitely is *not* a 100-yard cartridge, but it is nothing to shoot around recklessly with the idea that beyond the range of a few yards it is harmless. About the year 1922, our local police records showed that a woman shot herself with a .22 CB cap and died almost immediately.

At times, the killing power shown by a small .22 caliber bullet at low velocity, when it does not expand as it would at a higher velocity, thereby giving deeper penetration and greater effect, is far greater than the public is accustomed to believe.

As a comparison to the 720 f.s. velocity developed by this pifflin' cartridge, as some classify the .22 CB cap of today, consider the old .41 caliber Derringer rim fire cartridge which fired a 130-grain bullet. This latter had a muzzle velocity of only 520 f.s., and it was the favorite upsleeve and under-the-table gun by many gamblers. The CB bullet starts off 200 feet faster and is still jogging along some 85 feet faster at 100 yards than the speed at which the .41 Derringer bullet leaves the muzzle.

Today, the place of the .22 CB cap is primarily for indoor shooting in the basement or cellar of the average city home, where 25 to 50 feet can be used for a range and where noise is the big item to be considered. It is also a rather effective load at very short range, such as the killing of furbearing animals in a trap; muskrats, skunk (when caught by a front foot only), o'possums, mink and the like, where a shot through the head is desired with no risk of further damage to the fur, and when fired through some old singleshot rifle carried along in the trap bag, where no consideration need be given to chamber and throat erosion.

THE .22 SHORT

The story of .22 caliber rim fire sporting and target ammunition has engaged the attention of manufacturers, riflemen and writers through many generations. This is the metallic cartridge that started them off, the grandpappy of all ammunition as we know it today— Cartridge No. 1. For the .22 short, called merely by the name of No. 1 cartridge at the time of its development and introduction, was produced by Smith & Wesson in the year 1856, originally intended for use in a .22 caliber rim fire revolver. Frank Wesson chambered his singleshot Wesson rifles for this same .22 short cartridge in the year 1858, three years before the start of the American Civil War, or, as some know it, the War of the Rebellion. In fact, to be explicit, some others refer to it as the War Between the States, and the publisher tells of meeting one Unreconstructionist who always referred to it as the Yankee-American War.

From the start, the .22 short cartridge was gradually developed in the matters of accuracy, reliability and effect. Oldtimers in the J. Stevens Arms & Tool Company told the author that this .22 short cartridge was quite accurate in singleshot rifles prior to 1875, and this same claim was stated in Stevens' literature in 1900. It is a cartridge that has always been immensely popular and was, and still is, the most widely used shooting gallery cartridge in the world.

The .22 short was originally, and for many years thereafter, loaded with three grains of fine black powder and a 30-grain bullet. In 1910 the J. Stevens Arms & Tool Co. said, "We believe it is a fair statement to say that the .22 short, as made by the cartridge factories, will shoot as well as the marksman can hold the rifle." Previous to 1910 the .22 short had been brought out in both semi-smokeless and in smokeless loads, but the black and semi-smokeless assemblies were the most accurate and reliable for another 15 years.

Even previous to 1910, the .22 short was made also in hunting style and loaded with 27-grain hollow point or mushroom bullet and three grains of black powder; also by then in semi-smokeless and smokeless styles. Along about 1926, it was made with non-corrosive priming.

Millions of boys and men also used the .22 short to shoot sparrows and the smaller squirrels. It was extensively used for butchering hogs, and sometimes calves and beeves. But in the hunting field its limited range and moderate killing power caused it to be most generally superseded by the .22 long, which used the same weight bullet but in a longer case, and then by the .22 long rifle which was the .22 long case with a 40-grain bullet.

One of the more recent innovations in .22 short cartridges has been the High Velocity type, which appeared about 1928 and developed about the same muzzle velocity to the bullet as normally had been given by the .22 long. This, in fact, gave the cartridge a reasonably flat trajectory over 100 yards.

Today, the standard ballistics of the .22 short are as follows:

Western has a .22 short Kant-Splash greased bullet cartridge with synthetic bullet, which develops a muzzle velocity of 970 f.s. Their .22 short Super-X cartridge with wax coated 29-grain bullet develops a muzzle velocity of 1,130 f.s., of which 925 f.s. is retained at 100 yards, and the 100-yard trajectory is only 4.1″. It has a muzzle energy of 82 foot pounds and 55 foot pounds is still retained at 100 yards. This makes it a fairly powerful little cartridge. It has a Lubaloy coated bullet.

The Western Super-X Wax Coated cartridge with hollow point 27-grain bullet which is Lubaloy coated, is a little faster. It has a muzzle velocity of 1,155 f.s.—remember most .22 long rifle target ammunition had a muzzle velocity of 1,070 to 1,100 f.s. and some of it in ordinary type has even been below 1,000 f.s. according to report. This Western Super-X .22 short H.P. has 925 f.s. velocity remaining at 100 yards, develops 82 foot pounds of energy at the muzzle and still gives up 55 foot pounds of energy when it strikes at 100 yards. The trajectory over 100 yards is 4.1″.

Western also has a .22 short Expert cartridge, with lead bullet uncoated with anything but grease, which is lower velocity than others. It develops 1,030 f.s. muzzle velocity, has 860 f.s. remaining at 100 yards, produces or imparts to the bullet 68 foot pounds of energy at the muzzle and the projectile still retains 48 foot pounds at 100 yards. The remainder has been disseminated in the form of heat. The 100-yard trajectory of this cartridge is 5.1″.

Winchester Repeating Arms Company has similar lines in .22 short. Their .22 short Super-Speed H.P. hunting load, drives a 27-grain Kopperklad, wax coated expanding bullet at 1,155 f.s. muzzle velocity, it has the same energy as the corresponding Western load, and has a 4.1″ trajectory over 100 yards. Their Super-Speed .22 short with 29-grain solid bullet develops 1,130 f.s.m.v. In comparison, the Winchester .22 long Leader cartridge develops only 1,080 f.s.m.v. to its 29-grain bullet, in which instance we have a Super-Speed .22 short giving higher muzzle velocity, greater energy to the bullet and with a flatter trajectory over 100 yards, than the common .22 long, of the same or other makes. The 100-yard trajectory is 0.2″ flatter, for the Super-Speed .22 short. Winchester Spatterproof and Spotlight cartridges drive 26-grain bullets at only 970 f.s. muzzle velocity.

In the Remington line, they have a .22 short Gallery Special Spatterless containing a 28-grain lead bullet at 995 f.s.m.v. which develops 57 foot pounds of muzzle energy. They have a Kleanbore .22 short of intermediate velocity, driving a 29-grain lead bullet at 1,030 f.s.m.v. This has a 4.3″ trajectory over 100 yards, has 68 foot pounds muzzle energy and 48 foot pounds remaining at 100 yards.

In Kleanbore Hi-Speed, Remington has two cartridges in .22 short caliber. The 29-grain solid bullet cartridge at 1,130 foot pounds muzzle velocity, and the 27-grain H.P. bullet charge which develops 1,155 f.s.m.v. and has a 4.1″ trajectory over 100 yards—the same as the Western and Winchester loads of corresponding type.

In his younger days, the author has killed many sparrows, rats, a few cats, some squirrels and rabbits and similar game with the .22 short. Also, quite a few 150- to 350-pound hogs. The bullet will normally cleanly penetrate the skull from in front, go clean through the skull, and lodges in the fleshy part of the back of the head or the neck, and will most often do that even with the low velocity, solid bullet cartridge. Sometimes the bullet will be deflected or reversed in direction so that it turns over, in which case it will then be found in the brain or the skull.

The .22 short is never a cartridge to be lightly regarded because of its size, name, or a common belief held in some quarters that it is not deadly beyond 25 or 50 yards. It will stick in a board or may even cleanly penetrate the side of a small boat at 500 to 600 yards and the Hi-Velocity types of the .22 short will do damage at still greater distances.

It lacks power for field or woods hunting, and the .22 long rifle is a better hunting cartridge, but as made today, it can be used, and is a good cartridge for shooting small, non-dangerous trapped game.

THE .22 LONG

The .22 long rim fire cartridge was originally the .22 short bullet loaded ahead of five grains of black powder in a cartridge case longer than that of the .22 short.

The .22 long cartridge was developed by the makers of the Frank Wesson rifle (who made ammunition in those days) and was put out in Frank Wesson .22 long caliber rifles during the period of 1868–1870.

While Frank Wesson rifles were in rather common use in some

localities they did not reach other sections in quantity for quite a few years. Oldtime riflemen in the Philadelphia area, who were keen on target shooting, hunting, and rifle development, do not appear to have seen any .22 long rifles until about the time of the opening of the Philadelphia Centennial which was held in 1876. At least one of these rifles was used in Philadelphia during or about the year 1881. It was found about that time that re-chambered .22 short rifle barrels would not properly spin a longer or longer and heavier bullet than the .22 short bullet used in both .22 short and .22 long cartridges.

Rather early in the rim fire game Smith & Wesson disposed of the patents covering .22 rim fire and .32 rim fire cartridges and within a few years the Union Metallic Cartridge Company, the United States Cartridge Company, the Winchester Repeating Arms Company, and the Peters Cartridge Company were making such rim fire ammunition.

Beginning about the year 1896, the author shot hundreds and then thousands of rounds of .22 long cartridges, mostly for hunting. He first bought ammunition in small quantities and then in thousand round lots. It never seemed to last long. Shooting at dozens of stones, pieces of lime, clods of dirt across plowed fields and on hillsides in hilly country in Pennsylvania used up .22 long ammunition at a prodigious rate. There were enough pine squirrels and some gray squirrels, plenty of crows, a good many hawks and buzzards, and many ice cakes to shoot at in winter.

I shot English sparrows by the dozens around the houses of my father and my grandfather, also out in wheatfields in the summer where sparrows gathered in flocks and where they in those days destroyed considerable wheat. There were plagues of sparrows in those days—they "followed the horses"—you may recollect. The .22 long helped to harvest them and to keep their numbers within more reasonable bounds.

I do not agree with the many, mostly target shots, that claim that the .22 long cartridge had little or no merit. It was a good all around rim fire hunting cartridge. What helped out was that from five to seven, and sometimes eight of each ten shots from a box of .22 long cartridges would, at 50 or 60 yards, group almost as closely as the same best grouped shots from 10 .22 long rifle cartridges of those days. The off shots were spread out wider in the case of the .22 longs, but if anyone killed 40% to 60% of everything he shot at with a .22 rifle in those days, he thought he was doing very well —and he was. It was those closely grouped 70% of the shots which did nearly all of the killing.

We will not trace the development of the .22 long all the way up

A Semi-albino Chuck

A semi-albino woodchuck, a color phase of the Eastern *Marmota Monax*. Spots on left hip and flank, probably caused by fighting. Note four toes on front feet, five on rear feet. Note tail, which in this instance is darker toward tip.

Photo by C. L. Dewey

the line, because good smokeless loads, non-corrosive priming, semi-smokeless powder of King's Semi-Smokeless type, appeared in the .22 long about the same time as in the .22 short, and generally, in the later improvements, at the same time as in the .22 long rifle.

Cartridges in .22 long caliber today closely parallel in type, that offered in .22 short and in .22 long rifle calibers. Let us take the recent Remington line as an example.

The .22 long Remington Kleanbore standard velocity cartridge contained a 29-grain bullet but is no longer produced. Their intermediate velocity .22 long drives a 29-grain bullet of lead, at 1,080 f.s. muzzle velocity, which is 50 foot seconds faster than the corresponding Remington .22 short cartridge, but 150 foot seconds slower than their 40-grain .22 long rifle bullet of the intermediate grade cartridge. This .22 long has a remaining velocity of 900 f.s. at 100 yards, and a 100-yard trajectory of 4.3". That is 0.8" flatter than the .22 short's trajectory.

The Kleanbore Hi-Speed lead bullet .22 long cartridge develops 1,375 f.s. with its 29-grain bullet, which is the same as that of the .22 long rifle but the bullet of the .22 long rifle weighs 11 grains more. The 100-yard trajectory of the .22 long is 3.2" which is very good indeed.

The Remington Hi-Speed .22 long H.P. cartridge, which is the better hunting load, develops 1,395 f.s. muzzle velocity with a 27-grain hollow point (or H.P.) bullet, still retains 1,010 f.s. of this at 100 yards, it has 117 foot pounds of energy at the muzzle and still retains 61 foot pounds of this at 100 yards. It has a 3.2" trajectory height at 50 yards, when the rifle is sighted exactly for 100 yards, which means the bullet is 3.2" above the bore at 50 yards when the rifle is sighted for 100 yards.

A scope sight on the rifle makes the arm appear to shoot considerably flatter than this, and the proper sighting with scope is to sight in for about 70 yards, and you will not shoot more than about 1" above the line of sight at 40 yards, will group to the line of sight at 70 yards, and will then show considerable drop below the line of sight, at 80 to 85 yards. In case this sighting is found a little too high for squirrel shooting, sight for 60 yards and you will have a 70 to 75 yard deadly range with the one sighting.

Western X-Pert and Winchester Leader .22 long cartridges will give approximately the same ballistic results as the Kleanbore intermediate velocity load, and Western Super-X and Winchester Super-Speed .22 longs will duplicate the Remington Hi-Speed .22 long in trajectory and ballistics. The principal difference today between .22 long rifle and .22 long hunting ammunition ballistically, over the first 100 yards, is that the .22 long rifle cartridge is driving a bullet 10 to 11 grains heavier, in both solid and hollow point styles, and it is starting it five to 25 foot seconds faster, in most instances. The long never has an advantage in accuracy, except in very good individual lots, it might show this for a short time, at some one range, but the advantage in favor of the .22 long rifle often is quite considerable.

Nevertheless, the .22 long Hi-Speed, Super-Speed or Super-X cartridge especially in H.P. style, is a snappy little load, kills well when the bullet is placed, and very definitely should not be classed as a poor shooting load because without doubt it is more accurate, on the average within .22 long hunting ranges, than such cartridges as the average lot of .25–20 lead bullet ammunition, .30–30, .32 Special and .32–20, and is very much more accurate at 50 and 100 yards than such oldtimers in factory black powder or most smokeless cartridges like the .40–65, .40–60, .44–40 and .38–40, also it is much more accurate than the .32 short or the .32 long, rim or center fire ammunition. More care is used in making it or so it seems.

The modern .22 long smokeless loads can be used in many .22 singleshot and .22 repeating rifles which will not chamber and were not bored and rifled for the .22 long rifle cartridge. While the author does not suggest buying a new rifle for the .22 long, nevertheless, the ammunition will continue to be made and sold in large quantities and will have its place in supplying the older rifles which did not handle, or were not adapted to handling the .22 long rifle cartridge.

In the case of any arm made for the .22 long cartridge but not of a design or present condition to suggest using the High Speed .22 long cartridge in it, use the Leader, Expert or intermediate velocity .22 long Kleanbore cartridge in that rifle.

THE .22 LONG RIFLE CARTRIDGE

The introduction of the .22 short and of the .22 long rim fire rifle cartridges, and suitable rifles to fire them, brought about a demand for another rim fire cartridge, a longer-ranged .22 case which would have all of the good qualities of the existing .22 rim fires—convenience; inexpensiveness; the condition that a small, light, card container would hold a surprising number of rounds and could be carried readily on the person; and, also, that all the work and bother of loading or reloading be done away with when using such rim fire ammunition.

As the years passed this demand grew and shooters became more and more insistent that they be provided with a .22 rim fire rifle and cartridge that would perform at 50 and at 100 yards, in the manner the .22 short would shoot at 50 or 100 feet.

As is usually the case, experiments began with existing barrels, actions and cartridge cases. Even though the .22 short was developed in 1856, and the .22 long in 1868, and the .22 short began to show outstanding accuracy of shooting before 1875, nevertheless it was about 1889–1890 before the .22 long rifle cartridge was finally developed. It was simply the .22 *long* cartridge case fitted with a longer bullet which weighed 40 grains and was shot in a barrel of much quicker twist than was proper for the .22 short or the long cartridge.

It seems that many worked on the development of the .22 long rifle cartridge and rifle at much the same period of time and various individuals and firms have claimed to have developed this most remarkable .22 rim fire cartridge.

The late W. M. (U.M.C.) Thomas told the writer that he, Thomas, was the man who was responsible for and had developed the .22 long rifle cartridge.

J. Stevens Arms & Tool Company also claimed to have developed the .22 long rifle cartridge. Their earlier and the 1910 Stevens catalogs contained that claim; also that Stevens had developed the .25 Stevens Rim Fire and the .25–20 Stevens singleshot cartridges. There is no reason to doubt this. They and U.M.C. probably worked closely together on these matters. T. L. Hopkins, then Sales Manager of Stevens, discussed the early development of the .22 rim fires with numbers of their earliest employees and then wrote the author after these conferences: "The .22 long rifle cartridge was entirely a Stevens development." Old employees of Peters Cartridge Company claimed early participation in .22 long rifle manufacture. Their work was probably most closely tied in with Kings Semi-Smokeless in the .22 long rifle, in the period from about 1895 to 1910 and then especially about 1912–1914.

We must not forget the part of the United States Cartridge Company in the development of .22 rim fires. In the earlier days of ammunition manufacture in this country they were easily the principal competitor of U.M.C., especially in .22 rim fire cartridges.

I do know that Stevens experimented with the .22 long rifle about 1889 and the first .22 long rifle cartridges were made about 1891, and rifles followed in 1892. We must not overlook the Marlin Model 1892 rifle and their previous but not so successful 1889 Model which came along 1888–89, and then still later their Model 1897 which used all three cartridges, as apparently also did the 1892 Marlin. Many firms and individuals quite obviously contributed to the development and improvement of the .22 long rifle.

Today, there seems to be but little known about the exact date that Wurfflein and also Maynard made rifles for the .22 long rifle, or the first manufacture of Ballard rifles for the .22 long rifle.

John Dillin credits the year 1890 as the time the .22 long rifle Wurfflein came to hand. It was in 1892 that John took a Wurfflein to the Chicago World's Fair, and cleaned up with it at that Exposition at 200 yards offhand. He also had a No. 1½ Remington with which he did very good squirrel shooting in Kansas or Nebraska. Both of these were of .22 long rifle caliber.

The .22 long rifle U.M.C. ammunition of about 1905–1910 was uncrimped and loaded with black powder. It was remarkable shooting stuff in some lots, in comparison to other .22 rim fire ammunition, or any other caliber of factory ammunition of those days. International Indoor matches were being held about that period and this increased interest in super-accurate .22 rifle ammunition.

In the years 1912–1914, Dr. Henry A. Baker of Boston, and Adolph Niedner, who was then located at Malden, Massachusetts, were intensely interested in .22 rim fire rifle shooting. Baker and Niedner shot in the N.R.A. 50 and 100 yard postal matches of that period and did very well, many of their 99s being reproduced in *Arms & The Man*, along with an occasional possible at 100 yards, although these latter were not too common. World War I interfered with .22 ammunition manufacture for some years, then in 1919 Captain Laudensack showed up with about a dozen Model 52 Winchesters at the National Matches at Caldwell and later at Perry, and these were largely instrumental in reviving interest in small bore target shooting.

The U. S. Cartridge Company's N.R.A. target cartridge in .22 long rifle caliber held the center of the stage at that time, and especially in rather loosely bored rifles, of which there were plenty, it outshot the field and often quite badly. It did especially well in Pope and Hubalek barrels and in Petersons.

Soon Winchester began to make the grade with fine shooting lots of .22 long rifle Precision 200 and also of Precision 75 ammunition, and the Precision 200 packed in boxes with maroon-colored labels was particularly accurate, especially in normal small-sized barrels—the 52 barrels for instance.

Jim Burns' white priming mixture was going to town in the U. S./N.R.A. cartridge, and U. S. continued to maintain its accurate shooting for quite a few years until it was absorbed by Winchester.

In the 1919 era, and into the early 20s, Remington .22 long rifle ammunition was in comparison often very ordinary shooting stuff. But then they came out with an 07 PU Palma Match lot which really went to town. This was followed by other lots packed in boxes of a pinkish hue which ammunition shot consistently for many riflemen but would not shoot in my .22 barrels. It shot still worse in the best of them when tested in the Bridgeport ammunition plant. This helps to prove that a .22 rifle barrel should be fitted with its ammunition whenever possible, and those lots used which shoot best in it.

Non-corrosive .22 long rifle ammunition was introduced to the public generally about 1926 and did surprisingly well, even at first. The Remington Kleanbore cartridge came along then, as Jim Burns had transferred to Remington and with his priming compounds the stuff shot. As a matter of fact, locally purchased commercial lots of Kleanbore shot better for me at 200 yards in my 52 Winchester than any lot of special Remington match ammunition I ever used.

Palma Match VEEZ '33 was probably the most uniform batch of .22 long rifle Match Ammunition Remington ever marketed and VEEZ '34 was nearly as good, but from then on someone apparently lost the knack of uniformity. It could have been any one of dozens of things. All companies seem to have this difficulty—they have it, they lose it, they have it again and probably often they do not know exactly why.

Western was putting out wonderful shotgun shells and center fires in the period from 1919 through the 20s, but at first their .22 long rifle target cartridges had trouble making the grade.

However, in the more recent era Western Super-X hunting ammunition was one of the first to blaze the way in accurate, hard-hitting hunting ammunition of the high velocity type. Western Super-X bullets seemed to be fairly hard when they first came out, and were a little slow in expanding on game like gray squirrels, but the cartridge had a vicious crack and the bullet struck very hard; for a time it was probably loaded to faster speed than some of the others of similar persuasion before velocities became more fully standardized. That which I shot had a tendency to "plop" solidly when it struck game, and to knock it out of trees easily.

Western X-Pert came along as their medium price cartridge but the target load which helped raise a reputation for Western with .22 long rifle match ammunition was .22 long rifle Super-Match. This has greased bullets, is loaded most recently with a 40-grain lead bullet at 1,180 foot seconds muzzle velocity, has 995 foot seconds velocity still remaining at 100 yards, and develops 124 foot pounds of energy at the muzzle and retains 88 foot pounds at 100 yards. The 100 yard trajectory height is 3.8″. For hunting, the rifle should be sighted for 60 yards.

In more recent years, up to World War II which interfered with commercial ammunition manufacture, Western made their greatest reputation with .22 match ammunition with their Western Super-Match *Mark 11* ammunition. This load, in brass cases like the others, develops 20 f.s. *less* muzzle velocity than regular Super-Match. It also apparently shot much more consistently and received a much wider acclaim among top-flight .22 match shooters. This charge develops 1,160 f.s. muzzle velocity to its 40-grain greased bullet of lead and looks just about like the regular Western Super-Match cartridge, but the box which holds 50 cartridges is marked Super-Match Mark 11. This charge develops 120 foot pounds of energy at the muzzle, retains 86 foot pounds at 100 yards, and has a 3.8″ trajectory height over 100 yards. Both grades or types of Super-Match, regular and Mark 11, are loaded with smokeless powder and non-corrosive priming, and it (Mark 11) has a different priming compound than Mark 1, or regular Super-Match.

Of the Western .22 long rifle match ammunition for either target shooting or hunting, with solid bullets, this Super-Match Mark 11 cartridge is the one the author would suggest.

The Western Super-X cartridge, however, is a high velocity cartridge and makes a much better hunting cartridge where range is important. However, it has two faults—it cracks much louder than Super-Match Mark 11 and it gives more wind drift at long range when shot in strong side winds.

I would like to point out here a seeming analogy in .22 long rifle match and target ammunition. The High Velocity type, such as Super-X, gives a much lower trajectory, especially over 200 yards, the bullet does not rise as much above the line of sight, on the way out to the target, yet the wind drift, or sidewise deviation is almost exactly *twice* as great over 200 yards as with the target ammunition. One may wonder how a bullet, traveling 1,375 f.s. muzzle velocity, when it leaves the rifle, can drift about twice as much in the wind, going 200 yards, as a bullet which starts off at 1,160 f.s. muzzle velocity, which is 215 f.s. *less*. The most commonly-given reason is that at or near the velocity of sound, a .22 bullet glides through the air without very much disturbance and the waves given out by the bow and stern of the bullet, and any projecting portions of the bullet, are regular and uniform and the waves drive out in regular formation, outward and backward, but at a muzzle velocity about 200 f.s. to 300 f.s. higher muzzle velocity, which is 1,080 f.s. at 100 yards, when starting with 1,375, the bullet drives along through a medium as bumpy as the white caps on a river in a storm, and probably gives much the same result as a tenderfoot walking on sharp stones or coral rock. He gets there eventually, but what a time he has on the way over—up and down, side to side, seeking the easy spots. The bullet is not quite that erratic, but in hunting with high speed .22s as compared to standard velocity or intermediate velocity .22s, you will find you will have much less trouble with shooting over or under the object, but a good deal more in shooting to the side of it, if the wind is blowing sharply from one side. At 100 yards this might be 50% to 60% more, at 200 yards almost exactly *double*.

Friends of the author who have shot Super-X, Hi-Speed, or other high velocity .22 long rifle ammunition at 200 yards, in the hope of winning due to much *less* wind drift, have often been beaten badly and did not know why. This is *why!* Greater horizontal dispersion and also greater *average* horizontal drift.

The British, being more clever than we are in some things, seemed to find this out first. A. G. Banks, their most popular ballistic writer has also proven this to be so, with actual tests. Incidentally, the .22 Hornet factory load gives just 69% as much wind drift at 100 yards, in a moderately strong side wind, as the .22 long rifle standard velocity cartridge. You may find this convenient to remember sometime while hunting. Mr. Banks made these tests on his 100 yard range in England, shooting first in one direction and then in the exactly opposite direction and taking the mean of the two as the average result.

The best .22 long rifle Western hunting load is the Super-X Hollow Point. This develops 1,400 f.s.m.v. with a 37-grain Lubaloy coated lead bullet with a small hollow point in the nose. It has been my experience with these that the hollow point is more likely to close up at the nose than some others, and this should be opened before loading in the rifle, if jammed together, closed with grease which is hard and solid, or if the nose of the bullet appears almost solid. The Super-X H.P. long rifle load is wax coated, develops 161 foot pounds muzzle energy, still has 95 foot pounds of it at 100 yards. It has a 3.0″ trajectory over 100 yards. When using a telescope sight this will seem very much flatter. The rifle can be sighted for 75 yards with Super-X, and not shoot over 1″ above the line of aim, or slightly below it, between 15 and 75 yards. At 85 yards, it will be an inch or slightly more, below the line of sight. However, for squirrels and the like in woods at which the average shot is about 30 to 40 yards, then a 60 yard sighting is preferable. Most of your shots will be going about spine height, at 40 yards, if sighted for 75 yards.

Remington's best hunting load is their Hi-Speed .22 long rifle H.P. charge loaded in brass cases. Remington developed the brass case for the .22 long rifle and had almost a monopoly on this feature, at first. The brass case, if actually brass and not plated, is tough, hard, holds its shape, and does not puncture as easily as a copper cartridge case, if high pressures or a blow-back is to be expected, due to pressure or due to a very sharp firing pin point or a case head rested improperly when struck by the firing pin.

The author has used this load for squirrel and crow shooting for about eight years past. It is just about right for fox squirrels, kills excellently on crows, also on hawks, up to and including the red shoulder, goshawks and Coopers hawks. It is a bit excessive in tearing power for gray squirrels and black squirrels, and it is excessive in *report* for quiet shooting in settled areas. This cartridge should, if possible, be toned down in report for a hunting charge. Furthermore, Remington and other firms should again put out the standard velocity .22 long rifle Hollow Point load for it is true that it is a little lacking in killing power for body shots at gray squirrels, and it does not knock a squirrel out of a tree unless instantly killed, on the other hand, it was about as quiet in sound as the regular low velocity Kleanbore and in that particular it is so satisfactory that a conservative, experienced hunter using his head, can go in a dense woods, within 100 to 150 yards of a house (sometimes the law prescribes this) *face away from* the house, and can shoot a single shot once every hour or so without attracting practically any attention, assuming the wind is not blowing strongly from him to the house. This permits considerable hunting, by careful, considerate men, in many areas where farmers or estate owners and especially their women folks are either annoyed or frightened, as women often are, by the noise of firing. A man or boy who is considerate and thoughtful can often get a number of season's hunting in a woods using standard or low velocity ammunition, of .22 long rifle or .22 long caliber, who would be almost immediately chased out if using a 12 gauge shotgun, or a sharp-report rifle. However, you can *not* shoot around promiscuously, fire in the direction of the house or barn, corncrib or silo, do extensive sighting-in or target shooting, or plinking on such property and expect to remain there. Be neither seen nor heard is the idea. Do not shoot across a pasture filled with cattle. If the farmer or his hired man comes up, try to get him interested in your rifle and in a bit of expert rifle shooting, and "talk down" the idea of those who shoot wildly, make a lot of noise, and are not quiet, careful and mind their own affairs while hunting, like *you* do. It will not always work, but most times it may. Often it will. It is worth trying!

The Hollow Point Hi-Speed Remington Kleanbore cartridge in .22 long rifle size, develops 1,400 f.s. muzzle velocity, and 1,375 with solid bullet. Many use the solid bullet for squirrels. They strike just about as hard, and spoil less meat, especially on shoulder or rear quarter hits, but they do not make the instant kills, especially in shooting at running game, as does the H.P. load. Some barrels shoot this load very accurately. I have such a barrel, but it is not too accurate with target ammunition. The H.P. bullet just seems to fit it. It has a 2.9″ to 3.0″ trajectory over 100 yards.

It has been my experience that a small caliber bullet for gray squirrel and crow shooting should pack from 130 to 150 foot pounds of energy at the muzzle and a minimum of 80 to 90 at 100 yards. If 120 at 100 yards, so much the better. If it gives 400 foot pounds at the muzzle and 250 to 270 foot pounds at 100 yards, it will give slashing wounds, even if solid bullet, and will almost invariably knock squirrels out of a tree, regardless of where the bullet strikes solidly through the game.

Anyone using a cartridge developing materially less than 80 foot pounds at 100 yards, is going to lose a lot of cripples, and will knock very little game out of the trees, unless instantly killed.

Remington's intermediate velocity Kleanbore cartridge, which is *not* made in hollow point style, at this writing, develops 1,230 f.s.m.v. and 1,030 f.s. at 100 yards. It gives 135 foot pounds energy at the muzzle and 94 foot pounds at 100 yards. It has a trajectory of 3.8″ over 100 yards, .9″ more than the high speed. The standard low velocity cartridge has a 4.0″ trajectory over 100 yards.

The standard velocity .22 long rifle Kleanbore cartridge with 40-grain bullet develops 1,130 f.s. m.v. and still has 970 f.s. at 100 yards. It has 111 foot pounds of energy at the muzzle and 84 foot pounds remaining at 100 yards.

It is a quiet cartridge to shoot. It is not a good killer on body shots back of the shoulders, except through the heart or both lungs, on gray, black or fox squirrels. You will lose one every now and then, which will get into a hollow down log, crawl into a hole, or reclimb the far side of the tree, which you would have bagged if using a H.P. Hi-Speed bullet. But one can be fooled with that too.

One odd thing about squirrel shooting, is that a H.P. bullet driven full force into a squirrel's stomach when same is fully expanded with finely ground up nuts, will often kill him more instantly, on the spot than if shot through both lungs or the lower part of the heart. A squirrel shot through one lung or the lower part of the heart will often kick around very smartly, for a few moments, and may drag itself under an old leaf-covered fence rail, or even down a hole, if one be convenient to where he hits. But a squirrel shot in the middle of a well filled dinner basket seems to suffer severely from hydraulic shock or possible air or gas expansion in that tightly drawn sack. Rarely does he escape, although this effect is very likely to *not* happen if shot in the same spot, with solid, pointed bullet of 30 or 40 grains, at 1,080 to 1,500 f.s.m.v.

Remington has sold millions of rounds on the Kleanbore advertising. The residue of Kleanbore .22 long rifle ammunition, of which the author has shot many thousands of rounds is definitely not "clean." It is gray black and rather greasy, however, the non-corrosive qualities are good.

The reaction to .22 long rifle Kleanbore standard velocity ammunition among practical and expert shooters can in fairness be described as "mixed." The report of the shot is excellent and the odor indoors, or outdoors, is not offensive. Whether it will prove to be a very accurate and uniform cartridge in a .22 rifle in your hands, will depend, as it does with many others, on the fit of the bullet in the barrel. I wish they still made it in H.P. style. This would be more valuable for hunting than either the standard velocity or intermediate velocity solid bullet cartridge.

The Winchester .22 long rifles parallel the Western brands, and were made in the three velocities, but today the low velocity brands are not supplied. They have the Leader, which is a nice looking rifle cartridge, which drives a 40-grain bullet at the usual 1,180 f.s. and with a 100 yard trajectory of 3.8".

They still make their Precision Lesmok match ammunition which is low velocity, 1,100 f.s. m.v. and with a 100-yard trajectory of 4.3". This is the most accurate 200-yard match load Winchester ever produced, and in the years immediately preceding World War II, cleaned up small bore matches at 50, 100 and 200 yards, with monotonous regularity.

Winchester also has an All-X Match, which is a somewhat faster smokeless cartridge, driving the 40-grain bullet at 1,180 f.s. m.v. and with a 100 yard trajectory of 3.8". This, of course, is standard for the medium velocity loads.

Then they have their Super-Speed Kopperklad, wax-coated bullet cartridge with solid bullets at 1,375 f.s. and with 37-grain H.P. bullet at 1,400 f.s. For all practical purposes this is a duplicate of the Western Super-X hunting cartridge, in ballistics, but with Winchester priming, bullet and loading. There is a slight copper deposit on the bullet, probably placed there by electrolysis. How it could help in a hunting load, I am at a loss to understand, as it would certainly make the bullet slightly more difficult to expand.

Winchester's old standard .22 long rifle Staynless cartridge appears to have been taken off the market. The author found this cartridge abnormally annoying when shooting on indoor ranges, causing in my case severe inflammation of the eyes and back of the throat, resulting in bronchitis or laryngitis very promptly. Whether from primer, powder, or a combination of both, I do not know, but it certainly was not for me. Outdoors I had no trouble with it as the gas would be quickly disseminated.

The best Winchester .22 long rifle hunting load, is obviously the .22 Super-Speed H.P. and their crack target load for *outdoors*, Precision EZXS. If you want a very quiet, and a smokeless load, for either indoor or outdoor the All-X would be a good choice.

The outstanding .22 long rifle cartridges from all of the above, appear to be Winchester Precision EZXS for outdoor, long range, match shooting and for work on crows, hawks, and head shots on gray, fox or black squirrels. I rarely shoot at the head of a gray squirrel as they bleed for one or two hours, in a hunting coat pocket, after being so shot, even though dressed and allowed to air dry. The last new Duxbak pants I was able to buy acquired a blood spot about 5″ in diameter, on the front of the thigh, from a single gray squirrel shot at the butt of the ear, at long range too, because it only stuck its head up in a crotch in a hickory tree, and would not show more of itself, so I had to take what was presented. Unless you want to bloody yourself, back and front, avoid head shots on squirrels.

Another outstanding outdoor target cartridge is the Western Super-Match Mark 11, a smokeless cartridge for the same purpose. Remington put out a special dense smokeless pistol powder .22 long rifle hand gun cartridge they call Police Targetmaster. It gives 1,155 f.s. m.v., has 940 f.s. remaining at 100 yards, gives a 4″ trajectory over 100 yards, when used in rifles, and which was found to perform particularly well at 200 yards in rifles. The reason is obvious—the dense pistol powder burned quickly, uniformly and completely, within the barrel. This tends to eliminate drop shots. I would however, expect shorter barrel life with such cartridge loading. This load should be found entirely smokeless and quiet for woods shooting.

The Remington Hi-Speed .22 long rifle with greased lead bullet in brass cases, which bullet in H.P. style expands very promptly, is probably the most deadly of the outdoor hunting loads. Its drawback is its report in dense woods on a foggy morning—it sounds almost as sharp as a .22 Hornet. The Western Super-X is nearly as satisfactory as a killer, but expands a bit slower on squirrels. The Hi-Speed will tear a hole the size of a nickel to a quarter in a crow or a hawk, due to matting of the feathers before even the bullet emerges. In the fall of 1944 I killed four crows off a high tree, with successive cartridges with this load, one afternoon, and laid them out in a row on the ground. The average range was about 60 yards, and one was shot through the jugular vein and just sat there on the limb about 70 feet above the ground until it bled to the point of insensibility, then it fell off. It seemed to be paralyzed.

The Canadian riflemen, and many living in states bordering Canada, expecially those in the Detroit area, use a good many Dominion .22 long rifles. I have shot probably 10,000 of them. The most accurate in some arms, is their Bisley Match. This is a Lesmok match cartridge of splendid accuracy. It shoots like EZXS, more or less, but looks more like Palma Match. Dominion ammunition favors Remington ammunition more than any other of the U. S. makes. Dominion's Central-Vs is a smokeless .22 long rifle target cartridge, of good accuracy, but slightly inferior to Bisley Match, in my arms, although others differ, including company tests. It is better for indoor shooting, being smokeless and is a cartridge much like Palma Match or Kleanbore Palma.

Dominion's Whiz Bang is their High Velocity hunting load. It is made in both solid bullet and H.P. styles and in the latter they made for some years, a dry, cadmium-coated cartridge of which they reported most excellent accuracy. I had a carton or two of these but let most of them go to a friend who was stuck for hollow point .22s, wanted to shoot squirrels with the rifle, and could not get any locally. They had a fairly sharp report. The bullet had a good sized orifice in the point, and should have killed well.

Reports from many readers of my columns, who used this load, were generally quite satisfactory. It had, as I recall, a copper case and Dominion always claimed about 50 foot seconds or more, higher velocity with their Whiz Bangs than other loading companies. I have shot a good many Whiz Bangs in solid bullet type and while they shot well, they were not so accurate, in my barrels, as either Central Vs or Bisley Match. Central Vs and Bisley Match are graced with very handsome cartons and boxes for 50 cartridges, especially the latter, and they make an attractive appearance on counter or shelf. It is a company, up there near Montreal, which has always had the sense to write courteous and friendly letters that helps make friends for them. In addition, their promotion and sales managers have mostly been active shooters, which helps in practical things in the making and marketing of .22 rifle ammunition.

STANDARD ELEVATION CHANGES FOR .22 LONG RIFLE AMMUNITION

Remembering that one minute of angle, equals very slightly more than 1″ (inch) per 100 yards, and having found by actual shooting the exact elevation for any one measured range, the elevation reading for any other range may be found by adding or subtracting the following figures.

These Readings Are in Minutes

Range in Yards	.22 long rifle standard Velocity Ammunition	.22 long rifle Hi-Speed Super-X or Super-Speed
0	0	0
25	2	2
50	5	5.5
75	8	8.5
100	13	11.5
150	22	18.3
200	32.5	26.0
300		43.0

The Same as Above—But in ½ Minutes

25	4	4
50	10	11
75	16	17
100	26	23
150	44	36.6
200	65	52
300		86

The Same as Above—But in ¼ Minutes

25	8	8
50	20	22
75	32	34
100	52	46
150	88	73.2
200	130	104
300		172

Best single sighting for .22 long rifle Standard Velocity ammunition—set sights for 60 yards.

Best single sighting for .22 long rifle High Velocity ammunition—set sights for 75 yards.

Best single sighting for .22 long rifle Intermediate Velocity ammunition—set sights for 65 yards.

The .22 long rifle cartridge is the most rifle cartridge for the money ever placed on the market, among the rim fires, just as the .22 Hornet is the most center fire cartridge in value received. Their accuracy, uniformity and killing power, for their size, is astonishing and each is outstanding among .22s and is recommended without reservations.

THE .22 EXTRA LONG RIM FIRE

This cartridge was an attempt, away back in black powder days, to obtain higher muzzle velocity in a .22 rim fire cartridge by using a much longer cartridge case and filling it with black powder, then inserting the base of a 40-grain outside lubricated bullet. It looked like a super-.22 long rifle although actually the result was quite a disappointment, at least the modern loading gives only the same muzzle velocity as that of the standard velocity .22 short, and 100 f.s. *less* than that of the Super-X, Super-Speed and the Hi-Speed .22 short, although all these use only a 29-grain or 30-grain bullet.

It is not in it at all with the modern .22 long rifle. The extra long pushes its 40-grain lubricated lead bullet at only 1,030 f.s. m.v., the Leader and X-Pert types of .22 long rifle 1,180 f.s. m.v. and the Super-X and Super-Speed type 1,375 f.s. m.v., or 340 f.s. higher muzzle velocity.

The .22 extra long today has not a thing to recommend it; it was made as something to catch the eye of the young chap back in the early horse and buggy days, who bought his cartridges by *size*. In this instance size meant very little—today it means nothing.

The .22 extra long was shot, in the old days, in some of the small singleshot Winchester bolt actions, Maynards, and a few early Stevens which were bored for and chambered so you could use, the .22 short, the .22 long and the .22 extra long. This .22 extra long could not be used successfully in the .22 long rifle chamber, or pitch of rifling. It needed the slower rifling of the .22 long.

Why they scrapped the most useful .22 long rifle low velocity hollow point cartridge and continue to make this outmoded rim fire is one of those mysteries.

Frankly the cartridge has nothing to recommend it. It costs a great deal more than the .22 long or .22 long rifle, is not equal to either of them, and is normally marked away up per single box of 50, or two boxes aggregating 100 cartridges, which is what most boys can buy of this load, in most small country hardware, sporting goods and grocery stores. It is just an eye-arresting curiosity because of its length and because it *looks* as if it would be a long range cartridge, which it is not. Pass this one up for better sizes.

The trajectory over 100 yards is 4.9″, which is 2.0″ higher than that of Super-X—.22 long rifle.

This one came in with ostrich feathers and went out with the iron kelly.

Tell the little fellows who will be disappointed, to buy the .22 long, and they will have a higher velocity, better killing cartridge for those small .22 singleshot rifles it was made for. So far as the author recalls at the moment, it was never intended nor chambered for any of the .22 rim fire repeaters.

The .22 Winchester Rim Fire Cartridge

The .22 W.R.F., otherwise known as the .22-7-45, and by Remington as the .22 Remington Special, first appeared in the Winchester catalog of November, 1890. The .22 long also first appeared in the Winchester catalog of that date. The .22 W.R.F. was designed for use in the Model 1890 Winchester slide action repeating rifle, as a more powerful and better hunting cartridge of rim fire type.

The .22 Winchester rim fire used a 45-grain blunt point bullet made with small cannelures and inside lubricated. This made it a convenient and clean cartridge to carry loose in a hunting coat pocket, or if a box came open in the pocket and the cartridges spilled out there was no exposed lubricant to pick up grit and then rub off—the grease, not the grit.

The power of the original cartridge was just about right for squirrels and cottontail rabbits and also for ruffed grouse. The flat pointed bullet killed well, the cartridge was more snappy in sound than the .22 long and it also looked like a larger, more substantial cartridge. The Model 1890 rifle was not made for the .22 long rifle in those days.

The original .22 Winchester rim fire was loaded with 7 grains of black powder. Peters came along eventually with Kings semi-smokeless, and of course there have been numerous smokeless loads.

The Ideal Handbook gives the .22 W.R.F. Winchester barrels as having a groove diameter of .226″, with right hand rifling, one turn in 14″. Stevens rifles of this caliber, were bored with a groove diameter of .223″ to .224″ with right hand rifling of one turn in 14″. The Stevens rifling gave one the impression of being cut with somewhat shallower grooves than the Winchester barrels.

Ballistics of the .22 W.R.F.: The old standard velocity .22 W.R.F. cartridges were, and of course still are, loaded with 45-grain bullets at 1,100 f.s. muzzle velocity, as listed by Stevens, and 1,105 f.s. as listed by Winchester. Stevens gives the trajectory as 1.0″ over 50 yards and as being 4.4″ over 100 yards. Winchester lists it as 4.0″ over the same distance.

The W.R.F. Hi-Speed cartridge with 45-grain blunt point solid bullet, is listed by Stevens as giving 1,500 f.s. muzzle velocity, and a 50-yard trajectory of .5″ and a 100-yard trajectory height of 2.5″.

Winchester's .22 W.R.F. Super-Speed Kopperklad load develops 1,450 f.s. muzzle velocity and a 2.7″ trajectory over 100 yards. This cartridge, if zeroed at 50 yards for hunting, and if the rifle is fired at greater ranges with the 50 yard sighting, at 100 yards the bullet will strike 5″ low; at 150 yards, 22½″ low; and at 200 yards, 46″ low. In the latter case, with 50-yard sighting you would have to hold over nearly four feet to score on a crow, a buzzard or a woodchuck.

The Western Super-X .22 W.R.F. inside lubricated cartridge gives its 45-grain bullet 1,450 f.s. muzzle velocity, and the 100-yard trajectory height at midrange or 50 yards is 2.7″. It has 210 foot pounds of energy at the muzzle, 1,110 f.s. remaining velocity at 100 yards and 123 foot pounds of energy at 100 yards.

The best sighting for hunting, with any of these .22 W.R.F. high speed cartridges with muzzle velocity of 1,450 to 1,500 f.s., is to set the sights for 85 yards, with scope. The bullet then strikes 1.0″ high at 45 yards and also 1.0″ low at 100 yards. That makes an effective killing range of 100 yards with but one sight setting, provided you aim slightly low at 40 to 50 yards and 1″ high at 100 yards.

The .22 W.R.F. H.P. cartridge, is loaded with the 40-grain hollow point hunting bullet and today is only made in high speed style. Stevens gives the muzzle velocity as 1,525 f.s. and the 100-yard trajectory as 2.5″. Winchester gives their Kopperklad cartridge with H.P. bullet as developing 1,475 f.s. muzzle velocity and a 100-yard trajectory of 2.7″ for this Super-Speed hunting load. If sighted for 50 yards, at 100 yards the bullet will strike 5″ low; at 150 yards, 22½″ low; and at 200 yards, 47½″ low. Western gives about the same, with 210 foot pounds of energy at the muzzle and 123 foot pounds at 100 yards for Super-X H.P.

Those who have used the .22 W.R.F. ammunition extensively for hunting speak very highly of its killing power on squirrels and grouse—if the latter be shot through the butts of the wings. Those who have done most of their shooting with the various .22 long and .22 long rifle cartridges are little impressed and talk of better accuracy and more consistent tack hold bullseye punching. They figure it is better to hit a gray squirrel right where you want to than there, or thereabouts. The .22 W.R.F. clique claim there are not too many "thereabouts" and with good lots of ammunition probably no more than with ordinary .22 long rifle, especially with long rifle H.P.

Back in the not-so-gay 20s, when they were making lots of .22 long rifle match ammunition which would shoot the whiskers off a goat, and not make him drop his tin can, they had .22 long rifle H.P. standard velocity hunting ammunition which would often shoot

A WILD FOX

Only for a moment, but it is enough! Out of the shadows into the sunlight, walks a fox. He, too, is hunting. He, too, stalks small game. In many
Northern localities this makes the fox the most sought after prize of
the varmint hunter.

Photo by W. H. Morin, Courtesy: U. S. Forest Service

99 or 100 × 100 at 50 yards but you really had to be a rifle shot to shoot a 193 or a 194 with the same stuff at 100 yards, and if you happened to score 196 or 197 you called it a day right there. Such ammunition had to be reserved for hunting on the first day of the season. It was certainly nothing to plug into bullseye targets. The .22 W.R.F. hunting ammunition—none of it you know is target ammunition—is probably less likely to show as much difference between its accuracy, at least with solid bullets, between 50 and 100 yards, but, on the other hand, neither does it shoot quite as small groups at 50 yards.

Now the .22 long rifle, Super-X H.P. load gives its 37-grain bullet 1,400 f.s.m.v. and 1,075 f.s. velocity remaining at 100 yards with the corresponding energies 161 and 95 foot pounds.

The Western Super-X H.P. which is listed as having a 45-grain bullet also, still has 1,110 f.s. remaining velocity at 100 yards, and has an energy of 210 foot pounds at the muzzle and 123 foot pounds at 100 yards. That gives the W.R.F. bullet, either solid or H.P. an advantage of 35 foot seconds of velocity and 28 foot pounds of energy, at 100 yards over the .22 long rifle; in addition the bullet is eight grains heavier—there is eight grains more of it, and it has a flatter point. Consequently, if the two bullets hit the same spot, the .22 W.R.F. is sure to be a better killer for two—yes, for several reasons. It is traveling faster, it hits a harder blow, the bullet point being flatter will cause more laceration of tissue or bone, and the bullet is very slightly larger in diameter, hence for that reason also, will drill a slightly larger diameter hole.

But, the .22 W.R.F. ammunition costs materially more money than the .22 long rifle ammunition, is always more difficult to obtain even in times of ammunition plentifulness, and is almost entirely unobtainable in times such as existed between 1941 and 1946. Especially is it always more difficult to obtain in small country stores or in small towns, where they may have calls for only a very few boxes a year.

So there is a fair, accurate, and truthful comparison of the two cartridges. If smashing power is indicated, the .22 W.R.F. is the better choice if you can get ammunition. If you cannot get ammunition readily any rifle is merely an ornament—it is a gas engine without gas. You can nearly always get *something* that will crack, in the way of .22 long rifle ammunition, and if not that then .22 longs, which are not to be sneezed at as hunting cartridges.

One thing must always be borne in mind. You can *not* use .22 W.R.F. ammunition in any other size of .22 rim fire rifle, because the bullet and the cartridge are both larger in diameter. You also cannot use .22 short, .22 long, .22 long rifle or .22 extra long rim fire cartridges in the .22 W.R.F. rifle—and you cannot shoot any of them in a .22 center fire rifle. You would be surprised how many would be willing to try!

If a few shots a day are sufficient, if you can afford the ammunition, and can *get* .22 W.R.F. ammunition, you are all set for nice small game shooting and a good time, but always remember that this cartridge makes a louder, sharper report than the .22 long or .22 long rifle. This different report identifies the hunter as "you" because it is not at all likely that anyone else in your neighborhood, or not more than one other rifleman is shooting a .22 W.R.F. caliber rifle. Every empty cartridge you may cast aside thoughtlessly, proves at a glance that you were there and did the shooting. The .22 W.R.F. empty cartridge looks enough like a No. 6 or standard size blasting cap, or dynamite detonator, to attract the attention of farmers, miners, quarrymen and blasters to cause many to reach down and pick it up for examination, something they will rarely bother to do with other .22 rim fire empties.

THE .22 WINCHESTER AUTOMATIC CARTRIDGE

This was the original cartridge for which the Model '03 Winchester .22 automatic rifle was manufactured. This 1903 Winchester selfloading rifle is the handsomest little .22 rifle that the Winchester Repeating Arms Company ever marketed. Its action originally did not seem suitable to handle the .22 long rifle loads nor was the .22 long rifle cartridge of that day adapted for any autoloading rifle, hence it was a long time before this rifle was made to handle that cartridge. Today the .22 long rifle is the only cartridge for which it appears to be manufactured, at least upon regular order, but thousands of these Model 1903 rifles were made to handle the .22 Winchester auto cartridge only, and as they require ammunition, this cartridge is made today, in three styles by Winchester and Western, while other manufacturers have competitive ammunition.

It should be understood that the .22 short, .22 long and .22 long rifle cartridges should not be chambered in the Winchester 1903 and the .22 long rifle is the *only* cartridge that should be used in the Model 63 Winchester automatic rifle.

The .22 automatic cartridge is made today, regularly, in three styles. One is the .22 automatic with 45-grain inside lubricated lead bullet. It has a muzzle velocity of 1,055 f.s., 930 f.s. of this is retained at 100 yards, which is good; it develops 111 foot pounds of muzzle energy, and the bullet still retains 86 foot pounds of this out at 100 yards.

Trajectory is not so favorable. It is 4.6" over 100 yards, meaning the bullet is that much above the line of the bore at 50 yards, when perfectly sighted in for 100 yards. But, if you have the rifle properly sighted for 50 yards, at 100 yards the bullet would strike 8″ below the point of aim. In comparison, either the .22 long rifle Super-Speed or the .22 W.R.F. Super-Speed, so sighted, would strike only 5″ inches below the point of aim.

Winchester makes two other cartridges for this rifle. One has a 45-grain solid bullet copper coated by electrolysis, it is called Kopperklad, and the third cartridge is the same with 45-grain hollow point bullet, also Kopperklad; this last one is much the better hunting load. They all three have approximately the same ballistics and trajectory over the short hunting ranges at which this cartridge is generally used.

Western makes a solid bullet and also a H.P. bullet load, giving the same ballistics. Both have bullets Lubaloy coated in the same manner.

None of these loads is in the same class as the high velocity type of the .22 long rifle or the high velocity types of .22 W.R.F. in trajectory, in killing power, nor in accuracy.

The reason why the company had to bring this rifle out in .22 long rifle caliber is obvious—it made a much more effective rifle out of it. The only advantage the .22 auto cartridge had was that the bullet was inside lubricated.

The .22 Remington Auto, Inside Lubricated

This is very nearly the same cartridge as the above, but made special for the .22 Remington automatic, or rather semi-automatic rifle, and this cartridge is loaded by Western with a 45-grain bullet, which is inside lubricated, but the bullet is loaded only to 920 f.s. muzzle velocity, which is 10 f.s. less than the .22 Winchester Auto cartridge gives at 100 yards. The Western loading of the .22 Remington cartridge develops the same energy at the muzzle as the .22 Winchester auto cartridge still retains at 100 yards, in fact 2 foot pounds less, (84 to 86 foot pounds) so that this makes the .22 Winchester auto slightly more powerful at 100 yards than the .22 Remington auto is at the muzzle. This could be construed as a left-handed handshake which felt kind of weak and clammy, but let us see what the Remington ammunition does with it.

The Remington ammunition in .22 Remington autoloading caliber gives 920 f.s. muzzle velocity, exactly the same as the Western loading, with 45-grain bullet, producing the same muzzle and the same 100 yard energy figures as the Western load, with a 5.5″ 100-yard trajectory, and Remington also loads the .22 Winchester auto cartridge to 1,055 f.s. muzzle velocity, which suggests that the action of the .22 Remington auto rifle is not adapted to handling quite as high breech pressure as the other, although it works very well.

So, there we have two .22 auto rim fire cartridges—they are not the same in ballistics, and each had better be used in the rifle for which it was intended. Remember the difference.

As the .22 Winchester auto is, as mentioned, now made for the .22 long rifle ammunition, of either style, but greased, the long rifle is the cartridge you should buy for any new Winchester .22 auto you buy over the counter, unless you happen to get hold of one made for the old .22 auto inside lubricated cartridge, and that rifle does not handle the .22 rim fire ammunition of other types.

So far as the author ever could see these rifles have no advantage over a good .22 long rifle handoperated rifle, such as is made by Winchester, Remington, or Savage, except a very slight theoretical advantage in speed of fire—and excessive speed of fire, is exactly what the average boy or man learning to shoot a .22, should *not* have. He should train himself to the idea of trying to make every bullet hit center.

If the author were to buy a .22 rifle for any other .22 rim fire cartridge than the .22 long rifle, it would not be for the .22 auto cartridge of either style, it would be for the .22 W.R.F. cartridge, and he would shoot the high velocity 1,475 f.s. H.P. load in it. Speed of fire would mean little because most times, you need to shoot only once! At least, let us hope you are that kind of shot!

Early the next morning several groups were fired at 50 yards, prone, with an arm rest on a small cushion, on a measured rifle range. Both loads grouped better than I had expected. A quarter completely covered the first group. New targets were then put up, the test repeated, with nearly identical results. There was a shade of improvement.

As the day before had brought the opening of the squirrel season, I gathered my equipment and placed it in the car, and headed for a woods where a few squirrels could be shot if one were experienced in finding them. After I arrived at the woods the rifle was loaded with the hollow point cartridges and I headed up an old abandoned wagon trail which led deep into good gray squirrel territory.

In about ten minutes a squirrel began barking off to the left about 25 yards. As the glare of the morning sun was in my eyes I had to move around a bit to the right before he could be seen. It was a young squirrel sitting half way out on a limb of an old elm and vigorously voicing his feelings. He had his back to me. Resting an arm against the side of the tree, the crosshairs were placed a little low on his head, between the ears. When the rifle cracked he dropped, and upon picking him up it was found that the bullet had exploded when it hit, tearing out part of his tongue, breaking the jaw and knocking out a few of his sharp teeth. A fragment of the lead had entered the brain. The bullet struck him just below the base of the brain and came out of the mouth. This is the normal course for a bullet in the base of the skull, from the rear. That squirrel was placed in the Duxbak coat and hunting was resumed. The flesh of this squirrel was undamaged.

Rather soon another gray squirrel was noticed feeding on the ground at the base of a young hickory some 20 yards away. He was broadside and the result was a shoulder shot. This proved to be another young squirrel. The bullet shattered the shoulder and broke up, part of it piercing the heart and the lungs but without seriously damaging the flesh of the animal. Putting No. 2 in my coat the journey was resumed up the trail.

I had walked about 20 minutes when another gray was observed feeding on some red berries about 30 yards off. A hit in the stomach was desired, solely to observe the shocking effect and laceration given by a shot in that area delivered by a .22 Hornet bullet, fired from a reduced load. Consequently the range was shortened to 20 yards and the charge eased off after placing the crosshairs intersection on his middle. He fell to the ground, hard hit, and tried to get to a tree about three feet away. He managed to get up the trunk about two feet before I whacked him on the head. This time the bullet tore up the stomach, ribs and lungs. I then concluded that possibly it was better to use only head and shoulder shots. As this made three squirrels with the hollow points, I reloaded my rifle with soft points and then started to dress the last squirrel. While dressing the gray I heard a commotion behind me and looked around. I saw a large brown weasel running across a log, traveling away from me. Picking up the rifle, the thought occurred, "Will it be possible to obtain a shot?" Weasels are so destructive to game, especially quail, rabbits and squirrels, that I never lose an opportunity to kill one. All readers should do likewise.

The weasel stopped at the end of the log for it had smelled blood; so, placing the crosshairs on the back of his neck the trigger was pressed and at the report of the rifle it fell over dead. I ran over and picked him up. It was one of the largest weasels I have seen for years. The bullet had broken his neck and had emerged at the mouth, tearing off the tongue and breaking off several teeth. As the hide was worthless early in the season, the tail was cut off and placed in the pocket of the gunning coat.

The gunner then proceeded on his way. I saw two squirrels, one at about 25 yards, which barked and then popped into his hole. The other was racing along a rail fence as if he had an engagement, and it was pressing. It was then about lunch time, so I cut across the field toward the car. On the way I passed close to an old stump where I had previously seen a woodchuck sitting on a mound of dirt, before the den. Near the edge of the woods he was found, sitting up about three feet from his den mouth, and about 75 yards distant. He was facing the rifle. Resting an arm against the side of the tree, the crosshairs were placed a bit high on his chest. At the report, he fell over backwards, and then started slowly for his den. He stopped when half way there. His tail stuck up straight, waving back and forth in quick jerks, which, as any woodchuck hunter knows, is the "all in" signal. The curtain is going down, the final act of the show is over. The bullet had made a small but neat hole directly in the middle of the chest and blew up the lungs. A piece of the lead also pierced the heart. Another fragment of the bullet made a small, jagged hole, on its way out through the back. The chuck was carried to the car and on the way home it was given to a colored man who said he "would take very good care of it for me." He said, "Mister, here is one chuck that ain't gonna' get into no moh' trubble."

Early the next morning I drove to another woods, where a few grays had fallen to my rifle the previous season. After walking about ten minutes, along the edge of the woods which was next to a cornfield, I saw one feeding on an ear of corn about two feet from a cornshock, and about 20 yards off. I put the crosshairs on his shoulder and eased off the shot. The bullet bowled him over. This was a good sized gray squirrel. The bullet broke the shoulder, ranged through the heart and lodged in the other side of the animal. No meat was spoiled. Putting him in the coat the hunt was resumed.

About fifty yards farther on I spotted another squirrel, feeding on the top of a cornshock. This one offered a head shot. A lucky hit struck in the left ear. The bullet simply smashed the top of the head. This was a nice young buck gray squirrel. Continuing, I saw two more feeding in a tree about 30 yards off. One was missed and no shot could be obtained at the other.

I then entered the woods and followed the old bridle path. Soon another squirrel was observed about 25 yards ahead, on the path. I rested the rifle barrel against the side of a nearby tree and plugged this one in the neck. He was not quite dead when retrieved, but it was not long until he was gone. The bullet had made a neat hole, clear through, severing the jugular. I then decided I had enough for one day, and left for the car. We have killed plenty of game in our family, but have never made a practice of shooting more than needed, at any one time. There is always another day coming and where will be the thrill of walking into a woods which is without good timber and without squirrels?

On the way back to the car, a large Cooper's hawk stopped off in a tree almost overhead. The shot was an easy one, at not over 100 feet. The bullet struck directly in the breast without tearing, and the hawk, being a handsome bird, was taken home and mounted. Both loads appeared satisfactory for squirrels. The charge was 4.0 grains of No. 80, and a 45-grain expanding bullet, one soft point, the other hollow point.

About 15 years ago, we had the worst snow and ice storm, and the most severe blizzard that has come to this neighborhood within 25 years. The ice cap was two to four inches thick over everything. Snow also covered the ground in places to a depth of a foot. This snow and ice remained on the ground for five weeks. Toward the end of this siege of cold weather, due to alternate thaws and freezes, the ice seemed to become harder, low on the ground, and game birds, squirrels and rabbits became weakened from a lack of food. Squirrels could not dig down to the shellbarks, hickory nuts and acorns; the birds found their food to be under a solid sheet of ice. Game birds are accustomed to finding their food either slightly aloft, on weeds and grasses and grains, or else lying in the grass and leaves on the ground. Rabbits had trouble both getting out of and back into their dens, which were largely closed with ice.

It was a situation of real concern to all having any interest whatever in the local supply of small game.

From somewhere far up the Atlantic Coast line, probably, as

judged from newspaper accounts at the time, and word received on the subject from Gun Department correspondents of the author of this book, the hawks were migrating. Many of them had very large heads and curved beaks, most of them goshawks and similar destructive varieties, such migrating from Nova Scotia, New Brunswick and Labrador. It was a flight of exceptionally large and vicious hawks and some Arctic white owls, that came down along the coast at that time. These birds were seen in great numbers in flight first, along the coast of Maine, and for a very short distance inland. They swept down clear to the Carolinas, in some instances. Toward the end of the continuance of this ice cap, everything was so numb and worn down with hunger and weakness, that the birds of prey often sat around on very low limbs, or fence posts and even on stumps in many instances, especially on foggy days. And the small birds, tree squirrels and other game and insectivorous birds were an easy prey and, according to prominent game officials, Bob White quail were badly thinned out and almost exterminated, in the whole area, north of a line drawn through the center of North Carolina and West clear to Missouri. In Maryland, a prominent Game Official stated to the author that two years after this storm and ice cap, there were but two counties still containing a fair proportion of quail, so severe was the total effect. In Delaware, the result was just as noticeable.

During this ice cap and freeze we were set for a countrywide slaughter of game, and had it. Locally, we had some game on so-called Game Preserves but about all this meant was that some farms had signs to this effect, and the hawks and white owls were not observing the signs. Temperatures ranged 30° below normal and most persons were too busy hugging warm radiators and stoves to bother with protecting game. A few game wardens killed a very small number of hawks with shotguns, but there were no riflemen in the Game and Fish Department. As it was my vacation at the time, I felt it was an opportune period to hunt those hawks and crows, or legal game would be something that one only read about where we did our local shooting. I loaded up several hundred .22 Hornet reloads with 10.5 grains of No. 1204, using Peters hollow point bullets, Winchester cases and No. 116 primers. The rifle was my Savage 23-D sporter, equipped with Winchester 5A scope, in one half minute mounts. I sighted in for 100 yards, to hit the dot. This load, when tested, gave me a 9X possible at 100 yards, the tenth shot being out on the edge of the 10 ring at 9 o'clock.

From notes kept during the hunting period mentioned, some of the results obtained can be given. Ranges of course were unknown, but paced when at all possible, and one of the long shots could not be paced until daylight of the next day, when a sudden freeze enabled the shooter to cross a low and wet spot on the new ice, and pace from the point of shooting to the dead hawk. The pacing was done very carefully. Most of the shots were from an arm rest, when practical, such as may be obtained against a car, a tree trunk, fence post or fence rail, or whatever happens to be handy to aid in getting a perfect let off for a long range shot. Numerous shots, however, had to be taken strictly offhand.

The first hawk was spotted 150 yards off, sitting in a tall tree, well out in the open. From this point of vantage, his vision could take in quite a sweep. He overlooked the best pheasant thicket around; and also an inland pond upon which some wild ducks came in to visit to escape storms. One shot was fired at this hawk, piercing the breast. The bullet tore quite a hole through, as the feathers matted and caused unusual expansion. Further along, in the same district, a hawk was observed on an elm, at a range of about 40 yards. The bullet entered the left side and made a gaping wound where it came out. The hawk of course was killed. Another was seen shortly, a quarter of a mile or so, from the last one. The first shot was a miss. The second struck squarely in the back, making a mangled wreck of this harrier. He was a large red-tail, which type hunts the more open fields, has very large feet and tremendous claws, and can grab a squirrel, a pheasant, or a quail, whenever he may feel like it, and spots one. The theory that such feet and talons are used only for catching a few field mice is absurd. Nature does not make such mistakes. It is like using a 10-ton truck to haul a single sack of potatoes, or a 10-pound spike maul to drive brads. Under the conditions prevailing, it seemed that varmints felt like grabbing anything edible, and often did so. Under such circumstances, inoffensive and valuable meadow larks seemed to be one of the commonest victims after every early storm. They appeared to be totally unable to find protection from aerial dive bombers and their lemon yellow and the darker back feathers were to be found staining the snow, for the area of a two or three foot littered death-struggle location. That, in addition to the game that was destroyed. The destruction of meadow larks was extensive.

Near a large farm, on which we knew there was some game, a big hawk was shot which had a 47½" wingspread. It was killed at a range of 247 paces. This was a very large red-tail. In South Carolina they have been repeatedly proved to have killed good-sized wild turkeys—Henry E. Davis, of Florence, has commented upon this most vigorously. Harmless, certainly, until they become hungry and then they are as destructive as a gone-wild house cat under similar circumstances. In this shot, the bullet, even at 247 paces, broke a wing and entered the side, tearing quite a hole. It showed excellent expansion.

Some time later a small gray hawk, probably a small sharp-shin, with 33″ wingspread, arrived and was shot out of the top of the tree, at a range of 50 yards. It appeared to be watching something intently, beneath the tree, but before it could dive onto it, the hawk exploded in a puff of feathers, when the expanding bullet landed. While retrieving this one, I jumped *two* small rabbits about 20 feet from the trunk of the tree upon which the hawk had stopped and was sitting. This looked like a very close shave for those bunnies.

Another hawk was shot at 75 yards. Four shots were required to bag him; the first bullet struck the left wing, the second and third hit in the breast, while the fourth tore off his left leg, and tumbled him off the tree. He must have been frozen fast. I fail to recall when another hawk acted similarly, when shot up so badly. Upon retrieving this, it was measured as accurately as we could, along the length of the rifle, and it had a 59″ wingspread. My father got quite a kick out of that one.

Cutting across country, a large Cooper's hawk was spotted at 100 yards. Three hours later we shot another out of the same tree, which shows how another hawk appropriates a choice perch. They haul up there and sit and as soon as some prospective victim moves down below, they swoop, first wheeling in many instances, to get right over the victim.

Before long another hawk was spotted sitting on a rail fence, at 100 yards, and with a safe background. Smacked that one in the left side. At 100 yards, you do not merely kill your game with a .22 Hornet. You pick the spot on the game you desire to hit, and then hit that spot—like dotting a point in the center of a circle.

A very large gray hawk was seen sitting on the top of a tree, some 300 yards off. This is a *shot*, for a Hornet; or for any other medium velocity .22 center fire rifle for that matter! When I fired, he fell to the ground. It was exactly 310 paces to where we picked him up. The wingspread was 54½″. The bullet made a large, gaping hole in the breast. A Hornet bullet tears a very much larger hole in a large hawk than in a woodchuck. The reason is that the bullet expands in the tough, many layered feathers, and is expanded when it first enters the flesh.

Within two days I had shot three large hawks out of another tree, about 60 yards from the firing station. In another locality, four hawks were bagged out of one tree, showing definitely that after another migrating hawk comes along, the accipiter takes up its position in a good hunting locality—good hunting that is, for the hawk, and it keeps it until shot off, dispossessed, or until it migrates farther South or farther North. Shooting one hawk does not stop the slaughter of game birds, rabbits and insectivorous birds in a locality. Of course some rodents are picked off, but rodents can be controlled by the use of poisoned grain, as the Department of Agriculture has so often proved. And their damage is often tremendously exaggerated at best. It is like the claim that quail were worth $5.00 apiece to farmers, and which claim practically stopped quail shooting, in many localities for two or three years. It was only an estimate. Probably no one could prove it, and no one could disprove it. One might as well say that grasshoppers each do fifty cents or one dollar's worth of damage. Get that idea current and everyone will be out swatting grasshoppers. One might say that pheasants are each worth five dollars to a farmer because of the cutworms, insects and bugs they eat. Along would come some other chap and say that each pheasant destroyed five dollars worth of corn or wheat, and who could prove that *he* was wrong. So, the net worth or net damage done by any species or any individual winged or furred visitor or inhabitant, must be judged by what appears logical, sensible and practical, that it is likely to do if allowed to remain where it is. It is well known what hawks will do around any game farm, given opportunity. It is a constant battle to keep them away or shot, or trapped. In like manner, in the open game fields, damage done must depend upon circumstances favorable or unfavorable to the hawks, the game, and to the relative plentifulness of game. The more game present, the more that can be destroyed. It is useless to try to protect something which does not exist, and it is foolish not to protect game when one has it. To sportsmen, game is much more desirable and valuable than hawks, or the destruction of a few rodents. So we shoot them as and if they appear to need killing.

All four of the hawks mentioned above as being shot out of one tree, were badly mangled by hollow point bullets. The average range on these was 250 paces. At another place, two red-shouldered hawks were shot. One was at 125 yards, and was quite badly torn when picked up. Another was shot at 75 yards, while retrieving the first one. This one was hit on the bone of the left wing, tearing a large wound and then mangling the breast. The Hornet is very deadly on hawks and crows because of its great accuracy, sufficiently flat trajectory, and ample killing power.

Three crows were then shot in a meadow, at 100 yards; all were completely blasted. Another chance at 200 yards netted a black rascal. In a cornfield, near a pile of rubbish, two other crows were shot, one at 50, the other at 75 yards. Note how much closer the crows fell than the hawks. The hawks are much more wary. The following day a crow which appeared large enough, possibly, to be a raven, and looked much like one, was shot at 100 yards. The bullet made a very large hole in the breast. Out in the country farther, a hawk with a 60½″ spread was practically blown apart, at a distance of 150 yards. Note carefully that with a shotgun most persons would not have been able to get within gunshot of most of these hawks. It was necessary to use an accurate and flat-shooting rifle. And it was necessary to have an experienced rifleman handling it, or it was largely useless for a man to go after them with a rifle. They would fly before a man bearing a firearm could get close enough, unless he had the proper long range outfit and knew how to and *could* use it effectively. Most hawks fly before the average gunner can get close enough to hit them. Farmers and the like are generally helpless to do much in controlling such pests. Then too, they often appear when the farmer is busy, or out working away from the house and barn, or when he is in town. Most farmers are not riflemen, in the sense that they are skilled with and have a small caliber varmint rifle.

So, we will recount a few more rounds, and go to another subject. A shot at 150 yards, brought down a large hawk from a buttonwood. This bird was hit with a hollow point. Two of us took a trip down the state, partly for the ride, in part also to see what the varmint conditions seemed to be there and to pick up a bit of needed shooting. Four feathered migrants the size of wild turkeys, were all hard hit, and three crows and two hawks. In a period of five weeks, when the ground was covered with a sheet of ice, as detailed previously, I shot and killed 33 hawks with the rifle and about an equal number of crows. I believe this to have been the most effective game protection carried on in our locality at that time, because never within the memory of my father or myself have we been plagued with such an enormous migration of hawks. At one time, within this period, the temperatures having been within a range of 5° above zero, to 10° below zero, shooting was anything but comfortable. It was windy, and it was bitter cold and damp, and the Arctic weather seemed at times almost to congeal the blood in the body. But we made the shooting trips and believe that it was really helpful in net results. It also gave us much data on the accuracy and killing power of .22 Hornet loads on varmints.

WOODCHUCK SHOOTING WITH HORNET RELOADS

Early one summer afternoon I took the Savage Hornet equipped with 5A scope and handloaded ammunition containing hollow point bullets ahead of 10.5 grains of No. 1204 to my favorite woodchuck grounds. I set forth largely to see what results would be obtained on that tough little varmint of the clover fields. Some cherish chucks for their association and because they give life to an otherwise lifeless hillside. Others will not have them around because they cut down crop production and dig unneeded holes. The shooting in this instance was to be on the farm of a friend who wanted to have his woodchucks reduced.

The first chuck was seen sitting in front of a clump of briars at 150 yards. He dropped instantly to the shot, and examination showed the hollow point bullet had entered the throat. A fragment entered the brain. Throat shots are normally very deadly on chucks and upon any other animal.

Another woodchuck was fired upon at 50 yards. The bullet entered the right eye and he was as dead as a door nail when found. Notes made further along in the chuck hunting, show one killed at 265 paces. It was sitting more or less beneath a fence rail. The bullet luckily struck him in the left ear, tearing up the skull. Several others were shot at 100 yards; three of these were struck in the chest, the bullet piercing the heart or lungs. All were nice clean kills. One chuck at 165 paces was killed right on his doorstep. The bullet struck in the mouth, broke off several teeth, and separated into fragments. Parts of the jacket entered the brain. Still another chuck was shot squarely between the eyes. Only his head was sticking out of the hole. When shot he turned a complete back-flip and landed in his den. At first it appeared I had missed, but when I went up to look there he was, almost out of sight in the hole and quite dead.

Several were shot at 50 to 75 yards, all hit in the head. The bullet killed all of these cleanly. Chuck shooting results depend a great deal upon where you hit the chuck as well as what you use on him, as most experienced riflemen know. The Hornet is deadly on all shots forward of the middle, and hardly any rifle is a clean killer on woodchucks if the bullet strikes in back of the diaphragm.

One chuck was sitting 90 paces off. His paws were folded across his chest, or just hanging limp so as to appear so. The bullet went through one paw, entered high in the chest, and then ranged upward and back into the head. I had to cut up this animal considerably to follow the path of the bullet. It is always interesting to see exactly what the shot has accomplished. One day a woodchuck was put to rest at 70 yards, or so it seemed, but then when I walked up to pick him up he suddenly came to life. He snarled and sniffed and then turned and dove into his den mouth. That was one groundhog I will never forget! I had probably "creased" him.

One real wise old groundhog managed to stay out of range for about two seasons. His den had been dug in the middle of a large field, usually the safest place for a woodchuck to den, because he is

then hard to stalk within rifle range. This den was about 250 yards
from the nearest cover. One morning I visited the rifle range and
sighted the Hornet rifle for 300 yards. I then drove to the spot from
which I thought I might get a shot. Cover was found behind a log
and the rifle barrel rested upon it. I waited about twenty minutes
and there he was, sitting up looking things over. I very carefully
placed the crosshairs upon the mark and eased off the shot. Down
he went! Racing over to pick him up, I found he was probably the
largest groundhog I had ever shot. I estimated his weight at a good
15 pounds, but some seem to feel that this is beyond the weight attained by large woodchucks. On the other hand, weights up to 40
pounds have been claimed. Regardless, this was really a very large
and fat woodchuck.

In my experience of 20 years in hunting small game and varmints,
I have killed 500 to 600 woodchucks, and hawks, crows and squirrels in goodly numbers. During the 10 or 11 years I have used mine,
I have found the comparatively light Savage sporter 23-D to hold
its zero very well. Sometimes I wish for more weight of rifle, but
nevertheless prefer the Savage Hornet sporter to any other in my
gun cabinet. The rifle is exceptionally accurate, kills well, the ammunition reloads cheaply when reloading is possible, and in many
ways it has so many practical features for an area such as I live in
that, for its cost, it is rather difficult to find a more generally satisfactory rifle of that price range, both as to rifle and its ammunition.
The two should always be considered together.

In my father's home, nothing but hawk and crow heads, or chuck
or squirrel tails "count." You cannot go home with the claim that
you have shot something unless you have evidence to prove it.
Game which contains more than one bullet hole is not received
there with enthusiasm. A rifle which produces a loud report, has
excessive range, or gives ricochets which whine, is not desirable in
our type of shooting. Much of the best of it must be done carefully,
around where there are inhabitants. One of the longer ranged .22s
of the wildcat persuasion would of course give greater range and
more killing power, but they are also more expensive to load or
reload, give a much sharper report, crack louder as well, and have a
longer range when fired at objects on trees or above the level of the
ground. None of those features is an advantage in most settled or
semi-settled areas. The thicker the population per square mile, the
more elaborate the homes, the more exclusive and set-apart the
people imagine themselves to be, or wish to be regarded, the more
important these subjects become.

I have hunted halfway across the North American continent, I
have been in Canada quite a number of times, have driven over a

THIS IS WHAT A GRAY WOLF LOOKS LIKE

Two hundred, three hundred, maybe four hundred yards away, this gray wolf would make a difficult shot, even with a .22–4000 f.s. scope sighted rifle. The most certain spot for a kill, would be to rest the cross-hairs intersection on a spot on the shoulder just behind and beneath the right eye.

Photo by Bud Dalrymple

good many thousand miles of roads in New York, Pennsylvania, Ohio, Maryland, Delaware and other states, and have hunted and shot a good many gray and fox squirrels in Missouri, and have had opportunity at first hand to observe game conditions and shooting possibilities in quite a few localities. It is of no special import to mention that I have shot and killed 42 woodchucks within a week, and 33 hawks in five weeks, using a .22 Hornet rifle, for these were special occasions and were rather unusual. However, this may help to demonstrate and prove that the .22 Hornet rifle is an effective sporting rifle, also that it is a good clean killing arm on small game and varmints and it is a clean killer with handloaded ammunition normally easy and convenient to prepare, and not too expensive to load and shoot.

These are abnormal times in the handloading of ammunition, but such cartridges have kept many in the shooting game when otherwise they would have had to look into the merits of other outdoor pursuits and sports. I hope that a reading of these experiences may have been of assistance to other riflemen and will be more likely to suggest that they choose a .22 center fire rifle of not too much report, not too much range, not too much killing power and not too much expense. Few rifles using factory ammunition have been as useful in protecting small game here in the East.

It is useless to say that certain hawks pick out only the old, the decrepit and the sick and helpless to strike down. Would you? If game, to you, served no other purpose than to provide your choicest food, would you pick the poorest specimens for your own consumption? Then why try to argue that varmints will do so? Accidents do not happen only to the aged, the infirm, or the sick. They happen to all—the decrepit and the most vigorous. It is like that in the fields and the woods. The actions of the game itself, is the best possible proof that varmints of the air and varmints of the ground spare none. They strike down whatever they can pounce upon. The law of nature is, to some extent, the survival of the fittest. On the other hand many of the fittest, in the matter of age and bodily health, happen at times to be caught out from cover or shelter, and when this occurs often meet their end.

Nature simply provides a setting or background for the birds, animals and creatures of all different kinds, many of which, both large and small, prey upon each other. Man himself lives largely upon animal and bird life. He chooses the best whenever possible. So do winged vermin. The rest is merely propaganda. Watch the actions of wild animals and birds subject to attacks by hawks, as proof. Do you find only the old and decrepit seeking shelter when a hawk appears. Very definitely not. They *all* squat, run, or hide.

The rifleman is the most useful protector of small game from the varmints which so often feed upon and destroy them. The .22 Hornet rifle is probably the most useful and efficient firearm so far developed, using commercial ammunition, suitable for such shooting. It gives the most deadly results in proportion to the cost of its ammunition. It is adequate for most of the medium range work to be done, and when it is not a slightly larger and longer ranged .22 varmint cartridge of custom manufacture should be chosen but then only if the rifleman is prepared to supply his own ammunition, or has some ready means of obtaining it.

The matter of range, velocity, comparative wind drift, flatness of trajectory, should not be overdone nor overstressed. Especially, should it not be overstressed at the expense of accurate barrel life or neighborhood safety. The .22 Hornet appears to be the best caliber, larger than the .22 long rifle, which today suits the average shot, exceedingly well; My father; Edgar Burkins, probably the most expert and experienced woodchuck hunter in Delaware; and I, all agree that the .22 Hornet is about as long ranged and powerful a rifle as should be used generally, for sporting purposes, in this state. It is important that a rifle should not crack too loudly nor give a report which will carry for too great a distance. This condition is important in many other states and localities. I have traveled enough to find this so!

Finally, it comes down to a question—which *is* the best .22 rifle for you and me. I would suggest a .22 long rifle, a .22 Hornet, and if you need something materially more powerful, then another arm like the .22 Varminter, the .219 Donaldson-Wasp, the .219 Zipper Improved, or the .22 Lindahl Super-Chucker; but expect none of them to do the work of all three. The R-2 or the .22/3000 Lovell is a good compromise caliber, and it could be used here, but unless underloaded it is unnecessarily powerful and long ranged for most settled district small game, other than crows, hawks and woodchucks. At the present time, it is not supplied factory loaded, although it may be eventually. Rifles for the cartridge case from which it is made have not been manufactured in quantity for at least the past 15 years.

All calibers giving still higher velocities are still more powerful, crack sharper, their sound carries farther, and they will annoy more people. A rifle is in one respect, very much like the engine of an automobile. What it will do at its average speed should be regarded as its most important characteristic. The .22 Hornet, even the present Super-Speed and Super-X types are not too powerful, too sharp in report, or too expensive in factory ammunition, for the needs of most small bore riflemen who hunt in the field. But step up that velocity 500 to 800 f.s. and what is the result? Do you advertise yourself and your shooting more than you gain in range?

The .22 Hornet may therefore be regarded generally, as having a great deal on the ball for the man who expects and demands results, and yet who does not wish to conduct a small, personal ammunition loading plant, who will depend largely upon commercial ammunition in normal times, and yet who wishes match rifle accuracy. The .22 Hornet will give it to him.

Much of the success of the .22 Hornet cartridge can be credited to the fact that it has been supplied in three good bolt action rifles and in all of these it gave remarkable accuracy for factory loaded commercial ammunition at all ordinary sporting ranges up to 200 yards. Long shots, at considerably greater distances, are both practical and rather common, provided you can actually shoot a rifle in the field and have ability as a hunter and stalker of game and varmints.

These are conditions common to all successful rifle shooting in the field and unless you can put into practice your shooting and hunting skills when needed even a very fine shooting little cartridge like the .22 Hornet will not enable you to make a very high average of kills. The .22 Hornet, however, is quite sufficiently long ranged to enable a good rifleman to kill most varmints at a distance at which most such targets consider themselves safe. So as long as your rifle will do this you rarely need a longer ranged rifle.

In the .22 Hornet caliber, Remington puts out a 45-grain pointed soft point bullet loading at a claimed muzzle velocity of 2,600 f.s. which has a good deal to recommend it. It retains 2,210 f.s. at 100 yards, 1,860 f.s. at 200 yards and 1,550 f.s. at 300 yards, with energies of 675, 490, 345 and 240 ft. lbs. at the muzzle, 100, 200 and 300 yards respectively. This is 330 f.s. higher velocity at 300 yards, than is retained by the Remington 46-grain H.P. or mushroom load, which starts off with 2,650 f.s. muzzle velocity but has dropped to 1,220 f.s. at 300 yards as compared to the 1,550 f.s. of the soft point bullet at 300 yards.

The trajectory also is better, with the soft point 45-grain bullet. It is 0.8" over 100 yards, 3.5" over 200 yards (the same approximately as the .30–1906–2700 Springfield 150-grain service load) and is 10.0" over 300 yards. The 46-grain H.P. bullet, due to that open point which is moderately flat on the front end, gives a trajectory over 100, 200 and 300 yards, of 0.8", 4.0" and 12.5". In other words, as a bullet's total drop over a range is four times its midrange trajectory height, that 45-grain soft point bullet actually drops 10"; less over 300 yards than the 46-grain H.P. bullet, starting off 50 f.s. faster.

Another matter: the author has often felt that the soft point bullet killed quicker and more certainly, because it usually expanded faster and more certainly in shots through the ribs, where the going was relatively soft in a woodchuck. Also, the hollow point bullet is a good deal more likely to ricochet on hard, gravelly ground than the soft point bullet. Phil Sharpe, in his book on Handloading, tells of some experiments he made, in firing a Hornet rifle at small pine sticks on a hillside, in which instance about 60 per cent of the hollow point bullets *ricocheted* while *none* of the soft point bullets did so.

A good many farmers are more "tetchy" on the subject of ricochets than any other. You can shoot, so long as you do not attract the attention of too many persons. But start bouncing ricochets over cows, or the barn, or the sheep on a nearby hillside, and it is only a question of a very few minutes until someone will come rushing out of the farmhouse, shouting at least once each five yards, quoting volubly from the Koran in a voice that will carry 1,000 yards to two miles, depending upon the way the wind is blowing and how much breath he has left. I could mention specific instances of chaps becoming quite sensitive about anyone letting off a rifle shot within a quarter of a mile of where ewes in that condition known as "expectant" are grazing about lambing time. It appears that a lamb's mama-to-be is likely to drop her lamb a few days too soon, if startled suddenly and excited, and a whining ricochet will often get action from the ewes and from the lamb's foster Papa.

I want this to get past the censor, so do not shove me, but it is a subject upon which the reader could ponder for a few moments and maybe decide that in future he will try to use soft point bullets for shooting around most of those back pasture fields where you may find woodchucks, and where you may also find domestic stock. You will not find it advantageous to shoot anything which suddenly arouses the farm vote!

There is also the subject of not shooting at anything which looks like the head of a woodchuck until you are *sure*, yes doubly *sure*, that it *is* the head of a woodchuck and not the cap of a berry picker who is bent over picking dewberries or huckleberries on the far side of a line fence. Shooting accidents seem at times to run by neighborhoods. In a certain small area, in another state there seem to be more men shot in mistake for a woodchuck, over the course of five or ten years, than almost any other locality in this country. At least, newspaper accounts would so indicate. This is a neighborhood of rich farm valleys and gentle rolling hills. The author has been on a survey or two, running into that area and has also driven through that country repeatedly. In such woodchuck shooting, a .22 Hornet is quite sufficiently powerful for woodchucks, crows, hawks, and occasional head shots at gray squirrels as may come to hand in such hunting.

There is also the matter of being tripped up by a root, thrown by a dewberry vine, or of stumbling or slipping on a moss-covered rock, and of getting off an accidental shot that you did not anticipate. Rifles for the .22 Hornet are of a type in which this is unlikely, but it always can happen, and it pays to keep the safety at least halfway over when hunting, and of not setting the set trigger of a Schuetzen double set trigger rifle until actually about to shoot at game which has been positively identified—and of "unsetting" same immediately if you do not then make the shot. This is done by grasping the hammer with the thumb on the spur, releasing the trigger and letting the hammer down slowly, then re-cocking in the normal manner. This is the safe procedure in field shooting.

In the matter of a greatly reduced load in a .22 Hornet, Fred Ness once wrote of a Loverin bullet of 44-grains, known as No. 225438 which, with 3.0 grains of Hercules Unique or of Hercules Infallible, in W.R.A. .22 Hornet cases, with W.R.A. No. 116 primers, was used for squirrels. The charge averaged .38″ per 5-shot group at 50 yards, measuring inside to inside of shots farthest apart—which is not the usual way of measuring. My son tried 4.0 grains of No. 80 with 45-grain Peters H.P. bullet which gave a good squirrel load.

Hervey Lovell once wrote the author that he had given up trying to develop a charge for the .22–3000 Lovell for squirrels which would not tear them. He was using more than twice as much powder as required.

F. C. Ness reports that 8.8 grains of 1204 and the Sisk 35-grain F.M.P. bullet tears squirrels badly. On the other hand, Henry E. Davis states that he has shot probably over 100 squirrels with the same charge either of #1204 or of #4227 powder behind the same bullet, and that he has had no mutilation except in cases where the bullet struck a large bone. For some purposes, 8.3 grains of 2400 or 7.5 grains of 2400 are good game loads in the .22 Hornet, using the 45-grain Sisk bullet, although they are about double the required squirrel charge. They would do for jackrabbits, hawks, and crows at not too great distance.

Many large birds like hawks, buzzards and the like tear easily with expanding bullets because the bullet mats in the feathers before it enters the body. Most hunters are inclined to very greatly under-estimate the killing power, accuracy, and comparative flatness of trajectory of the .22 Hornet over 150–175 yards. Remember always that the bullet has the trajectory of the Springfield or the Garand service rifle over 200 yards, and with soft point bullets will rarely or ever throw lead after the bullet hits turf. It often strikes down a woodchuck so suddenly that on a number of occasions I have shot at them running and at ranges around 100 yards and, due to the forward velocity of the animal's body, have made hits in the ribs or the middle when I had aimed about the end of the nose or the head and fired when the chuck came up with the crosshairs. The animal so shot simply slides forward on its nose, kicks a few times, frenziedly raises and whips its tail, and that is the end of it until you walk up and examine a bullet hole oozing blood, which orifice is about the size of a dime to a nickel and the animal's lungs when prodded with the foot, go "oosh!" It bleeds heavily inside.

At 100 yards, the .22 Hornet 2,600 f.s. soft point bullet strikes a blow just a bit over *five times* as hard as the .22 long rifle Super-X H.P. bullet delivers at the same distance. I have personally been along and seen eight consecutive clean kills on woodchucks, at an average range of 100 yards, and with no one of them very far from that 100 yards distance, using a .22 Model 1897 Marlin rifle with H.P. long rifle ammunition. When someone complains bitterly therefore when he loses shot after shot at 100 yards with a Hornet, I am convinced that one of two things is wrong. His rifle is either not sighted properly for 100 yards; or, he cannot hold the crosshairs steadily at the exact moment he lets off the shot. Concentrate on those two details and you will be surprised how your opinion of the killing power of the Hornet rifle and cartridge will improve. The most important thing about rifle shooting is the exact spot on which you land the bullet. This Remington soft point 45-grain, non-ricocheting bullet delivers almost exactly one-quarter ton of kinetic energy at 100 yards, every time you press the trigger of a .22 Hornet rifle. The rest is entirely up to you!

CHAPTER 25

Telescope Sights

THE POOREST ECONOMY IMAGINABLE IS TO INSTALL A CHEAP AND POOR quality telescope on a good rifle. Our modern good grade rifles are engines of precision and efficiency, and deserve the sight equipment that will enable them to perform to the limit of their capacities. A cheap telescope is certainly not such equipment. In addition, it introduces a certain amount of eye strain, and to say the least this is no recommendation for any form of rifle sight. Hence in this chapter very little will be said about, and nothing commending, such telescopes.

Since the close of World War II has come a perfect deluge of new telescopes by both old and new makers, and the end is not yet in sight. Each month witnesses the advent of a new instrument, sometimes by an old established firm and frequently by a newcomer in the field. A recent scope is the new variable power 2½X to 4X hunting telescope with a special mount for both windage and elevation put out by Bausch & Lomb Optical Company and announced in May, 1948. While this great concern is one of the two largest American optical companies, the making of rifle telescope sights is an entirely new venture on its part. Indeed the list of new telescopes is so long and imposing that no attempt will be made to catalogue, much less, describe them. Hence the discussion in the main will be confined to the old and well established lines.

LYMAN TELESCOPES

Shortly after World War I The Lyman Gun Sight Corporation, of Middlefield, Connecticut, decided to add a line of glass sights to its already well-known line of iron sights. To this end it purchased the telescope sight business of the Winchester Repeating Arms Company and also that of the J. Stevens Arms & Tool Company.

For many years the most generally useful and satisfactory rifle telescope of American manufacture was the Winchester A5. This was of five power, with a three-fourth inch tube 15⅞" long. Focusing for various ranges was accomplished by a knurled graduated ring on the objective end of the instrument. An error was deliberately built into the optical system, the error in one lens being corrected by that in another. The purpose of this, so it was claimed, was to prevent fraudulent imitations.

The rear mount was of the four point suspension type, with plungers and graduated screw thimbles for elevation and windage. Contact of the tube with the elevation plunger was maintained by a double armed wire spring frequently called a "grasshopper" spring. While the movements for elevation and windage were reliable, there were too many protrusions on the mount, and the spring frequently did not function, thus allowing the tube to stick or hang up.

Shortly after acquiring the rights to the A5, Lyman redesigned its optical system and substituted a new and reliable three point suspension rear mount, with graduated thimbles giving one-fourth inch minute click movements for both elevation and windage. The revamped telescope had a field of view of 18' at 100 yards, an eye relief 1¾", an objective lens of five-eights inch free aperture, and was equipped with Bausch & Lomb lenses. This redesigned telescope was renamed the 5A, and as such was manufactured and sold by Lyman for a number of years until the company finally rendered it obsolete and supplanted it with the 6X Junior Targetspot.

Externally no changes were made in this scope by Lyman, and after it had been revamped it could anywhere be recognized on sight, having as much individuality as a Winchester Model 97 shotgun. Whether made by Winchester or by Lyman, this was a good and reliable all-around telescope. The power was just about right for most shooting, and it was pretty near fool-proof, both in the field and on the range, for the chap who would sight in carefully and then have sufficient courage and common sense to let the mounts alone. Both as a shooter and as a statistical office official at many Sea Girt small bore shoots, I noticed time and again that while the users of 5A scopes might not make quite as high top scores as those using Lyman and Fecker scopes of larger sizes and higher powers, neither did so many of them make foolish errors and every now and again miss the whole target for shot after shot when changing from one range to another. Another matter of interest was that the shooter who had not had the advantage of technical or engineering training was usually able to take a 5A, work things out for himself, and use it efficiently right from the start.

For many years I have been using a 5A on my favorite Winchester-Hoffman Model 52 rifle, and it has always given thorough satisfaction. I could ask for nothing better on a rifle of that caliber.

This telescope is rather short for use on a rifle with a long receiver, like the Model 52, and by installing three telescope bases on the barrel I have solved the problem this presents. Others have solved it by installing the rear base on the receiver bridge and the front base on the barrel six inches on centers in front of the rear base. On many Model 52 rifles this means substituting a Lyman 48 rear sight for the factory sight and sweating in the rear sight slot a matted blank on which the rear base is placed. On my rifle the rear base is on the barrel and abuts the receiver ring, the next two bases are on the barrel and are spaced on centers 3⅞″ and 5⅞″, respectively, from the center of the rear base. This gives me nearly a six inch intermount spacing for prone shooting and nearly a four inch intermount spacing for offhand shooting and woods hunting. I wish the latter was more, but a greater spacing is impractical on this rifle.

Always remember that a scope with three mount bases will have one set of readings for the prone position when using the rear and forward bases, and an entirely different set of readings all the way out from 20 to 300 yards when using the rear and middle bases for the offhand, the kneeling and perhaps the sitting positions. Keep these readings separated in your pocket notebook with each set correctly labeled, otherwise disaster will surely follow.

In recent years, the 5A has been almost entirely superseded by the Junior Targetspot. Optically the latter is a better instrument, but it is not in such practically universal focus for hunting, and it is not so readily used effectively by a tyro. It is only superior when it is used properly.

THE TARGETSPOT MODELS

In the later part of 1937, Lyman developed and put on the market a new telescope equipped with Bausch & Lomb lens, and called it the Junior Targetspot. The company continued to make the 5A for several years, but finally abandoned such manufacture. The Junior Targetspot is made in 6X, 8X and 10X, and is 21¼″ in overall length. The tube is three-fourths inch in diameter, but the ends are slightly enlarged, the objective distinctly so, since it carries a cell that houses a lens having a three-fourths inch (19 mm) free aperture. Like all Lyman target telescopes, this one is fitted with a Pope nonrotating rib, and is equipped with the Lyman standard target mounts in which the rear mount is of the three point suspension type with one-fourth inch minute click adjustments for elevation and windage.

The Junior Targetspot has in 6X a field of 16′ at 100 yards, in 8X 14′ at 100 yards, and in 10X 12′ at 100 yards, and a two inch normal eye relief in all powers. It weighs, with mounts, 22 ounces. Everything considered, this telescope in either six or eight power is one of the best, if not the very best, of all telescopes obtainable by a rifleman today for open country shooting of woodchucks, gophers, prairie dogs, foxes, coyotes, prairie chickens, crows, hawks, and other varmints. In 6X it is fine for woods hunting of squirrels, crows and hawks, but is a little slow for picking up squirrels feeding on the ground.

Among the many admirable features that should be mentioned are the clarity of the field, the brilliancy of the lenses, the exceptionally good resolving power, the light gathering properties, the fine finish of the parts, the distinctness and accuracy of the gradations on the focusing sleeve, and the ease of adjusting the mount quickly and accurately for taking shots at different ranges. It is rather long, and if 2¼″ shorter would be about as near perfect for its purposes as anything mechanical ever gets to be.

As has been pointed out, a short telescope, like the 5A, requires the location of three bases on the barrel of the rifle, or some other device, in order to use it effectively in the usual shooting positions assumed in hunting. This is not at all necessary with the Junior Targetspot. With the bases spaced apart six inches, or even 7.2″, the distance recommended by Lyman to give one-fourth minute of angle movements of the bullet per 100 yards of range, the rear lens of this telescope can be located at exactly the right distance from your aiming eye when shooting off-hand or otherwise, and locking by tightening the screw of the adjustable collar on the outside of the telescope tube makes this location exact and permanent. In fact, all this could be obtained by a telescope of 19″ length, and this is the reason that shortening this model was suggested above.

The 6X glass can be set to mean ordinary range for hunting, but for best results and maximum clarity of lenses when woods hunting it should be set for the range at which shots are usually obtained. It will be found a bit slow and hard to hold steady when picking out a squirrel, crow, or hawk in the dense foliage of a large tree, but it will be much better for such use than would be one of the larger and heavier glasses of higher power. On the other hand, in the 6X it is most excellent for shooting squirrels, crows and hawks off bare trees at long range, especially when some form of rest can be utilized.

The Lyman Company makes in 8X and 10X another similar telescope called the Targetspot. It weighs two ounces more and is three-fourths inch longer than the Junior Targetspot, and has an objective of 1⅛″ (28 mm). This too is a quality instrument with lenses of the greatest brilliancy and the highest resolving power. In short, its optical qualities are superb. On the target range this telescope is all that could be desired, but it is too bulky for any sort of hunting except long range rest shooting of pests with powerful .22 caliber rifles.

The same may with emphasis be said of the Super-Target line also put out by the Lyman company. These big heavy telescopes two feet long with $1\,1\frac{1}{32}$" (34 mm) objectives, and coming in various power from 10X through 20X, are among the finest and clearest target glasses ever built, but they belong on the target range and nowhere else.

LYMAN CHALLENGER

The Lyman Challenger is a 4 power hunting scope for big game rifles primarily. It is also a good woodchuck scope and for coyotes, if you can get it set with sufficient accuracy to the rifle zero. This depends upon the mounts. The Challenger is really a Lyman Alaskan in 4X and was something Henry Lyman often spoke of to the author for years before it appeared on the market. I often suggested it to him, and also to others.

The weight of the Lyman Challenger is 13 ounces; it is approximately $11\frac{1}{2}$" in length; the field of view at 100 yards is 27 feet, the same as that of the Hensoldt Dialytan 4X; eye relief is just short of 4"; outside diameter of eyepiece, $1\frac{1}{2}$", and the tube diameter is 1"; objective is 1.3". This glass works well in Griffin & Howe mounts of the proper diameter ring, and it should also be made with target style mounts with the knobs not sticking out too far, so that still finer adjustments could be possible. It is a first class glass and has many uses. Running shooting can be done with a 4 power glass of large field, and it has sufficient resolving power for accurate coyote, fox, woodchuck and squirrel shooting.

OTHER LYMAN TELESCOPES

For some years the Lyman company put out a cheap telescope in the $10.00 class called the Expert. It was all right for boys and for those who could not afford a good instrument. But some men who should have known better and could have afforded the best used it on real good rifles. It was discontinued in 1945, and the shooting world was none the poorer thereby. The same is true of the Lyman 438, which was a 4X telescope acquired in the deal with the Stevens company. It cost much more than the Expert, but was no more efficient. Happily, it also left the market in 1945.

The Lyman company manufactures one other very high grade telescope that should be mentioned. This is the all-weather Alaskan hunting telescope in $2\frac{1}{2}$X, which is regarded by many as the best hunting telescope that has ever been produced. It is 10½″ long, weighs without mounts 11 ounces, has internal adjustments for both elevation and windage, has a noncritical eye relief of approximately five inches and a field of view of 40′ at 100 yards. It has great light gathering ability, universal focus, and brilliant luminosity, which shows to best advantage when the visibility is poor, and is practically waterproof. It is at this time probably the most popular big game scope in all this country. Near the close of World War II a number of select Garand rifles were fitted with this scope in special Griffin & Howe mounts as sniper outfits. They saw but little, if any, actual service, but were pronounced by those competent to express an opinion to be the only real sniper rifles America had in that war. Regardless of all this, the Alaskan is not adapted to varmint shooting with .22 caliber rifles of any sort. It belongs to the big game field, and is out of place for shooting such as described in this book.

FECKER TELESCOPES

J. W. Fecker, who obtained his early training in Europe and also with Bausch & Lomb Optical Company, which is one of the two largest manufacturers of lenses in the United States, the other being the American Optical Company, was one of the most skilful, successful and highly regarded makers of telescopes in America. I roomed with "J. W." at various Sea Girt small bore tournaments, and in this way came to know and have a very high regard for this quiet unassuming gentleman and master craftsman. To the great loss of the rifle shooting fraternity, he passed away at the age of 54 in November, 1945. However, the business he founded in Pittsburgh, Pennsylvania was incorporated, and since his death the firm has carried on and has added new models to the line.

The Fecker telescopes are of two types, the target and the small game. The target type is put out in three styles, as follows: First, three-fourths inch objective in 4.5, six, eight and 10 powers, in 20″ length (or on order, this scope will be built in 18″ length); second, 1⅛″ (now 1¼″) objective in six, eight, 10 and 12.5 powers, in 22″ length; and third, 1½″ objective in eight, 10, 12.5 and 16 powers, in 25″ length. All of these are equipped with a central graduated focusing sleeve with lock rings, which move the erector lens instead of the objective lens as in the Lyman and Unertl. All have an eye relief of three inches, and a smaller field than other high grade telescopes of similar power, that of the 4.5X being 17′ at 100 yards, and that of the 6X being 12′ at 100 yards, as against 16′ for 6X Lyman, which has only a two inch eye relief.

These telescopes can generally be converted by the factory from smaller to larger objectives. Also a cell containing a higher power ocular can be obtained, thus enabling a shooter to have a scope say of regular 6X and a special 8X. These are not too satisfactory and the higher magnification should not be used on anything except rifles of low recoil on account of the short eye relief.

The small game telescopes are made in 2¼, three and four powers, 10″, 12″, 14″, 16″ or 18″ long overall, with diameter of objective 1¹⁄₁₆″, diameter of eye-piece three-fourths inch, eye relief two inches, and field of view 26′ at 100 yards. Telescopes of this type focus by loosening the rings and two set screws on the central collar, and sliding the collar and then tightening the screws and the rings at the ends of the collar—a very poor mechanism.

Fecker puts out two styles of mounts, both made of Duralumin alloy. The rear mounts are of the three-point suspension type, and the front mounts are identical, being made to take the Pope rib characteristic of these telescopes. In the cheaper mount, the ends of the thimbles bear against the scope tube, and they adjust by graduations and not by clicks. In the best grade mount, the thimbles bear against the scope tube through square straight edge bars, and the adjustments are by one-fourth or one-half minute clicks. This is one of the best target mounts ever designed, is made with precision, and gives sure movements. Both front and rear mounts are securely clamped to the bases by heavy transverse screws.

Fecker unquestionably was responsible for beginning the general marketing in the United States of high grade rifle telescopes with large objectives. For years his telescopes swept the boards at the Sea Girt and Camp Perry small bore rifle target matches. Then came along Lyman, Unertl and other high grade makers to garner some of the honors with their products of similar design.

A number of small bore riflemen use the regular Fecker 6X target telescope with 1⅛″ objective for small game hunting, especially woodchuck, coyote and gopher shooting. The Fecker glass with objective of this size takes in 2⅛ times as much light as does the three-fourths inch objective.

My friend and shooting companion Edgar F. Burkins, who has been over the years probably the most successful woodchuck hunter in Delaware, employed for many years a Fecker 1⅛″ objective target scope with three interchangeable eye-pieces in eight, 10 and 12 powers, but he nearly always used the eyepiece of lowest power. His specialty was head shots on chucks, and for such shooting he used either a .30–06 or a .22 Hornet, always the latter if loud reports were objectionable. With the latter he once ran 13 straight kills on chucks. Burkins, like a great many others, has specialized on Fecker scopes for both hunting and target shooting. He uses the single crosshair exclusively, and in either the medium or the finer sizes.

The author has used a Fecker 4X scope in Fecker click mounts for some years. It is a very fine hunting scope, and the light gathering qualities are most excellent. It has a very clear, distinct field, and the reticule is well made and sharp. However, he has never been able to do as well with flat top post reticules as with medium or coarse single crosshairs, probably due to his engineering training and experience, in which class of work crosshairs are used exclusively.

In the Spring of 1947, J. W. Fecker, Inc., announced the "Woodchucker," a new rifle telescope of 16″ length with 1.2″ objective, in four, 5.5 and seven powers in new dehorned micrometer mounts. This should be a most excellent scope for varmint shooting, but owing to its shortness the same difficulties in the spacing of the bases as were above mentioned in discussing the Lyman 5A will be encountered except in rifles like the Model 70 where the rear mount is on the receiver bridge.

Shortly after that the same company placed on the market a larger target telescope with 1⅝″ objective and in from 10 to 24 powers. In December, 1947, the Fecker company announced that it was putting on the market a new target scope with 1¼″ objective to replace the former 1⅛″ objective, with exclusive one-fourth minute micrometer mounts. By late summer of that year it was advertising that it was making rifle telescopes of from four to 30 power.

This completes the review of the Fecker line up to June, 1949. Throughout their history, Fecker telescopes have been fine glasses, and the workmanship thereon has always been of the highest order. An objection to their use in the hunting field has been the prominence of the adjustment thimbles on the rear mount, but these have been more theoretical than actual. With the coming of the new dehorned mounts, this objection vanishes.

J. W. Fecker and his company deserve a great deal of the credit for the accuracy developments of .22 caliber rifles and ammunition and for the improvement of rifle telescopes generally in this country.

UNERTL TELESCOPES

After World War I, John Unertl, a German-born and trained optical engineer, came to this country and entered the employ of J. W. Fecker. After a few years, he set up his own business in Pittsburgh. In appearance his telescopes bear a marked resemblance to those of Fecker, and are put out in the same two general types for target and small game. In addition he makes 3X and 4X hunting telescopes. His focusing adjustment on the target scope is on the front of the instrument after the manner of the Lymans.

In 1936 he put on the market a target type telescope made in six, eight and 10 powers, with 1″ clear objective, and an overall length of 21⅜″. This is of the same type as the Lyman Junior Targetspot, and since it has a larger objective is equal, if not superior, to that excellent instrument. In 6X or 8X it should be as fine a telescope as can be found for general varmint hunting with .22 caliber rifles.

He supplies telescopes of target type with 1¼″ objective and 24″ length in powers of eight through 12, all of which are fine glasses but, long and heavy for anything but the target range. In fact, the Unertl line of big target scopes now features instruments of various sizes of large objectives, the largest being two inches, and the powers run as high as 24X.

The Unertl small game scope is almost identical with the Fecker, but is made only in 18″ length. One notable difference among others is that it is supplied in 6X while the Fecker is not.

The standard Unertl mounts are quite similar to the Fecker, and are of the best quality. Originally the operating thimbles could not be locked, but this has now been changed and the set screw common to the Lyman and Fecker mounts has been supplied. They can be obtained separately.

Unertl announced in March, 1947 what he termed a new special varmint telescope in 6X and 8X with new dehorned mounts with one-fourth minute clicks to fit standard target type bases. A 10X scope in this model was added the following year. This new scope has a heavy tube of .875″ diameter, is 19.5″ long, with outside ocular diameter of 1.25″ and outside objective diameter of 1.5″, 16 foot field at 100 yards in 6X, and 2.8″ eye relief. The dehorned mounts have one-fourth minute click adjustments for both elevation and windage. Optically this scope is wellnigh perfect, and for rest shooting on varmints should be all that can be asked. It would seem too heavy for general field use.

The general high quality of Unertl scopes, and particularly the clearness and sharpness of the lenses and the lack of color fringe place them in the very front rank, and in the opinion of some render them even better than the Lyman and Fecker lines. The mounts of all three are graduated much the same although there are minor differences, and the scopes themselves are of the same general size and style. Choice among the three lines is a matter of personal taste, as all three are definitely quality telescopes. Nearly all Unertl telescopes have 2¼″ eye relief.

In recent months John Unertl has put out three new scopes. The first is the Falcon, of 2¾ power; as the power is low, the field of view at 100 yards is quite large taking in 37½'. Eye relief is long, being 4⅓", fine for hard kicking rifles or when your scope happened to be mounted a bit too far forward, or too far to the rear, to exactly suit your eyes—and your neck length; you can not stretch that too much and live, and you cannot shrink it. The Falcon weighs 7½ ounces without mounts, the tube diameter is 1" and the eyepiece 1.4".

The Unertl Hawk, a 4X hunting scope, but claimed by one reviewer to be 3 power, has a 29-foot field of view at 100 yards; diameter of tube is 1" and of the objective (outside diameter) is 1.4"; weight is 8 ounces and tube length 11.56". This glass greatly resembles the Lyman Challenger and the Hensoldt Dialytan 4X, except the field is 2' wider at 100 yards, the scope weighs less due to the use of a Duralumin or other very light weight alloy tube instead of steel, which has a higher specific gravity. These light-weight tubes are strong but they do not always take as pleasing or as lasting an outside finish.

The Unertl Condor is a 6 power hunting scope of somewhat greater over-all size than the others just mentioned. Why John should have named this after the South American vulture is unknown, but there also is a South American gold coin of the same name, and also an airplane so he may have had one of these in mind. Because of the higher power, the field of view is reduced to 16½' at 100 yards, but the diameter of the tube remains the same; at 1" the outside diameter of the objective is the same, 1.4"; the weight is only 9 ounces, and the length is 13¼".

OTHER TARGET TYPE TELESCOPES

High grade target type telescopes similar in appearance to those already discussed are put out by several other American makers.

In March, 1947, the Edwards Sight and Optical Company of Union City, Indiana, announced its fine Model V scope for varmint rifles in six, eight and 10 powers. This is 15" long overall, and has one inch ocular, with long eye relief and 1¼" objective, and is equipped with target type dehorned three point suspension mounts. This should be the last word in a varmint scope for a rifle of the Model 70 type where the rear base can be put on the receiver bridge.

The following July, R. A. Litschert, of Winchester, Indiana, advertised his "Targeteer" line, with four different objectives in the same general style. These appear to be quite similar to the Lyman "Targetspot" line but are shorter. The smallest, with seven-eighths inch objective, is only 18" long. They are equipped with target type

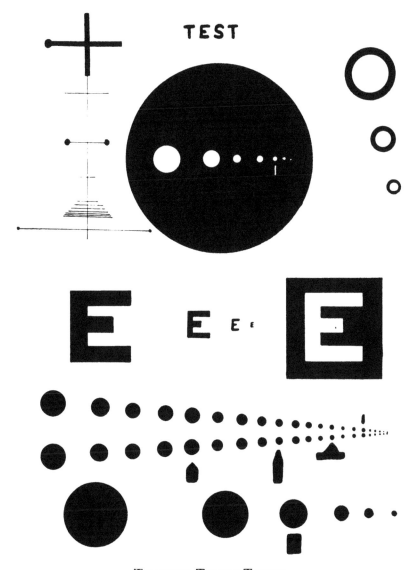

TELESCOPE TESTING TARGET

Above shows a most suitable test sheet for comparing different rifle telescopes and for the accurate focusing of same.

This reproduction is about half the size to which the actual target should be made. Make two of them and keep one lying on the testing bench for ready comparison with what you think you see through the scope.

click mounts both in regular and dehorned styles. The smallest of these should be ideal for varmint hunting. It is just about the right weight and length.

Litschert announced in February, 1948, a new "Spotshot" 1¼″ objective target and vermin scope 10X and 12X. This is a cheaper instrument, but is equipped with the same one fourth minute click mounts. Its power is too high for a hunting rifle. In fact, Litschert makes target scopes up to 24 power in the very highest grade, as well as a full line in lower grade. He is more widely known, however, for his attachments for increasing the power of hunting type telescopes.

WEAVER TELESCOPES

For some years the Weaver Model 330, made by W. R. Weaver Company, of El Paso, Texas, was probably the best selection on the American market for a hunting scope on a light six pound side ejecting repeater in .22 long rifle caliber. The power was only 2½, the field was 35′ at 100 yards, and the lenses were clear and bright to the very edge. So clear was this glass that in using it you appeared to be looking out of a window surrounded by a thin round rim.

The other high grade telescope produced by Weaver prior to World War II was the Model 440 in about 3½X. It was quite similar to the Model 330, but inferior to it optically. It, however, is an excellent scope on a .22 caliber rim fire rifle.

The best low priced model put out by Weaver was the 29S, in 3X, which, notwithstanding the fact that it did not have the corrected achromatic lenses of the two models above mentioned was a very good glass. In the opinion of many it was the best scope of its class sold in this country.

In World War II a number of two groove barrel Springfield rifles manufactured by Remington were equipped with Model 330 scopes in Redfield mounts and issued as snipers' rifles. They proved unsatisfactory for many reasons. The soldiers who were to fire them were not sufficiently trained to use and care for such outfits, and the rifles were inaccurate. The telescope proved too fragile for hard usage and was not waterproof, and the mount was in the way for clip loading. The army gunsmiths who worked on these outfits in the field declared that water always poured out of the telescopes when they were brought in for repairs. So the Model 330, while satisfactory in the hunting field, could not stand the gaff of modern warfare.

Shortly after World War II, Bill Weaver decided to scrap his entire line of telescopes and to substitute therefor entirely new models in every grade and type. He announced in June, 1948 that this conversion had been completed. The models now being currently manufactured are: K1, K2.5, K4, K6, J2.5, J4, J6, G4, G6. The figure in each instance indicates the power of the scope. The maker states that the J2.5 replaces the old Model 330, but that it is a better all-around instrument. He likewise states that the J4 takes the place of the old Model 440, but with its larger objective is far superior to that model. The J6 is a new scope, which was put out to meet a demand for a six power glass in small game shooting.

The G series are the lowest price glasses now made by the Weaver Company and are of the same class practically as the old 29S.

The K series are all new telescopes and differ radically from anything previously put out by their maker. These are all instruments of the very highest quality, and are in the class of the best telescopes manufactured in this country. The lenses are all bright and clear, free from color fringe, and the images are sharp and distinct. For hunting big game the 2½ power is to be preferred, but the four power is perhaps best on all small game rifles through the Hornet class. The six power will be preferred for long range varmint shooting. In fact, for anyone who likes a short compact telescope in sturdy smooth-lined mounts, nothing better can be obtained.

While making very fine telescopes, the Weaver Company has not to this date put out any mount worthy of a place on a good rifle. Fortunately, however, we have quite a number of excellent mounts that are adapted to these telescopes. Among others may be mentioned the various bracket types, like the Griffin & Howe, and the bridge type like the Mashburn, the Redfield, Jr., and the Stith. A specially good mount for these telescopes is the Hill, the advantage being that regular type bases can be used with it. In fact, the good mounts are legion, and further attempt to list them will not be made.

The latest to the Weaver line is a new rifle and shotgun telescope of IX, or *no* magnifying power. The author received one, which sells for about $35.00 at this writing, in the middle of June, 1949. Quite a few years ago, Weaver put out an IX scope which was used a good deal on shotguns by Tackhole Lee. Also, he used it successfully for trap shooting in competitions. The old model has been retired and the greatly improved new model is now available.

While this scope is intended primarily for use on shotguns, including 12 gauge guns, and for high power rifles, yet due to its very long eye relief it could likely be used without much chance of accident on even .300 and .375 Magnums, provided the hunter did not get too excited or slip at the moment of firing, and have his gun butt recoil back either above his shoulder or through the opening at the armpit, beneath the arm and shoulder. This has occurred oftener than you might think. The wife of a now deceased Gun Editor once lost her right eye when using a relatively light recoil rifle in British Columbia, when she slipped on a rock while firing at mountain game and a tang peep sight whacked her in the right eye when the rifle fired. There was of course *no* eye relief in that instance.

This K-I Weaver is 9½″ long; has a 1″ very heavy steel tube; the eyepiece is 1.24″ in outside diameter. The Weaver mounts are light, steel, ring type mounts, for either side mounting or top-of-barrel and receiver mounting, or usually top-of-receiver mounting, as desired. Nos. 6 and 7 mount bases for side mounting, came with the scope—the No. 7 being the wider—and there are plenty of screw holes in both. Scope and mounts are blued and oddly enough, probably due to lack of magnification, you can see clearly and sharply through *either* end of the scope. This may cause some parties to put the scope on the rifle or shotgun hind end first, because when they pick up the scope, they of course see clearly through the first end they look through. The side mounts should be placed on the *left* side of the gun, the graduations on top, and right side and the large *eyepiece to the rear*.

Many aging and aged men, and also many chaps in their 20s, are abnormally nervous and cannot hold a scope sighted rifle to the shoulder with only normal movements due to heart action, breathing and nervous reactions. The hands of some men, in fact of *many* men, tremble abnormally. As the *motion* which is seen when aiming with a rifle telescope is always magnified by the power of the telescope—a 4X scope magnifying the actual movement—the movements of the hands and body, or the movement of the game itself, by four, and a 6X scope by 6—this is why 8X, 10X and 12X scopes are very difficult for most men to use well in the field. Thus we have a situation in which the very trembly and nervous man can use *only* the IX or the 2X to 3X scopes with certainty. Not only for big game, but for woodchucks, squirrels, and crows, the elderly man who is farsighted and who has correctly fitted eyeglasses, and can see like nobody's business at long range but who cannot read a telephone book with his distance glasses, or no eyeglasses, will find even the IX scope possibly of material help to him.

He can hold the K-I scope sighted rifle just as steadily as most men with normal nerve control, can hold a rifle sighted with a 6X to 10X scope, insofar as *apparent* jump in the scope is concerned.

Another case where the K-I would come in good is when gray squirrels or red squirrels are feeding on densely leaved beechnut trees, and while every other tree in the woods, maples, oaks, hickories either have the leaves all on the ground, or they are turned light yellows, reds and browns by frost, the beeches will still have dense, dark green leaves on the whole tree, thick as hair on a dog, and impenetrable to sight if the light is poor, as in early morning or late evening. In September and October this condition is abnormally aggravating because every gray squirrel around will be feeding on the beechnuts until the hickorynuts and sweet acorns are ripened. Green hognut hickorynuts are abnormally bitter and the squirrels will not feed on them extensively until they are well ripened *if* beechnuts are available. These may grow in wet ground, scattered here and there in the woods, or they may grow on tops of small knolls in the woods. Later in the fall the beechnut trees often become very bare and *then* you can see your squirrels. Before that time, you sit for a half an hour, or even an hour or two, on dark days, see the leaves shake where they are feeding, or jump, from one branch to another, see the squirrel move for a foot or two around the trunk, or when coming down or going up the tree, but try to get aim at it with a rifle—just *try!* A man who is slow in his reactions and has poor eyesight, and who also trembles, will be badly out of luck, until the squirrel moves over into a more open and lighter colored locality or a bare tree. If he has a high power scope or no sights but poorly defined iron sights, especially peep sights with too small an aperture he will likely get no shooting at all, because the game will disappear again before he takes aim and lets off the shot.

The K-I scope has friction lock adjustments. Each graduation changes adjustment ½″ for each 10 yards—not for each 100 yards but for each 10 yards. This is for shotguns, thus, one graduation equals 1″ at a 20-yard range; 2″ at 40 yards; 3″ at 60 yards; 5″ at 100 yards. You can get mounts having closer change graduations for rifle work, if you want them.

Most of these scopes come with coarse single crosshairs, and a rather large round dot, like a big Lee Dot, at the crosshair intersection. They will also be made with only coarse single crosshairs and with square block, which latter can be fitted special—maybe by Lee, if by no one else.

In friction lock Weaver adjustments, adjusting screws are turned with a coin or screw driver. Do not disturb the knurled lock nuts to make adjustments and turn only the screws which are *friction tight.* If the screws turn too freely use pliers to tighten the lock nuts to increase friction.

When using click adjustments the screws are turned with the fingers and are fitted with graduated discs. After sighting in, the discs can be set at zero by loosening the small screw in the center of the disc. Settings for long range can be marked on the disc.

The *elevation screw* is at the top of the scope. When turned in the direction marked by the arrow, with the word UP the point of impact of bullet strike is *raised*—and vice versa.

The *windage screw* is on the right side. When turned in the direction of the arrow, with the letter L the point of impact of bullet strike is moved to the left—and vice versa.

As the slightest movement of scope or mounts will cause the gun or rifle to shoot to a different point of impact, everything must be tight—lens cells, base screws, scope clamping screws, turret screws, or mount *base* screws on other target types of scopes, other than the Weaver—so turn screws tightly and keep them tight.

All Weaver scope and base screws are hardened, turn them as tight as you can with a screw driver having a medium large handle and a well-fitting hardened blade. If necessary grind the blade to fit the screw heads—do *not* try to open the screw slots to fit the existing blade.

OTHER TELESCOPES

The No. 1 Malcolm telescope made by Malcolm Telescope Company, of Auburn, New York, was an exceptionally good sight, especially when mounted in the Malcolm heavy Mann V type mounts. These mounts hold a scope rigidly to the same degree day after day, year after year, better than any other scope mounts I have ever used. My Winchester 54 Hornet was fitted with a Malcolm 3¾X No. 1 scope in these mounts, and was most certain to kill its game on the first shot of any rifle I ever owned.

I have a friend who uses on a Hornet rifle a similar Malcolm 5X scope in Lyman one-fourth minute mounts. His principal game is woodchucks, and the field of the glass is particularly good. In fact I have heard similar reports on these Malcolm telescopes during the past 30 years.

Recently this company sold its business to P. O. Ackley Company, of Trinidad, Colorado, and I do not know what the plans of the purchaser are as to continuing the production of these excellent telescopes.

HUNTING TYPE TELESCOPES

Up to World War II, aside from the Lyman Alaskan, the Weavers, the special Unertl, and the Noske, most of the hunting type telescopes used in this country were of foreign make. Zeiss, Hensoldt, Goerz, Kahles and Ajack were perhaps the best known.

The big Zeiss Zielvier was perhaps the finest four power telescope that has ever been produced. Its center tube was 26.5 mm. in diameter, and it weighed 13¾ ounces without mounts. A feather-weight model was also produced.

The Zielklein in 2¼ power was made by the same company. It had a length of 10⅛", weighed eight ounces, and had a 34½ foot field at 100 yards. It was widely ballyhooed in this country by one gun editor for big game shooting, but in my opinion was vastly overrated. I have examined possibly 20 of them, and comparatively few of the number were really good glasses. Other heavy and high powered glasses were also put out by Zeiss, some of them of variable power.

Hensoldt put out two excellent small telescopes of 2¾ power, and also two excellent four power telescopes. The heavier of these, called the Dialytan, was of the same grade as the Zeiss Zielvier.

The war interfered materially with the production of these foreign telescopes, and since its close the demand for such instruments has been supplied by American makers. In fact, these makers seem to have vied with each other in putting on the market practically as many hunting type telescopes as the target type makers have of the high power target models. In addition to the new Weavers, the Lyman Alaskan and the Unertl 4X Hawk, we have five special models from 2½ power to six power made by Maxwell Smith Company, of Los Angeles; two models, one 2½X and the other 4X, by Rudolph Noske, of Santo Carlos, California; a 2½ power by Norman Ford Company, of Tyler, Texas; a 2¼ power by Leupold & Stevens Instruments, of Portland, Oregon; and the Eagle 4X by R. A. Litschert. In addition, Weaver makes several special models for Stith, the mount manufacturer of San Antonio, Texas. Maxwell Smith Company has recently added to its force a number of men who were trained in the Zeiss and Hensoldt factories in Europe, hence it has the unusual advantage of having a personnel of very highly trained technical men.

As a rule, these hunting type telescopes except in the highest powers are not to be recommended for use on anything but big game rifles.

Hensoldt Dialytan

This 4 power hunting scope is very similar to the Lyman Challenger in power, in field of view and in eye relief, which is 4"; the objective lens gives a 0.1" larger unobstructed width; eyepiece and tube are about the same diameter as the Lyman 4X and the Hensoldt is about ½" shorter over-all. The two ends are abrupt in outline and have parallel sides to the tube and taper down more sharply to the body of the scope than does the Challenger. Optically both are much the same.

THE SWISS WILD SCOPE

The Swiss Wild—a fine 4X glass, has quite a short outside tube, this being only 10¼″ over-all; the eyepiece has a quite large outside diameter of 1.6″; and the tube diameter is a trifle over 1″; eye relief is about 4″. The amount it can be moved forward and backward in the mount rings is very limited due to the shortness of the scope barrel, the presence of a focusing ring which is about 40% of the distance from the rear to the front end, and thus the mounts and mount bases must be placed on your rifle where they exactly fit your physique and eye relief. Therefore, it is not a suitable scope for using on different rifles of varying stock length, but as a scope for use on one rifle, and when exactly mounted to suit you, it is very satisfactory as a big game hunting scope and for coyotes, chucks, foxes, deer, antelope, remembering in this regard, the limitations of exact sight setting of the average hunting scope mount.

THE LEUPOLD SCOPE

The Leupold combination rifle telescope and mount, for high power bolt action rifles, made with a lifetime service guarantee by Leupold & Stevens, of Portland, Oregon, is a $60.00 combination at this writing.

The Leupold Pioneer scope is factory sealed with nitrogen, and thus is claimed to do away with the possibility or the likelihood of condensation of moisture and fogging due to changes in altitude or temperatures; also to changes of moisture in the air, which with some scopes can condense on the inside of the tube and onto the lenses. On the outside of the lenses, front and rear, such condensation of moisture can be wiped off, provided you have soft tissue or a very soft handkerchief with which to do this, but when inside the scope tube your day is spoiled.

The Leupold scope weighs only 4½ ounces, due to the use of a lightweight tube and the scope mounts are made of Beryllium copper—an alloy which is used today for many light and very tough metal fishing rods. The light, tough tube is quite a weight saver, although but two or three ounces at most, is probably not quiet as important, except for mountain climbing, as many other things about your equipment. For instance, almost all hunters wear footwear which is too heavy, and too rugged, and excessive weight on the feet is felt far more before the day is done, than a couple of ounces in a rifle scope. Too, many hunters weigh themselves down with five times the ammunition they are likely to shoot that day, a heavy belt axe, a heavy hunting knife instead of a light one, a pistol or revolver, which they rarely need and which is not as effective as a reduced load in the rifle, so that a slight weight reduction is not as important as complete 100% moisture sealing of the scope tube, which *is* highly important.

The Leupold mount is adaptable to very low mounting on the rifle, especially on most bolt actions having a low or turned down bolt handle. A feature of this scope is ½ minute built-in micrometer adjustments in the mount.

Once sighted in, it is claimed adjustments stay put and the scope was built to last a lifetime. It is made and sold by Leupold & Stevens Instruments, 4445 N. E. Glisan Street, Portland, Oregon. The scope tube is only 10″ long and you will want to mount that one carefully, too, as to exact position on the rifle; tube is ⅞″ in diameter; magnification is 2½X and all lenses are hard-coated. Incidentally, in tests the writer has made himself, sighting at freshly painted houses of different colors, in a village one third of a mile off, from the West windows of his house, and making the test on a nice, bright, sunny day, houses which were painted a deep *brown*, showed up better with rifle scopes and spotting scopes which had lenses which were *not* coated. Other colors showed up better with the coated lenses. Much game is a deep brown or reddish-brown or gray or gray brown. You are sighting on the game, not the background.

Field of view at 100 yards is about 35′ in diameter; eye relief just under 4″; power 2½. It is a scope which you would use where you might prefer a reconnaissance transit, due to its small size and light weight—in other words, in high altitudes where the ground or rock is rough, the climbing tough, and every piece of equipment must be super-light or—shed.

Both scope and its mounts are among the lightest on the market, also, among the best of the type.

RETICULES

The most important feature of a rifle telescope outside of the mounts is the aiming device or reticule. My own preference, at least until recent years, has been the standard coarse crosshairs. Some, however, prefer the flat top post or the picket post with a horizontal hair. For those who like them, this may be all right in hunting type telescopes, but are not nearly as good as crosshairs for use in varmint hunting.

The only real improvement in reticules I have found is the Lee Black Dot placed at the intersection of the crosshairs. This is installed by T. K. Lee in his shop in Birmingham, Alabama. He has been an important figure in the sport of .22 caliber rifle shooting since about 1908. Between that date and 1918 he excited considerable interest nationally in the matter of long runs and consecutive possibles, both in outdoor and indoor matches.

Only two styles of the Lee Dots will be here considered. The most useful is the No. 1, which is a perfectly round coal black dot placed exactly at the intersection of the horizontal and vertical hairs, and hence in the middle of the telescope field. The No. 2 is the same as the No. 1, but with an additional smaller black dot on the vertical hair placed below the middle dot so as to give the approximate elevation for a distant shot at some predetermined range. The center dots are furnished in various sizes to cover so many inches per 100 yards of range. Usually the No. 1 is sufficient for all purposes, but it might be well to have a No. 2 installed in a telescope that is to be used on a long range rifle.

In hunting telescopes or other telescopes of low power for use on .22 rim fire rifles, a dot covering two inches at 100 yards will probably be best, but on a long range rifle a dot covering $\frac{3}{4}''$ to $1''$ at 100 yards is preferable.

The Lee Dot is so black that it can be seen distinctly against the plumage of a crow or a buzzard or against a black squirrel, and is adapted to telescopes of many makes, sizes and powers. It is a definite help in hunting, and one chap claims that he killed 45 coyotes with 48 shots out of a rifle sighted with a scope fitted with this dot.

Several concerns are now putting in similar dots, but to date none better have been installed than those by Lee himself, and you can be sure of a proper job if the installation is entrusted to him.

COATED LENSES FOR RIFLE TELESCOPES

One of the real outstanding achievements of World War II was the successful development of the coating of lenses used in all optical instruments. Long before that time, it had been known as a scientific fact that the treating of the surface of a lens with a fluoride salt reduced the surface reflection of light. During the war a process of coating lenses with magnesium fluoride, a crystalline powder which resembles common salt, was perfected. A microscopically-thin film of this magnesium fluoride is deposited on the lens by an electrical process, and as a result the amount of light transmitted to the eye by such lens is increased to a very large extent. This coating causes telescopes, binoculars and similar instruments equipped with such lenses to give much sharper and clearer images. All telescopes produced in recent years have this improvement, and the older instruments of fine quality can be improved by having their lenses treated in the same manner by firms that specialize in this technical work. There is no comparison between the effectiveness of a telescope with coated lenses and one without them.

SPECIAL ADJUSTMENTS

Two American makers, R. A. Litschert and Edwards Sight & Optical Company, feature special adjustments to be installed on the objective ends of the lower power hunting telescopes, and thereby raise them to six or eight power. These are very practical, and by the use of such an adjustment a rifleman can have the advantage of a 2½ power telescope, such as the Weaver K2.5, for big game hunting and a six power in the same instrument for varmint shooting.

THE USEFULNESS OF A TELESCOPE SIGHT

The mounting of telescope sights on rifles, or of scope mount bases on the rifle barrel or receiver, or receiver and barrel, should be entrusted only to the maker of the telescope, or to some custom gunsmith fully experienced in such work. Even so, the job should not be accepted and paid for if the mount bases having flat tops are not put on level. If even one of the screws is the least bit loose and you can not tighten it so that it will lock the base to the rifle and the mount to the base with perfect rigidity, the rifle will be erratic in its shooting and the job should be rejected. Your mounts and mount bases are the gun carriage locking and aiming devices of your rifle, and unless they are rigidly and securely attached and in the proper place, with the eye relief of the scope exactly right for your eyes, satisfaction will not be complete and really good shooting will not be possible. It is not probable that your scope will be put on other than correctly by a custom gunsmith, but some terrible jobs of scope sight base fitting have been turned out on unsuspecting customers, even by large arms companies. I have received one or two such, and you should be on guard for such occurrences.

All scopes should be adjusted for parallax and for focus of the eyepiece. The maker always provides instructions with his scope and if these have been lost write the maker for a new set of instructions. Read all your instructions a couple of times, before trying to put a rifle telescope on a rifle, or before trying to tighten the bases or change the focus of the scope. Do not take a rifle telescope apart and try to clean the lenses yourself. You will very likely tear or break the crosshairs—let this wait for a man with experience.

A rifle telescope is a tremendous help to anyone with failing or faulty vision and will add years to the shooting life of such persons.

To anyone, even with 20–20 vision, a good rifle telescope is a *great* help in small game shooting, especially when the game is in cover and you are more in the open.

One well-known chuck shooter claims he uses a very large, heavy, target type rifle telescope of 20X for shooting woodchucks, and that he shoots them offhand at 200 yards with this outfit, and that he does this right along. Others have objected to such statement most violently.

Most of us must be much more conservative, both in the weight of the rifle, telescope, and ammunition, and in the power of the telescope. You must of course, be able to *see* the game and to have sufficient resolving power to see its details, to be able to aim at a *vital* spot. On the other hand, when you want to be able to shoot with success at *moving* game you need a wide field and not too much apparent movement in the field of the telescope. The happy medium is usually between the two extremes.

In this chapter I have discussed principally the *latest* dope in scopes. No one type, power, weight, or size of rifle telescope will suit everyone equally well or be equally useful for shooting at game of different sizes, colors and types, under varying shooting conditions. One day is dark, another is light and bright; one week visability is high, next week you can scarcely see at all in the woods, with the same telescope; the third week the sun is again out bright and hot.

Some days your vision is excellent and at other times, due to eyestrain, overwork, exhaustion, or maybe worry, or probably because your glasses do not suit you exactly, under such conditions, you could not see to hit the fat end of an elephant with a double barrel shotgun—not even with a K-I scope on it, although the K-I will likely be found more adapted to slide-action, repeating shotguns.

I have never met but one man, who really *tried* hard to learn to use a rifle telescope, who was habitually unsuccessful and who simply could *not* learn to shoot a scope sighted rifle as well as an iron sighted rifle.

The author has used telescopes on transits, wye-levels, theodolites, and on rifles, for 45 to 50 years or more. So long as the supports which hold that scope are rigid, so long as the lenses are tight in their cells, are not fogged by rain, fog or dampness, and the various relationships between lenses, cells, and tube are correct, and as long as the shooter is in sufficiently good physical shape so that he can *see* things where nature placed them; so long as he can read English, remember a portion of what he reads, and has sufficient intelligence to feed himself and has sufficient nerve control to drink a cup of coffee, he ought to be able to quickly learn how to shoot a scope sighted rifle in the hunting field. Only by personal experience will the reader discover what a great help to almost everyone the high grade rifle telescope can become.

A rifle telescope, contrary to popular opinion among those who do not know better, does not "bring the game up closer," does not give you "an unfair advantage," and does not make the shooting of small game or varmints as are ordinarily found in the wilds a simple matter. But it does enable many to shoot a rifle with real accuracy for the first time, and a good outfit of this sort will enable you to get everything out of your rifle and ammunition they will produce. It will soon prove whether there is ground for the supposition that you are a rifleman. It gives many men past the age of 42 another 20 to 30 years, or more, of satisfactory and accurate rifle shooting. What better investment could you make of less than $100.00?

That is the real value of a good rifle telescope sight, properly mounted. It gives you perfect vision of the object at which aim is taken and with sufficient magnification of details to permit a perfect delivery of each shot fired. The rest is up to you—make the best of it!

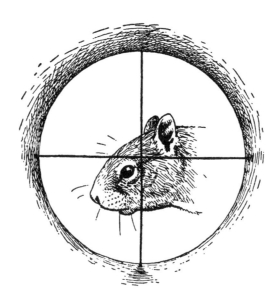

CHAPTER 26

Elevation Readings for the .22 Long Rifle Cartridge—50 to 300 Yards

ONE OF THE MOST DIFFICULT THINGS FOR MANY RIFLEMEN TO DO, especially for riflemen of little experience, or those who have never had extensive match shooting experience on measured rifle ranges, is to know where to set their sights for a long range shot.

This is not merely an academic problem; nor is it just a lesson in physics and ballistics. It is a very real everyday determination with which they are faced every time they go hunting, or want to do a little long range target shooting at small stones in a plowed field, on a hillside, along a creek where there is a convenient backstop, or on a target range.

Suppose you are sitting out there somewhere watching a couple of groundhogs or woodchucks, maybe a colony of prairie dogs, or you may be in the woods where squirrels come out to feed and play and crows and hawks come along and sit on the top of an old snag, and the crows will nearly always caw and annoy you. You have a rifle which is sighted for 25, 50, 75 or 100 yards, if sighted at all. How much are you going to raise the sights for each distance, and have you definite grounds for the belief that the sighting you will try will be the correct one? In other words, is there reason to assume that if you do raise your rear sight or move the scope mounts for a 200-yard shot, that you will be more likely to score a kill, than if you had left the sights alone and made a good guess (On the quiet this should read, a careful *approximation*. Sounds more highbrow, like a graduate of M.I.T. or the Yale Scientific School would phrase it).

Raising the sights may help, but if you raise them an incorrect amount you will actually be more certain to miss than if you left them alone and held over—sometimes you *will* guess right, that way. You may have remembered the midrange trajectory height over 200 yards of the .22 cartridge you are about to shoot, and you may have recalled from having been told a number of times that the total drop of the bullet is four times its midrange trajectory height. So, assuming your rifle is sighted for zero range, which it seldom is, when firing at long range without raising the sights, hold over the target just four times the midrange trajectory height, minus the sighting rise to 50 yards. If this midrange height is 12″, your hold over will be 48″—minus that small correction. This will unfortunately, sound too much like a "by gosh and by guess" correction to those with technical training, so we should have a more accurate set of sight readings to use in the field.

About the year 1920, one of the most active, likeable, and successful shooters in the small bore target game was Robert V. R. Reynolds of the National Capital Rifle Club of Washington, D. C. He shot with the best of them at both Camp Perry and at Sea Girt, and he has been following the small bore game closely ever since. R. V. concluded he would do another useful favor, so he conferred with his old club mate, R. H. McGarity, one of the best known match shots attending Sea Girt Tournaments and between them they compiled a table to show the differences in sight readings when changing from one range to another. They included dope from different riflemen, on different rifle ranges, firing in different barometric and temperature conditions, and to prove that this matter of raising the rear sight for a long shot with a .22 does include a very large number of imponderables and variables.

Differences in Elevation Required by Different Riflemen

.22 Long Rifle Hi-Speed Ammunition
(*Graduations in ½ Minutes*)

Yards	The Gun Handbook	R. V. Reynolds (*Kleanbore*)	R. H. McGarity (*Kleanbore Match*)
50–100 yards	11.6	12	11
100–150	13.4	13	12
150–200	14.8	16	16
200–250	16.0	19	22
250–300	17.4	23	26
Rise 50–300 yds.	73.2	83	87
50–200	39.8	41	39
200–300	33.4	42	48

In examining and using this table, remember that these two men were among the most expert in the game, for many years of competition, and today could hit a woodchuck in the head, using a .22 high velocity rifle, at 100 or 200 yards, or farther, with sufficient consistency to make the matter not merely a factor of luck.

Reynolds was using a Savage 23AA with 23" barrel, which is standard for that rifle, fitted with Fecker telescopic sight bases or blocks, situated at 7.2" apart, (so as to give ½-minute changes of impact, with each raise or lowering of one small graduation on the scope mount barrel). The telescope sight was a Winchester 5A. The range on which Mr. Reynolds fired was well protected from the wind, but the 300-yard firing point was on a hill, perhaps 40" above the general level. This should have cut down the elevation a bit.

McGarity was using his old Sea Girt match rifle, a Model 52 Winchester with scope mount bases set at the factory, presumably 7.2" apart, his sight likely was a Fecker; both men shot prone.

One thing Reynolds wished to bring out here was that both he and McGarity required considerably more elevation at ranges beyond 200 yards than given in the published table. Another thing that showed up was that at Sea Girt the elevations required were greater than on many inland ranges. This bears out the experiences of the author to a T, that at sea level and with sea level atmospheric conditions, one does at times require materially higher elevations than inland. On the other hand, the Sea Girt range is hotter, requiring less elevation because of its temperature. However, the elevations on a range near Washington D. C. would not likely be very far above tidewater.

This should drive home to the shooter one fact, that tables of elevations can only be the *starting point* for your calculations, just as a table of loads for a .22 wildcat caliber can only be a starting point for the determination of the loads *you* will use in *your* rifle.

REFERENCE TABLES FOR RIFLEMEN WHO ARE USING .22 LONG RIFLE FITTED WITH TELESCOPIC SIGHT THE BLOCKS OR BASES FOR WHICH ARE PLACED 6" BETWEEN CENTERS.

The following are sight readings and actual elevation differences expressed in one half minutes of angle on the graduated micrometer thimble of a 5A scope, but give greater deflections per division due to having been 6" instead of 7.2" between centers. This 6" length with a short scope is better for hunting, or fits men built wide across the chest and shoulders and with short, heavy neck. In such instance, 7.2" inter-base distance places the ocular lens too far from the eye, unless the glass is a long barrel Lyman, Unertl or Fecker target scope.

Table of Sight Raises—Sea Girt Range—6″ Inter-Mount Distance

50 yards–100 yds.	14 graduations	Kleanbore
50–100	13–14½ "	Different lots Palma
100–150	19 "	Kleanbore
100–200	33–36 "	Kleanbore
50–200	52–53 "	Kleanbore

Shooting at Sea Girt from June 30 to late September. Range not protected from sun or wind. Usually quite windy from 9 A.M. to 4 P.M. Fine light on target in late evening. Most morning shooting, in fog and mist. Sun quite bright and glaring on sunny days. Light dull on rainy days.

Rifle—Same Winchester-Hoffman Model 52, Standard Weight Barrel Fitted with 5-A Winchester Scope and mounts. Bases 6″ between centers.

Shot by C. S. Landis on Todd's Cut Range, Wilmington, Delaware. Range open and exposed, normally sunny. Range 250 yards. Firing toward north.

Range	Elevation Readings	Windage	Ammunition
50 yards	104–105	96	Kleanbore
		Score	
100 yards	118	96 (99–97–100)	"
150 yards	131	97 (75–75–25 Vs)	"
175 yards	142 Smoke and low temp. necessitates greater elevation reading	87 (50 × 50.) Temp. 50°, strong 8 o'clock wind. Very smoky)	Palma Match
175	140	97	Kleanbore
200	150	97	Kleanbore
250	170	93 Temp. 80° F.	Kleanbore (S.G. Lot)
250	172	91	Red Box Palma Match
250	179	86 (Five straight 5s on 200 yard target at 250 yards—PUO7)	Palma Match

BACK IN THE GOOD OLD DAYS

Bob Cat and Coyote Skins from Wyoming. Note the scope sighted .22 Krag High Velocity rifle shown near centre of picture.

Photo by Dalrymple

RIFLE, WINCHESTER 52 WITH HEAVY HOFFMAN SPORTER-TARGET STOCK, 5A WINCHESTER SCOPE, SHOOTING BY C. S. LANDIS ON SEA GIRT, N. J. RIFLE RANGE

Range	Elevation Readings	Windage Reading	Ammunition
50 yards	104–105 Once 108½	96	Kleanbore
50 "	107½	96	PUO7 Palma
50 "	106–108	96	Prec. 200
100 yards	118	97	Kleanbore
100 "	121	94	PUO7 Palma Match
100 "	120 Strong windage	102	Pink Box Palma
200 yards	150	104	Kleanbore
200 yards	150	102	Palma Match
200 "	156 This had higher zero at 50 yards	97	Winchester Prec. 200.

TABLE OF RANGE CORRECTIONS

Bases 6" apart. *Todd's Cut Range—Firing Points higher than butts.*

50 to 100 yards	Raise 13 divisions	Kleanbore
100 to 150 yards	" 13 "	"
150 to 175 yards	" 9 "	"
175 to 200 yards	" 10 "	"
200 to 250 yards	" 20 to 22 divisions	"
50 to 200 yards	Raise 45 divisions	"
50 to 250 yards	" 67 "	"
		Palma Match
50 to 250 yards	" 73 "	(PUO7)

With 6" interbase distance, three complete turns of the rear mount graduated thimble will raise elevation from 50 yards to approximately 270 yards. This is equal to 75 divisions. This assumes you make three complete turns from the 50 yards zero. If the zero is 104 and you raise the elevation three turns, your new reading is 179, at which point due to wind out at the target, you may also require a good increase in the windage reading. Be sure it is in the right direction. This is given merely to show you how you make a very large correction for a very long range shot.

Same Winchester-Hoffman 52 rifle

Centreville, Delaware, New Range. Firing south west in late evening. Range dark, calm, poor light. Sun too bright to shoot against in mid-afternoon.

50 yards zero when firing North East on same grounds.

50—	104–105	96
200 yards.	156	92 to
	156	102—up to 20 mile wind.

Elevation rise, 50 to 200 yards, shooting against light, 50, 51 to 52 graduations, but high zero sometimes and greater rise on dark evenings.

Centreville, Delaware, old 200-yard Range. Firing North, up shallow hollow, wind protection from North West, North, and East. No shade. Best 200-yard range author ever shot on.

Elevation Readings	Windage	Score	Ammunition
149	94½	(50–49–49)	Kleanbore
150	96	90° temp.	"
150	94	(249 × 250—with 37	"
		Vs. Author never heard of a better 200-yd. score in Vs, up to that time.) Also shot a 250 × 250. Absolute zero, cloudy.	
150	104	49–50. 15 mile 2 o'clock wind.	

Shellpot Range—Wilmington, Delaware. Firing S. E. Range protected and rather shaded in late afternoon.

	Elev. Readings	Windage	Score	Ammunition
50 and 100 yards				
50 yards	108	95	(100–100–99–100)	Palma
100 yards	122½	93	(99–100)	Palma Match PUO7

70°, dead calm. Dark, dull. Absolute zero for this range. Both distances.

Rise—50 to 100 yards, 14½ divisions. Faster cartridge would take less.

DIRECTIONS FOR MOVING GRADUATED THIMBLE OF REAR MOUNT OF WINCHESTER 5A, LYMAN 5A, FECKER, LYMAN TARGETSPOTS, UNERTL, AND SIMILAR RIFLE TELESCOPES WHEN MOUNTED ON .22 RIFLES.

The top thimble is the *Elevation* thimble. The thimble on the right side, is the *Windage* thimble. Be certain to remember this. Unless you are *certain* which thimble to move, and the proper *direction* in which to move it, move *nothing*. You cannot well go so far wrong, by holding off, what you think is the proper amount. Remember, your scope acts the same as the rear sight and your shot will go in the direction in which you move your scope barrel.

INCREASING OR DECREASING ELEVATION

Increasing the elevation reading on the top thimble or mount graduation, *increases* your rifle's elevation. Example, if you raise the elevation from 100 to 105, your next shot should go correspondingly higher. The exact amount it will be raised is determined entirely by the distance between the centers of your telescope mounts. This assumes the scope mounts are well made and move the exact theoretical amount they are supposed to when the thimble is turned. If you cut down the reading from 100 to 95, the shot will go an equal amount or distance *lower*. Always pull your scope tube back the full distance, and upward and to the right before firing a shot, if the scope barrel has been moved.

MAKING A CHANGE IN WINDAGE

Here is where many shooters make mistakes. They forget the scope thimbles represent the rear sight. The shot always goes in the direction in which you move your rear mount thimble. Suppose you look out at the target, and notice that a good strong breeze is blowing from the right. Obviously, you want to move the bullet to the right, so that as it drifts with the wind it will curve just the right amount and hit the center of the target, regardless. So, you decide to put on 10 points of windage. If, your windage reading is now 85 (three complete turns plus 10) you *increase* the reading to 95, and your shot moves to the right automatically, 10 points, and the crow or woodchuck or whatnot which did not know you could shoot either an outcurve or an incurve with a rifle bullet, sits up there as unconcerned as a steeplejack and suddenly you hit him right on the button! But suppose you move that windage thimble *in the wrong direction*—you miss him by just twice as much as if you had left it alone.

Too, suppose the wind is blowing from the left—what then? In that case *decrease* the windage reading, in this case, by 10 points, and your new reading is now 75, and instead of feeding him an outcurve, you now feed him an incurve, just chin high, and of course he is waved out by the umpire because he did not see that bullet curving in toward him in time to duck!

But, suppose it is cold as Hell, and last time you were out hunting you had summer temperatures. Your elevation reading was 105, maybe 106, and the temperature was up around 80 even in the shade, in the woods. What to do—and, what will happen?

Let us take a look in the little old scorebook. Right under the directions in the front of the scorebook telling the owner how *he* shall move the elevation or windage thimbles in case *he* becomes exhausted, is too tired to think, and cannot remember whether to turn the windage thimble forward or backward, is a reading penciled carefully to remind the author that the proper elevation and windage reading for 50 yards sighting, with the temperature down to 28° F.—four degrees below freezing, at which temperature a man gets cold easily, if he stands still, his ears get numb, his feet get numb, his eyes water, and maybe he—if sufficiently tired as well —just does not give a hoot! In that case, here is the reading in the book—elevation 107½, windage 96. Score made one day to be sure it was the proper readings, 100–100–100–100–400 × 400 at 50 yards. Yes, it can be and was done at 28 F. on the old Centreville 50–100 yard range—wearing wool shirt, heavy coat and three pairs of wool socks inside a roomy pair of Bean's Maine hunting boots. Keeps the toes nice and cozy.

TURNING THAT WINDAGE THIMBLE

Anyone the least bit forgetful—*when tired*, will just as sure as shooting forget which way to turn those windage graduations. Remember this, and put it down, *write* it down legibly, in your little pocket scorebook, which you will carry with you while hunting, the following: "Turning the windage screw *away from you*—the thimble on the right side of the telescope barrel is the one to turn now, moves the windage to the *left*." This decreases the readings.

Turning the windage thimble *backward* or toward you, increases the reading and moves the shot to the right. Higher reading— bullet goes to right; lower reading, bullet goes to left. As simple as that, but not everyone remembers out in the woods when he is looking around hunting game, has probably been straining his eyes for four or five hours, has walked five or 10 miles, or maybe only one-half mile which is a long distance to a man who seldom walks anywhere except to the curb and his car, and so, that little pocket scorebook should go hunting with you *every* time you take out your .22 caliber squirrel or varmint rifle.

What to do, when you cannot remember what to do? Do absolutely nothing—sit down and rest and maybe the thought will come back to you, after a while. Remember that if you move the scope mounts or the iron sights on a rifle, in the *wrong direction*, you are twice as badly off as if you had not moved them at all. It is like starting a fight. Starting a fight often is not at all serious, but starting a fight with the wrong man, and especially with the wrong woman, can be tough! Think back a little.

Let me drive home just one last thought: Move your sight in but one direction at a time, and be certain you are moving it in the right direction.

Riflemen by the tens of thousands, have paid real money to obtain rifle telescopes with 1¼″ to 1½″ objectives, to give good definition of the target. They have mounted them in three-point ¼-minute click mounts, made and adjusted almost like a Swiss watch, to give X-ring accuracy, and so they can exactly superpose the group upon the bullseye. When they get it all added up and mounted ready to shoot, they find themselves possessed of an outfit costing up to $300.00 today and then they go hunting and see a very long range shot and under the excitement of the moment cannot remember *which direction* to move either the elevation or windage to score a hit. This happens to the best of them, and even to the most experienced, and it happens oftener than many would like to admit. Especially is it difficult for many to recall in which direction they should move the windage thimble, because so many of them are not marked with an arrow to show in which direction moving that thimble moves the bullet.

Possibly it should be brought out here, that there are two schools of riflemen in the field. One type moves the mounts for every shot at a different range or with an increase or decrease in the wind. The other school rarely moves the sight but hold off for both elevation and windage.

I have moved the mounts, of the rifle I use most for hunting, but *once in the last three years* and now to start another season I have increased the elevation just one-half minute as it was shooting a bit too low. Once I get a rifle adjusted so that it shoots on a tack at the distance of the average shot—that is, the average fairly long shot—I let it alone. Nevertheless, I always carry my little notebook containing the sight readings for different ranges and you should do the same. Better men than you or I have made mistakes in the field so be sure to put down in easily read typing or lettering in the easiest found page in the book, the direction it moves the shot, when you move the windage so as to increase the reading. Increasing the reading on the elevation thimble *always* raises the point of strike, but millions will find themselves unable to remember this, or to figure it out instantly even though carefully instructed how to do so. It is like using a compass in the woods. Tens of thousands carry a compass to use in case they become lost, yet very few of these know how to use that compass. For instance, nearly everyone thinks it is important to know in which direction is north. It is of not a bit of use to know the direction of north unless after knowing this, you can figure out the direction in which you should travel to get from where you are, to where you want to go. Knowing the direction of south, or of east, is just as valuable as knowing the direction of north but a surprising number of people will immediately start to walk north, instead of stopping to calculate the angle from magnetic north in which they should walk to reach their objective.

The use of the rifle telescope, and the setting of its mounts, are of the same order of intricacy and puzzlement to many riflemen. The idea is that your present sighting—*is north*. Now then, what you want to do is to figure out quickly but accurately, the amount of change, and most especially the *direction* of change, so that you can deflect or divert the bullet from the direction in which it is now aimed, due to the sight setting, to the new direction so that it will be fired in the exact deflection from the previous reading to cause it to center your target.

Every rifle has two base lines, just as every survey must have a base line. One is drawn horizontally through your vertical zero. The other is drawn vertically through your horizontal zero. All your sight settings are measured from these two lines, and are recorded as plus or minus sight readings—plus or minus from your zero. Artillery must have a zero-zero to work from, in other words, base lines. So must every instrument which propels a projectile or it will be impossible to sight it accurately.

Remember, when you go hunting in the backwoods with a rifle, to carry at least 10 cartridges somewhere where you will not ordinarily use them; an extra pair of socks; a small compass which is accurate, and then know how to use that compass; a few matches, a sharp knife, and if you forget everything else, carry your rifle scorebook or sight setting notebook in your shirt pocket, so that if you take off your coat, and leave it in the car, or leave it at home, you will still have that notebook with you.

The importance of knowing your zero readings for any range, is that your sights, if metallic, may loosen due to temperature change or a knock or a fall. Your scope thimble may be turned by the rifle rubbing along your coat sleeve or the side of your coat, while carrying it. To check before shooting, look in your notebook. If it checks both ways, you are ready to fire. If it does not, you have moved the mounts accidentally, or because you took a long range shot and forgot to move them back immediately.

It is always handy to know that with high velocity .22 long rifle ammunition, the average scope sighted rifle will shoot about a

2¾″ trajectory height above the line of scope sight at 50 yards, when sighted for 100 yards. Remember that with standard velocity ammunition, you should sight for 60 yards, and with high velocity .22 long rifle you *can* sight for 75 yards, and not fire out of a 1″ up and down variation between the 15 yard point and the point suggested. And with the .22 W.R.F. high velocity loads you can make this sight setting for 85 yards. With the .22 Hornet you can sight in 1″ high at 100 yards, and be on the dot at 150 yards. With the K-Hornet or the .22–3000 you can sight in 1″ high at 100 yards and be on the dot at 175 to 200 yards—and hit what you are shooting at, any place in between. Carrying these few items of ballistic knowledge in your head makes your field shooting problems, so much simpler, and makes it possible to make many more long runs of straight kills on game or varmints.

Men of different eyesight, and of different physical build and of varying types or methods of holding a rifle and of different sling tension, will all require different sight readings for any one of the longer ranges, and the greater the range, the more this reading may vary from some generally accepted standard. Consequently, because some table says that if your rifle is sighted for 50 yards, and you should raise the rear sight readings by 40 half minutes or 20 whole minutes, or actually 40″ on the target, and you do so, and there is apparently a dead calm, you get off a perfect shot, and the crow or hawk maybe does not even fly, but looks sharply around at the direction of the bullet which suddenly whizzed past its whiskers and which sounded like a black hornet in an awful hurry to get home—do not worry. That does not prove that you are no shot or that you are too stupid to set a rifle sight, it simply means that with the calculated theoretical sight setting for you, you either had a bullet traveling with a different muzzle velocity to start it, or it had a different coefficient of form, and ranging ability, or something else went haywire, and you missed—badly. Do not feel too low, once you do get the proper sight setting business will pick up like time, over where that hawk or crow is sitting.

Quoting from memory, which may be mistaken at the moment on the exact number of shots fired, but on one occasion the author saw a large chicken hawk sitting up close to the top of a bare stub on a cliff across the Conodoguinnet Creek in Cumberland County, Pennsylvania and where the wind was blowing strongly. The hawk sat there unconcerned while the bullets whizzed past at some unknown level and windage. However, with a change in holding the hawk suddenly struck out savagely to his left just about on a level with his head, as two or three shots buzzed by, one after another. So, we held another foot into the wind and at the next shot, which, as I recall now was the 33rd shot, the bullet landed with a resounding "splat" and down the face of the cliff, with a whirling end over end fall, went the hawk. I could not get across the creek which was very wide and very deep, in those days a famous black bass stream, and it was a very long distance, around by the nearest bridge, with no boat handy, so I did not go over to get him, but that was a shot, and it was also a most annoying experience until I did get the range and windage guessed absolutely correct. The hawk was just a lot farther off and the wind was blowing the bullet a foot or more farther to the side than I calculated as the hawk sat up there on that very prominent limb, visible for a quarter mile or more in any direction.

With a high velocity .22 wildcat, killing that hawk would only have been a matter of a shot, or a few shots at best, but with the .22 long rifle, which in those days as now, had quite a rainbow trajectory and which has a wide winddrift at 200 yards and more, it was a problem of putting the ball over the middle of the old home plate. On another shot equally difficult, I might have dropped him the first shot, and likely within two or three shots, but in those days we had fewer known facts to guide a rifleman trying to learn the intricacies of shooting the small bore rifle.

Make up a table of elevation corrections from this, keep a copy in the upper left hand pocket of your hunting coat, or shirt, and have it with you. Many a time it will help you to tumble a hawk or crow which otherwise will sit up there defiantly, until the crack of doom! Only the shots that hit are shots that count—the misses are merely part of past history.

CHAPTER 27

Small Bore Rifles and Small Game Shooting of the Future

ACCURACY, WITH THE .22 LONG RIFLE SQUIRREL AND MATCH RIFLE, or with the .22 Wildcat for chucks, hawks and coyotes, is not based upon one characteristic, such for instance, as excessively tight chambering, but upon all of the closely coordinated, scientifically designed parts, machined to 1,000th or 10,000th of an inch, that are required to give long life and "bumblebee" accuracy.

Development includes: Priming compounds and smokeless powder, each selected after many careful chemical and physical tests; much better ignition and cartridge design; the study of the flow or passage of heated powder gases through cartridge case shoulders having different slopes, such as 5°, 10°, 15°, 17°, 20°, 25°, or 35°, as one experimenter after another tries out what he believes may be best. Sharp slopes prove best with light bullets, gentle slopes with heavy projectiles.

There seems to be no end to the number of ideas which are proposed and tested, and many of them work. More surprising still, many of them work which appear to be diametrically opposite in characteristics. It so happens that nearly all of the most accurate .22 center fire wildcats and even some of the factory loads, have been privately designed and developed, at least during their major stages; and so, also, have many of the worst. The .22 long rifle was strictly a factory development.

The airplane industry has had a tremendous expansion and development and this has come about after unlimited experimenting. Many ideas tested in that industry will prove successful with bullet contours, desirable velocities and case neck slopes and shapes. Many of these scientific improvements have occurred as a result of the knowledge of thousands of the best trained men who acquired their technical start at Cornell, Lehigh, Penn State, M.I.T., Yale, Leland Stanford, Michigan, and a host of other good Universities and Schools of Technology. These trained men have been employed in the war-industry laboratories, drafting rooms and engineering offices, ballistic stations, and all the other places helping in staffing the great melting pot of war. The aggregate knowledge and skills of many men, plus the ingenuity of the confirmed rifle crank, may be expected to gravitate, little by little, experiment by experiment, idea by idea, into better cartridges, better priming, better bullets, better lubricants, bullet jackets and cores, tougher brass, more resilient steel cartridge cases, better powders, longer lasting and tougher barrel alloys, and better designs, all to result in better firearms and a higher degree of accuracy.

The world was not made in one summer, nor has man been developed over night. Time has gone on for millions of years. Recorded history covers more than 6,000 years, although any coal mine will prove "known" history is only the last few chapters. We may expect better lenses, including coated lenses, better telescopes, better mounts, better everything in time, except better riflemen. They may be some time coming, but better tools to shoot with, we will eventually design and produce.

While we are talking and thinking about scientific advancement in the field of rifle building and rifle shooting, we must not forget those many practical tests conducted by the multitude of riflemen who have had their principal technical training, and who have received their diploma, on the beechnut ridges, the chestnut flats, and the knolls or wooded hills where the hognut hickory grows. We must not overlook any of those who have made of themselves knights of the grooved bore in the back pasture, or who have modest but effective testing ranges hidden away in the quiet of a creek bottom where the light of an evening is soft and still, and the wind is low.

We must not forget those who, after men snap on the lights of an evening, gather in the cellar shop of some mechanically-minded man whose place is adorned with tools which chip and cut and draw in wood and in steel, and where the work bench and the walls are piled with gadgets and adorned with targets, each carefully selected and alike in one particular—each is minus most of its X-ring!

We must not forget the obscure shop of the careful private gunsmith who is a wizard with chambering reamer, rifling machine, checkering tool, micrometer calipers and parts-fitting files. We must not overlook the rifles standing there along the wall, and in corners, each waiting its turn to be converted into that twist and this caliber, so that progress in the attainment of accuracy, and experiment can go on. All of this came in the development in the breeding of .22 "Wildcats" which now spit out a .22 bullet with tremendous speed, and then, almost immediately a small hole appears like magic in the V-ring in the target out there at 200 yards.

We should not forget the love and patience of the many who over the long years have been kind and understanding, while we riflemen have arisen two or three hours before dawn, have of course aroused the household, and after a quick but substantial breakfast have made off at full speed for the mountain to be well settled there in a favorite cover, and again breathing evenly, half an hour before the first blush of morning bursts forth in the East. We must never forget to give credit to those who have lost sleep, while we tossed around waiting for the alarm clock to ring, so that the shooting could go on. A rifleman, especially a small bore rifleman-hunter is not always on time at meals, especially is this true in the earlier days of each hunting season. In the evening, after work, he is often late getting home from the range, because the light then is soft and even, and the wind has gone down. Time flies, but no one notices. So he keeps on shooting. When he arrives home, dinner has been waiting two hours, but if he is lucky, maybe *she* does not complain. It is *his* fault if the mashed potatoes are flat. She is used to waiting, so that she too, has her place in shooting. If he went out for a nine on the forty-third shot, she might even be sorry!

We should not forget those seven or eight, who, by Gun Department advice and counsel, and by developed correspondence with shooting cranks, by collected evidence, or by ballistic range development, have passed on the knowledge of bullet, powder, and primer combinations, that have given other riflemen throughout the land, their best results. Boone, and Crockett, and other old time woodsmen, plainsmen and riflemen had none of these helps. We must not forget to give credit to *all* those who have helped to make the .22 caliber rifle and its ammunition what they are today.

The .22 caliber, or any one, well known cartridge, is not the work of any single experimenter, but of many. Without the efforts and the work of them all, none of our fine .22 rifles and cartridges of today, would be what they are now. Look back 40 years, and note the difference—the .22 long rifle was just getting into stride, there were the .22 W.C.F., the .22-15-60, the .25-21 and the .25 Stevens rim fire. Not many others were there which greatly tempted the small bore rifleman or the woods hunter of furred game. The progress of the .22 rifle and its cartridges has been the result of the lifetime experiment of many, not only of the few.

But let us turn to another side of the picture. "What about the Human Element in small bore rifle shooting?" as Cap Richard once asked through *Arms & The Man*, back in the twenties. The shooter was born, he was sent to school, he was fed with sufficient food, he was encouraged to develop himself, he was, if fortunate, educated in the sciences, he was given opportunities. But has he come along in proportion to the developments in engineering and in chemistry? The Army says he has not. In fact the Army suggests very frankly, that in far too many cases, he has developed little if at all. In too many cases, he is not in the same class as an all-day walker, a hunter, or as a rifle shot with his father, his grandfather, or his great grandfather. He has not *trained himself* to be a rifleman!

So let us leaf over another page and look again into the future of the rifle and its shooting. The fine wildcat varmint rifle of 1960, 1970 or the year 2000, may be, and very likely will be, a wonderful piece of engineering design, plus the finest of mechanical finish and workmanship, providing we are then handling a *quality* rifle. Its ammunition should be a marvel of chemical, metallurgical and ballistic achievement. We may even by then, be able to design bullets which will do better in bucking wind currents and sound waves in air just above the velocity of sound in the atmosphere, which is one of our worst headaches today. We have with us the ballistic anomaly of one .22 long rifle cartridge developing approximately 100 per cent more wind drift than another giving 250 f.s. *lower* velocity.

By one of the future dates just mentioned, many men may understand the Einstein theory, if it is then worth understanding. Riflemen may be able to score a pinwheel at more than double present ranges, with small bores, but the *skill* to shoot such a rifle, designed, engineered and built, like an engineer's transit must be developed by *riflemen,* or arms development will be useless because the human element is unable to apply it.

Riflemen will have to advance as physical specimens, and as shooters, or otherwise, within a very short time, 20 years, probably, or else rifles and cartridges will have outstripped those who shoot rifles. Man must train himself so that he can let off a shot at exactly the right moment, with regard to light, wind and aim, so as to center the target. The author recently had the privilege of examining the rifle *score book* kept by a Japanese soldier, and brought home from the South Pacific area. His shots were all plotted carefully on bullseyes, and, except for the Japanese writing, were surrounded by neat, marginal notes, all in Japanese characters exactly like those we have in our rifle score books. Consequently, it was obvious at first glance, that if that soldier's rifle and ammunition was worth anything at all, he was still about five years away from being truthfully classed as a sniper. It was not at all difficult to deduce *why* that Jap's score book had fallen into the hands of some American soldier. He just could not shoot a rifle! All his hits plotted on some pages, were what the English call "outers." In some instances, very much so!

Accuracy, practically perfect accuracy, at the longest ranges, is still the goal of all true riflemen. I am afraid such accuracy has never been the aim of those who have been proclaiming from the house tops, that riflemen, "expert" riflemen can be produced in quantity, with three weeks training on the target range and that further practice is largely a waste of effort.

If the whole truth be told, in most such instances where men have shown promise of real ability in that short preparatory period, it is almost certain that they have had at least five or 10 years previous experience with air rifles, .22s, and other firearms, but were simply *claiming* they were new at the game. This thing of playing dumb and innocent of ability or previous experience, is one of the oldest dodges in the shooting game. In addition, it is also most unfortunately true, that range target shooting, or even practice on a peace-time or base camp sniping range, can never include more than the *primary* training of a rifleman. Field and woods hunting is very different from range shooting. On the range, nearly everything happens at a given signal and within a certain time limit which is known. In hunting almost nothing happens according to schedule, and you get your shots at the most unexpected times, usually when you are so dog tired your tongue is ready to smack your knees, your eyes are dull, and your gun is either on your shoulder, is standing safely against a rough-bark tree just *out* of reach, or the game gets up too close to a house or the background must be watched carefully. You stand or sit in the woods, scanning the trees for hours, and you see nothing, and just after you have changed your position from a good secure rest to a place out in the open, *there is one*, looking at you, 80 yards off, and all set to run or fly. Take it or leave it!

The game fields are full of experienced trap shots, many of whom are not, and never have been, good game shots. The traps are often visited by many who will never be consistent trap shots. They have not been trained on that sort of targets. I recall distinctly the finest live pigeon shot in matches I knew in my home district when a youth. I have seen that man, a big, powerful, kindly dispositioned truck farmer, kill 48 out of 50 *trained* live pigeons in a match that meant a good deal to him, and shortly thereafter, I had seen the same man, using the same Parker trap gun, *miss* 49 out of 50 clay targets, from 16 yards, at *known* angles and shot at from a trap set right out in the open, in a field, with a clear sky background. I have seen another man, with some hunting experience, break the first clay target, stick his tongue out at the audience, say, "Yah—they're easy!" And then, *miss the next 24 straight*, amid of course, the ribald laughter of his friends.

I could mention cases of highly educated men, most excellent match target shots, with rifled firearms, who actually hunted for two or three years in the company of experienced hunters, without killing a single game animal or game bird, due in large measure to apparently being unable to get into action fast enough, when game flushed or moved, or came into view, to score a kill. Or else suffered the same sort of paralyzing nervousness or buck fever, which so often curses those of us who have done a lot of match target shooting. The man or woman who has *never* been nervous in match target shooting, is very rare, although some are afflicted much worse than others, and the harder they try to avoid this, the worse the attack.

In the field, there are also many who cannot go into swift and certain wing shooting stance, and get off the shot with deadly accuracy and at once, when shooting rising game birds like grouse, pheasants or quail. Still others become uncontrollably slow and nervous when faced with a shot at a squirrel, a rabbit or a deer. A man must be trained as a woodsman, a hunter *and* a rifleman, before he can expect to be successful in small game rifle shooting in the field, day after day, at all ranges, and under different circumstances. A man must learn this largely for himself. He can be coached, he can be taught caution in stalking game, how close to approach and when and how to aim and fire, but essentially a man must *develop* as a hunter, especially as a woods hunter, by days of experience in the woods. He must develop a woodsman's *eyes*—eyes that can spot game instantly, in dense foliage, or in underbrush. No book ever written can do this for a hunter. It takes a city man at least seven to 10 days before he starts to *see* game in cover. He must see it in time, and as it happens to be located. I have myself, often noticed that some years it has taken me three to five days before I began seeing rabbits *sitting* in cover, or hawks or crows hidden in dense green leaves, in tree tops, or squirrels feeding on hickory nuts, if there was still much foliage on the trees, and *after* I had been working steadily for a year or so, either at close range on a drafting board, or in writing. One of the most difficult things for many men is to get the eyes accustomed to woods backgrounds, and their ears to woods sounds, when they have not been in the woods for months at a time.

I do not believe it is possible to make a "rifleman" within a very short time, and I do not expect any young friends, to develop as expert squirrel or woodchuck hunters with a rifle, the first season. Certainly I do not expect a wing shot to develop his first November in the wheat stubble and the cornfields. A man must expect to serve his apprenticeship in the fields and the woods with the rifle, before he begins to acquire the ability to *sense* where game may be found, and to be there at the right time to find it. Squirrels or chucks, for instance, are inclined to be at a certain place, feeding, at a given time or times of day, and it is often useless to be there at any other time of the period between daylight and dark, and expect to get a shot. They will be sleeping, or else feeding in another locality, not too far away.

The author is fairly well convinced that a good woods rifle shot, or an equally good wing shot, is largely "born" rather than made. In nearly all instances, such experts began young, each had good tutoring at an age when the advice sank in, and remembered to *watch* the tactics of his shooting instructor. It is not just by accident that a veteran sits down to watch 40 yards from a group of young hognut hickories which are being fed upon by gray squirrels, as proved by "cuttings" beneath these trees and on the highest stumps nearby. It is not by accident that a woodchuck hunter picks out the most likely chuck dens to watch, first time he looks over the hillside. The most fortunate gift a woods hunter can have, is the ability to size up the shooting grounds, the probable game therein, and where it is most likely to be found within the coming hour. Time wasted in watching areas unproductive of shots, is time totally thrown away, except for the pleasure of being afield.

Squirrel, woodchuck, and crow shooting with a .22 rifle, requires patience which has been carefully developed beyond normal. It requires both feeding and denning-habit information, it requires first class equipment kept in tiptop shape, well oiled where the hands touch; clean, free of rust, and perfectly sighted in for the most effective distance for which that arm *should* be sighted. It requires match grade ammunition, if possible; the ability to decide almost instantly, the *moment to shoot*, and then the courage and skill to get off the shot with a center hold at that instant. That means, you have to begin your aim, take up the slack if any, in the trigger pull, let the rifle muzzle sway slowly and evenly back and forth over the game, and start letting off the shot just *before* your crosshairs intersection or bead covers the spot to be hit. The only time you can hold dead on game, is when the game is not moving and your rifle muzzle is not moving.

Do not fire too hurriedly and too nervously if the game appears unafraid and inclined to sit and visit. Game often does. It is often slightly combative, resents your presence there, and is nearly always curious. On the other hand do not wait on a squirrel feeding on the ground, coming *down* a tree, or one which is going up a tree very rapidly and apparently badly scared. Shoot as you have opportunity and do not forget to lead the game slightly.

Remember that game, particularly squirrels or woodchucks, or gophers, is likely to be attracted by other game of the same species, or frightened by a natural enemy like a hawk or any sort of larger predator. Rabbits will be on the watch for weasels, mink, cats, dogs, hawks, eagles, or foxes. Recall to mind, as you sit by yourself and watch for game to come out, that game often moves around, for no apparent reason, or may be simply traveling through an area, on its way to or from, a feeding or denning ground. Or it may just decide on the spur of the moment, for no apparent reason, to go in, to come out, or to go elsewhere. These sudden changes of plan, may often cause you to lose a shot. On the other hand, game like gray squirrels, woodchucks, or a crow on a watch post, may sit there or remain in sight for an hour or two, and give you plenty of time to choose your shot at the exact instant the *position* of the game, horizontally or vertically, gives you the most promise of an instant kill. The .22 rifleman should always note this particularly, as his bullet has a high trajectory.

Hawks when seen, and when they know you have spotted them, are very much inclined to fly from one to three seconds only before you can raise your rifle, take steady and careful aim, and fire with deadly effect. The author's son is the most deadly hawk shot he has ever hunted with because he shoots the instant, almost, he sees a hawk, and that simply "busts" a lot of hawks which one to three seconds later would be soaring on their way. I have seen him or known him to kill as high as 33 hawks in a year, in a locality in which the killing of one or two hawks a year, by the average good shot, using either shotgun or rifle, is to be expected.

A man, who regardless of college education, position in the world, or wealth, who by reason of his business experience is inclined to think over a matter carefully for a moment or two, before making a reply or acting, is *not* going to be a successful woods shot with a rifle, on many occasions. A man must keep his mind strictly on his hunting, not moon over this or that problem, of business, taxation, politics, or home life, while out shooting. Game is here this instant and gone the next. A man can lose so many good shots, within a week or ten days of hunting, by simply being absent-minded, too deliberate, or too slow, that those lost shots would be sufficient to provide good hunting for a different man, keenly alive to what is going on around him, and who wheels into action almost instantly. It is possible to lose more shots, by dallying on the trigger, than the kills made per day, simply by being asleep at the switch. I do not believe in snap shooting with a .22, on most small game animals or varmints, but neither can one mull over his next week's schedule before taking aim and shooting. Make slow and deliberate movements while shooting squirrels, chucks and hawks, which obviously are wild and about to change position, but on the other hand, do not dally around making up your mind. Take aim and shoot, and if you think you are fairly certain to miss from where you are, watch your footing before changing position.

Take a man with no woods or field experience with rifles and hunting sights, give him three weeks of range instruction and practice, at known ranges only, and at big easy-to-hit targets, and then suddenly transport him to some distant post where one morning he looks out over the trench at an enemy. That enemy is an experienced rifleman, armed with a scope sighted sniper's rifle. The tyro who has just come up in the line, possibly had little sleep the night before, maybe had a hard march on the way up, or anyhow he is nervous, excited, his heart is hammering, his eyes dim up on him, and frankly, he cannot see a great deal of what is going on over there. All the advice, and usually all the orders that man receives or has received will be immediately forgotten so that he can up and make one of the dozen or so boners a tyro is likely to make under such circumstances. Sticking up his head farther, so that he can see what is probably occurring across the way, exposing his shoulders or his arm, or what has he that he can do wrong! He will be pretty sure to make some sort of break within the first half hour. The enemy immediately notices it, senses that it is a move a veteran would not make, sizes him up as a *safe* target at which to fire, and when the rifle cracks, there is an immediate call for the meat wagon, or another early job for the burial squad. In the woods, a man who is inexperienced, and some who are experienced, make the same breaks, no one shoots at him, but the game spots him, and off it goes. Either a man has the natural qualifications and actions of a hunter, or he has not. There is no middle ground. You are either a good hunter, or not so good!

The public has been ballyhooed in recent years on the subject of "fire power," "tons of bombs dropped," and atomic energy until the average young chap, and many older ones who ought to know better, have forgotten all about the subject of accuracy of fire, and the importance of killing with the first shot fired, of doing that, or of not shooting at all.

Mighty few farmers today, are going to invite you, or even permit you to come back to hunt another day, if you fire two or three boxes of ammunition in an afternoon. Maybe two or three rounds are fired at game, the rest at rocks, stones, knots, cans, clods of turf, or some object out in a field. That is very poor tactics. The farmer probably thinks you are either shooting all the game on the place, or his chickens, or his cows, maybe. If he hears a dozen or so bullets go screaming and whirring off into the distance, most definitely he will be relieved when you go home. You would form similar conclusions were you the farmer. Also, do not smoke in dry woods, and I do not think it a good idea to smoke at all, when hunting. A good strong pipe will be noticed at quite a distance by squirrels or woodchucks, both of which have a keen sense of smell, simply as indicating the presence of a *strange* man. The farmer, they probably pay little attention to, because they are accustomed to his presence daily.

The small game hunter using a .22 rifle, should be properly equipped in the matter of rifle, sights, ammunition, and *clothing*. His shoes or footwear should be soft, quiet on leaves and in undergrowth and reasonably water repellent. Rubber soles are fine for mornings when the grass and leaves are wet but very hot in the middle of the day, when the sun comes out and dries off the undergrowth. If going hunting by car, take two kinds of footwear along. Rubber-bottomed or rubber soled hunting shoes for early wear, comfortable leather shoes for mid-day. If a hunter is dressed too warmly, or with insufficient warm clothing, depending upon the temperature and the precipitation, if any, he may become so uncomfortable after a time that not only does he not enjoy the hunting, but he will not likely shoot well. His personal discomfort, from cold fingers, cold ears, cold feet, or a chilled spine, or exhaustion from hard hunting in excessive heat, when wearing a Duxbak or other waterproof and hot hunting coat, will tell upon his ability to *hold*. A man may start to cough, and will cough repeatedly and almost constantly, if his throat becomes inflamed. This is surely fatal to most chances in squirrel or woodchuck shooting. A man also, must have a rifle which will kill the game over the long range chance as well as the short distances.

When the author was quite young, his cousin kept a small sporting goods and general store, and had the local agency for Remington double barreled shotguns and Remington .22 caliber rifles. He was a remarkably capable duck shot, a good squirrel hunter, a fine bass fisherman, and loved to talk about hunting and shooting. He knew his stuff, too. He was an excellent instructor in nearly all kinds of small game hunting and shooting.

In that town we had a well educated and scholarly man who was also a very vigorous and determined man. He owned an old Springfield musket with which he insisted upon hunting gray squirrels. He was a very enthusiastic and tireless hunter, he *found* many squirrels but he *killed very few*, simply because they were all located on the mountain, five to 10 miles away, always very wild both from the surroundings and from generations of hunting. The timber was mostly old chestnut, 60 to 90 feet tall and there was plenty of it and plenty of feed. Squirrels did not have to go far for feeding, and they kept back in the flat, and along the edge of the ridge, at the foot of the mountain, and on the flat and mountain it was very rocky, and squirrels are almost invariably wild and difficult to approach, under such circumstances, particularly from either above or below their position level.

This sort of hunting required a rifle or shotgun with range, accuracy, and in the case of the shotgun, killing power at long range. This hunter's old Springfield just did not have it. It lacked pattern, and it was not well choke bored. But, he was a very strong-willed man, most unusually so, "stubborn" most persons called him, and he had made up his mind to kill squirrels with that old Springfield, (the Musket, not the .30–1906), and kill them he would. He wore out a lot of shoe leather, but that was about all. Never, to his dying day, would he fit himself out with an *adequate* firearm, and that too, though my cousin would have sold him a hard-shooting 12 gauge single barrel shotgun, full choke, for as low as about $3.75. Yet this teacher would get up away before daylight, walk five, six or seven miles to the mountain, cruise around as he felt like it, on the mountain, all day long, regardless of whether it was sunny or was raining hard. He even hunted many times in sleet or when it was snowing. Yet he would *not* spend the money for an adequate gun or rifle.

There are a surprising number of men today, who will not buy a *good* rifle. It is also true, that there are far too many comparatively affluent and well educated and in other things *generous* and kindly men, for there are many such, who will not buy their own son or daughter, a *proper* firearm with which to go hunting. Eight to $10 may be their self-imposed limit. Yet they may buy the same child a $2,000 automobile, and the gas and oil and tires to run it.

It all, does not make sense. It is not *fair* to the child. If you expect your son to be a rifleman, be certain he is supplied with the arms of a rifleman because to supply him with the arms of a small boy, is needlessly to humiliate him before his fellows. This work attempts to show you and him both, what *can be* and *has been done* with *rifles*, not toys. This book is not fiction.

But let us get back to the main subjects of this chapter. We have digressed to give instances to show you some of the numerous ways to *fail* in trying to become a rifleman.

There is not the least question, that to hundreds of thousands of people who love the outdoors, the woods, and the chuck-denned hills, rifle shooting at small game and varmints is the most interesting of all sports. The only thing which compares to it, in the author's opinion is wing shooting at the most clever of upland winged game, meaning quail and ruffed grouse.

Hitting the butt of the ear of a chuck, or the brain pan of a coyote, at 200 to 400 yards, requires accuracy, it requires great care, consummate skill, perfect timing, absolute coordination of eye, ear, nerves and the muscles of the hands and chest (in breathing). It requires a good knowledge of ballistics and one's fair share of luck!

Let us hope that in the years to come, perfection of rifle and ammunition may come gradually, and *not too fast*. If 100 per cent accuracy is achieved in anything, if actual *perfection* is accomplished at all, in any science, pursuit or sport, there is then no spot at which to aim—no goal left for which to strive. Competitions are without point. Everyone makes the same score. The averages are all 100 per cent.

Perfection, and also, improvement, has arrived slowly in the small bore rifle game. Those of us, of sufficient years, that we can look back and recall the .22 accuracy of former years recollect that we had .22 ammunition that would group nicely at 100 yards, about 1908–09. It was the U.M.C. *black powder* .22 long rifle cartridge with uncrimped bullets. Then there was some improvement about 1912–14, when Dr. Henry Baker and A. O. Niedner were shooting well at 50 and 100 yards, around Boston. Next time there was good .22 ammunition was in 1919, and it stepped up nicely again in about 1922–23. We also had good stuff again about 1927–29. There have been many good lots since, and some ordinary. The average, however, has been surprisingly good in .22 long rifle caliber. What the future may bring, is anyone's guess. I expect more development in the wildcats and in .22 long rifle hollow point hunting ammunition.

I shot many a 50-shot score of 485 to 490, and some over 490 up to 495, at 50 yards, with .22 long rifle hollow point cartridges around 1922 to 29. See old issues of *Arms & The Man* and *American Rifleman*, as proof. Also, in those days, a 20-shot score of 193 at *100* yards, for .22 long rifle, *hollow point*, standard velocity .22 long rifle was *very* difficult to make. Anything over 188 took real holding and a much better than average rifle. At 50 yards, however, two to four possibles in a row, were likely, most any good, quiet evening.

Today, it is very little better, although some better at 100 yards. The match ammunition of recent years will *shoot*, although it will not shoot as well as advertised in many good barrels. I have owned barrels which shot wonderfully with ordinary commercial lots of .22 long rifle and less than one half as good with the *best* lots made by the same firm. Ed Burkins and the author once got a lot of Remington commercial ammunition from a small distributor in Southern New Jersey, with which the author scored 47 straight 10s at 50 yards, while Burkins scored 57 straight bulls at 200 yards, simultaneously, or at least in part; both in advertised Re-entry matches, and both on the same range. Scores appeared in *The Rifleman*, and the 57 straight was the longest run made at 200 yards up to that time, by any known man. This was back in the 20s.

Those of us who have shot a good many years, can look back to the remembrance of the old black powder .22–13–45 and the .22–15–60 Stevens when both were reasonably popular among the same sort of chaps who shoot the .22 Wildcats today, made mostly from the .25 Remington, .303 British, .30–40 Krag, .22 Savage H.P. 250–3,000, .30–1906 or .219 Zipper cases necked down or changed in some manner, like neck slope or length. The fellows who today, shoot the Hornet or the Wasp, shot the .25 rim fire or the .22 W.R.F. *then*. They fitted some neighborhoods better. They still do! Being overgunned is worse than being undergunned in many places.

As we look forward into the future of .22 caliber rifle shooting, let us be wise enough to try to enjoy it as it materializes, but never let us come to that time, or the time when we must visit a rifle range and see nothing but 20X possibles or 20V possibles on every score board and on every score card! Never let us know the time when we will go hunting in the woods and *never* miss a chance or a shot, or that none of us will miss!

The struggle to excel, to perfect, to gain, to achieve, and to hold what modest progress we manage to obtain or attain, is what helps, encourages, pushes, impels, and even propels the human race. And especially does it impel its most enthusiastic and fanatical rifle cranks to hold 'em, point 'em, and direct 'em, toward the target so that the bullet will cut the middle out of the X-ring on the target range, or perform its counterpart in the tree tops.

Down through the ages have come the traditions and the precepts that have guided riflemen. Even the mythical "Natty Bumppo," had them. For the future and for the shooters as yet unknown, it is given to a few of us to set down part of the record of the achievements of many who have developed our rifles, our ammunition, and our sport.

CPSIA information can be obtained
at www.ICGtesting.com
Printed in the USA
BVHW092158170119
538104BV00006B/50/P